MASS MEDIA

Second Edition

In a Changing World

MASS MEDIA

Second Edition

In a Changing World

HISTORY   INDUSTRY   CONTROVERSY

George Rodman

Brooklyn College of CUNY

Boston   Burr Ridge, IL   Dubuque, IA   Madison, WI   New York   San Francisco   St. Louis
Bangkok   Bogotá   Caracas   Kuala Lumpur   Lisbon   London   Madrid   Mexico City
Milan   Montreal   New Delhi   Santiago   Seoul   Singapore   Sydney   Taipei   Toronto

Higher Education

Published by McGraw-Hill, a business unit of The McGraw-Hill Companies, Inc., 1221 Avenue of the Americas, New York, NY, 10020. Copyright © 2008 by The McGraw-Hill Companies, Inc. All rights reserved. No part of this publication may be reproduced or distributed in any form or by any means, or stored in a database or retrieval system, without the prior written consent of The McGraw-Hill Companies, Inc., including, but not limited to, in any network or other electronic storage or transmission, or broadcast for distance learning.

Some ancillaries, including electronic and print components, may not be available to customers outside the United States.

This book is printed on acid-free paper.

1 2 3 4 5 6 7 8 9 0 DOW/DOW 0 9 8 7

ISBN: 978-0-07-351190-0
MHID: 0-07-351190-0

Vice President and Editor-in-Chief: *Emily Barrosse*
Publisher: *Frank Mortimer*
Sponsoring Editor: *Suzanne S. Earth*
Senior Development Editor: *Thomas B. Holmes*
Editorial Assistant: *Erika Lake*
Senior Marketing Manager: *Leslie Oberhuber*
Senior Project Manager: *Christina Thornton-Villagomez*
Art Manager: *Robin Mouat*
Design Manager: *Laurie J. Entringer*
Interior design: *Maureen McCutcheon*
Cover design: *Cassandra Chu and Maureen McCutcheon*
Manager, photo research: *Brian J. Pecko*
Media Project Manager: *Magdalena Corona*
Associate Media Producer: *Christie Ling*
Senior Production Supervisor: *Carol A. Bielski*
Permissions Editor: *Marty Moga*
Composition: *10/12 Adobe Garamond, Thompson Type*
Printing: *#45 Pub Matte Plus, by R.R. Donnelley/Willard*
Cover Credit: *© Lonny Kalfus/Workbook Stock/Jupiter Images*

Credits: The credits section for this book begins on page 559 and is considered an extension of the copyright page.

Library of Congress Cataloging-in-Publication Data
Rodman, George R., 1948–
    Mass media in a changing world : history, industry, controversy / George Rodman.
    2nd ed.
        p. cm.
    Includes bibliographical references and index.
    ISBN-13: 978-0-07-351190-0 (softcover : alk. paper)
    ISBN-10: 0-07-351190-0 (softcover: alk. paper)
    1. Mass media. I. Title.
P90.R596 2008
302.23—dc22   2006047075

The Internet addresses listed in the text were accurate at the time of publication. The inclusion of a Web site does not indicate an endorsement by the authors or McGraw-Hill, and McGraw-Hill does not guarantee the accuracy of the information presented at these sites.

www.mhhe.com

Dedication
To my constants in the vortex of change:
Linda, Jennifer, Alexandra and Dean.

About the Author

George Rodman

George Rodman is professor and chair of the Department of Television and Radio at Brooklyn College of the City University of New York. He has taught on the college level

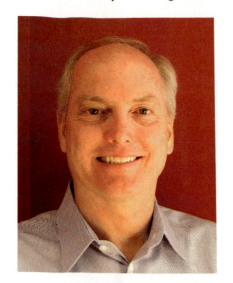

since he was 21, which was many, many years ago. His enthusiasm for media studies, however, has never diminished.

Rodman is the author, coauthor, and editor of several books, including nine editions of *Understanding Human Communication* (with Ron Adler, Oxford University Press), four editions of *Mass Media Issues* (Science Research Associates and Kendall/Hunt), *Making Sense of Media* (Allyn & Bacon, 2001), and four books on public speaking, including *The New Public Speaker* (Harcourt Brace, 1997), a book that features the role of public speaking in the media–information age. He has written for newspapers, magazines, journals, film, television, radio, and multimedia programs.

Rodman has been listed in *Who's Who in Entertainment* and *Who's Who in Education*. He serves as the faculty adviser to *The Excelsior,* one of a pair of competing campus newspapers that were named third in the nation by the *2005 Princeton Review of America's Best Colleges.* In 2005 he was named the Bernard H. Stern Professor of Humor and was awarded the Brooklyn College Award for Excellence in College Citizenship. He has been voted "Favorite Teacher" by graduating seniors several times, most recently in 2006.

In a way, Rodman is genetically predisposed to an interest in mass media. His grandmother was a first cousin to, and grew up with, Hollywood mogul Cecil B. DeMille. His grandfather was a personal lab assistant to Thomas Edison, and was later president of the Radio Manufacturers Association. His father's start-up business ventures included importing European recording equipment, printing, and computer manufacturing.

Rodman lives on Garden City, New York, with his wife Linda and three children: Jennifer, Alexandra, and Dean. Maintaining the family interest in media careers, Jennifer has worked as a movie extra, Alexandra as an actress in television commercials, and Dean as a model for textbook illustrations.

Brief Contents

Contents

PART 2 THE PRINT INDUSTRIES

PART 3 THE ELECTRONIC INDUSTRIES

PART 5 MEDIA LAW AND ETHICS

List of Boxes

Preface

Understanding media in today's world is more than a scholarly exercise; it is a necessary survival skill in a world that has been utterly changed by mass communication. All students, whether they will be practitioners, critics, or consumers, have to be able to analyze the ways in which mass media are being used to change the world. This book provides the tools they need to accomplish that analysis.

KEEPING CURRENT

This edition is shaped by two forces: The first is the progression of events that have shaped media and been shaped by media in the two years since the first edition was published, and even in the one year since the updated 2007 edition appeared. The second is a dedicated group of instructors who found the first edition effective and made suggestions about how to make it even better.

Both of these forces have lead to a complete update, which now covers trends that were barely a blip on the screen a year ago, such as the huge popularity of online social networks, and events that cry out for explanation, such as the riots in response to the Danish cartoons depicting the prophet Muhammad. Research, examples, and cases have been updated throughout, and the revised tables and figures make this year's statistics and industry data accessible, relevant, and up-to-date.

You'll find that the new material in this edition is in the form of analyses that students can sink their critical teeth into. This material is exemplified in the new chapter openers, which still catch student interest and introduce the content of the chapter, and now include:

- A meditation on the new generation of young people who have grown up in a digital world, examining how it has shaped them and prepared them to shape the world of the future (Chapter 1).

- An analysis of the crisis faced by the newspaper industry as news and advertisers move online (Chapter 4).

- An analysis of the similar crisis faced by movie theater owners as new media transforms movies from a big-screen theatrical event to a small-screen home and mobile experience (Chapter 6).

- An analysis of the social significance of the huge popularity of the social networking sites such as MySpace and Facebook (Chapter 10).

- A look into the significance of Katie Couric's ascendancy to the solo anchor position at *CBS Evening News* (Chapter 11).

- An examination of the public relations aspect of the ongoing national debate over immigration reform (Chapter 12).

- An analysis of the ethical implications of a Danish newspaper's decision to publish cartoons depicting the prophet Muhammad (Chapter 15).

Throughout, you will find an increased focus on the possibilities of new media, including a new model of converged media communication in Chapter 1. You will also find new information about industry consolidation, following a year in which the Big Seven movie studios have become the Big Six (Dreamworks has gone to Paramount) and the Big Five record labels have become the Big Four (with the merger of Sony and Bertelsmann to form Sony BMG).

There are new sections in Chapter 5 on photojournalism and on the art of magazine covers. In Chapter 6, a new Close-Up on Industry box about the job title "producer" explains the controversy following the 2006 Best Picture Academy Award for *Crash*. In Chapter 7, a new section on royalties and performance rights organizations helps clarify that area of the recording industry. Chapter 8 contains new material on public broadcasting and a new Close-Up on Industry box on the commercialization of public radio. A new section in Chapter 9 examines the significance of public access channels. New Close-Up boxes in Chapter 10 look at the impact of Google, in all its ramifications, and at the controversy surrounding online predators. Another new section in Chapter 10 deals with online commercialism versus public service, including a discussion of such issues as community Wi-Fi and Net neutrality. The chapter ends with an expanded discussion about the reliability of online information. Chapter 12 has new material on the use of video news releases as "fake news," and Chapter 13 includes new material on product placement as an advertising strategy. Even the history sections are updated, such as the new section in Chapter 9 on how early television changed family life.

Finally, instructors of this course have suggested that we move the chapter on effects, research, and theories to the introductory overview part of the book, to allow students to become grounded in those areas before they begin the in-depth examination of the individual media industries. Because so many instructors of this course have already adapted their course outlines in this way, it made sense for me to move the chapter for their convenience. For the same reason, sections on video recordings have been moved from the chapter on recordings to the chapters on movies and television. As in earlier editions, the chapters can still stand alone and be assigned in any order.

Although the changes we have made are significant, we have retained this book's innovative approach, which includes:

- A unique three-part narrative structure in which each chapter is organized around the topics of history, industry, and controversy.
- A synthesis of industry and critical points of view.
- An organization that allows for both comprehensiveness and maximum comprehension.
- An integration of unique multimedia ancillaries that lend meaning and relevance to the themes of every chapter.

THREE-PART NARRATIVE APPROACH

Mass Media in a Changing World has a unique three-part narrative structure in which every chapter is divided into sections on history, industry, and controversy. This structure makes clear the way industry practices developed historically and how those practices have resulted in today's issues. This is the story of where the media came from, why they do what they do, and why those actions cause controversies.

Dealing with history, industry practices, and controversies in each chapter creates a narrative flow that helps readers understand and remember essential concepts. This organizational scheme creates a recognizable structure for students, providing them with a conceptual framework that breaks up the story of media into progressive chunks of easily mastered material.

The book also takes a middle path between industry and critical approaches, providing a survey that is useful not just to those students who want to enter the industry as practitioners, but also to those who plan to be critics, and to those who will continue to be media consumers (a category that includes all students).

This is the story of where the media comes from, why they do what they do, and why those actions cause controversies.

ORGANIZATION OF THE TEXT

Because the breadth of content in this course can be overwhelming, *Mass Media in a Changing World* is organized for simplicity as well as comprehensiveness. Introductory chapters set the stage by introducing the essential concepts that are developed in later chapters. In Parts 2 and 3, each mainstream medium is discussed in its own chapter. In Part 4, electronic news, public relations, and advertising are given chapters of their own so that students may become aware of the influence and interaction of information and persuasion industries. The final two chapters, in Part 5, organize and complete the discussions of media law and ethics. In various places in the book, therefore, issues such as violence, stereotyping, and censorship are examined both as general issues and from the perspective of different media. Because ethics is dealt with throughout the book in this way, the final chapter provides an especially effective wrap-up for the content of this course.

SPECIAL FEATURES OF THE TEXT

To help students attain a clear understanding of all the important facets of this extensive field of study, *Mass Media in a Changing World* makes use of a number of important learning tools.

Chapter Highlights

Each chapter begins with a list of learning points that are covered in the history, industry, and controversies sections of the chapter. These highlights represent learning objectives that help students organize their reading and concentrate on key concepts.

Chapter-Opening Vignettes

Each chapter opens with a brief media-related story. These high-interest vignettes introduce the central theme of each chapter in such a way that the student enters a chapter with open eyes and an open mind.

Mass Media History

The history of mass media is an important element of any survey course on mass communication. *Mass Media in a Changing World* presents history using three easily assimilated features:

- *History section.* Each chapter contains a history section to centralize the discussion of key events in mass communication history.

- *Milestones.* A list of milestones appears at the end of the history section of each chapter. Each list summarizes the most important events in a chapter, providing the student with a set of priorities to guide them through their review of the history section.
- *Timeline appendix.* The book contains an extensive timeline in an Appendix, which gathers in one place all the historical milestones discussed in the text (see page 551).

Close-Up Boxes on History, Industry, and Controversy

These boxed features reinforce the three-part structure of every chapter. Each deals with an interesting example or trend that drives home an important concept in that section of the chapter. In the chapter on radio (Chapter 8), for example, the Close-Up on History box deals with the 1938 *War of the Worlds* broadcast and ensuing public panic. In the chapter on movies (Chapter 6), the Close-Up on Controversy box looks at the social effects of motion pictures that glamorize cigarette smoking. In the chapters on media impact (Chapter 2), media law (Chapter 14), and media ethics (Chapter 15), the Close-Up on Industry box has been recast as a special Close-Up box covering key issues affecting those areas of study.

Self Quiz Questions

Another unique feature of this text is the self quiz questions that run in the chapter margins. These questions enable students to reinforce their comprehension of the material while it is still fresh in their minds. They also highlight the most important points for key passages in a chapter and make an effective review tool.

Consider This Questions

Critical-thinking questions headed "consider this" are also placed in the chapter margins. They pose thought-provoking questions to stimulate student thinking and to foster discussion. The instructor may also use these questions as discussion points for class or as writing assignments.

Fact Files

Fact Files are illustrations or tables providing snapshots of important data for a given industry, such as industry leaders, revenue figures, market share, and consumer trends. They are designed to help students reinforce their understanding of important industry facts and trends. The unique visual design of the Fact Files makes the data easy to understand and retain.

Key Terms

Understanding the vocabulary of mass media is an important part of the introductory course. *Mass Media in a Changing World* reinforces mass media vocabulary by providing key terms and definitions in the margins of each chapter. Between 30 and 35 essential concepts are introduced in each chapter. These concepts, all of which are useful in areas of the liberal arts and sciences besides media studies, are set in boldface, carefully defined in the running narrative, and then amplified with examples chosen to stimulate student interest. In addition, the end of each chapter includes a list of that chapter's key terms, with page reference numbers.

Summing Up

An end-of-chapter summary recaps the essential points of the chapter in narrative form. It assists students in reviewing important themes, events, controversies, and concepts.

Global Perspectives Map

The global perspectives map found on the inside front cover illustrates where concepts from the book extend into various parts of the world. This map helps students synthesize mass communication as a global phenomenon that relates to all areas of media studies.

Electronic Excursions

Each chapter concludes with an integrated set of media-related activities using the student DVD and Web site developed especially for the text. These include the following for each chapter:

- *Web Excursions.* Recommended Web sites related to the chapter are coupled with critical-thinking questions to help the student assess the content of a given site.
- *DVD Excursions.* These activities point the student to specific, relevant tracks found on the DVD that accompanies the book. These include segments from *Media Tours* and *Media Talk,* which are further described in Integrated Electronic Resources below.

Notes

A comprehensive list of source notes is organized by chapter and included at the end of the book.

Full Glossary of Key Terms

A concise master glossary of essential vocabulary is included at the end of the book. These terms are also page-referenced in the index.

Complete Timeline of Mass Media Milestones

This complete timeline, located in the back of the book, integrates all the media milestones from each chapter and other important dates from the book into one comprehensive format. It provides a single place to view, compare, and contrast the historical developments of key mass media. The complete timeline is an effective study aid for the student who wishes to brush up on key historical events. There is also an interactive version of the timeline, on the companion Web site, that uses simple quizzing techniques to further reinforce the study of media history.

Integrated Electronic Resources

Mass Media in a Changing World is more than a text. Its accompanying *Media World* DVD and its Online Learning Center Web site work together as an integrated learning system to drive home the basic concepts, history, industry practices, and controversies surrounding mass media. This comprehensive system, using a combination of print, multimedia, and Web-based materials, meets the needs of instructors and students with a variety of teaching and learning styles.

For the Student

Each chapter is supported by unique content located on the accompanying Online Learning Center (OLC) Web site for the book (www.mhhe.com/rodman2). The OLC includes the following:

- Student self tests for each chapter, providing a comprehensive set of review questions not found in the book.
- Electronic timeline study guide, based on the Complete Timeline of Media Milestones from the text.
- Web Excursions activities and links for each chapter.
- Additional Internet exercises for each chapter.
- Recommended readings, movies, and documentaries for each chapter.

The *Media World* DVD is produced exclusively by McGraw-Hill. It includes video materials to reinforce the student's understanding of the mass media industry and practices. *Media World* content is highlighted in the chapters so that students and instructors can integrate it with the total learning experience. The *Media World* DVD includes:

- *Media Tours* videos, providing virtual field trips that give students an inside look at the day-to-day operations of real media organizations.
- *Media Talk* videos, featuring newsworthy interviews about important developments in mass media from the NBC News Archives.

For the Instructor

Additional electronic resources have been developed with the instructor in mind. The Instructor's Online Learning Center (OLC), at www.mhhe.com/rodman2, features the following:

- An Instructor's Manual with optional activities for each chapter.
- A Computerized Test Bank. McGraw-Hill's EZ Test is a flexible and easy-to-use electronic testing program. The program allows instructors to create tests from book-specific items. It accommodates a wide range of question types, and instructors may add their own questions. Multiple versions of the test can be created, and any test can be exported for use with course management systems such as WebCT, BlackBoard, or PageOut. EZ Test Online is a new service that gives instructors a place to easily administer EZ Test–created exams and quizzes online. The program is available for Windows and Macintosh environments.
- PowerPoint presentations for each chapter.
- Downloadable Interactive Classroom Question Bank. This resource consists of a question bank for the Classroom Performance System (CPS). CPS is a revolutionary wireless response system that gives instructors immediate feedback from every student in the class. CPS units include easy-to-use software and hardware for creating and delivering questions and assessments to your class. Every student simply responds with his or her individual, wireless response pad, providing instant results. CPS questions for classroom use are included on the Instructor's OLC for those instructors who choose to adopt this technology, which is available from your school's McGraw-Hill service representative.

Media Tours is available as a VHS tape that includes the same profiles of real media companies included on the student DVD. The videotape is provided upon request for instructors who prefer to show the clips in class using a videotape player. *Media Talk Lecture Launcher* is a series of VHS tapes that include the same newsworthy interviews from the NBC News Archives that are included on the student DVD. The videotape is provided upon request for instructors who prefer to show the clips in class using a videotape player.

The author of this text also hosts an electronic discussion group for instructors and students in the basic course in mass media. This group, active since 1997, has been a handy device for distributing up-to-the-minute course updates, as well as serving as a forum for discussions about the nature of this course. You can join the group by sending a blank e-mail message to MediaProfs-subscribe@yahoogroups.com. Messages addressed to the author individually can be sent to grodman@brooklyn.cuny.edu.

Acknowledgments

A number of people helped make this book possible. If any errors or omissions have slipped though this process, they are entirely of the author's doing, probably because he failed to follow the advice of someone on this great team. Much of what is good about this book, however, is attributable to the following people: Thom Holmes, my senior developmental editor and favorite tennis partner, was an incredible support system throughout the development of this book. Thom was more like a co-author than an editor of this book, and I couldn't have completed it without him. We were strangers when we began this project, but I am proud to count him among my friends today. Betty Whitford, on the other hand, my former McGraw-Hill service representative, has been my friend for years and would always stop by to see me on her campus visits, even though I was often in competition with the authors she represented. It was Betty who suggested that I pitch this project to McGraw-Hill and who smoothed the way for my introduction to Phil Butcher, my original sponsoring editor and publisher. Betty insisted that I would like Phil, and she was right. He turns out to be one of the straightest shooters that I've run across in this or any other business. Christina Thornton-Villagomez and Christina Gimlin, my project managers (production), have been incredibly patient and thorough, and Alice Jaggard was an extraordinary copy editor. Leslie Oberhuber, the marketing executive for this book, has been a source of practical suggestions since my earliest meetings with McGraw-Hill.

I'd especially like to thank Brian Pecko for his incredible photo research, Laurie Entringer for her fantastic design work, Carole Quandt for her excellent proofreading, and Erika Lake for her comprehensive editorial coordination.

I'd like to thank those who developed the excellent ancillary materials for this book, including Mark Stephens (PowerPoints), Susan Bachner (Web site content, CPS questions), and Robin Mouat (art and screen captures).

I'd like to thank the members of my MediaProfs e-group, who have provided guidance by sharing with me their problems and solutions in teaching this course. Of these members I am especially indebted to Beth Grobman, who also authored the outstanding Instructor's Manual and Test Bank for this book.

Finally, I'd like to thank my students in my Introduction to Media courses at Brooklyn College. We are blessed with a responsive breed of student at BC, and they haven't been shy about letting me know what does and doesn't work in this book.

A panel of expert reviewers was instrumental in shaping the book you hold in your hand today. I am indebted, therefore, to each of the following:

Ed Adams, *Brigham Young University, Utah*

Katrina Bell-Jordan, *Northeastern Illinois University*

Thom Botsford, *Pensacola Junior College, Florida*

Michael R. Brown, *University of Wyoming*

Lawrence Budner, *Rhode Island College*

David Bullock, *Walla Walla College, Washington*

Rich Cameron, *Cerritos College, California*

Jerry G. Chandler, *Jacksonville State University, Alabama*

Robert B. Clark, *Lane Community College, Oregon*

Joan Conners, *Randolph Macon College, Virginia*

Dana Eugene Creasy, *Office of the Governor of Pennsylvania*

Eric J. Danenberg, *Northern New Mexico Community College*

J. Laurence Day, *University of West Florida*

Linda K. Fuller, *Wilmington College, Delaware*

Valerie Greenberg, *University of the Incarnate Word, Texas*

Beth Grobman, *De Anza College, California*

Louisa Ha, *Bowling Green State University, Ohio*

Tracy Halcomb, *Southeastern Louisiana University*

Kirk Hallahan, *Colorado State University*

Margot Hardenbergh, *Fordham University, New York*

Robin Hardin, *University of Tennessee*

Murray Harris, *Flagler College, Florida*

David Holman, *Tacoma Community College, Washington*

James L. Hoyt, *University of Wisconsin, Madison*

Kathy Merlock Jackson, *Virginia Wesleyan College*

Dwight Jensen, *Marshall University, West Virginia*

Carla Johnson, *St. Mary's College, Indiana*

Chris R. Kasch, *Bradley University, Illinois*

Carl L. Kell, *Western Kentucky University*

Teresa Lamsam, *University of Nebraska, Omaha*

Kim Landon, *Utica College, New York*

Nanci LaVelle, *Lane Community College, Oregon*

Curtis D. LeBaron, *Brigham Young University, Utah*

John A. Lent, *Temple University, Pennsylvania*

Charles Lewis, *Minnesota State University, Mankato*

Carol Liebler, *Syracuse University, New York*

Annette M. Magid, *Erie Community College, New York*

Robert Main, *California State University, Chico*

John N. Malala, *University of Central Florida*

Linda Martin, *Louisiana State University, Shreveport*

Walter F. McCallum, *Santa Rosa Junior College, California*

W. Bradford Mello, *Trinity College, Washington DC*

Denis Mercier, *Rowan University, New Jersey*

Debra Merskin, *University of Oregon*

Nancy Mitchell, *University of Nebraska, Lincoln*

David D. Moser, *Butler County Community College, Pennsylvania*

Alfred G. Mueller II, *Pennsylvania State University*

Michael D. Murray, *University of Missouri, St. Louis*

Diana Peck, *William Paterson College, New Jersey*

Jerry Pinkham, *College of Lake County, Illinois*

Joan B. Ramm, *Delta College, Michigan*

Eric S. Reed, *Owens Community College, Ohio*

James E. Reppert, *Southern Arkansas University*

Lynn Robertson, *Delgado Community College, Louisiana*

Joseph A. Russomanno, *Arizona State University*

Karon Speckman, *Truman State University, Missouri*

David Syring, *St. Mary's University of Minnesota*

Robert L. Terrell, *California State University, Hayward*

Dan Tinianow, *La Sierra University, California*

JoAnn Valenti, *Brigham Young University, Utah*

Mary D. Vavrus, *University of Minnesota*

Hazel G. Warlaumont, *California State University, Fullerton*

Gary M. Weier, *Bob Jones University, South Carolina*

Hans-Erik Wennberg, *Elizabethtown College, Pennsylvania*

George Whitehouse, *University of South Dakota*

Shelly A. Wright, *State University of New York, New Paltz*

REVIEWERS OF THE 2007 UPDATE AND THE SECOND EDITION

Arje-Ori Agbese, *Salve Regina University, Rhode Island*

Herbert Amey, *Ohio University*

Nancy Arnett, *Brevard Community College-Melbourne*

Frank A. Aycock, *Appalachian State University, North Carolina*

Sean Baker, *Towson University, Maryland*

Julie Beard, *Lindenwood University*

Ralph Beliveau, *University of Oklahoma*

Robert Bellamy, *Duquesne University, Pennsylvania*

Charlyne Berens, *University of Nebraska, Lincoln*

Rick Boeck, *Consumnes River College, California*

Matthew Bosisio, *Northwest Missouri State University*

Karen Burke, *Southern Connecticut State University*

Joseph L. Clark, *University of Toledo, Ohio*

Adrienne E. Hacker Daniels, *Illinois College*

Juliet Dee, *University of Delaware*

Lori Demo, *Ball State University, Indiana*

Mike Dillon, *Duquesne University, Pennsylvania*

Samuel Edelman, *California State University, Chico*

Colleen Fitzpatrick, *University of Wisconsin*

Bradley Freeman, *Marist College, New York*

Peter Galarneau, *West Virginia Wesleyan College*

Harry W. Haines, *Trinity University, Texas*

Arthur S. Hayes, *Fordham University, New York*

Troy Hunt, *College of Eastern Utah-Price*

John Jenks, *Dominican University, Illinois*

Robert Kagan, *Manchester Community College, Connecticut*

Michael L. Larson, *St. Cloud State University, Minnesota*

J. Douglas Lepter, *Trevecca Nazarene University, Tennessee*

Louis Lucca, *LaGuardia Community College, New York*

Robert Main, *California State University, Chico*

Donald Meckiffe, *University of Wisconsin, Fox Valley*

Steven Miller, *Rutgers, the State University of New Jersey*

Susan Moeller, *University of Maryland*

Frank Nevius, *Western Oregon University*

Sandra Nichols, *Towson University, Maryland*

Hanna Elise Norton, *Arkansas Tech University*

Charlotte Petty, *University of Missouri–St. Louis*

Thomas P. Proietti, *Monroe Community College, New York*

Heather Ricker-Gilbert, *Manchester Community College, Connecticut*

Karen Ritzenhoff, *Central Connecticut State University*

Brian Rose, *Fordham University, New York*

Thomasena Shaw, *University of Tennessee*

Victoria Smith-Ekstrand, *Bowling Green University, Ohio*

Steve H. Sohn, *University of Connecticut*

Michael Spillman, *Ball State University, Indiana*

Carol Terracina-Hartman, *American River College*

John Weis, *Winona State University*

Your Visual Preface Preview

Innovative Three-Part Structure

Every chapter is divided into sections on history, industry, and controversy. The three-part structure makes clear the way industry practices developed historically and how those practices have resulted in today's issues.

Intriguing Vignettes

Chapter-opening stories effectively introduce the central theme of each chapter and are analyzed so that the student enters a chapter with open eyes and an open mind.

Close-Up Boxes

These boxed features reinforce the three-part structure of every chapter. Each deals with an interesting example or trend that drives home an important concept in that section of the chapter.

This is the story of where the media came from, why they do what they do, and why those actions cause controversies.

Milestones

A milestone chart, which appears in each chapter, summarizes the most important historical events for the chapter and provides students with a set of priorities to guide them through their reading.

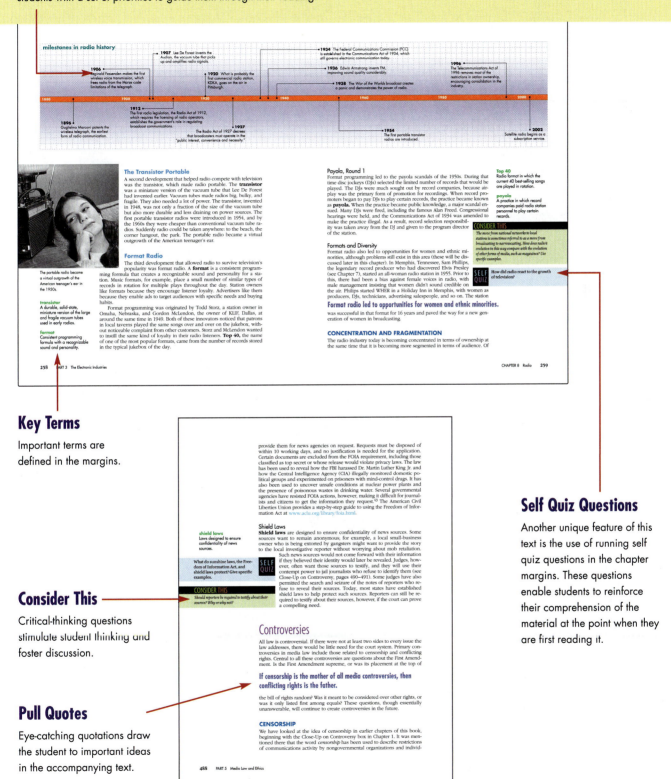

Key Terms

Important terms are defined in the margins.

Consider This

Critical-thinking questions stimulate student thinking and foster discussion.

Pull Quotes

Eye-catching quotations draw the student to important ideas in the accompanying text.

Self Quiz Questions

Another unique feature of this text is the use of running self quiz questions in the chapter margins. These questions enable students to reinforce their comprehension of the material at the point when they are first reading it.

Smart Visuals

Revealing visual aids are used to convey the history of mass communication and its economics, as well as the influence of mass media on culture.

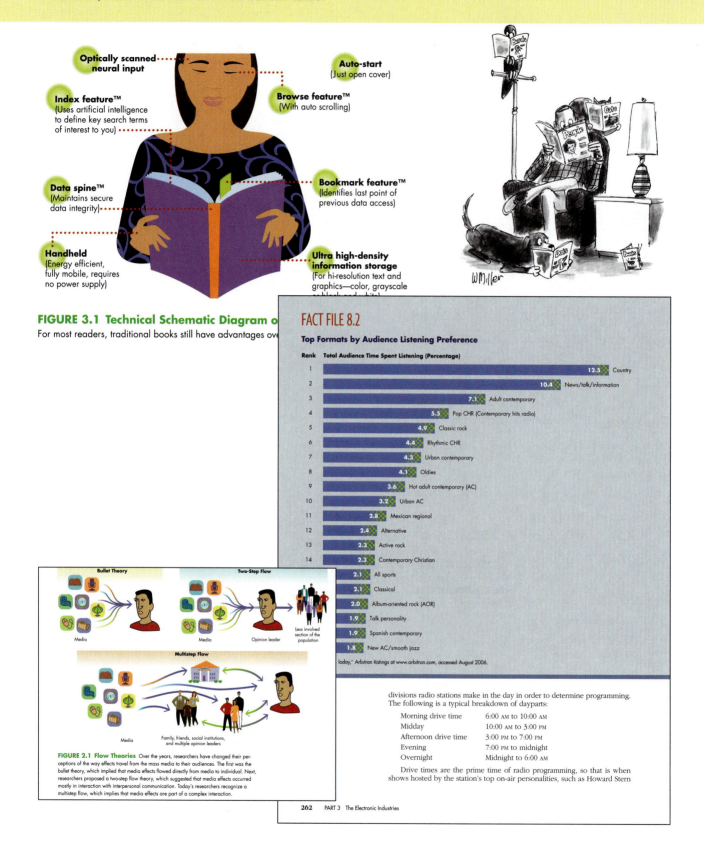

Optically scanned neural input

Auto-start (Just open cover)

Index feature™ (Uses artificial intelligence to define key search terms of interest to you)

Browse feature™ (With auto scrolling)

Data spine™ (Maintains secure data integrity)

Bookmark feature™ (Identifies last point of previous data access)

Handheld (Energy efficient, fully mobile, requires no power supply)

Ultra high-density information storage (For hi-resolution text and graphics—color, grayscale or black and white)

FIGURE 3.1 Technical Schematic Diagram o

For most readers, traditional books still have advantages ov

FACT FILE 8.2

Top Formats by Audience Listening Preference

Rank	Total Audience Time Spent Listening (Percentage)	
1	12.5	Country
2	10.4	News/talk/information
3	7.1	Adult contemporary
4	5.5	Pop CHR (Contemporary hits radio)
5	4.9	Classic rock
6	4.4	Rhythmic CHR
7	4.3	Urban contemporary
8	4.1	Oldies
9	3.6	Hot adult contemporary (AC)
10	3.2	Urban AC
11	2.8	Mexican regional
12	2.4	Alternative
13	2.3	Active rock
14	2.3	Contemporary Christian
	2.1	All sports
	2.1	Classical
	2.0	Album-oriented rock (AOR)
	1.9	Talk personality
	1.9	Spanish contemporary
	1.8	New AC/smooth jazz

Today," Arbitron Ratings at www.arbitron.com, accessed August 2006.

Bullet Theory

Two-Step Flow

Media

Media

Opinion leader

Less involved section of the population

Multistep Flow

Media

Family, friends, social institutions, and multiple opinion leaders

FIGURE 2.1 Flow Theories Over the years, researchers have changed their perceptions of the way effects travel from the mass media to their audiences. The first was the bullet theory, which implied that media effects flowed directly from media to individual. Next, researchers proposed a two-step flow theory, which suggested that media effects occurred mostly in interaction with interpersonal communication. Today's researchers recognize a multistep flow, which implies that media effects are part of a complex interaction.

divisions radio stations make in the day in order to determine programming. The following is a typical breakdown of dayparts:

Morning drive time	6:00 AM to 10:00 AM
Midday	10:00 AM to 3:00 PM
Afternoon drive time	3:00 PM to 7:00 PM
Evening	7:00 PM to midnight
Overnight	Midnight to 6:00 AM

Drive times are the prime time of radio programming, so that is when shows hosted by the station's top on-air personalities, such as Howard Stern

Media World Student DVD

Media World, a DVD set produced exclusively by McGraw-Hill, includes video materials to reinforce the student's understanding of the mass media industry and practices.

Media World includes:

- *Media Tours* videos, providing an inside look at the day-to-day operations of real media organizations.
- *Media Talk* videos, featuring newsworthy interviews from the NBC News Archives about important developments in mass media.

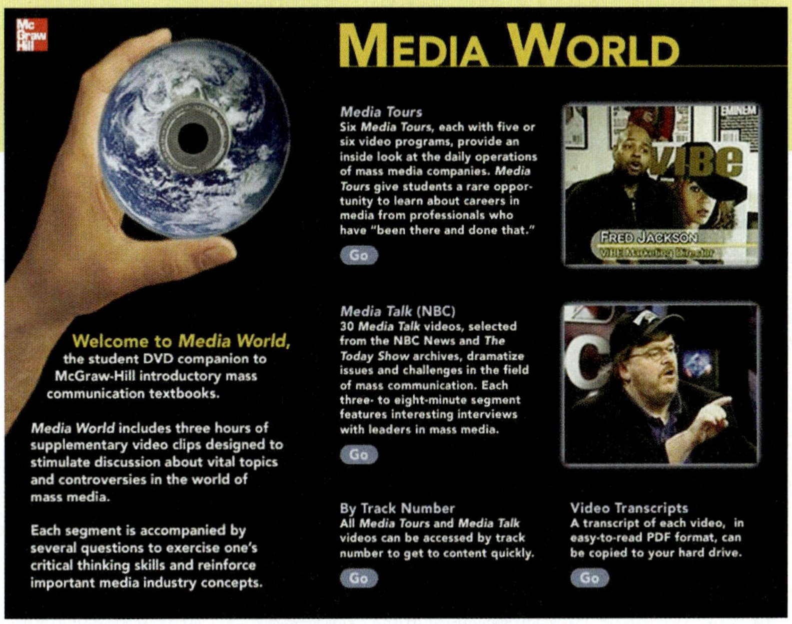

Mc Graw Hill
MEDIA WORLD
Welcome to Media World, the student DVD companion to McGraw-Hill introductory mass communication textbooks.
Media World includes three hours of supplementary video clips designed to stimulate discussion about vital topics and controversies in the world of mass media.
Each segment is accompanied by several questions to exercise one's critical thinking skills and reinforce important media industry concepts.
Media Tours
Six Media Tours, each with five or six video programs, provide an inside look at the daily operations of mass media companies. Media Tours give students a rare opportunity to learn about careers in media from professionals who have "been there and done that."
Go
VIBE
FRED JACKSON
Media Talk (NBC)
30 Media Talk videos, selected from the NBC News and The Today Show archives, dramatize issues and challenges in the field of mass communication. Each three- to eight-minute segment features interesting interviews with leaders in mass media.
Go
By Track Number
All Media Tours and Media Talk videos can be accessed by track number to get to content quickly.
Go
Video Transcripts
A transcript of each video, in easy-to-read PDF format, can be copied to your hard drive.
Go

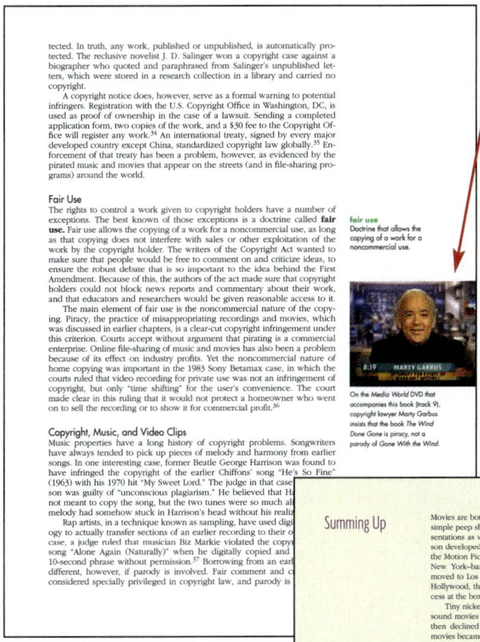

tected. In truth, any work, published or unpublished, is automatically protected. The reclusive novelist J. D. Salinger won a copyright case against a biographer who quoted and paraphrased from Salinger's unpublished letters, which were stored in a research collection in a library and carried no copyright.

A copyright notice does, however, serve as a formal warning to potential infringers. Registration with the U.S. Copyright Office in Washington, DC, is used as proof of ownership in the case of a lawsuit. Sending a completed application form, two copies of the work, and a $30 fee to the Copyright Office will register any work.[34] An international treaty, signed by every major developed country except China, standardized copyright law globally.[35] Enforcement of that treaty has been a problem, however, as evidenced by the pirated music and movies that appear on the streets (and in file-sharing programs) around the world.

Fair Use

The rights to control a work given to copyright holders have a number of exceptions. The best known of those exceptions is a doctrine called **fair use.** Fair use allows the copying of a work for a noncommercial use, as long as that copying does not interfere with sales or other exploitation of the work by the copyright holder. The writers of the Copyright Act wanted to make sure that people would be free to comment on and criticize ideas, to ensure the robust debate that is so important to the idea behind the First Amendment. Because of this, the authors of the act made sure that copyright holders could not block news reports and commentary about their work, and that educators and researchers would be given reasonable access to it.

The main element of fair use is the noncommercial nature of the copying. Piracy, the practice of misappropriating recordings and movies, which was discussed in earlier chapters, is a clear-cut copyright infringement under this criterion. Courts accept without argument that pirating is a commercial enterprise. Online file-sharing of music and movies has also been a problem because of its effect on industry profits. Yet the noncommercial nature of home copying was important in the 1983 Sony Betamax case, in which the courts ruled that video recording for private use was not an infringement of copyright, but only "time shifting" for the user's convenience. The court made clear in this ruling that it would not protect a homeowner who went on to sell the recording or to show it for commercial profit.[36]

fair use
Doctrine that allows the copying of a work for a noncommercial use.

On the *Media World* DVD that accompanies this book (track 9), copyright lawyer Marty Garbus insists that the book *The Wind Done Gone* is piracy, not a parody of *Gone With the Wind.*

Copyright, Music, and Video Clips

Music properties have a long history of copyright problems. Songwriters have always tended to pick up pieces of melody and harmony from earlier songs. In one interesting case, former Beatle George Harrison was found to have infringed the copyright of the earlier Chiffons' song "He's So Fine" (1963) with his 1970 hit "My Sweet Lord." The judge in that case [illegible] son was guilty of "unconscious plagiarism." He believed that H[illegible] not meant to copy the song, but the two tunes were so much al[illegible] melody had somehow stuck in Harrison's head without his realiz[illegible]

Rap artists, in a technique known as sampling, have used digi[illegible] ogy to actually transfer sections of an earlier recording to their o[illegible] case, a judge ruled that musician Biz Markie violated the copyr[illegible] song "Alone Again (Naturally)" when he digitally copied and [illegible] 10-second phrase without permission.[37] Borrowing from an earl[illegible] different, however, if parody is involved. Fair comment and c[illegible] considered specially privileged in copyright law, and parody is [illegible]

Media World videos are fully integrated with the text, providing another dimension to the learning experience.

End-of-Chapter Features for Easy Review

Helpful Chapter Summaries and Key Terms

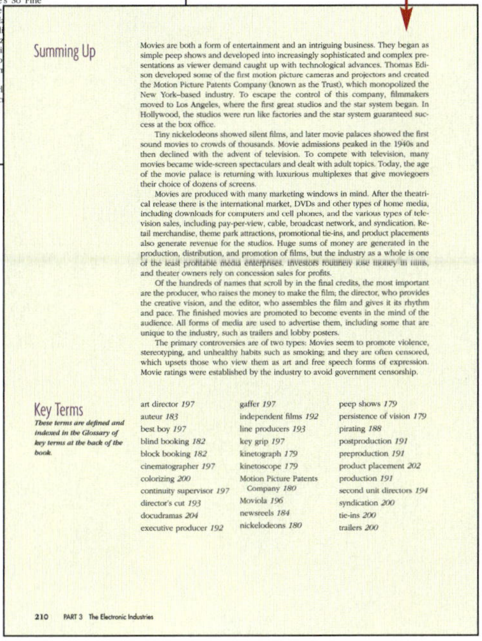

Summing Up

Movies are both a form of entertainment and an intriguing business. They began as simple peep shows and developed into increasingly sophisticated and complex presentations as viewer demand caught up with technological advances. Thomas Edison developed some of the first motion picture cameras and projectors and created the Motion Picture Patents Company (known as the Trust), which monopolized the New York–based industry. To escape the control of this company, filmmakers moved to Los Angeles, where the first great studios and the star system began. In Hollywood, the studios were run like factories and the star system guaranteed success at the box office.

Tiny nickelodeons showed silent films, and later movie palaces showed the first sound movies to crowds of thousands. Movie admissions peaked in the 1940s and then declined with the advent of television. To compete with television, many movies became wide-screen spectaculars and dealt with adult topics. Today, the age of the movie palace is returning with luxurious multiplexes that give moviegoers their choice of dozens of screens.

Movies are produced with many marketing windows in mind. After the theatrical release there is the international market, DVDs and other types of home media, including downloads for computers and cell phones, and the various types of television sales, including pay-per-view, cable, broadcast network, and syndication. Retail merchandise, theme park attractions, promotional tie-ins, and product placements also generate revenue for the studios. Huge sums of money are generated in the production, distribution, and promotion of films, but the industry as a whole is one of the least profitable media enterprises. Investors routinely lose money in films, and theater owners rely on concession sales for profits.

Of the hundreds of names that scroll by in the final credits, the most important are the producer, who raises the money to make the film; the director, who provides the creative vision, and the editor, who assembles the film and gives it its rhythm and pace. The finished movies are promoted to become events in the mind of the audience. All forms of media are used to advertise them, including some that are unique to the industry, such as trailers and lobby posters.

The primary controversies are of two types: Movies seem to promote violence, stereotyping, and unhealthy habits such as smoking; and they are often censored, which upsets those who view them as art and free speech forms of expression. Movie ratings were established by the industry to avoid government censorship.

Key Terms

These terms are defined and indexed in the Glossary of key terms at the back of the book.

art director *197*	gaffer *197*	peep shows *179*
auteur *183*	independent films *192*	persistence of vision *179*
best boy *197*	line producers *193*	pirating *188*
blind booking *182*	key grip *197*	postproduction *191*
block booking *182*	kinetograph *179*	preproduction *191*
cinematographer *197*	kinetoscope *179*	product placement *202*
colorizing *200*	Motion Picture Patents Company *180*	production *191*
continuity supervisor *197*	Moviola *196*	second unit directors *194*
director's cut *193*	newsreels *184*	syndication *200*
docudramas *204*	nickelodeons *180*	tie-ins *200*
executive producer *192*		trailers *200*

210 PART 3 The Electronic Industries

Electronic Excursions

These meaningful resources include Web-based exercises, links to media essays and articles, and additional *Media World* videos.

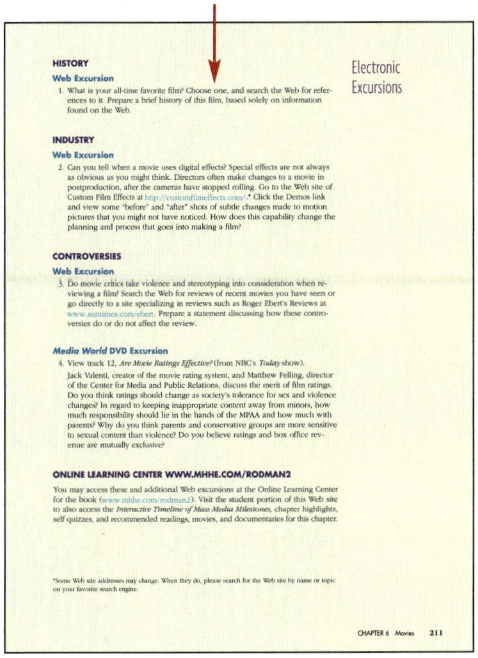

Electronic Excursions

HISTORY

Web Excursion

1. What is your all-time favorite film? Choose one, and search the Web for references to it. Prepare a brief history of this film, based solely on information found on the Web.

INDUSTRY

Web Excursion

2. Can you tell when a movie uses digital effects? Special effects are not always as obvious as you might think. Directors often make changes to a movie in postproduction, after the cameras have stopped rolling. Go to the Web site of Custom Film Effects at http://customfilmeffects.com/.* Click the Demos link and view some "before" and "after" shots of subtle changes made to motion pictures that you might not have noticed. How does this capability change the planning and process that goes into making a film?

CONTROVERSIES

Web Excursion

3. Do movie critics take violence and stereotyping into consideration when reviewing a film? Search the Web for reviews of recent movies you have seen or go directly to a site specializing in reviews such as Roger Ebert's Reviews at www.suntimes.com/ebert. Prepare a statement discussing how these controversies do or do not affect the review.

***Media World* DVD Excursion**

4. View track 12, *Are Movie Ratings Effective?* (from NBC's *Today* show). Jack Valenti, creator of the movie rating system, and Matthew Felling, director of the Center for Media and Public Relations, discuss the merit of film ratings. Do you think ratings should change as society's tolerance for sex and violence changes? In regard to keeping inappropriate content away from minors, how much responsibility should lie in the hands of the MPAA and how much with parents? Why do you think parents and conservative groups are more sensitive to sexual content than violence? Do you believe ratings and box office revenue are mutually exclusive?

ONLINE LEARNING CENTER WWW.MHHE.COM/RODMAN2

You may access these and additional Web excursions at the Online Learning Center for the book (www.mhhe.com/rodman2). Visit the student portion of this Web site to also access the *Interactive Timeline of Mass Media Milestones,* chapter highlights, self quizzes, and recommended readings, movies, and documentaries for this chapter.

*Some Web site addresses may change. When they do, please search for the Web site by name or topic on your favorite search engine.

CHAPTER 6 Movies 211

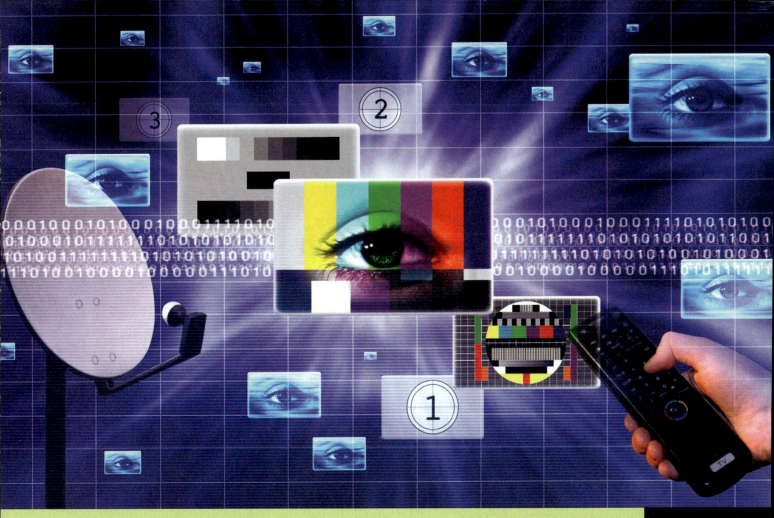

PART ONE

Overview

This first part of *Mass Media in a Changing World*, consisting of two chapters, introduces some of the key terms and concepts that will be dealt with throughout the book. The first chapter explains why we study media and places the study of media in the context of the rest of the field of communication. It provides a brief introduction to media history, industry structure, and controversies, all of which will be expanded upon in subsequent chapters. The second chapter introduces the concept of media impact and includes a history of media research, an overview of media theory, and a consideration of the controversies that arise when theory, criticism, and industry clash.

Introduction

Media in a Changing World

1

Chapter Highlights

MEDIA LITERACY: The introductory course in mass communication has two primary objectives: to sharpen students' critical skills and to prepare students for careers in mass media. Critics and practitioners often take opposite sides in media controversies.

BASIC TERMS: Mass communication is just one form of mediated communication. It differs from interpersonal communication in a number of essential ways.

HISTORY: New media technologies often change society in subtle and unexpected ways.

INDUSTRY: The U.S. media dominate globally; other countries sometimes resent this dominance. Reasons for the growth of media corporations include economies of scale, synergy, and global competition.

CONTROVERSIES: Media controversies are based on impact, legal, and ethical issues. In many ways, these are related issues.

The Convergence Generation

Sociologists call them Millennials and define them as those born since 1980. They are the babies of the baby boomers, the huge generation born after World War II. By 2010, Millennials will outnumber all other generations in the 18-to-49 age category that advertisers love because of their free-spending habits.

Not all members of this or any other generation are the same, but one thing that distinguishes the Millennials is the way that most

Today's young people are especially adept at using digital media, and it affects how they communicate one-on-one.

"Come pick me up. This is going nowhere."

of them use media. They are the most technologically savvy generation in history. Thanks to the Internet, handheld computers, and cell phones, Millennials have billions of facts literally at their fingertips. They like to watch television, but they barely recognize the concept of prime time; instead, they download their favorite shows (without commercials) to TIVOs, laptops, video iPods, and cell phones.

They almost never buy newspapers or magazines; nearly all their information comes from the Internet or from their network of electronic contacts. They take broadband Internet access for granted.

This is a generation weaned on computer technology. They tinker comfortably with digital media—from creating Web sites and blogs to mixing their own music files—and they have constant access to their friends through instant messaging and online networking. "It consumes my life," said one college senior. "If I'm not texting my friends over the cell phone, I have my laptop with me and I'm IM'ing them. Or I'm doing research on Google. Honestly, the only reason any of

my college friends use the library is for group meetings."[1]

The Millennials find entertainment and information (and one another) through a wide variety of new media, including the newest versions of iPods, Treos, and BlackBerries. Many of these new media are products of convergence, the integration of previously separate forms of media.

Millennials are highly skilled at multitasking and working in teams. Shaped by the end of the cold war, the explosion in technology, a new global economy, the terrorist attacks of September 11 and the terrorism that continues, they tend to be more sober-minded than those who came before them and more willing to work within the system to effect change. Millennials are focused on achievement and have a respect for authority. They are less violent and less inclined to participate in risky behavior than their parents were at the same age. Millennials drink less alcohol, use fewer recreational drugs, and smoke fewer cigarettes than earlier generations. They are more likely to go to college.[2]

It's no wonder that experts expect great things from this gen-

eration. As one group of authors predicts: "The Millennial Generation will entirely recast the image of youth from downbeat and alienated to upbeat and engaged—with potentially seismic consequences for America."[3]

Not all the traits of Millennials are positive, however. Their English teachers feel that they've lost touch with the nuances of grammar and punctuation. They tend to possess notoriously short attention spans. One researcher coined the term *grasshopper mind* to describe the Millennials' inclination to leap quickly from one topic to another.[4] Under intense pressure from their parents to succeed and faced with a new, more competitive world economy, they also feel more stress than earlier generations. Millennials are more prone to childhood obesity and depression.[5]

Perhaps more than anything else, the Millennials stand as proof that the media have affected young people—and that these same young people are poised to change the world. These impending changes make a great argument for the idea that everyone needs to understand today's media.

Media Literacy

If the Millennials stand as evidence of the effects of media, then questions related to this argument get to the heart of the concept of media literacy. Just as literacy is the ability to read and write, **media literacy** is the ability to understand and make productive use of the media in your life. Media literacy involves understanding the effect media can have on you and on the society around you. For some, media literacy is the difference between being victimized by and being in control of media's influence.

media literacy
The ability to understand and make productive use of the media.

There are at least two different but related perspectives to media literacy: media criticism and career preparation.

MEDIA CRITICISM

Media criticism is the analysis used to assess the effects of media on individuals, on societies, and on cultures. Media criticism doesn't necessarily have to be negative, but it does have to consist of analysis based on well-reasoned argument.

media criticism
The analysis used to assess the effects of media on individuals, on societies, and on cultures.

Many students are interested in media criticism in their roles as consumers, and some are concerned about their present or future roles as parents. In the primary grades, instruction in media criticism centers on making children careful consumers of media messages; the goal is to help them realize that they can react logically to the emotional messages of the media. At this level, media criticism lessons are designed to teach children that advertisements really do sometimes try to sell them things they don't need. On the secondary level, high school students begin to learn about how the various media influence society and how media messages can contribute to a teenager's self-image. High school media studies might deal with how movies tend to make smokers look cool or how an excessively skinny body is promoted as an ideal.

On the college level, instruction in media criticism goes a step further in providing tools for the in-depth analysis of the messages of mass communication. In the introductory course in media criticism, college students begin to examine the relationships among media history, current industry practices, and controversies, as well as how laws and ethics relate to the impact of media. Many students find that an increased awareness of the inner workings of their favorite media makes their use of those media more interesting and more significant. Using media is something most people will do for the rest of their lives, so the prospect of making that use more meaningful is often compelling. Students who have taken media for granted, and have accepted a view that is essentially uncritical and unreflective, often find the introductory course in mass communication to be an eye-opener.

CAREER PREPARATION

Part of media literacy is learning how to use media. Practical use is of most interest to students who want to explore media careers. These might be careers in the media spotlight—as a newscaster or reporter, for example—or behind-the-scenes employment in film production, book editing, advertising, Web site creation, or scores of other careers. This book provides an overview of the various industries in mass communication and suggests career possibilities by giving a general blueprint for how the various industries work.

Even students who have their eyes set on a career in a particular medium—film production or newspaper journalism, for example—often find it helpful to learn how the other media operate. A surprising number of students aiming for a particular career in mass communication wind up in a different but related field (such as the many journalism students who find themselves in public relations jobs), so a well-rounded study of media fields in general often turns out to be useful. In addition, many nonmedia careers turn out to have a media component. Many a corporate executive, for example, learns that a successful career will involve working with the media to get a business message out to the public.

THE CRITIC VERSUS THE PRACTITIONER

The two different approaches to the study of media—as criticism and as career preparation—lead to different ways of looking at media. Often media professionals will find media criticism to be unduly harsh and unrealistic, whereas media critics will find the bottom-line approach of professionals to be simplistic and detrimental to society. This book tries to present both sides of this dichotomy, so you will often read here the phrases "critics say" or "critics believe" as well as "media practitioners say" or "media professionals believe," to introduce ideas and explanations from the two points of view. Students are invited to reach their own conclusions about which side is right in each controversy. The important goal is to analyze media through well-informed critical thinking. That skill will be of great value to both future practitioners and future critics.

BASIC TERMS

We begin the study of mass communication by defining some terms that will concern us throughout this book. As you will see, even such basic terms as *media* and *mass communication* are in a process of constant change.

Communication

Before we begin to look at media, we need to consider the concept of communication. This term has many meanings, and has been used to refer to interaction between animals and machines as well as among people. For our purposes, however, **communication** refers to the process of human beings sharing messages. The messages might be entertainment, information, or persuasion; they might be verbal or visual, intentional or unintentional. In fact, they might have a different meaning to the people sending them than they do to those who receive them. Courses in interpersonal, group, public, and mass communication are all given on the college level. Interpersonal communication usually refers to individuals interacting face-to-face and includes the study of intrapersonal communication, or the thought patterns that make up our internal conversations. Group communication is also called small group communication when there are few enough members to interact face-to-face, and organizational communication when the groups are large enough to need to communicate through devices like e-mail and telephones. Public communication focuses on public speaking, a subject that has been taught at the college level since ancient times. All of these types of communication are represented by a basic model of the communication process, in which one person (a source) sends a message through a channel, to another person (a receiver). **Feedback** is defined as messages that return from the receiver of a message to the source of that message. Anything that interferes with this process is called **noise,** which includes psychological noise when it occurs internally, such as daydreams, worries, or being offended by the mes-

communication
The process of human beings sharing messages.

feedback
Messages that return from the receiver of a message to the source of that message.

noise
Anything that interferes with the communication process.

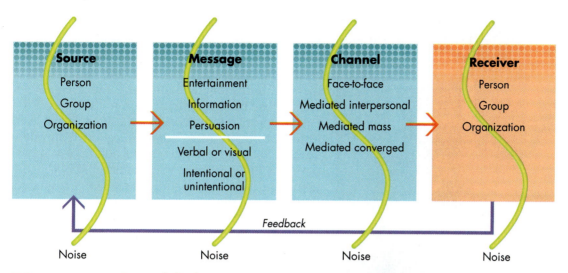

FIGURE 1.1 Basic Model of Human Communication This basic model of human communication shows how components such as source, message, channel, receiver, feedback, and noise are interrelated.

sage, and environmental noise when it occurs externally, such as a younger sibling screaming across the room. If these terms sound rather technical, it is because they were originated by mathematicians working on formulas for types of electronic communication.[6] This model (see Figure 1.1) is used to explain all types of communication. It helps clarify, for example, how a message sent out by a source might be interpreted differently by a receiver because of noise.[7]

Mediated Communication

Mediated communication is any type of sharing of messages conveyed through an interposed device, or **medium,** rather than face-to-face. **Media,** the plural form of *medium,* refers collectively to the print media (books, magazines, and newspapers); broadcast media (television and radio); digital media (sometimes referred to as *new media,* including the Internet, cell phones, and any other medium that uses computer-based technology); and the entertainment media (all of these, plus movies, recordings, and video games). The word *media* is sometimes used in the singular, as in "The media provides little of value" or "The media is a wonderful source of entertainment." Most experts believe that such usage not only is grammatically incorrect but also suggests a lack of understanding about how diverse the various media are.

When most people talk about "the media" they are referring to the channels of mass communication, such as television and radio. However, not all media are used to reach mass audiences. Although mediated communication includes mass communication, it also includes mediated interpersonal communication and communication through converged media that are both mass and interpersonal. (*Convergence* is discussed later in this chapter.)

Mass Communication

Mass communication consists of mediated messages that are transmitted to large, usually widespread audiences (see Figure 1.2). Mass communication differs from interpersonal communication (interaction between individuals) in several ways.

mediated communication
Messages conveyed through an interposed device rather than face-to-face.

medium
An interposed device used to transmit messages.

media
Plural of *medium.*

mass communication
Mediated messages transmitted to large, widespread audiences.

Gatekeepers determine which images will represent chaotic news events, such as Hurricane Katrina's devastation of New Orleans in 2005.

gatekeepers
Those who determine what messages will be delivered to media consumers.

Mass Media Do Not Talk Back

First, mass communication differs from interpersonal communication in that the former allows little or no contact or interaction between the sender of the message and individual audience members. Feedback, those messages that return to the source of a message from the receiver of a message, is restricted in most forms of mass communication. You might be able to write a letter to the editor of a newspaper or the creator of your favorite Web site, but you could wait a long time to receive a response. Furthermore, the editor or creator would feel less pressure to respond to you than in a face-to-face encounter. Most feedback in mass communication is indirect; advertisers, for example, gauge the impact of their messages by tracking sales of advertised products, and television producers depend on ratings data such as the Nielsen ratings.

Gatekeepers Determine Which Messages Are Sent

A second important difference between mass and interpersonal communication is that most messages that succeed in gathering large, diverse audiences are usually developed, or at least financed, by skilled professionals working for large organizations. The producers of mass messages are often called **gatekeepers,** because they determine which messages will be delivered to media consumers, how those messages will be constructed, and when they will be delivered (see Figure 1.2). Sponsors, editors, producers, reporters, and executives all have the power to influence mass messages. These messages are shaped by a wide range of economic, ethical, and legal considerations that will be discussed later in this chapter as well as throughout this book.

Mass Media Have Wide Impact

Finally, mass communication has the potential for far greater impact than interpersonal communication, if only because of the larger audience and the professional nature of the messages. This impact might be seen in audience pleasure or buying behavior, or it might be seen in an unintentional effect, such as a young child's imitating the violent behavior seen in a favorite TV show or video game. As the model of mass communication in Figure 1.2 suggests, this impact becomes part of the feedback sent to the source, perhaps as news reports about studies into the effects of media. We will continue our examination of the impact of the media in Chapter 2 of this book.

Mediated Interpersonal Communication

Mediated interpersonal communication is the sharing of personal messages through some form of interposed device. We speak to close friends over the telephone, we e-mail friends and send text messages across the nation and around the world. Mediated interpersonal communication does not involve face-to-face

In what ways does mass communication differ from interpersonal communication?

SELF QUIZ

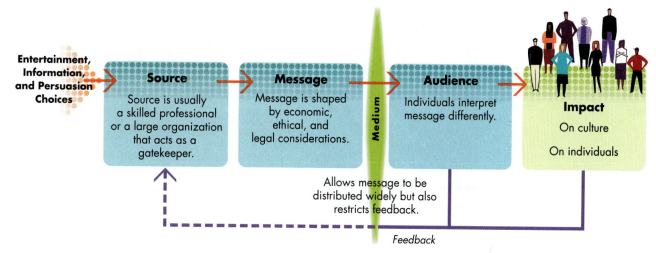

FIGURE 1.2 Traditional Model of Mass Communication This model emphasizes the role of the gatekeeper and the restricted nature of feedback in mass communication. The gatekeeper chooses from the unlimited array of entertainment, information, and persuasion that audience members might be exposed to. Feedback from audience members is restricted. Media impact affects both individuals and entire cultures, and also acts as a form of feedback.

contact; even with a webcam, you are talking to merely a facsimile of another person. Mediated interpersonal communication is also different from mass communication. In mediated interpersonal communication, a message doesn't go out to a large audience, it isn't produced by professionals, and it allows a considerable amount of interaction and feedback (although not as much as face-to-face communication).

Converging Communication Media

The distinction between mass and interpersonal communication is much fuzzier today than in the past. Digital technology is creating a new kind of mediated communication. The word *convergence* refers to any type of coming together. In media studies, **convergence** refers to three types of mergers: those involving technologies, industries, and content.

The convergence of technologies refers to the merging of computer, telephone, and mass media technologies, such as in BlackBerries, Treos, and multiuse cell phones. The convergence of industries refers to corporate mergers that allow companies to combine their media technologies, such as when a cable TV company acquires Internet and telephone divisions.

mediated interpersonal communication
The sharing of personal messages through an interposed device.

convergence
The merging of technologies, industries, and content, especially within the realms of computer, telephone, and mass media.

The era of convergence is seen in the superdesk of the Tampa (Florida) *Tribune.* News is distributed to the company's Internet, TV, and newspaper outlets from the starship-like deck.

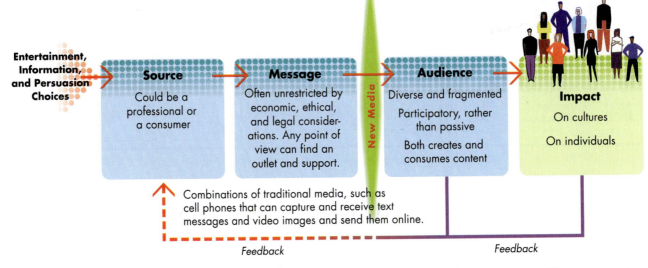

Entertainment, Information, and Persuasion Choices

Source
Could be a professional or a consumer

Message
Often unrestricted by economic, ethical, and legal considerations. Any point of view can find an outlet and support.

New Media

Audience
Diverse and fragmented

Participatory, rather than passive

Both creates and consumes content

Impact
On cultures

On individuals

Combinations of traditional media, such as cell phones that can capture and receive text messages and video images and send them online.

Feedback   *Feedback*

FIGURE 1.3 Converged Media Model of Communication New media have changed the traditional model of mass communication, especially in terms of the diversity of messages and the function of the audience.

The convergence of content is a natural extension of technological convergence. It involves bringing together mediated interpersonal messages, including telephone and e-mail, with the messages of traditional mass communication, such as text and television. The social networking site Facebook, for example, combines traditional yearbooks with community Web sites, e-mail, blogs, bulletin boards, audio, and video. Figure 1.3 provides a model of converged media communication and its implications.

In fact, the Internet—or, more precisely, the communication network known as the World Wide Web—is a prime example of a converging medium. On the one hand, the Web is used for interpersonal communication. It is our conduit for e-mail, chat groups, and instant messages. Electronic discussion groups, organized by and for people with a specific interest, address an astonishing range of topics, from antique cash registers to Lithuanian literature to hip-hop music. But the Web is also a mass medium. Both individuals and organizations can create Web sites that have the potential to reach millions of users. Elaborate Web sites created by professionals include the sites of major corporations such as Microsoft, Time Warner, and Yahoo. We will focus on both traditional mass media and converged media throughout this book. Converging media are creating important changes, and we can learn a lot about what to expect from these changes by examining how media have changed in the past.

MEDIA HISTORY

Each chapter of this book will contain a brief history of the topic under consideration. We study media history because very often an understanding of today's media practices can be found there. We also examine this history because the development of each medium changes society, sometimes in subtle and unexpected ways, such as the way the telegraph changed journalistic writing (see the Close-Up on History box). A brief overview of some important dates in media history is provided in the Milestones in Media History on pages 14–15. We will expand on these events in subsequent chapters, each of which will have its own Close-Up on History and Milestones in History boxes.

SELF QUIZ What is meant by *convergence*, and why is it important in mass communication?

Understanding Today's Media *Industries*

Media industries exist on a number of different levels—including local (the small-town newspaper), regional (radio station groups that cover several states), and national (the broadcast television networks)—but it is the global level that is key to understanding today's media business. Travelers abroad are often surprised to see advertisements for such U.S. products as McDonald's hamburgers and Coca-Cola, and to see U.S.-style advertisements for local products, not to mention *The Simpsons, The OC,* and countless other television programs dubbed into the language of the country they are visiting. Many global media trends, such as big-budget, action-adventure movies and rap music, start in America. The United States is the only country in the world that is a net exporter of mass media products, such as movies, recordings, TV programs, and books—it sends out far more media materials to other countries than it imports. The U.S. trade surplus in media is in the tens of billions of dollars. The American domination of world media products has been so strong and so long-lasting (it was true for most of the 20th century) that global mass media has been called the American Empire.[8]

AMERICAN DOMINANCE OF WORLD MEDIA

There are several reasons why American media products dominate the global scene. One is the English language, which is spoken by more people

Technology and Change: The Telegraph

New media technology has changed society at many points in history. Technological events have ranged from the invention of the printing press in the 15th century to the adoption of the World Wide Web in the 1990s. The introduction of the telegraph in 1844 is especially instructive because it contributed to a new style of journalistic writing and established wire services for newspapers.

Samuel Morse, a well-known artist and inventor, worked on his telegraph throughout the 1830s, and by 1844 he had talked the U.S. Congress into financing a line from Baltimore, Maryland, to Washington, D.C. Morse's first message to Congress, sent in the code of dots and dashes that he had invented, was "What hath God wrought!" Telegraph lines carrying messages in Morse code were soon spreading across the country.

By increasing the speed of long-distance communication from that of a team of horses to that of an electric impulse, the telegraph transformed the way Americans exchanged information and did business.

News from faraway places was available very quickly, and could affect everything from a banker's choice of investments on Wall Street to an Iowa farmer's decision to plant soybeans or corn. The telegraph even changed the way people wrote, not only in journalism but also in literature. The lean, "telegraphic" writing style that the new medium encouraged eventually became fashionable and replaced the flowery, wordy writing of the 19th century. The inverted-pyramid style of newswriting—in which the most important facts (the who, what, when, where, why, and how) are squeezed into the first paragraph of the story—began because of the telegraph's lack of reliability. Reporters using the telegraph had to make sure that the most important information would be transmitted before the line went down.

The telegraph made possible the formation of wire services, which were organizations that sent local newspapers stories from far away. The Associated Press of New York, the first wire service, was formed in 1848 when six New York newspapers, all of which had

worldwide than any other language. English isn't the most spoken first language (Mandarin Chinese takes that honor), but it is by far the most spoken second language, which makes it easier to export U.S. media products. There are several English-speaking countries, however, and none of them have America's global media dominance. There are three primary reasons for this dominance: freedom of expression, audience diversity, and big business's ability to produce big-budget popular entertainment.

Freedom of Expression Has Worldwide Appeal

The freedom available to U.S. media practitioners allows them to create a wide range of movies, books, and other media products on a variety of topics, with limited interference by the government. Also, the American notion of freedom that is evident in so many of its media products has been embraced internationally, especially by young people, with freedom's inherent

The United States sends out far more media materials to other countries than it imports.

appeal to those who wish to rebel against tradition, oppressive rules, and the status quo. Many critics consider media freedom in the United States a

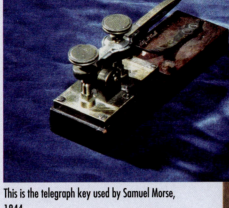

This is the telegraph key used by Samuel Morse, 1844.

correspondents in Boston, agreed to share one correspondent in order to save money. The enterprise worked so well that the Associated Press (AP) became a nationwide association in which hundreds of papers shared their local news and correspondents. Before the AP, America still had a partisan press, which meant that most papers had a decidedly political point of view. With the formation of the AP, however, each paper had to make its articles appropriate for other papers, on all sides of the political spectrum. Thus began the journalistic ideal of **objectivity,** the writing style that separates fact from opinion.

Samuel Morse, in an 1866 oil over photograph by Mathew Brady.

mixed blessing, however, especially when it goes too far, such as when it exposes children to violence and pornography. Religious fundamentalists around the world have been especially offended by sexual representations in American media products. Many other cultural critics have complained about the glorification of criminal behavior and crass materialism in U.S. products.

objectivity
Writing style that separates fact from opinion.

Partisan Press: Papers that had a decidedly political point of view.

Producing for a Diverse Audience

U.S. media producers have to make products for a diverse audience that incorporates a wide range of backgrounds and tastes. American movies, recordings, books, and magazines must be sold to various ethnic, racial, and religious minorities, and to women as well as men. To this end, media producers have increasingly involved people with different backgrounds in production decisions. There is still progress to be made, however. In many media industries, women and minorities are underrepresented as employees. Many critics believe that media have also been, and continue to be, used as powerful instruments for preserving the social order in which women and minorities have been relegated to subordinate positions in American society. Still, with the progress that has been made, the likelihood that U.S. media products will be successful overseas is far greater than that for the media products of less diverse societies.

1456 In Germany, Johannes Gutenberg's printing press allows books to be mass-produced, and sets in motion a revolution in the way people learn and think.

1741 The first magazines in America are published, creating a new medium that has greater durability than a newspaper, but fewer pages than a book.

| 1450 | 1500 | 1550 | 1600 | 1650 | 1700 |

1690 *Publick Occurrences*, the first newspaper in America, is shut down by the government after one issue.

American media continue to be popular overseas. This is the German poster for *Over the Hedge* (2006).

cultural imperialism
The displacement of a nation's customs with those of another country.

Big Business and Popular Entertainment

The big-business structure of the American economy makes it possible to finance and produce expensive media products. Furthermore, the large size of the American market encourages big-budget productions. Critics contend that these impressive budgets do not always correlate to high quality, but media practitioners point out that they do seem to produce the most popular entertainment worldwide.

CULTURAL IMPERIALISM

The global dominance of American media is often resented overseas. Many countries dislike America's incursion into their native cultures, accusing the United States of **cultural imperialism,** that is, the displacement of their traditional culture with American culture. France and Canada, for example, have both imposed limits on the importation of U.S. television programming.

A fear of cultural imperialism is often blamed for anti-Americanism overseas. In 2002, the Pew Research Center for People and the Press conducted a Global Attitudes Survey and found that "America is nearly universally admired for its technological achievements and people in most countries say they enjoy U.S. movies, music and television programs." However, the survey also found that "the spread of U.S. ideas and customs is disliked by majorities in almost every country included in this survey. That sentiment is prevalent in friendly nations such as Canada (54 percent) and Britain (50 percent), and even more so in countries where America is broadly disliked, such as Argentina (73 percent) and Pakistan (81 percent)."[9]

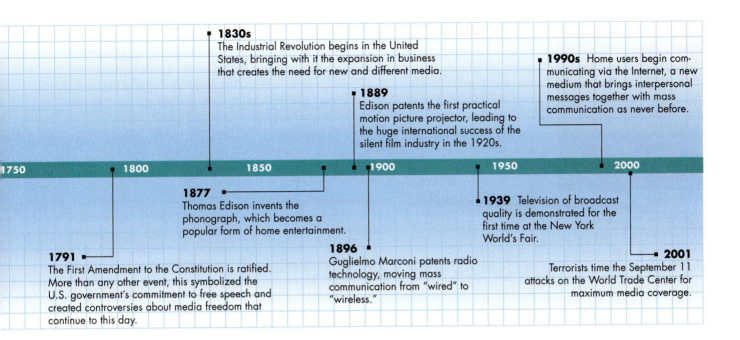

1830s
The Industrial Revolution begins in the United States, bringing with it the expansion in business that creates the need for new and different media.

1889
Edison patents the first practical motion picture projector, leading to the huge international success of the silent film industry in the 1920s.

1990s Home users begin communicating via the Internet, a new medium that brings interpersonal messages together with mass communication as never before.

1750   1800   1850   1900   1950   2000

1877
Thomas Edison invents the phonograph, which becomes a popular form of home entertainment.

1939 Television of broadcast quality is demonstrated for the first time at the New York World's Fair.

1791
The First Amendment to the Constitution is ratified. More than any other event, this symbolized the U.S. government's commitment to free speech and created controversies about media freedom that continue to this day.

1896
Guglielmo Marconi patents radio technology, moving mass communication from "wired" to "wireless."

2001
Terrorists time the September 11 attacks on the World Trade Center for maximum media coverage.

Indonesian Muslims protest the local edition of *Playboy* in Jakarta in April 2006. The poster reads, "Declaration of war against *Playboy* and porn magazines."

Thomas Edison events the phonograph in 1877

This would suggest a serious downside to the popularity of American cultural products overseas. For example, one expert pointed out that American movies "are seen by a lot of foreign countries as the ultimate propa-

Many countries accuse the United States of cultural imperialism: the displacement of their traditional culture with American culture.

ganda weapon, and a device to corrupt their cultures."[10] One study of teens from 12 countries found that many of the teens considered Americans materialistic, sexually immoral, and often criminal people who seek to dominate other cultures. That study found popular media at least partly to blame for that perception.[11]

On the *Media World* DVD that accompanies this book (track 19), Tom Brokaw investigates why the United States is viewed negatively overseas.

FOREIGN MEDIA IN THE UNITED STATES

In spite of the global dominance of U.S. media, the foreign media have had great influence in the United States. Films from other lands, including France, Italy, and China, are often of exceptional quality and inspire American directors, many of whom come from abroad. British groups have been extremely influential in the pop music scene, and you only have to watch Public Broadcasting Service (PBS) channels to see the British influence in U.S. television programming. Also, in commercial TV, hits such as *American Idol* and *Who Wants to Be a Millionaire* all began in England.

The globalization of media businesses is also by no means one-way. Foreign companies have purchased a considerable portion of America's media. Four of the top five book publishing houses are now owned by overseas companies. Japan's Sony Corporation owns a major movie studio (formerly Columbia Pictures) and a major U.S. music producer (formerly called CBS Records). Five of the six largest recording companies are foreign owned. News Corporation, which is owned by Rupert Murdoch, an Australian, owns dozens of U.S. newspapers and magazines, as well as the Fox television and movie operations. Several foreign corporations own advertising companies in the United States.

Many critics are less concerned about foreign ownership of U.S. media than they are about the sheer size of international media conglomerates. It is important to understand both why media businesses grow large and who owns them.

REASONS FOR CORPORATE MEDIA GROWTH

Simply stated, media businesses have a tendency to grow large because they can make more money that way. The three primary reasons why growth is profitable involve economies of scale, synergy, and global competition.

Economies of Scale Increase Profits

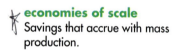

economies of scale
Savings that accrue with mass production.

Economies of scale are the savings that come with mass production. When large numbers of units are produced, each unit costs less. Not even the richest show-off in the world would pay $60 million to watch a movie, yet that is the cost of the first copy of a typical Hollywood movie today. Each subsequent copy costs only a few thousand dollars and is viewed by thousands of people. In the same way, the first copy of the typical daily newspaper costs tens of thousands of dollars, but after thousands of copies are made, each copy costs pennies. This rule of first-copy cost is true in all media. The first book, magazine, recording, or television program has an enormous cost, including payments to creative personnel such as writers, editors, and actors.

A company that is big enough to make lots of copies of something is able to make those copies cheaply and earn high profits on them. Thus, a newspaper that buys up a competitor is probably buying that paper's customers more than its equipment, real estate, and personnel. If the company can simply sell the same paper it was originally producing to twice as many customers, it can often double its profit. This is one reason why media takeovers and mergers are frequently accompanied by news of massive layoffs of employees—those people are part of the "savings" in economies of scale. Right after AOL and Time Warner merged in 2001, for example, 2,000 people were immediately laid off. When NBC merged with Universal in 2004, the new conglomerate announced similar potential savings.

Synergy: Parts Working Together

Synergy, which comes from the Greek word meaning "to work together," refers to any combination of forces that results in a whole that is more than the sum of its parts. One form of synergy is seen in the creative bonus that results from combining personnel with different types of knowledge or skills. This kind of synergy can be seen in a college environment when a group of students works together on a class project. Such a group allows people with different talents to inspire each other to new levels of creativity and productivity; they produce more as a group than they could as individuals working alone.

Businesses merge with other businesses to take advantage of this phenomenon. NBC Television had synergy in mind in 2001 when it bought Telemundo, a Spanish cable network; NBC wanted to combine its programming executives with Telemundo's experts in reaching the international Spanish-speaking audience. Not all plans for synergy work out, however. When AOL merged with Time Warner in 2001, both sides were looking for the synergy that would result when AOL's Internet experts began working with Time Warner's information and entertainment experts. The merger cost stockholders billions of dollars when AOL's business lost value and Time Warner could do nothing to help it. (AOL's profits came mostly from providing dial-up Internet connections, which became less popular when high-speed connections became available.)

Another form of synergy results when selling the product in one form promotes sales of the product in some other form, a process sometimes called **cross-merchandizing** or cross-promotion. Book companies published some of the earliest magazines and used them to promote their products. Movie studios buy publishing houses so that they can sell their stories in both movie and print forms. Many movies are made from books, and a movie's success will increase sales of the book significantly. All media are related in this way. Television networks purchase much of their programming from movie studios, and radio stations are largely dependent on recorded music.

synergy
A combination in which the whole is more than the sum of its parts.

cross-merchandizing
Promoting a product in one form to sell it in some other form.

Global Competition Favors Larger Companies

Another reason media companies seek to grow large is to confront global competition. Disney competes with Time Warner and Sony not just in the United States but all over the world; these companies believe that they have to be big to compete on the global stage. Competition is especially fierce in media industries, in which a large percentage of new products have a tendency to fail. Most movies lose money, as do most books, recordings, and television programs. Most new magazines fail within a year or two. New products have to be developed constantly, and when one of them becomes a moneymaker, the corporation has to exploit it in as many markets as possible. When the Harry Potter books became fantastically successful, for example, Time Warner was able to produce blockbuster films and sell related toys throughout the world.

SELF QUIZ What are the reasons for corporate media growth, and how does each reason relate to media products?

PATTERNS OF OWNERSHIP

As media businesses grow, they become structured in various patterns of ownership, including groups, conglomerates, monopolies, and oligopolies.

Groups and Chains

One way that media companies grow is through **group ownership** (also called chain ownership), a system in which one company owns the same

group ownership
The acquisition of the same type of business in more than one market area by one company.

TABLE 1.1 Vertical Integration Vertical integration occurs when companies own both production and distribution facilities, as in any of the *columns* in this table.

Books	Newspapers/ Magazines	Movies/ Television	Recordings/ Radio	Internet
Literary agencies	News services/ syndicates	Talent agencies	Talent agencies	Web site designers
Publishing houses	Publishers	Studios	Record labels	Web portals
Printers/paper mills	Printers/paper mills	Film/video manufacturers	Recording manufacturers	Information services
Book clubs	Subscription/ delivery services	Distributors/networks	Record clubs/networks	Internet service providers
Bookstores	Newsstands	Theaters/television stations	Record stores/ radio stations	E-commerce sites

YOU'VE GOT MAIL! ALSO, TIME, CNN, HBO, ICQ, WARNER BROS., NETSCAPE, SPORTS ILLUSTRATED, PEOPLE, AOL INSTANT MESSENGER, AOL MOVIEFONE, TBS, TNT, THE CARTOON NETWORK, WARNER MUSIC GROUP, SPINNER, WINAMP, FORTUNE, ENTERTAINMENT WEEKLY, COMPUSERVE, DIGITAL CITY, AOL.COM, AND LOONEY TUNES!

© The New Yorker Collection 2000
Mick Stevens from cartoonbank.com.
All Rights Reserved.

conglomerates
Large companies that own many different types of businesses.

vertical integration
A business model in which a company owns different parts of the same industry.

antitrust laws
Laws that prohibit monopolistic practices in restraint of trade.

type of medium in more than one market area. Many newspapers are part of a group; the Gannett Corporation, which publishes *USA Today,* owns a group of 90 newspapers. Television stations are also owned in groups (including the Gannett group, which owns 22 of them), as are radio stations (Clear Channel owns 1,200); movie studios (Disney owns four); and movie theaters (General Cinema, Cineplex-Odeon, and United Artists each own thousands).

Conglomerates

Conglomerates are large companies involved in many different types of businesses. Conglomerates form in various ways. One way is through vertical integration.

Vertical Integration Includes Parts of the Same Business

Vertical integration is a business model in which a company owns different parts of the same industry, thus controlling both production and distribution facilities (see Table 1.1). When a newspaper publisher buys a paper plant, an ink plant, a trucking company, and a string of newsstands, that company becomes vertically integrated. NBC integrated vertically when it bought Universal Studios, giving it both the Universal production facilities and the NBC television network and cable channels (including Bravo and Telemundo) to distribute the programming that Universal produces.

There is nothing illegal about vertical integration as long as it is not used to compete unfairly against other companies. When a firm vertically integrates for the sole purpose of making it impossible for other companies to compete with them, however, **antitrust laws** are activated. In the 1940s five large movie studios bought up 70 percent of U.S. movie theaters and collaborated to control which films were shown, where, and for how long. They made it impossible for competitors' films to be shown anywhere. The government

TABLE 1.2 Horizontal Integration Horizontal integration occurs when a company owns many different types of businesses, as in any of the *rows* in this table.

Books	Newspapers/ Magazines	Movies/ Television	Recordings/ Radio	Internet
Literary agencies	News services/ syndicates	Talent agencies	Talent agencies	Web site designers
Publishing houses	Publishers	Studios	Record labels	Web portals
Printers/ paper mills	Printers/paper mills	Film/video manufacturers	Recording manufacturers	Information services
Book clubs	Subscription/ delivery services	Distributors/ networks	Record clubs/ networks	Internet service providers
Bookstores	Newsstands	Theaters/ television stations	Record stores/ radio stations	E-commerce

prosecuted the studios for antitrust violations and forced them to sell their theaters. In that case, the government found that the movie studios were using their vertical integration "in restraint of trade," which is legal jargon for "to destroy the competition," which, according to the antitrust laws, is illegal. A more recent example involved Clear Channel, the largest owner of both radio stations and concert productions. When the company was accused in 2004 of keeping off its radio playlists artists that signed with other concert promoters, the government initiated an antitrust lawsuit against Clear Channel.[12]

Horizontal Integration Involves Different Types of Businesses

Another way conglomerates form is through **horizontal integration,** which occurs when a company buys many different types of businesses (see Table 1.2). In the case of horizontal media integration, the newspaper company doesn't buy a paper mill; it buys a radio station or a TV station. Horizontal

horizontal integration Corporate growth through the acquisition of different types of businesses.

Concentration of media ownership can result in one company's having too much power to sway public opinion.

integration occurs in media businesses when one company wants to sell its properties and products across different types of media. When a television network buys a publishing company to produce books about its television shows, it is integrating horizontally.

A broader form of horizontal integration occurs when a company owns businesses outside of the world of communication. For example, NBC is owned by General Electric (GE), which makes not only lightbulbs but also engines for the F-16 Fighter jet, the Abrams tank, the Apache helicopter, the U2 Bomber, and the Unmanned Combat Air Vehicle (UCAV). Critics are especially concerned about this broader type of horizontal integration, because it means that GE's journalism units are reporting on a wide variety of topics (such as debates about military spending) that affect the conglomerate's other businesses.

Combined Integration Is Most Common

Most conglomerates combine horizontal and vertical integration. The Disney Corporation, for example, owns not only a group of movie studios but also

movie theme parks where cartoon movie characters such as Mickey Mouse and Snow White are featured and the topics of the movies become attractions. In fact, the *Pirates of the Caribbean* movies were based on a long-standing Disney theme park ride. Disney also owns recording studios that sell movie soundtracks and publishing companies that produce books and magazines about its movies and movie characters. It even owns a professional hockey team, the Mighty Ducks, which was a subject of one of its movies. These are classic forms of horizontal integration. But Disney also owns the ABC television network and several cable channels that show its movies, as well as video companies that distribute those movies in video form. It also owns a chain of retail stores that sell its videos, recordings, and books. Because these businesses are involved in both the production and distribution of Disney films, they are classic forms of vertical integration. Both vertical and horizontal integration of large conglomerates worry critics who believe that concentration of media ownership results in one company's having too much power to sway public opinion.

Monopolies

A **monopoly** is an economic situation in which one company dominates an entire industry. Monopolies can occur locally, regionally, nationally, or globally. The Microsoft Corporation currently has a global monopoly in computer operating systems: More than 90 percent of all computers are equipped with one of Microsoft's Windows systems. AT&T was a national telephone monopoly until 1984, when it was broken up into regional companies following a lengthy government antitrust action. Many local newspapers are monopolies in their communities. Some monopolies, such as local cable and telephone systems, were planned in conjunction with local governments. To entice companies to build the initial system, the community granted them the monopoly, promising that no competing company would be allowed in. Most planned monopolies are regulated in some way. Early telephone and cable companies, for example, had regulated rates. A monopoly becomes illegal only when it performs an action in restraint of trade, which, as mentioned earlier, is defined as unfairly seeking to destroy another company.

Oligopolies

An **oligopoly** is a economic situation in which a small number of companies dominate an industry. Many media industries today are essentially oligopolies. Six movie studios receive 90 percent of American film revenues, and four major music studios receive 80 percent of recording revenues. There are just six major book publishers, and the television industry was an oligopoly of three networks—ABC, CBS, and NBC—from the 1950s through the 1970s. Television has diversified since then, especially because of cable, but today it is still mostly an oligopoly of five companies: Disney/ABC,

monopoly
An economic situation in which one company dominates an entire industry.

CONSIDER THIS

Media conglomerates are getting bigger and bigger, with more and more media companies concentrated in fewer hands. Is this a positive or a negative trend? Why?

oligopoly
An economic situation in which a small number of companies dominate an industry.

Viacom/CBS, NBC Universal, Time Warner, and News Corporation (see Fact File 1.1).

Entrepreneurial Start-Ups

As powerful as media conglomerates are, not all media are in the hands of giant corporations. Some are owned by entrepreneurs (from the French for "enterpriser"). An **entrepreneur,** defined as an individual who invests the time and money to start a new business, is usually someone who is willing to take a considerable risk on a new idea. Some media, such as broadcast, cable, or satellite properties, are now so expensive that only the richest individuals or corporations could own them, and even then the majority of start-ups fail. There is still some opportunity for entrepreneurial start-ups, however.

entrepreneur
An individual who invests the time and money to start a new business.

When large corporations buy up their successful competition, it often creates opportunities for entrepreneurs to step in and fill a need. Entrepreneurs have started successful local newspapers and book publishing houses. They start up hundreds of new magazines each year. Entrepreneurs have formed small movie companies and made successful films for a small fraction of what a Hollywood film costs. There have been numerous entrepreneurial start-ups in the advertising business, where small boutique agencies have been established in living rooms. The computer and Internet industries have tended to be extremely entrepreneurial. Steve Jobs and Steve Wozniak started Apple Computer out of Job's garage, and two graduate students, Jerry Yang and Dave Filo, created Yahoo! in a tiny trailer office at Stanford University. Many students get their start in media industries through entrepreneurial activities (see the Close-Up on Industry box).

SELF QUIZ What are the primary forms of media ownership, and what are the main characteristics of each?

MEDIA AND GOVERNMENTS AROUND THE WORLD

The ways the media serve the public are highly dependent on the type of relationship media organizations have with government. Several types of media–government relationships exist in the world today.

Government Ownership

At one extreme, a system calls for the government to own and operate the media. Communist countries such as China, North Korea, and Cuba tend to follow this model, as did Afghanistan under the Taliban. The idea behind government control over mass communication is that media exist to serve the government. Truth and public service are both determined by what government officials decide is good for society.

Private Ownership, Government Control

A slightly less extreme system of media control allows the media to be privately owned but still requires media organizations to be controlled by the government. This is the media–government relationship preferred in dictatorships such as that in Iraq under Saddam Hussein. Just as in the system of government ownership, the government determines the information, entertainment, and persuasion that will be presented through the media. Generally, in such a system, voices that might challenge government authority are censored. The majority of countries today have either a government-owned or a government-controlled media system.[13]

Media Conglomerates

These five media conglomerates control an enormous number of well-known properties. They are all products of both vertical and horizontal integration.

Company	Some Holdings of Interest
Time Warner (www.timewarner.com)	**Movie studios:** Warner Bros., Castle Rock, New Line **Television:** Time-Warner Cable, Road Runner, television production studios, HBO, CNN, Cinemax, Cartoon Network, TBS, TNT, Court TV, CW Television Network (with CBS), PrimeStar Satellite TV, CNN Airport Network, AOL-TV **Sports teams and events:** Atlanta Braves, Atlanta Hawks, Goodwill Games **Magazines:** *Time, Life, People, Sports Illustrated, Essence, Fortune, Entertainment Weekly, In Style, Money, Popular Science, Yachting, Mad Magazine, DC Comics,* and 135 others **Book publishing:** Time-Life Books, Book-of-the-Month Club, Sunset Books, Bookspan **Internet companies:** AOL, AIM, CompuServe, AOL International (with services in 10 countries and 5 languages); Netscape, ICQ (an instant messaging system), Digital City, Moviefone, MapQuest, Amazon.com (partial) and dozens of other major partnerships; CNN.com, Spinner.com, Winamp, and others
Viacom/CBS (www.viacom.com, www.cbs.com)	**Viacom** **Movie studios:** Paramount Pictures, Dreamworks, and Paramount Home Video **Movie theaters:** National Amusements, 1,300 screens **Video rentals:** Blockbuster Video stores **Television:** Paramount Television, Spelling Entertainment, and Big Ticket Television **Cable networks:** MTV, Nickelodeon, VH1, BET, Logo, TV Land, Spike TV, Comedy Central, Country Music Television (CMT) **Book publishing:** The Free Press, Pocket Books **Theme parks and rides:** Paramount Parks **Internet:** iFilm.com, NeoPets.com, Xfire online gaming platform, gametrailers.com. **CBS** **Television:** CBS Television Network, CW Network (with Warner Bros.), 39 local stations; King World syndication **Radio:** CBS Radio (179 radio stations and the CBS, NBC, and Westwood One networks, among others) **Cable networks:** Showtime, The Movie Channel, FLIX, Sundance Channel **Internet:** CBS.com, CBSNews.com, CBS Sportsline.com, UPN.com. **Book publishing:** Simon & Schuster **Billboards and transit advertising:** CBS Outdoor

Libertarian

At the other extreme, a third type of system, the libertarian system, calls for media to be privately owned and to be free of government control. A purely libertarian system, however, exists only in theory. The United States probably comes closest to this ideal, but because of the nature of broadcast media and the power of media in general, no country allows its media to be entirely unregulated. In fact, most countries have a mixed model.

Mixed Model

Most countries today have varying degrees of government control and ownership of media. In China, for example, most media are government owned and operated, but private ownership of some media is now being allowed. The United States also has a mixed model. Although most U.S. media are pri-

Company	Some Holdings of Interest
The Walt Disney Company (www.disney.go.com)	**Movie studios:** Walt Disney Pictures, Touchstone Pictures, Hollywood Pictures, Miramax Film Corporation, Buena Vista home video **Television:** ABC Television Network, 10 owned stations **Cable networks:** ESPN, Disney Network, ABC Family, Toon Disney, SOAPnet **Radio:** 72 stations and Radio Disney, ESPN Radio, and ABC News Radio networks **Music labels:** Walt Disney Records, Buena Vista Records, Hollywood Records, Lyric Street Records **Sports teams:** Anaheim Mighty Ducks, Anaheim Angels **Theme parks and resorts:** Disney World, Disneyland, Disneyland Paris, Tokyo Disneyland, Disney Vacation Club, Disney Cruiseline, a Broadway theater **Book publishing:** Hyperion Books **Consumer products:** Disney Toys, The Baby Einstein Co.
News Corporation (www.newscorp.com)	**Movie studios:** 20th Century Fox Studios and Fox Studios **Television:** Fox Television Studios, Fox Television Network, 35 owned television stations; DirecTV and satellite and cable systems on five continents; Fox News Channel, Fox Movie Channel; Fox Sports Channels; FX, National Geographic Channel; Speed Channel **Internet:** MySpace.com **Magazines:** *TV Guide, The Weekly Standard,* and others **Newspapers:** world's leading publisher of English-language with operations in the United Kingdom, Australia, Fiji, Papua New Guinea and the United States, totaling more than 175 different newspapers that print more than 40 million papers a week, including the *New York Post* **Book publishing:** HarperCollins, William Morrow, Avon books, and others
NBC-Universal (www.nbcuni.com)	**Movie studios:** Universal Pictures, Focus Features, Rogue Pictures, Universal Studios Home Entertainment **Television:** NBC and Telemundo television networks, 26 owned television stations, Universal Television studios **Cable networks:** CNBC, MSNBC, USA Network, Sci Fi Channel, Bravo, Trio **Theme parks and resorts:** Universal theme parks and resorts, including Universal Hollywood **Other:** NBC is part of the General Electric (GE) conglomerate, which manufactures a complete line of home appliances, consumer electronics, and a variety of high-technology products, including electrical utility equipment, health care equipment, and aircraft engines. GE also provides financial services to businesses and consumers (including credit services to customers, retailers and auto dealers in over 35 countries).

Sources: Company Web sites as listed.

vately owned, the government owns and operates several media outlets, such as the U.S. Government Printing Office, the Armed Forces Radio and Television Network, Radio Free Europe, and Radio Free China. The U.S. government also regulates the privately owned broadcast media, although it does so in a much less repressive way than a government such as China's.

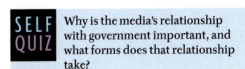

SELF QUIZ — Why is the media's relationship with government important, and what forms does that relationship take?

The U.S. Model

The American media and the American government are interrelated in three important ways: (1) Media businesses are subject to government regulation, (2) the media act as a potential watchdog or "fourth estate" of government, and (3) the media are the principal channels through which political campaigns take place.

Breaking into a Media Career

The DVD that accompanies this book contains a series of "Media Tours" that will take you inside several media companies. For those who are interested in pursuing careers in the media, here is a handful of guidelines and suggestions:

1. *Extracurricular activities.* First, take advantage of on-campus opportunities related to your field of interest. If you are interested in journalism, volunteer to work on your campus paper. Many campuses today also have radio stations and television studios where students can work. Some also have advertising and

> **Employers look for three things in prospective employees: good communication skills, good computer skills, and a well-rounded general education.**

public relations offices that will accept student volunteers or part-time workers. Sometimes a campus work experience will show you what area of a field you are interested in; other times, it might show you that you aren't really interested in that career, and guide you toward your true calling instead.

2. *Coursework.* Choose courses that develop the skills that are in demand. Most employers, in most types of companies, look for three things in prospective employees: good communication skills, good information technology (computer) skills, and a well-rounded general education. Courses in media-related

areas are also important, but not for the reasons you might think. Media employers (with the exception of most newspaper editors) usually do not believe you are going to learn how to perform a specific job in your college classes. The industries change too quickly for that, and employer needs tend to be too specific. Managers know they are going to have to train you to perform the functions they need done. However, coursework in media areas shows that you are interested in their industry, and that you have a general knowledge of what that industry is all about. These courses also enable you to work on special projects that you can list on a résumé and show to a potential employer. If you apply at a movie studio, for example, there is a good chance that an executive there might be interested in the research you did into new movie technologies or movies on the Web.

3. *Internships.* Take advantage of internship opportunities. Many colleges now offer the opportunity for students to work in a local industry and earn academic credit for doing so. Generally, the internship has to be set up both with the local company and with the college department. You should begin planning for your internship several months before you plan to take it. Find out what the policies are at your college and which local media companies are available. You can inquire at the employment or human relations department of the company to find out about their policies on internships.

Regulation

Government regulation of the media has always been minimal in the United States because of fears of censorship. **Censorship** is a broad term that includes any action that prohibits an act of expression from being made public (see the Close-Up on Controversy box, pp. 30–31). In spite of the fact that the free circulation of both political and artistic ideas is important in a democracy, the idea of dangerous speech has real meaning when that speech is delivered via mass media. For example, Geraldo Rivera, serving as a war correspondent for Fox News during the early days of the 2003 war in Iraq, drew a diagram in the sand to show where his unit was and how they would engage the enemy forces. The U.S. military felt this act endangered

censorship
Any action that prohibits an act of expression from being made public.

4. *Off-campus work.* Consider a part-time or temporary job at a local media company, such as the town newspaper or an Internet start-up. This type of job often does not involve college credit or the supervision of an academic adviser, but it does have the advantage of generating income and helping you gain valuable experience. Also, if there are no internships or jobs available, or if you are the type of person who likes to work for yourself rather than an employer, consider the entrepreneurial route. There are many media fields that lend themselves to self-starters. You could help save a failing barber shop, for example, by organizing an advertising and public relations campaign that includes raffles for free haircuts and circulars delivered to neighborhood homes. Working on a percentage of new business generated, you could earn a fair commission as well as invaluable experience to tell a future employer about.

5. *Networking.* In this sense the word *network* means to develop contacts with and open up lines of communication with industry professionals. They are usually busy people, but they often don't mind offering advice to college students. You might meet industry professionals when they come to your school as guest speakers, or you might arrange to interview media practitioners, if only over the telephone or by e-mail, for college projects and papers. Also, make a habit of reading the professional publications in your field of interest. Organizations such as the National Association of Broadcasters and the Newspaper Publishers Association of America have student branches; ask your professor about these, or find them through the Internet. Participating in conferences of student media organizations is also good for networking. If you happen to find a media professional you particularly admire and get along with, you might want to ask him or her to mentor you. A mentor is a professional you can seek out for advice on a regular basis.

6. *Outside reading.* Browse in your local library or bookstore for books about the media areas you are interested in. Useful books include Peterson's *Breaking into . . .* series, such as *Breaking into Television,* and books written by industry veterans, such as Dan Rather's *The Camera Never Sleeps.*

On the *Media World* DVD that accompanies this book (track 3.1, *Radio: Getting a Job*), Kevin McNeil, DJ and Production Director at WKNE-FM in Keene, NH, discusses the value of college media courses.

the lives of soldiers in the field, since enemy intelligence had access to Rivera's report. The correspondent was asked to leave the country (although later he was allowed to return).

Adversarial Relationship

While the U.S. government does have some regulatory control over the media, the media act as an unofficial watchdog of government actions. The founders of the United States—people such as Thomas Jefferson and Benjamin Franklin—envisioned the American media as a **fourth estate,** or unofficial fourth branch of government, designed to observe and report on the executive, legislative, and judicial branches. The media were supposed to

fourth estate
The press as an unofficial fourth branch of government.

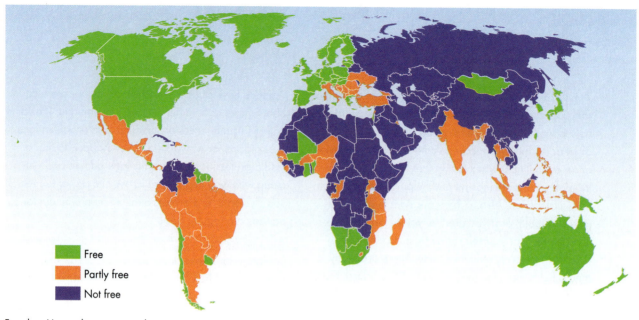

Free

Partly free

Not free

Freedom House does an annual survey of press freedom in the world. On their 2006 map, 73 countries (38 percent) were rated Free, 54 (28 percent) were rated Partly Free, and 67 (34 percent) were rated Not Free.

adversarial relationship
A relationship in which two parties contend with or oppose each other. In the United States, the media are expected to have an adversarial relationship with the government so that they can serve a watchdog role.

keep citizens informed about the actions and decisions of their elected representatives. In doing so, the media were expected to have an **adversarial relationship** with government, one in which the press followed objectives different from the objectives of those in power. An adversarial press is not supposed to act as a cheerleader or perform public relations for governmental administrations. Alexander Hamilton, one of the architects of the Constitution, pointed out that it is the duty of the press to examine each new law proposed by government. If the law is found wanting, Hamilton said, "it is essential to say, not only that the measure is bad and deleterious, but to hold up the person who is the author, that, in this our free and elective government, he may be removed from the seat of power."[14]

Some critics contend that today's press goes too far in its watchdog role, especially during times of war. President George W. Bush, for example, complained that the press was concentrating too much on the violence that followed the declared end to major conflict in Iraq in 2003. Others, however, say the press does not go far enough in its watchdog role. Many critics, in fact, felt that the press was too lenient in examining the Bush administration's motivations for invading Iraq in the first place.[15] Other critics point out that journalists knew about the abuse of Iraqi prisoners by Americans long before it became a major scandal in 2004, but failed to report it.[16]

Elections
Modern mass media, especially television, have reshaped American politics by allowing candidates to go directly to the people rather than working their way up through the ranks of the two major political parties. Some observers believe that much of this change is for the better: Candidates are no longer chosen solely by party leaders meeting in private, and political deals unknown to the public are less likely to be the basis of their candidacy. More Americans than ever before are exposed to what the candidates have to say. Critics, however, claim that media coverage has reduced political campaigns to sportslike contests, in which short, sensational sound bites distract voters from the substance of issues, while 30-second negative commercials cause voters to distrust all candidates.

One of the problems with "horse race" campaign coverage is that news organizations often rush to be the first to declare the winner, which leads to situations such as that of the 2000 presidential election, when both George W. Bush and Al Gore were declared winners on election night, only to have the election results placed in limbo for more than a month. Other critics say that media coverage gives inexperienced celebrities too great an advantage in elections, as when Jesse Ventura, a former professional wrestler, was elected governor of Minnesota, and Arnold Schwarzenegger, an actor, was elected governor of California. At the very least, most critics agree that under the current system only those rich enough (or skilled enough at fund-raising) to finance a highly publicized campaign, complete with tens of millions of dollars for television advertising, can win public office.

MEDIA AND THE AUDIENCE

An important yet often forgotten part of any media system is the audience. The audience determines the final meaning for any media message. It also determines whether a particular media product, or even the medium itself, will survive.

The Audience Is the Final Arbiter of Meaning

The producers of mediated messages—the writers, editors, directors, and so on—might have a particular message in mind, but it is the audience who decides what the final meaning is. In many cases, for example, the directors intended the films to be deadly serious, but the audience found them to be unintentionally funny. This was true of some of the campy science fiction movies of the 1950s.

The audience's perception of what a message means is notoriously unpredictable and varied. For example, the character Archie Bunker in the 1970s sitcom *All in the Family* was famous for spouting ethnic and racial slurs. The producers of that program intended for the audience to consider Archie's bigotry worthy of revulsion. A part of the audience, however, saw Archie as a man who spoke the truth, someone who said aloud what other people only thought. Thus, a character meant to expose and ridicule bigotry became a reinforcer for members of the audience who were already prejudiced.

Audiences have found some films to be unintentionally funny, even when the producers intended them to be frightening.

The Audience Has Economic Clout

The tendency of the audience to determine the meaning of media content is important because of the audience's economic clout. All media products, from book titles to Web sites, survive by audience preference. The print media's advertising rates are determined by circulation figures; television programs live and die by Nielsen ratings. Advertisers depend on the most basic audience vote of all: buying behavior. In fact, many critics consider audience influence too great today. These critics say that the media are continually giving audiences what they want, rather than what they need, what is good for them, or what is of an inherently high quality.

Audience Acceptance Establishes New Technology

The audience also plays a major role in the acceptance or rejection of new media technology. Even in their primitive stages, many new technologies evoked enough wonder in enough people to create a demand for advanced forms. Often the first reactions were pure curiosity: Voices from the air! Moving pictures from a piece of living room furniture! When stereophonic sound came out in the 1950s, the most popular records were simple sound effects, like crowd noises or thunder, moving from one stereo speaker to another. People were happy to watch test patterns on early TV, just as early scribes stood in awe of the first pages to come off the printing press.

There has been, however, considerable resistance to and fear of each new medium as well. Books were threatening to the religious leaders of the 15th century because they would allow the spread of literacy and thus undermine the church's unique authority. Radio's rock-and-roll music in the 1950s was considered a dangerous influence on youth, and that fear continues in reference to some of today's rap music. In the 1930s perceptions of the movies' violence and immorality fueled calls to ban certain films. Similar fears were heightened at various points in later decades when the same type of entertainment entered the home through television, video games, and the Internet.

Audience preferences will determine if handheld devices such as the Treo will become a viable medium for movies and television programs.

In what ways do audiences influence media industries?

Organized Audience Members Can Make a Difference

Audience members concerned about media content have wielded a considerable amount of power when they have banded together as consumer groups. Activist groups that have had a notable impact include the National Consumers Union, various religious and environmental groups, and racial and ethnic organizations. One group, Action for Children's Television, led by Peggy Charren, influenced the passage of the Children's Television Act of 1990, which required television broadcasters to schedule three hours a week of educational children's programming.

Activist groups have shown that audience members can have an impact. In fact, even one consumer can make a difference. Terry Rakolta, a midwestern housewife who became upset about the quality of television programming, led a boycott that prompted two advertisers to pull their ads from the

SELF QUIZ

sitcom *Married with Children*. These examples illustrate the potential influence of the media audience. They also lead to a consideration of the types of controversies that affect mass media today.

Media Controversies

There are many ways to look at the controversies that media create in today's society. Some controversies exist only in a particular medium. The transmission of computer viruses, for example, is a controversial issue that relates solely to users of computer networks such as the Internet. In fact, we will look at media controversies in the next eight chapters of this book on a medium-by-medium basis. Alternatively, many of these controversies can be organized into three separate types: impact issues, legal issues, and ethical issues.

IMPACT ISSUES DEAL WITH MEDIA'S INFLUENCE

Impact issues deal with media effects: how the media affect society and how they affect individuals within society. When we discuss impact issues throughout this book, our conclusions will be informed by various findings from the world of media research, designed to explain how various media distort reality and what effect these distortions have on society. You should also gain an enhanced understanding of the complexity of media impact and learn why overly general blanket criticisms don't make sense. The statement "Media violence causes increased violence in society," for example, is far too simplistic to apply in all matters of public policy. To truly understand media impact, you will need to know the findings from a variety of different types of research. We will address those in Chapter 2.

Violence, like that shown in this scene from the television program *The Shield*, tends to be an impact issue. Many researchers have tried to determine whether or not there is a link between violence in the media and violent behavior.

First Amendment
The part of the U.S. Constitution's Bill of Rights that guarantees freedom of speech.

LEGAL ISSUES DEAL WITH MEDIA LAW AND REGULATION

Legal issues deal with media practices—such as those in the areas of libel, invasion of privacy, and antitrust actions—that are governed by law. When discussing media law, we will look at the way basic tenets of the U.S. Constitution, especially those inherent in the **First Amendment,** have resulted in conflict. For example, the right of news media to report on trials and the right of the defendant to a fair trial are constantly at odds. Many conflicts are based on differing definitions of censorship (see the Close-Up on Controversy box). We will deal with media law throughout this book and focus on it specifically in Chapter 14.

ETHICAL ISSUES DEAL WITH THE MORALITY OF MEDIA

Numerous controversies deal with the basic idea of whether certain media practices are right or wrong, from a moral point of view. Truth telling as opposed to deception in media, for example, is usually an ethical issue. Ethics takes on a special importance in media studies because many observers believe that the media are at least partially to blame for the confusing state of today's morals. Conflicting messages confuse people about what's right and what's wrong. Many media products seem to glorify ethical behavior. The blockbuster *Spider-Man* movies, for example, exalted bravery, selflessness, and the nobility of the common person, while television magazine shows such as *60 Minutes* make a practice of uncovering and bringing down unethical people and practices. But other media products seem to promote the low end of the ethical continuum even more enthusiastically: television sitcoms, even innovative ones such as *Curb Your Enthusiasm,* smirk at white lies and manipulation, and prime-time cartoons such as *The Simpsons* appear to celebrate antisocial behavior by both children and adults. Meanwhile, in the world of popular music, gangsta rappers have been accused of bragging about rape, assault, and the murder of police officers, while they insist they are just depicting the reality of inner-city neighborhoods.

The Many Meanings of *Censorship*

We will look at the idea of censorship repeatedly in this book. In fact, it will become something of a recurrent theme, from the censorship of classic books such as James Joyce's *Ulysses,* to the censorship of films, radio shows, and Web sites.

Criticism is not censorship. Censorship is prior restraint or prosecution of communications activity by the government.

One of the things that make censorship such a big issue is the fact that it is defined differently by different people and therefore includes a wide range of behaviors. For a legal purist, censorship involves **prior restraint,** that is, forbidding or restricting a form of expression before it is made. Certainly the severest form of censorship, prior restraint by the government is also extremely rare in the United States. It has been attempted only a few times, and the courts have generally found it to be unconstitutional.

For some, governmental prosecution of communications activity after the fact is also a form of censorship. Thus, when some municipalities prosecuted theaters that exhibited Martin Scorsese's 1988 film *The Last Temptation of Christ* because they found it sacrilegious, there was a wide uproar. A judge overturned those prosecutions.[1] In Oklahoma, video store operators were prosecuted for renting out the German film *The Tin Drum* (1979) because of a two-minute scene in the film that suggested sexual conduct involving minors. This legal action also touched off an uproar and was overturned.

For others, censorship includes any restriction of communications activity, whether or not on the part of government. For these critics, infringements on the right of free speech are too serious to be ignored no matter who commits them. This is why, for example, fans of radio celebrity Howard Stern complained of censorship when Stern's show was taken off six radio stations owned by Clear Channel Communications in 2004. From a legal scholar's point of view, however, that was not censorship but merely a business decision

Some critics believe that popular television programs such as *The Simpsons* are guilty of ethical faults.

When discussing ethics, we will look at what the world's philosophers have told us about various ethical points of view. We will also look at the various codes of ethics that each media industry espouses, and we will consider how well the industries conform to those codes. We will deal with ethical issues throughout this book and focus specifically on them in Chapter 15.

THE INTERRELATIONSHIP OF IMPACT, LEGAL, AND ETHICAL ISSUES

Impact, legal, and ethical issues are interrelated. Laws are written to protect citizens from harmful media effects; for example, pornography involving child actors is outlawed. Ethically, it is considered wrong to present something to an audience that could have a harmful effect on them. This is essentially the argument used against portrayals of violence that might be viewed by children. You might say that ethical issues take impact and legal issues one step further, to a basic philosophical understanding of what the impact or law means in moral terms.

Because they are interrelated, some controversies can be analyzed from all three perspectives. Analyzing issues from the impact perspective, you might deal with these questions: "Does media violence cause violence in society?" or "Does the concentration of ownership of American media lead to less freedom of speech?" From a legal perspective, you might ask: "Should it

that Clear Channel had every right to make, in view of the fact that Stern's programming put the company at risk for heavy fines from the Federal Communications Commission.

For some media practitioners, any criticism of the media is considered a form of censorship. This is why the Southern Baptists, for example, have been accused of trying to impose censorship for saying that Walt Disney's films promote immorality. As one First Amendment expert has pointed out: "Technically, legally, only an agent of the state can censor. But the term has been loosened to mean that if you criticize somebody's work, and you imply in the course of the criticism that it should be done away with, people by and large would call that censorship."[2] From a legal point of view, of course, criticism is not censorship. Legally, censorship is prior restraint or prosecution of communications activity by the government.

Inherent in the controversy over censorship laws is the idea that freedom of speech involves a freedom to hear as well as a freedom to express. Thus when the Bush administration edited out information about global

Church members circle a bonfire of Harry Potter and other books outside a church in Alamogordo, New Mexico. The church's pastor called the books by author J. K. Rowling a "masterpiece of satanic deception." Some media practitioners consider this type of protest to be a form of censorship.

warming on an Environmental Protection Agency report in 2003, critics called that censorship, because the public no longer had access to that information.

[1]"Judge Overturns Ban on Film," *New York Times*, September 11, 1988, p. 34.
[2]Nat Hentoff, columnist for the *Village Voice* and author of many books on freedom of speech, quoted in William F. Powers, "War of the Words: But Bob Dole & Co. Are onto Something. The New Censorship: A Manifesto," in Thomas Beell, ed., *Messages 4: The Washington Post Media Companion* (Boston: Allyn & Bacon, 1997).

 SELF QUIZ What are the different definitions of *censorship*? What is the legal definition?

be legal to produce programs that might cause additional violence in society?" or "Should it be legal for media businesses to become so big that freedom of speech is threatened?" And from an ethical perspective, you might ask: "Is it morally right to produce programs that might cause additional violence in society?" or "Is it morally right for media businesses to become so big that the diversity of voices is lessened?"

prior restraint
Prevention of publication by the government.

SELF QUIZ How do impact issues, legal issues, and ethical issues differ? How are they related?

Mediated communication consists of mass communication, mediated interpersonal communication, and communication through converged media. Mass communication consists of messages that are transmitted through a medium to large, usually widespread, audiences.

Media companies tend to concentrate into large corporations and conglomerates for three profit-oriented reasons: economies of scale, synergy, and global competition. The ownership of today's media fits into several patterns: Group, or chain, ownership occurs when one company owns the same medium in different market areas; conglomerates form when companies buy up different types of businesses, in the form of either vertical or horizontal integration; monopolies are individual companies

Summing Up

that dominate a particular industry; and oligopolies occur when just a few companies dominate an industry. Entrepreneurs are risk-taking individuals who often start new companies to fill a niche left unserved by large corporations.

Governments are always key players in a nation's media. In the United States the media are regulated by government, act conversely as a watchdog over government, and form the channels through which election campaigns are conducted. The final component of a media system is the audience. The audience determines the final meaning of media content. The audience has economic influence, even in terms of the acceptance and rejection of new types of media. The audience also plays a key role in generating media controversies by protesting and forming groups to lobby against media practices.

Controversies tend to be based on three concerns. Impact issues concern how the media affect both individuals and society; common issues in this area involve violence and sex in movies, television, and recordings. Legal issues—such as libel, privacy, and antitrust laws—deal with media practices that have been prohibited or required by legislation. Ethical issues such as truth telling deal with the basic idea of whether media practices are morally right or wrong.

Key Terms

These terms are defined and indexed in the Glossary of key terms at the back of the book.

adversarial
   relationship *26*
antitrust laws *18*
censorship *24*
communication *6*
conglomerates *18*
convergence *9*
cross-merchandising *17*
cultural imperialism *14*
economies of scale *16*
entrepreneur *21*
feedback *6*

First Amendment *29*
fourth estate *25*
gatekeeper *8*
group ownership *17*
horizontal integration *19*
mass communication *7*
media *7*
media criticism *5*
media literacy *5*
mediated
   communication *7*

mediated interpersonal
   communication *9*
medium *7*
monopoly *20*
noise *6*
objectivity *13*
oligopoly *20*
prior restraint *31*
synergy *17*
vertical integration *18*

Electronic Excursions

HISTORY

Web Excursion

1. In your opinion, what are the major technological breakthroughs in American media history? Search for media history sources on the Web, or go directly to the Media History Project at www.mediahistory.umn.edu. Access the timeline and image gallery, and choose five scientific breakthroughs that seem to you to be most important.

   There is no single right answer to this question; be sure to explain why you selected the events you did.

INDUSTRY

Web Excursion

2. Search for sites devoted to media ownership, or go directly to Who Owns What, *The Columbia Journalism Review*'s guide to media companies at www.cjr.org/tools/owners/.* Who owns the media that you use most? Find the owners of your favorite newspaper, magazine, radio station, TV station, cable

service, and Web site. Any surprises? Any possible conflicts of interest? What could be the possible effect of that ownership?

Media World DVD Excursion

3. **Media Talk**—On the DVD that accompanies this book, view *Media Talk* track 7, *Media Professionals Discuss the State of the Media* (from NBC's *Today* show). In this clip, Steven Brill, editor of *Brill's Content;* Larry Sabato, a professor at the University of Virginia; and Cynthia Tucker, Editorial Page Editor of the *Atlanta Journal Constitution,* discuss media standards and ethics. What does Steven Brill mean by his statement, "We've gone from meat-and-potatoes journalism to hot-fudge-sundae journalism"?

CONTROVERSIES

Web Excursion

4. Search the Web for sites devoted to media criticism, or go directly to Cursor at www.cursor.org, to Alternet at www.alternet.org, to AIM at www.aim.org, or to FAIR at www.fair.org. Select a current media issue that you find noteworthy, and describe how it could be seen from all three perspectives (as an impact, a legal, and an ethical issue) discussed in the "Controversies" section of this chapter.

Media World DVD Excursion

5. **Media Talk**—On the DVD that accompanies this book, view *Media Talk* track 15, *Michael Moore Discusses Columbine and Mass Media.* On a visit to NBC's *Phil Donahue Show*, filmmaker Michael Moore discusses his views on the American media. One of Moore's arguments is that increased violence in the media leads to increased violence in our society. What are your thoughts on this argument?

ONLINE LEARNING CENTER WWW.MHHE.COM/RODMAN2

You may access these and additional Web excursions at the Online Learning Center for the book (www.mhhe.com/rodman2). Visit the student portion of this Web site to also access the *Interactive Timeline of Mass Media Milestones,* chapter highlights, self quizzes, and recommended readings, movies, and documentaries for this chapter.

*Some Web site addresses may change. When they do, please search for the Web site by name or topic on your favorite search engine.

Media Impact

Understanding Research and Effects

2

Chapter Highlights

HISTORY: A look at some of the early studies of media effects can help explain today's theory and research.

THEORY AND RESEARCH: Research findings have led to the development of various theories. When you look at a combination of these theories, the complexity of today's media effects becomes more apparent.

CONTROVERSIES: Media effects are not as straightforward and clear-cut as some observers have made them out to be. This has led to arguments, disagreements, and debates about the impact of media.

Grand Theft Auto: Theory and Research

A recent version of the Grand Theft Auto video game is set in a Miami-like virtual city during the 1980s. It features the voices of movie actors Ray Liotta and Dennis Hopper, as well as Phillip Michael Thomas, star of the 1980s television series *Miami Vice*. It took a staff of 50 employees two years to develop the game, which is perhaps the most realistic "first-person shooter" video game ever made.

Grand Theft Auto, or GTA as fans affectionately call it, allows players to smash windows, steal cars, sell cocaine, and distribute porn. It also allows them to kill police officers and to hire prostitutes for sex and then kill them, steal their money, and dump their bodies. Along the

Critics of Grand Theft Auto worry that it might bring out aggressive impulses in young people.

way, players can also kill pedestrians in drive-by shootings. The more people they kill and the more crimes they commit, the better they do at the game.

Critics of GTA worry that it might bring out aggressive impulses in young people. They believe it desensitizes kids to real-life violence, making it more likely that they will commit violence themselves. One U.S. senator said, "Games like Grand Theft Auto are particularly troubling because they go beyond just celebrating violence generally, and actually reward players for engaging in organized crime, murdering innocent people and other forms of perverse, antisocial behavior."[1]

There is certainly enough anecdotal evidence to support the critics' point of view. Two Tennessee teenagers told police that they were copying the game action of GTA when they carried shotguns to the interstate highway near their home and shot at passing traffic. They killed one motorist and seriously injured two others. A gang of teenagers in California who were charged with plotting carjackings and murders told police that they were inspired by the game. Another group of young people told police they played GTA before going out and robbing and killing random victims on the street.[2] Families of two people shot by teenagers who were avid players of the game are suing its manufacturer for $246 million.

You would think that the effects of this game are clear-cut, but they are not. They are the subject of a debate, and each side has cited research that supports its point of view. Critics of the game point to a study conducted at Iowa State University that supports the idea that violent video games lead to aggressive behavior. But video-game manufacturers point to studies by the Australian government and by Washington State University that find no connections to real-world violence.[3] The Entertainment Software Association, which represents the video-game industry, also points to research showing that youth crime has gone down even as video games have proliferated. There is even research to support the idea that video games like GTA are good for kids—at least one study has shown that they help kids develop visual attention.[4]

Some researchers are even interested in the lessons educators could learn from video games like GTA. As one researcher recently explained: "I'm interested in how games use learning principles. Think about it. Your standard computer game can take 50 hours to play. Imagine if a student loved spending 50 hours learning a language. We have a lot to learn from video games."[5]

Most parents and teachers, however, take a different point of view. As one mother said: "With all those images that flicker and flash, how will they be able to sit down and work with something that takes time to understand?"[6]

It's no wonder that people get confused about what research on media effects really means.

A gang of teenagers in California who were charged with plotting carjackings and murders told police that they were inspired by Grand Theft Auto.

This chapter examines the impact that media have on individuals and society. We will look at the history of media research, at current theories about media impact, and at some of the controversies surrounding both research and theory. As the opening example about Grand Theft Auto suggests, making sense out of media theory and research can be confusing. Do violent entertainment media cause violence in society? Do print media contribute to moral decline? Can you become addicted to Internet use? The answers to questions like these begin with a look at the history of media research.

A Brief History *of Media Research*

The history of media research provides some interesting insights into the effects of today's media. Because early studies were conducted in times when both the media and the methods of studying them were simpler, the answers they uncovered seem more straightforward than those presented in today's complex studies. Looking at these historic studies as a whole provides an excellent foundation for an understanding of media effects in today's media-saturated world.

EARLY STUDIES

Concerns about the impact of media are as old as the media themselves. Fifteenth-century church leaders thought printed Bibles would corrupt society; scholars and parents felt the same way about the first novels. Systematic research into media effects, however, did not begin until the 1920s. This early research was a reaction to the propaganda used during World War I. During the war, **propaganda** (information spread for the purpose of promoting a doctrine or cause) had been so blatant, and apparently so useful, on the part of both the Allies and their enemies, that people feared the media had become powerful enough to brainwash innocent people by influencing them in ways that they did not realize.[7] Experts in media research have identified

propaganda
Information that is spread for the purpose of promoting a doctrine or cause.

Early research into the effects of mass media was a reaction to the propaganda used by both sides during World War I. The German war poster on the left, from 1917, says "Help Us Win! Subscribe to the War Loan." The American poster is from around the same time.

When did people become concerned about the effects of media? When did systematic research into media effects begin?	SELF QUIZ

a number of early studies that made major contributions to the understanding of media effects.[8] The first of these were the Payne Fund studies.

The Payne Fund studies influenced public support for the 1930 Motion Picture Production Code, which limited the amount of sex and violence in movies. *Lucky Star* (1929) was exactly the kind of movie that worried parents at the time.

The Payne Fund Studies

Conducted in 1929, the Payne Fund studies were the first large-scale investigations into the effects of media. Specifically, these studies consisted of 13 separate investigations into the influence movies had on the behavior of children. At the time, children went to the movies once a week, on average, and many experts and laypeople alike were concerned that moviegoing children seemed to be picking up antisocial habits through a phenomenon known as **modeling.** The Payne Fund, an independent philanthropic organization, recruited the best-known social scientists of the day to study these effects.

Some of the studies involved **content analysis,** a research method in which observers systematically analyze the subject matter presented through a given medium. Today, content analysis is commonly used to count such things as violent acts in television programming. The Payne Fund studies classified movies into several categories and demonstrated that the vast majority dealt with crime, sex, and love. They looked at more specific content as well and demonstrated, for example, that the use of liquor was openly portrayed in most movies, in spite of the fact that the sale of alcoholic beverages was illegal at that time (prohibition was the law of the land from 1920 until 1933).

Some of the Payne Fund studies were laboratory experiments. In a **laboratory experiment,** the scientific method is used to isolate variables (such as sexual scenes) in a controlled environment (such as a classroom or

Researchers found that sex scenes in movies "blew the sixteen-year-olds off the graphs."

 modeling
The imitation of behavior from media.

 content analysis
A research method in which observers systematically analyze media subject matter.

laboratory experiment
Scientific method of isolating and observing variables in a controlled environment.

survey methods
Research methods that rely on questionnaires to collect research data.

the researcher's office) so that the effect of those variables on individuals can be measured. The Payne Fund studies used modern technology that seemed like science fiction at the time. Researchers attached electrodes to viewers to record their skin responses and breathing patterns, much in the manner of today's lie detectors. These experiments suggested, among other things, that romantic and erotic scenes did not have much effect on young children, who took little notice of them. The scenes had little effect on adults, also, because adults saw them as fiction. However, the scenes with sexual content had a noticeable effect on teenagers. In fact, the researchers pointed out that sex scenes "blew the sixteen-year-olds off the graphs."[9]

Some of the Payne Fund studies used **survey methods,** which rely on questionnaires administered to participants. The results of surveys administered to young movie viewers, their parents, and their teachers, as well as to teenagers who were asked to recall the effects that early movie viewing had on them, suggested that movie viewing was harmful to a child's health (in that it disturbed sleep), contributed to an erosion of moral standards, and had a negative influence on the child's conduct. Movie fans were seen by their teachers as badly behaved when compared with their classmates who did not attend movies frequently. Heavy moviegoers also had worse reputations, did worse in school, and were not as popular as their classmates. The surveys that asked teenagers to recall whether movies had affected their behavior showed that they had "imitated the movie characters openly in beautification, mannerisms, and attempts at love-making."[10]

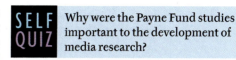

The Payne Fund studies remain one of the largest scientific studies of the influence of media ever undertaken. However, some of their experimental methods would be judged primitive by today's standards. Today, researchers would not ask subjects simply to recall effects. Effects investigators have learned that subjects often say what they think the researcher wants to hear; today's studies use more sophisticated types of analysis that keep the subject blind to the true intent of the study. The Payne Fund studies did, however, establish media research as a serious form of scientific inquiry. They also had considerable political influence and were instrumental in developing public support for the 1930 Motion Picture Production Code, which limited the amount of sex and violence in movies.

The Invasion from Mars Study

Following the panic caused by *The War of the Worlds* broadcast of October 30, 1938 (see Chapter 8), social scientists were eager to discover why the radio broadcast had the effect it did. News reports suggested that there had been a widespread panic, with large portions of the population believing that an invasion was actually taking place. Rumors of suicides and attempted suicides were rampant. A team of researchers at Princeton University sought to determine what the true extent of the panic was, why this broadcast frightened people when other science fiction broadcasts did not, and why it frightened some people but not others.[11] Ratings services estimated that 32 million people were listening to their radios that night. By examining those data and comparing them with other sources, the Princeton researchers were able to estimate that 6 million people listened to at least part of the play, and that 1 million of those listeners actually believed the invasion to be real. There were no suicides, and reported attempts of suicide were unconfirmed.

Those who were frightened by the *War of the Worlds* broadcast had been fooled by its dramatic techniques, such as simulated on-the-spot reporting and interviews with "experts." The researchers found that many of these listeners had accepted radio as their primary and most credible source of breaking news. Those who had practiced "dial twisting" had had heightened fear—while they were sampling other networks, deciding which program they liked best, they had missed the introductory disclaimer announcing that the play was not a news report. Of equal importance, however, were the sociological conditions of the times. Americans had endured years of economic insecurity during the Great Depression and were facing the threat of being drawn into political battles around the globe. This was an audience that already felt itself to be on the edge of disaster, and they believed anything could happen at any time.

As to why some people were frightened while others were not, the researchers found that those who were not good at critical thinking, logic, analysis, and reasoning were most likely to be alarmed by the broadcast. Also, those with strong religious beliefs, those who were emotionally insecure to begin with, and those who listened with others who believed the broadcast were more likely to be fooled. This part of the Princeton study made it one of the first investigations into what kinds of differences might exist within an audience and how those differences might allow the same

SELF QUIZ

message to have different effects on different people. The study also had a significant historical importance—most of what we know about the 1938 panic comes from this study. Without it, the various rumors surrounding the panic might be accepted as true today.

The People's Choice Study

The People's Choice study was an examination of how media affected voter behavior in the 1940 presidential election.[12] Franklin Delano Roosevelt, a Democrat, was running for a third term, which was legal then, although no one had attempted it before. There was little doubt that he would win. Roosevelt was extremely popular; most voters saw him as having brought the country out of the Great Depression. His Republican challenger was Wendell Willkie, a business leader who had never been elected to public office. Roosevelt was also recognized as a master of radio, the primary medium of his day. He had been able to win both of his previous presidential elections without much support from the print media. Many newspaper publishers, in fact, editorialized against him.

Random Samples

random sampling
Method that ensures that every member of the population being studied has an equal chance of being chosen.

Erie County, Ohio, was chosen as the site for the People's Choice study because its voters were representative of the United States in general and because they had deviated very little from national voting patterns in earlier elections. Subjects were chosen randomly, which is an important part of the scientific method. In **random sampling,** every member of the population being studied has an equal chance of being chosen. Randomness was assured by visiting every fourth house in the county. Subjects were studied over a six-month period of the campaign to see how their voting choices changed.

Psychological Consistency

selective exposure
Process by which people seek out messages that are consistent with their attitudes.

selective perception
Process by which people with different attitudes interpret the same messages differently.

selective retention
Process by which people with different views remember the same event differently.

The researchers in the People's Choice study noted that the effect of the media changed depending on several psychological factors. For example, people wanted to feel that their ideas were balanced and in harmony both with the ideas of those around them, and with their own self-image. This need for psychological consistency led to selective exposure, perception, and retention. **Selective exposure** (sometimes called selective attention) is the process by which people seek out messages that help them feel consistent in their attitudes. Republicans would avoid messages that seemed to support Roosevelt, while Democrats would tend to seek out these messages. **Selective perception** is the process by which people with different attitudes interpret the same messages differently. Thus, Republicans could hear one of Roosevelt's fireside chats on the radio and interpret it as evidence of his incompetence and duplicity; Democrats would interpret the same message as evidence of Roosevelt's great abilities and integrity. **Selective retention** (sometimes called selective recall) is the process by which people with different views remember the same event differently. They would remember information that was consistent with their attitudes and tend to forget information that conflicted with those attitudes. Thus, Republicans would tend to forget an inspiring fireside chat, while Democrats would burn it into their memory.

The Findings: Reinforcement, Not Conversion

The researchers in the People's Choice study found that the main effect of the campaign was reinforcement, in that the media strengthened attitudes

The People's Choice study examined the presidential election of 1940, which was won by the radio-savvy Franklin D. Roosevelt without much help from newspapers, as seen in this editorial cartoon of the period.

that were already held by the voters. In fact, fully 53 percent of the voters were affected only through reinforcement, although the researchers were quick to point out that this effect was important because at least these voters did not change their minds and because they made sure to cast their votes on election day. A lesser effect of the campaign was the activation of those who were less interested in politics to actually get out and vote (14 percent). The smallest effect was the actual conversion of voters from one side to another—only 8 percent of the voters appeared to be affected in this way. The media therefore did not seem to have the kind of direct, powerful effects that had been suggested in earlier studies.

 SELF QUIZ What were the primary findings of the People's Choice study?

Opinion Leaders

The most important finding of the People's Choice study, however, was that voters in all categories received a great deal of their information and influence directly from other people. Certain well-informed members of families, neighborhoods, and peer groups tended to be **opinion leaders,** who kept up on media reports and tended to be sought out by others as sources of information. Opinion leaders thus created what the researchers called a **two-step flow** of communication: Ideas, they said, "often flow from radio and print to the opinion leaders and from them to the less active sections of the population."[13]

opinion leaders
Well-informed people who help others interpret media messages.

two-step flow
Communication process in which media effects travel through opinion leaders.

The American Soldier Studies

In 1942 General George C. Marshall, chief of staff of the U.S. Army, asked Frank Capra, who had already become famous directing movies such as *Mr. Smith Goes to Washington* (1939) and *Meet John Doe* (1941), to produce a series of documentary films for the orientation and training of army recruits. The result was the *Why We Fight* films, which were full-budget, top-flight movies that can still be appreciated today. Prominent social scientists

The American Soldier studies were based on Frank Capra's documentary film series *Why We Fight*, which included newsreel footage like this, in which German officers showed artillery pieces to young boys.

were brought in to study the effect of these films on the soldiers, with the full support of the War Department.[14] The researchers had unprecedented control over their subjects, as well as a substantial amount of background information on them from army records.

Movies as Educators

The basic method of the American Soldier research was to measure knowledge and opinions before the soldiers saw the films and then to assess changes afterward. The researchers found that the films had a major effect on the acquisition of factual knowledge. For example, few of the recruits truly understood the complex international events that had brought the United States into World War II before viewing the films, but follow-up tests confirmed that they had mastered this material. The studies therefore established film as a powerful teaching aid. In fact, from this point on, films became an integral part of the American public school curriculum.

The researchers in the American Soldier studies also looked at how the films shaped attitudes. They wanted to know whether the films could improve a recruit's acceptance of military duties and the sacrifices necessary to achieve victory. They found that the films were clearly ineffective in this regard. Like the findings of the People's Choice study, these results suggested that media did not always have direct, powerful effects, such as those that would be needed to change deeply held beliefs.

The studies made extensive use of the soldiers' records to examine individual differences. They found, for example, that the soldiers with higher educational attainment learned more from seeing the films than the soldiers with less education. Furthermore, men of lower intellectual ability were prone to change their opinion because of appeals that men of higher intellectual level did not regard as particularly valid. The less educated, in other words, were easier to sway with propaganda.

How did the American Soldier studies affect American education?

The Nazis had somehow led Germany, one of the most literate and best-educated nations of its time, into unspeakable acts of aggression and genocide.

Following the American Soldier studies, the analysis of mass communications became an important area of academic study. The world had been shocked by what German chancellor Adolf Hitler and his minister of propaganda, Josef Goebbels, had been able to accomplish through strict control of the German media. The Nazis had somehow led Germany, one of the most literate and best-educated nations of its time, into unspeakable acts of aggression and genocide. Postwar America had a great belief in science, so courses designed to study propaganda were taught mostly from the social science perspective, which we will examine later in this chapter.

applied research
Media investigations devoted to practical, commercial purposes.

Applied Research: Conducted by Industry

Increasingly, the techniques of academic research were also adapted by industry for **applied research,** which is research devoted to practical, commercial purposes. Examples of applied research include radio and television ratings (see Chapters 8 and 9), public relations research (see Chapter 12), and the research performed by ad agencies (see Chapter 13). All media industries eventually began to use scientific techniques to determine how best to attract an audience and maximize their advertising profits. Advertising and public relations agencies began to establish research departments that hired people who had earned doctoral degrees in media research and were seeking work outside academia.

In spite of advances in scientific research, some unscientific studies published in the popular press often received more attention. This was true of Dr. Fredric Wertham's studies into the effects of comic books (see the Close-Up on History box), which did great damage to the comics industry of the 1950s.

SELF QUIZ What's the difference between applied and academic research?

STUDIES INTO THE EFFECTS OF TELEVISION

In the 1950s and 1960s television's apparent influence over children alarmed many parents, teachers, and legislators. Surveys revealed that watching television reduced the amount of time that children spent playing, helping with chores, and reading. It became popular for politicians to blame television for contributing to many of society's ills, and research money began to flow from both the government and various foundations to get to the bottom of the problem.

Television and Children

The first major study into the effects of the new medium, *Television in the Lives of Our Children,* was conducted by Wilbur Schramm and his colleagues at Stanford University in the late 1950s.[15] Thousands of schoolchildren and their parents were interviewed, surveyed (through questionnaires and diaries), and tested. The researchers looked at how children used television and how that use affected those children.

Viewing Time

The researchers found that, on average, children began to watch television around age two and were regular viewers by age three. Three-year-olds

"From ages three through sixteen children are likely to devote more time to television than to any other activity except sleep." —Wilbur Schramm

watched 45 minutes a day, and viewing time increased until age 12, when kids were averaging three to four hours a day. They then tapered off in adolescence, as social contacts became more important. Thus, Schramm pointed out, "from ages three through sixteen children are likely to devote more time to television than to any other activity except sleep."[16]

Children with high IQs tended to be heavy viewers when they were young but became lighter viewers as they grew older. Less intelligent children showed the opposite pattern. Children from dysfunctional families and those who had problems with their peer groups watched more, probably as a form of escape. Most children began watching adult programs at an early age. Content analyses revealed that television content during the "children's hours" of 4:00 to 9:00 PM was extremely violent, including such shows as

Seduction of the Innocent: The Effects of Comic Books

Although decidedly unscientific, Dr. Fredric Wertham's studies into the effects of comic books were extremely influential in the 1950s. Comic books had been around since the mid-1930s, when one of the companies that printed comics for newspapers came up with the idea of producing them in magazine form. They became extremely successful, especially the action comics featuring characters such as Superman, Tarzan, and Buck Rogers. By 1948, when Wertham began looking at the new medium, 60 million comic books were being sold across the United States each month.

Wertham, a psychiatrist, was concerned about the way children became absorbed in comics. Some children spent two or three hours a day reading comic books. Many took them to bed with them, walked along busy streets reading them, or read them in school. Health care professionals warned that children would find it difficult to distinguish such an attractive entertainment from real life. Their fears seemed to be confirmed in 1948 when a young boy wrapped a Superman cape around his neck and jumped from the window of his apartment house to his death.[1]

Wertham argued that comic books not only presented children with a distorted and dangerous view of life but also contributed to juvenile delinquency. To prove his point, he conducted a content analysis that documented the gory details found in comics. He reproduced the cover of one comic, for example, that depicted two men being dragged, tied up and facedown, behind a speeding car. There were two hood-lums in the car, one saying, "These -%*@^# gravel roads are tough on tires!" and the other answering, "But ya gotta admit, there's nothing like 'em for ERASING FACES!"[2]

Wertham provided examples of what he said were the many ways comics taught kids techniques for committing crimes. "If one were to set out to show children how to steal, rob, lie, cheat, assault, and break into houses," he wrote, "no better method could be devised."[3] He also showed examples of how women were stereotyped as possessions of men, to be used and abused. Women, he said, were typified by "the pretty young blonde with the super breast."[4] People of color were also stereotyped, as inferiors or villains. Women of color were shown with their breasts fully exposed, although white women never were. Wertham claimed that this portrayal inaccurately suggested that races are fundamentally different in regard to moral values and that one is inferior to the other.

Along with his content analysis, Wertham reported on case studies of mentally ill children whose problems he associated with their use of comic books. He told of an 11-year-old boy who killed a woman in a holdup. Police who arrested the boy found him surrounded by comic books. His 21-year-old brother said: "If you want the cause of all this, here it is: It's these rotten comic books. Cut them out and things like this wouldn't happen."[5] Wertham also told of several cases of children hanging themselves, with comic books open beside them depicting a hanging.

Gunsmoke, The Lone Ranger, and *Dragnet.* More than half the program hours consisted of shows in which violence played an important part.

Summary Finding:
Some of the Children, Some of the Time

Schramm's work resulted in several hundred pages of findings on increasingly specific areas of children's use of television, which he summarized as follows:

> For some children, under some conditions, some television is harmful. For other children under the same conditions, or for the same children under other conditions, it may be beneficial. For most children, under most condi-

Wertham published his findings in popular magazines such as *Ladies' Home Journal* and *Reader's Digest* in the early 1950s, and in a best-selling book entitled *Seduction of the Innocent* in 1954. These works created intense public interest and led to Senate hearings into the problem. The attendant publicity (along with the advent of television) helped end the huge success of the comic book industry. Parents began to forbid their children to buy comics.

In spite of their influence, Wertham's studies were not supported by scientifically gathered data. Wertham gave no statistical proof, for example, that his content analysis was representative of all comics. He simply collected the most extreme and offensive examples he could find. The participants also were far from a random sample. The children were all being seen in psychiatric clinics, and many had been referred there because of extreme behavioral problems. Wertham took these children's statements at face value as long as they could be used as evidence of the harmful effects of comic books. According to researchers who later reexamined Wertham's findings, "It would have been a very dull child, indeed, who attended Dr. Wertham's clinic and did not discover very quickly that most of his or her problem behavior could be explained in terms of the comic books."[6]

Dr. Frederick Wertham's book, *Seduction of the Innocent*, blamed comics like this one for juvenile delinquency.

[1]Norbert Muhlen, "Comic Books and Other Horrors: Prep School for Totalitarian Society?" *Commentary*, January 1949, p. 80.
[2]Fredric Wertham, *Seduction of the Innocent* (New York: Rinehart, 1954), p. 164.
[3]Ibid., p. 157.
[4]Ibid., p. 101.
[5]From Wertham, *Seduction*, cited in Shearon Lowery and Melvin DeFleur, *Milestones in Mass Communication Research: Media Effects* (New York: Longman, 1983), p. 246.
[6]Lowery and DeFleur, *Milestones*, p. 264.

tions, most television is probably neither harmful nor particularly beneficial.[17]

Schramm's overall conclusion, as stated, was accurate, scientifically valid, and honest. To many, however, it suggested that experimental research was no way to uncover the true effects of media. Many academics began to take a less scientific, and more critical, look at media effects.

MARSHALL McLUHAN AND CULTURAL STUDIES

Many academic researchers of the 1960s became interested in a type of research that came to be known as **cultural studies.** Cultural studies depend

cultural studies
Research based on careful observation and thought rather than on controlled experiments or statistics.

not on controlled experiments or statistics, but rather on careful observation and thought. One of the best-known researchers (although by no means the first) in the cultural tradition was Marshall McLuhan.[18] A Canadian professor of English literature, McLuhan wrote that it was the nature of the communication technology itself, rather than the content that was carried on it, that changed society in radical ways—or, as he famously put it, "The medium is the message."

For McLuhan, the idea that television could be either good or bad, depending on how it was used, was the stance of a technological idiot. Regardless of its content, he said, a medium like television tends to deaden the critical faculties of individuals. Print at least encourages logical thought, because it requires a rational, step-by-step decoding. Television, on the other hand, encourages irrationality by providing information all at once, without logical order and in an emotional, visual way rather than a rational, linear way.

McLuhan was a great believer in technological determinism, the theory that the introduction of new technology changes society, sometimes in unexpected ways (see Chapter 3). He advanced his ideas as near-mystical "probes" rather than testable theories. His axioms were puns rather than straightforward statements. At one point, "The medium is the message" became "The medium is the massage," suggesting that mass media gently massages its user into a state of oblivion that destroys rationality and critical thinking. McLuhan also advanced the idea of the **global village,** in which information about people of different cultures, in different countries thousands of miles away, becomes as meaningful to media consumers as things happening in their own neighborhoods.

McLuhan wrote more than a dozen books, the best known of which is *Understanding Media: The Extensions of Man* (1964), which some critics have described as "so densely written as to be unreadable."[19] Because of the profound nature of much of what he said, McLuhan was referred to as a media guru during his lifetime. After his death in 1980, many called him a media prophet because his suggestions seem to have special significance to the contemporary world.[20]

global village
Marshall McLuhan's idea that modern communications technologies will bring together people of different cultures.

Who was Marshall McLuhan, and why is he important to the study of media?

SELF QUIZ

Television and Violence

Even though cultural research became popular among academics, social scientific studies continued unabated. By far the most popular research topic became the effect of mediated violence. Interest in the effects of television violence reached a new high during the 1960s. This was a turbulent decade. Protests against the war in Vietnam and for civil rights often turned violent. Major cities erupted in large-scale urban riots. John F. Kennedy, Robert Kennedy, Malcolm X, and Martin Luther King were all assassinated. The Federal Bureau of Investigation reported a 100 percent increase in crime during the decade.[21] Public concern grew about the relationship between violence portrayed in the media and violence in everyday life.

In 1968, following riots in Detroit and Newark, President Lyndon Johnson appointed the National Commission on the Causes and Prevention of Violence. One part of the commission's report dealt with violence and the media, especially television.[22] This was a huge undertaking, involving both summaries and original research studies. In summarizing past research, the study reaffirmed both short-term and long-term effects that other researchers had established. In the short term, audience members might model acts of violence they see in the media, especially if they expect to be rewarded for it. In the long term, they might experience **desensitization,** a process by

desensitization
A process by which viewers of media violence develop callousness or emotional neutrality in the face of a real-life act of violence.

which viewers of media violence develop callousness or emotional neutrality in the face of a real-life act of violence. Desensitization became a popular explanation for the failure of onlookers to come to the aid of mugging victims in major cities. Critics today worry that violent video games will desensitize players to violence in general.

The commission's original research consisted of a content analysis of portrayals of violence in prime-time television programs and a nationwide survey of the actual violent experiences of Americans. The two worlds were then compared. The content analysis, conducted by a team led by Professor George Gerbner of the University of Pennsylvania, found that around 80 percent of all programs contained one or more violent incidents. However, the violence shown was far from realistic. For example, television beatings produced little visible pain, and the details of physical injury were shown in only 14 percent of all programs. Such portrayals made it difficult for viewers to appreciate the downside of violent behavior. Violence, rather than the rule of law, was depicted as the solution to problems in 80 percent of the cases.

In investigating the actual world of violence, the commission found that only a tiny percentage of the population had any real experience with violence as a victim, assailant, or observer. From this, the researchers concluded that violence was depicted unrealistically on TV when compared with real life. Television, they said, exaggerates the probability of being directly involved in violent acts. It also misrepresents who would be involved in those acts. In real life, most violence occurs between family members, friends, or acquaintances, while on TV the majority of violence occurs between strangers.

Lawmakers continued to fund studies of television violence with government grants. Extensive surgeon general's reports were issued in 1972 and 1982. A third major report, the National Television Violence Study, conducted for three years with government support, was released in 1996. All of these

In 1968, following riots like the one that caused this damage in Detroit, President Johnson appointed a commission to study the causes of violence. One area they looked at was media violence.

In real life, most violence occurs between family members, friends, or acquaintances, while on TV the majority of violence occurs between strangers.

reports found that most television programming contained at least some harmful violence that helped children learn how to behave violently, that desensitized them to the harmful consequences of violence, and that made them more fearful of being attacked. When Congress was again considering another major violence study in 1999, one leading researcher summarized the effects of media violence as follows:

SELF QUIZ What were the major findings concerning television violence?

Not every child who watches a lot of violence or plays a lot of violent games will grow up to be violent. Other forces must converge, as they did recently in [the school shootings in] Colorado. But just as every cigarette increases the chance that some day you will get lung cancer, every exposure to violence

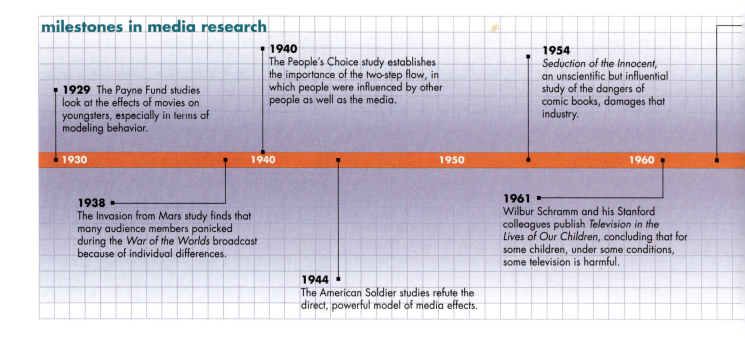

milestones in media research

1929 The Payne Fund studies look at the effects of movies on youngsters, especially in terms of modeling behavior.

1940 The People's Choice study establishes the importance of the two-step flow, in which people were influenced by other people as well as the media.

1954 *Seduction of the Innocent,* an unscientific but influential study of the dangers of comic books, damages that industry.

1930   1940   1950   1960

1938 The Invasion from Mars study finds that many audience members panicked during the *War of the Worlds* broadcast because of individual differences.

1944 The American Soldier studies refute the direct, powerful model of media effects.

1961 Wilbur Schramm and his Stanford colleagues publish *Television in the Lives of Our Children,* concluding that for some children, under some conditions, some television is harmful.

increases the chances that some day a child will behave more violently than they otherwise would.[23]

CURRENT RESEARCH

Politicians and media professionals continue to argue about the effects of mediated violence (and we will discuss some of those arguments in the "Controversies" section later in the chapter), but media researchers have moved on to literally hundreds of different areas of study. A quick perusal of any of the Web sites devoted to media research, such as the Communication Institute of Online Research (www.cios.org), reveals the wide range of topics studied today.

Many of these deal with the effects of proliferating media. For example, some studies suggest that modern media encourage social fragmentation rather than social unity.[24] The older media, which included three national TV networks and a handful of popular general interest magazines such as *Look, Life,* and the *Saturday Evening Post,* were "society-making media," in that they encouraged a sense of communality. Newer media, which include hundreds of cable and satellite TV channels, the unlimited resources of the World Wide Web, and the incredibly diversified and specialized print media, are "segment-making media" because they encourage audience fragmentation.

Other studies look at the effect of media on social life. They note that people are losing their connections with the group and political life of their communities as television watching and Internet surfing increases. These researchers note a decrease in informal socializing and visiting; they even observe an increase in bowling alone instead of in leagues.[25]

Other researchers have zeroed in on specific effects that would escape the notice of everyday people. One theorist insists that today's media have resulted in a lost "sense of place" for many people.[26] According to this theory, media enable average people to be everywhere, instantaneously. But to be everywhere is to be nowhere—to have no sense of place. Others look at how media have changed the concept of childhood,[27] forcing children to confront adult information early in life.[28]

CONSIDER THIS

Do industry professionals have the ethical responsibility to produce society-making media rather than segment-making media? Why or why not?

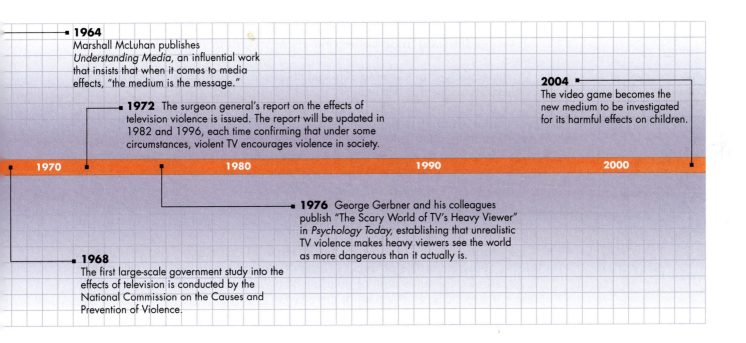

1964
Marshall McLuhan publishes *Understanding Media,* an influential work that insists that when it comes to media effects, "the medium is the message."

1972 The surgeon general's report on the effects of television violence is issued. The report will be updated in 1982 and 1996, each time confirming that under some circumstances, violent TV encourages violence in society.

2004
The video game becomes the new medium to be investigated for its harmful effects on children.

1970   1980   1990   2000

1976 George Gerbner and his colleagues publish "The Scary World of TV's Heavy Viewer" in *Psychology Today,* establishing that unrealistic TV violence makes heavy viewers see the world as more dangerous than it actually is.

1968
The first large-scale government study into the effects of television is conducted by the National Commission on the Causes and Prevention of Violence.

Understanding Today's *Media Theory and Research*

Research in the area of media effects has led to the development of various theories. A **theory** is a set of related statements that seek to explain and predict behavior. Whereas theories arise from research, they are in turn tested and modified through further research. Our review of the history of media

> **theory**
> A set of related statements that seek to explain and predict behavior.

The media do not have the kind of direct, powerful effect on voting behavior that was once believed.

research indicates that investigators moved over time from a powerful-effects, to a minimal-effects, to a mixed-effects theory of media influence.

The Payne Fund studies supported the **powerful-effects model,** which predicts that media will have an immediate and potent influence on their audiences, causing teenagers, for example, to change from good behavior to bad following the viewing of a movie. Later studies, including the People's Choice study and the American Soldier study, led to the **minimal-effects model,** which predicts that media will have little influence on behavior, as when they fail to change voting behavior in an election campaign. Today, researchers accept a **mixed-effects model,** which predicts that sometimes media will have powerful effects, sometimes minimal effects, and sometimes—depending on a complex variety of contingencies—a mixture of powerful and minimal effects.

The mixed-effects model makes the most sense. We know that an effective ad can make a product fly off the shelves, and that a news report can fuel a riot. In fact, in 2005 we saw fatal riots erupt overseas because of a one-sentence item about the desecration of a Koran, and again in 2006 because of the publication of cartoons depicting the prophet Mohammed in a Danish newspaper. These certainly prove powerful effects. Yet we know that most children can watch violent television and movies, and listen to violent recordings, without becoming violent. That fact suggests minimal

> **powerful-effects model**
> Model that predicts that media will have swift and potent influence.
>
> **minimal-effects model**
> Model that predicts that media will have little influence on behavior.
>
> **mixed-effects model**
> Model that predicts that media can have a combination of influences.

effects. The mixed-effect model, however, predicts that a small percentage of children will, indeed, become more violent from their use of violent media.

The history of media research also shows an evolution of **flow theories,** or theories about the way effects travel from the mass media to their audiences. Early powerful-effects studies developed an approach later termed the **bullet theory,** which implied that media effects flow directly from media to individual—like a bullet.[29] According to the bullet theory, people who watch violent movies would become violent, and those who read "immoral" comic books would become immoral. Later research, such as the People's Choice studies, suggested a two-step flow in which media effects occur mostly in interaction with interpersonal communication. You might or might not buy an advertised product, for example, depending on what your friends say about it.

Even though the bullet theory has largely been discredited as too simplistic, some examples of direct effects do occur. A new blockbuster movie, for example, can earn tens of millions of dollars in box office receipts in its first weekend simply because of advertising and publicity. For the great majority of mediated messages, however, effects depend on interpersonal communication. After the movie's first weekend, its box office will likely be determined by word-of-mouth communication.

Today's media researchers recognize a **multistep flow** in which effects are part of a complex interaction.[30] On one level, opinions are shaped by opinion leaders, who in turn have their own opinion leaders. You might be your friend's opinion leader about what sort of computer to buy, for example, which would influence how much effect ads and articles about computers would have on that friend. But you probably have your own opinion leaders, people who know more about cell phones than you do and therefore affect how you will react to the information about cell phones that you encounter in the media. At the same time, a wide range of other influences—family, friends, school, church—act as filters of media information and therefore affect how individuals will react to mediated messages (see Figure 2.1).

flow theories
Explanations of the way effects travel from the mass media to their audiences.

bullet theory
Theory that implies that media effects flow directly from the media to an individual.

multistep flow
A complex interaction of media effects.

What are flow theories, and what do they tell us about the process of mass communication?

SELF
QUIZ

There really is no general, simple answer to the question of how media affect behavior. The best answer is usually "It depends."

The complexity of the mixed-effects and multistep models makes it seem that very little can be said about media effects—and it is true that there really is no general, simple answer to the question of how media affect behavior. When it comes to this question, the best answer is usually "It depends."[31] Several key theories seek to explain the next logical question: Just what does it depend on? These theories look at the effects that media have on both individuals and societies. They are categorized as two types: social science perspectives and cultural perspectives.

SOCIAL SCIENCE PERSPECTIVES

Media theories based on the social science perspective have developed from research featuring controlled laboratory experiments and content analyses. There are hundreds of these theories, but some of the best known involve the concepts of social learning, individual differences, cultivation, agenda setting, and uses and gratifications (see Figure 2.2).

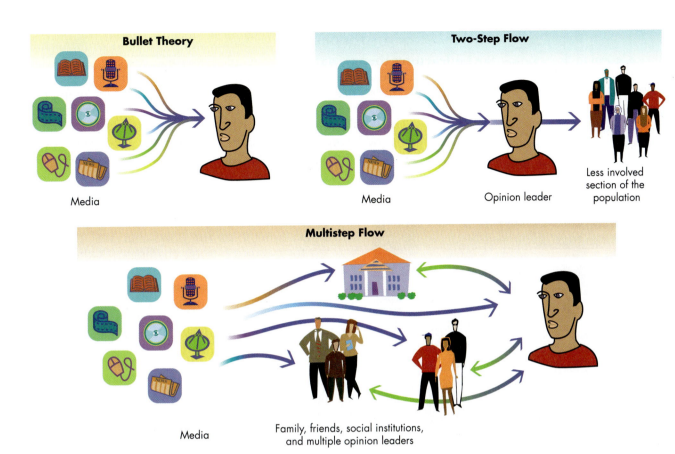

Bullet Theory

Media

Two-Step Flow

Media

Opinion leader

Less involved section of the population

Multistep Flow

Media

Family, friends, social institutions, and multiple opinion leaders

FIGURE 2.1 Flow Theories Over the years, researchers have changed their perceptions of the way effects travel from the mass media to their audiences. The first was the bullet theory, which implied that media effects flowed directly from media to individual. Next, researchers proposed a two-step flow theory, which suggested that media effects occurred mostly in interaction with interpersonal communication. Today's researchers recognize a multistep flow, which implies that media effects are part of a complex interaction.

Social Learning Theory

People learn how to behave by observing others, including those portrayed in the mass media.

Individual Differences Theory

Mass media will affect different media users in different ways.

Cultivation Theory

The media will shape and distort how people view the world.

Agenda-Setting Theory

The mass media influence what you think about and your perception of what is important.

Uses and Gratification Theory

Media users actively choose and use media to meet their own needs.

FIGURE 2.2 Media Effects: Social Science Perspectives Theories of the social science perspective have developed from research featuring controlled laboratory experiments and content analyses.

Social Learning Theory

social learning theory
Theory that people learn by observing others.

socialization
Process by which children learn the expectations, norms, and values of society.

Social learning theory, also known as modeling theory, is based on the assumption that people learn how to behave by observing others, including those portrayed in the mass media. Social modeling is considered an important part of the process of **socialization,** in which a child learns the expectations, norms, and values of society. This theory developed from many studies, including the Payne Fund studies and the surgeon general's reports. It was introduced to the general public largely through the experiments of Albert Bandura in 1963.[32]

In Bandura's most famous studies, nursery school children watched films in which an adult encountered Bobo, a three-foot-tall pop-up clown. One group of preschoolers saw a version of the film in which the adult beat up Bobo and was then rewarded for being a "strong champion." Others saw versions in which the adult assailant was scolded for being a bully and was spanked with a rolled-up magazine. After watching the film, the children themselves then had a chance to play with Bobo. Bandura discovered that the children who had seen the adult being rewarded treated the Bobo doll more violently than those who saw the adult being punished.

The movie *Get Rich or Die Tryin'*, starring the rap artist 50 Cent, was blamed for an increase in gang shootings. Two shootings occurred in a mall where the movie was being shown; one shooting followed a fight that took place inside the theater as the movie was being screened.

Social learning theory would suggest that critics are right to be concerned about the stereotyping of women and ethnic and racial groups in the media. Content analyses consistently indicated that women are portrayed as submissive and dependent and that African Americans and Hispanics are portrayed as criminal perpetrators. According to the theory, these depictions not only teach audiences to accept the stereotypes but also teach women and minorities to behave in the ways they are depicted.[33]

Two other theories are closely related to social learning theory. Both *aggressive stimulation* and *catalytic* theories suggest that media might be one of several factors that could cause someone to act out in an antisocial way.[34] Both theories would suggest, for example, that a young person who was angry and depressed about his or her social life, and who also had a bad day at school or work, might be pushed over the edge into violent behavior by the depiction of violence in entertainment media, especially if that violence is rewarded rather than punished.

Individual Differences

individual differences theory
Theory that predicts that people with different characteristics will be affected in different ways by the mass media.

diffusion of innovations theory
Theory that different types of people will adopt new ideas at different times.

As its name suggests, **individual differences theory** looks at how media users with different characteristics are affected in different ways by the mass media.[35] Some types of users are more susceptible to some types of media messages than others are. For example, a viewer with a high level of education tends to be more susceptible to a message that includes logical appeals than would a viewer with a low level of education. Other individual differences include age, sex, geographic region, intellectual level, socioeconomic class, level of violence in the home, and a wealth of other demographics. The Invasion from Mars study supported individual differences theory, at least that part of it that sought to discover why *The War of the Worlds* fooled some listeners but not others. The American Soldier study also looked at individual differences, especially between men of different intellectual levels.

More subtle psychological characteristics also distinguish media users. **Diffusion of innovations theory,** for example, explains that there are five types of people who have different levels of willingness to accept new ideas from the media.[36] These types also predict who will be first to use and become competent in new media:[37]

1. *Innovators*—These are venturesome people who are eager to try new ideas. They tend to be extroverts and politically liberal. They are the first to try out and become competent in new media and new technology.

2. *Early adopters*—Less venturesome than innovators, these people still make a relatively quick but informed choice. This tendency makes them important opinion leaders within their social groups.

3. *Early majority*—These people make careful, deliberate choices after frequent interaction with their peers and with their opinion leaders. They seldom act as opinion leaders themselves, however, and tend to adopt an innovation when it has reached a critical mass of the general population.

4. *Late majority*—These people tend to be skeptical and accept innovations less often. When they do adopt an innovation, they often do so out of economic necessity or increasing peer pressure.

5. *Laggards*—These people tend to be conservative, traditional, and resistant to any type of change. Their point of reference tends to be the past, and they tend to be socially isolated. Today, these are the people who are mystified by the World Wide Web and might not even use a computer.

Dr. George Gerbner was the theorist who gave us cultivation theory. On the *Media World* DVD that accompanies this book (track 14), Gerbner discusses the implications of violence in the media.

Cultivation Theory

According to **cultivation theory,** advanced by George Gerbner and his associates at the University of Pennsylvania, the media shape how people view the world.[38] This theory helps explain how a person's perceptions of the world are shaped and sometimes distorted by media. Cultivation theory predicts that, over time, media use will "cultivate" within users a particular view of the world.

Gerbner's research found that heavy television viewers had a markedly different view of reality than light viewers. Heavy viewers overestimated their chances of being involved in some type of violence, overestimated the percentage of Americans who have jobs in law enforcement, and found people in general to be less trustworthy than did light viewers. Cultivation theory suggests that one of the primary effects of television is to give heavy viewers a perception that the world is less safe and trustworthy, and more violent, than it really is. Recent research suggests that violent video games have a similar effect.[39]

cultivation theory
Theory that the media shape how people view the world.

Agenda-Setting Theory

Another important approach to media effects—**agenda-setting theory**— was posited by researchers in the 1970s.[40] Studying the way political campaigns were covered in the media, these investigators found the main effect of media to be agenda setting, telling people not what to think, but what to think *about.* In other words, the amount of attention given to an issue in the media affects the level of importance the public assigns to that issue.

The main thrust of agenda setting is that media content might not change your point of view about a particular issue, but it will change your perception of what is important.[41] For today's researchers, the important point to make about agenda setting is that once issues capture people's attention, they have a tendency to influence government policy.[42] Televised pictures of the corpses of whole families of Kurds in northern Iraq helped

agenda-setting theory
Theory that predicts that the amount of attention given to an issue in the media affects the level of importance assigned to it by the public.

Agenda setting: Pictures of the gassing of 5,000 Kurds by Saddam Hussein (left) helped set the agenda for the U.S. invasion of Iraq. Later, pictures of abused Iraqi prisoners at Abu Ghraib prison (right) helped turn some Americans against U.S. involvement there.

make the case against the Iraqi dictator Saddam Hussein in the years leading up to the American invasion of 2003. Later, pictures of Iraqi prisoners being abused at Abu Ghraib prison helped turn public opinion against American involvement there. Agenda setting is also important when one considers that a small number of conglomerates such as Time Warner and Viacom/CBS set the agenda for what other media outlets report.

Many theorists disagree with the agenda-setting approach. One opposing theory, known as **cumulative effects theory,** suggests strongly that media do, in fact, tell us how to think. Developed by Elisabeth Noelle-Neumann, cumulative effects theory holds that media messages are driven home through redundancy and have profound effects over time. According to this theory, a "spiral of silence" occurs when individuals with divergent views become reluctant to challenge the consensus opinion offered by the media. Historians point out that this is what happened in Germany in the 1930s, when many people who disagreed with the Nazis failed to speak out against them.

Uses and Gratifications Theory

Uses and gratifications theory is based on the ways media consumers actively choose and use media to meet their own needs.[43] Uses and gratifications research doesn't regard consumers as passive creatures whose behaviors are controlled by the media industry. Instead, it views them as decision makers who choose—sometimes deliberately and sometimes less consciously—which media to use and how to use them. Scholars who study uses and gratifications ask questions different from those posed by media effects researchers. Instead of asking "What effects do media have on people?" uses and gratifications researchers ask, "What do people do with media?"

Researchers who study uses and gratifications continually find new ways people use media. Some of the most common are surveillance (keeping informed about the world), diversion (escaping from the pressures of the real world through entertainment), conversational currency (keeping up-to-date on topics to talk about), and social integration (connecting with others by using shared knowledge acquired through the media).

cumulative effects theory
Theory that media have profound effects over time through redundancy.

uses and gratifications theory
Theory that looks at the ways media consumers choose media to meet their needs.

What are some of the theories that have derived from the social science perspective, and what are the main ideas of each?

SELF QUIZ

CULTURAL STUDIES

All the theories we have discussed so far stress the media's effect on individuals; these same media also appear to have significant long-term effects on entire cultures. The role that the media play in changing entire societies is difficult to measure. Rather than relying on statistical analyses and controlled experiments, cultural studies (like those of Marshall McLuhan, mentioned earlier) rely on "close readings" of messages from the mass media. In a close reading, cultural researchers examine the meanings, both surface and hidden, of these mediated messages, and then use logic and insight to come to certain conclusions about the effect those messages might have on their audiences. Cultural studies examine, for example, the role that media play in reflecting and shaping society's most widely and deeply held values in areas such as class, ethnicity, and gender.

Cultural studies are also known as critical studies because they are based on the careful, logical analysis of critical thinking. Some cultural theorists are critics in another sense, because they abandon the goal of impartiality that characterizes the social sciences, criticizing some social practices and suggesting what they believe are better alternatives. These theorists explore the invisible ideologies, or underlying ideas about culture, that are embodied in media programming. They look at the media as an environment of culture; in fact, one school of cultural study calls itself **media ecology** to suggest that media make up an ecological system for humans similar to the one nature provides for animals and plants. An ecological system can either nourish or poison the humans who are part of it. Among the wide range of cultural approaches are gender analysis and political/economic analysis.

"Is there no escape from escapism?"
© The New Yorker Collection 2002 Alex Gregory from cartoonbank.com. All Rights Reserved.

media ecology
School of cultural study that suggests that media make up an ecological system for humans.

Gender Analysis

Gender studies examine how the media construct and perpetuate gender roles. A culture's assumptions about how males and females should think, act, and speak are continually presented in mediated messages. For example, researchers Caren Deming and Mercilee Jenkins examined the gender roles advanced in the classic television sitcom *Cheers* by conducting a close reading of the premiere episode. They found that the show contradicted certain gender stereotypes through dialogue and visual imagery. The study showed how the character Diane Chambers (played by Shelley Long) used humor as a tool of resistance and succeeded in asserting her individuality in the face of attempted domination by Sam Malone, the leading male character (played by Ted Danson). Deming and Jenkins demonstrated how a sitcom like *Cheers* can refute the rules that subjugate people and thus have a liberating effect on its audience.[44] Several other gender theorists have looked at the effects of different types of media, including computer games.[45]

gender studies
Research that looks at how the media deal with male and female roles.

 SELF QUIZ What's the difference between social science and cultural approaches to media research?

Political/Economic Analysis

Much of **political/economic analysis** is based on the work of the philosopher Karl Marx (1818–1883). To Marxist media critics, Marx was a humanist whose argument was essentially a moral one. Marx believed that the economic system of a nation (in the case of the United States, capitalism) influenced

political/economic analysis
Theory that predicts that a culture's exchange system will influence its values.

Media's Influence on Language: Speaking the Previously Unspeakable

Different theories of media effects would explain changes in society in different ways. The way language is used in society, for example, has certainly changed in recent years.[1] Terms that were once considered obscene have become commonplace. Evidence of changing language patterns abounds in everyday conversation. During the Bill Clinton–Monica Lewinsky scandal, oral sex became dinner-party conversation. With the publicity surrounding Viagra and other male potency drugs, erectile dysfunction was suddenly being discussed in mixed company. It's hard to believe that a few years ago it was considered bad form in certain circles to speak of a breast of chicken.

Most experts believe that media have played a role in this transformation. Years ago, the media encouraged the use of only "proper" language. For many years, the word *pregnant* was not uttered on television, even by Lucille Ball, whose character on *I Love Lucy* was obviously in that condition. Married couples in sitcoms occupied twin beds, and television comedy writers were prohibited from using the word *penis* on the air.[2] Today, words that used to be considered bad enough to get a kid kicked out of school—

words such as *sucks, bites,* and *blows,* used as verbs of criticism—can be heard routinely on Saturday-morning cartoons. Worse can be heard on late-night programs such as Comedy Central's *South Park.*

How would the various theories explain media's role in the way language has changed?

- The findings from social learning research would suggest that these changes in language usage occurred as people imitated the language they heard in movies and on TV.

- Individual differences theory would suggest that the same language will affect different people in different ways, and that perhaps only segments of the population who were predisposed to it would adopt the new language use.

- Cultivation theory would suggest that media language use slowly changes individuals' worldviews, perhaps convincing them that society in general has become more coarse and that such language use is therefore acceptable.

- Agenda-setting theory would suggest that news coverage of sexual scandals and crimes made sexual

the values of the entire culture (in the case of the United States, encouraging materialism, which is the craving for money and what it can buy).

Political/economic analysis therefore looks at how media become the means by which the haves of society gain the willing support of the have-nots to maintain the status quo. Marxist theorists believe that media help create a "false consciousness" within the working class that enables the wealthy to manipulate and exploit them. The mass media distract people from the realities of their society (poverty, racism, sexism, and so on) by clouding their minds with the ideas that powerful commercial forces want them to have, ideas such as I feel better when I buy something.

Marxist theory has led to many interesting insights about mass media. For example, two researchers looking at Muzak, a trademarked name for a type of "functional music" piped into elevators and department stores, pointed out that it was originally used in factories to control and regulate work and is now used in stores and malls to control and regulate consumption.[46] The mindless, relaxing nature of Muzak, they say, puts people in a positive frame of mind to spend money.

What are some of the theories that have derived from the cultural perspective, and what are their main ideas?

SELF QUIZ

MEDIA THEORY: A COMPLEX WHOLE

When taken together, the various theories of media impact demonstrate that it is usually ill-advised to make blanket statements about

affairs part of the national agenda and therefore grist for everyday conversation.

•   Cumulative effects theory would suggest that language use changed slowly as more and more mediated messages contained coarser language. This theory would also suggest that a change occurred when those who believed in using only socially acceptable terms became silent in the face of continual mediated use of obscenity.

•   Uses and gratifications theory would suggest that people have attended to media messages with this type of language because it performs some function for them, perhaps freeing them from societal restraints that they found repressive.

•   Gender analysts might see these changes in language use as a way for women to seek equality with men, or perhaps as a form of oppression against women.

•   Political/economic analysts might regard the new language use as a successful assault on the repressive status quo.

All of these theories provide insights into media effects. They might be different insights, but taken as a

110

Media have played a role in changing language norms. In this 2001 episode of *South Park*, the uncensored word "shit" was used 162 times in less than 30 minutes. Each time the word was used, the counter in the lower left corner of the screen recorded it.

whole and treated with logic and critical thinking, they begin to help us make sense out of the question of how media affect behavior.

[1]See Ellen Goodman, "Becoming Desensitized to Hate Words," *Boston Globe*, June 6, 1995. This column also appears in Ronald B. Adler and George Rodman, *Understanding Human Communication*, 7th ed. (Fort Worth: Harcourt, 2000), p. 91.
[2]Janny Scott, "Speaking the Unspeakable (No Blushing is Required)," *New York Times*, June 6, 1998, p. A1.

media effects. It is not completely accurate to say "Violent television causes violence in society" or even "Skinny models in magazine ads encourage girls to be anorexic," without qualifying that statement with words like *some* or *sometimes*. Each of the theories discussed in this section, as well as many others, has revealed that the uses and the effects of media are many and complex (see the Close-Up on Media Theory box). That complexity is part of what has made the idea of media impact controversial.

CONSIDER THIS

In your opinion, which theory of media effects is most useful in explaining media impact? Why?

Controversies

Media research was designed to help solve social problems by determining the links between media use and harmful behavior. As we emphasized in our examinations of media research history and current theory, the answers that have been found are not as straightforward and clear-cut as some observers would like. This has led to continual arguments, disagreements, and debates about the impact of media. These controversies arise between different members of the research community, the media professions, the government, and the public.

RESEARCH VERSUS CONVENTIONAL WISDOM

Media research promotes a reasoned, rational point of view about media's effects on society. However, that point of view often conflicts with conventional wisdom, the view held by the average person on the street. Some media experts insist that in spite of all the findings of research, most people hold an inflexible powerful-effects point of view. This perspective assumes, among other things, that media are a malignant, cancerous force within society; that they have the power to reach out and directly influence the minds of average people; and that they are capable of producing social problems on a vast scale.[47] In other words, researchers may have moved from a powerful-effects to a minimal-effects to a mixed-effects model, but the conventional wisdom still believes in powerful, direct, and mostly negative media influences.

In different times and places, this conventional wisdom has won out and encouraged an oppressive governmental control of the media. The powerful-effects theory was the prevailing view in Germany before World War II, and it helped lead to Adolf Hitler's total control over the media, allowing only Nazi messages to be heard. The powerful-effects theory also seems to arise in the United States with every new medium, becoming the rallying cry for those who would place restrictions on it.

Isolated examples and anecdotes are used to support the conventional wisdom. Every day brings a new example of a criminal who copied a mediated crime in real life or a child who modeled media behavior to some disastrous effect. Determining effects by anecdote, of course, is extremely unscientific, but it is one of the reasons that the conventional wisdom persists.

Another reason for the disparity between research and public opinion is that most people cannot keep up with the thousands of media studies that are published. These studies are conducted in a variety of academic fields, including communication, sociology, history, literature, and anthropology. Studies are produced by graduate students to earn their degrees, by faculty members to earn promotion and tenure, and by various organizations that want to prove a point.

Even if they were able to keep up with all this research, most people would be hard pressed to understand it. Academic research uses highly specialized methods and jargon, and much of it deals with concepts that only specialized researchers understand.

LIMITATIONS OF RESEARCH

Even for those who follow and understand media research, its limitations further confuse the conventional wisdom. Some limits arise from academic infighting: Social scientists tend to dismiss cultural studies as unscientific. These studies, they say, tend to rely on interpretations that are a matter of literary sensitivity rather than hard evidence. Also, the social scientists say, cultural critics tend to see all problems in terms of their specialties: Marxists see everything in terms of economic oppression, gender theorists see everything in terms of sexism.

Cultural researchers, for their part, point out the limitations of social science research, which sometimes finds it difficult to mix scientific control with the complexity of human subjects. For example, several studies have noted that a majority of Americans said that they did not approve of either the amount or kind of violence that was portrayed on TV. The researchers concluded that the public was not getting the type of programming it wanted. But other researchers pointed out that those responses were given in personal interviews, in which there would be a tendency for respondents to give socially desirable responses to sensitive questions. Thus, respondents could say they disapproved of violent shows while at the same time watching them with pleasure.[48] Or perhaps this result was a simple contradiction in human behavior—while the researchers concluded that the public was not getting the type of programming it wanted, perhaps the subjects actually "wanted" programming that they "disapproved" of! Perhaps this helped them feel superior to others in society or gave them a gratifying taste of forbidden fruit.

Cultural critics like to point out that statistical studies reduce big questions to little variables that can be easily measured but that have little relevance to real life.[49] Measuring violence, for example, has always been a problem. Do you include violence in cartoons? Do you also include mere threats of violence? Television producer Dick Wolfe, in the DVD that accompanies this book (track 16), complains that "in some of these studies a pie in the face is considered violence."

The limitations of social science research also include problems with conflicting interpretations and causation.

The *Media World* DVD that accompanies this text (track 29) examines *The Physical Effect that Violent Video Games Have on Children.*

Conflicting Interpretations

Even if studies produce reliable results, those results can still be interpreted in different ways. For example, research that associates violence in the media with violence in real life is usually open to at least three conflicting interpretations:[50]

1. The viewing of violence leads to aggressive tendencies.
2. Aggressive tendencies led to the choosing of violent viewing.
3. Aggressive tendencies and the viewing of violence are both products of some third condition or set of conditions, such as personality factors, intelligence, socioeconomic status, or violence in the home.

Conflicting interpretations of research findings have led to the development of conflicting theories (see the Close-Up on Controversy box). The most famous conflict is that between the theory of catharsis and the the-

"For every psychologist who insists that there is a causal link between violent entertainment and violent crime, there are others who argue the opposite."

ory of violent stimulation. **Catharsis theory** is the idea that viewing violence actually reduces violent behavior because it satisfies a person's aggressive drive. Catharsis theory derives from classical drama; it was originally articulated by Aristotle to explain the audience's reaction to Greek tragedies performed on the stage. This theory, however, is not supported by modern research. In spite of this lack of proof, the idea of catharsis remains popular. As one journalist

The catharsis theory, which suggests that audiences use media violence to defuse their own violent actions, is popular within the entertainment community.

catharsis theory
The idea that viewing violence actually reduces violent behavior.

Michael Moore is the producer of films such as *Bowling for Columbine* and *Fahrenheit 9/11*. In the *Media World* DVD that accompanies this book (track 15), he discusses how the media deal with violence.

correlation
A situation in which two things occur at the same time, or in close succession, more often than chance would lead you to expect.

 SELF QUIZ
What are some of the limitations of social science research?

who has reported on the issue pointed out, "For every psychologist who insists that there is a causal link between violent entertainment and violent crime, there are others who argue the opposite—that the graphic material can actually help defuse aggressive impulses."[51] The catharsis theory is especially popular within the entertainment community. Typical of those feelings are those of Jamie Lee Curtis, the star of the *Halloween* horror movies. As Curtis points out: "There's an audience of people who love this genre who are not violent. In fact, they sort of use it to vent their violent nature so they don't have to act it out in real life."[52]

Causation and Correlation

Another drawback to the popular understanding of media research is that most people find it difficult to distinguish between causation and correlation in research findings. When you prove that two things occur at the same time, or in close succession, more often than chance alone would lead you to expect, you prove only **correlation.** Correlation does not equal causation, but it can produce some impressive statistics. Studies have shown, for example, that about 80 percent of those who commit sex-related murders, have a taste for violent pornography.[53] That sounds like an impressive number, but it does not prove that the violent pornography caused the violent behavior; 100 percent of those killers might also drink milk or use aspirin—but those factors don't necessarily cause them to be murderous.

THE INDUSTRY'S RESPONSE

Violence has been a primary focus of media effects controversy, so industry professionals have taken pains to respond to the charges. When assailed for saturating their products with images of violence, many media producers reply that dramatic violence is as old as the great classics. Shakespeare's *Hamlet* contains no fewer than seven murders, and in the Greek tragedy *Medea* a woman tears her children to pieces as revenge against her husband. Violence is action, and action holds audiences' attention. It is used appropriately when it is essential to plot or character.

Besides, the entertainment executives say, they are simply reflecting the fact that society itself is violent. Violence reflects real life, even if (as numerous content analyses have proved) it reflects only the extreme parts of real life. Network and movie studio executives, as well as producers and writers, argue that the link between viewing violence and behaving violently found in media research is far too small to warrant the attention paid to it. The size of the effect, they say, is especially tiny when compared with other factors, such as the availability of guns, the pressures of poverty, or the problems of child rearing in single-parent and working-parent households. Mediated violence might adversely influence a disturbed viewer, they say, but entertainment should not be overly concerned with that small segment of the population. Reactions of the entertainment community are reflected in the comments of Steve Tisch, producer of *Forrest Gump* (1994) and *Cowboys and Aliens* (2006). "What's more troubling," Tisch asks, "a kid with a sawed-off shotgun or a kid with a cassette of *The Basketball Diaries*? It's not just movies. Lots of other wires have to short before a kid goes out and does something like [a school shooting]. It's a piece of a much bigger, more complex puzzle."[54]

SELF QUIZ
What is the industry's typical response to the charge that violence in the media causes violence in society?

Does Pop Culture Make Us Smarter?

In spite of the huge amount of research that has been done into media's effects, the findings remain controversial. There's always a different way to look at things. For example, by examining IQ tests over the years, social scientists have determined that people are getting smarter. In fact, a person whose IQ score placed him or her in the top 10 percent of the American population in 1920 would today fall in the bottom third.[1] Most scientists attribute that rise in IQ to economic progress, better nutrition, and better education.

In the book *Everything Bad Is Good for You,* author Steven Johnson proposes that what is making us smarter is precisely what we thought was making us dumber: popular culture.

Take television, for example. Johnson points out that story lines are much more complex and challenging than they were 30 years ago. An episode of *Starsky and Hutch,* in the 1970s, followed a simple, single story line: Two characters solve a relatively uncomplicated problem, moving toward a fairly obvious solution. An episode of one of today's dramas, such as *The Sopranos* or *Grey's Anatomy,* might follow 5 or 10 narrative threads, involving a dozen characters who weave in and out of the plot. (Johnson calls this "multi-threading.") Today's comedies are also more complex, such as a *Simpsons* episode that typically contains numerous allusions to politics, classic cinema, or postmodern philosophy. In fact, Johnson says, because the industry now makes so much money on DVD sales, program creators have a vested interest in producing shows that can sustain multiple viewings, so that people can discover new facets of a production each time they watch it.

Johnson makes the same argument about video games. Unlike old-fashioned games such as chess or Monopoly, which have a clear set of rules, video games require the player to discover the rules as the game is being played—again, a much more complex challenge. This, Johnson says, is why older people are baffled by most video games; those same games, however, make kids smarter by teaching them how to think on the fly and solve complex problems.

Johnson admits that popular culture makes us smarter only in terms of certain kinds of intelligence. Reality shows, for example, increase our emotional

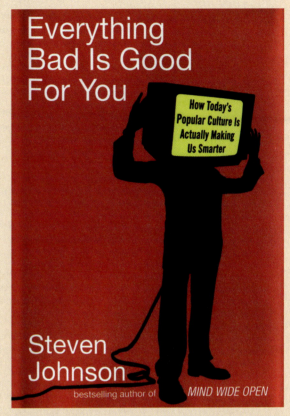

intelligence. To be smart enough to engage in a sustained argument based on ideas, you still need books. As a case in point, Johnson reminds us that he is presenting his own argument in the form of a book, not a video game.

Critics, however, are generally no more convinced by Johnson's claims than by the industry's long-term response that this is all just entertainment and we shouldn't take it so seriously. One critic summarizes his feelings this way: "Video games and TV—from *The Sopranos* to *The Simpsons* to *Grand Theft Auto*—may indeed be helping to make us smarter, and in surprising ways, just as Johnson argues. But the nagging and unanswered fear is that they may not be making us better people or helping us create a better society."[2]

Note: See the *Media World* DVD, track 31, for an interview with author Steven Johnson.

[1]Malcolm Gladwell, "Brain Candy: Is Pop Culture Dumbing Us Down or Smartening Us Up?" *The New Yorker* online, May 16, 2005.

[2]Suneel Ratan, "Everything Bad's Not Bad," *Wired* online, May 24, 2005.

Summing Up

The history of media research provides some interesting insights into the impact of today's media. For example, the Payne Fund studies looked at the effects of movie viewing, and found that kids copied the behavior of movie stars they identified with. The Invasion from Mars study showed that only some types of people panicked during the *War of the Worlds* radio broadcast. The People's Choice study, which looked at voter behavior in the 1940 presidential election, found that some media effects traveled in a two-step flow, from media to opinion leaders and then to other people. The American Soldier studies looked at the effects of army training films and found that media did not have the direct, powerful effects that earlier studies had suggested.

Later large-scale studies into the effects of television viewing on children established that for some children, under some conditions, some television is harmful. Around the same time, cultural researchers, such as Marshall McLuhan, were warning that media like television could have far-reaching effects that could not be discovered by the kind of experiments social scientists had been conducting.

Several theories help explain the complex nature of media effects. Some of these theories grew out of experiments conducted from the social science perspective. Social learning theory predicts that people learn how to behave by observing role models in the media. The predictions that derive from social learning theory make the most sense when you also consider individual differences theory, which states that media users with different characteristics are affected in different ways. A similar theory, diffusion of innovations, explains that different types of people will have different levels of willingness to accept new ideas from the media.

One of the more sophisticated theories of media effects, cultivation theory, predicts that media shape our view of the world more than our behavior. Heavy viewers of television, for example, tend to see the world as less trustworthy and more dangerous than do light viewers. Agenda setting is a theoretical approach that suggests that the main effect of the media is telling us what to think about; therefore, the amount of attention given to an issue in the press affects the level of importance assigned to that issue by consumers of mass media.

Cumulative effects theory predicts that media's influence will build up over time, leading to a "spiral of silence" when people fail to challenge the consensus opinion offered by the media. Uses and gratifications theory looks at the ways media consumers actively choose and use media to meet their own needs.

Cultural studies look at the long-term effects of media on society in general. Rather than relying on experiments, cultural studies are built on a close analysis of mediated messages. Gender analysis examines how the media construct and perpetuate gender roles. Political/economic analysis looks at how media affect the relationship between the economic system of a nation and the values that the nation holds.

All of these theories, when taken together, provide a broad understanding of the many different effects of media in the lives of individuals and in society overall. Understanding these theories can help you appreciate why the most accurate answer to questions about whether and how different media affect people is often "It depends." This apparent ambiguity has created a number of controversies. One of these is based on the difference between the research perspective, which considers a complex array of different types of impact, and the conventional wisdom, which continues to see media as having direct, powerful effects. Other controversies arise between types of researchers: Social scientists say that cultural studies lack hard evidence, and cultural studies researchers point out the limitations of social science research, including conflicting interpretations and theories, and problems with establishing causation instead of correlation. Other controversies arise between industry professionals and researchers. In the case of violence, for example, industry professionals insist that the effects suggested by research are overstated.

Key Terms

These terms are defined and indexed in the Glossary of key terms at the back of the book.

Electronic Excursions

HISTORY

Web Excursion

1. Search the Web for sites related to current media research, or go directly to the Communication Institute for Online Scholarship at www.cios.org* or the Freedom Forum at www.freedomforum.org.* Access one of the research reports posted on the site. In your opinion, how does the research compare with the historical studies cited in this chapter? Does it seem to be more or less meaningful, more or less specific, more or less sophisticated? When compared with the studies cited in this chapter, did the contemporary study break new ground? Why or why not? Write a brief summary of your findings.

INDUSTRY

Web Excursion

2. What is the state of media studies at your own college? Access your school's Web site and search for "media studies." Look under appropriate departments (Communication; Radio, Television and Film; Journalism) and under faculty interests. Now choose a second college you are familiar with, and access its Web site in the same way. You might want to go directly to a college department such as the University of Florida Communications Research Center at www.jou.ufl.edu* or Ithaca's Center for Research on the Effects of Television at www.ithaca.edu/cretv/.* How do the colleges compare in terms of the types of media research being conducted?

CONTROVERSIES

Web Excursion

3. One criticism is that media studies are not written for public comprehension. Search the Web for contemporary research reports, or go directly to one of the sites listed in Web Excursion 1. Find a report and analyze it. How would you present this report to the public? Acting as a journalist, write a brief article about the study.

Media World DVD Excursions

4. View track 14, *Debating the Effects of TV Violence* (from NBC's *Today* show). Dr. George Gerbner, Dean of the Annenberg School of Communications at the University of Pennsylvania and Dr. Jonathan Freedman, a psychology professor from the University of Toronto, talk with Bryant Gumble about the effects of violence on television. What does Dr. Gerbner mean by the "mean world syndrome"? If TV is supposed to reflect reality, should violence be represented accurately?

5. View track 16, *Violence in the Media and Its Effects on Children* (from NBC's *Today* show). With school violence constantly in the news, the debate over violence in the media became a central concern for the country. Is network television actually less violent than ever in its history? Should parents be responsible for what their children watch?

ONLINE LEARNING CENTER WWW.MHHE.COM/RODMAN2

You may access these and additional Web excursions at the Online Learning Center for the book (www.mhhe.com/rodman2). Visit the student portion of this Web site to also access the *Interactive Timeline of Mass Media Milestones,* chapter highlights, self quizzes, and recommended readings, movies, and documentaries for this chapter.

*Some Web site addresses may change. When they do, please search for the Web site by name or topic on your favorite search engine.

PART TWO

The Print Industries

This part of *Mass Media in a Changing World* will examine the book, newspaper, and magazine industries—their history, their current structure, and the social issues that create controversy about them. These are the oldest media, but they continue to be culturally influential. The Internet and other new media formats are challenging print industries, which, so far, are adapting and remain profitable.

Books

The Durable Medium

3

Chapter Highlights

HISTORY: Books have changed in form throughout history. They have also changed the world, especially through their encouragement of literacy.

INDUSTRY: Types of books include trade, educational, reference, professional, and specialty books. The players include authors, editors, publishers, booksellers, and readers.

CONTROVERSIES: Major debates arise today about the censorship of books and about the industry's obsession with blockbuster titles.

Da Vinci Decoded

The plot of *The Da Vinci Code* is hard to summarize, especially if you don't want to give away the ending to the few people who haven't read the book or seen the movie yet. Basically, a mild-mannered college professor is called to a crime scene to decode a secret message left behind by the victim. Before long the professor realizes that the police believe that *he* is the murderer, and he is about to be arrested. To save himself, the professor has to flee with his new love interest and solve the crime himself.

This leads to a dizzying number of plot turns and twists, betrayals and reversals that unravel a mystery, finally, based on the idea that Jesus Christ was married to Mary Magdalene (who

A city councilor in a small town on the outskirts of Rome holds the cover of a copy of Dan Brown's bestseller *The Da Vinci Code* after setting it on fire during a 2006 demonstration against the book and the film by the same title.

66

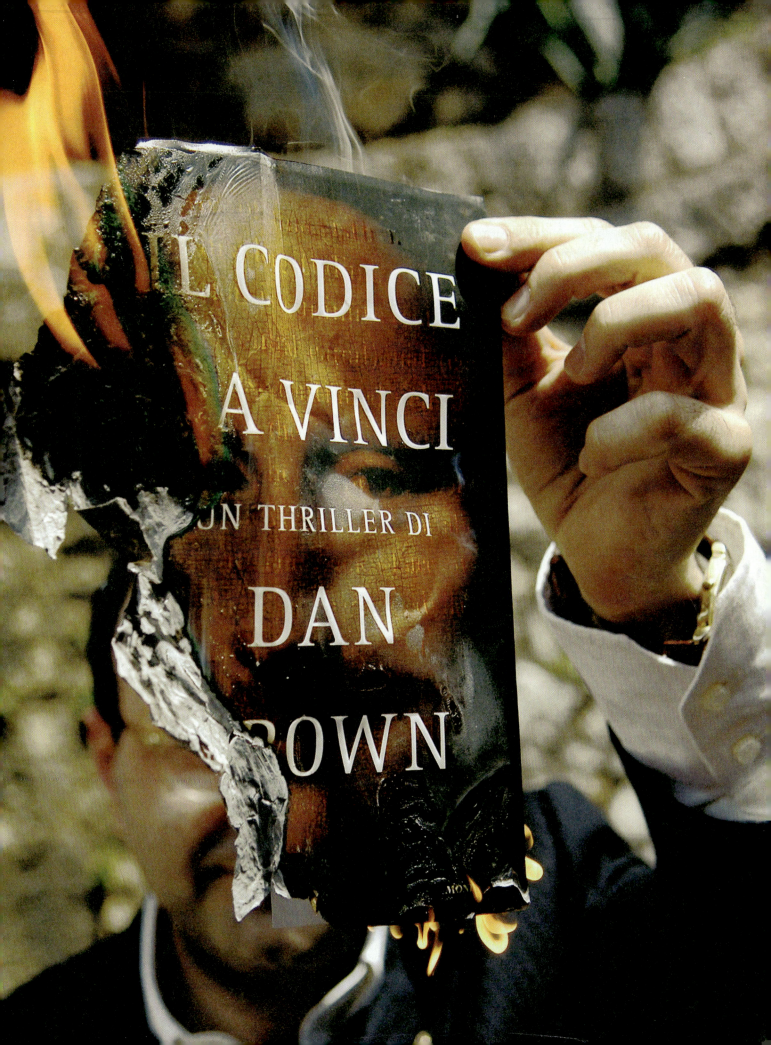

was actually of royal blood, not the harlot that history has come to portray) and that Jesus had a child with her. As one character in the book claims: "Jesus was the original feminist. He intended for the future of His Church to be in the hands of Mary Magdalene."[1]

The secret of Mary Magdalene, hidden by an underground society for 2,000 years, involves a number of historical figures and artifacts, including Leonardo Da Vinci, Isaac Newton, the *Mona Lisa* painting, and the Holy Grail (the chalice that Jesus drank from at the Last Supper, which knights throughout history have devoted their lives to finding).

The Da Vinci Code, published originally in 2003, has sold more than 40 million copies in 44 languages. It has spent more than two years on the *New York Times* bestseller list. It has made its author,

Dan Brown, a very wealthy man and landed him on *Time* magazine's list of the 100 most influential people in the world and on *Forbes* magazine's list of the most influential celebrities.

The Da Vinci Code has become part of the world's culture wars.

The book has been nothing short of a pop culture phenomenon. It has become a major motion picture. It has inspired the writing and publication of more than a dozen other books that promise to break, crack, unlock, or decode its secrets. Churches mentioned in the book have seen a huge increase in visitors, with many of them clutching one of the guides and decoding manuals based on the book. At least one university reports a resurgence in student interest in art history based on the book.

The book has also been controversial. It has been banned in

Lebanon, which allows no books to defame a religion of any kind. (The movie has also been banned in several countries as an insult to Christianity.) An Italian cardinal branded the book as being full of "cheap lies."[2] According to other church leaders, many readers believe Brown's claims and say his novel has challenged and changed their beliefs. One research study, conducted in Canada, found that one in three readers believed the story told in the book.[3] "The belief in Jesus' marriage to Mary Magdalene," said one pair of church scholars, "has been popular in feminist circles for several decades. It forms a central part of a strategy to undermine Church teaching about priestly celibacy and women's ordination."[4]

Thus *The Da Vinci Code* has become part of the world's culture wars, proving how successful and how controversial the book industry can be.

The controversy surrounding *The Da Vinci Code* points to some significant changes in today's book publishing industry. People tend to think of this industry as stable and unchanging, but a look at its history suggests that the only constant has been change. One of the most profound changes deals with the very definition of the word *book*. Bound and covered pages, numbered consecutively, containing material that took years to write once defined it. As we'll see in this chapter, however, that hasn't always been the case, and each of these characteristics is now changing again.

A Brief History *of Books*

Books, with their in-depth organizing of knowledge and information, have endured since ancient times as our primary repositories of culture. It has been through books that the wisdom of one age has been passed on to the next. Great ideas, it seems, need book-length explanations. Three of the world's great religions grew around books—the Christian Bible, the Muslim Koran, the Jewish Torah—and widespread social and political systems have grown out of theories developed in books. The truly educated person is still the person who knows books and the ideas they contain.

EARLY FORMS

Today's books seem to be rapidly changing in form, appearing as everything from audiotapes to digital files. You might be surprised to learn, however, that books have been changing in form through most of their 6,000-year history. Most scholars agree that the first books were actually clay tablets from around 4000 BC, found in Mesopotamia, the ancient land that is now Iraq. The book evolved into its familiar form of today through the development of paper.

Papyrus

The earliest paper was invented around 3000 BC. It was made from **papyrus,** a type of reed that grew alongside the Nile River in Egypt. The word *paper* is derived from *papyrus*. The Greeks, who borrowed paper-making knowledge from the Egyptians, preserved their papyrus books, including the works of Plato and Aristotle, in long scrolls that were attached to wooden rods on both ends; when we scroll though a computer file today, we are essentially perusing data in the same way the Greeks did with the original scrolls. Scroll selling and collecting flourished in ancient Greece; scrolls were produced by hand, and copying was a profitable trade. The royal library at Alexandria, founded in the third century BC, is said to have housed 700,000 scrolls.

papyrus
A type of reed used to make an early form of paper.

Parchment

Papyrus eventually gave way to **parchment,** which was made from dried animal skins. Parchment's extreme durability allowed some ancient books to survive until modern times. The first book to resemble today's familiar form was produced on parchment by Romans in the first century AD. Called a **codex,** it had parchment pages that were cut and bound on one side. The writing was done by hand, and making copies was therefore difficult and time-consuming.

parchment
An early form of paper made from animal skins.

codex
A book written on parchment pages that were cut and bound on one side. Developed by the Romans in the first century AD, the codex was the first book to resemble today's familiar form.

Asian Contributions

Around the time of the ancient Greeks, several Asian cultures, including the Chinese, the Korean, and the Japanese, were fashioning books out of long strips of wood tied together in bundles. Asian books were also printed on rice paper with a technique called woodcutting, in which carved wooden blocks were inked and then pressed onto the page; woodcuts, which could consist of either text or images, were reusable. Europeans later adopted the woodcut technique, but it

SELF QUIZ What are the major changes in form that books have taken through time?

wasn't until the invention of movable metal type that printing revolutionized the world of books.

THE PRINTING REVOLUTION

Johannes Gutenberg grew up in a region of Germany that was known for its goldsmiths and jewelers. He began working with metal at an early age and came upon the idea of a type mold for movable metal type. The type mold he fashioned was one of the world's earliest precision instruments and one of the prototypes of mass production. The metal mold enabled the production of exact multiple replicas of the letters of the Latin alphabet, and those type pieces made possible the mass production of printed documents. Gutenberg sought to exploit his invention by becoming a printer and producing Bibles of great accuracy and beauty. He was indeed an artist, though not much of a businessman. His Bible-printing business went bankrupt. In spite of Gutenberg's business failure, his invention sparked a revolution.

technological determinism
Theory that states that the introduction of new technology changes society, sometimes in unexpected ways.

oral culture
A culture in which information is transmitted more by speech than writing.

Encouraging Literacy

The way the printed book changed literacy, and literacy in turn changed the world, is one of the great examples of **technological determinism,** a theory that states that the introduction of every new technology changes society, sometimes in unexpected ways. Printing led to a fundamental shift in the world from oral culture to literate culture.

Oral Culture

Before printing, people in all parts of the world lived in an **oral culture,** one in which information was transmitted more by speech than by writing. Oral cultures depended on local experts to interpret the few hand-copied books that were available and disseminate that information to the masses. Scholars would travel great distances to read these books and then would return to their towns and villages to discuss them in meeting halls, universities, and houses of worship. In fact, today's religious sermons and college lectures are both derived from these oral traditions.

Some aspects of oral culture survive to this day. Here, the town crier of Tepu, in Surinam, uses a megaphone to present the local news.

Print Culture

Print media, however, changed things. With printing, books and other materials could be mass-produced, and people were able to read ideas from far away and from ancient times on their own. Facts could be validated, ideas could be transported from place to place, and learning could be handed down from generation to generation. In this way the technology of printing led to the Enlightenment in Europe during the 17th and 18th centuries. During the Enlightenment, which was also called the Age of Reason, great books attacked superstition, ignorance, social injustice, and tyranny. Most historians believe that these books helped lead to the American and French revolutions of the late 1700s. Teaching people to think for themselves, it seems, threatened the traditional authority of kings and religious

CONSIDER THIS

Many scholars believe that we have now moved from living in a print culture to living in an electronic media culture that is in many ways similar to an oral culture. They argue that people now get their most important information from the "conversations" of radio and television. Would you agree or disagree?

leaders, whose power was based at least in part on their ability to think for the people.

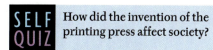

SELF QUIZ How did the invention of the printing press affect society?

THE BOOK IN AMERICA

The Spanish established the first press in the Americas, in Mexico City in the 1530s, to produce texts to teach Spanish to the Indians. The presses of New England, however, had the most influence in the development of the future United States. The Puritans who settled in New England in the early 1600s were avid readers and book collectors. Miles Standish, captain of the militia that accompanied the *Mayflower* and a leader among the early colonists, had a library of 50 volumes, which was considerable for its day. By 1645 there were 145 college graduates in the American colonies, 100 of them from Cambridge University. This created a higher percentage of educated people in the colonies than could be found in any community of comparable size in Europe.[5]

Colonial Publishers

Many of the early colonial publishers were escaping repression in England, where the king had carefully controlled any type of publication. The English monarchy realized how dangerous books could be to its power. Printers who operated without the king's permission were often punished, sometimes by imprisonment, torture, or hanging. This repressive restraint was in place from the beginnings of English book publishing until well into the 1690s.

Printers came to America seeking freedom, which included not just the freedom to express ideas but also the freedom to make money. Printers could make more money in the colonies than in England because fewer printers were available in the colonies and printed material was much in demand there. Printing presses were hard to come by, though, because England restricted the importation of machinery that might compete with its own industries. In the early colonial years, therefore, most books were imported from England.

The First Colonial Books

The first press capable of producing books in the colonies was set up in 1638 in Cambridge, Massachusetts, at Harvard College. It produced the first book printed in America, the *Bay Psalm Book*. In the years that followed, other printers tried to satisfy some of the demand for printed work with a product known as a **chapbook,** an inexpensive early form of paperback containing mostly stories to be read for pleasure. Colonial printers also printed booklets and pamphlets developing philosophical and political ideas that became important forces in the American Revolution.

By the time books were produced in America, parchment had given way to paper made from cotton and linen fibers. Even if it was made from rags, paper was still expensive. Cloth of all kinds was scarce in the colonies, and paper was therefore relatively costly and rare. In the paper business today, the best papers still have a certain amount of cotton or linen fiber, which is referred to as **rag content.**

From Bookstores to Libraries

In an early example of the vertical integration mentioned in Chapter 1, most colonial printers also ran bookstores. These combination printing shops and

chapbook
Inexpensive early form of paperback containing mostly stories to be read for pleasure.

rag content
Proportion of cotton or linen fiber in high-quality paper.

McGuffey's Eclectic Readers,
first published in 1836, were
extremely influential in
promoting literacy.

bookstores became meeting places and educational centers. The importance of such a meeting place was not lost on early printers like Benjamin Franklin. With some of his associates, Franklin founded one of the first public libraries in 1731. Called the Library Company of Philadelphia, its purpose was to collect books and promote reading. It was the first library open to the public.

Universal Education

One of the radical ideas promoted by Franklin's Library Company and in early colonial books was that of free, taxpayer-supported, universal education. As this idea began to catch on, the schoolhouse became a fixture in early colonial villages. In 1642 Massachusetts became the first colony to pass a law requiring that every child be taught to read.

Universal education became law in the United States in the 1820s. One series of textbooks, *McGuffey's Eclectic Readers,* was extremely influential in promoting literacy. First published in 1836, the books used pictures to reinforce vocabulary. By the end of the 1800s *McGuffey's Readers* were standard in most schools—there were more than 120 million copies in print.

THE INDUSTRIAL REVOLUTION

As America grew, education became increasingly important. Workers had to be prepared for advances in science, business, transportation, and political thought. The Industrial Revolution of the late 18th and early 19th centuries ushered in a number of technological advancements that allowed more books to be published less expensively than ever before. First there was machine-made paper, produced from inexpensive wood pulp instead of cotton and linen fiber. Then came the steam-powered high-speed rotary press, followed by the lithography process that made it possible to produce high-quality illustrations at high speed. By the 1880s, pages no longer even had to be typeset by hand—Linotype machines set type automatically from a typewriter-like keyboard.

As book publishing grew, distribution became a problem because the U.S. government refused to grant book publishers the same low postage rates it gave to newspapers and magazines. Publishers tried to disguise books as both newspapers and magazines, but the government fought them until 1914, when Congress, finally realizing that the distribution of books was good for the country, established a special postal book rate.

Books that spoke out against slavery (see the Close-Up on History box) helped lead to the Civil War, after which the American publishing industry grew steadily. Scientific and industrial advancements had to be explained, and workers had to be educated to take their places in the new technological society. By the 1920s, publishing was a large and profitable business. Then some enterprising entrepreneurs thought up a new way to sell books: book clubs. The Book-of-the-Month Club was first, in 1926, followed by the Literary Guild in 1927. The idea behind the book club was to use experts to

Books and Slavery

Before the Civil War, American slaves were deprived of both books and education. Slaves who attempted to learn how to read were subjected to severe punishment. One former slave recalled, "The first time you was caught trying to read or write you was whipped with a cow-hide, the next time with a cat-o-nine tails and the third time they cut the first joint off your forefinger."[1] Punishment was even more severe for slaves who tried to teach others to read: Hanging was common for such an offense.

Several freed and escaped slaves wrote books that were important contributions to the literature of their time. In fact, the first American best seller in England, published in the 1790s, was a book of poems written by a freed black woman named Phillis Wheatley. Later, the books of Frederick Douglass were important in the abolition movement, especially his 1845 autobiography, *Narrative of the Life of Frederick Douglass,* which both told of the horrors of slavery and demonstrated the intellectual possibilities of

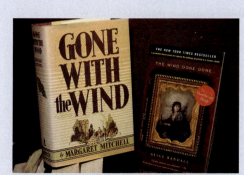

Books about slavery by African Americans continue to both create turmoil and raise awareness. In the *Media Talks* DVD that accompanies this book, author Alice Randall discusses the difficulty she had publishing her book *The Wind Done Gone,* a parody of Margaret Mitchell's *Gone With the Wind* told from the slaves' point of view.

African Americans. Douglass was born a slave, but his owner's wife had taught him the alphabet. His ability to read helped him to plot his escape from slavery using forged seaman's papers. Once he became a free man, Douglass went on to become one of the best-known abolitionists and black leaders of his day.

Another important book in the fight against slavery was Harriet Beecher Stowe's *Uncle Tom's Cabin.* Published in 1851, this novel was America's first national best seller. It brought the realities of slavery to the consciousness and imagination of the American people, although it was not appreciated everywhere. At the University of Virginia, students held a public book burning, and peddlers were run out of southern towns if they tried to sell it. Nevertheless, books were influential in bringing the harsh realities of slavery to public attention.

[1] Alberto Manguel, *A History of Reading* (New York: Viking, 1996), p. 280. See especially the chapter "Forbidden Reading."

---

suggest new books to club members. The clubs grew rapidly and soon began to influence the country's literary tastes.

 SELF QUIZ How did the Industrial Revolution affect book publishing, and vice versa?

PAPERBACK BOOKS

The modern mass-market paperback appeared in the 1930s. There were, however, two precursors of modern paperbacks: chapbooks and dime novels.

Early Paperbacks

Colonial chapbooks, mentioned earlier, were a type of paperback, but they had a limited audience, were expensive to produce, and were too costly to distribute before the days of book rate postage. **Dime novels** became popular in the 1860s, especially with Civil War soldiers, who carried them into the field. They actually sold for 10 cents and were also known as **pulp novels** because of the cheap paper on which they were printed. By 1885, one-third of all U.S. books were dime novels. This early paperback boom didn't last

dime novels
Inexpensive fiction, popular in the 1860s, that sold for 10 cents; also called pulp novels.

pulp novels
Paperback books printed on cheap paper made from wood pulp; another name for dime novels.

long, however. Because many of the dime novels were pirated from foreign editions, the Copyright Act of 1891, which made such pirating illegal, ended the business.

By 1900 a book, in most people's minds, had a hard cover and was relatively expensive. Books were sold mostly to the upper classes at traditional bookstores that were usually located in upscale neighborhoods. The modern mass-market paperback movement changed that.

Mass-Market Paperbacks

What were the earliest forms of the paperback book?

Mass-market paperbacks were introduced to the United States by Pocket Books of New York City in 1939. Pocket Books' products included not only recycled best-selling novels but also nonfiction works such as Dr. Benjamin Spock's *Baby and Child Care* (1946) and Dale Carnegie's *How to Win Friends and Influence People* (1940). To keep costs down, paperback publishers often printed works in the **public domain** (the realm embracing works, such as classics, on which the copyright has expired, meaning no royalty payments have to be made) or works by unknown authors who wrote for a low flat fee. Publishers also kept the cost of mass-market paperbacks low by using pulp paper, a small page size, and huge publishing runs that created substantial economies of scale. Retailers could thus charge just 25 cents a book, which was well within most people's entertainment budgets.

public domain
The realm embracing works on which the copyright has expired.

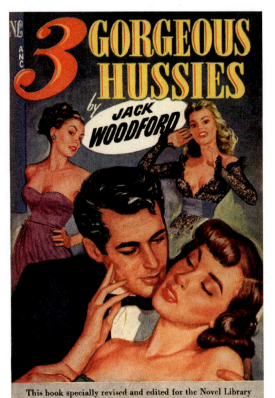

This book specially revised and edited for the Novel Library

The formula for the mass-market paperback novel consisted of a human interest story, a sexy cover, a low price, and mass distribution.

The Paperback Formula

The formula for the mass-market paperback novel consisted of a human interest story, a sexy cover, a low price, and mass distribution. Such novels often featured violent crime or tales of great heroism. The full-color cover illustrations added to the sensationalism of the story lines; they often featured attractive, scantily dressed women and men in romantic or dramatic poses, accompanied by cover lines such as "They were the cover girls on the book of temptation. This is their intimate story."[6]

Marketing the Paperback

As important as the sex-and-violence formula was, the real secret behind the success of the mass-market paperback was its distribution. Paperbacks were sold principally through periodical distributors—the wholesalers of newspapers and magazines, who knew where every little stall and kiosk was. The distributors got them into the racks in newsstands, drugstores, bus stations, and eventually airport terminals. At first the large chain stores such as Woolworth's were put off by the covers and refused to carry the books, but they finally relented and overall sales increased sharply. Soon mass-market paperbacks appeared in most department stores and even in the Sears catalog.

Before modern paperbacks came along, only the rarest of books sold more than 100,000 copies and the Bible was the only book that sold in the millions. The mass-market paperback changed the economics of book ownership. Suddenly books could reach millions of readers, many of whom had never owned a book before.

Cultural Impact of the Paperback

Many readers feared that paperbacks would be the death of real literature, but the opposite proved true in the long run. The wide dissemination of fictional materials in paperback encouraged working-class people to take up the reading habit. This in turn increased literacy, and soon more people were reading literary classics. In a way, people had to learn to "walk" through sensational human interest stories before they could "run" to the classics.

SELF QUIZ What were the keys to the success of the mass-market paperback?

The Action–Adventure Novel

The 1950s saw a boom in the paperback industry, made up mostly of mysteries, westerns, and thrillers.[7] These heavily formulaic books featured no-nonsense heroes who had high-action adventures in which the good guys ultimately triumphed over one-dimensional villains.

The Romance Novel

While action–adventure novels appealed primarily to men, the women's market was becoming increasingly important. By the 1960s women were entering the workplace in increasing numbers and paperback novels were the reading of choice on buses, trains, and planes. At the same time, paperbacks were being sold in supermarkets, where the majority of shoppers were women. Perhaps even more important, male–female relations were in the process of change during the 1960s. The growing women's movement was creating controversies about the role of women in society. It was a dynamic, sometimes confusing time, and the formula provided by romance novels seemed to provide the solace of order and stability from an earlier time. The basic formula for a romance novel was "girl meets boy, girl loses boy, girl gets boy back, and they live happily ever after."

Most publishers of romance paperbacks could afford neither to advertise nor to promote a single title heavily. Harlequin, a Canadian company founded in 1949, decided that it could market its romances in the same way as regular household products were marketed—that is, by building a brand name. Harlequin put its advertising and promotion dollars into a dependable, consistent formula quickly identifiable to a loyal group of readers. The critic Kenneth C. Davis describes the formula this way:

> The Harlequin romance invariably involves a vulnerable young woman, usually in some subservient position, who meets the man of her dreams, usually older and somewhat callous. Their stormy affair is never consummated but always brought to the dangerous borders of passion until the climax (no pun intended) in which the couple marry and the woman gives up her job.[8]

Trade Paperbacks

In the 1970s American publishers introduced a new kind of book called the **trade paperback.** Also known as quality paperbacks, trade paperbacks had a larger trim size than the standard mass-market paperback. They also had heavier covers and were made from better-quality paper. Today, trade paperbacks make up the majority of paperbacks sold in the United States.

trade paperback
A quality paperback book with a larger trim size than the standard mass-market paperback.

CONGLOMERATION AND GLOBALIZATION

Like other media industries, book publishing in the later half of the 20th century concentrated into conglomerates and went global. Very often these

FACT FILE 3.1

Top Publishers of U.S. Books

Five publishers dominate U.S. book sales, and four of them are foreign owned.

Publisher, Home Country, Web site	Companies Owned
Bertelsmann AG, Germany, www.bertelsmann.com	Anchor, Ballantine, Bantam, Broadway, Crown, Delacorte, Dell, Del Rey, Dial, Doubleday, Everyman's Library, Fawcett, Knopf, Modern Library, Pantheon, Random House, Schocken Times Books, Villard, Vintage
Pearson, England, www.pearson.com	Addison Wesley, Allyn & Bacon, Dutton-Putnam-Berkeley, Longman, Penguin, Prentice Hall, Signet Plume, Simon & Schuster's educational and reference divisions, Viking
News Corporation, Australia, www.newscorp.com	Avon, HarperCollins, William Morrow
Time Warner, United States, www.timewarner.com	Book-of-the-Month Club; Little, Brown; Sunset Books; Time-Life Books; Warner Books
Holtzbrinck, Germany, www.holtzbrink.com	Farrar, Straus & Giroux; Henry Holt; St. Martin's Press

Sources: Company Web sites.

two trends occurred at the same time, as the conglomerates that bought up publishing houses were headquartered or had interests in other countries.

By the 1960s, conglomerates both in the United States and overseas became interested in American publishers. The managers of these bottom-line-oriented conglomerates believed that American publishers were not

Five corporations dominate American book publishing. Four of these companies are foreign owned.

operating as real businesses and that much of their profit potential was remaining unrealized. Publishing houses were still mostly family owned and were still nurturing young, unproven writers with no sales records. Figuring they could do better, conglomerates began to buy up the old-name U.S. publishing houses. By 2006, five corporations dominated American book publishing; four of these companies were foreign owned (see Fact File 3.1).

When Bertelsmann AG, a huge German conglomerate, bought Random House, one of the largest and most established American publishing houses, a worried critic observed wryly, "The history of publishing began in Germany; perhaps it will end there."[9]

Global conglomerates' decision-making process differs from that of small publishing houses. Sometimes, for example, executives in one country base decisions on business and political concerns elsewhere. This has been especially true for HarperCollins, a publishing house owned by Rupert Murdoch's News Corporation of Australia. In 1996 News Corporation was trying to develop various business interests in China, including a satellite–cable TV service. That same year, HarperCollins published a biography of the Chinese

Why are international conglomerates attracted to mergers with American publishing houses?

SELF QUIZ

president Deng Xiaoping, written by his daughter. The book was blatant propaganda, and badly written at that, but News Corporation launched it with a massive publicity campaign that included star-treatment personal appearances by the author throughout the United States. Later, HarperCollins canceled a book by Chris Patton, Hong Kong's last British governor; it was well written and objective but was critical of China's human rights record. It is widely believed that both decisions were made because of Murdoch's desire to curry favor with Chinese leaders.[10]

NEW FORMS OF THE BOOK

As mentioned at the beginning of this chapter, books have taken various physical forms over the years. Along with traditional hardcovers and paperbacks, their current forms include audiobooks and e-books.

Audiobooks

Books on tape, books on disc, and downloadable podcasts, collectively called **audiobooks,** originated to allow people with vision problems to enjoy coherent collections of written information. Today they are popular with commuters who find themselves stuck on highways several hours a day, runners and others who seek to improve their minds as they tone their bodies, and people who just enjoy listening rather than reading.

Publishers produce both full-text and condensed audiobooks, many of which are recorded by the author or by a professional actor who can change voices for dozens of characters. Even in an abridged version, the audiobook of a best seller can run from three to six hours. Audiobook enthusiasts led this medium to grow to nearly $2 billion in annual retail sales by 2007.

E-Books

The term **e-books** refers to books that exist as digital files. Several companies now sell e-book devices, called readers, that are laptop computers roughly the same size and shape as a printed book. Handheld personal organizers such as the Palm and Treo are also used as e-book hardware. Buyers usually download e-books from the Internet. Some are formatted for specific hardware readers, but some can be read on any computer.

A few years ago, e-books were seen as the wave of the future in the publishing industry. Although they failed to achieve their initial promise, there has been some progress. E-books on CD-ROMs have been used as college textbooks, and some people are beginning to read novels and nonfiction books on their handheld organizers. Many students have found that classic books for literature courses can be downloaded free from Web sites such as Project Gutenberg or the University of Virginia's Electronic Text Center.

The biggest advantage of e-books for students is that one reading device can replace dozens of traditional books, which could make overloaded backpacks considerably lighter. Many e-books have built-in dictionaries, animated illustrations, and unlimited search capability. When read online, digital books also allow readers to browse around in areas of interest through hyperlinks.

E-book technology has the potential to make books less expensive to produce and distribute. It could also make more books available to buyers, because no book will need to go out of print. Several companies, in fact,

Harlequin Romances now offers novels that can be downloaded to cell phone screens. The new Harlequin On the Go series comes in daily installments, each intended to be read in 5 to 10 minutes.

audiobooks
Books recorded on tape or some other medium.

e-books
Books that exist as digital files.

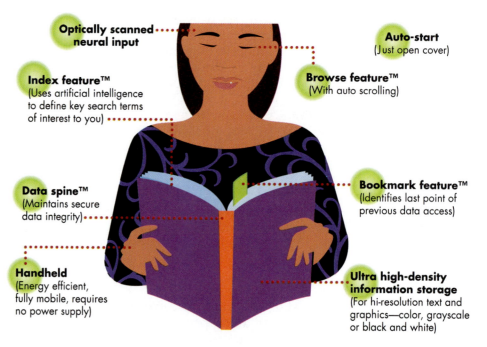

FIGURE 3.1 Technical Schematic Diagram of a Traditional Book
For most readers, traditional books still have advantages over e-books.

now specialize in printing books on demand from electronic files. For $100 or so, a company can have a book scanned into a digital library. From that point on, it costs only about $5 to print out a high-quality copy of the book from the e-book.[11] This technology is being used for both new and out-of-print books and is allowing authors to self-publish books that major publishers don't want to publish.

E-books could also be used to circumvent censorship. Governments around the world routinely ban books that threaten them in some way. Protestors can now place an entire book on the Internet so that people all over the world can read it.

Finally, the e-book has the potential to change the book as a medium. For example, interactive **hypertext fiction** can allow readers to change the plot to their liking. The first interactive novel, William Gibson's *Agrippa (A Book of the Dead),* was released on floppy disk in 1992.

E-books also have several disadvantages. The readers are relatively expensive, and often the e-books produced for one reader are incompatible with others. Another disadvantage is that most people still prefer to read on paper (see Figure 3.1). Bound books are easier on the eyes than computer

CONSIDER THIS

Do you think e-books are the wave of the future? Why or why not?

hypertext fiction
Interactive stories that allow the reader to change the plot as the narrative is read.

E-book technology has the potential to make books less expensive to produce and distribute, but most people still prefer to read on paper.

screens are. Black print on a white page provides great contrast and high resolution, which together make it comfortable to read a book on a beach.

Traditional books are convenient, lightweight, portable, and inexpensive. They don't need electric power, they don't have to be booted up, and they don't crash. With a book, you can immediately see how much you have read and how much you have left to read. Books are durable to the point of being practically unbreakable, which means that you can entrust them to a fifth grader with the reasonable expectation of getting them back in working condition.

SELF QUIZ

What are the advantages and disadvantages of e-books?

Understanding Today's Book Publishing *Industry*

Books are humanity's storehouse of culture. They are the means through which a society teaches its members everything from the basics of its government to the doctrines of its major religions. But books are also products sold by companies, and the need for those companies to make a profit often conflicts with the cultural purpose of books. Our examination of today's book publishing industry will look at the realities of the world of books, including the types of books that are published and the people who publish, market, and read them.

TYPES OF BOOKS

There are many different types of books, and many different ways to categorize them. Libraries, schools, and bookstores all have labeling systems designed to help people find the books they want. The publishing industry itself, however, categorizes them as trade, educational, reference, professional, or specialty books (see Figure 3.2).

Trade

Trade books consist of fiction and nonfiction books that are sold to the general public. They can be hardbound, trade paperback, or mass-market paperback books. Trade books include both adult and children's books, and they account for the largest share of books sold by publishers. Most bookstore titles are trade books.

trade books Fiction and nonfiction books sold to the general public.

Trade	Educational	Reference	Professional
General interest fiction and nonfiction sold to the public	Texts for elementary, secondary, college, and vocational schools	Collections of facts and information for general research	Information for specialized occupations, such as law, medicine, or engineering

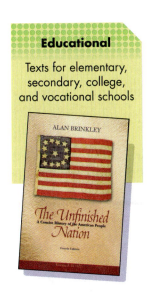

FIGURE 3.2 Types of Books The publishing industry categorizes books according to these four broad categories, as well as a fifth category, "Specialty," which includes everything from religious titles to college yearbooks.

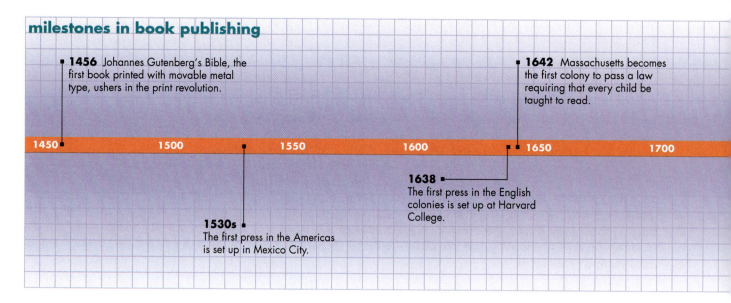

milestones in book publishing

1456 Johannes Gutenberg's Bible, the first book printed with movable metal type, ushers in the print revolution.

1642 Massachusetts becomes the first colony to pass a law requiring that every child be taught to read.

1450   1500   1550   1600   1650   1700

1638
The first press in the English colonies is set up at Harvard College.

1530s
The first press in the Americas is set up in Mexico City.

Educational

Compared with sales of trade books, those of educational books are reliable and easy to predict: They have grown steadily throughout U.S. history, and many believe that educational books will be the great growth industry of 21st-century publishing. Educational books include textbooks for elementary, secondary, college, and vocational schools.

Elementary/High School Textbooks

Elementary/high school, or el-hi, texts are sold directly to school systems throughout the United States and sometimes to state adoption boards. The especially powerful boards in Texas and California can influence textbook content for the entire nation because publishers are often willing to alter text content to encourage big sales. State boards that include religious conservatives, for example, have been able to expunge discussions of evolution from science texts.

College Textbooks

Publishers market college textbooks to professors, who in turn require students to buy the texts through the college bookstore. The required nature of the purchase, as well as ever-increasing costs, have made the price of college texts controversial.

An interesting development in the college textbook industry is the idea of the custom text. Professors can now order specific chapters of a textbook, which the publisher will custom-bind. They can also mix and match chapters from several different textbooks.

Cultural Importance of Educational Books

On the global level educational books greatly influence culture, and that has made them controversial in recent years. To cite just one of many examples, some critics have said that textbooks in Islamic countries helped lead to the terrorist attacks of September 11, 2001. In these countries—which include Saudi Arabia and Pakistan, supposedly allies of the United States—the only texts in some schools were 17th-century versions of the Koran. Students

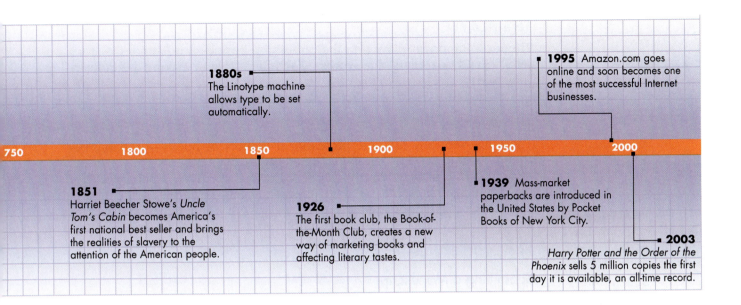

1880s
The Linotype machine allows type to be set automatically.

1995 Amazon.com goes online and soon becomes one of the most successful Internet businesses.

750   1800   1850   1900   1950   2000

1851
Harriet Beecher Stowe's *Uncle Tom's Cabin* becomes America's first national best seller and brings the realities of slavery to the attention of the American people.

1926
The first book club, the Book-of-the-Month Club, creates a new way of marketing books and affecting literary tastes.

1939 Mass-market paperbacks are introduced in the United States by Pocket Books of New York City.

2003
Harry Potter and the Order of the Phoenix sells 5 million copies the first day it is available, an all-time record.

were not exposed to critical thinking or modern subjects. As a result, without other books to serve as comparison, the ancient text could be interpreted to condemn all non-Muslims as infidels deserving of death. Several critics have pointed out that such indoctrination in religious schools led to a wide recruitment among anti-American terrorist networks.[12]

Reference

Reference books, such as encyclopedias, dictionaries, atlases, and almanacs, are used for looking up facts and information. Today's reference works, especially encyclopedias, are as likely to appear on the Internet or on CD-ROMs as on paper. Although expensive to originally produce, reference works remain profitable because they come out in new editions periodically and much of the content is recycled. Also, there are no big-name authors who must receive advances. The more expensive multivolume reference works, such as the *Encyclopaedia Britannica* are sold mostly to libraries; smaller general interest reference books, such as the *World Almanac and Book of Facts* and the *Information Please Almanac,* are sold to the general public through bookstores.

Professional

Professional books are those that contain the information people need for specialized occupations, including law, business, medicine, and engineering. Not intended for general readers, these books include manuals, original research, and technical and scientific reports. E-books have already realized some success as professional books.

Specialty

The specialty classification includes any type of book that doesn't fit into one of the categories above. It consists of religious books, mementos such as high school and college yearbooks, and anthologies of cartoons and comics (although comic books are categorized as magazines).

SELF QUIZ What are the five basic types of books?

THE PLAYERS

The most important players in the publishing business are authors, editors, publishers, booksellers, and readers. Each has a role in making the industry profitable.

The Author

There are very few full-time professional authors of books—probably between 100 and 200 for the entire United States. Most authors do something else, in addition to writing books, to earn a living. They teach, work for newspapers or magazines, or work as entertainers—celebrities make up one of the largest classes of authors. Noncelebrities who want to become authors generally establish their credentials in other forms of writing, such as newspaper and magazine articles for nonfiction, and short stories for fiction.

Submitting a Manuscript

Publishers receive many unsolicited manuscripts. In the business these are said to "come in over the transom" (after the openings at the top of old-style office doorways), and they often land in "slush piles"—stacks of manuscripts that may be thrown away without being read. To avoid this fate, an aspiring book author should complete one or two sample chapters and then send a query letter to a carefully selected agent or editor at a publishing house. If interested, the agent or editor will read the sample chapters and then work with the author as the book is written. An agent's or editor's input can give the finished book a better chance of being financially successful.

Contracts and Royalties

An author writes in one of two ways: either on speculation **(on spec)** or under contract. To write on spec means to finish a book without a commitment from a publisher. First-time novelists, for example, usually write on spec because they have to prove what they are capable of before a publisher will take a chance on them. Established authors and celebrities typically write under contract.

For a nonfiction trade book or a textbook, a potential publisher will send chapters out to prepublication reviewers who can provide insight into whether the idea for the book is sound and whether there is a market for it. If the reviewers say that revisions are necessary, the publisher might ask the author to make those changes before a contract is drawn up.

The contract usually involves an advance (an up-front payment) against royalties to provide the author with income as the project is completed. **Royalties** are the author's share of the net amount of the work's revenues. Authors' royalties usually run anywhere from 5 to 15 percent of the publisher's revenue for the book, although a star author like Stephen King can command up to 25 percent. If the book "earns out" more than his or her advance, the author collects the additional royalty.

Celebrity Authors

There are two types of celebrity authors: (1) established writers like Stephen King and J. K. Rowling and (2) people who become celebrated in other areas—entertainment, sports, politics—and write books about themselves. This second type of celebrity has changed the definition of what it means to be an author. Today, publishers sign celebrities to multimillion-dollar con-

---

on spec
On speculation; in the publishing industry, finishing a work without a contract guaranteeing that it will be bought.

royalties
The author's share of the net amount of a work's revenues.

The Harry Potter Phenomenon

It's certainly not the first time that a handful of books has changed the world. It's just that these books were unlikely candidates.

The Harry Potter books. They seem to have changed the world of publishing. Sales of children's literature have picked up markedly since Potter's U.S. debut in 1998. The publishing industry loves the books because they bring people, including adults, into bookstores, where other titles might catch their eye. The *New York Times* was forced to establish a new best-seller list, exclusively for children's literature, because Potter books were taking up too much of the adult list. The new list brought fresh attention to children's books in general.

By the time the sixth book in the series, *Harry Potter and the Half-Blood Prince,* hit the bookstores in the summer of 2005, more than 270 million copies of the first five books had been sold. Sales of *The Half-Blood Prince* reached 6.9 million copies in its first 24 hours, eclipsing the record of 5 million copies held by the previous Potter book. That was an average of 287,000 copies sold per hour. Most authors could retire on a couple of hours' worth of Harry Potter sales. The first three books in the series had been made into blockbuster movies, while the fourth was in postproduction. The books' influence was truly global—they had been translated into 55 languages and were available in 200 countries.

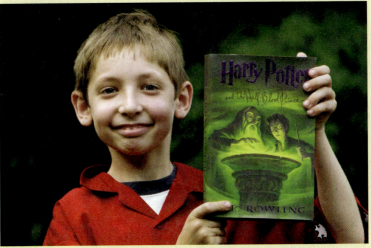

Harry Potter books have changed the world by getting children—even boys—interested in reading.

The Harry Potter books have made J. K. Rowling, their author, the wealthiest woman in England—wealthier than the queen. Not bad, when you consider that Rowling was a single mother on welfare when she began writing the first book in the series.

The most important way the Harry Potter books appear to have changed the world, however, is that they have gotten children to read—even boys ages 9 to 12, the segment of the population least likely to read anything. Boys dive into the Potter books, even the 890-page *Order of the Phoenix,* as if they were the latest video game. They like the characters Rowling has created, and they like to talk about them in the schoolyard the next day. For that, many parents and teachers believe that Rowling deserves a Nobel Prize.

tracts and then go looking for ghostwriters or collaborators to actually write the book. In this star system of publishing, books are sold on the author's name value in much the same way as a movie star guarantees the box office for a blockbuster film. Thus Fabio Lanzoni, a model who became famous after posing for the covers of romance novels (and who is known simply as Fabio), "wrote" several novels with an established author.

Critics say that celebrity authors are a natural outgrowth of the fact that publishers look not for the best writer but rather for the author who can sell the most books. An author might have this potential because he or she is "promotable." Perhaps he has a compelling story—as did John Grisham,

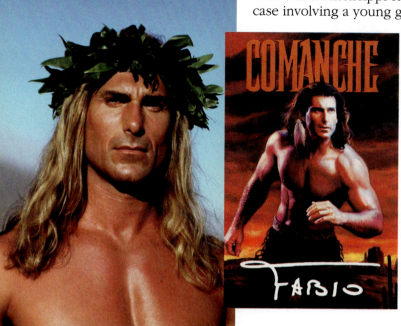

In one of the stranger turns on celebrity authorship, the paperback romance cover model Fabio became an author of romances, "in collaboration with" established author Eugenia Riley.

who was a Mississippi state legislator and a criminal lawyer when a local case involving a young girl inspired him to write his first novel, *A Time to Kill* (1988). Grisham, like Tom Clancy, Stephen King, and J. K. Rowling, is now a "seamless sell," which is what publishers call an author who always has a book coming out, either in hardcover or paperback. Authors who are seamless sells are easy to promote. Publishers also look for authors who are attractive and can hold their own in polite conversation, making them naturals for the talk-show circuit. One critic claims that publishers also give preference to good-looking authors because they will look better on the back flap of dust jackets.[13]

The Editors

There are several different types of book editors, including acquisition editors, developmental editors, production editors, and copy editors.

Acquisition Editors

An **acquisition editor** is responsible for obtaining (acquiring) books to be published. Sometimes acquisition editors choose an over-the-transom book suggested to them by an intern or assistant whose job it is to pull manuscripts from the slush pile. Usually, though, acquisition editors solicit particular manuscripts. Perhaps an article in a magazine or a short story in a literary journal will interest an editor, who will contact the author to propose that the article or story be expanded into a book. Generally, acquisition editors keep in touch with several authors and author's agents to see if any interesting projects are in the works. Often they will meet, perhaps over lunch, with authors and agents to toss ideas around and see if they can figure out a new approach for a book that would have sales potential. The actual decisions about what to publish, however, are made by publishing committees, which include financial and marketing people. The acquisitions editor will present the project to the group in a formal presentation.

acquisition editor
An editor who obtains books to be published.

About 75 percent of editors are women.

developmental editor
An editor who works directly with the author during the writing of a book, going over each chapter and suggesting major revisions.

copy editor
An editor who polishes a manuscript line by line and prepares it for typesetting.

Developmental Editors, Production Editors, and Copy Editors

Once the manuscript is acquired, the acquisitions editor might stay in touch and act as the author's intermediary with the publisher, but he or she usually does not work on the manuscript itself. That is the work of the developmental editor, the production editor, and the copy editor. The **developmental editor** works with the author, going over each chapter and suggesting any major revisions, including new directions for the author to take, sections to add and passages to cut. When the manuscript is complete, it goes into production, where the production editor oversees the process of turning the manuscript into a bound book. Part of the production team is the **copy editor**, who carefully polishes the manuscript line by line and prepares it for typesetting.

Authors

Professional writers

Experts in other fields

Celebrities

Publishers

Major publishers

Independents

University presses

Small presses

Vanity presses

Editors

Acquisition editors

Developmental editors

Copy editors

Booksellers

Chains

Megastores

Independents

Online booksellers

Readers

Bibliophiles

Casual readers

Required readers

Aliterates

Illiterates

FIGURE 3.3 Players in the Book Industry These are the most important players in the book publishing business.

According to the Association of American Publishers, about 75 percent of editors are women. Ethnic minorities are less well represented in publishing; only around 5 percent of editors are African Americans, and 9 percent are other ethnic minorities, including Hispanics and Asians.

The Publisher

Although the top five publishers (see again Fact File 3.1) garner a large portion of U.S. book industry revenues, there are between 10,000 and 20,000 other publishers in business. This number fluctuates because many small publishing endeavors are started by eager entrepreneurs who fail quickly and fade from the scene. Some publishers specialize in a particular type of book, such as trade, educational, reference, professional, or specialty. Others publish only a particular **genre** (that is, a type of writing), such as romance or mystery novels. Figure 3.3 lists the major players in the book publishing industry.

genre
Type of writing, such as romance or mystery.

Minority Publishers

There are numerous small, independent book companies that target particular minority audiences. Pleasant Company Publications, for example, specializes in fiction and nonfiction for girls, and Just Us Books, Inc., publishes stories for young black readers. Cinco Punto Press in El Paso, Texas, publishes books for children and adults from the Mexican border area and throughout the southwestern United States. Odd Girls Press publishes books for gay, lesbian, bisexual, and transgendered audiences, and New Victoria Publishers targets lesbian audiences.

University Presses

A **university press** is a publisher affiliated with an institution of higher education that produces mostly academic books, especially original research by college professors. University presses are often subsidized by their institutions and are able to publish low-profit, low-print-run books. Professors are willing to review the manuscripts of these books free of charge, authors don't expect much in terms of royalties, and libraries buy enough copies to keep the press in business. There are around 100 university presses in the United States.

Small Presses and Others

A **small press** is a publisher with a few employees and minimal facilities. Many small presses try to publish serious books, especially the poetry and avant-garde fiction that tends not to interest big publishers. A big publisher would find it very difficult to make a profit on a book that sold just 1,000 to 5,000 copies, but a small press would consider that a successful run. One type of publisher, known as a **vanity press,** requires its authors to pay the full cost of producing their own books. **Online publishers** such as iUniverse.com provide "supported self publishing," in which editorial help is provided through a Web site and only the books that are ordered and paid for will be printed. Online publishers tend to be less expensive than a vanity press as a way to publish books that do not catch the interest of publishing houses owned by conglomerates. The U.S. government is also a publisher, through the U.S. Government Printing Office, which prints many book-length government reports.

Book Promotion

The publisher is also concerned with the promotion of the finished book. In some ways, this job is like the promotion of any other product. The pub-

iUniverse is an online publisher that helps authors self-publish and then prints only those books that are sold.

lisher has to decide what media the book should be advertised in and what approach that advertising should take. Publishers have experimented with dramatic TV commercials that make books look like movies, and with billboards, placed near bookstores, that make authors look like movie stars. A standard promotional item in publishing is a large cardboard point-of-purchase display, called a dump when it includes a bin to hold copies of the book. Publishers also coordinate a force of sales representatives. Sales reps for trade books travel to bookstores and speak to buyers. In the educational market, sales reps visit professors and introduce them to the new texts their houses are publishing.

Publishers also have at their disposal several methods of promotion that are unique to the book industry:

• *Jacket blurbs*. Publishers will send manuscripts to well-known writers, critics, and experts in the topic area of the book, asking for brief laudatory comments, or **blurbs,** that can be placed on the cover of the book. Blurbs can be rich with hidden meaning. Exaggerations like "One of the most significant books ever published" are not uncommon, but sometimes the blurb can be subtly noncommittal, such as "Never in my life have I read such a book." Sometimes a blurb is taken from a critic's review of one of the author's earlier books. Other times friends who are on a first-name basis with the author provide the blurb. Dave Barry satirized this trend when he provided the following: "Tony Kornheiser is the funniest writer in world history. And I do not say this because he is my close personal friend. I say this because I am a pathological liar."[14]

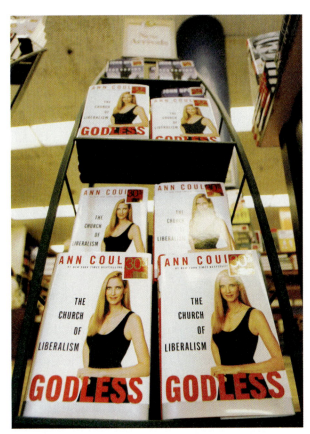

Ann Coulter often promotes her books with heated rhetoric. In *Godless: The Church of Liberalism,* she said of the widows of the September 11, 2001, terrorist attacks: "These broads are millionaires, lionized on TV and in articles about them, reveling in their status as celebrities and stalked by grief-arazzis. I have never seen people enjoying their husband's death so much." Coulter promptly went on the talk-show circuit to defend her point of view.

• *Magazine and newspaper reviews*. Book reviews are extremely important in book promotion. Book buyers are readers, and they take to heart the reviews in their favorite magazines and newspapers. To make sure that reviewers have enough time to read the book before it comes out, publishers send them the book three or four months ahead of publication, as either bound or unbound galleys, which are samples of the book made after typesetting but before final proofreading (and without the final cover). Periodicals such as *Kirkus Reviews, Publishers Weekly,* and *Booklist* can be extremely important to sales, because bookstores, libraries, and schools use them to make decisions about purchases.

blurb
Brief laudatory comments that can be placed on the cover of a book.

• *Excerpts*. The publisher hopes that putting a fragment of the book in a magazine or newspaper, or on a Web site, will get readers to want more of the same and eventually buy the book. Excerpts also add to the "buzz," or hype, that says that something big is being published. Publishers used to be able to sell excerpts to magazines for tens of thousands of dollars, but as magazines realized the promotional role they played by printing excerpts, they demanded lower prices, usually just a few thousand dollars. Whole chapters are now routinely made available on the author's, publisher's, or bookstore's Web site, as well as through direct mail and as booklets inserted into newspapers.

Book signings are a time-honored form of book promotion. Here, former Vice President Al Gore signs copies of his book on global warming, *An Inconvenient Truth*, at a Nashville, Tennessee bookstore.

• *Book tours*. On a traditional book tour, the author travels to bookstores where the book is being sold and signs copies that customers buy. Book tours continue to be popular with publishers and booksellers, who get publicity, and with book buyers, who get a signature that increases the book's value. Today's book tour includes appearances on television and radio talk shows. Publishers have a symbiotic (that is, mutually beneficial) relationship with these shows. The shows want celebrity authors, and the publishers want publicity, especially on television. Oprah Winfrey's television program, for example, has been a significant force in book sales since the start of Oprah's Book Club in 1996.

Of course, some blockbusters make their own rules when it comes to promotion. When *Harry Potter and the Half-Blood Prince* went on sale precisely at midnight on Friday, July 16, 2005, bookstores stayed open for the event. Some threw parties and invited kids to show up in costume as characters from the Harry Potter's world. The boxes of books were carefully guarded during shipment, sometimes by armed guards. To preserve the surprise of the story, the publisher allowed no advance reviews and sent no excerpts to magazines or newspapers.

The Bookseller

Books are sold in many different and unlikely places, and the number of outlets is growing. There are an estimated 13,000 bookstores in the United States today, about 75 percent more than in the 1980s. About 17,000 other outlets, including drugstores, department stores, pet shops, discount clubs, supermarkets, office product stores, and computer retailers also sell books. Book sales are generated in clothing stores and movie theaters as well, but the majority of sales occur in one of three places: chains, independent bookstores, and online.

Chains and Megastores

Although they are facing some serious competition from online booksellers, chain bookstores such as those owned by Barnes & Noble and Borders still take in more than half of the money from U.S. book sales, and other countries such as England and Germany are following this trend. Many chain stores are small, mall-based outlets, but some are superstores, also known as **megastores.** Megastores feature around 100,000 book titles as well as live readings by authors, activities for children, coffee bars, and numerous racks of magazines and out-of-town newspapers. In some locations, including some college towns, these stores are becoming a kind of intellectual gathering place, reminiscent of colonial print shops, only bigger.[15]

Many book lovers see megastores as a threat to the publishing industry. The clerks aren't paid much and often don't know a lot about books. The managers stock books strictly by the numbers rather than by any concept of worth or quality. The computerized inventory systems of the chains and megastores let managers know what books are and are not selling. Unsold books are quickly returned to the publisher. In fact, booksellers return around 35 to 40 percent of the books they order.[16] Many of these books become "remaindered," which means essentially that the publisher has given up on full-price sales. Remainders are returned to the bookstore as "bargain

megastores
Large bookstores that feature around 100,000 book titles and offer various amenities such as coffee bars and live readings.

Amazon.com is the leading bookstore in cyberspace. Here workers are gathering books for shipment inside one Amazon warehouse.

books" to be sold at a fraction of their original price. Chains also charge publishers to have their books displayed in prime space. Front-of-store and end-of-aisle displays throughout the chain can cost a publisher $10,000 a month per title.[17] The power of the chains and megastores also means that book-buying decisions are being placed into fewer hands. This has become especially true with the demise of many small, independent bookstores.

Independent Bookstores

Independent bookstores are not owned by a chain and are not part of a larger company. They often specialize in a particular type of book. Some focus on a cultural niche, such as women, African Americans, Hispanics, or gays and lesbians. Others sell only religious books, self-help books, or books on health. Many independent bookstores, finding it difficult to compete with chains, have gone out of business, but other independents have begun to fight back. Through their trade group, the American Booksellers Association (ABA), the independent bookstores have sued publishers and forced them to give small bookstores the same discounts they give to the large chain stores.

independent bookstores
Booksellers not owned by a chain and not part of a larger company.

Online Booksellers

Rather than outmoding books, the Internet has made them easier to attain. Amazon.com is the leading bookstore in cyberspace. Jeff Bezos, who founded the company in 1994, reasoned that bookselling would be a natural for Internet commerce because book sales could benefit from the huge amount of

Although facing serious competition from online booksellers, chain bookstores still take in more than half of the money from U.S. book sales.

information that a Web site could offer. No book clerk can be an expert on all subjects, and no physical bookstore can stock every book in print. Amazon invited book enthusiasts with Web pages to become "associates," recommending books on their Web pages and receiving an 8 percent referral fee for each sale they generated. Amazon also developed a powerful search program and a database program called Bookmatcher that recommends books based on a customer's other preferences. It also has a "search inside" feature that allows customers to electronically hunt for a particular topic in a book.

Other online booksellers include Barnes & Noble, Alibris, and more than 250 independent and specialty sites. Used books are now part of most online sales.

The Reader

Readers are the most important players in the book publishing game, because they determine what is published. Critics complain about the number of trashy celebrity biographies and romance novels that are published, but if readers didn't purchase them, publishers wouldn't publish them for long. Publishers notice trends in readership, and they react to them. When they saw that 70 to 80 percent of fiction buyers are women, they went out of their way to publish books written by women as well as books (by women or men) that have a strong woman as a central character. Publishers have also noticed the markets represented by ethnic minorities. In recent years, for example, black authors such as Terry McMillan (*Waiting to Exhale*) and Toni Morrison (*Beloved*) have consistently topped best-seller lists.

Types of Readers

There have always been different types of readers. The most enthusiastic are known as **bibliophiles**—book lovers who consume 50 or more books a year and devote time to reading that others might spend socializing, watching TV, or surfing the Web. Bibliophiles started the phenomenon of neighborhood book groups, in which friends and acquaintances gather to discuss a book that they all have read. **Casual readers** are those who enjoy reading but find the time to read only a few books a year. **Required readers** might read extensively, but they read only what they have to for their job or studies. Many students on both the high school and college levels are required readers. Textbook sales would be nonexistent without students, and the sales of classic literature are highly dependent on college students.

Types of Nonreaders

Just as there are different types of readers, there are also different types of nonreaders. The two main categories of nonreaders are illiterates and aliterates. **Illiterates** are those who can't read because they never learned how. Some experts suggest that as many as one in five Americans are functionally illiterate—they may have some basic skills but cannot read even a simple children's story with comprehension. **Aliterates** are those who can read but don't. They include people who dislike the act of reading and people who just never picked up the habit. Some experts estimate that as many as 15 percent of Americans are aliterates. According to Gallup polls, fewer books are read in the United States, per capita, than in any other English-speaking country.

Even in this age of conglomerates and megastores, the book industry is in the business of creating readers by lifting nonreaders into the ranks of casual readers and casual readers into the ranks of bibliophiles. According to

© The New Yorker Collection 2002
C. Covert Darbyshire from
cartoonbank.com. All Rights
Reserved.

bibliophiles
Book lovers; heavy readers.

casual readers
Those who enjoy reading but find the time to read only a few books a year.

required readers
Those who read only what they have to for their jobs or studies.

illiterates
Those who can't read because they never learned how.

aliterates
Those who are able to read but do not.

a number of surveys, the industry seems to be succeeding, because book reading is on the rise. Readers have been cutting down on newspapers, but they have been spending more time reading books—about 100 hours a year on average.[18]

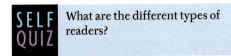
SELF QUIZ What are the different types of readers?

CONSIDER THIS
What type of reader are you? What effect has your reading style had on your education and your life?

Controversies

In an era of X-rated cable TV and movies with body counts the size of the population of small countries, it seems strange to speak of books and the book industry as controversial. And yet books can cause controversy, mainly because of their enormous influence. As enduring repositories of culture, books have direct and powerful effects on their readers. Children acquire part of their outlook on the world from textbooks, and adults seek life's meaning in the books they read. It is because of the power of books that legislators, religious leaders, teachers, and parents have always been concerned about their content, and this concern has led in some cases to censorship.

BOOK CENSORSHIP

The First Amendment to the U.S. Constitution restricts government interference with free speech, so any act of government censorship tends to be a serious issue. Books, however, have often been the targets of censors. In fact, many books now considered classics have been censored at one time or another. James Joyce's *Ulysses,* considered by many to be the best novel ever written, was banned by the U.S. government from 1920 until 1933 because of its close examination of the sex life of its main characters. Even journal editors who tried to print excerpts were jailed on charges of obscenity.[19] Joyce's case hinged on how to define obscenity, pornography, and art—questions we still grapple with today (see Fact File 3.2).

Censorship by quasi-governmental agencies such as public schools and libraries has also been extremely controversial over the years. The Los Angeles Public Library pulled Edgar Rice Burroughs's *Tarzan* from the shelves in 1929 because the title character was living with a woman (Jane) to whom he was not married. In recent years, school libraries have removed children's books such as *Heather Has Two Mommies* and *Daddy's Roommate* from their shelves because of their depiction of gay lifestyles. Libraries have removed books dealing with drugs, the occult, and suicide, as well as books containing profane language or sexual themes, such as J. D. Salinger's *Catcher in the Rye.* They have also removed books that contained ethnic slurs and other forms of insensitivity. Mark Twain's classic *The Adventures of Huckleberry Finn* has been removed from many libraries because of its use of the word *nigger.*

Censorship as Unintentional Promotion

Ironically, challenging a book usually provides publicity that stimulates sales. "Banned in Boston" was a sales pitch

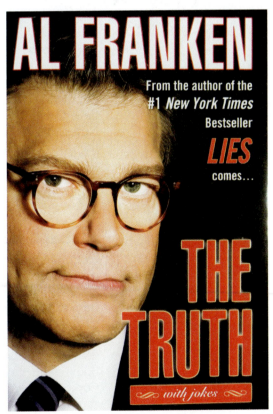

Al Franken is one of the authors who have gained publicity from attempts to censor their books.

FACT FILE 3.2

Most Frequently Banned Books

The following were the most frequently challenged books in the United States during 2005, as compiled by the Office of Intellectual Freedom of the American Library Association.

1. *It's Perfectly Normal* for homosexuality, nudity, sex education, religious viewpoint, abortion, and being unsuited to age group.

2. *Forever* by Judy Blume for sexual content and offensive language.

3. *The Catcher in the Rye* by J.D. Salinger for sexual content, offensive language, and being unsuited to age group.

4. *The Chocolate War* by Robert Cormier for sexual content and offensive language.

5. *Whale Talk* by Chris Crutcher for racism and offensive language.

6. *Detour for Emmy* by Marilyn Reynolds for sexual content.

7. *What My Mother Doesn't Know* by Sonya Sones for sexual content and being unsuited to age group.

8. Captain Underpants series by Dav Pilkey for anti-family content, being unsuited to age group, and violence.

9. *Crazy Lady!* by Jane Leslie Conly for offensive language.

10. *It's So Amazing! A Book about Eggs, Sperm, Birth, Babies, and Families* by Robie H. Harris for sex education and sexual content.

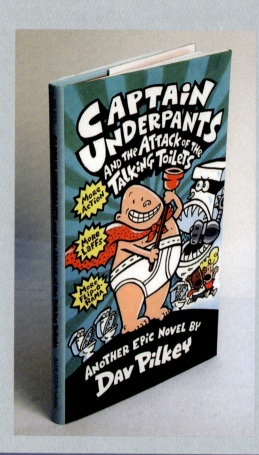

The Captain Underpants books are among those most often challenged in schools and libraries by parent and religious groups.

in the 1950s for books such as D. H. Lawrence's *Lady Chatterly's Lover.* In recent years, a minister's protest against *Heather Has Two Mommies* and *Daddy's Roommate* increased sales of those books when protestors went out, bought copies, and donated them to local libraries. Some observers believe that lawsuits against publishers are a form of censorship, but when Fox News sued Al Franken in 2003 for using the phrase "fair and balanced" in the title of his book *Lies and the Lying Liars Who Tell Them: A Fair and Balanced Look at the Right,* the publicity became a windfall for the publisher as millions of readers who might not have otherwise heard of the book became aware of it.[20]

Global Censorship

Examples of U.S. censorship tend to be rare, but book censorship occurs all over the world, usually on far stricter terms than in the United States. When novelist Salman Rushdie's *Satanic Verses* was banned in Iran in 1989, the Iranian leader issued a death sentence against the author. Rushdie, a British citizen living in Paris at the time, was forced to live in hiding to escape the order. Recent travelers to Vietnam have been surprised to have their travel guides confiscated because they referred to Vietnam's 1978 invasion of Cambodia—the Vietnamese government took exception to the word *invasion.* Copies of *The Rough Guide to Morocco* were confiscated in that country because they included a map showing a border with Western Sahara, which Morocco claims is part of its own country. Books are routinely banned in

China, although in recent years pirated copies of banned books have become best sellers there.

In Praise of Censorship

Censorship of any kind tends to make people immediately take a side. Those who might call themselves free speech advocates gather on one flank and those who might call themselves child protection advocates gather on the other. Free speech advocates often complain about the censorship of fiction, pointing out that a novel is not an instruction manual and that the existence of controversial issues in a book does not mean that readers will adopt negative behaviors. Child protection advocates find it difficult to accept this argument, however, when the book *is* an instruction manual, one that apparently advocates some kind of violence. Paladin Press, for example, publishes over 600 books, including *Hit Man: A Technical Manual for Contractors, Breath of the Dragon: Homebuilt Flamethrowers,* and several books on how to make explosives at home. These kinds of books have been implicated in school violence.

Irving Kristol, a conservative intellectual who served as editor of *The Public Interest* magazine and as an adviser to President Ronald Reagan, once pointed out, "If you believe that no one was ever corrupted by a book, you

> **"If you believe that no one was ever corrupted by a book, you have also to believe that no one was ever improved by a book."—Irving Kristol**

have also to believe that no one was ever improved by a book. You have to believe, in other words, that all art is morally trivial, and that, consequently, all education is morally irrelevant."[21] Kristol also spoke of the relationship of censorship to democracy. He insisted that if you truly believe in democracy, you have to believe in censorship. "The desirability of self government depends on the character of the people who govern," he said, and these people should take care "not to let themselves be governed by the more infantile and irrational parts of themselves." Kristol underscored his belief in the importance of censorship by saying, "What is at stake is civilization and humanity, nothing less."[22]

SELF QUIZ In what ways has censorship affected the book publishing industry?

CONSIDER THIS

When, if ever, is book censorship justified? Use examples to explain your answer.

THE BLOCKBUSTER SYNDROME

Another recurrent controversy in the book publishing industry is the blockbuster syndrome. The term **blockbuster** refers to all types of huge events, especially in terms of media products. The word comes from a type of bomb used in World War II that was capable of wiping out entire blocks of buildings. It is ironic that in today's parlance *bomb* is the opposite of *blockbuster*.

Publishers have always been interested in publishing blockbusters, but today's obsession with them controls the economics of the industry. If the publisher believes the public will be interested in a story, the sky seems to be the limit. After Bill Clinton left office, his publisher gave him a $10 million advance for his unwritten memoirs. Hillary Clinton was given $8 million for hers.

Critics contend that the huge advances paid for potential blockbusters leave little money left over to publish more challenging or literary works, or to publish books by new and promising talent (see the Close-Up on Controversy box). Others hypothesize

blockbuster
All types of huge events, especially in terms of media products.

SELF QUIZ What is the blockbuster syndrome, and what are its effects?

A Victim of the Blockbuster Syndrome?

Critics believe that one effect of the blockbuster syndrome is the freezing out of young talent. An early example of this was the case of John Kennedy Toole, who in the 1960s wrote a novel called *A Confederacy of Dunces*. Toole submitted the manuscript to a long list of publishers, but none of them thought the novel, about a group of oddball characters in New Orleans, had commercial potential. After years of rejection, Toole lost hope and committed suicide at the age of 31. His mother, in despair, decided that she would take up her son's cause.

Over a period of 10 years she sent the manuscript to eight different publishers, all of whom rejected it. She then took the book to the well-known novelist Walker Percy, who was teaching at a university nearby. Like most successful writers, Percy was often asked to read the works of writers hoping for publication. Authors are usually able to read only a page or two before dismissing the work being thrust upon them. But this book was different. Percy read the first pages and then the first chapters; before he knew it, he had read the entire book. He loved it, and he convinced the Louisiana State University Press to publish it. Like most university presses, Louisiana's had little money for promotion or large printings, but Toole's *A Confederacy of Dunces*, finally published in 1980, became a best seller anyway. It also won the 1981 Pulitzer Prize for fiction and eventually was translated into a dozen foreign languages. Unfortunately, however, the book's success came far too late to be of any use to its author.

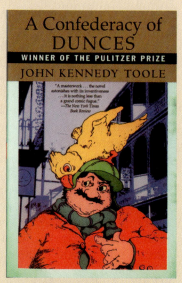

A Confederacy of Dunces became a best seller too late for its author to enjoy his success.

that the greatest works of literature from the past would never be published as new books under today's economic conditions. If that is true, the loss to global culture would be considerable.

Authors who write books that have literary merit but doubtful commercial potential are known in the publishing world as **midlist authors.** Midlist authors don't make it to the best-seller lists but still have respectable sales, usually between 10,000 and 15,000 copies. Many famous authors would be considered midlist authors today. William Faulkner and John Irving had small sales for their early books. Henry David Thoreau sold only 2,000 copies of *Walden*.

The quest for blockbusters has led to "books by crooks." In fact, so many publishers began to sign convicted criminals to write books about their lurid crimes that many states have passed laws prohibiting a criminal from profiting from book sales about his or her crime. The most famous of these statutes was New York's Son of Sam law, named after an infamous serial killer.

Another problem that has been associated with the quest for blockbusters is a decline in quality, particularly a decline in accuracy in works of nonfiction. According to some critics, publishers scrimp on editing and fact-checking to pay for big advances. Critics contend that lack of editorial control has led to an enormous number of factual errors published as truth.

midlist authors
Authors who don't make it to the best-seller lists but still have respectable sales.

What are the major controversies in today's world of books?

SELF QUIZ

A related problem has been a number of books that have turned out to be hoaxes or that have been plagiarized. One celebrated case was that of Kaavya Viswanathan, a Harvard sophomore who published a novel in 2006 entitled *How Opal Mehta Got Kissed, Got Wild, and Got a Life*. The book was about an Indian American girl struggling to get into Harvard. Because of her youth, her Harvard pedigree, and the apparent autobiographical basis of the book, it was heralded as a sure best seller and the premiere of a promising literary career. The book was on the shelves only a few days, however, when readers noticed that passages had been copied from three other novels by two different authors.[23] The publisher withdrew the book from publication.

Another 2006 scandal involved yet another first-time author, James Frey, who had published a memoir about his struggles to overcome alcoholism and drug addiction. The book, *A Million Little Pieces*, caught the attention of Oprah Winfrey, who featured it on her television book club. As is typical of a book promoted by Oprah, this one soared onto the best-seller lists. In fact, it sold more than two million copies in the three months following the author's appearance on Winfrey's show, making it the fastest-selling book in the club's 10-year history. The Smoking Gun, an investigative Web site, then reported that it had found multiple discrepancies between Frey's life and his account in the book. Among the site's findings were that Frey had spent only a few hours in jail, not nearly three months as he had written, and that he lied when he claimed that he had received a root canal without anesthesia because the dental center prohibited the use of novocaine.

The author James Frey was rebuked by Oprah Winfrey for lying in his memoir, *A Million Little Pieces*.

Oprah defended Frey on *Larry King Live*, but then changed her mind and brought him back onto her television show to rebuke him for lying about his past and portraying the book as a truthful account of his life. "I feel duped," she told him. "But more importantly, I feel that you betrayed millions of readers."[24] She also apologized to her viewers for defending Frey earlier, saying, "I made a mistake and I left the impression that the truth does not matter. And I am deeply sorry about that, because that is not what I believe."[25]

Many book lovers hope that online publishing can help solve the block-buster syndrome, at least partially. While publishers will probably continue to seek out blockbusters for the great profits they promise, more books of merit could be marketed online with low overhead.

Summing Up

The history of books shows how they have changed in form over the years: from handwritten papyrus scrolls and parchment codexes to printed books. The development of printing in the 15th century had a huge impact on society. As people learned to read for themselves, they began to question many of the established truths and authorities of their day. The Enlightenment of the 17th century was due in part to the widespread availability of printed books. In America, books affected people's feelings about everything from the American Revolution to the idea of universal education. In fact, printed books changed society so much that they are a good example of technological determinism.

Early publishing houses tended to be family businesses that prided themselves on helping new authors. They were not the most profitable of businesses and very often had to merge with other publishing houses to stay alive. The accumulation of scientific and technical knowledge made possible by books helped bring about the Industrial Revolution, whose advances in turn helped the book publishing business grow. One new product that resulted from the Industrial Revolution was the dime novel, a precursor to the modern mass-market paperback.

The continual growth of the American book publishing industry led to conglomeration as large multifaceted corporations bought up the old publishing houses. Conglomeration has led to globalization, as international owners provide overseas markets with American books. The book has also continued to take on new forms, including audiobooks and e-books.

Books today are classified by type: trade, educational, reference, professional, or specialty. The players of the publishing world include the author, who writes either on spec or under contract; various types of editors; the publisher, whose major considerations include the promotion and distribution of the finished book; and the booksellers, which include chains, megastores, independent bookstores, and Internet booksellers. In the long run, the reader determines what books will be published.

Major controversies within the book industry today include censorship, especially when carried out by government and quasi-governmental organizations such as schools and libraries, and the blockbuster syndrome, which is defined as the publishing industry's obsession with "big books" that will have sales in the millions.

Key Terms

These terms are defined and indexed in the Glossary of key terms at the back of the book.

acquisition editor *84*

aliterates *90*

audiobooks *77*

bibliophiles *90*

blockbuster *93*

blurb *87*

casual readers *90*

chapbook *71*

codex *69*

copy editor *84*

developmental editor *84*

dime novels *73*

e-books *77*

genre *85*

hypertext fiction *78*

illiterates *90*

independent
  bookstores *89*

megastores *88*

midlist authors *94*

on spec *82*

online publisher *86*

oral culture *70*

papyrus *69*

parchment *69*

public domain *74*

pulp novels *73*

rag content *71*

required readers *90*

royalties *82*

small press *86*

technological
  determinism *70*

trade books *79*

trade paperback *75*

university press *86*

vanity press *86*

Electronic Excursions

HISTORY

Web Excursion

1. The history of the book has become a hot topic in academia. Search the Web for this topic, or go directly to the Society for the History of Authorship, Reading & Publishing at www.sharpweb.org/. Go to Exhibits, find one specialized area of book history, and write a brief report outlining its major eras or events and their significance.

INDUSTRY

Web Excursion

2. Which online bookstore has the best software for the potential book buyer? Go to www.amazon.com,* look up three books, and critique the software that is used to access them. Then try another site, such as www.barnesandnoble.com* or www.varsitybooks.com,* and compare its software in terms of such characteristics as ease of selection and information provided about the book. Also compare the ease of finding and accessing books online with finding books in traditional bookstores.

CONTROVERSIES

Web Excursion

3. Search the Web for sites concerning book censorship, or go directly to Banned Books Online at http://digital.library.upenn.edu/books/banned-books.html* or the Banned Books and Censorship page at www.booksatoz.com/censorship/banned.htm.* Find one book that has been censored, and present a brief argument condemning or supporting that censorship.

Media World DVD Excursion

4. View track 9, *Publisher of "The Wind Done Gone" Ordered to Stop Publication* (from NBC's *Today* show). Author Alice Randall, publisher Wendy Strothman, and attorney Marty Garbus, who represented the estate of *Gone With The Wind* author Margaret Mitchell, discuss the controversial court order to stop publication. Where is the line drawn between parody and piracy? What lasting effects could this decision have on the publishing industry as a whole?

ONLINE LEARNING CENTER WWW.MHHE.COM/RODMAN2

You may access these and additional Web excursions at the Online Learning Center for the book (www.mhhe.com/rodman2). Visit the student portion of this Web site to also access the *Interactive Timeline of Mass Media Milestones,* chapter highlights, self quizzes, and recommended readings, movies, and documentaries for this chapter.

*Some Web site addresses may change. When they do, please search for the Web site by name or topic on your favorite search engine.

newspapers

Where Journalism Begins

4

Chapter Highlights

HISTORY: Newspapers played a pivotal role in the formation and growth of the United States. The history of the newspaper industry tells the story of how the concept of journalism and the meaning of news evolved.

INDUSTRY: Concentration of ownership in the newspaper industry is altering the way news is covered. This chapter looks at who owns today's papers, how they are staffed, and what changes are occurring in readership patterns.

CONTROVERSIES: Two challenges facing today's newspaper industry are how to practice good journalism in an era of corporate ownership and how to bring diversity into newsrooms.

Outrunning the Boulder

There's a crisis in the newspaper industry, one that veteran journalists describe as trying to outrun a boulder going downhill. One veteran sums up the issue by asking his colleagues, "Do you think we can outrun this thing?"[1] The "thing" is the tendency for both readers and advertisers to migrate to the Internet, where news is largely free and classified advertising can be purchased more cheaply than in the local paper. This migration represents profound changes in both the newspaper industry and society, and those changes are creating something of an identity crisis in the world of newspapers.

"Have you considered the possibility that I don't _want_ the paper?"

Newspaper circulation has been declining for years, and the decline is accelerating. Even established readers are becoming less willing to go to the trouble of actually obtaining a newspaper. As one longtime reader noted: "Once, I would drive across town if necessary. Today, I open the front door and if the paper isn't within about 10 feet I retreat to my computer and read it online. Only six months ago, that figure was 20 feet. Extrapolating, they will have to bring it to me in bed by the end of the year and read it to me out loud."[2]

The loss of circulation has led to a loss of revenue caused by a decline in local advertising by such traditional clients as auto dealers, travel advertisers, and hotels. The Ford Motor Company, for example, says that 80 percent of its customers now shop online, doing everything from their initial research to setting up test drives and getting quotes from dealers.[3]

At the same time that advertising revenue is down, the costs of producing the newspaper are up. P. Anthony Ridder, chairman and chief executive of the Knight-Ridder newspaper chain, explained it this way: "Newsprint costs are up significantly. Wages and health benefits are up. So you have the cost pressure on the one hand and the lack of revenue growth on the other."[4]

Ridder knew what he was talking about. Shareholder pressure forced him to sell all 32 papers in the Knight-Ridder chain in 2006. The buyer, the McClatchy Company, turned around and sold 12 of the 32 papers. All these new owners will try to increase profits by cutting back on expenses. They will join the owners of the majority of metropolitan papers who have announced job cuts, often in the hundreds, in the last two years. And often the employees don't have to be laid off. When a buyout was offered at the *Washington Post,* there was a rush for the doors.[5]

Examining these cost-cutting measures, the editors of the *Columbia Journalism Review* observed: "This can work for a while, but at some point it has to erode the quality of the product, which further erodes readership, because who needs a paper when the reporters producing it are too rushed to get beneath the surface? When editors are too fearful and squeezed to be creative?"[6]

Another editor, trying to be optimistic, said it this way: "That doesn't mean newspapers are toast. After all, they've got the brand names. You gotta trust something called the 'Post-Intelligencer' more than something called 'Yahoo!' or 'Google,' don't you? No, seriously, don't you? OK, how old did you say you are?"[7]

And throughout the industry, the boulder gathers speed.

The newspaper industry might be changing in profound ways, but newspapers are still culturally powerful because other media follow their lead. Workdays at radio, television, and Web newsrooms around the world begin

Newspapers are still culturally powerful because other media follow their lead.

with the staff's reading and quoting from "the papers." In the United States, those papers include the *New York Times,* the *Washington Post, USA Today,* and the *Wall Street Journal.* Even the writers for television's late-night comedy programs begin their workday by scanning newspapers, which is interesting when you consider that more than 20 percent of young people use these programs as one of their main sources for news.[8]

Of course, the editorial offices of most major newspapers keep their televisions on, especially during breaking news. And their computer terminals access Internet news services throughout the business day. But who influences whom in the world of the news media is not a chicken-or-egg type of question; the process starts at the newspapers. Even the subjects of magazine articles and movies often start out as newspaper articles. News gathering is what newspapers do. A major newspaper employs far more news reporters and editors than other media outlets do. The *Los Angeles Times,* for example, employs a few thousand people in a news-gathering capacity, compared with the few hundred at CNN or NBC. Most Internet news services have no more than a dozen or so employees.

This chapter takes an in-depth look at the changing world of newspapers. First, it examines the history of this medium, a history that helped form all that media are today. It then analyzes the contemporary industry, which is reinventing itself to meet changes in its readership. Finally, it looks at some of the controversies that occur in this industry, controversies based on business and societal changes, and what they mean to the changing relationship between newspapers and their readers.

SELF QUIZ What is meant by this statement: "Newspapers lead the news process"?

A Brief History *of Newspapers*

In oral cultures, town criers were the first professional deliverers of news. This tradition started with the ancient Greeks and was well established in early colonial America. The town crier was often a well-educated and respected member of the community who would read the news in front of a tavern and then nail it to a doorpost. This is the derivation of the expression *posting a notice,* and it is why so many newspapers today are called the *Post.*

Town criers didn't think too much about what was and wasn't news— they just shouted out what their leaders told them to. Answers to the basic question of journalism—What is news?—developed with the growth of the newspaper industry.

THE FIRST NEWSPAPERS

The first newspaper probably appeared in China, printed from woodcuts, more than 1,200 years ago. News at that time consisted of bits of wisdom from religious leaders and official notices of government decrees, directed toward a few dozen wealthy merchants and members of the imperial court. In Europe, Johannes Gutenberg's printing press, developed in the 15th century, eventually allowed documents of all kinds to be mass-produced, and Gutenberg's fellow Germans pioneered newspaper production in the early 1600s.

As other European countries began developing newspapers in the following years, the word *news* came to mean information that a large audience would be interested in—although a large audience at that time would be 100 or 200 literate people in a good-sized city. By the 1640s, newspaper editors had discovered the sales potential of human interest stories, and Italian newspapers were already covering local fires and murders. These papers sold for a small coin called the *gazetta,* which is where we get the word *gazette* that some newspapers use in their names.

Benjamin Franklin (1706–1790) as a young printer's apprentice. Illustration by an unknown artist, early 20th century.

THE NEWSPAPER IN EARLY AMERICA

By the time the newspaper arrived in America, editors and legislators were already arguing over both the nature of news and its regulation.

America's First Newspaper: *Publick Occurrences*

Benjamin Harris was a bookseller and publisher in London who got in trouble with the authorities for selling religious pamphlets. He spent two years in prison before moving to America. His "newes-paper," *Publick Occurrences both Forreign and Domestick,* which he began publishing in Boston in 1690, was the first newspaper in America (though it lasted only one issue).[9] As if predicting the interactive news media of the future, Harris printed stories on only three pages of his four-page paper. The fourth page was reserved for readers to add their own news before passing the newspaper on to others.

Harris's paper was arguably also the first tabloid. *Publick Occurrences* featured a number of articles of which today's *National Enquirer* would be proud. There were stories about a kidnapping, a suicide, and a fire, as well as a story accusing the king of France of sleeping with his son's wife. The colonial government, not pleased, closed down Harris's paper, thus treating the press the way it had been treated in England. In fact, in England, newspapers were banned outright from 1632 until 1641 and were tightly controlled long thereafter so that they would publish nothing that would upset the king.

What was America's first newspaper, and how long did it last?

SELF QUIZ

The *Boston News-Letter*

John Campbell's *Boston News-Letter,* the first American paper to last more than one issue, appeared in 1704. Campbell, the postmaster of Boston, started by writing out his newsletter by hand and sending it to subscribers. When he had too many subscribers to service by hand, he made a deal with a printer and the *Boston News-Letter* was born. Although Campbell barely made a profit with his paper, he had a secure monopoly with the only paper in the colonies for 15 years, until the *Boston Gazette* was published in 1719.

Early Government Control: Licensing and Seditious Libel Laws

The *Boston News-Letter* was published by authority of the colonial government, which meant that Campbell had a license to publish. Everything he wrote was submitted to local authorities before it was printed, and had he printed anything they didn't like, he would have lost his license. Licensing laws died out in just a few years, but the authorities found another way to control printers: They established **seditious libel laws,** which made it illegal to print derogatory or potentially inflammatory remarks about the government or its members. Several colonial publishers spent time in jail because of this law.

seditious libel laws
Laws established in colonial America that made it illegal to criticize government.

Characteristics of Early American Newspapers

The *Boston News-Letter,* like most early American papers, was published weekly at best; the first daily newspaper didn't appear until 1784, after the United States had won its independence from Great Britain. The weeklies were only about four pages long because paper was expensive, and difficult to come by, and the type had to be set laboriously by hand. They were also relatively expensive at a few pennies a copy, so community opinion leaders, acting as gatekeepers, would buy them and read the stories aloud at the local tavern.

SELF QUIZ
Describe the characteristics of early colonial newspapers.

Although expensive, early American papers tended to be inaccurate because their publishers were basically printers, not reporters or editors. They would publish anything that seemed to them to be news, including rumors. Moreover, what information they could find was usually hopelessly out of date. Transportation was slow in those days, and communication was tied directly to transportation. It could take several weeks for a ship to arrive with news from England, and news from around the colonies arrived with travelers on slow-moving stagecoaches.

The Zenger Case and Freedom of the Press

Before the American Revolution, royal authorities continued to crack down on newspapers that spoke out against the government, but a milestone in press freedom occurred in 1735 with the trial of John Peter Zenger. Zenger was the publisher of the *New York Weekly,* a paper that liked to point out the failings of the royal governor of New York, William Cosby. Zenger accused the governor of, among other things, stealing land. Most of what Zenger published was true, but the law of seditious libel made any criticism of the government and its agents illegal, whether it was true or not. In fact, true criticism was often considered more libelous than the false kind.

When Zenger was put on trial, his lawyer argued that no matter what the law said, it ought to be permissible for a newspaper to publish the truth. The jury agreed with him and went against the law by finding Zenger not guilty. This established the idea that, as far as the American settlers were concerned, newspapers had the inherent right to publish the truth about government actions. This idea became officially sanctioned in 1791, in the First Amendment to the U.S. Constitution, although it was not fully realized in practice for many years.

SELF QUIZ
Why was the Zenger case important to the development of press freedom?

Women in Early Newspaper Publishing

While John Peter Zenger was in jail awaiting trial, his wife, Anna Zenger, took over as publisher of the *New York Weekly*. In doing so, she became one of a handful of women who became prominent in colonial publishing. Women of the time were not encouraged to work outside the home, but newspapers were generally family businesses and women could become unofficial apprentices by helping out the men in their family. Often they proved to be more adept at publishing than the men, and when they had to take over, as Anna Zenger did, some of them achieved considerable success in terms of both profitability and quality. Newspaper publishing therefore became one area that led, albeit slowly, to women's changing roles in American society.

Newspapers and the American Revolution

partisan press
Newspapers owned or supported by political parties.

By 1765, the colonies had more than 30 newspapers, most of which formed a **partisan press**—that is, newspapers owned or supported by political parties. The partisan papers chose one side or the other about issues related to the American Revolution and the formation of the new nation.[10] Political parties, including the Whigs, who resented British control and favored independence from Britain, and the Tories, who were loyal to Britain, each owned their own papers and had their own readers. A smaller but thriving **mercantile press** provided news of business and shipping. Both Whig and Tory newspapers tended to decry the commercial restraints that had been placed on the colonies by the mother country. British rulers did not want the colonies to develop industry; it wanted them to remain dependent on England for manufactured goods. Printers, suffering from a scarcity of presses and type, were quick to point out that these limitations had been imposed by Parliament but that Americans had no voice in that governing body. The cry of "no taxation without representation" might never have been heard without the printers.

mercantile press
Newspapers that provided news of business and shipping.

This hand-colored woodcut depicts a protest in colonial New York opposing the Stamp Act, which levied a tax of one cent on every copy of every newspaper.

The Stamp Act

Resistance against taxation without representation reached a peak with the imposition of the Stamp Act in 1765. This act levied a tax of 1 cent on every copy of every newspaper. Publishers saw the act as an attempt to put them out of business. Parliament repealed the tax the following year, after rioting in Boston in which the governor's house was burned. But repealing the act didn't satisfy the colonial editors; the great majority of them were now united in their desire for independence.

Fanning the Flames of Revolution

Colonial newspapers fanned the flames of what eventually became the American Revolution. They played a major role in publishing the clandestine pamphlets of patriots such as Thomas Paine and Samuel Adams that advanced the argument for independence. Furthermore, much of the fervor for fighting was encouraged by the sensationalized coverage of early confrontations between the British and the colonists. When an unruly Boston crowd threatened a group of British soldiers who in turn fired on them, killing five, it became the "Boston Massacre" in the colonial papers, an act of pure evil, and the threatening mob became innocent bystanders.

The Federalist Papers

After the Revolutionary War, newspapers played an important role in the ratification of the U.S. Constitution. As the new country was being formed, many of the settlers were opposed to the idea of a strong federal government. Alexander Hamilton, James Madison, and John Jay wrote a series of essays that explained the concept of the new federal government and published them serially in several New York newspapers. These essays came to be known as the **Federalist Papers.** They were extremely important to the nation-building process, as they helped convince citizens of the importance of a strong but democratic central government. Many believe the U.S. Constitution would not have been ratified without them.

SELF QUIZ

What role did the newspaper industry play in the American Revolution and the formation of the new nation?

CHANGES IN THE CONCEPT OF NEWS

The partisan press continued well into the 1800s. Gradually, however, editors of major credible papers began to standardize their definition of news. The **editorial page,** for example, became the place for properly labeled opinion pieces. Rumor, innuendo, and political propaganda began to disappear from the **hard news** of the front page, which was made up of stories about current events that had an impact on people's lives. **Feature news,** also known as soft news, was not necessarily either current or important; it was directed more toward human interest and curiosity.

The Beginnings of the Ethnic Press

The **ethnic press,** which is made up of newspapers aimed at particular cultural groups such as African Americans, Hispanics, and Native Americans, has played an important role in the history of the United States.

Foreign-Language Press

Early ethnic papers were published in foreign languages for immigrants and people already living in territories into which the United States expanded. Benjamin Franklin published one of the first German-language newspapers in 1732. The first New Orleans newspaper, *Moniteur de la Louisiane,* was published in French in 1794. The first newspaper in Texas, *La Gaceta,* which appeared in 1813, was printed in Spanish. By 1914 there were some 1,300 foreign-language newspapers in the United States.

Native American Press

Despite the existence of some foreign-language papers, the mainstream press often disregarded the poorer cultural minorities whom advertisers had little interest in reaching. The Native American press began in 1828 as a reaction to this lack of coverage, with the publication of the *Cherokee Phoenix,* a bilingual newspaper published by Elias Boudinot, a Cherokee who saw literacy as the root of the white man's power.

African American Press

In the early 1800s the largest minority community not being served by mainstream papers consisted of African Americans. The northern states had abolished slavery in 1804, but the African American population was largely invisible in the pages of local newspapers. African Americans' weddings, births, anniversaries, and deaths went unreported, and their concerns, especially their point of view about the struggles for nationwide emancipation, went largely unheard. To combat this, *Freedom's Journal,* the first black newspaper, was established in 1827. Its editors were John Russwurm and

Federalist Papers
Essays that explained the new federal government to early Americans.

editorial page
Section of newspaper reserved for statements representing the opinion of the newspaper.

hard news
Stories about current events that have impact on people's lives.

feature news
Stories directed toward human interest and curiosity; also known as soft news.

ethnic press
That part of the newspaper industry aimed at particular cultural groups.

The African American population was largely invisible in the pages of the mainstream press.

Samuel Cornish. Russwurm was the first black to graduate from a college in the United States (Bowdoin, in 1826), and Cornish was a Presbyterian minister. Although the paper lasted only two years, it proved that such an endeavor could succeed in spite of the poverty and forced illiteracy of much of its audience. Between 1827 and the end of the Civil War, 40 additional African American newspapers began publication.

The Penny Press

The **penny press** appeared in the 1830s and began the era of inexpensive, advertiser-supported newspapers. The Industrial Revolution of the early 19th century made the penny press possible. Printing technology had advanced to the stage where newspapers could be produced inexpensively. Newly developed steam presses could reproduce copies rapidly and eventually could even cut and fold the papers. An inexpensive type of paper known as **newsprint** had been developed as well. Newspapers, however, which sold at about six cents a copy, were still beyond the means of the average reader. (At the time six cents could buy three loaves of bread, a pound of beef, or a pint of whiskey.)

penny press
Inexpensive, advertiser-supported newspapers that appeared in the1830s.

newsprint
Inexpensive paper used for newspapers.

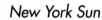
SELF QUIZ

What was the penny press, and what was its significance to future media?

news hole
Total amount of space in a newspaper that can be devoted to editorial content versus advertising.

sensationalism
Use of exaggeration and lurid elements to produce a startling effect.

New York Sun

Benjamin Day is credited with creating the penny press; his *New York Sun,* which sold for one penny, appeared in 1833. Day, an ambitious 23-year-old, proved that a newspaper could make a profit solely on advertising income, as long as its content appealed to a wide enough readership. The audience was there because many people had learned to read. And the advertising revenue was there because manufacturers now needed to reach a wide audience that included the common people. As far as advertisers were concerned, circulation—the total number of copies delivered to customers—was what was important. The *Sun* began the practice, standard today, of determining the size of the **news hole**—the total amount of space that can be devoted to editorial content—according to the amount of advertising sold.

Human Interest and Sensationalism

Benjamin Day set about attracting the readership of the common people by stressing human interest stories over hard news. His brand of journalism, called **sensationalism,** used exaggeration and lurid elements to produce a startling effect. Day achieved this effect by stressing scandals and bloody police reports. The upper classes saw the sensational stories in the *Sun* as vulgar and trivial, but Day didn't care.

The *Sun* featured mostly local stories, but also ran stories about such national celebrities as Daniel Boone, Davy Crockett, and Wild Bill Hickock. In the search for sensational stories, truth was often brushed to the side. One series of front-page stories in the *Sun* featured new scientific evidence that

"What could I do? It jumped off the newsstand."

"proved" that there was life on the moon. The stories were later exposed as a hoax.

Personal Journalism

The success of the *New York Sun* encouraged the founding of many other penny papers. Although these papers continued to stress sex and violence to reach a large audience, some of them became the great news gatherers of their day. They began by using the pony express, and then the telegraph when it became available, to gather news from distant places. These papers came to include the *New York Herald,* published by James Gordon Bennett in 1835; the *New York Tribune,* published by Horace Greeley in 1841; and the *New York Times,* published by Henry J. Raymond in 1851.

These influential publishers and others like them are remembered today as presiding over an era of personal journalism, in which the beliefs and eccentricities of the owners were as big a determinant of what went into the paper as anything that could be called news value. Joseph Medill, the publisher of the *Chicago Tribune,* was typical of this type of owner. Medill believed in simplified spelling, so his paper used words such as *telegrafed* and *favorit.* For years, Medill believed in the power of sunspots to affect everything from weather to human behavior, and their potential effects had to be mentioned in news stories. One day, Medill read about microbes and decided that they were the true cause of natural phenomena. When a reporter in Egypt sent in a story about how a plague there was probably caused by sunspots, Medill went through the story and changed each appearance of the word *sunspots* to *microbes.*

Joseph Medill, the legendary publisher of the *Chicago Tribune,* was typical of the influential publishers who injected their beliefs and eccentricities into the news.

The Civil War Years

The establishment of the Associated Press (AP) in 1848 led to a more objective brand of journalism, as both political and personal viewpoints had to be tempered to fit in a wide range of papers. The AP also made the presentation of national news more timely, which became important during the Civil War as citizens sought the latest news from the front. Several journalistic conventions changed and developed during the war. For example, the element known as a **byline**—the line at the beginning of a news story giving the author's name—was virtually nonexistent before the war. For editors of that period, it was the news that was important, not who wrote it. During the Civil War, bylines were established by order of the Union Army, whose leadership wanted to know where reporters had received their information. Reporters and editors got used to the practice of printing writers' names and continued it after the war.

byline
A line at the beginning of a news story giving the author's name.

The Inverted Pyramid

The **inverted pyramid** style of hard news writing was also developed during the Civil War period. In this style (which, as noted in Chapter 1, followed the invention of the telegraph in 1844), writers packed the most important information into the first paragraph of the story. Because the telegraph lines

inverted pyramid
News style that packs the most important information into the first paragraph.

were undependable and might be cut by opposing forces at any time, reporters placed the "five Ws and one H" of *who, what, when, where, why,* and *how* at the very beginning of the story so that the facts had a better chance of getting through before the line went down.

The inverted pyramid style of hard news writing was developed during the Civil War.

The inverted pyramid style was, at first, used mostly for short news stories transmitted by telegraph but also became popular for longer news stories in the following decades as knowledge exploded and people felt the need to get to the heart of reported information quickly. Most papers still use the inverted pyramid style for hard news, whereas features and human interest pieces might build up to the basic facts slowly, taking the time to establish atmosphere first.

The industrial advances in the years following the Civil War created boom times for American newspapers. Manufacturers and retailers bought up advertising space to build the customer bases they needed for their mass-produced goods. Newspapers throughout the United States helped build the country during the periods of postwar reconstruction and westward expansion; their stories glorified the West, and their ads touted cheap land and travel.

Yellow Journalism

yellow journalism
A style of reporting characterized by unprecedented sensationalism; it reached its peak in the Hearst–Pulitzer circulation wars of the 1890s.

The successes of the penny press era led to the **yellow journalism** era, in which increased competition among newspapers gave rise to unprecedented sensationalism. Yellow journalism reached its height in the Hearst–Pulitzer circulation wars of the 1890s. William Randolph Hearst, a successful San Francisco publisher, moved to New York to publish the *New York Journal* and compete with Joseph Pulitzer's *New York World*. Both papers used any device they could in attempts to increase their own circulation and put the other paper out of business. Such devices included everything from sensationalistic stories to the halftone printing of photographs on newsprint. Another gimmick was color comics, a technological marvel of the time, from which arose the terms *yellow journalism* and *the yellow press* (see the Close-Up on History box).

What was yellow journalism? Where did the name come from?

SELF QUIZ

William Randolph Hearst (1863–1951), newspaper publisher, photographed around 1922. His circulation war with Joseph Pulitzer helped lead the United States into the Spanish-American War.

The Yellow Kid

The Yellow Kid was the main character of one of the first newspaper comic strips, *Hogan's Alley,* published by Joseph Pulitzer's *New York World* in 1895. The kid was a street urchin from the slums whose real name was Mickey Dugan. He had a distinctive appearance:

HOGAN'S ALLEY FOLK HAVE A TROLLEY PARTY IN BROOKLYN.

The Yellow Kid of Hogan's Alley gave yellow journalism its name.

He was jug-eared, buck-toothed, and bald, his head having been shaved to rid him of lice. His most striking characteristic was his bright yellow nightshirt, a hand-me-down from his sister. R. F. Outcault, the artist who created the kid, was a master of layout, able to fill a page with dozens of humorous details based on keen observation. Common people liked the kid because he and his fellow tenement dwellers often mocked high-society manners in events such as "The Horse Show as Reproduced at Shantytown," and activities such as "Golf—The Great Society Sport as Played in Hogan's Alley."

Critics denounced the strip for the violence it often portrayed, such as in a Fourth of July panel showing children being blown into the air, dogs running with firecrackers tied to their tails, and flaming skyrockets hitting women and children as they fell down fire escapes while fleeing burning tenements.

In 1896, Hearst lured Outcault away from Pulitzer with a much higher salary, and the Yellow Kid moved from the *World* to the *Journal.* Pulitzer, however, retained the title *Hogan's Alley* and hired another artist—a friend of Outcault's—to continue drawing the panel. For a while, the two Yellow Kid comics were published at the same time.

The Spanish-American War

In both the *New York Journal* and the *New York World,* lurid headlines would sometimes take up half of the first page, often conveying false impressions. This tendency reached a high pitch in the days leading up to the brief Spanish-American War of 1898. Many historians blame Hearst and Pulitzer for encouraging the United States to undertake this conflict, which began with a local rebellion in Cuba against Spanish rule. Both Hearst and Pulitzer sent squadrons of reporters and artists to cover the revolt, and the *Journal* and the *World* exaggerated Spain's actions against the rebels, at one point claiming that a quarter of Cuba's population had been wiped out by the Spanish, when in fact there had been only a few casualties. Still, it seemed unlikely that the United States would become involved in the conflict, so the noted artist Frederic Remington, who worked for the *Journal,* asked to be relieved of his Cuban assignment. "Please remain,"

> **CONSIDER THIS**
>
> *Read the Close-Up on Controversy box in Chapter 11 (pp. 380–381), and compare Rupert Murdoch's actions regarding the war in Iraq with William Randolph Hearst's actions regarding the Spanish-American war. Was Murdoch's influence similar to Hearst's? Why or why not?*

Hearst is said to have cabled him. "You furnish the pictures and I'll furnish the war."[11]

When the U.S. battleship *Maine* mysteriously blew up in Havana harbor, Hearst and Pulitzer declared the event another Spanish atrocity. As soon as the United States finally declared war on Spain, Hearst chartered a ship, outfitted it with a printing press and composing room, and personally set sail for Cuba with a staff of reporters and photographers. Hearst even took up reporting duties for a reporter who was wounded in a battle. Later, Hearst told the reporter, "I'm sorry you're hurt, but wasn't it a splendid fight? We must beat every paper in the world!"[12]

THE MAKING OF THE MODERN PRESS

Today's newspapers pride themselves on investigative reporting, responsibility, and respectability. It may be hard to believe that these attributes existed in the era of yellow journalism, but they did take root and grow even alongside the sensationalism of the time.

Investigative Journalism

Some publishers in the era of yellow journalism, Pulitzer especially, began to combine good reporting with their cheaper tricks.[13] Following the lead of magazine journalists, certain newspaper reporters began to champion the causes of the common people and fight against corruption in high places. This was the beginning of **investigative journalism,** a style of reporting that uncovers information that sources—including governments, corporations, and other powerful groups—have tried to conceal. Investigative reporting was known for a time as muckraking, a style of writing we will examine further in Chapter 5.

investigative journalism
Reporting that uncovers information that sources have tried to conceal.

Nellie Bly

One of Joseph Pulitzer's most famous investigative reporters was a young woman named Elizabeth Cochrane, who wrote under the pen name Nellie Bly. One of Bly's first assignments with Pulitzer was to go undercover at a lunatic asylum. She pretended to be mentally ill to get herself committed. The resulting headlines shrieked, "10 Days in a Madhouse," and the series of articles helped bring about reforms in the treatment of women in mental facilities. In other investigations Bly posed as an unwed mother to expose a black-market baby operation and stole $50 from a woman's purse to get arrested and report on how women were treated in city jails. Another one of her famous exploits was her trip around the world in 72 days, to beat the record of Jules Verne's fictional hero in *Around the World in Eighty Days*. Bly was one of the first reporters to place herself at the center of her stories. She was also the first and one of the most famous practitioners of **stunt journalism,** in which a reporter would perform some spectacular exploit to gain publicity for his or her story. Nellie Bly remains a model for both investigative reporters and tabloid journalists.[14]

stunt journalism
Reporting that includes a spectacular exploit to gain publicity for the story.

Ida B. Wells-Barnett

Another important early investigative reporter was Ida B. Wells-Barnett. Wells-Barnett was a schoolteacher until she was fired for writing about the injustices suffered by African Americans. As a full-time journalist she became co-owner of *Free Speech,* an African American newspaper published in Memphis, Tennessee. She joined the investigative movement after one of her friends, a black grocer whose store had been successful against white competitors, was lynched. In 1895, she published *A Red Record,* first as a series of newspaper articles and later as a book, exposing the long history of lynch-

So incriminating was her series of articles about lynching that Ida B. Wells-Barnett's paper was mobbed and she herself was nearly lynched.

ing in the United States. So incriminating was her series that Wells-Barnett's paper was mobbed and she herself was nearly lynched. Wells-Barnett was acclaimed for her investigative skills and the thoroughness with which she compiled her evidence, and her reporting eventually led to the end of lynching in Memphis for several decades.

Responsibility and Integrity in Journalism

Quality journalism began to squeeze out the excesses of yellow journalism at the end of the 19th century. As the market became saturated with sensational news, people felt the need for a more responsible press, one they could trust for information and not just use for entertainment and titillation. Of course, sensationalism stayed around, but for a while it became relatively unprofitable and moved to the background of journalistic practices. Helping to cool down the yellow journalism period was the responsible reporting of three newspapers of the time: the *New York Times,* the *Wall Street Journal,* and the *Christian Science Monitor.*

New York Times

Adolph Ochs had bought the nearly bankrupt *New York Times* at the height of the yellow journalism period, in 1896. He was convinced that his paper could succeed commercially by offering an alternative to the sensational, trivial news that other papers were reporting. Under Ochs, the *Times* became the U.S. newspaper of record, the "gray lady of American journalism," a paper that printed, as it still proclaims on its front page, "All the News That's Fit to Print."

Along with fact-based, carefully researched reporting on the important events and issues of the day, the *Times* offered essential information such as stock quotes, business reports, analyses of governmental actions that would affect society, and full-text transcripts of important speeches and bills. Ochs also lowered the price of the *Times* to a penny. Today, the *New York Times* continues to enjoy its reputation as the newspaper of record. The *Times* also stands at the center of a huge corporation that includes 27 newspapers, a wire service, and one of the best online news sites.

Wall Street Journal

Charles Dow and Edward Jones, two New England financial reporters, established the *Wall Street Journal* in 1889. Their paper was dedicated to battling the excesses of yellow journalism in the financial and business community. At that time, stock market manipulators floated rumors that drove the market up or down as they saw fit—rumors that the yellow papers were only too happy to print. The *Wall Street Journal* carried no large headlines or photographs but soon established a reputation for providing honest and reliable information.

Today the paper is more influential than ever. The international business community relies on its information, advertisers rely on the prosperous national audience it delivers, and political conservatives rely on the influential voice of its editorial pages.[15] It is the centerpiece of the huge international Dow Jones financial publishing empire, which brings readers the Dow Jones Industrials average from the stock market each day.

Christian Science Monitor

The *Christian Science Monitor* was first published in 1908, also as a reaction to the yellow press. It was started by Mary Baker Eddy, the founder of the Christian Science religion. Eddy was understandably put off by Joseph Pulitzer, who campaigned against her and her church. Eddy's belief that many diseases could be cured by faith rather than by medical treatment seemed to particularly incense Pulitzer, who used all his editorial influence to try to have Eddy declared insane. Eddy was even subjected to a formal sanity hearing, which was quickly dismissed.

Afterward, she set up the *Christian Science Monitor* as an objective source of news independent of commercial as well as political interests. She insisted that the *Monitor* was not to be a religious paper but rather a real newspaper that happened to be published by a church. Everything in the *Monitor* would be hard news and nonreligious features, except for one religious article that would appear each day in the Home Forum section. The *Monitor* became a respected newspaper that never wavered from its public service philosophy. It stands today as a monument to Eddy, who founded the paper against incredible odds at a time when women didn't even have the right to vote in the United States. The *Christian Science Monitor* still strives to be an independent voice, maintaining its own news bureaus in 13 countries. Ironically, considering its founder's battles with Joseph Pulitzer, the paper has won six Pulitzer prizes.

Originally called the *Illustrated Daily News,* the *New York Daily News* was the first tabloid. This is the front page of its first edition, June 26, 1919.

Jazz Journalism

The formation of respectable papers like the *New York Times* did not mean sensationalism had died out. The journalistic environment heated up again after the end of World War I. In fact, the 1920s are remembered as the era of **jazz journalism** because the energy of the newspaper business paralleled that of the music of the era. As the decade began, the number of U.S. newspapers had peaked at 2,600 dailies and 14,000 weeklies, all of which reflected the hot atmosphere of the Roaring Twenties. Many households subscribed to both a morning and an afternoon paper. Papers would hold the presses for breaking stories and print extra editions for important happenings. The news vendor's cry of "Extra! Extra! Read all about it!" became the harbinger of major events.

jazz journalism
Style of news presentation of the 1920s that paralleled the music of the era.

The Tabloids

The era of jazz journalism is most significant because it saw the birth of the tabloid newspaper. The *New York Daily News,* founded in 1919, was the first of this kind of paper. **Tabloids** repeated the sensationalism of the yellow press but added two new features. The first was the abundant use of photographs, with a single image often taking up the entire front page. The other innovation was the tabloid format itself: a smaller page than the traditional broadsheet papers, and a single fold, both of which made the paper easier to handle on the street and on public transportation.

Strangeness and novelty became important facets of a tabloid story. Two-headed births were apparently more important than major treaties; an insane person's descent into cannibalism got more space than a president's policy speech. Jazz journalism died out toward the end of the 1920s, but the tabloids are still with us.

tabloids
Newspapers characterized by a smaller size than a standard newspaper, a single fold, and abundant photographs.

The Canons of Journalism

In 1923, in a reaction to jazz journalism and the tabloid press, a group of journalists formed an association that they called the American Society of Newspaper Editors. They adopted an ethical code called the Canons of Journalism that same year.[16] The canons stressed the following:

1. *Responsibility.* Journalists must always consider the public's welfare.
2. *Freedom of the press.* First Amendment rights are to be guarded as vital and unquestionable.
3. *Independence.* Independence from sources, politics, and advertisers is essential.
4. *Sincerity, truthfulness, accuracy.* These three qualities are to be the foundation of all journalism.
5. *Impartiality.* News reports should be free from opinion or bias of any kind.
6. *Fair play.* Opposing views should be solicited on public issues and accusations; papers should publish prompt and complete corrections of mistakes.
7. *Decency.* Papers should avoid "deliberate pandering to vicious instincts" such as details of crime and vice.

CONSIDER THIS
How well do today's newspapers honor the canons of journalism? Which ones are most and least respected? Back up your answer with examples.

CONCENTRATION INTO CHAINS

Around the beginning of the 20th century, American newspapers began to concentrate into chains. The **chain,** defined as one company that owns the same type of company in more than one market area, was not a new idea. Benjamin Franklin started the first newspaper chain in the United States when he owned both the *Pennsylvania Gazette* and the *New England Courant* in 1729. Many other publishers followed Franklin's lead in the early years, but the first one to make it work on a large scale, and therefore the one who is today considered the founder of the first modern newspaper chain, was Edward Wyllis Scripps.

The basic idea behind all chains, including Scripps's, is to take advantage of economies of scale on administration, production, and distribution costs. Newspapers in a chain are able to share reporters, for example, for both features and hard news, and they can sell advertising space to all their papers at once. Scripps began his chain in Cleveland in 1878. His formula was to buy or start a newspaper in a promising community and then find talented, hardworking young people to run it for him. By 1914, he had a chain of 33 newspapers.

chain
One company that owns the same type of business in more than one market area.

William Randolph Hearst, of *New York Journal* fame, became the next great chain owner. He owned 20 daily papers by 1922, along with two wire services, the largest newspaper feature syndicate, a newsreel company, and a motion picture production company. Many other chains followed. By 1900, around 10 percent of U.S. dailies were chain owned. Critics at the time decried the fact that 1 in 10 papers was held by one of the "press barons," but the trend continued. By the 1980s, the figure had reached 40 percent. Today it is 80 percent.

As mentioned at the beginning of this chapter, in 2006 one of the great chains, Knight-Ridder, was sold because of stockholder demand. Another chain, the McClatchy Company, bought Knight-Ridder and immediately sold off 12 of its 32 papers. Another milestone occured in 2006 when the Gannett chain purchased *The FS View & Florida Flambeau,* the student newspaper of Florida State University. This was the first time that a college paper had been bought by a major chain, but media industry analysts said that because the big chains want to attract young readers, it might not be the last. This purchase made the Florida State paper a sister publication of *USA Today.*

Some of today's top chains are listed in Fact File 4.1.

LEADING THE NEWS PROCESS

The U.S. newspaper has particularly been the medium in which journalism begins in the reporting of political events. Newspapers led the way in reporting the 1960s civil rights struggle in the southern United States, as well as the civil unrest surrounding the Vietnam War during the 1960s and early 1970s. The *New York Times* and the *Washington Post* especially uncovered many stories about the government's policies regarding the war in Vietnam and in 1971 published a set of leaked government documents known as the Pentagon Papers. These documents proved that the U.S. government had been less than honest with the American people about the conduct of the war.

Watergate Coverage

Perhaps the best modern example of newspapers taking the lead over other media in the news-gathering process comes from the Watergate scandal of 1972–1974. When police caught burglars breaking into the Democratic National Committee headquarters, located in the Watergate apartment complex in Washington, D.C., two young *Washington Post* reporters, Bob Woodward and Carl Bernstein, were assigned to the story. On the advice of an administration source identified only as Deep Throat, Woodward and Bernstein followed the money that had been paid to the burglars and found that it had come from the Committee to Reelect the President (CREEP). They also traced the burglars back to the Central Intelligence Agency and the Nixon administration, unearthing a massive cover-up by Nixon and other top officials.

Further reporting provided increasing proof of Nixon's guilt, and Congress finally resolved to impeach him in 1974. The pressure led to Nixon's resignation in August of that year, an ironic end for a once-popular president who had campaigned on a strict law-and-order platform.

In the *Media World* DVD that accompanies this book (track 36, *Woodward and Bernstein on Deep Throat*) Bob Woodward and Carl Bernstein discuss ex-FBI official Mark Felt, who admitted in 2005 to being Deep Throat.

FACT FILE 4.1

Top U.S. Newspaper Chains, by Daily Circulation

Rank	Chain and Daily Circulation (millions)	Total Dailies Held	Examples of Newspapers Owned
1	**Gannett;** Arlington, Virginia • www.gannett.com — 7.3	90	*USA Today, The Arizona Republic, The Cincinnati Enquirer, The Des Moines Register, The Detroit News, The Honolulu Advertiser, The Indianapolis Star, Louisville Courier-Journal, Montgomery Advertiser, Rochester Democrat and Chronicle, The Tennessean* (Nashville), *Tucson Citizen*
2	**The McClatchy Company;** Sacramento, California • www.mcclatchy.com — 3.3	32	*The News and Observer* (Charlotte, NC), *Star Tribune* (Minneapolis), *The Sacramento Bee, The Kansas City Star* (Missouri), *The Wichita Eagle, Fort Worth Star-Telegram, The Miami Herald, The Charlotte Observer* (North Carolina)
3	**Tribune Company;** Chicago • www.tribune.com — 3.2	11	*Baltimore Sun, Chicago Tribune, The Hartford Courant, Los Angeles Times, Newsday* (Long Island, NY), *Orlando Sentinel*
4	**Newhouse/Advance Publications** • www.newhousenews.com — 2.9	26	*The Birmingham News, Plain Dealer* (Cleveland), *The Oregonian* (Portland), *The Star-Ledger* (Newark, NJ), *The Times-Picayune* (New Orleans), *The Trenton Times*
5	**The New York Times Company;** New York • www.nytco.com — 2.4	18	*The Boston Globe, International Herald Tribune, The New York Times*
6	**Dow Jones;** New York • www.dowjones.com — 2.4	8	*The Wall Street Journal*
7	**MediaNews Group;** Denver, Colorado • www.medianewsgroup.com — 1.8	34	*The Denver Post, L.A. Daily News, Long Beach Press-Telegram, Oakland Tribune, Salt Lake Tribune*
8	**Hearst Corporation;** New York • www.hearstcorp.com — 1.7	12	*Albany Times Union, Houston Chronicle, San Antonio Express-News, San Francisco Chronicle, Seattle Post-Intelligencer*
9	**E. W. Scripps Company;** Cincinnati, Ohio • www.scripps.com — 1.5	20	*The Albuquerque Tribune, Birmingham Post-Herald, The Cincinnati Post, The Commercial Appeal* (Memphis), *The Knoxville News-Sentinel, Rocky Mountain News* (Denver)
10	**Cox Newspapers;** Atlanta, Georgia • www.coxnews.com — 1.2	17	*Austin American-Statesman, Dayton Daily News, Rocky Mount Telegram* (North Carolina), *The Atlanta Journal-Constitution, The Palm Beach Post* (Florida), *Waco Tribune-Herald* (Texas)

Source: Company Web sites, updated October 2006.

Providing Context

Newspaper reporters continue to work around the clock to cover developing news stories and to provide background and meaning for both readers and other news media. This role of providing context has been especially important in the aftermath of the terrorist attacks of September 11, 2001; the invasion of Afghanistan in 2002; and the war in Iraq that began in 2003.

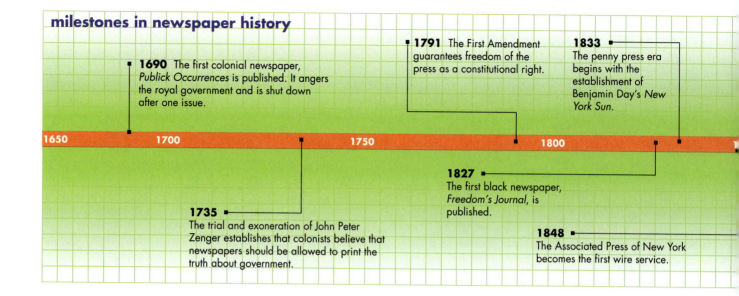

milestones in newspaper history

1690 The first colonial newspaper, *Publick Occurrences* is published. It angers the royal government and is shut down after one issue.

1791 The First Amendment guarantees freedom of the press as a constitutional right.

1833 The penny press era begins with the establishment of Benjamin Day's *New York Sun*.

| 1650 | 1700 | 1750 | 1800 |

1827 The first black newspaper, *Freedom's Journal*, is published.

1735 The trial and exoneration of John Peter Zenger establishes that colonists believe that newspapers should be allowed to print the truth about government.

1848 The Associated Press of New York becomes the first wire service.

CHANGING PUBLICATION PATTERNS

Before the 1960s, most newspapers were printed in afternoon or evening editions; since then, they have shifted to mostly morning editions. There are several reasons for this shift. Up until the 1950s, people had little time for a morning newspaper—they had to leave the house for their factory and farming jobs at dawn. Today's service jobs give people time to read the paper in the morning, and commuters can take their newspapers with them. Also, production and delivery became more expensive (and thus reduced newspapers' profits) as afternoon traffic congestion worsened in urban areas.

Other sociological trends also worked against afternoon and evening papers. Rather than heading home to eat dinner and read the paper, Americans began using their after-work time in different ways, such as stopping at the gym. Competition from other media forms, especially the evening television news, also helped spell the death of afternoon newspapers.

The Web is being embraced even by small local newspapers, as seen in the comprehensive Web site of the *Devils Lake Journal,* the hometown paper of Devils Lake, North Dakota (www.devilslakejournal.com). Devils Lake Journal. Used with permission.

ADAPTING TO NEW MEDIA

Although newspapers have suffered from the competition of other media, they have also adapted to technological innovations. For years, pundits have declared that various new media would spell the death of the newspaper industry. First there were newsreels, shown in movie theaters, with their dramatic visual impact and their large captive audiences. But newsreels on Saturday afternoon only whetted audience appetites for that week's papers.

Newspapers are preparing for a future in which Web-based news will be a major source of income.

Then came radio, which was seen as a threat in the 1930s. But again, radio's on-the-spot coverage seemed to encourage listeners to seek out the fuller coverage of newspapers.

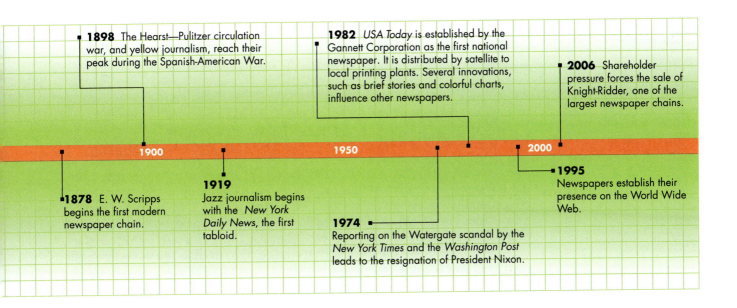

1898 The Hearst—Pulitzer circulation war, and yellow journalism, reach their peak during the Spanish-American War.

1982 *USA Today* is established by the Gannett Corporation as the first national newspaper. It is distributed by satellite to local printing plants. Several innovations, such as brief stories and colorful charts, influence other newspapers.

2006 Shareholder pressure forces the sale of Knight-Ridder, one of the largest newspaper chains.

1900   1950   2000

1878 E. W. Scripps begins the first modern newspaper chain.

1919 Jazz journalism begins with the *New York Daily News*, the first tabloid.

1974 Reporting on the Watergate scandal by the *New York Times* and the *Washington Post* leads to the resignation of President Nixon.

1995 Newspapers establish their presence on the World Wide Web.

With television, pundits again predicted that soon no one would need newspapers. But television turned out to be mostly a headline service, once again whetting the public's appetite for in-depth news arranged in a way that enabled them to find and read what they wanted. When a further challenge was presented by cable television, with its multiple channels devoted to news, several newspapers embraced the new technology by setting up their own cable news programs. Newspapers in general also adapted to television news by becoming more like it—that is, by using color photographs and other visuals and shorter, more interesting stories. This trend was encouraged by the establishment of *USA Today* in 1982 (discussed later in this chapter).

Today's biggest challenge to newspapers comes from the World Wide Web, but newspapers are again facing this threat by embracing it. By 1995, newspapers were pumping millions of dollars into their own Web editions. Though they have very little income yet to show for it, newspapers have been preparing for a future in which Web-based news is expected to be a major source of advertising and database income. By 2004, nearly every U.S. newspaper, including most small-town weeklies, had some kind of Web presence.

Will the newspaper of the future move to the Web? For many industry executives, it doesn't matter. They consider themselves in the news business, not the newspaper business. According to Arthur Sulzberger Jr., publisher of the *New York Times* and chairman of the Times Company: "We will follow our readers where they take us. If they want us in print, we will be there in print. If they want us on the Web, we will be there on the Web. If they want us on cell phones or downloaded so they can hear us in audio, we must be there. At the end of the day, it is the audience we collect and the quality of that audience that is the critical factor, not the means by which we collect it."[17]

New e-paper devices would like to become the iPods of the newspaper business. This experimental e-paper is thinner than a regular newspaper but is actually a digital screen that allows access to thousands of pages.

Online news, along with radio and television news, will be examined in Chapter 11. That chapter will also take a further look at the current definition of the word *news* itself.

Understanding Today's Newspaper *Industry*

The newspaper industry is changing radically, and those changes are altering the way news is covered. And yet, the newspaper industry continues to be profitable, often more so than other industries. The 12 major public newspaper companies in the United States routinely post profit margins of more than 20 percent—which means that for every dollar of revenue they bring in, 20 cents is pure profit. That's more than double the average profit margin of the Fortune 500.[18]

Understanding this industry requires knowing who owns today's papers; the types and varieties of papers that exist; the way newspapers are staffed; which support services, such as wire services and feature syndicates, newspapers use; and the kind of relationship newspapers have with their readers.

THE OWNERS

In the 1980s, chains began to acquire newspapers at a furious rate. The price of newsprint had gone down, advertising rates were going up, and newspapers looked like a better investment than ever. Plus, chains were making record profits, and if they used those profits to buy more papers, they avoided corporate income taxes.

During a typical year, 75 to 100 U.S. daily newspapers will change hands. Most pass from one chain to another. The concentration of news-

During a typical year, 75 to 100 U.S. daily newspapers will change hands.

paper ownership into giant chains has been extremely controversial, as many critics believe that business values and news values often conflict. We will discuss these controversies in the final section of this chapter.

THE NEWSPAPERS

A wide variety of newspapers make up today's industry, but newspapers are generally categorized as either dailies, weeklies, or special interest papers.

Dailies

As the term suggests, daily newspapers are those that come out every day, at least Monday through Friday, although most of them publish weekend editions as well. Dailies are usually classified according to their geographic reach: national, metropolitan, or suburban.

National Dailies

Four newspapers today are published for the national market and also have significant amounts of international distribution. The *Wall Street Journal,* the *New York Times,* and the *Christian Science Monitor* were discussed in the history section of this chapter. A relative newcomer, but a highly influential

FACT FILE 4.2

Largest U.S. Newspapers, by Daily Circulation

Rank	Circulation (millions)	Publication Name and Publisher
1	2.199	**USA Today,** Gannett Company Inc., Washington, DC
2	2.070	**Wall Street Journal,** Dow Jones & Co. Inc., New York, NY
3	1.136	**New York Times,** New York Times Company, New York, NY
4	.908	**Los Angeles Times,** Tribune Publishing Company, Los Angeles, CA
5	.752	**Washington Post,** Washington Post Company, Washington, DC
6	.736	**New York Daily News,** New York Daily News, New York, NY
7	.678	**New York Post,** News Corporation, New York, NY
8	.575	**Chicago Tribune,** Tribune Publishing Company, Chicago, IL
9	.528	**Houston Chronicle,** Hearst Newspapers, Houston, TX
10	.469	**San Francisco Chronicle,** Hearst Newspapers, San Francisco, CA

Source: Fact Pack 2006, Supplement to *Ad Age* magazine at www.adage.com

one, has been *USA Today* (see the Close-Up on Industry box). Several other papers—such as the *Los Angeles Times,* the *Washington Post,* and the *Chicago Tribune*—are essentially local papers but publish a national edition as well. Fact File 4.2 lists the largest U.S. newspapers.

USA Today was the first newspaper to be designed from its inception for national distribution, and the first to distribute its content to printing plants around the United States each day by satellite.[19] Its colorful, graphic approach has had a significant influence on the design and layout of other newspapers (see Figure 4.1).

SELF QUIZ How does *USA Today* differ from earlier newspapers?

Local Dailies

Most newspapers are local; their strength lies in presenting the in-depth local news, information, and advertising that the other media don't handle as well. Local dailies can be major metropolitan papers such as the *Houston Chronicle* or small suburban ones such as the *Democrat Reporter* of Linden, Alabama. Even the great metropolitan papers are mostly local in flavor and have relatively small circulations by international standards. The U.S. newspaper industry's local tradition is based largely on the importance of local government, which is involved in everything from how garbage is collected to how much schoolteachers are paid. In other countries, where those decisions are made at the national level, national papers became the norm.

Weeklies

In today's world of fast-breaking news, there may seem to be no place for weekly newspapers. Many such papers do exist, however, and they take up the slack left by the dailies. In small towns and suburbs, where there

USA *Today* Changes the Face of Journalism

USA Today changed the face of journalism by appealing to a national audience through a colorful design, short articles, and snappy graphics. The paper was introduced by the Gannett Corporation in 1982. It was the brainchild of Al Neuharth, the hard-driving Gannett chairman who had built the chain into a colossus and made it highly profitable. *USA Today* was by far his boldest move, involving innovations in concept, design, distribution and marketing.

14 percent minorities. Nancy Jane Woodhull became the founding editor and helped shape the identity of the paper. Loaners, or reporters from the other Gannett papers, came from 29 different states.

USA Today's design seemed to be influenced by television. Like TV, it was highly visual and flagrantly colorful. The weather map jumped off the page, with a variety of colorful graphics. Neuhath admitted, "This is a direct, absolute steal from Willard Scott and other

Its critics immediately labeled *USA Today* "junk-food journalism" and "McPaper." It was the news equivalent of fast food, attractive and tasty but not particularly good for you.

Only a chain the size of Gannett, and a chairman as powerful as Neuharth, had the resources to create such a paper. Neuharth borrowed some of the most talented reporters, editors, and graphics designers from the papers of the Gannett chain for *USA Today*, but the chain's more important support was financial. This was the most expensive newspaper debut in history, costing its parent company tens of millions of dollars during its first year—and the paper lost money for 10 years. In fact, one of its distinctions is that it lost more than any newspaper in history, hundreds of millions of dollars, before becoming financially successful in the 1990s.

The paper was designed from the beginning to appeal to a national, rather than a local, audience. In fact, a large percentage of its readers are travelers, and most of its copies are sold at newsstands, convenience stores, hotels, and airports. To grab the attention of these travelers, page 1 would have a carefully selected mix of hard news and features, all of which were chosen for wide human interest. Stories and artwork would represent various minorities and both genders. Inside the paper, there would be a full page of weather news covering the entire country. A two-page center insert, "News from Around the Nation," would feature one or two brief, high-interest items from each state. In hiring, Neuharth strove for a diversity of viewpoints by staffing 39 percent women and

TV Weathermen."[1] Even the vending boxes were designed to look like television sets. Like local TV journalism, the paper would favor good news with happy endings, and would not be opposed to front-page pictures of children washing their pets. Even important news stories would be boiled down to quick bites. Whenever possible, bulleted lists and charts would be used instead of conventional stories.

Its critics immediately labeled *USA Today* "junk-food journalism" and "McPaper." It was the news equivalent of fast food, attractive and tasty but not particularly good for you.

The paper began making a profit in 1992. By 1996 the editors noticed that sales jumped whenever breaking news was put on the front page, so *USA Today* began doing more hard news and investigative reporting, and running longer stories. By 2003 it actually received high praise from a competitor, *Time* magazine, which said, "*USA Today* does better than ever a hard thing that looks easy—making news brief but not dumb—through efficient, informed stories that lay out the facts without calling attention to themselves."[2]

[1] Peter Prichard, *The Making of McPaper: The Inside Story of USA Today* (Kansas City: Andrews, McMeel & Parket, 1987).
[2] James Poniewozik, "The People's Paper: Read by Millions, Often Ignored by Peers, the U.S.'s Biggest Newspaper Wants to Add Prestige to Its Popularity," *Time*, July 21, 2003, p. 48.

Left ear:
Promotes sports stories and gives scores of hot games.

Newsline:
A digest of the day's news and an index of inside stories.

Breaking news:
Based on current TV reports.

Talker:
Human interest story people will be talking about.

Snapshot:
Statistical look at life in the USA; often pegged to a study released that day.

Right ear:
Promotes feature story on inside page.

Cover story:
Major feature article that might continue on page 2.

Lead:
Top news of the day, with a bold headline.

Main color art:
At least one half appears "above the fold," the top part of the page that readers see in the window of the newsrack.

Boxed sidebar:
Brief, high-interest story-within-the-story.

Simplified graphic:
Designed for quick impression.

Sidebar tease:
Promotes sidebar on inside page.

Photo tease:
Promotes news story on inside page.

Color band:
Front-page ad.

FIGURE 4.1 Sample Front Page of *USA Today* The front page of *USA Today* shows the flashy, colorful, and brief features that have influenced the layout of other newspapers.

isn't enough news to justify a daily, weeklies supply a chronicle of local events. Some weekly newspapers, known as **shoppers,** are free-distribution newspapers that consist mostly of ads but that also contain some news and entertainment to attract extra readers. Some major dailies publish their own weekly shoppers.

shoppers
Free-distribution newspapers consisting mostly of ads.

Special Interest Newspapers

When we speak of dailies and weeklies, we usually refer to general interest newspapers that are designed to reach a wide and diverse audience. There is also a thriving industry of special interest newspapers, including organizational papers, alternative papers, and ethnic papers.

The Organizational Press

organizational papers
Newspapers published as part of an organization's communication with members.

Organizational papers include all those published by business entities, religious and educational institutions, and social groups as an integral part of their organizational communication with members. Companies may put out a weekly paper for their employees; industries and labor unions may support industrywide papers; and nearly every college publishes its own newspaper, as do many religious groups.

Many organizations send out a free newsletter to their members. Others send out specialized information for which people are willing to pay. For example, a thriving medium today is the newsletter that supplies premium information to investors who want to know about potentially successful companies that haven't been discovered by other investors yet. Many investor newsletters charge their subscribers up to $2,000 a year for eight pages of typeset text weekly, or its equivalent delivered by fax or e-mail. The *Kiplinger Washington Letter* is one of the oldest and most respected business newsletters. It began publishing in 1923 and now has an annual circulation of more than 275,000.

The Alternative Press

alternative press
Publications that provide a different viewpoint on the news, usually one that is politcally radical or otherwise out of the mainstream.

The term **alternative press** suggests to many people the underground papers of the 1960s, but the classification is broader than that. Alternative papers are those that provide a different viewpoint on the news, usually one that is politically radical or otherwise out of the mainstream. Some alternative papers are targeted toward cultural groups. For example, most major cities have at least one gay and lesbian publication such as the *Houston Voice* (www.houstonvoice.com) or New York's *LGNY* (www.lgny.com). One such publication, *Outweek,* published nationally in the early 1990s, gained notoriety for its practice of "outing" public figures who were secretly gay or lesbian. There have been several papers put out by prison inmates, and also newspapers by and for the homeless, such as *Street News* in New York (www.othersides.com/streetnews.htm) and *Real Change* in Seattle (www.realchangenews.org). In fact, many smaller markets now carry papers for the homeless, such as the *Dark Night* of Cedar Rapids, Iowa, and *Art's Garbage Gazette* of Madison, Wisconsin. As an alternative to panhandling, vendors sell these papers with the goal of raising funds to get themselves, and others who work on the publications, off the street. Foundation grants and donations finance most homeless papers until they become profitable.

CONSIDER THIS

Is your school newspaper an organizational paper or an alternative paper? Why?

underground press
Alternative newspapers of the 1960s and 1970s that passionately criticized cultural and political norms.

Some underground papers, and others like them, do still exist. The **underground press** of the 1960s and 1970s offered a radical view of politics and tended to question mainstream, middle-class values as well as many governmental practices. The original underground papers supported many activities that were illegal at the time, such as abortion; today's versions also advocate some illegal activities, such as recreational drug use.

New York City's *Village Voice* (www.villagevoice.com), begun in Greenwich Village during the beat era of the 1950s, was the first underground newspaper. Others, such as the *Berkeley Barb,* appeared on and around college campuses in the 1960s. The *Boston Phoenix* (www.bostonphoenix.com),

Chicago's *Reader* (www.chireader.com), and San Francisco's *Bay Guardian* (www.sfbg.com) are well-known alternative papers. Some of these have survived their alternative days very successfully and have become mainstream newspapers today. The alternative papers are often advocates for minorities and minority opinions, which is a role that has also been fulfilled by the ethnic press.

The Ethnic Press

Today's ethnic press continues to include foreign-language newspapers and papers written in English but aimed at a particular ethnic group, such as African Americans, Hispanics, or Native Americans. It continues to play an important role in the lives of new immigrants, although there are far fewer foreign-language papers today than in earlier days. The 1,300 foreign-language newspapers of 1914 now number only 500, mostly due to assimilation. Many readers have slipped into America's English-speaking mainstream, lured away by television and other media. Ethnic radio and television stations have also cut into the readership of these papers. In addition, today's immigrants can keep in touch with their native countries by inexpensive global communications; contact is not nearly as difficult as it was years ago.

One alternative newspaper, *The Onion*, is so "alternative" that it isn't a newspaper at all. Like *The Daily Show with Jon Stewart* on TV, *The Onion* is a parody of real news.

The following are included in the ethnic press:

- *The Hispanic press.* By far the biggest segment of the foreign-language press is Hispanic, with 200 papers reaching 10 million readers. Hispanic papers include major urban dailies such as Chicago's *El Mañana Daily News*, Los Angeles's *La Opinión*, and New York's *Hoy* and *El Diario–La Prensa*. Hispanics are the fastest-growing segment of the U.S. population, and the Spanish-language press is growing in circulation and influence with it. Hispanics are a diverse group, coming from many different countries. The **Chicano press,** which targets Mexican Americans, makes up the majority of Hispanic papers.

- *The Native American press.* The Native American press is now published almost entirely in English. This segment has struggled over the years, but during the 1990s, more than 50 new tribal newspapers started up, bringing the total to almost 120. The papers are almost all owned by tribal governments and are financed in large part by gambling revenues, the sale of natural resources, and cash settlements from land disputes. The *Navajo Times* (www.thenavajotimes.com), for example, is the weekly newspaper of the Navajo Nation.

- *The African American press.* Today there are more than 170 black newspapers, including New York's *Amsterdam News,* the *Chicago Defender,* and Baltimore's *Afro-American.* Like all ethnic papers, the African American newspapers record the daily happenings of their communities: births, deaths, weddings, new businesses, community functions, and so on (items often not covered in the mainstream press), while their editorials fight for the rights of that ethnic group.

What are the different types of newspapers, and how is each unique?

Chicano press
Part of Hispanic American newspaper industry that targets Mexican Americans.

publisher
In print industries, the person who runs an individual company and acts as its chief representative.

THE STAFF

While newspapers vary in terms of size and readership, most have a similar staffing organization. As in other print industries, the **publisher,** who is often at least a part owner, runs the individual newspaper and acts as the paper's chief representative-in-residence. The publisher makes all the major decisions about the business and editorial directions that the paper will take.

For example, the publisher might decide to stress responsible rather than sensational stories, or to try to increase circulation by reducing newsstand and subscription prices.

Carrying out the publisher's general orders is the work of the editorial and business staffs. All papers have the two basic divisions of editorial and business, with the editorial side making editorial decisions, such as which stories to cover, and the business side making business decisions, such as how to attract more advertisers. (See Figure 4.2.) Most journalists believe it is important to keep the two divisions separate. The separation between the two sides is so important that most journalists refer to them as "church and state."

The Editorial Staff

The editorial staff includes editors and reporters. The head editor is usually called the editor in chief or executive editor, and various other editors report to that office. For example, there is usually a managing editor who oversees the day-to-day operations of the newsroom. There is also an editorial page/op-ed page editor who oversees the unsigned editorials that express the paper's point of view, and the **op-ed** pieces that are signed columns, opinion pieces and guest editorials. The op-ed page gets its name from its placement in the paper, which is generally "opposite the editorial page."

Larger papers employ several other editors, such as the city editor and the sports, business, and features editors. At the larger papers these men and women sometimes do little actual editing; they are instead managers who hire and fire reporters, assign stories, and approve finished copy. At other papers they do indeed edit: They question facts and phrasing. They rearrange paragraphs and often rewrite leads for maximum impact. Other employees, called copy editors, make smaller changes in style, grammar, and spelling before trimming the copy to fit a space and writing a headline. Wire service editors coordinate the dispatches from the Associated Press and other wire services; and art, graphics, and photo editors are becoming increasingly important now that papers are becoming more visually oriented. And there are even more specialty editors at a major paper like the *New York Times,* which employs 6,000 people. Of course, many other papers employ only a handful of workers, and sometimes just a mom and a pop, so individuals have to undertake multiple editorial functions.

A major paper also employs several types of reporters. All of them seek out stories and write the early drafts. **General assignment reporters** can cover anything, while **beat reporters** are assigned to particular areas, such as technology, businesses, or city hall. Much of the reporting is done in teams, including pairs of reporters and photojournalists, the photographers who supply the photos published in the paper. With the Internet and specialized databases, computers are an essential tool for most reporters.

The *Navajo Times* is the weekly newspaper of the Navajo Nation.

op-ed page
The section of the newspaper "opposite the editorial page" reserved for signed columns, opinion pieces, and guest editorials.

general assignment reporters
Journalists who can find and write stories in any area.

beat reporters
Journalists who find and write stories in a specialized area.

FIGURE 4.2 The Newspaper Staff The separation between the editorial and business departments is so important to most journalists that they refer to the two sides as "church and state."

The Business Staff

The business side of a newspaper's staff includes the advertising, production, and circulation departments.

Advertising

Newspaper advertising departments include sales representatives for both display and classified ads, as well as layout people who work with display ads. Like the news stories themselves, classified ads seldom appear on paper now before the newspaper is actually printed. The salesperson takes the information and keys it into a computer file that is sent to the composing room. Because newspapers rely on advertising revenue to make money, this department is of great concern to the publisher. It was advertising departments that lobbied for, and won, specialty sections in newspapers on real estate, food, automobiles, and so on in order to create an amenable environment for ads for related products.

Production

The production department at a newspaper runs the presses, which are becoming increasingly sophisticated as papers become more visual. The finished page is photographed directly from the editor's computer file onto a special plate by **photo-offset printing,** in which the negative image holds the ink and transfers the image onto the newsprint as it flows through the press. Technology has led to a considerable amount of automation in the printing process. At many plants, large robot devices move the giant rolls of newsprint automatically from a warehouse into the press position, and the flow of the ink and the speed of the paper are both controlled by computer.

photo-offset printing
Technique in which a photo negative transfers ink onto paper.

Circulation

In any print media company, the **circulation department** is the division that manages distribution and sales. A newspaper's circulation department arranges for the delivery of the finished papers from the printing plant to newsstands and homes, as well as to grocery stores, bookstores, and vending machines. This department makes sure that the papers get out on time

circulation department
The division of a print media company that manages distribution and sales.

and keeps track of the unsold copies that are returned. It is also in charge of promotions to increase circulation and readership, such as college programs in which students are given half-price subscriptions for newspapers that are used in classes.

What are the major staff positions on a newspaper, and what are the responsibilities of each?

SUPPORT SERVICES

Newspapers make use of a wide range of supplementary services that support their operations, including wire services, syndicates, and the Audit Bureau of Circulations.

Wire Services

The Associated Press (AP) is the world's best known and most prolific wire service, with hundreds of bureaus collecting news in a hundred different countries and distributing it in half a dozen different languages. The AP is a cooperative, which means that reporters at its member news organizations (including television, radio, and online outlets as well as newspapers) send local stories in if they have potential regional or national appeal. The editors at AP decide if those stories will go out along with those of its own reporters. Historically, the AP's biggest competitor was United Press International (UPI), which was formed in 1958 when E. W. Scripps's United Press merged with William Randolph Hearst's International News Service. Both of these services had been formed in the early 1900s to compete with the AP. They merged because neither was profitable; but despite its combined resources, the UPI continued to experience financial troubles. Today, the UPI is owned by the Rev. Sun Myung Moon, the charismatic leader of the Unification Church,[20] and provides news only to Internet news organizations.

Other major international wire services include Agence France-Presse (AFP), headquartered in Paris, and Reuters, of London, which is developing an American market for online news. There are also several specialized and supplemental news services, including Dow Jones, the New York Times News Service, and the Washington Post/Los Angeles Times Service. Some chains, such as Gannett, also have their own wire services. Some supplemental wires, such as the Business Wire and the Public Relations Wire, supply free commercial news to newspapers.

Feature Syndicates

Feature syndicates act as brokers for newspaper feature items such as comic strips and crossword puzzles. Feature syndicates also carry columns by well-known writers such as Larry King and Liz Smith, as well as games, horoscopes, serialized books, and editorial cartoons. The papers pay for each item used, which enables them to run material from cartoonists and columnists that they could never afford to hire full-time. The biggest feature syndicates are United Media (owned by Scripps-Howard), King Features

feature syndicates
Brokers for newspaper entertainment and specialty items.

Cartoons became a newspaper editorial device in the years following the Civil War, and they quickly showed their power. Today, they are must-sees for many readers, and they often set the tone for the entire editorial page. Often, they present images that can be more devastating than words. The cartoon [on the left], by Charles Green Bush from the *New York World*, 1903, shows Theodore Roosevelt "taking" Panama. Paul Szep's 2004 cartoon [on the right] accuses George W. Bush of using the same type of heavy-handed foreign policy. *By permission of Paul Szep and Creators Syndicate, Inc.*

(started in 1914 by William Randolph Hearst), Tribune Media Services (owned by the Chicago Tribune chain), North American Syndicate (owned by Rupert Murdoch), and Universal Press Syndicate.

Audit Bureau of Circulations

The **Audit Bureau of Circulations** supplies an extremely important service to newspapers by verifying circulation figures for advertisers. The bureau was established in 1914 as a not-for-profit association by advertisers, advertising agencies, and publishers (including magazine publishers) who came together to establish standards and rules for circulation reporting. They created the association to verify circulation reports by audit and to provide independent, and therefore credible and objective, information to the buyers and sellers of print advertising. The bureau also audits Web sites. Most newspapers and magazines are members, along with most major advertising agencies.

Red Eye is a condensed version of the *Chicago Tribune* that is designed to attract younger readers.

THE READER

There are two ways to characterize newspaper readers. The first is to recognize that different newspapers attract different types of readers. A clever list of types of newspaper readers that circulated recently on the Internet read, in part, as follows:

1. The *Wall Street Journal* is read by the people who run the country.

2. The *New York Times* is read by people who think they run the country.

3. The *Washington Post* is read by people who think they should run the country.

4. *USA Today* is read by people who think they ought to run the country but don't really understand the *Washington Post*. They do, however, like their smog statistics shown in pie charts.

5. The *Los Angeles Times* is read by people who wouldn't mind running the country, if they could spare the time, and if they didn't have to leave L.A. to do it.

Such a list might or might not be accurate, but it does point out that when we talk about "the newspaper reader" we are talking about a diverse audience. Still, there are certain things we can say about the typical reader, including the fact that patterns of readership have changed over time.

Changing Patterns of Readership

In colonial days, tavern readership of newspapers was marked by interaction and argument, in which news stories served as what one historian describes as "gambits, provocative first moves in a game the reader would then play."[21] Newspapers of the 19th century were usually read to the family and interpreted by the man of the house. Twentieth-century news saw the TV anchor assume that role, and some observers believe that today's Internet news returns us to the spirit of the tavern as people discuss news items in forums of various types.

Changes in readership naturally affect the structure of the industry. Over the years, for example, readers moved from the cities to the suburbs, and the industry followed as city papers died and new suburban papers were born. As mentioned earlier, afternoon papers died as work schedules changed, leaving more time for morning reading, and people began to look to television for their evening news.

CONSIDER THIS

Toward what type of reader is your local newspaper directed? Provide examples of specific stories to back up your answer.

Younger Readers

From the newspaper industry's point of view, an alarming trend among changing patterns of readership is a generally lower circulation and, more ominously, a lower readership among young people, who are failing to take up the newspaper-reading habits of their parents. The average age of today's newspaper reader is 53.[22] The industry worries about its future readers, especially since many advertisers want to sell to people ages 18 to 25.

Younger readers might still use newspapers to figure out movie times or to catch up on sports scores, but not for the kind of in-depth analysis of news that the papers do best. Newspapers are, however, making extra efforts to connect with today's increasingly distracted and time-pressed young readers. The *Kansas City Star,* for example, has developed a section written by and for teenagers. Other papers have beefed up their coverage of rock bands, youth-oriented movies, college life, and social issues of interest to young people. Several publishers have put out free condensed papers in a tabloid format designed to attract younger readers.

Public Journalism

Another trend designed to be of interest to the younger reader is **public journalism.** An innovation of the 1990s, public journalism, also called civic journalism, calls for newspapers to become involved in, rather than just cover, community issues. Public journalism might lead a newspaper to organize citizen focus groups about community problems, to sponsor town hall meetings to address local concerns, or to join with radio and television stations to promote civic projects like cleaning up vacant lots or building playgrounds.

public journalism
Reporting that becomes involved in, rather than just covers, community issues.

Critics contend that public journalism not only blurs the traditional distinction between reporting and editorializing but also creates a conflict of interest because newsrooms that become directly involved in civic improvement are in fact shaping the local news that they should be reporting objectively. Proponents of public journalism say that anything that strengthens the bonds be-

PORTER

Public journalism is alive and well in the college press. In the *Media World* DVD that accompanies this book (track 10), NBC News reports on a group of college journalism students whose investigation freed a wrongly accused death row inmate.

tween newspaper and community, and encourages readers to become more involved in their own communities, is a good thing that should be encouraged.

Controversies

The debate over public journalism is just one of the controversies that the modern newspaper industry engenders. Other major controversies affecting the newspaper industry derive from the ways that the industry is changing in reaction to changes in media economics and society. Two such changes involve concentration of ownership and diversity in the newsroom, both of which are controversial because they affect the way news is covered.

CONCENTRATION OF OWNERSHIP

There are many advantages and disadvantages to chain ownership. Critics point out that chains tend to create local newspaper monopolies because the most powerful chain-owned paper in the community tends to kill off its competitors. In fact, the great majority of communities now have just one daily newspaper, most likely owned by a chain.[23] Critics fear that this reduces the diversity of opinions that readers have available to them. The chains respond that they are interested in profits, not editorial policy, so most of them allow their editors and reporters to develop their own opinions. Also, they say, with the great diversity of news outlets today—includ-

The relentless bottom-line attitude of a typical newspaper chain can mean poorer-quality journalism.

ing broadcast, cable, and Internet sources—no one need worry about access to a diversity of viewpoints. Finally, the chains argue, in many cases the community also benefits, with a better paper that can afford to practice a higher level of journalism.

Critics respond that in some small cities with a chain-owned newspaper, none of the local television or radio stations have the resources to provide much local news, so in fact the chain-owned paper is the dominant voice on local news. There may well be a diversity of information available on national and international news through television and the Internet, but chain-owned papers do choke off the competition for local news—and rarely with "a better paper that can afford to practice a higher level of journalism."

In fact, according to most critics, the typical chain's relentless bottom-line business orientation will mean poorer journalistic performance. After all, chains are famous for continually demanding higher profits from their owned papers. To reach these levels of profitability, most chains will lay off a large number of staff members when they first take over. Sometimes, they will require all the staff members to reapply for their jobs. The chain will then replace highly paid veterans with young staffers right out of college who can be paid as little as possible. When these staffers gain experience, they are encouraged to move on so that the paper can hire someone even less experienced at an even lower salary.

Some chains like to garner national journalism prizes such as Pulitzers for publicity purposes, so they support some talented veterans who work on major pieces. Even that, however, leaves few resources for local news. Critics complain that new chain owners are sometimes not sufficiently acquainted with the community to know who is prominent enough to merit an obituary or who is corrupt enough to warrant an investigation (see the Close-Up on Controversy box). The managers of newspaper conglomerates, however, insist that chains often use

What are the arguments, both pro and con, for chain ownership of newspapers?

their substantial outside resources to stand up to local corruption and have won many prizes for doing so.

LACK OF DIVERSITY IN THE NEWSROOM

A second controversy attracting considerable heat is the lack of diversity in the newspaper newsroom.

The Need for Diversity

In the 1970s, following several urban riots, the National Commission on the Causes of Violence pointed out that the lack of a minority viewpoint in the nation's press was partially to blame for the alienation from society many ethnic groups felt. Minorities and nonminorities saw the world differently. Minority communities felt that white reporters were insensitive to the nuances of racial slights and ethnic stereotypes. They were often offended by subtle changes in wording, pictures, and story placement. White reporters critically covering a black politician, for example, would often do so in ways that blacks considered racist.[24] Minority reporters tended to choose different sources for their stories than white male reporters did and had different ideas about when it was appropriate to identify someone by color.

Attempts to Increase Diversity

In an attempt to make newsrooms more diverse, the American Society of Newspaper Editors (ASNE) resolved in 1978 that minority employment in newsrooms should match the percentage of minorities in the population. Minority employment slowly increased for more than 25 years, but by 2004

Only about 13 percent of daily newspaper journalists are African American, Hispanic, Asian American, or Native American.

only 13 percent of local newspapers had a percentage of minority employees that matched the percentage of minorities in their community. Critics of the slow progress pointed out that many papers were still mostly white in communities that were largely minority. The *Independent* in Gallup, New Mexico, for example, had an all-white newsroom and a community that was 92 percent nonwhite.[25]

Overall, a little less than 13 percent of daily newspaper journalists were black, Hispanic, Asian American, and American Indian in 2004, while the U.S. Census Bureau reported that nearly 32 percent of the U.S. population belonged to those four groups.[26] Women fared somewhat better, making up around 40 percent of the newspaper workforce, but even that number seems inadequate when you consider that women make up 70 percent of the student body at journalism schools and university communication departments.[27]

The Industry Response

Newspaper publishers have responded to the controversy over diversity by saying they have difficulty attracting qualified minorities, especially to small papers that don't pay very well. Publishers say they are indeed concerned; they want their newsrooms to be more diverse, not only as a matter of basic fairness but also because a more diverse staff will help win new readers

The Power of the Independent Press

Critics contend that chains often cut down on local news to save money and often avoid controversial issues so as not to offend advertisers. What may be lost in that bargain can be seen in communities that still have an independent press. One such community is the tiny town of Linden, Alabama, population 2,500. Linden had a big problem. Their county sheriff was running a corrupt department, but everyone was afraid to speak up—everyone, that is, except for the editor of the local weekly paper, Goodloe Sutton, and his star reporter, Jean Sutton, who was also his wife.[1]

The Sutton family had owned the *Democrat Reporter* since 1917. In all that time it had never been taken over by a chain because it was so small that no chain ever noticed it. When the Suttons started to print stories about the corrupt sheriff, they began to receive threats. One came anonymously and said, in part, "I wonder how brave you will be when someone catches you in a place where there are no witnesses." Other threats were delivered in person, by the sheriff's deputies who routinely stopped the Suttons whenever they drove their car. One of the deputies warned them that if they didn't stop publishing stories about the sheriff they were going to find some drugs planted in their house and be arrested for possession. The sheriff

also began to spread rumors. He told people that the editor was a drunk, that his wife was having affairs, and that his two sons used drugs.

In spite of his unconventional approach to law enforcement, the sheriff was well liked in the town of Linden. He had friends and family in local government and business. Some of the Suttons' biggest advertisers stopped advertising in the paper, and many readers canceled their subscriptions. But the Suttons were not deterred. When they found out the sheriff had bought his daughter a pickup truck with county funds, they published the story. When they discovered that the sheriff had embezzled funds, they published a page of his ledger as proof. When they uncovered the fact that he had stolen checks from the county mental health center, they published copies of the canceled checks. They exposed everything from extortion to the protection of drug dealers, and they sent every piece of evidence they collected to state authorities. Unfortunately, they received no reply from the state.

Figuring that the sheriff's powerful friends were protecting him, the Suttons nevertheless continued to publish their stories. What they didn't know was that a U.S. attorney in the state capital had started an undercover investigation when his mother sent him copies of

among members of minority communities. Some papers have appointed diversity committees made up of reporters, editors, and outside consultants that do annual "content audits" to assess how minorities and women are portrayed in pictures and print. Most say they aggressively recruit minorities. But, they say, it is difficult to raise the numbers when minority reporters move on to better-paying jobs in related fields such as public relations. Journalism schools produce only around 750 minority journalists annually, about the same number that leave the profession each year.

Conservative critics say that the newspaper industry is too interested in attracting minority reporters. They point out what happened in the Jayson Blair case, in which a young black reporter was caught plagiarizing and fictionalizing a number of stories. These critics say that editors at the *New York Times* gave Blair too many chances because they were too concerned with keeping their newsroom diverse and not concerned enough about quality journalism.

Minority Organizations

Because of the problems minorities have faced in getting hired and working in the newsroom, a number of organizations exist to promote their interests.

some of the Suttons' first articles. He couldn't tell the editor or his wife about the secret investigation, though, so they continued to publish their stories without any knowledge of action or protection from the authorities. Finally, the state authorities swept in and made arrests; in 1997 the sheriff and his deputies were all sent to prison. The U.S. attorney who won the case summed up the Suttons' fight by saying, "Never get in an argument with a man who buys his ink by the barrel."[2]

[1]Jean Sutton died in 2003.
[2]Rick Bragg, "Small Alabama Newspaper Prevails in Crusade to Expose Corrupt Sheriff," *New York Times,* June 1, 1998, p. A10.

Goodloe and Jean Sutton took on a corrupt local sheriff and won.

These include the National Association of Black Journalists (www.NABJ.org), the National Association of Hispanic Journalists (www.NAHJ.org), the Asian American Journalists Association (www.AAJA.org), the Native American Journalists Association (www.NAJA.com), and the National Gay and Lesbian Journalists Association (www.NGLJA.org).

OTHER CONTROVERSIES

Newspapers deal with other controversial issues every day. Throughout this chapter we have referred to controversies about the way news is covered, from the days of the partisan press to the establishment of *USA Today.* This will be a recurrent theme throughout this book and will be dealt with in some depth in later chapters. Political bias and news as entertainment, for example, will be discussed in Chapter 11, which looks at the various forms of electronic news. Fairness, accuracy, and sensationalism are topics in Chapter 15. Advertiser influence over newspaper content will be dealt with in Chapter 13, and legal issues such as libel and invasion of privacy are discussed in Chapter 14.

 SELF QUIZ

Why is the lack of diversity in the newsroom a major issue?

Summing Up

Newspapers are where journalism begins, in the sense that most news stories that are picked up by other media originate with newspaper reports. The newspaper industry continues to thrive in spite of competition from new technologies. A look at its history provides insight into how this industry has become both profitable and culturally powerful.

Early colonial newspapers tended to be tightly controlled by the government, but they began to gain a measure of freedom with the vindication of John Peter Zenger in 1735. They played a pivotal role in both the American Revolution and the formation of the new nation. Benjamin Day's *New York Sun* marked the beginning of the penny press in 1833, when it established advertising as its main form of support. Competition increased during the penny press era, leading to the Hearst–Pulitzer circulation wars of the 1880s and the era of yellow journalism.

Soon, several papers—such as the *New York Times,* the *Wall Street Journal,* and the *Christian Science Monitor*—helped establish journalistic responsibility and integrity, but a tug-of-war between responsible and irresponsible journalism continues to this day. The economics of the newspaper industry made it inevitable that ownership would concentrate into chains that took advantage of economies of scale. E. W. Scripps began the first modern newspaper chain in 1878. Today, chains are the dominant force in the industry; 80 percent of all daily newspapers are owned by chains.

A wide variety of types of papers make up today's newspaper industry. Dailies include national dailies such as *USA Today,* as well as metropolitan dailies and suburban dailies. Weekly papers include small-town papers and free-distribution shoppers, as well as special interest papers. Special interest papers can include organizational papers, alternative papers, and ethnic papers, which include the foreign-language press.

The staff of the modern paper is divided into editorial and business functions. The publisher oversees both sides, while editors and reporters work the editorial side and the production, advertising, and circulation staffs work the business side.

Newspapers also make use of a wide range of supplementary services, including wire services that provide national, international, and specialized news; syndicates that provide features, columns, and entertainment items such as comics and games; and the Audit Bureau of Circulations, which verifies the paper's circulation claims for its advertisers.

The final major player in today's newspaper industry is the reader. Most trends within the industry can be traced back to the people who buy and use the newspaper. These trends include the shift from afternoon to morning newspapers and from metropolitan to suburban papers. The most alarming trend from the industry's point of view is lessening readership; papers are combating this trend with various features and practices that seek to involve readers, especially younger readers, with their local newspapers. One such practice is public journalism, a movement that calls for papers to become involved in, rather than just cover, civic issues.

One of the major newspaper controversies is the effect of the concentration of ownership, including the creation of local newspaper monopolies and an emphasis on profits rather than solid journalism. A second major controversy involves the idea of diversity in the newsroom. Newspapers say they find it difficult to attract minority reporters, while some minorities insist they are not hired because of discrimination.

Key Terms

These terms are defined and indexed in the Glossary of key terms at the back of the book.

Electronic Excursions

HISTORY

Web Excursion

1. Take a closer look at one era of newspaper history and report on what you find. Search the Web for your specific topic, such as penny press, yellow journalism, jazz journalism, or 19th-century press. How do the journalistic practices of your selected era compare with the ones of today? Write a brief summary of your findings, detailing at least five major changes, similarities, or differences.

INDUSTRY

Web Excursion

2. Some college newspapers seem to be part of the alternative press, whereas others are very much organizational papers. Organizational papers tend to present news from the administration's point of view, while the alternative paper will do it from a student, and often an anti-administration, point of view. Most college papers will be a mixture of the two types. Analyze your campus paper to answer the question, Is it organizational, alternative, or mixed? Then compare your campus paper with one or two online student papers, such as those linked to the Web site of the *Daily Beacon,* the campus paper of the University of Tennessee, at http://dailybeacon.utk.edu/.*

Media World DVD Excursions

3. View track 2, *Newspapers: Inside The Record.* This track explores the daily operations of a local newspaper. Are newspapers your primary source of news? If so, why? If not, why not? What are the three areas of advertising newspapers target? Which do you think is the most important?

4. View track 2.5, *Issues: Facing the Future.* This track looks at the competition newspapers face. Do newspapers seem to be at risk of becoming obsolete? What are the advantages and disadvantages of newspapers' adopting online versions?

CONTROVERSIES

Web Excursion

5. Is diversity in the newsroom important? Search the Web for pages devoted to this issue, or go directly to *Slate* magazine's analysis of today's papers at http://slate.msn.com.* Prepare a brief statement explaining how newsroom diversity might have affected the ways an event is covered by different papers.

Media World DVD Excursion

6. View track 11, *College Newspaper Under Fire for Controversial "Advertorial"* (from NBC's *Today* show). Student journalists from Brown University find themselves in the center of a firestorm over their decision to run a controversial ad in their newspaper. Should student newspapers be held to standards different from those of mainstream publications? Should ads be rejected if there is a risk that certain groups would be offended?

ONLINE LEARNING CENTER WWW.MHHE.COM/RODMAN2

You may access these and additional Web excursions at the Online Learning Center for the book (www.mhhe.com/rodman2). Visit the student portion of this Web site to also access the *Interactive Timeline of Mass Media Milestones,* chapter highlights, self quizzes, and recommended readings, movies, and documentaries for this chapter.

*Some Web site addresses may change. When they do, please search for the Web site by name or topic on your favorite search engine.

Magazines

The First of the Specialized Media

5

Chapter Highlights

HISTORY: Magazines were the last of the print media to become popular, but they became the first national medium. They also became the first of the specialized media, following an evolutionary pattern that all media tend to follow.

INDUSTRY: Today's magazine publishing industry is built primarily around consumer and trade magazines. The players in this industry consist mostly of those in editorial, advertising, and circulation departments.

CONTROVERSY: To become successful, magazines resort to techniques that lead to a number of controversies. In this chapter we will look at the impact of the industry's photographic images, along with truth and accuracy, editorial independence, and marketing schemes.

The Birth of *Latina*

"I didn't know that I couldn't do it,"[1] says Christy Haubegger, explaining how, at the age of 27, she came to be the founder of *Latina,* the first lifestyle magazine for bilingual Hispanic women.

Growing up as a Mexican American adopted by Anglo parents, Haubegger always wondered why the magazines at the checkout counter in the supermarket never had people on the cover who looked like her. As a teenager, she says, she couldn't help noticing that "you never saw anyone with brown eyes in *Seventeen* magazine."[2]

When she was 10, she started to dream of creating a magazine and kept it in mind while she

Having grown up as a Mexican American adopted by Anglo parents, the founder of *Latina* wanted a magazine with people on the cover who looked like her.

Visit us at latina.com

Latina

10th Anniversary Special!

Jennifer Lopez

Our original cover girl on her first Spanish album and being crazy in love with Marc

10

- secrets for dressing 5 pounds lighter

- real women on how they lost weight & kept it off!

- things every woman should do in her lifetime

PLUS:

The hottest new Latin music and movies

What's a normal Latina? Our survey of Hispanic women

finished her education. She earned a degree in Spanish and philosophy at the University of Texas and graduated from Stanford Law School.

Fresh out of law school, she decided to make her dream a

she told her potential investors, "we may only be 11 percent of the country, but we buy 16 percent of the lipliner."[4]

Her magazine would contain not only beauty and fashion articles but also cultural pieces for

stand next to Claudia Schiffer and say she looks just as good—if not better."[6]

Along with her initial five investors, Haubegger looked for a backer who knew something about the magazine business. She found such a backer in Edward Lewis, the founder and owner of the black women's magazine *Essence.* Lewis already knew the ins and outs of ethnic marketing, and he knew how to attract advertisers. Before long, Haubegger had signed up such big-name accounts as General Motors, Tommy Hilfiger, Honda, Revlon, and the Gap.

"It's very important for us to see Jennifer Lopez on the newsstand next to Claudia Schiffer and say she looks just as good—if not better."

reality—or at least to try. All she had at first was a 75-page business plan and the editorial concept for a magazine for second-generation Latinas like herself. She would need investors, and she began her search for them in Silicon Valley, in the same venture capital firms that were funding dot-com start-ups. "I knocked on 105 doors," Haubegger says, "And I got five yeses."[3] To get those yeses, she stressed that Hispanics were the fastest-growing minority group in the United States (in fact, by 2003 they had become America's largest minority group). They also had buying power: "Remember,"

Latinas who were battling stereotypes and walking a fine line between the Old World and assimilation. It would contain celebrity profiles of such role models as basketball star Rebecca Lobo and Mexican American astronaut Ellen Ochoa. "I wanted to create a magazine for Hispanic women where they would see beautiful and capable women like themselves," said Haubegger.[5] The ads would feature Latina models as well as familiar Anglos like Cindy Crawford and Christy Turlington. "It's very important for us," Haubegger explained, "to see Jennifer Lopez on the news-

She launched *Latina,* and its circulation grew to more than 200,000 within a year, a success by any standard. Her advice to others who might want to start their own magazine? "You have to feel really passionately about the magazine and about the audience. Women pick up this magazine and it's like they're looking in the mirror for the first time. And smiling."[7]

Magazines are our most diverse print medium. Along with the hundreds of specialized titles like *Latina,* they include newsmagazines like *Time* and scholarly journals like *Critical Studies in Mass Communication.* They include women's magazines like *Ladies' Home Journal* and men's magazines like *Maxim.* They include fashion magazines like *Elle* and trade magazines like *American Sweeper,* a periodical for the U.S. power-sweeping industry. They include Sunday newspaper supplements such as *Parade* and the *New York Times Mag-*

azine. They include literary magazines with circulations that are so small they are referred to as little magazines, and self-published magazines, called zines, that are even smaller.

By definition, a **magazine** is a collection of reading matter, issued regularly. "Issued regularly" generally means nondaily but at evenly spaced intervals, such as weekly, monthly, or quarterly. Because of this regular-interval stipulation, the word **periodical** is used in place of the word *magazine.* "Collection of reading matter" usually refers to a variety of stories, articles, and ads.

A Brief History of *Magazines*

Magazines were the last of the print media to become popular, after books and newspapers had already taken hold. In spite of this, they became the first of the truly national media. In fact, magazines are a good example of the evolution of the typical mass medium.

MAGAZINE EVOLUTION

Most historians agree that media go through three stages of development over time. First, they have an **elite stage,** in which only the richest and best-educated members of the population make use of them. Next, they have a **popular stage,** in which a truly mass audience takes advantage of them. And then they have a **specialized stage,** in which they tend to break up into segments for audience members with diverse and specialized interests. Historians have seen parallels with each medium, but magazines demonstrate the elite–popular–specialized cycle most clearly.

SELF QUIZ What are the three stages of media development, and what occurs in each stage?

The First Magazines

The first magazine, *Edifying Monthly Discussions,* appeared in Germany in 1663, nearly 200 years after printing technology had been used to produce books. Edited by Johann Rist, a poet and theologian, *Edifying Monthly Discussions* was what we would today call a literary journal and was targeted to an elite, literate audience. As opposed to early newspapers, which were edited by printers, the editors of early magazines were mostly writers. In fact, the three most influential literary journals in England early in the 18th century were Daniel Defoe's *Review,* Sir Richard Steele's *Tatler,* and Steele and Joseph Addison's *Spectator.* Defoe would go on to write *Robinson Crusoe,* considered by many to be the first English novel; Steele was a playwright, and Addison was the most famous essayist of his day.

The first periodical to actually use the word *magazine* in its title was Edward Cave's *Gentleman's Magazine,* which appeared in England in 1731. This was a magazine in the true sense of the word, a storehouse of excerpts from other sources, a precursor to *Reader's Digest.* Samuel Johnson, who would become Great Britain's foremost poet and literary critic, wrote for *Gentlemen's Magazine* as a young man.

The First American Magazines

American magazines were slow to appear. Even if people had wanted magazines, they didn't have the leisure time to read them. People in the early days of colonial America mostly worked from sunup until sundown, with reading time reserved for the Bible and an occasional newspaper.

Still, the first magazines in America foreshadowed how competitive the industry would become. More than 100 years after the first printing press had been established in America and more than 50 years after the first newspaper had been published, two publishers in 1741 suddenly decided the time had come for magazines. The first was Andrew Bradford's *American Magazine,* followed within three days by Benjamin Franklin's *General Magazine.* Franklin had originated the idea, but Bradford heard about it and beat him to press. Both publications were collections of essays on literary and newsworthy items of the day.

These two endeavors also foreshadowed how difficult it would be to establish a successful magazine. Bradford's lasted for just three monthly issues; Franklin's lasted for six. They failed because of the same reasons that it took so long for them to appear in the first place. Books and newspapers were considered necessities, but magazines were seen as a luxury. In fact, many of the first magazines were designed to be bound and added to private libraries, as some people do with *National Geographic* today. In fact, both Bradford's and Franklin's magazines were expensive, selling for a shilling, which was about half a day's wages for a working person, plus the cost of postage, which was also expensive. Magazines were heavy, and the mail rates were based on letters by the ounce, with no special discounts for bulk matter. Mail had to be carried by human or horse, neither of which made a distinction between 50 pounds of magazines and 50 pounds of letters carried over roads that were often no more than muddy trails through the forests.

Bradford's and Franklin's magazines were also the first attempts to build a national medium. Because the population was small and spread out over too large a territory, the colonies weren't ready for such a medium, and wouldn't be for another century. But that didn't stop quite a few colonial editors from trying. By 1776, a hundred magazines had started and failed. Most of them did not circulate far from where they were printed and were in fact published for their specific colony, with names like *Pennsylvania Magazine, Massachusetts Magazine,* and *New-York Magazine.* Many of these early magazines plagiarized stories and essays from British publications, taking advantage of the absence of copyright laws.

What were the factors that worked against the success of colonial-era magazines?

SELF QUIZ

Early Specialized Magazines

America's growing magazine industry during the late 18th and early 19th centuries was made up of small, specialized publications, often based on religion or literature. Specialized magazines also served various professions, including farmers, doctors, lawyers, and teachers. Fewer than 100 American magazines were published in 1825. By 1850, there were more than 600.

Women's Magazines

One factor in the growth of magazines as America's first national medium was a particular kind of specialized magazine: the women's magazine. Women's magazines had been around since the earliest periodicals, at least since 1693, when *Ladies' Mercury* was published in London.

In the United States, of the early attempts to establish a magazine for women, none were as successful as *Ladies' Magazine,* which began publishing in 1828 under the editorship of Sarah Josepha Hale. In 1822 Hale was left a widow with five children. She took up writing and editing to support her family and made *Ladies' Magazine* a significant success within its first two years.

The magazine caught the eye of publisher Louis Godey, who established a competing magazine, *Godey's Lady's Book,* in 1830. After seven years of head-to-head competition, Godey bought *Ladies' Magazine,* mostly to acquire the talents of Sarah Hale. He merged the two magazines in 1837, keeping his own title, and named Hale as editor. It was a position she held for 40 years, and she used it to fight for women's rights and education. *Godey's Lady's Book* was the first to offer color illustrations—which, because of the limitations of the printing technology of the day, had to be tinted by hand. Hale hired 150 women for this process.

Godey's Lady's Book was the predecessor for other women's magazines, the most famous of which is the *Ladies' Home Journal* (see the Close-Up on History box).

GENERAL INTEREST MAGAZINES

The *Ladies' Home Journal* attracted a large audience, but it was still a special interest magazine, one aimed at specific readers with specific concerns and curiosities—in this case, women. The first magazine to achieve a general interest, mass audience was the *Saturday Evening Post.* The *Post,* which could trace its lineage all the way back to Benjamin Franklin's newspaper, the *Pennsylvania Gazette,* had been founded in 1821 and was about to go out of business when Cyrus Curtis bought it in 1897 for $1,000—with a $100 down payment. Curtis originally designed the magazine for a male readership, hoping to parallel his success with the *Ladies' Home Journal.* He edited the magazine with a variety of features that would be of interest to men, including the best fiction of the day. Men brought the *Post* home and, in the tradition of newspapers, read it aloud to their families. It turned out that women were as interested in its features as men were, and the *Saturday Evening Post* slowly evolved into a middle-class family magazine, complete with its own section for women. Targeted for a national audience, it became America's longest-lived magazine.

Godey's Lady's Book was the first magazine to include color illustrations. Each one was individually hand painted.

 SELF QUIZ How did *Godey's Lady's Book* and *Ladies' Home Journal* change women's magazines?

The Golden Age of Magazines

The *Saturday Evening Post's* success signaled the dawn of the age of the general interest magazine and a golden age of American magazines that ran from 1885 to 1905. During this period, the number of magazines published doubled, from 3,500 to 7,000. These magazines became important in shaping public opinion and providing a forum for the discussion of important ideas, including everything from Charles Darwin's ideas about evolution to Susan B. Anthony's ideas about women's rights.

Magazines also became a national advertising medium, something that manufacturers in the burgeoning economy needed. Technical changes came rapidly as woodcuts gave way to modern lithography, and color illustrations

Ladies' Home Journal Invents the Modern Women's Magazine

The best-known and most long-lived women's magazine is *Ladies' Home Journal,* founded in 1883 by Cyrus Curtis. Cyrus and his wife, Louisa, had been publishing a weekly magazine called the *Tribune and Farmer.* Curtis was in charge of the editorial aspects of the magazine, and Louisa handled the business end. The magazine had a women's department, but Cyrus chose all the articles, and Louisa couldn't stand them. They spoke down to women, instructing them in various household duties as if they were children. Louisa came to Cyrus's office one day and said, "I don't want to make fun of you, but if you knew how funny this material sounds to a woman, you would laugh, too."[1]

Louisa Curtis knew that women's role in society was beginning to change, with women becoming both more literate and more independent. Louisa took over the women's department, and that section of the magazine became so popular that Cyrus issued it as a separate publication. The *Tribune and Farmer* soon failed, but the *Ladies' Home Journal* went on to transform the field of women's magazines, expanding the idea of women's interests and including sheet music and popular fiction by authors such as Louisa May Alcott. By the 1890s the *Journal* had a circulation of a half million, which made it the best-selling magazine in the country.

Edward W. Bok, the Curtises' son-in-law, took over as editor of the *Ladies' Home Journal* in 1889 and built on Louisa Curtis's success. He hired women editors and campaigned against a variety of social problems, including the killing of birds to decorate women's hats and the use of unsanitary public drinking cups. He published the best and best-known authors he could find, including Mark Twain and Rudyard Kipling. Bok was also the first magazine publisher to offer advertisers an **adjacency,** the opportunity to place an ad near a particular article, at an extra cost.[2] Under Bok, the *Ladies' Home Journal* became one of the first magazines ever to reach a circulation of 1 million, a milestone it reached in 1903. Women's magazines like the *Ladies' Home Journal* provided information to women that they often could not obtain elsewhere, such as articles about birth control, sexually transmitted diseases, and patent medicines.

[1]Helen Damon-Moore, *Magazines for the Millions: Gender and Commerce in the Ladies' Home Journal and the Saturday Evening Post, 1880–1910* (Albany: State University of New York Press, 1994).

[2]Charles P. Daly, Patrick Henry, and Ellen Ryder, *The Magazine Publishing Industry* (Boston: Allyn & Bacon, 1997), p. 16.

adjacency
The opportunity for an advertiser to place an ad near a particular article, at an extra cost.

Edward W. Bok hired some of the most talented artists and illustrators of the day to create covers for *The Ladies' Home Journal.* This one was painted by Frank Godwin in 1919.

and photography became increasingly important. The look of magazines changed as new cover images were used each month. For the first time, special

As the nation's first national mass media, magazines became important in shaping public opinion and providing a forum for important issues.

commemorative issues were published for big events like the turning of the 20th century, and premiums and gifts were used to spur subscription sales.

Several events made this golden age possible. First, the United States had made a commitment to free universal education, which resulted in an increase in literacy. Second, the Postal Act of 1879 reduced magazine rates to a penny a pound, making it economical for magazines to be distributed by mail. Third, the Rural Free Delivery postal system was established in the 1890s, enabling magazines to be delivered to out-of-the-way farms and country homes. Perhaps most important, the price of magazines came down as the industry caught up with the idea of the penny press and realized the profit potential of lowering copy and subscription costs.

Advances in high-speed printing technology and in photoengraving, which was much less expensive than woodcuts, had helped bring the costs of production down. It was now in the magazine's interest to sell more copies to defray the fixed, first-copy costs; writers, editors, typesetting, and illustration layout cost the same for one copy as they did for a million.

SELF QUIZ What events toward the end of the 19th century enabled general interest magazines to become mass circulation magazines?

Munsey's Magazine: Lower Cost and Wider Circulation

Most magazines cost 35 cents a copy during the 1880s, which meant that they were still luxury items. The first publisher to cut prices was Frank Munsey, who found himself broke and desperate after the economic panic of 1893, which was one of America's worst depressions. With his credit dried up, Munsey had to do something. In October 1893 he ran an ad in the *New York Sun* announcing that *Munsey's Magazine* would be dropping its price to 10 cents, and its annual subscription fee from $3 to $1. The magazine at the new price was an immediate hit, and Munsey was able to set his advertising rate according to a strict **CPM,** or cost per thousand, guideline (the *M* stands for *mille,* Latin for 1,000). Munsey's CPM was $1 a page. Munsey later estimated that the 10-cent magazine had tripled the size of the magazine-reading public, from 250,000 to 750,000.[8] Within a short time several other popular magazines—*McClure's, Collier's, Century,* and *Cosmopolitan*—were all selling for 10 cents, and advertising had become the chief source of revenue for the magazine business. One last thing was necessary for magazines to become a mass circulation medium: articles that caught the imagination of the public. That final ingredient was added by a group of investigative reporters who came to be known as muckrakers.

CPM
Cost per thousand; guideline for the price of each exposure of a customer to an ad.

The Muckrakers: Journalism That Inspired Social Change

At the beginning of the 20th century, newspapers and magazines got serious about crusading for social reform. Magazines, however, were most effective in bringing about in-depth investigations. Many of them had already fought for everything from large issues such as women's education to smaller issues such as Edward Bok's stands against feathered hats and public drinking cups. Before the Civil War there had been an entire class of magazine devoted to the abolitionist movement. The former slave and well-known writer

Frederick Douglass, for example, published *Douglass's Monthly* to argue the case against slavery. Later, Elizabeth Cady Stanton edited *Revolution* specifically to argue for woman's suffrage and other feminist reforms.

The new movement that came to be known as muckraking, however, was taken up by a variety of general interest magazines, not just the ones founded by crusaders. By 1900, the landscape of America was changing. Businesses were consolidating, sometimes by using ruthless tactics and by cutting corners that put corporate workers and customers in danger. A small group of highly successful businessmen, such as John D. Rockefeller and Andrew Carnegie, were becoming extremely powerful politically and were thus coming to be known as "robber barons." What business was doing to America became the story of the day, and many of the best magazines took it up with a vengeance, assigning top reporters to investigate the situation and write it up for publication.

Ladies' Home Journal and *Collier's* investigated and fought against fake patent medicines—a brave stance, considering that manufacturers of these products were the magazine industry's major advertisers. *McClure's* magazine was also famous for its investigative reporting. Journalist Ida Tarbell wrote articles for *McClure's* attacking Rockefeller's monopolistic practices; these were later collected into her book *The History of the Standard Oil Company* (1902). Similarly, *McClure's* editor Lincoln Steffens's collection *Shame of the Cities* (1904) exposed municipal corruption in several cities. Other magazines began to look into poor working conditions, government corruption, and unsanitary practices in food industries. Still others fought for an income tax, thought to be a great benefit for poor people, because the robber barons didn't pay any taxes on their income.

Muckraking articles helped lead to child labor laws, workers' compensation laws, and the first congressional investigations into business practices.

Who were the muckrakers, and what did they do?

muckraking
Investigative journalism conducted with the goal of bringing about social reform.

By 1906 Teddy Roosevelt, believing the magazines had gone too far, named them muckrakers, after a character in John Bunyan's epic poem *Pilgrim's Progress* who delighted in raking up filth. The magazines and their investigative reporters wore the title with pride, and **muckraking** came to be known as investigative journalism conducted with the goal of bringing about social reform. The newspapers of the day also took up the practice. Muckraking articles of this period helped lead to child labor laws, workers' compensation laws, and the first congressional investigations into business practices. Congress passed the Pure Food and Drug Act in 1906 partially because of the influence of muckrakers' reporting.

MASS CIRCULATION MAGAZINES

With the muckrakers, the age of the great mass circulation magazines had begun. The mass audience was made up of different types of people, with diverse interests. Everyone was reading magazines now, and the field of general interest magazines grew to include cultural magazines, digests, and newsmagazines, many of which grew to huge circulations through low-cost subscriptions and healthy newsstand sales.

Cultural Magazines: Trends in Modern Living

Cultural magazines covered all aspects of modern life; they observed trends and reflected them back to their readers. They included magazines of high culture, such as *Harper's* and *Atlantic,* but they also included style maga-

Condé Nast founded *Vogue* magazine and the Condé Nast chain.

zines and entertainment magazines, called **pulps** because of their cheap paper, where the cultural reach was fairly low. Pulp magazines included *True Romance* and *True Confessions,* which are still published today. Most of the cultural magazines, however, represented middle-class culture, in the manner of the *Saturday Evening Post* and *Collier's.*

One notable cultural magazine is the *New Yorker,* founded by Harold Ross in 1925. It immediately established itself as a powerful influence in literature. It has published stories and serialized books by such authors as Saul Bellow, James Thurber, E. B. White, Edmund Wilson, Rachel Carson, and John Cheever. It also covers politics, sports, movies, fashion, art, concerts, and plays, and is famous for its cartoons, which provide a wry commentary on life (the cartoons on pages 3 and 99 are *New Yorker* cartoons).

Condé Nast was another influential publisher of cultural magazines. Born in St. Louis, Nast trained to be a lawyer but found legal work boring. He began working in advertising and soon became advertising director for *Collier's.* He bought the struggling society- and fashion-oriented *Vogue* in 1909 and redesigned it for a certain quality, rather than quantity, of readers. The audience he sought included the rich and stylish urbanites that advertisers were willing to pay extra to reach. *Vogue* succeeded, and with his earnings from this success, Nast purchased *Vanity Fair* and *House & Garden,* thus founding the Condé Nast chain, which is part of Newhouse's Advance Publications today.

pulps
Magazines produced on cheap paper with a low cultural reach, such as *True Romance* and *True Confessions.*

Digests: Excerpts from Other Media

Digests, the second type of general interest, mass circulation magazine, are composed mostly of material excerpted from other sources, including books, newspapers, and other magazines. Digests are part of a long tradition of magazines borrowing content from other sources. The *Literary Digest,* begun in 1890, achieved a circulation of more than 1 million in the 1920s. The king of all digests, however, is *Reader's Digest,* which Dewitt and Lila Wallace began in 1922, publishing it out of their New York City apartment. *Reader's Digest* specializes in brief versions of articles that are informative and well written, and that stress conservative, middle-class values. Other digests emerged, including *Coronet, Pageant, Jet,* and *Children's Digest,* all of which copied *Reader's Digest's* pocket-sized format.

Newsmagazines: Pictures of Current Events

The first newsmagazine was *Time,* founded by Henry Luce in 1923. Soon after graduating from college, Luce and a partner had the notion that readers would respond well to a magazine that presented the news of the world in an easy-to-read, summarized format. They were right, and the magazine they founded went on to define the field of newsmagazines. In fact, the terms *newsmagazine, photojournalism,* and *photo essay* all originated with *Time,* as did new methods of reproducing vivid photographs for print. Other newsmagazines followed, including *United States News* (which would later merge with *World Report*) and *Newsweek,* which were both founded in 1933. Luce went on to found three more of Time-Life's core magazines, all outstanding successes: *Life,* which was one of the great general interest magazines, and two special interest magazines, *Fortune* and *Sports Illustrated.* Today, these magazines are cornerstones in the Time Warner conglomerate.

SELF QUIZ What are the three types of mass circulation magazines, and what are the characteristics of each?

The Golden Age of Photojournalism

Photojournalism had been around since the days of the Civil War, but early cameras required their subjects to be still for a long period, so most of the photojournalism of that day is either stiffly posed portraits of army personnel or pictures of battlefield casualties. Matthew Brady's work of that era is famous largely because his photos of the dead were so poignant.

The true golden age of photojournalism began in the 1930s with the introduction of the 35 mm Leica camera, which made it possible for photographers to move with the action, taking shots of events as they were unfolding. The newsmagazines and magazines such as *Life* and *Sports Illustrated* quickly took advantage of this portability and began to develop reputations for great action shots. Magazine photographers such as Robert Capa, Alfred Eisenstaedt, Margaret Bourke-White, and W. Eugene Smith be-

The photojournalism of Margaret Bourke-White is classic and timeless. On April 28, 1945, she captured this image of half-starved, emaciated male prisoners during the liberation of Buchenwald concentration camp by American forces.

came household names. The glossy paper and high-quality ink and engraving in magazines were perfect for photojournalism. *Life* often published a UPI or an AP photo that had been widely reproduced in newspapers; the quality magazine version, however, appeared to be a different photo altogether. The golden age of photojournalism lasted until the decline of the great general interest magazines.

THE DECLINE OF GENERAL INTEREST MAGAZINES

Magazines were America's only national medium from the 1890s until the 1920s, when the radio networks were established. Radio didn't hurt the growth of the magazine industry because advertisers still wanted to present the colorful, visual ads that magazines could provide. The age of the mass circulation magazines actually peaked in the postwar boom of the 1950s, but by the 1960s advertisers who were interested in reaching the wide and diverse audience that general interest magazines like *Life, Look,* and the *Saturday Evening Post* offered were moving to television instead.

Why did several mass circulation magazines die out in the 1970s?

As advertisers withdrew their support, mass circulation magazines learned that they could be killed by their own success. Since the cover price was less than the cost of production and distribution, without strong advertiser support the magazines were losing money with every copy. They therefore purposely trimmed their subscriber lists—by charging more and by stopping promotions—but they continued to lose money. The *Saturday Evening Post* finally died in 1969; *Look* followed in 1971, *Life* in 1972, and *Coronet* shortly after. *Life* and the *Saturday Evening Post* eventually came back as specialized "nostalgia" magazines with smaller subscription lists and a new target audience: older people who yearned for the times when these magazines ruled the newsstand.[9] The layout and typography of the new versions remain the same as they were in the 1940s; even the *Post's* covers are reminiscent of those produced by Norman Rockwell in the magazine's heyday. Stories tend to focus on older people and olden times.

THE RISE OF SPECIAL INTEREST MAGAZINES

In the latter part of the 20th century, both advertisers and readers began to turn to **special interest magazines.** These magazines offered their readers information they could not find anywhere else, but there were many other reasons for their success. Society had changed. The United States had begun to emphasize its cultural diversity, and people who identified with their racial and ethnic background wanted to read about issues affecting their particular group. The economy had changed also, with the postindustrial information age requiring specialization and special knowledge in work, which caused business magazines to flourish. Because the U.S. economy tended to be a successful one, good times and bad times notwithstanding, Americans had the money to develop diverse recreational interests, along with the necessary leisure time. Because of the First Amendment, Americans also had the freedom to develop a variety of interests that might not even be allowed in other cultures. Through its commitment to broad liberal arts education, the United States had further encouraged this diversity of interests.

Magazine specialization enables this industry to serve the diverse population of the United States. The hundreds of titles range from *Filipinas,* written for Filipino Americans, to *Latvian Dimensions,* published

special interest magazines
Magazines aimed at specific readers with specific concerns and tastes.

© The New Yorker Collection 1987 Warren Miller from cartoonbank.com. All Rights Reserved.

by the American Latvian Association. Magazines also serve minorities that don't immediately spring to mind, such as left-handed people (who have

Magazine specialization enables this industry to serve the diverse population of the United States.

Lefthander Magazine). Ethnic minorities are supplied with information tailored to their occupational and recreational interests rather than just their gender or ethnic identification. The industry serves many types of women (with offerings like *Working Woman* and *Woman Runner*), instead of just the stereotypical housewife of early women's magazines. African Americans are served by dozens of glossies, from *Black Scholar* to *Black Professional* to *Black College Sports Review*. A wide array of Hispanics are served with titles like *Hispanic Business* and *Hispanic Engineer*. These publications tend to hire women and minorities, who are generally underrepresented in the management staffs of more mainstream publications.

Specialized magazines are breaking up into ever more specific segments. Where there were once merely golf magazines, there are now golf magazines for women and seniors, golf magazines to help you improve your play and tell you where to play, and golf magazines devoted to specific areas of the country.

What were the factors that made magazine specialization successful?

Technology has now advanced to the point that, with computer-programmed presses, it is possible for one company to put out dozens of glossy, full-color magazines, coordinating their distribution for maximum efficiency. These companies find it extremely profitable to produce several highly specific magazines.

ADAPTING TO NEW MEDIA

Magazines have always adapted to new media. When movies became popular, the industry embraced them with magazines about movies and cover stories about movie stars. With the advent of television, magazines not only covered the new medium but also branched out into it. Playboy Enterprises today makes more money from its cable and video divisions than from its magazines, and *Time* magazine works together with CNN, also owned by Time Warner. Magazines have also embraced computers and the Internet, with hundreds of magazines covering these topics. Several computer magazines and professional journals appeared on CD-ROMs almost as soon as the technology became available.

Magazines have further embraced digital technology by going online. The *New England Journal of Medicine,* the first periodical on the Internet, has been available there since 1984. By 1995 dozens of major magazines had some kind of Web presence. Today, they nearly all do. Magazine publishers are venturing onto the Internet because of its economic advantages: no investments in paper, ink, presses, or postage; no worries about printing overruns or underruns; and no demands from distributors.

Interactivity with Readers

The interactivity that is possible with a Web site, in which readers can react to the content of the magazine and tell something about themselves, is appealing to advertisers. So is reaching young upper-income consumers who are hooked up to the Web. So far, Web versions of print magazines have tended to be supplements rather than replacements, but there have been some interesting signs of change. Some businesspeople, for example, have shown that they are willing to pay extra for Web versions of controlled-circulation trade magazines that they receive free in their print versions. The Web versions enable them to get necessary information faster.

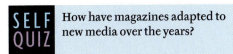
SELF QUIZ How have magazines adapted to new media over the years?

Webzines

The Internet has also spawned a number of Web-only magazines, which are known as **webzines** or e-zines. *Slate* and *Salon* are two of the best-known webzines, although hundreds of special interest webzines exist, such as the *Motley Fool* (for financial advice) and *Hotwired* (for technology).

webzines
Magazines that appear only on the Internet, such as *Slate* and *Salon*; also called e-zines.

GLOBAL ENDEAVORS

The magazine industry is thriving in most industrialized countries. *Ulrich's International Periodicals Directory* lists over 165,000 serials published throughout the world. Many U.S. publishers are moving to international editions to take advantage of new markets for their magazines, especially in former iron curtain countries, such as Poland and the Czech Republic, where the demand for American products is strong, and in Latin American countries that have brought inflation under control.

Most of these international editions are offered in translation, although sometimes only slight changes are necessary. When *Condé Nast Traveler* started its British edition, it changed the spelling to *Traveller*, the way the British prefer. *Good Housekeeping* is known as *Buenhogar* in Latin America. Several versions of *Men's Health* are printed in translation in Latin America, Germany, and South America, as well as alternate English versions in Britain, South Africa, and Australia. There are now 50 versions of *Cosmopolitan*, including editions in Latvia and Kazakhstan. In South America, *Reader's Digest, Fortune, National Geographic,* and *Glamour* are best sellers. The Spanish version of *Reader's Digest* is the best-selling magazine in both Argentina and Chile, where it is called *Selecciones;* the Brazilian edition of the *Digest* (in Portuguese, called *Selecoes*) is the best-selling magazine in Brazil.

The new Chinese edition of *Vogue* is betting that it will be able to define the fashionable Chinese woman's sense of style.

Understanding Today's Magazine *Industry*

The specialization of the magazine industry continues today and is expected to go even further. Because of this, those interested in a career in magazine publishing will find a many-faceted industry with a potential niche for everyone. Those who are more likely to interact with this industry as consumers or critics will do so with greater proficiency if they understand how this industry works. The first step in understanding magazine publishing is to familiarize yourself with two broad areas: the types of magazines and the industry players.

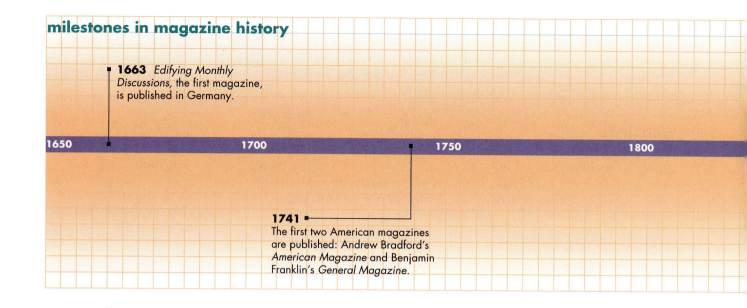

milestones in magazine history

1663 *Edifying Monthly Discussions*, the first magazine, is published in Germany.

1650 1700 1750 1800

1741
The first two American magazines are published: Andrew Bradford's *American Magazine* and Benjamin Franklin's *General Magazine*.

Consumer Magazines

Target members of the buying public

Advertise consumer products

Cover consumer products and the consumer lifestyle

Trade Magazines

Target those in specific businesses and industries

Advertise products and services that those industries need

Public Relations Magazines

Target a corporation or institution's employees, customers, stockholders, and dealers

Enhance the corporation or institution's prestige

Miscellaneous Magazines

Target various types of readers, and include:

Professional and academic journals

Little magazines

Comic books and zines

FIGURE 5.1 Types of Magazines The magazine industry classifies its publications according to these four broad categories.

TYPES OF MAGAZINES

A quick look at the types of magazines that are published gives you a feel for the scope of this industry (see Figure 5.1). Magazines are generally classified as consumer, trade, or public relations. Of the United States' estimated 22,000 total print periodicals, 4,000 are consumer, 8,000 are trade, and 10,000 are public relations magazines. In spite of these huge numbers, only around 160 of these periodicals could be called majors—that is, magazines with a circulation of over 500,000 and revenues of over $1 million.[10] All the majors are consumer magazines.

Consumer Magazines

consumer magazine
Any magazine that advertises and reports on consumer products and the consumer lifestyle.

According to industry standards, a **consumer magazine** is a periodical released at least three times a year, with a circulation of at least 3,000 general (nonbusiness) readers, and containing at least 16 pages of editorial (as opposed to advertising) content.[11] Some industry professionals point out that consumer magazines are the magazines that advertise and report on consumer products and the consumer lifestyle. *Bacon's Magazine Directory* lists

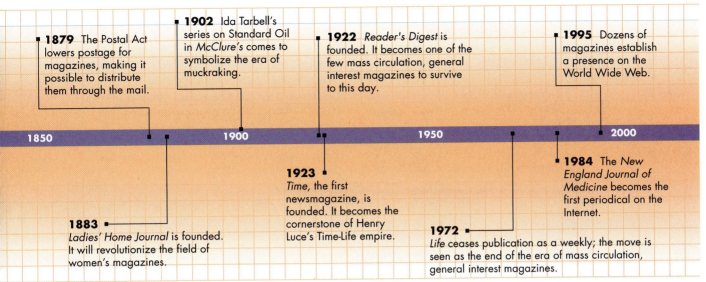

1879 The Postal Act lowers postage for magazines, making it possible to distribute them through the mail.

1902 Ida Tarbell's series on Standard Oil in *McClure's* comes to symbolize the era of muckraking.

1922 *Reader's Digest* is founded. It becomes one of the few mass circulation, general interest magazines to survive to this day.

1995 Dozens of magazines establish a presence on the World Wide Web.

1850   1900   1950   2000

1923 *Time*, the first newsmagazine, is founded. It becomes the cornerstone of Henry Luce's Time-Life empire.

1883 *Ladies' Home Journal* is founded. It will revolutionize the field of women's magazines.

1984 The *New England Journal of Medicine* becomes the first periodical on the Internet.

1972 *Life* ceases publication as a weekly; the move is seen as the end of the era of mass circulation, general interest magazines.

225 different market classifications for consumer magazines, from aerobics to yachting.[12] Fact File 5.1 lists the major types. Fact File 5.2 lists the top 10 magazines by revenue, and Fact File 5.3 lists the top 10 by circulation.

Trade Magazines

Trade magazines are those that focus on a particular business and are usually essential reading for people in those businesses. *Billboard* is the trade magazine for the music industry, while *Variety* and *Backstage* are the trades for performing arts professionals. The more than 500 U.S. farming journals are also considered trade magazines. Like consumer magazines, trade magazines are numerous and very specialized. Hog farmers, for example, can subscribe to *Hogs Today, Hog News, National Hog Farmer, Pig Farming, The Pig Journal, Pig International, Pig-World, Pork Magazine,* and several others.

Some trade magazines tackle the problems in their industries and aren't afraid of offending potential advertisers. Others tend to be boosters rather than critics. Trades that go as far as to allow ad salespeople to provide the content for the stories come very close to being public relations magazines.

Public Relations Magazines

Public relations magazines are put out by organizations, corporations, and institutions with the sole intent of making their parent organizations look good. They are often nicely bound, glossy, high-quality magazines. Their target audience might be employees, customers, stockholders, dealers, or a combination of all four. *Colors* was a public relations magazine for Benetton clothing. Designed to associate the Italian clothier with a sense of social responsibility, its early editions featured images of poverty and dying AIDS patients.

Public relations magazines are often designed and produced by publishers of consumer magazines while being paid for by the corporate sponsor.

Many colleges publish public relations magazines to stay in touch with their alumni. This is an example from Illinois State University.

trade magazines
Magazines that focus on a particular business and are usually essential reading for people in that business.

public relations magazines
Magazines produced with the objective of making their parent organizations look good.

FACT FILE 5.1

Major Types of Consumer Magazines

Magazine Type	Selected Examples
Women's	*Better Homes & Gardens, Family Circle, Good Housekeeping, Ladies' Home Journal, McCall's, Redbook, Woman's Day, Vogue, Glamour, Cosmopolitan, Harper's Bazaar, Elle, Savvy, Self, Working Woman, Brides, Essence, Latina*
Sports and Outdoors	*Sports Illustrated, ESPN the Magazine, Sport Magazine, Sporting News, Balls and Strikes, Volleyball, American Angler, Wildfowl, Field & Stream*
Hobbies	*Road & Track, Car and Driver, Hot Rod, Popular Photography, American Photo, Quilting, Model Railroading*
Entertainment	*TV Guide, People, Entertainment Weekly, Rolling Stone, Spin, Vibe, Interview, US*
Home	*Architectural Digest, Country Living, House Beautiful*
Men's	*Playboy, Penthouse, GQ, Esquire, Details, Men's Journal, Maxim, Stuff, FHM, Men's Health, Popular Mechanics, Family Handyman*
Youth	*Highlights for Children, Humpty Dumpty's Magazine, Jack and Jill, American Girl, Boys' Life, Seventeen, Teen, Teen Beat, YM* (See Close-Up on Industry, page 156.)
Political	*American Spectator, Commentary, Foreign Affairs, Mother Jones, National Review, The Nation, New Republic, The Progressive, Boycott Quarterly, The Militant, Off Our Backs*
Ethnic	*Ebony, Essence, Jet, Emerge, Image, Latina, Hispanic Magazine, Hispanic Times, Native Peoples*
Regional	*Arizona Highways, Midwest Life, New York, Los Angeles*

Name the three main types of magazines today, and give characteristics of each.

SELF QUIZ

That way, the corporate sponsor is able to put out a magazine that looks, feels, and reads like a typical magazine rather than a catalog of praise for the corporation's products. The custom publishing unit of the Meredith Corporation, the publishers of *Better Homes & Gardens* and *Ladies' Home Journal,* creates three magazines for the Dodge, Jeep, and Chrysler brands of DaimlerChrysler. Six million copies of the magazines are delivered to the owners of these automobiles, filled with lifestyle features on topics ranging from architecture schools to rock music.

Other Types: Journals, Comic Books, and Zines

Various other types of magazines include professional and academic journals, comic books, and zines.

Journals

professional journals
Periodicals that doctors, lawyers, engineers, and other occupational groups rely on for information in their fields.

Professional journals are periodicals that doctors, lawyers, engineers, and other professionals rely on for the latest research and information in their fields. Professional journals are sometimes confused with trade magazines, but the differences are considerable. Trade magazines support themselves through advertising, while professional journals often do not accept ads because they don't want to compromise their credibility in the eyes of their

There are around 4,000 U.S. consumer magazines. Some megastores seem to carry them all. The DVD that accompanies this book (track 35, *Celebrity Magazine Wars*) looks at those that feature gossip about well-known people.

readers. Trade magazines are often sent free to eligible subscribers, but professional journals are usually expensive. For example, journals for medical professionals and researchers include *Brain Research* (annual subscription $14,919) and *Mutation Research* ($7,378 a year). These journals are becoming increasingly difficult for students to find because many libraries are cutting back on them to save money to reinvest in online databases instead. Libraries are also cutting back on **academic journals,** also called scholarly journals, which publish research in a variety of academic fields.

A close cousin to the scholarly journal is the small literary magazine, which is known as the **little magazine.**[13] These magazines publish promising and established poets and authors of literary essays and fiction. Most of them have tiny circulations. Some of the best known are the *Antioch Review,* the *Kenyon Review,* and the *Paris Review*.

Comic Books

Comic books, such as the superhero monthlies published by Marvel and D.C. Comics, have a smaller revenue stream than the rest of the magazine industry because they don't contain much advertising. But comics have long been an important part of American culture. They began during the Great Depression as an inexpensive way for Americans, especially American children, to escape from their economic woes. They became extremely popular in the 1930s and 1940s—*Superman* was a sensation when it came out in 1938. At Army bases during World War II, comic books outsold all other magazines 10 to 1. Parents and educational groups worried that comics were polluting the minds of America's young people (see the Close-Up on History box in Chapter 2, page 44). These groups were somewhat mollified when Classics Illustrated began publishing in 1947, bringing historical and literary classics to young people who might never have been exposed to them otherwise.

Zines

Zines, often called fanzines, are small, inexpensive publications put out by people who are enthusiastic about a topic, usually an obscure one. Zines typically have print runs of 200 or less and production costs of around $500. They are devoted to a wide variety of topics, including science fiction, music, celebrities, and radical political movements. Very few of them make any money. Zines were important parts of the beat movement of the 1950s and the hippie subculture of the 1960s. They are primarily a form of uncensored

academic journals
Periodicals that publish research in a variety of scholarly fields; also called scholarly journals.

little magazines
Industry term for literary magazines with small circulations.

zines
Low-cost self-published magazines put out by fans on a variety of topics; also called fanzines.

The Changing Face of Teen Magazines

For decades, three magazines led the field of magazines for teenage girls: *Seventeen, Teen,* and *YM.* These magazines are far from young themselves. *Teen* was founded in 1967; *Seventeen* began in 1946; and *YM,* which originally meant *Young Miss* and was later changed to *Young and Modern* but now means *Your Magazine,* was founded in 1932. And these industry leaders were far from alone. A complete list of their competitors would number more than 100, including magazines such as *Tiger Beat* and *Teen Style.*

> **"We have to give girls tools that they have not needed in past generations. The intricacies of being a teenager have definitely changed."**

With such a crowded field and well-entrenched industry leaders, it would seem almost foolish to attempt to break into this market. But in recent years several brand-name magazines have rolled out teenage versions, including *CosmoGirl* and *Teen Vogue. Teen People* and *Elle Girl* moved to web-only versions in 2006.

The reason for the growing list of competitors is simple: Teenagers are important to advertisers. Most of their income is disposable, since Mom and Dad pay the rent and the grocery bill. Teenagers' spending grew by 41 percent from 1997 to 2001, with the average 16-year-old now spending more than $100 a week.[1] They have more time to read magazines than grownups do, they are very brand conscious, and they are influenced by the kind of advertising magazines provide. And today's teen population, which marketers have labeled Generation Y, is growing. These babies of the baby boomers are considered prized lifetime acquisitions for advertisers. In short, advertisers feel that they can win long-term brandname recognition and support if they can catch this market segment early.

The new teen magazines are subtly different from their older counterparts, however, because their audience is changing in personality as well as in number. Covers still feature teenage idols and articles about complexion problems and hairstyles, but now these staples are joined by articles about sexual harassment at school, eating disorders, racism, and depression—along with dozens of other topics that were once reserved for adults.

One industry expert points out that teens have more options and are more confused about their identities than they were 20 years ago: "Teenage girls today have to sort through so many messages. They don't know if they're supposed to grow up to be corporate working women and conquer the world, or stay-at-home moms, or Miss America or Hillary Clinton. The typical teenage girl isn't quite sure whether to worry about her pimple or whether to go out and win a Pulitzer. That's in part why you can have so many magazines."[2] Atoosa Rubenstein, the 25-year-old editor of *CosmoGirl,* sums up the trend by saying, "We have to give girls tools that they have not needed in past generations. The intricacies of being a teenager have definitely changed."[3]

Today's teens are considered prized lifetime acquisitions by magazine publishers and their advertisers.

[1] Teenage Research Unlimited, a market research firm based in Northbrook, Illinois, quoted in David Carr, "Coming Late, Fashionably, *Teen Vogue* Joins a Crowd," *New York Times* online, January 13, 2003.

[2] Jane Rinzler Buckingham, the president of Youth Intelligence, a market research firm that studies the buying habits of teenagers, quoted in Alex Kuczynski, "In Age of Diminishing Innocence, Magazines for Teenagers Shift Focus," *New York Times* online, April 2, 2001.

[3] Kuczynski, "In Age of Diminishing Innocence."

FACT FILE 5.2

Top Magazines by Revenue

Total revenue includes advertising, subscriptions, and newsstand sales.

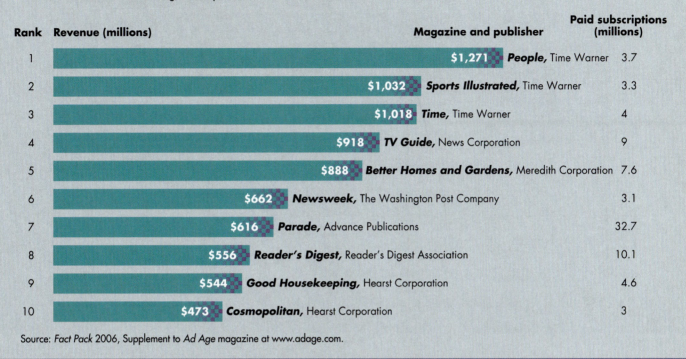

Rank	Revenue (millions)	Magazine and publisher	Paid subscriptions (millions)
1	$1,271	**People,** Time Warner	3.7
2	$1,032	**Sports Illustrated,** Time Warner	3.3
3	$1,018	**Time,** Time Warner	4
4	$918	**TV Guide,** News Corporation	9
5	$888	**Better Homes and Gardens,** Meredith Corporation	7.6
6	$662	**Newsweek,** The Washington Post Company	3.1
7	$616	**Parade,** Advance Publications	32.7
8	$556	**Reader's Digest,** Reader's Digest Association	10.1
9	$544	**Good Housekeeping,** Hearst Corporation	4.6
10	$473	**Cosmopolitan,** Hearst Corporation	3

Source: *Fact Pack* 2006, Supplement to *Ad Age* magazine at www.adage.com.

expression for their editors and contributors, who are often a quirky and independent bunch. Today's zines continue to be self-published outlets for counterculture voices, but they are now produced with **desktop publishing,** which enables one person to act as editor, publisher, and writer through the use of a personal computer. Hundreds of zines have been devoted to little-known musical groups. One, called *Yoko Only,* is devoted to Yoko Ono, the wife of the late Beatle John Lennon.

Many zines exist only on the Web today. In fact, weblogs, the online diaries that we will discuss in Chapter 10, are an online version of what zines used to be.

desktop publishing
Using a personal computer to act as editor, publisher, and writer.

THE PLAYERS

There are many players in the magazine business. We will look at three broad categories here: magazine publishers, the staffs they employ, and the readers they seek to attract.

The Publisher

As in the newspaper industry, when we talk about the publisher in the magazine industry, we could be talking about a person or a company. The magazine publisher-as-person is often most important, because she or he gives the magazine its character and individuality, much as Christy Haubegger gave *Latina* its personality, as discussed at the beginning of this chapter.

Entrepreneurs: Individual Risk Takers

Many magazine publishers are entrepreneurs with a deep interest in a particular topic, a small amount of money (often borrowed from friends), and a

FACT FILE 5.3

Top Magazines by Circulation

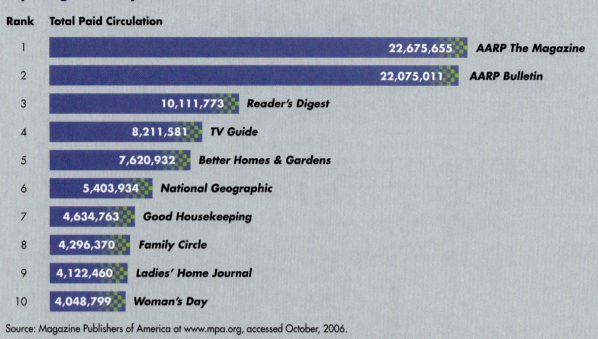

Rank	Total Paid Circulation	
1	22,675,655	AARP The Magazine
2	22,075,011	AARP Bulletin
3	10,111,773	Reader's Digest
4	8,211,581	TV Guide
5	7,620,932	Better Homes & Gardens
6	5,403,934	National Geographic
7	4,634,763	Good Housekeeping
8	4,296,370	Family Circle
9	4,122,460	Ladies' Home Journal
10	4,048,799	Woman's Day

Source: Magazine Publishers of America at www.mpa.org, accessed October, 2006.

high tolerance for risk. Between 500 and 1,000 new magazines are launched each year, but fewer than 20 percent survive into a second year. Jan Wenner started the music magazine *Rolling Stone* with a few thousand dollars borrowed from friends. For several years he had to make enough money with each issue to pay for the next issue, or he would have gone out of business.

A magazine's mission statement is a guiding force in its growth and development.

mission statement
A brief explanation of how the magazine will be unique and what will make it successful.

sponsored magazines
Magazines published by associations, such as *National Geographic*.

The publisher is often the magazine's founder. The founder's first task is to decide on a focus and a target audience for the publication. Both of these should be expressible in a **mission statement,** which is a brief accounting of how the magazine will be unique and what will make it successful. The mission statement can be shown to investors, editorial staff members, and potential advertisers

Here is Hugh Hefner's mission statement for *Playboy:*

Playboy is an entertainment magazine for the indoor man—a choice collection of stories, articles, pictures, cartoons, and humor selected from many sources, past and present, to form a pleasure-primer for the sophisticated, city-bred male. We hope it will be welcomed by that select group of urbane fellows who are less concerned with hunting, fishing and climbing mountains than good food, drink, proper dress, and the pleasure of female company.[14]

The editor in chief of *Essence* stated her magazine's mission statement like this:

CONSIDER THIS

Compose a mission statement for your favorite magazine. Whom does it seek to serve, and in what way does it attempt to be unique?

Essence looks at the world from black women's perspectives, and celebrates their beauty and intelligence. We proclaim a new pride and unity of purpose in black women and help define who we are and how we should be represented. We help black women push back any boundaries—real or perceived—that limit our lives. *Essence* calls sisters to honor our history and culture and to reject the distorted and disrespectful ways in which America has misinterpreted us.[15]

The magazine's mission statement becomes a guiding force in its growth and development. Often, the publisher will have a copy hanging on the wall of the editorial offices, in case any staff members forget it.

Celebrity Publishers

A recent trend in publishing has been for celebrities to found magazines, usually with the backing of a well-established magazine corporation. The publications are called eponymous celebrity magazines because they are named after the celebrity. That name, and often a cover picture of the celebrity, helps the magazine stand out on the magazine rack in our celebrity-obsessed culture. *Martha Stewart Living* was one of the first in this category, and *O, The Oprah Magazine* has been one of the most successful. The Mexican pop singer Thalía announced the founding of her magazine, *Thalía,* in 2004.

In 2002 the magazine *Rosie* folded after the celebrity founder Rosie O'Donnell argued with her corporate parent about the publication's mission. *Martha Stewart Living* considered changing its title when Stewart encountered legal troubles in 2004. Both incidents point to the fact that magazines founded by celebrities can be problematical. Celebrity can be fleeting, and celebrities themselves can be fickle. As one magazine expert pointed out, "It's a dangerous gamble naming a magazine for just one person. But no one is thinking about these publications as institutional magazines. Everyone wants to make a quick buck and get out. We're going to see a lot of publications heading in that direction."[16]

Essence looks at the world from a black woman's perspective.

Corporate Publishers

Some founders are now forgotten men and women in a corporate structure. Several successful women's magazines, for example, were started by supermarket chains. *Family Circle* was founded in 1932 by Piggly Wiggly markets and was given away to shoppers until 1946. The grocery chain A&P started *Woman's Day* in 1937. Although there were some articles, these magazines were at first mostly ads. Other magazines are ventures put together by huge publishing conglomerates. Holding different types of magazines gives the conglomerates economies of scale at the same time that it spreads their risks over several products. Fact File 5.4 lists the largest magazine conglomerates.

Sponsored Magazines

Some magazines are published by associations and are therefore known as **sponsored magazines.** *National Geographic* is a sponsored magazine. The National Geographic Society was formed in 1888 to finance and promote explorations and adventures, but most people join the society to get the magazine. This is also true for *Smithsonian,* published by the Smithsonian Institution. The opposite is the case for *AARP The Magazine,* however, which is sponsored by AARP, formerly known as the American Association of Retired Persons. Most people join the AARP for its benefits,

Latin singer Thalía at an in-store appearance to sign copies of her new magazine. American Media publishes the magazine, and Thalía (Thalía Sodi) is editorial director and has full approval over content.

FACT FILE 5.4

Top Magazine Corporate Publishers

Rank	Magazine Revenue (billions)	Publisher (headquarters)	Well-Known Titles
1	**Time Warner** (New York) • www.timewarner.com — $4.85		140 titles, including *Time, Life, Sports Illustrated, People, Fortune, Money, Entertainment Weekly, DC Comics, Mad Magazine, Parenting*
2	**Advance Publications/Conde Nast** (Newark, NJ) • www.condenet.com — $2.42		22 titles, including *Allure, Architectural Digest, Bon Appétit, Bride's, Details, Glamour, GQ, Mademoiselle, The New Yorker, Vanity Fair, Vogue, Wired, Parade*
3	**Hearst** (New York) • www.hearstcorp.com — $1.84		17 U.S. titles (115 international), including *Cosmopolitan, Good Housekeeping, House Beautiful, Esquire, Harper's Bazaar, Popular Mechanics, Redbook, O, the Oprah Magazine, Seventeen*
4	**Meredith Corporation** (Des Moines, IA) • www.meredith.com — $1.53		17 titles, including *Better Homes and Gardens, Country Gardens, Ladies' Home Journal, Traditional Home*
5	**Primedia** (New York) • www.primediainc.com — $1.21		250 titles, including *American Baby, New York, Soap Opera Digest, Teen Beat, Tiger Beat, Popular Hot Rodding, Hot Bike, Volleyball, Classic Trucks, Fly Fisherman, Crafts Magazine, American History, Cats*
6	**Reader's Digest Association** (Pleasantville, NY) • www.rd.com — $.917		*Reader's Digest* (19 languages), *Walking, The Family Handyman, American Woodworker*
7	**International Data Group** (Boston, MA) • — $.755		15 titles, including *Computerworld, GamePro, InfoWorld, MacWorld, PC World*
8	**McGraw-Hill Companies** (New York) • www.mcgraw-hill.com — $.687		*BusinessWeek*, several business, energy, construction, aerospace, and defense trade magazines
9	**Reed Elsevier** (New York) • www.reed-elsevier.com — $.594		*Variety, Broadcasting and Cable*, medical, scientific, business, and professional journals
10	**Hachette Filipacchi Media U.S.** (New York) • www.hfmus.com — $.552		17 titles, including *Car and Driver, Elle, Home, Popular Photography, Road and Track, Woman's Day*

Source: *Fact Pack 2006*, Supplement to *Ad Age* magazine, at www.adage.com; accessed October 2006.

Name three types of publishers, and give characteristics of each.

SELF QUIZ

including senior discounts on a wide range of goods and services, and feel that the magazine is just part of the package.

The Staff

Most magazine publishers have three primary staff departments: editorial, advertising, and circulation (see Figure 5.2). Other departments include production, promotion, and new product development.

Editorial Staff

The magazine industry has the same kind of diversity of editors as the newspaper industry does (see Chapter 4), but with some variation in title. The

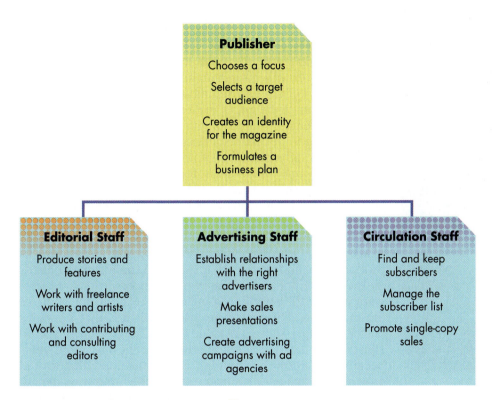

FIGURE 5.2 The Magazine Staff Each department in a magazine company contributes in its own way to the success of that magazine.

person in charge overall is called the editor, the editor in chief, or the executive editor. The editor is in charge of the overall direction of the magazine and usually gives final approval of each issue before it goes to press. There is usually a managing editor, and there might be several deputy editors, senior editors, or associate editors, all of whom provide an extra organizational level between the editor and the day-to-day operations and interactions with the staff. These editors work on three issues of the magazine at once: the one that's about to go on sale, the one in preparation, and the one in its planning stage.

Unlike their counterparts in the newspaper industry, magazine editors work mostly with freelance writers. At the *Atlantic Monthly* the masthead lists dozens of editors and staff members but only one staff writer. Only the largest magazines have full-time writers, and only the newsmagazines have primarily full-time writers. The title of **contributing editor,** sometimes referred to as a consulting editor, is generally given to the magazine's highest-paid freelance writers. Contributing editors might get to edit other people's pieces or supply general advice to the editors, but mostly they are writers who are known well enough that they lend some prestige to the magazine's masthead. At *Harper's,* Tom Wolfe is listed as one of the contributing editors; Ann Beattie is one of the contributing editors at *The American Scholar.* Both are well known and highly respected authors.

contributing editor
Title given to a magazine's highest-paid freelance writers, who sometimes polish others' work.

Advertising Staff

Most magazines will live or die by their advertising sales staffs. Magazine publishing is an extremely competitive business, and usually advertisers will not come looking for salespeople. Relationships must be established, presentations must be made, and proof of potential effectiveness must be established.

revolve
THE COMPLETE NEW TESTAMENT

"Are You Dating a Godly Guy?" and other Quizzes

BEAUTY SECRETS You've Never Heard Before!

RADICAL FAITH WHAT SCRIPTURE REALLY MEANS

200+ BLAB Q & A'S

HOW TO Get Along With Your Mom AND OTHER RELATIONSHIP NOTES

100+ WAYS TO APPLY YOUR FAITH

GUYS SPEAK OUT ON TONS OF IMPORTANT ISSUES

The magazine style of layout and images has affected the design of other print media, including religious books. This is a New Testament Bible designed for teen girls who find the traditional Bible intimidating.

circulation department
The division of a magazine company charged with finding and keeping subscribers, managing the subscriber list, and promoting single-copy sales.

blow-in cards
Postcard-sized business reply cards, usually containing subscription solicitations, that are inserted into magazines during the production process.

subscription fulfillment companies
Businesses that specialize in soliciting magazine subscriptions.

Part of that proof is in the cost per one thousand people reached (CPM—again, the *M* stands for *mille,* or thousand), which is verified by the Audit Bureau of Circulations. CPM alone, however, will not sell an advertising account. Members of the sales staff have to sell the personality of the magazine and the worth of the target reader, but first they have to find the right advertiser. The sales staff at *Vegetarian Times,* for example, will go after manufacturers of tofu and homeopathic tea remedies, advertisers who are not likely to buy space in *Cigar Aficionado.* Advertisers for *Divorce* include lawyers, therapists, hair and makeover stylists, moving companies, and even forensic accountants, whose specialty is uncovering a spouse's hidden assets or unexplained hotel expenses.

Advertisers and magazines need each other in a variety of ways. The advertiser needs the magazine to enhance its product sales and its overall image, and the magazine needs the advertiser for content as well as income. Most readers want ads for the specific products that relate to the topic of the magazine. The magazine also needs ads that go along with the image of the magazine. When Hugh Hefner started *Playboy,* he didn't solicit advertising for the first three years because he knew he couldn't attract the kind that would enhance the image of his magazine. In the same way, the advertising staffs of most magazines have to try to solicit advertisers whose products and ads blend with the image and personality of their magazine. This is particularly true in fashion magazines, in which the advertising makes up the bulk of the content.

One final consideration for the advertising staff is that, no matter what else happens, a certain number of ad pages have to appear in each issue. Magazines boast of ad page volume in an effort to lure more advertising. A full complement of ad pages enhances the magazine's image in this respect. To fill the advertising pages, sometimes ad staff members must make special considerations, such as discounts.

The power that advertisers wield over magazines leads to potential ethical problems, which we will discuss in the final section of this chapter.

Circulation Staff

The **circulation department** has three primary functions: to find and keep subscribers, to manage the subscriber list, and to promote single-copy sales. Finding subscribers is done mostly by sophisticated direct mail operations, many of which offer free trial issues that the customer may receive before any bills are paid. Publishers also use **blow-in cards,** the familiar postcard-sized business reply cards that are inserted into the magazine during the production process. Most publishers also rely on **subscription fulfillment companies,** which are agencies that specialize in soliciting magazine subscriptions, such as Publishers Clearing House and American Family Publishers. Publishers receive little or no portion of the subscription fees collected by these agencies. They are willing to do this because their own methods of producing subscribers are quite expensive. Through the agencies they receive a free subscriber, one whom they can sell to advertisers and whom they might be able to renew on their own terms. The circulation department also maintains lists of subscribers and sells them to direct mail marketers.

FACT FILE 5.5

Where Magazines Are Sold

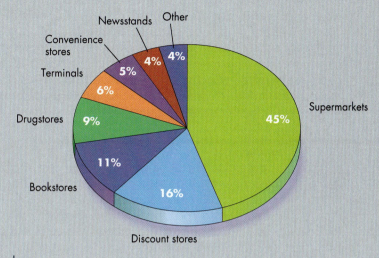

Source: Center for Media Research.

Sales of mailing lists are an important revenue source for magazines, and have been blamed for an increase in junk mail going out to consumers.

The magazine's management of its subscriber list can become quite complex, with new subscribers starting and old ones expiring or canceling every day. On top of that, many magazine publishers now put out demographic and regional editions, known as **split-run editions. Demographic editions** of the same magazines go out to different zip codes and to subscribers with different occupations. Copies that go to zip codes that are considered wealthy will contain ads for luxury items, subscribers who are identified as doctors will receive ads for the latest prescription drugs, and so on. **Regional editions** allow local advertisers to run ads in prestigious national magazines. *Time* and *Newsweek* each run more than a hundred split-run editions weekly.

The circulation department promotes single-copy sales by tracking the returns from newsstands, supermarkets, and bookstores to provide the optimum number to each point of purchase (see Fact File 5.5). This has become important in recent years, because only around 35 percent of single copies are sold; the rest are returned to distributors. Magazines such as *Woman's Day, Star,* and the *National Enquirer* survive primarily on these point-of-purchase sales. Some magazines produce different covers for newsstand and subscriber sales. For example, *Money* magazine might have one cover for its subscribers, who are assumed to be investors, with a cover feature such as "Your Six Best Investments Now." For newsstand buyers, who might be less wealthy and looking for a way to make extra money, the magazine might feature "How You Can Make $100,000 at Home" on the cover.

Of course, single-copy sales are mostly of interest to **paid circulation magazines,** those for which readers actually shell out subscription fees and newsstand charges. There is another type of circulation, called **controlled circulation,** in which the magazine is sent free to readers who qualify. *American Baby,* for example, has a controlled circulation of more than 1 million new mothers; their names are purchased from a company that specializes in collecting information about new births from municipal records.

split-run editions
Slightly different versions of the same magazine, as in demographic and regional editions.

demographic editions
Slightly different versions of the same magazine that go out to subscribers with different characteristics.

regional editions
Slightly different versions of the same magazine produced for different geographic areas.

paid circulation magazines
Magazines for which readers actually pay subscription fees and newsstand charges.

controlled circulation
A system of distribution in which magazines are sent free to desired readers.

Distributing the magazine free is economical for these publishers because the cost of identifying subscribers and then convincing them to pay for a subscription far exceeds the cost of simply compiling a subscriber list and sending the magazine out. Advertisers like the system because they can reach an entire target audience. Postal regulations, however, require that the publication be directly requested by at least 50 percent of the recipients to be eligible for lower, second-class postage rates. A high request rate is also used as proof of effectiveness for advertising sales, so publishers of controlled circulation magazines will send out renewal cards asking subscribers to check a box specifically requesting the magazine.

SELF QUIZ

What are the three main departments in a typical magazine company, and what are the responsibilities of each?

Production

The production department coordinates the actual printing of the magazines with outside companies, including those that specialize in high-speed color printing and the use of glossy paper. This department also coordinates the delivery of the content to the printing plants, which is sometimes complicated by editorial decisions. For example, the editors might decide to change articles at the last minute to take advantage of breaking news.

Promotion

Most magazines have a separate publicity department, and many of them hire outside publicists to get the name of the magazine into the news. The publicist's job is to make headlines in newspapers, radio and television programs, and Internet news services with the headlines from the cover of the magazine's current issue. This news coverage will in turn enliven newsstand sales, attract new subscribers, and catch the attention of advertisers.

Publicists perform their service not just by sending out news releases but also by planning parties, devising publicity stunts, planting items in gossip columns, and positioning the magazine as a newsmaker and expert so that its staff will be interviewed on air. The news releases are still important, of course. Sometimes these will announce a genuine breakthrough, such as when an article in the *Journal of the American Medical Association* established that eating fish could lower the risk of sudden cardiac death by 50 percent. Other press releases will announce that celebrities have said something newsworthy in that month's issue, or the magazine has run a survey about some interesting aspect of public behavior (the percentage of husbands who admit to having had affairs, for example). Other publicity-generating features might include a ratings list such as *Blender*'s list of the "50 Worst Songs Ever," which received massive publicity in 2004.[17] Awards of almost any type, such as *GQ*'s Men of the Year Awards or the Essence Awards, are also effective at generating publicity. Parties are often planned around special events, such as a magazine's anniversary celebration.

Sometimes, rather than sending a formal news release, the publicist will plant the news in a gossip column by giving it to the columnist as an exclusive story. One publicist pointed out how effective an item in a gossip column can be: "A magazine with one million circulation can sell 30,000 to 40,000 copies off a good item: 'Madonna reveals in *Harper's Bazaar*,' 'Sharon Stone admits in *Vogue*.'"[18] Publicists will also pitch future stories to TV programs, approaching a station months in advance with story ideas that

SELF QUIZ

What are some of the techniques that are used to promote magazine sales?

are still in the planning stages. This practice, in fact, has led to joint magazine/TV ventures such as *Good Housekeeping*'s arrangement to have its articles featured on *Primetime Live* on ABC and *People*'s similar deal with *Dateline* on NBC. Publicists also spend a great

FACT FILE 5.6

Top Magazine Covers

Some magazine covers have been honored as works of art, and some have been controversial. Often, these have been the same covers. Chain stores and supermarkets have stopped selling some magazines because of racy covers (see Close-Up on Controversy, page 169), and others have placed the magazines in bags that obscured the covers. But covers have also been an important key to magazine sales. In 2006 *People* magazine reportedly paid more than $3 million for its exclusive photo of Angelina Jolie and Brad Pitt's newborn baby. The photo paid for itself, however, in increased newsstand sales and extra advertising.[1] In 2005 the American Magazine Conference picked the 40 greatest magazine covers of the last 40 years. Here are the top 10 from that list:

1. *Rolling Stone,* January 22, 1981. The cover photo shows a nude John Lennon curled into a fetal position atop a fully clothed Yoko Ono. The shot was taken just hours before Lennon was shot and killed.

2. *Vanity Fair,* August 1991. The cover photo features a naked and very pregnant Demi Moore.

3. *Esquire,* April 1968. The photograph of Muhammad Ali with six arrows in his body was styled after the famous painting of St. Sebastian, a patron saint of athletes. The cover appeared after Ali was stripped of his title for refusing to be inducted into the U.S. Army because of his religious beliefs.

4. *The New Yorker,* March 29, 1976. Saul Steinberg's "View of the World from 9th Avenue" came to represent the typical New Yorker's perception of the country beyond the Hudson River.

5. *Esquire,* May 1969. This spoof of pop art showed Andy Warhol drowning in an opened can of Campbell's tomato soup.

6. *The New Yorker,* September 24, 2001. The cover featured a ghostlike black-on-black depiction of the twin towers of the World Trade Center.

7. *National Lampoon,* January 1973. This was the infamous "If You Don't Buy This Magazine, We'll Kill This Dog" cover, an early satire of good taste and political correctness.

8. *Esquire,* October 1966. An all-black cover with just the headline in white letters—"Oh my God—we hit a little girl"—referred to a cover story that helped changed the American public's perception of the war in Vietnam.

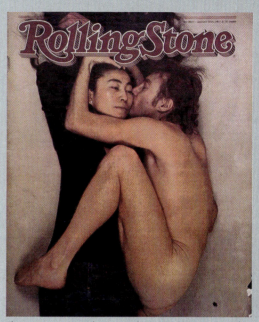

This cover was number 1 on the American Society of Magazine Editors' list of top magazine covers.

9. *Harper's Bazaar,* September 1992. Supermodel Linda Evangelista represented the "era of elegance" on this 125th anniversary issue. *Harper's Bazaar* was America's first fashion magazine when it debuted in 1867.

10. *National Geographic,* June 1985. The striking cover image featured the haunted eyes of a 12-year-old Afghan girl, a refugee from her war-torn homeland.

You can view all the high-resolution images of the winning covers at www.magazine.org/Editorial/Top_40_Covers/.

[1]Maria Aspan, "For Tender Moments, Product Placement," *New York Times,* online, June 19, 2006.

amount of time positioning their magazines as newsmakers so that TV stations will come to them for sound bites, commentary, and interviews.

New Product Development

New product development departments seek to generate innovative alternative sources of revenue. These new products, known as brand extensions in the industry, might be based on a different form of media, such as cable television or video. Some new product departments search for ways to license the magazine's name, either for editions in other countries or for products like *Field & Stream*'s fishing lures collection. *Better Homes & Gardens* has licensed its name to a greeting card line, a real estate service, and garden centers. *Maxim* has licensed its name to a new $1.2 billion hotel and casino in Las Vegas.[19] Magazines also generate income by renting out their subscription lists as mailing lists for companies with complementary products, by selling reprint rights to the articles and illustrations they own, and by developing book projects based on those materials. The *New Yorker,* for example, produces cartoon books, such as *The New Yorker Book of Cat Cartoons* and *The New Yorker Book of Lawyer Cartoons,* as well as a cartoon desk diary. Magazines also provide custom publishing services, such as a magazine or newsletter produced for one advertiser. Trade magazines generate extra income by organizing conferences, seminars, and trade shows for professionals in their field.

The Reader

pass-along circulation
Readership beyond the original purchaser of a publication.

Americans read a lot of magazines. In fact, the magazine industry claims that 90 percent of American adults read 12 issues a month on average,[20] and that the more education and income people have, the more magazines they read. Magazines also have a healthy **pass-along circulation,** which means that several more people than the original buyer or subscriber typically read them. Furthermore, the industry says that heavy magazine readers are light television viewers on average and that magazine readership, unlike newspaper readership, is increasing. Finally, readers tend to be highly involved in their magazines; 95 percent of U.S. adults cite magazines as their primary source of insights and inspirations.[21] This is one reason that even small circulation journals such as *Foreign Affairs* are influential, because political leaders who are influenced by their ideas read them.

The industry might be putting the best possible spin on those numbers. Glancing at the magazines in the doctor's office, for example, is counted as a "read." There can be no doubt, however, that magazine readers affect the content of the magazines they read. Publishers, in conjunction with the Audit Bureau of Circulations, constantly measure how many people read each issue. They also collect feedback on what readers like and dislike, to find clues as to how they can increase their readership and better satisfy their current readers. The larger magazines have their own research departments, but they still rely on objective outside organizations such as Simmons Market Research Bureau and Mediamark Research Inc. to run their major studies.

Controversies

Our examination of magazines makes it clear that this industry became specialized for one reason: That was the best way for publishers to make money. Segmentation increases competition: Thousands of periodicals vie for a limited number of advertising dollars. To become successful, magazines resort to techniques that lead to a number of controversies. They strive to produce striking images on their pages, and critics worry about what kind of impact those images will have on young people. Magazines also try to uncover events and information that will amaze and enlighten, but sensationalism often leads to controversies about truth and accuracy. The competition for advertising dollars also leads to questions of editorial independence, as stories are molded to please advertisers and sources such as celebrities who bring in the large readership that advertisers want. The quest for that large readership has also led to some controversial marketing schemes, such as misleading sweepstakes promotions.

THE IMPACT OF IMAGES

Magazines have been important to U.S. cultural life since the 19th century, when abolitionists used them to argue the case against slavery, feminists used them to argue for woman's suffrage, and muckrakers used them to stir up reform. Even at this early stage it was becoming obvious that people had a special relationship with their magazines. In a way, the magazines partially defined their readers and told them who they were. But something new happened in the 1850s, when magazines began to feature photography. People began to see photographs of celebrities for the first time; they placed these images in their personal photo albums, sometimes on the same pages as photos of family and friends. People began to see themselves differently, to compare themselves with the actresses, socialites, and ballet dancers in the photographs.[22]

The photographic images in the magazines were often on the cutting edge of social acceptability, constantly expanding the boundaries. In 1903, readers were shocked when *National Geographic* ran photographs of bare-breasted African women. Many subscribers protested, but they apparently failed to notice that fashion magazines were expanding boundaries in ways that would have even more impact on the lives of women. These magazines began to encourage women to be as glamorous as possible, especially by using products such as corsets and cosmetics. Subtly, through both ads and articles, they played on women's insecurities about the way they looked.

In fact, the image of the ideal woman changed in these magazines over the years. At first, the women in the photographs had roughly the same body shape and size as the general population. By the 1960s, the average model in a fashion magazine was around 10 percent thinner than the average woman; by the 1990s, models were 30 percent thinner than the average, which placed many of them in the anorexic range.[23] At the same time, the average real woman was becoming heavier, making the gap between magazine ideal and reality continually wider.

The magazine ideal is an illusion, of course (see Figure 5.3). It requires hours of work by highly paid professionals to get models to look as they do. Today, the ideal female beauty as defined by the fashion magazines tends to be a woman with perfect facial features, long legs, a long neck, and terrific body tone; most important, she is 5 feet 10 inches tall and weighs less than 120 pounds. This is a body size that is extremely difficult to find within the general population, where the average woman is around 5 feet 4 inches tall and weighs 144 pounds. The rarity of the body size, in fact, is reflected in the high wages models receive.

As fashion magazines continue to promote this unrealistic body size and shape, survey after survey shows that women are increasingly unhappy with their bodies. When asked what one thing would make them happy, most women answer, "to lose weight," a more frequent response than even romantic or professional success. Even the recent "superwoman" image of a woman who has status, accomplishment, and independence still tends to stress her physical attributes, especially how thin she

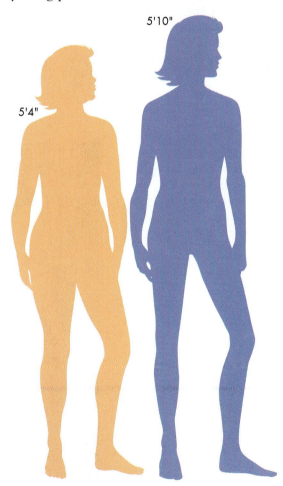

5'10"

5'4"

FIGURE 5.3 Outline of an Average Woman's Body versus Outline of a Model's Body

is. At the same time, there has been an explosion of cosmetic surgery techniques such as liposuction and breast augmentation. As a film documentary

As fashion magazines continue to promote an unrealistic body size and shape, surveys show that women are increasingly unhappy with their bodies.

maker who has studied the problem pointed out: "In an age when women are free for the first time to operate in the world outside the home, to grasp the beginnings of economic and political power, it is a peculiar irony that we have never felt more pressured to define ourselves through the way our bodies look."[24]

Teen magazines have been especially criticized for their obsession with beauty and thinness. Girls read these magazines as early as first grade. Many of these girls diet secretly, without telling their parents, a practice that stunts body growth and, ironically, results in a shorter and heavier adult because it essentially trains the body to store fat.

Women, however, are not the only victims. Often as a ritual part of their growing up, young men read skin magazines that range from the mildly sexually explicit *Playboy* to its raunchier competitors. Many critics insist that men's ideas about women are shaped not just by the images such as *Playboy*'s centerfold but also by the editorial content such as the "Penthouse Forum."[25] According to many observers, skin magazines are a form of sex education that encourages young men to view women as sexual objects only. They have been blamed for contributing to everything from date

Why is the impact of images a major controversy in the magazine industry today?

SELF QUIZ

CONSIDER THIS

Analyze the images in your favorite magazine. Would any of them be of concern to media critics? Have magazine images affected your own life in any way?

Early-20th-century magazine advertising encouraged women to change their natural body shape through corsets that gave them a wasp-waisted form. In later years such corsets became less fashionable, but the models became thinner.

Wal-Mart versus the Lads

When Wal-Mart announced in 2003 that it would stop selling three men's magazines—*Maxim*, *Stuff*, and *FHM*—the industry was understandably concerned. After all, Wal-Mart is the United States' biggest retailer of magazines. As a chain, it sells 15 percent of all the single-copy magazines in America.

These magazines came to be called the lads in England, where they originally appeared. Their publishers imported them to America, where their mix of scantily clad starlets and short pieces of bawdy humor (the kind of humor usually associated with junior high school boys) became a huge success with young American men and the advertisers who sought them. American publishers, who had previously believed that advertisers wouldn't be interested in appearing next to such sophomoric material, seemed to be caught unaware by the success of these magazines.

Still, they weren't happy when Wal-Mart dropped them. It was bad enough that Wal-Mart had occasionally declined to sell particular issues of some magazines, including one edition of *InStyle* featuring an artfully arranged nude photo of the actress Kate Hudson. Wal-Mart also took exception to a single photo in a compilation of *Sports Illustrated* swimsuit issues and decided not to sell that one-time publication.

Publishers, who always walk a fine line of editorial independence from advertisers, didn't want a retailer to dictate editorial policy. The problem was that single-copy sales of national magazines had dropped 40 percent in the last decade, thanks to competition from cable television and the Internet. To fight back, publishers were turning to more adult content—exactly the type of content that Wal-Mart objected to in the lads.

Many critics pointed out that Wal-Mart might be slightly hypocritical in its holier-than-thou attitude toward the men's magazines. As one observer pointed out: "Wal-Mart is neither strait-laced nor consistent. The store carries a full line of condoms, guns, Secret Treasures see-through panties, *Cosmopolitan* magazine, and even an Ozzy Osbourne line of toy cars for kids. There are CD's by the rap artist 50 Cent and computer games like Marine Sharpshooter, with the slogan, 'One Shot, One Kill.' Sometimes you get the impression that Wal-Mart is like a lot of parents these days, who have vague intimations but don't really want to know what their teenagers are listening to, because it would be such a hassle to try to shut it all down."[1]

Other critics pointed out that today's women's magazines tend to be just as sexy as men's magazines. In fact, it is often difficult to tell where the men's section ends and the women's section begins, since they both feature barely clothed models and cover lines about sexual topics. As if in response to these critics, Wal-Mart announced that it would start covering up the cover headlines on *Cosmopolitan*, *Redbook*, *Marie Claire*, and *Glamour*.

[1]David Brooks, "No Sex Magazines, Please, We're Wal-Mart Shoppers," *New York Times* online, May 11, 2003.

The industry worried when Wal-Mart decided to stop selling three racy men's magazines, including *Stuff* and *FHM*.

CONSIDER THIS

Are today's magazine covers too raunchy for supermarket checkout lines and other areas where children have access to them? Support your answer with examples.

rape to everyday difficulties in male–female relationships. See the Close-Up on Controversy box for how one retailer has taken on the men's magazines known as the lads. Magazine industry professionals insist that they are not to blame for these societal trends. In fact, they say, they merely reflect the trends that are already there. The truth is probably a middle ground: Like all media, magazines both reflect and affect society. Professionals also point out that the magazine industry has recognized the problem and is taking steps to correct it. Several magazines, such as *BBW* and *Extra Hip* are directed toward plus-sized women and stress that large women can be healthy and happy. *YM* announced in 2002 that it would use normal-sized models and no longer publish diet tips for girls. *O, The Oprah Magazine* refuses to advertise diet drinks like SlimFast.

TRUTH AND ACCURACY

Credibility is a magazine's primary asset, even in an industry that includes *Star* and the *National Enquirer.* Legally, magazines are expected to be even more diligent about truth and accuracy than newspapers are. Magazines have a longer amount of time to work on stories. Although they have deadline pressures, those deadlines are not as constant as the ones imposed on newspapers, and the law takes this difference into consideration. For example, it is assumed that magazines have more time to check statements for libel. When the actress Carol Burnett brought a libel suit against the *National Enquirer* for saying she had been drunk and disorderly in a restaurant, she won her case—whereas she might not have done so against a newspaper.

Besides the legal considerations, it can be extremely embarrassing for a magazine, especially a newsmagazine, to be caught making a factual mistake. In 1998 *Time,* in a joint investigation with CNN, reported that the U.S. Army had used lethal nerve gas during the Vietnam War on U.S. deserters. The U.S. government quickly refuted the story with *Time*'s own witnesses, pointing out that the magazine had edited testimony to "prove" an untrue allegation. *Time* was forced to issue a quick retraction and an apology.

About the same time that *Time* was wording its apology, the *New Republic* was experiencing some problems of its own. One of its writers had been accused of fabricating facts. The editors investigated and found that the writer, 25-year-old Stephen Glass, had indeed been taking shortcuts by making things up, describing people and even entire organizations that did not exist—such as "Truth in Science, a Christian organization skeptical of global warming," and the "Association for the Advancement of Sound Water Policy." Similar fictions had appeared in some 25 articles that Glass had written over a three-year period.

Critics say these examples prove that the magazine industry is too casual with the truth. The industry responds by saying that it does its best in a world with too much information and too many unreliable sources.

EDITORIAL INDEPENDENCE

Another potential threat to magazines' credibility is any indication of a lack of editorial independence, especially from advertisers.

Independence from Advertisers

Some magazines have a long history of separating advertising and editorial matter. *Ms., Consumer Reports,* and *Consumers Digest* take no ads, and *Reader's Digest* refuses all cigarette ads. Some critics insist that magazines that do take ads have often been all too willing to compromise their magazine's content for ad revenue. They cite cases such as that of the *Saturday Evening Post,* which in its final

Andrea Rosengarten, the managing editor of *Vibe* magazine, discusses the pressures that advertisers put on magazines in the *Media World* DVD that accompanies this book (track 1.5).

days as a mass circulation magazine promised to feature Henry Ford on its cover in exchange for $400,000 worth of Ford advertising.

Advertisers will often press for **complementary copy,** or editorial material designed to enhance nearby advertising, especially in women's magazines. In addition, they expect the magazine to speak well of their products. Some advertisers make it a point to withdraw ads from any issue that contains a potentially negative article. For years, Chrysler required magazines to notify the company in advance of articles that were negative about Chrysler or the automobile industry so that it could withdraw its ads from those issues.[26]

Independence from Subjects and Sources

Editorial independence usually refers to a magazine's independence from its advertisers, but it can also refer to its independence from the people it writes about and the people who supply it with information. Ethical quandaries arise in the way magazines treat celebrities. Most magazines are so desperate for stories and photographs, especially cover photographs, that they allow celebrities to be in charge. For example, Madonna agreed to pose for *Rolling Stone*'s 30th anniversary cover story on women in rock only if she could approve the layout, approve the photographs, and own the copyright to the photographs. This is all perfectly understandable from the star's point of view. After all, stars want control over how their images are presented to the public. But critics insist that this destroys the magazine's credibility in

> **Madonna agreed to pose for *Rolling Stone*'s 30th anniversary cover story on women in rock only if she could approve the layout, approve the photographs, and own the copyright to the photographs.**

terms of how it presents celebrities' ideas, work, and lifestyles. Celebrities are culturally important because people model their behaviors and try to be like them. When a magazine can't step back and say that a celebrity's statements about the meaning of life are actually drivel, real cultural damage could be done.

Many interviewers have allowed celebrities to read a piece about them in advance and correct it. Some critics consider this just as unethical as allowing an advertiser to preapprove articles about its business. Some editors have dealt with the controversy by simply dispensing entirely with reporters in celebrity profiles and simply allowing the stars to interview themselves. At least this way the articles can be presented accurately. Two examples are "Nobody Does it Better: Sharon Stone on Herself" in *Harper's Bazaar* and "The Unbelievable Truth About Mel Gibson. By Mel Gibson" in *US*.

SELF QUIZ
What is meant by editorial independence, and why is it controversial?

MARKETING SCHEMES

Controversy surrounds certain marketing schemes magazines use to sell subscriptions. In the highly competitive marketplace, magazines and their subscription fulfillment companies are constantly looking for innovative ways to sell. For years, schools, scout troops, and charities have been enlisted in magazine drives in which young people compete for "valuable prizes." Some companies use marketing techniques in which customers are told they have won a special prize and will receive free magazines—all they have to pay is a postage and handling fee. The "postage and handling fee," however, happens to be the same price as the magazine subscription.

Sweepstakes

For many years, sweepstakes run by several magazines and by subscription fulfillment companies like Publishers Clearing House and American Family Publishers seemed particularly misleading to many observers. The direct mail solicitations made it look like the potential subscriber has already won. Sometimes the mailings included a "check" for millions of dollars. Elderly people, in particular, were vulnerable, subscribing to dozens of magazines that they neither needed nor could afford on their fixed incomes. Critics said this practice was unethical; magazine subscription companies insisted they were just trying to get the consumer's attention in a world in which there was a glut of messages vying for that attention.

The courts came down on the side of the consumer, however. *Time* magazine was forced to refund nearly $5 million to consumers who were fooled, *Reader's Digest* was forced to return $8 million, and Publishers Clearing House was made to reimburse subscribers $18 million. Along with other companies that had used the sweepstakes technique, these companies had to agree that in all future mailings they would disclose the odds of winning, explain that a purchase would not increase the chance of winning, and make it clear that the customer had not necessarily won any prize.

Summing Up

Magazines were the last of the print media to become popular. In America they began in 1741 and were characterized for the first 50 years or so by a long series of failures. The first big successes were in women's magazines, such as *Godey's Lady's Book* and *Ladies' Home Journal*. These led to the first general interest magazines, such as the *Saturday Evening Post* and *Collier's*. A number of events helped these general interest magazines become mass circulation magazines, including increases in literacy, decreases in postal rates, advances in printing technology, lower cover prices, and muckraking investigations that caught the interest of a wide readership.

The great majority of mass circulation magazines of the 20th century tended to be cultural magazines, such as *Life* and *Look;* newsmagazines, such as *Time* and *Newsweek;* and digests, such as *Reader's Digest.* The era of the circulation giants peaked in the 1950s but died out during the 1970s, mostly because of television's greater appeal to advertisers who were looking for a large general audience. The magazine industry adapted by becoming an industry of mostly special interest magazines. Other important trends include the industry's adaptation to new media, such as the Internet, and investments in global publishing.

Today's magazine publishing industry is built primarily around three types of magazines: consumer magazines, trade magazines, and public relations magazines. Other types of magazines include professional and academic journals, comic books, and zines.

The players in the magazine industry include the publisher, perhaps an entrepreneur or a corporation. The staff of the magazine consists of those in editorial, advertising, and circulation departments. Editorial consists mainly of editors who produce each issue, usually working with freelance writers. Advertising staff find the appropriate advertisers for the magazine, and circulation departments build and maintain subscriber lists and stimulate single-copy sales. Other departments include production, promotion, and new product development.

Controversial issues within this industry include the impact of images, such as those in fashion magazines that stress extreme thinness or those in skin magazines that encourage young men to treat women as sexual objects; truth and accuracy of the facts presented; editorial independence, especially from advertisers; and marketing schemes such as those used by subscription fulfillment companies.

Key Terms

These terms are defined and indexed in the Glossary of key terms at the back of the book.

Electronic Excursions

HISTORY

Web Excursion

1. Magazines were the last of the print media to become popular, but they became the first national medium. Search the Web for the home pages of some of your favorite magazines. Review the content thoroughly. Write a brief essay explaining why, in your view, magazines are more or less effective as a national medium as opposed to television, radio, or the Internet.

INDUSTRY

Web Excursion

2. Today's magazine publishing industry is built primarily around consumer and trade magazines. Search the Web for the top-grossing magazines, or go directly to the Web page of *Ad Age,* www.adage.com,* and identify the top five magazines by circulation. Why do you think these magazines are the most successful? Explain.

Media World DVD Excursion

3. View track 1, *Inside Vibe Magazine*. You will be introduced to the various departments that make a magazine work. The director of photography and design director, together, are responsible for the look of the magazine. How important do you feel design and photography are to the profitability of a magazine? Do you think you would read the magazines you read today if the photos were in black and white and the text always looked the same?

CONTROVERSY

Web Excursion

4. Advertising and marketing are traditionally supposed to be separate from editorial. But in the magazine industry the two sides seem to be merging. Search the Web for the major publishing groups, or go directly to www.condenast.com,

www.hearst.com, or http://www.hfmus.com/HachetteUSA/interfaceframe.html.*
On these sites, do advertising promotions outweigh the editorial content? What
about on the magazine home pages themselves (such as those above)? Explain
your findings.

Media World DVD Excursion

5. View track 1.5, *Issues: Church and State.* This track explores the issue of
church and state, which in publishing means maintaining independent editorial and advertising policies and practices. How realistic is it to maintain a
balance of church and state in today's publishing industry? What is the importance of editorial integrity?

ONLINE LEARNING CENTER WWW.MHHE.COM/RODMAN2

You may access these and additional Web excursions at the Online Learning Center
for the book (www.mhhe.com/rodman2). Visit the student portion of this Web site
to also access the *Interactive Timeline of Mass Media Milestones,* chapter highlights,
self quizzes, and recommended readings, movies, and documentaries for this chapter.

---

*Some Web site addresses may change. When they do, please search for the Web site by name or topic
on your favorite search engine.

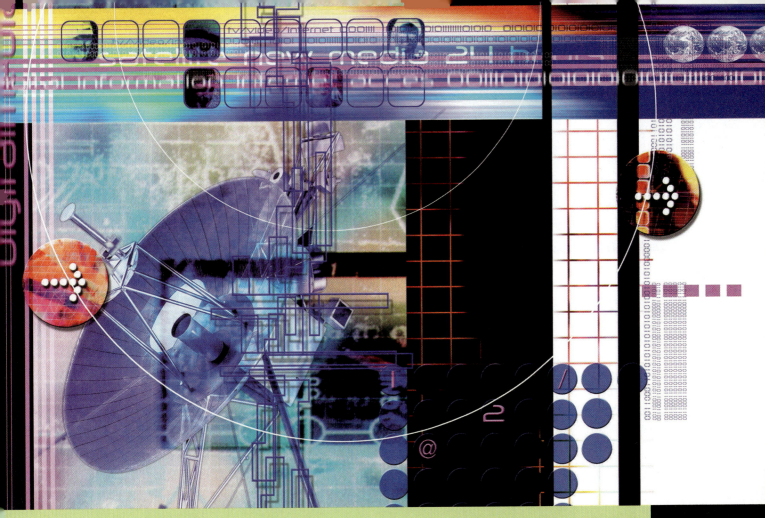

PART THREE

The Electronic Industries

This part of *Mass Media in a Changing World* will examine the movie, recording, radio, television, and Internet industries, once again looking at their history, their current structure, and the social issues that create controversy about them. With their electronic reach, these are considered the most powerful of the media. They are also rapidly converging into one digital, interactive format.

Movies

Magic from the Dream Factory

6

Chapter Highlights

HISTORY: The history of movies is the history of a technology, an art form, a business, and a cultural force.

INDUSTRY: Movies are produced for various markets, including international and home video. Each member of the production team plays an important role.

CONTROVERSIES: Movie controversies derive from their cultural power. Movies seem to promote violence, stereotyping, and unhealthy habits such as smoking; and they are often censored, which upsets those who view them as artistic forms of free expression.

The Monster That Ate the Movie Theater

There's a monster running rampant through the movie industry. It is a monster as terrifying to theater owners as any seen on the screen, and it goes by the name of home theater. Each year, movie attendance is decreasing and large-screen home HDTV ownership is increasing. The monster is transforming movies from a big-screen theatrical event to a small-screen home experience. By 2006, less than 15 percent of studio domestic revenues were earned from movie ticket sales, while more than 85 percent came from licensing or selling movies for use in the home.[1]

Despite some signs of life, such as the popularity of *Pirates of the Caribbean: Dead Man's Chest* (2006), many critics and media practitioners say the theatrical film business is in big trouble.

And the home theater monster is hardly alone. *Los Angeles Times* columnist Patrick Goldstein points out that it has lots of help:

> The era of moviegoing as a mass audience ritual is slowly but inexorably drawing to a close, eroded by many of the same forces that have eviscerated the music industry, decimated network TV and, yes, are clobbering the newspaper business. Put simply, an explosion of new technology—the Internet, DVDs, video games, downloading, cell phones and iPods—now offers more compelling diversion than 90% of the movies in theaters, the exceptions being "Harry Potter"-style must-see events or the occasional youth-oriented comedy or thriller.[2]

Goldstein goes on to point out that even the teenage audience members that have traditionally been the theaters' best customers can no longer be relied on to battle the monster: "It's become cool to dismiss movies as awful. Wherever I go, teenagers say, with chillingly casual adolescent contempt, that movies suck and cost too much—the same stance they took about CDs when the music business went into free fall."[3]

Theater owners are reacting to the monster by trying to squeeze more profit out of their captive audience through selling in-theater, on-screen advertising. Many moviegoers are becoming increasingly annoyed by 20 minutes of commercials, often played at an ear-shattering volume so customers will pay attention.

Even with snack sales and on-screen advertising, theater owners find it difficult to make ends meet in an era of declining movie attendance. Operating a theater is expensive, and includes the costs of ushers, cleaning staff, and projectionists. So now there are fewer ushers, which means there never seems to be one around to tell the guy behind you to stop yakking on his cell phone. And the theater doesn't get cleaned as often or as thoroughly, so the floors are often sticky.

Theater owners have even cut down on projectionists to save money. One projectionist now has to service up to eight movies. This leaves several movies unattended at any one time, which runs the risk that they might momentarily snag in the projector and get burnt by the lamp. To prevent this, projectionists expand the gap between the gate that supports the film and the lamp, even though this puts the film slightly out of focus. To save even more money, theater owners delay changing projector bulbs, which cost more than $1,000 each. They use the old bulbs even if they do not produce the optimum level of brightness to produce a perfect picture on screen. They seem to get away with it. As one movie chain executive pointed out: "I've never heard a teenager complain about PQ [picture quality]."[4]

Blasting commercials; out-of-focus, underlit movies; sticky floors and guys on cell phones—all erode the moviegoing experience, making it even less likely that theaters will fill up this weekend. One studio executive summed up the effects of the monster this way: "Each weekend, there's more blood in the water."[5]

Along with its theater attendance problems, the movie industry is also blamed for some of the worst ills of society, from violence to teen pregnancy to smoking addiction. Whether that blame is justified or not, it is clear that movies can have a powerful effect. Audiences for this medium experience an almost dreamlike state. The moviegoer enters a darkened theater (or home theater) and willingly suspends disbelief to enter the world created on the screen. Movies are obviously changing as a business, but they continue to be powerful as a cultural force.

A Brief History *of Movies*

Fascinated audiences have considered movies to be magical from their very beginning. The magic started with 19th-century experiments in making pictures move and continued through the eras of silent films, sound films, and the digital moviemaking of today.

EARLY MOVIE TECHNOLOGY

Any magician will tell you that the heart of a magic show is clever illusion. The same is true for the magic of movies, which is based on the **persistence of vision**—an aspect of human vision in which the brain retains images for a fraction of a second after they leave the field of sight. In the early 1800s, makers of some popular toys used their understanding of this aspect of vision to create optical illusions. At first these were simple toys, such as books of still pictures that could be thumbed through to create the illusion of movement. By the 1860s **peep shows,** which consisted of rolls of still pictures contained in a box and hooked up to a crank, were popular attractions at amusement parlors.[6] When the viewer peered through a set of eyeholes in the box and turned the crank, the pictures appeared to move, providing both entertainment and modest exercise.

This actor from *The Great Train Robbery* was uncredited. His real name was Max Aronson, and he went on to appear in more than 300 films under a variety of names, most notably as Gilbert M. "Broncho Billy" Anderson. Today he is considered the father of the movie cowboy and the first Western star.

Photography of Motion

Photography was invented in 1839, but movies had to await the development of the first successful photography of motion in 1872. That year California governor Leland Stanford asked an English photographer named Eadweard Muybridge to photograph a running horse. Stanford was trying to win a bet—he maintained that when a horse galloped, all four of its feet would occasionally leave the ground. Muybridge rigged a series of cameras with strings attached to their shutters and ran the strings across a track. When the horse ran by, the strings tripped the shutters and triggered a series of photographs. Not only did Muybridge help Stanford win his bet (some of the photos did show all four of the horse's feet off the ground), but when viewed in sequence, the photos created the illusion of motion.

From Peep Shows to Projection

A few years after Muybridge's demonstration, several inventors in the United States, France, and Great Britain were working at the same time to develop techniques for filming and projecting motion pictures. American inventor Thomas Edison and two French brothers, Louis and Auguste Lumière, made the first breakthroughs in this field. Edison perfected his **kinetograph,** a camera to take motion pictures, and **kinetoscope,** the device to show them, in 1889, using the flexible celluloid camera film that George Eastman had invented that same year.[7] (Glass plates had been used before that instead of film.)

SELF QUIZ What was Eadweard Muybridge's contribution to the development of motion picture technology?

persistence of vision
An aspect of human vision in which the brain retains images for a fraction of a second after they leave the field of sight; this allows for the illusion of movement from a series of still pictures.

peep shows
Amusement parlor boxes containing moving rolls of still pictures.

kinetograph
Early motion picture camera invented by Thomas Edison.

kinetoscope
Early motion picture viewer invented by Thomas Edison.

Auguste Lumiere (1862–1954) and Louis Jean Lumiere (1864–1948) at work in their laboratory at Lyon, France. The Lumiere brothers invented the Lumiere process of color photography and an early motion picture camera.

Edison's kinetoscope was designed along the same principles as the earlier peep shows, but instead of seeing a series of paper illustrations, the viewer would see an image created by a spool of film run over a lightbulb. Edison opened a kinetoscope parlor in New York City in 1894, with two rows of machines that showed bits of vaudeville and some brief original films that Edison had made in a tiny studio in West Orange, New Jersey. It was there that Edwin Porter made *The Great Train Robbery* in 1903. Porter's movie was the first to use editing—cutting together various shots—to tell a story. It was also the first western, and the first movie to contain a chase scene. *The Great Train Robbery* was around 12 minutes long.

Edison had not filed for international patents on his camera or viewer, so many people overseas copied and tinkered with both inventions. Louis and Auguste Lumière were among those who improved on Edison's equipment. The Lumières (the name, incidentally, means "light" in French), began exhibiting short films to groups of people in Paris in 1895. These are considered the first paid public showings of motion pictures.

SELF QUIZ

What was Thomas Edison's role in the development of the motion picture industry? Who else filled essential roles?

Nickelodeons

It took Edison a while to catch on to the idea of projecting movies to the public. He had envisioned motion pictures as a visual accompaniment to the phonograph, which he had invented in 1877. In this way he was truly thinking ahead of his time, to the eras of televisions and VCRs in the home. When Edison finally premiered his first theater projector, the Vitascope, in 1896, it was a sensation. Before long, small theaters were cropping up everywhere. They were called **nickelodeons** because the admission was a nickel and *odeon* was the Greek word for theater.

nickelodeons
Small early movie theaters.

THE TRUST

Once Edison realized the potential popularity of motion pictures, he moved to corner the market on the movie business. He rounded up the primary patent holders and film producers of the United States and France, and created an organization called the **Motion Picture Patents Company,** which came to be known simply as the Trust. George Eastman, who had the patent on movie film, signed an exclusive agreement to sell his film only to the Trust, which also acquired most of the existing film distributorships, the businesses that delivered the films to the theaters. Film producers who were not willing to pay the Trust's patent use fees were simply not allowed to make movies. If they attempted to use a camera, or film, the Trust would get

Motion Picture Patents Company
Company founded by Thomas Edison to control the movie equipment business; known as the Trust.

Early moviemakers left New York City for California, where they could escape the grip of Edison's monopoly.

a court order to raid the studio and destroy the equipment. The owners would then be prosecuted for patent infringement.

The Trust had the power to improve the quality of motion pictures in the same way that Microsoft improved the quality of computer operating systems during the late 20th century. The lack of competition allowed standards to emerge quickly. This helped make the American film industry strong, but it also made it expensive to produce movies. To escape the Trust, filmmakers left the industry's center in New York City with an eye toward a new promised land: California.

CONSIDER THIS

Some would say that Edison's Motion Picture Patents Company made it difficult for competitors to get started in the movie business, but others might point out that it standardized and advanced movie technology. In your opinion, was Edison's establishment of the Trust an ethical action on his part?

THE MOVE WEST

While southern California was a comfortable distance from Edison's New York lawyers, aspiring filmmakers moved west for several other reasons as well. California had great weather for outdoor shooting all year long. It also had varied scenery—locations for mountains, beach, desert, and plains could all be found in close range. This made it perfect for the typical low-budget pictures of the day, which were shot mostly outdoors with only natural sunlight. The little village of Hollywood, in particular, was attractive to filmmakers because it had a supply of huge old barns that could be converted to studios for interior shots.

The first modern feature film was D. W. Griffith's Civil War epic *The Birth of a Nation*, made in Hollywood in 1915. In it, Griffith improved the art of motion picture storytelling and perfected such techniques as the close-up, the flashback, the fade-out, and the montage. The film was a huge theatrical success, and from that point on, movies became big business. Unfortunately, the film was also a racist depiction of blacks and it glorified the Ku Klux Klan. Today it is considered an omen of the kind of power that films would have to promote antisocial messages.

D. W. Griffith's *The Birth of a Nation* was a huge theatrical success but also glorified the Ku Klux Klan.

The U.S. government forced Edison's Trust to go out of business in 1917. The courts found that the Trust was the type of vertically integrated monopoly that operated in restraint of trade, making it impossible for others to compete. Hollywood, however, continued to be the center of the film industry, and by the 1920s the studios there were thriving. Each studio was set up like a factory. All employees, from carpenters to stars, were put under exclusive contracts, and movies were cranked out on a regular schedule.

Savvy businessmen from the East were attracted to the movies' profitability, and soon the studios became powerful enough to monopolize the film industry. The studios did not try to control the technology, as Edison did, but they did try to vertically integrate both production and exhibition. By owning most of America's largest movie palaces, which held up to 6,000 patrons each, studios during the 1920s and 1930s were able to control 90 percent of all film revenue.

SELF QUIZ

Why did the U.S. movie industry move from New York to Los Angeles?

THE STAR SYSTEM

The star system was created in the 1920s when audiences began to demand to see popular actors. There were no "stars" before this time; early films did

SELF QUIZ

not even list the actors in the credits. In fact, the actors were expected to help the carpenters build the sets, just as the carpenters were expected to fill in as actors when needed. Moviegoers, however, would write to the production companies to ask for information about their favorite actors. Early producers kept quiet about the letters at first because they did not want actors to ask for more money. After all, actors were already being paid $10 to $15 a day, well above average for skilled workers in the early 1900s. Nevertheless, when the theater owners started to demand the actors that their customers were asking for, the studio heads knew they were on to something. To help guarantee box office success, studio executives created stars by placing actors and actresses under contract and promoting them heavily.

One technique the studios used to develop new talent (and to increase profits and keep the factories busy) was **block booking.** Under this system, the owners of independent theaters—those theaters not owned by the studios—were required to show movies with unknown stars in order to get the movies with the established stars. This practice was combined with **blind booking,** in which the studios forced theater owners to take their movies without previewing them first. These practices enabled studios to make money from what they called B movies, which were low-cost films whose actors were "stars in training."

U.S. stars went international when World War I interrupted European filmmaking and audiences in other countries turned to American films. Silent films were easily adapted to the international audience by replacing the English dialogue cards. The silent stars of this era, such as Charlie Chaplin, Mary Pickford, Douglas Fairbanks, and Rudolph Valentino, enjoyed huge international celebrity.[8]

block booking
Forcing theater owners to show movies with unknown stars in order to get movies with established stars.

blind booking
Forcing theater owners to reserve movies without previewing them.

GLOBAL INFLUENCE ON THE ART OF FILM

Although American films were, and continue to be, extremely popular internationally, influence has always flowed both ways. Early film was an integral part of several well-known European art movements, and each of these movements has influenced American films.

German Expressionism

German expressionism began in the 1920s as a style in painting, sculpture, and theater as well as film. It was a dark style, reflecting the pessimistic mood of the German people following their defeat in World War I. Expressionism used symbolism to represent inner psychological states, especially terror and horror. The source of the internal terror was often the characters' inability to distinguish what was real from what was imaginary. *The Cabinet of Dr. Caligari* (1919), directed by Robert Wiene, is the best-known film of this movement and very typical of its characteristics. It uses shadows for dramatic effect, with nightmare-like sets designed by expressionistic painters. *Metropolis* (1926), a science fiction classic

The Cabinet of Dr. Caligari is the best-known film of the German expressionism movement and very typical of its style of using symbolism to represent inner psychological states.

by Fritz Lang, is another example of the genre. Expressionism influenced American films that dealt with the psychology of individuals, such as Alfred Hitchcock's *Psycho* (1960) and *Frenzy* (1972).

Soviet Social Realism

Soviet social realism was a reaction to expressionism, and its opposite in several respects. Social realist filmmakers focused on the masses rather than the individual and on external problems rather than internal psychological states. The hero of the story tended to be a group. Many of the films were blatant propaganda for the Communist Party. Directors often used amateurs instead of professional actors to emphasize the "group hero" mentality. The best-known example of this school was Sergei Eisenstein's *The Battleship Potemkin* (1925), which deals with the failed Russian Revolution of 1905. In this film, a group of sailors and the citizens of the town of Odessa are the collective heroes. One sequence, known as the Odessa steps montage, is the most-studied strip of celluloid in the history of higher education. Social realism influenced many presentations of violence in films, such as the famous slow-motion death scene in *Bonnie and Clyde* (1968) and the stark torture scenes of *The Passion of the Christ* (2004).

French Surrealism

French surrealism, which was extremely influential in the 1930s, rejected social standards of good taste and acceptability. The movement rejected the "tyranny of reason" and embraced the unconscious, the irrational, and the passionate. The most famous film of this school is *An Andalusian Dog* (1928), which was a collaborative project of Luis Buñuel, a filmmaker, and Salvador Dalí, an artist. The title is meaningless, as is typical in surreal films; the film is 25 minutes long and filled with vivid, brutal images. A man (Buñuel) slashes a woman's eye; ants swarm out of a hole in a man's palm; the decayed carcasses of two donkeys are dragged across a living room. The influence of French surrealism is seen in the heavily symbolic violence of many American films, including the Kill Bill movies and the X-Men movies.

Italian Neorealism

Italian neorealism arose at the end of World War II as a reaction to films made by the Italian fascists. It was much like Soviet social realism but without the propaganda. It used real people along with professional actors in stories that dealt with everyday problems. Neorealism featured recognizable social environments like the gritty streets and ruined neighborhoods of postwar Italy. Roberto Rossellini's *Rome, Open City* (1945) and Vittorio De Sica's *Bicycle Thief* (1948) are the best-known films of this movement. Neorealism has influenced many American movies that deal with social problems, from *The Grapes of Wrath* (1940) to *A History of Violence* (2005).

French New Wave

In the French new wave films influential in the 1960s and 1970s, the director's vision was paramount. Many of the directors had previously been film critics, and they tried to establish a "signature" style in their films. A director with a distinctive style would be called an **auteur,** which literally translates as "author" but has the added connotation of "artist." Two of the best-known films of the French new wave were François Truffaut's *The Four*

auteur
A movie director with a distinctive style.

CONSIDER THIS

What is your favorite film? Does it seem to have been affected by any of the global influences mentioned above?

Hundred Blows (1959) and Jean-Luc Godard's *A Woman Is a Woman* (1961). The influence of this school is seen in the way many contemporary directors—Quentin Tarantino, George Lucas, M. Night Shyamalan—seek to establish a style of their own and maintain it across all their films.

THE GOLDEN AGE

Along with the efficient studio system and the global influence of film art, the development of sound and color in the 1930s marked the beginning of the golden age of motion pictures. Some of the best movies ever made were produced during this period (see the Close-Up on History box), which lasted from 1930 until around 1950. During these two decades, going to the movies became a weekly ritual for most Americans. Moviegoers were offered double features, newsreels, cartoons, and door prizes. By 1946, 90 million people—almost 75 percent of the population—went to the movies every week. Today's weekly attendance is only 20 million, or 7.5 percent of the population.

From Silents to Talkies

Before movies could talk, public address systems had to be improved. Both Edison and AT&T's Bell Labs started working on the problem in the 1890s, and by the 1910s the technology was ready. Many movie producers, however, were not enthusiastic about the idea of sound. After all, they were making fortunes with silent film. Some directors also resisted the idea, fearing that the gimmick of sound would destroy the art of film. Theater owners took their time warming to the idea because equipping theaters with sound was expensive. By the mid-1920s the only sound films were shorts distributed as novelties to the few state-of-the-art theaters that could show them.

newsreels
Film clips covering current events that were shown in theaters before the advent of television.

The breakthrough year for sound was 1927. Enough theaters were equipped by then that 20th Century Fox studios began to add sound to **newsreels,** which showed news events and items of special interest. The precursors of television news, newsreels were extremely popular with movie audiences, and those theater owners that had not already done so quickly installed sound equipment to show them. All this made it obvious to the studios that it could now be profitable to produce a full-length sound feature. That film was Warner Bros.' *The Jazz Singer,* which was released in 1927 just a few months after the talking newsreels had debuted. *The Jazz Singer* featured Al Jolson, a popular vaudeville star. It was still mostly a silent film, with only 354 words of spoken dialogue, along with a few songs. Still, it established both the technology and the popularity of sound. Some audiences stood and applauded when they heard the dialogue.

Culture and Color

Throughout the 1930s and 1940s, as the film industry thrived and moviegoing became part of American culture, the movies in turn began to reflect that culture. During the 1930s, for example, gangster films such as *Little Caesar* (1930) and *Scarface* (1932) became popular, reflecting the influence of organized crime during the Prohibition era. Other popular movies, such as *I Am a Fugitive from a Chain Gang* (1932), dealt with the economic conditions of the Depression era.

To escape their real-life problems, people flocked to such supernatural horror films as *Dracula* (1931), with Bela Lugosi, and *Frankenstein* (1931),

Best American Films

The American Film Institute picked its list of the 100 greatest American movies of all time in 1998, in honor of the 100th anniversary of American filmmaking. The following are the top 10 titles from the list:

1. *Citizen Kane,* 1941. Orson Welles's classic about the rise and fall of a media titan was based loosely on the life of William Randolph Hearst (see Chapter 4). This film was made when Welles was only 25. It was not a commercial success, at least in part because Hearst used his power as a newspaper magnate to demand negative reviews and to force theater owners to boycott the film.

2. *Casablanca,* 1942. Humphrey Bogart and Ingrid Bergman star as two sides of a lovers' triangle in World War II Morocco. This film won Oscars for best picture, best director, and best screenplay.

3. *The Godfather,* 1972. Francis Ford Coppola's epic tale of the violent life and times of a Mafia family. It won Oscars for best picture, best actor (Marlon Brando), and best screenplay (Coppola and Mario Puzo, from whose novel the film was adapted).

4. *Gone with the Wind,* 1939. Produced by David O. Selznick, this magnificent soap opera set during the Civil War won eight Oscars, including best picture, best actress (Vivien Leigh, as Scarlett O'Hara), best director (Victor Fleming), and best screenplay (Sidney Howard).

5. *Lawrence of Arabia,* 1962. David Lean's sweeping, literate blockbuster starring Peter O'Toole as the adventurer T. E. Lawrence won Oscars for best picture, best director, best cinematographer, best score, best editing, and best art direction.

6. *The Wizard of Oz,* 1939. Victor Fleming directed this fantasy based on L. Frank Baum's story. Judy Garland's song "Over the Rainbow" won an Oscar.

7. *The Graduate,* 1967. Mike Nichols's anthem to the 1960s included actor Dustin Hoffman's breakthrough role as a naive college grad who has affairs with both a childhood friend (Katharine Ross) and her mother (Anne Bancroft as Mrs. Robinson). Paul Simon and Art Garfunkel provided the musical score; Nichols won the Oscar for best director.

8. *On the Waterfront,* 1954. Marlon Brando stars as a misfit in a New York City harbor union. The film garnered eight Oscars, including best picture, best director (Elia Kazan), best actor (Brando), and best screenplay (Budd Schulberg).

9. *Schindler's List,* 1993. The story of real-life war profiteer Oscar Schindler, who saved more than 1,000 Jewish people during World War II, earned seven Oscars, including best picture, best director (Steven Spielberg), and best screenplay.

10. *Singin' in the Rain,* 1952. Gene Kelly directed and starred in this movie musical about Hollywood's transition to sound movies, featuring Jean Hagen as Kelly's silent-screen costar, who was having a difficult time getting into the new industry because her voice could shatter glass.

The American Film Institute's list of the 100 best American films was controversial. Critics pointed out that only four silent films made the list, three of them starring Charlie Chaplin, and that Kevin Costner's *Dances with Wolves* (1990, number 75) made the list, but D. W. Griffith's *Intolerance* (1916) did not. Still, most critics agree about these top 10.

The Godfather, starring Al Pacino and Marlon Brando, is number 3 on the American Film Institute's list of the greatest American movies.

with Boris Karloff. Screwball comedies like the Marx Brothers' *Duck Soup* (1933) also became popular diversions from hard times. Color was perfected in films such as *Gone with the Wind* and *The Wizard of Oz*, both produced in 1939. (Primitive forms of color had been used experimentally from the beginning of the industry. George Melies's famous silent film of 1902, *A Trip to the Moon*, contained scenes that had been hand painted, frame by frame.) Special effects came into their own in movies such as *King Kong* (1933) and *The Invisible Man* (1933).

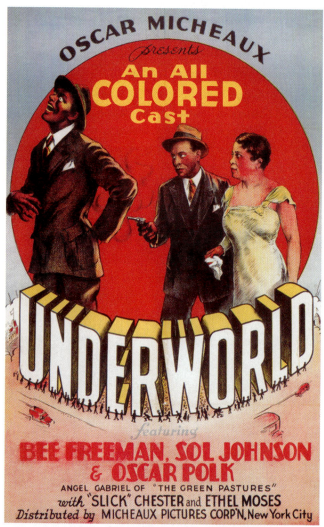

Oscar Micheaux (pronounced "Me-shaw") was the first African American to produce a feature film and one of the best-known filmmakers of the separate African American industry that emerged during the golden age of movies. *Underworld* was released in 1937.

African American Films

Unfortunately, the stereotyping of minorities, especially African Americans, continued during the golden age of motion pictures. There were also many segregated theaters throughout the United States, especially in the South, where blacks were not allowed in "white" theaters. A separate African American movie industry emerged to serve this market. Centered in New York City's Harlem, these films featured all-black casts and were shown in theaters in black neighborhoods throughout the country. Oscar Micheaux, who produced, directed, and distributed 46 movies, was one of the best-known African American filmmakers of the time. The Johnson brothers, Nobel and George, were also successful black producer/directors.

After the golden age, the long civil rights struggle to integrate the country was paralleled by the struggle of African Americans to direct and star in mainstream movies. Sidney Poitier was one of the first mainstream black stars, in movies such as *Guess Who's Coming to Dinner* (1967) and *In the Heat of the Night* (1967), which dealt with themes of racial intolerance.

The End of the Studio Monopoly

The golden age of movies ended with the demise of the big studio monopoly. Throughout the 1930s and 1940s competitors of the established studios complained to the government that it was impossible for new studios to get started. In a classic case of the abuse of vertical integration (see Chapter 1, page 18), studios such as Paramount and Metro-Goldwyn-Mayer (MGM), which owned the theaters, refused to show competitors' films. Following a 10-year lawsuit, the U.S. government forced the studios to sell their movie theaters in 1948. The practices of blind booking and block booking were also banned. This case, called the Paramount decision, dealt a severe blow to the studios. They would not be able to own theaters again until the 1980s, under the Reagan administration's policy of deregulation. The movie industry's greatest enemy, however, would be television.

When was the golden age of movies, and why was it considered golden?

SELF QUIZ

REACTING TO TV

Movie attendance peaked in 1946, and there were many reasons for the decline that followed. One was the exodus of families from American cities. In the post–World War II boom, couples moved to the suburbs to raise their children, leaving the huge old movie palaces behind. Suburbanites were working long hours to support their lifestyles. Free time and discretionary income were more likely to be spent on car polish and lawn mowers than on the movies.

The biggest reason for the decline in movie attendance, though, was that people were staying home and watching television. Television ownership grew steadily during the 1950s, and more than 90 percent of American homes had television sets by the early 1960s. Movie attendance plummeted. Big-city movie theaters were going out of business at an alarming rate.

Competing with the Small Screen

To compete with television, the motion picture industry had to redefine itself. Small suburban theaters emerged, as did drive-ins, which allowed suburbanites to watch movies in the automobiles that had become so important to them.[9] The technology of the movies also began to change. Sound systems were improved, and wide screens began to be used. These screens had futuristic names like Cinemascope, with a screen two-and-a-half-times as wide as it was high, and Cinerama, which was a curved, wraparound screen that required multiple projectors.

The style of movies began to change as well. Color became standard, to gain an advantage over television's black-and-white picture. Hollywood also began to produce spectaculars, which were high-budget films with lavish sets and costumes, that often had "a cast of thousands." *Quo Vadis?* (1951),

Movie studios now produce the majority of prime-time TV programming.

a typical spectacular, had 5,500 extras in one scene. Other movies were produced with special gimmicks, such as 3-D effects that required special glasses that were given out at the door, and Smell-o-Vision, which used fans and scent liquids to waft odors into the theater.[10]

The themes of movies changed as well, as they tried to deal with topics that couldn't be handled by television, including sex, violence, and disturbing social issues. Otto Preminger's *The Moon Is Blue* (1953), for example, made fun of virginity, and his *Man with the Golden Arm* (1956) dealt with drug abuse. By 1968, the graphic portrayal of violence and sex in movies led the Motion Picture Association of America to establish a ratings system, a form of industry control that will be discussed in detail in the Controversies section of this chapter.

If You Can't Beat Them, Join Them

Although they fought hard to compete with television, the movie studios also began to embrace the new medium as a way to make money. In 1949, a subsidiary of Columbia Studios began producing programs for television, including *Ford Theater* and *Father Knows Best*. In 1953, the networks switched from live to filmed production, and the movie studios became more active in producing programming. In 1955, Hollywood began releasing its old films to TV, and by the late 1960s the studios were making made-for-TV movies. Today, each of the studios

SELF QUIZ How, and why, did the movie industry change after the advent of television?

is a major producer of television programming. In fact, movie studios now produce the majority of prime-time TV programming. In an echo of an earlier time, many of the studios are owned by the same companies that own the television stations.

The movie industry continued to decline until 1975, when Steven Spielberg's *Jaws* ushered in the era of the special-effects blockbuster. The movies of the 1980s and 1990s featured $20-million-per-movie action stars such as Arnold Schwarzenegger and Sylvester Stallone, and on-screen violence and sex increased annually.

ADAPTING TO NEW MEDIA

Television, of course, was not the last new technology to which the movie industry had to adjust. It had the same kind of paranoid reaction to home VCRs (videocassette recorders) when they were introduced in the 1970s. By the early 1980s the industry was convinced that home videotaping would lead to its ruin. The Motion Picture Association of America fought several legal battles to stop the sale of home VCRs. Finally, in 1983, in what has come to be called the Sony Betamax case, the Supreme Court ruled that video recording for private use was not an infringement of copyright. The outcome of the Betamax case was that most families bought VCRs, and although they did use them to record programs, they also used them to play rented or purchased tapes, which created a huge profit area for movie studios.

By the time DVDs (digital video discs) were introduced in 1996, the movie industry saw them as a replacement for tapes and didn't resist them as much, especially in their original read-only format. When DVDs became recordable and people started downloading movies, however, the industry realized it had a problem.

Movie Downloading

Downloading from the Internet made **pirating** films and distributing them illegally over the Internet easy to do. Pirates worked in a variety of ways: Sometimes a print of the studio film was stolen; sometimes the movie was secretly taped using a video camera during a theatrical showing. Other times, DVD copies that were sent out to members of the Academy of Motion Picture Arts and Sciences for Oscar consideration wound up in the hands of pirates and were put online for file sharing.

In 2003 the movie industry declared war against file sharers. To avoid the types of losses suffered by the music industry, the movie companies distributed advertisements designed to dissuade people from downloading films and devised methods for encrypting DVDs so they couldn't be copied. They also brought lawsuits against file-sharing services such as Morpheus and Kazaa. They even hired private detectives to track down those who put films online, and they assisted law-enforcement officials in crackdowns on file sharers, which included several raids on college campuses.

The film industry fought international pirating by lobbying foreign governments to enforce international copyright agreements. The studios also developed a "fingerprinting" system that encoded serial marks, invisible to the naked eye, on every print of a film. This allowed enforcement teams to track down the theaters at which copies were made and resulted in several arrests.

At the same time, the studios were working on alternate movies-on-demand systems that would make it easier to pay for a download than to steal it. Online services such as MovieLink, which is owned by the major studios, now allow consumers to download some movies for as little as 99 cents.

Movies on demand can now be downloaded to cell phones.

pirating
The illegal copying and selling of movies.

The studios also struck deals with cable television and even cell phone companies to download movies on demand.

Digital Technology in Movie Production

In the early 1990s studios begin to use computers for digital editing and special effects. Disney's *Toy Story* (1995) was the first movie to be produced entirely on computers. Today, digital editing is used in all Hollywood movies, and many of them (*X-Men, Superman Returns*) would be impossible without it.

The studios have also started to experiment with digital distribution. In 1999, *Star Wars: Episode I—The Phantom Menace* was digitally distributed to a few theaters. If it becomes the norm, digital distribution could offer big economic advantages for the studios. Film copies cost around $1,500 each, plus the cost of shipping them to each of the world's 150,000 screens (35,000 in the United States, 115,000 in the rest of the world). Studios stand to save a few billion dollars each year if they no longer have to copy and ship film prints and can instead transmit them as electronic files through high-speed data links.[11]

Digital Technology in Theaters

Digital distribution would have advantages for theater owners also. Digitally projected movies will be easier to use. To prepare a standard 35-millimeter film at today's multiplex, employees must physically splice the film to the preview trailers the night before the first show. By contrast, to prepare a movie for digital projection, an operator selects the film title and the accompanying trailers from a list on a computer screen and adds them to the night's play list for as many screens as warranted. Digital projection will also enable theaters to regularly show live events, such as concerts or sporting events, making them entertainment complexes rather than just movie houses. Several experimental showings of such events have proved that audiences are willing to pay for them. Some industry people think that digital projection could help the theater business remain economically viable.

SELF QUIZ What are the advantages and disadvantages of the digital distribution of movies?

Technically, the industry has been able to transmit and project movie images digitally for more than a decade. The only thing holding back the conversion now is the argument between theater owners and studios over who will pay for the equipment.

GLOBAL DIMENSIONS

Today, the American film industry collects more than 80 percent of the world's film revenues, although it produces only around 15 percent of the world's films.[12] Brazil, China, Japan, and India are among many countries that have thriving film industries. India produces more movies than any other country, around 800 a year, which is almost twice as many as America does in an average year. In fact, so many movies are made in Mumbai (formerly Bombay) that the international film community refers to that city as Bollywood.

Although movies from around the world continue to influence American filmmakers, their impact pales in comparison with that of Hollywood's output on the rest of the world. The films of other countries are often clever remakes of Hollywood films, rewritten to adjust to local culture. For example, in India family ties are an integral part of a person's identity; so a lone man in India is essentially incomprehensible to the audience. The first thing an

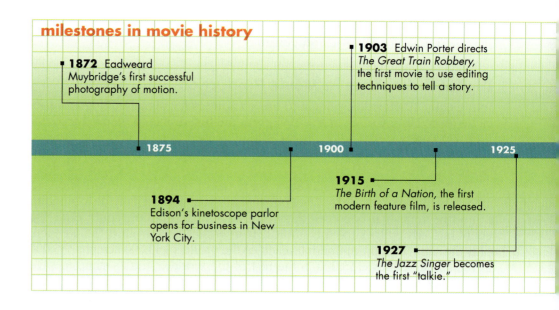

milestones in movie history

1872 Eadweard Muybridge's first successful photography of motion.

1903 Edwin Porter directs *The Great Train Robbery,* the first movie to use editing techniques to tell a story.

1875

1900

1925

1894 Edison's kinetoscope parlor opens for business in New York City.

1915 *The Birth of a Nation,* the first modern feature film, is released.

1927 *The Jazz Singer* becomes the first "talkie."

Bollywood/Hollywood was a Canadian film that used some of Bombay's hottest actors and actresses (along with typical Bollywood songs and a typical Bollywood plot line) to tell the story of an Indian family living in Toronto, and the effect that Bollywood movies continue to have on them.

Indian scriptwriter does is to give the antisocial detective or the solitary gunslinger a father and mother and usually a sister. Sometimes, American story lines are lifted in their entirety, adapted for popular local actors speaking in the native idiom. *Chachi 420* (1998), for example, was a popular Indian remake of *Mrs. Doubtfire* (1993). A film industry as large as India's has a significant international influence of its own. In Pakistan, for example, scriptwriters unabashedly lift story lines from Indian films.

Understanding Today's Movie *Industry*

Moviemaking is an extremely volatile industry, one in which a company's balance sheet is only as healthy as the box office receipts of its most recent

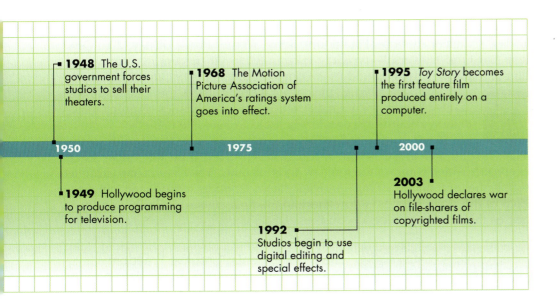

1948 The U.S. government forces studios to sell their theaters.

1968 The Motion Picture Association of America's ratings system goes into effect.

1995 *Toy Story* becomes the first feature film produced entirely on a computer.

1950   1975   2000

1949 Hollywood begins to produce programming for television.

2003 Hollywood declares war on file-sharers of copyrighted films.

1992 Studios begin to use digital editing and special effects.

releases. The average cost of producing and marketing a Hollywood film is now more than $96 million.[13] Many big-budget studio releases cost much more than the average. *X-Men: The Last Stand* (2006) cost $210 million to

The average cost of producing and marketing a Hollywood film is now more than $96 million.

make.[14] Major studios typically release between 15 and 20 movies a year. They can quickly run up hundreds of millions of dollars in losses if they do not have any big hits. Even in a good year, the movie business is not a very profitable industry for its investors. One studio chief estimated that the industry's overall rate of return on capital invested is about 3 percent.[15] Since the bulk of the profit goes to a handful of major studios, most of the people who invest in films lose money. The glamour of the industry and the lure of the occasional highly profitable blockbuster, however, keeps them coming.

You can begin to appreciate the economics of filmmaking by looking at its three major areas: production, distribution, and exhibition.

PRODUCTION

There are three stages of the production part of the movie business. **Preproduction,** the planning phase, includes script development, casting, budgeting, scheduling, set and costume design, location scouting, set construction, and special effects design. **Production** is the actual shooting phase, a point at which the activity becomes very hectic and expensive as the cast and crew swell into the hundreds and producers have to consider everything from caterers to day care for the star's poodle. **Postproduction** includes the film and sound editing, soundtrack scoring, special effects integration, and technical improvements to the film, such as color correction. To handle these three stages, the production business has two primary components: the production companies, and the people in the credits.

The Production Company

Today's movie business revolves around two types of production companies: the major studios and the independents.

preproduction
The planning phase of moviemaking.

production
The actual shooting phase of moviemaking.

postproduction
The final phase of moviemaking, which includes editing and other technical improvements to the film.

The Major Studios: The Big Six

Today, six major studios—Paramount, Sony, Warner Bros., Disney, 20th Century Fox, and Universal—typically take in 80 to 90 percent of commercial film revenues. Each is owned by a conglomerate. Two of the majors (Sony and Fox) are owned by corporations outside the United States. Many of them own smaller studios as subsidiaries. Further information about the six majors is listed in Fact File 6.1.

SELF QUIZ

What percent of movie revenues are earned by only six companies?

Movie studios today differ significantly from the studios of the 1920s to the 1940s. They still produce movies, but they no longer keep everyone under contract for long periods of time. They are more likely to simply finance and distribute movies for independent producers. In fact, each of the major studios is now more in the financing and distribution businesses than in the production business.

There are many independent film studios, including one at the University of Texas at Austin, where investors and the university have joined forces to produce films for profit. Here a graduate student works in the department's film editing lab.

SELF QUIZ

What's the difference between an independent studio and a major studio?

The Independents: Creative Freedom

Independent films are those that are not made by one of the major studios. They are usually made with lower budgets but allow their makers more creative freedom than major studios do. They also rely less on stars and special effects and more on subject matter and dialogue. If independent production companies do their jobs well, they are often bought by one of the majors, but can retain their independent character. Filmmakers like Spike Lee and Robert Rodriguez, who might not otherwise be noticed by major studios, made their marks as independent filmmakers.

Independent films range from student productions made with a few hundred dollars to multimillion-dollar productions made by subsidiaries of the studios. Films from Disney's Miramax studio, such as *Kill Bill* (2003) and *Shakespeare in Love* (1998), are considered independent productions.[16] Many critics and moviegoers believe these independent/studio hybrids are the best movies being made today. They take risks, but they have adequate financing and therefore decent production values. Demand for small independent films has increased because of cable channels (such as the Independent Film Channel) and the DVD market.

The People in the Credits

The people involved in making films are listed in that long scroll of personnel that most moviegoers ignore as they file out of the theater (see Figure 6.1). A basic understanding of the industry, however, requires an awareness of what the primary players do.

The Producer

Producers are usually classified as either executive producers or line producers. The **executive producer** finds the financing for the film and puts the package together, including the story, the script, the stars, and the director.

independent films
Movies that are not made by one of the major studios.

executive producer
The person who finds the financing for a film and puts the package together.

FACT FILE 6.1

Top Hollywood Studios

Studio/Web Address	Ownership Structure	Notable Releases
Paramount Pictures www.paramount.com	Owned by Viacom; owns Dreamworks	*World Trade Center* (2006), *Mission: Impossible 3* (2006), *War of the Worlds* (2005, co-produced with Dreamworks), *Mean Girls* (2004), *Titanic* (1997, co-produced with Fox), *Forrest Gump* (1994), *Raiders of the Lost Ark* (1981), *Beverly Hills Cop* (1984), *The Godfather* (1972)
Sony Pictures www.sonypictures.com	Owns Columbia, Tri-Star, and partial interest in Phoenix and Mandalay, as well as a chain of theaters and retail stores	*All the King's Men* (2006), *The Da Vinci Code* (2006), *Hitch* (2005), the Spider-Man movies, *Men in Black* (1997), *Ghostbusters* (1984), *Air Force One* (1997), *Charlie's Angels* (2000)
Warner Bros. www.warnerbros.com	Part of Time Warner; owns Castle Rock and New Line; owns and operates multiplex theaters in over 12 countries; owns retail stores	*The Departed* (2006), *The Dukes of Hazzard* (2005), the Harry Potter movies, the Matrix movies, the Lord of the Rings movies, the Batman movies, the Terminator movies
Disney www.disney.com	Owns Walt Disney Pictures, Buena Vista, Touchstone, Hollywood, Caravan Pictures, retail stores, and the famous theme parks	*Cars* (2006), *Herbie: Fully Loaded* (2005), the Pirates of the Caribbean movies, *Finding Nemo* (2002), *The Lion King* (1994), *Beauty and the Beast* (1991), *Dinosaur* (2000)
20th Century Fox www.foxmovies.com	Owned by News Corporation	*The Devil Wears Prada* (2006), *Robots* (2005), *The Day After Tomorrow* (2004), *Titanic* (1997, co-produced with Paramount), the Star Wars movies, the Alien movies, the Die Hard movies, *Independence Day* (1996), *Mrs. Doubtfire* (1993)
Universal www.universalpictures.com	Owned by NBC, a division of General Electric	*The Black Dahlia* (2006), *The 40-Year-Old Virgin* (2005), *Van Helsing* (2004), *E.T. the Extra-Terrestrial* (1982), the Jurassic Park movies, *Jaws* (1975), *Twister* (1996, co-produced with Warner Bros.), *Liar, Liar* (1997)

Line producers, who are sometimes called production managers, do much of the actual day-to-day work. The line producers in demand are those who can complete films on time and within budget.

Many producers are also writers and directors, at which point they become "hyphenates" (for the hyphen in whatever combination of producer-director-writer they are.) The title *producer* has become increasingly controversial. (See the Close-Up on Industry box.)

The Director

Film is a director's medium. Directors provide the creative vision and translate the written script into a finished product. They usually get involved in the project early in the preproduction phase and oversee everything in production and postproduction. During production, directors set up shots and work closely with the actors, using a variety of techniques to inspire their best performances. During postproduction, directors work directly with the editors. At the end of postproduction they deliver to the producer a **director's cut,** which represents the director's creative vision and often disregards

line producers
People who lead the actual day-to-day work of making a film.

director's cut
Version of film the director delivers to the studio.

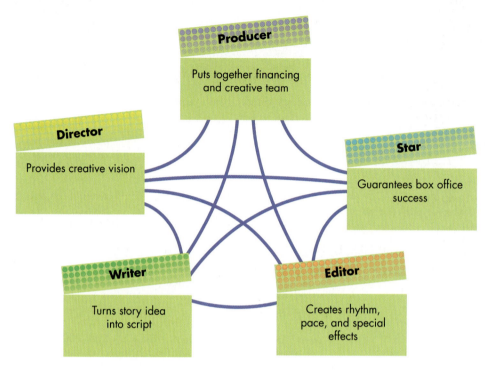

Producer
Puts together financing and creative team

Director
Provides creative vision

Star
Guarantees box office success

Writer
Turns story idea into script

Editor
Creates rhythm, pace, and special effects

FIGURE 6.1 The Production Team The many professionals who make up the production team help make moviemaking one of the most expensive, and least profitable, of all media businesses.

commercial considerations. In most cases the producer can recut the film if it is not satisfactory to the studio. Only the most sought-after directors have the right to determine the final cut.

Some directors are discovered right out of film school. Robert Rodriguez, the director of the *Spy Kids* movies, made his debut film, *El Mariachi,* for $7,000 in 1992. Others learn their craft over years in the business, starting out in lowly technical positions and working their way up to be first and second assistant directors or **second unit directors,** those who shoot the scenes that do not require the stars.

The Writer

Every movie begins with an idea—sometimes a star's, sometimes a producer's, sometimes a writer's. Frequently, the idea comes from a novel or nonfiction magazine article. Whatever its source, it is the writer's job to turn that idea into a script. Fact File 6.2 lists the top 10 screenplays, according to the Writers Guild of America.

Scripts today are often written by committee. One writer is brought in to spice up the humor, another for the romance, another to create strong female characters.[17] Studio executives justify this approach as a form of insurance. They are often spending $100 million or more, so they want to know that every word in the script is as good as it can be. To the studio's way of thinking, the script is far less a piece of creative writing than it is a business plan for a multimillion-dollar start-up company.

The Star

In today's Hollywood the star system is as strong as ever—studios still rely on the big names to guarantee box office success. However, the studios

second unit directors
Movie directors in charge of shooting the scenes that do not require the stars.

Just What Does a Producer Do?

The title "producer" has always been controversial. There's considerable confusion about what it means to be a producer, as opposed to a line producer (who manages the production process day to day) or an executive producer (who raises the money and puts the initial team together).

The producer credit is extremely important to Hollywood types, because it's the producer who picks up the Oscar for best picture at the Academy Awards. In the past, many people who didn't deserve the producer credit claimed it. In one case the star's personal manager received a "produced by" credit at the insistence of the star, and in another, a star's hairdresser and a producer's chauffeur both received billing as producers.[1] While not all the indiscretions were that blatant, the stage was still becoming crowded during presentations for best picture.

In 2006 the Producers Guild of America agreed to decide who was rightfully a producer, and the Academy of Motion Picture Arts and Sciences, the organization that awards the Oscars, agreed to honor the guild's decision. The agreement was meant to ease the controversy; instead, it seemed to fan it.

The guild declared that a producer had to be the driving force behind the film from the beginning all the way to the end, and it devised a checklist of 46 tasks to decide whether a producer deserved the credit. The guild called these tasks "parenting issues."[2]

Crash had six listed producers, but only two, Cathy Schulman and Paul Haggis, were eligible under the new rules. Bob Yari, a real estate tycoon turned producer, was one of the four who were denied credit. He filed a lawsuit against the guild and the Academy of Motion Picture Arts and Sciences five days before the Oscar ceremony.

Yari claimed, in both his lawsuit and the full-page ads he took out in industry trade publications, that he was a true producer. But the guild said 15 people who worked on *Crash* testified and did not substantiate Yari's account of his contributions.

Yari then insisted that he wanted to know who these people were. He said he wanted "due process," with the evidence and the reason behind the credit determination made clear to him. The "secret process," he said, was unfair.

But the Producer's Guild insisted that the identities of those testifying before the guild's panel had to remain secret. As one of the lawyers explained: "There is no way you could have credit determinations if producers and studios could bear down on the little people who testify. They know that if they testify against a Bob Yari, they're never going to do lunch in this town again."[3]

Bruce Davis, executive director of the Academy of Motion Picture Arts and Sciences, summarized the case against Yari: "He clearly played a crucial role, but he functioned as an executive producer, not a producer."[4] Yari's lawsuit was dismissed three months later. The judge said that Yari's case was based mainly on his subjective perceptions of fairness, which cannot be taken into consideration in a court of law.

Producers Cathy Schulman and Paul Haggis accept the Academy Award for Best Picture for *Crash* in 2006.

[1]Bernard Weinraub, "Only Where It's Due: Producers Want Credit," *New York Times,* June 26, 1997, p. C13.

[2]David Carr, "Nominations Highlight the Sticky Issue of Credit," *New York Times* online, February 1, 2006.

[3]George Hedges quoted in Sharon Waxman, "The Lawsuit over Producer Credit for 'Crash' Gets Personal," *New York Times* online, March 9, 2006.

[4]Quoted in Sharon Waxman, "The Lawsuit over Producer Credit."

are no longer in control of the star system. Now agents, managers, and the stars themselves run the system. Agencies—such as Creative Artists, International Creative Management, and William Morris—and managers who work directly for the stars promote and develop actors into celebrities much as the studios once did. In spite of all their best efforts, however, around every 20 years there is a changing of the guard among major stars. Few stars remain in the public consciousness for more than a small number of years. Public tastes change, and the industry is constantly searching for younger, fresher faces. In fact, the actor Ricardo Montalban, who starred in *Star Trek: The Wrath of Kahn,* once quipped that there are five stages of Hollywood celebrity:

Year 1. Who is Ricardo Montalban?

Year 2. Bring me Ricardo Montalban.

Year 3. Bring me a Ricardo Montalban type.

Year 4. Bring me a younger Ricardo Montalban.

Year 5. Who is Ricardo Montalban?[18]

The Editor

The editor's work, essential to the creation of the film, is invisible to most moviegoers. The editor chooses the shots and places them in sequence. He or she creates the rhythm of the film and the pace at which it moves, boiling down literally miles of celluloid into the finished product. For example, the editor who cut Francis Ford Coppola's *Apocalypse Now* (1979) handled 1.25 million feet of film, which works out to around 230 hours of shots. The finished film ran 2 hours and 35 minutes.

Before the early 1990s, editors cut and glued films by hand on a noisy little machine called the **Moviola,** which was basically two reels on which film was spooled over a small light so that the editor could view it as it was cut. An editor working on a Moviola would trample miles of film underfoot.

Moviola
Simple editing machine made up of two reels on which film is spooled over a small light.

Any special effects, including such basics as a fade-out (in which the picture turns to black) or dissolve (in which an image is slowly replaced with another image) would require the film to be sent off to an optical shop—from which it wouldn't be returned for several days.

Most editing is now done on a computer, which allows the editor to plan out the sequence of the film digitally and minimizes the physical cutting and pasting of film stock. Special effects can be accomplished on the same computer system; a few dozen extras, for example, can be multiplied into thousands through the use of specialized software. Computers are in fact allowing several different jobs—such as film editing, sound editing, special effects, and animation—to converge into one, called digital effects editing. Editing is still a demanding, time-consuming profession, however, even with computers. Frame-by-frame editing is often required just to erase wires, replace skies, and remove blemishes from the face of a film's star.

Other Members of the Production Team

Several other members of the production team play important roles. The **cinematographer,** who is the director of photography, is in charge of the cameras and works with the director to set up shots. The **art director** designs the visual look of the film and oversees the set design, wardrobe, makeup, lighting, and everything else that contributes to that look. The **continuity supervisor,** sometimes called the script supervisor, makes sure that each day's shots match up. If an actor has beard stubble and a stained shirt in one day's shot, he has to have the same stubble and stain the next day if those shots are going to be cut together in the finished film. Since movies are shot out of sequence, with all the scenes at a particular location shot at the same time, scenes from the same day in the film might actually be shot a month or more apart.

Several mysterious-sounding job titles appear on movie credits. These include the **key grip,** who sees that the cameras are set up and moved; the **gaffer,** who is in charge of lighting; and the gaffer's assistant, who is known by the wildly sexist term **best boy.**

DISTRIBUTION

Distribution is probably the least understood aspect of the movie business. Just a few years ago distribution primarily involved the copying and delivery of prints of the film to theaters. While copying and delivery are still involved, distributors (who are usually part of a major studio) today are involved in marketing the film to every venue from giant IMAX theaters to individual cell phones. The easiest way to explain this area of the business is to look at marketing windows and film promotion.

Marketing Windows

A marketing window is an opportunity to sell, rent, or license a product to a different type of customer. Marketing windows for movies include domestic

In *King Kong* (2005), Naomi Watts is filmed against a plain green screen, and the scenery and giant ape hand are inserted digitally during editing.

 SELF QUIZ What are a gaffer, a key grip, and a best boy?

cinematographer
The director of photography.

art director
The person who designs the physical look of a film.

continuity supervisor
Film crew member in charge of making sure shots match up; sometimes called the script supervisor.

key grip
Member of film crew who sets up and moves cameras.

gaffer
Lighting director.

best boy
The gaffer's (lighting director's) assistant.

Domestic Theatrical	**Overseas Theatrical**	**Home Media**	**Television**
First run in U.S. theaters might last anywhere from one weekend to six months.	Usually begins several weeks after domestic debut.	Usually three to six months after domestic release.	Anywhere from three months (pay-per-view) to several years (syndication) after domestic release.

FIGURE 6.2 Motion Picture Marketing Windows Marketing windows are opportunities to sell, rent, or license a movie to a specific type of purchaser.

theatrical, international, home media, and various types of television (see Figure 6.2). These windows will continue to change as distributors experiment with ways to increase profits.

Domestic Theatrical

Domestic theatrical is the industry term for the release of movies to U.S. theaters. For this marketing window, distributors negotiate with theater owners about when a movie will be released, the length of run, the amount of lobby advertising, and the division of box office receipts. The box office split is typically 70/30 in the first few weeks of the run, with 70 percent going to the distributors and 30 percent to the theater owners.[19] The split is negotiable, however. For a star-filled blockbuster that the theater owner really wants to have, the split might be as high as 90/10 for the first two weeks. For longer runs the split becomes 50/50.[20]

Film studios now make more from movie theaters in other countries than they do from those in the United States. In Germany the tag line "Take a Stand" for *X-Men: The Last Stand* became "On Which Side Do You Stand?"

International

Up until the 1970s, domestic theatrical accounted for most of a feature film's revenue. Since then, box office revenues from Europe, Latin America, and Asia have become increasingly important. In fact, film studios now make more from movie theaters in other countries than they do from those in the United States. *Titanic* earned more than $1.1 billion internationally in 1998.

Concerns about potential international sales influence what kinds of movies are made. Action, special effects, and big-budget star vehicles are very popular in the international market. This is true even in countries such as India and China that have thriving film industries of their own. Producers can presell action films to the foreign market on the basis of the stars alone. Sometimes, this presell can cover production costs.

Culture and politics often become factors in international sales. *Babe,* the family movie that featured a lovable talking pig, was initially banned in Malaysia because of the Islamic prohibition on eating pork. *Anna and the King* (1999) was banned in Thailand because Thais believed it was critical of their kings. China, in particular, likes to throw its political weight around with U.S. film distributors, knowing that its 1.2 billion potential theatergoers represent a huge market for Hollywood films. China threatened to curtail Disney's business opportunities there if the studio went ahead with plans to make *Kundun* (1997), a film about the Dalai Lama, the religious leader of Tibet who disputes China's claim to ownership of that country. Disney did not give in to the Chinese demands, but the public threat gave notice to all studios that China would not tolerate films about issues it viewed as delicate.[21]

Home Media

DVD versions of movies have become extremely popular. DVDs are easy to use and contain a wealth of additional material, such as scenes that were deleted from the original movie, documentaries about the making of the movie, and director commentaries.

One of the most successful DVD rental companies is NetFlix. NetFlix is a mail-order service that allows its customers to pick out titles on the Web and rent three movies a month for a fixed monthly fee. Customers can keep the movies for as long as they like with no late fees. Netflix stocks about 60,000 different DVD titles, and on the average day sends out 35,000 to 40,000 of them. This means that every day, almost two of every three movies ever put onto DVD are rented by a Netflix customer.[22] This is an inventory that no video store or cable on-demand system can match. By 2006, Netflix had five million customers.

As mentioned earlier, movie studios are also arranging legal downloading services to take advantage of the home market, but illegal downloading and pirating continue to be major industry concerns. Pirating often puts a poor-quality copy of the movie on the streets long before the studio is willing to release it. This has a significant effect on the international market. The film industry reports that in some countries, such as Vietnam, nearly all DVDs are pirated, sometimes with government help. China also has a thriving trade in bootlegged movies. Because of pirating, studios now release their DVD versions 3 months after the movie's theatrical release; a few years ago, 12 months was standard. And the studios have experimented with even shorter distribution windows. In fact, in 2006, *Bubble,* a low-budget murder mystery directed by Steven Soderbergh, appeared in theaters, on cable, and on DVD—all on the same day. This strategy, called universal release, undercuts film pirates and also takes advantage of the marketing efforts for the theater release.

Meanwhile, Hollywood studios continue to make progress with their own online distribution systems, such as MovieLink and iMovies. Hollywood's downloading option, by whatever device it may be realized, is one more part of the transformation of movies from a big- to a small-screen experience and from a theatrical to a home—or even mobile—product. The real issue for the Hollywood studios is how they can dig into this potential gold mine without undermining their existing revenue streams.

Bubble (2006), a low-budget murder mystery directed by Steven Soderbergh, appeared in universal release—that is, in theaters, on cable, and on DVD, all on the same day.

Television

Television sales of movies begin with pay-per-view and on-demand cable and satellite services. Pay-per-view, the older service, provides showings on a set schedule, while digital on-demand services offer movies at any time. Both services offer movies for a one-time fee. In some cases, such as hotel services, movies can be sold to pay-per-view while they are still in general release. Pay-per-view for home customers starts around three months later. After another three months to a year, the feature is sold to premium cable

What is a marketing window? What are the marketing windows for movies?

SELF QUIZ

services such as Home Box Office (HBO), which might have exclusive rights to show the film for two or three months. Then the feature is sold to broadcast television, usually to one of the networks. Each of these marketing windows can be lucrative. ABC, for example, paid $60 million and $70 million, respectively, for the network rights to the first two Harry Potter movies.

When a movie is sold to broadcast television, it is edited to remove obscene dialogue and nudity, to achieve the proper length, and to insert spaces for commercials. Some distributors took editing for television a step further in the 1980s by **colorizing** their classic black-and-white films, a process that was controversial because it changed the original atmosphere and style of the film.

colorizing
Adding color to black-and-white films.

syndication
The process of selling media content to individual outlets.

After the network run, the movie is sold to individual stations on a market-by-market basis, a practice known as **syndication.** By the time the movie is syndicated, it is usually three to five years old.

The Studio Library

After all the original marketing windows have been exploited, the movie returns to the studio's library and becomes a permanent asset that can continue to generate profits virtually forever. Sometimes marketing experts will come up with new windows; individual musical numbers from Disney's cartoon features, for example, are cut up and marketed as compilations of sing-along home videos. Most experts predict that movies on the Internet will be a significant window as soon as the studios can figure out a way to prevent their piracy.

Publicity and Promotion

Another part of the distribution business is publicity and promotion. The basic idea is to make the movie an event, to create a buzz, to make people talk about it. Most publicity campaigns include setting up screenings for reviewers, sending the stars out on the talk-show circuit, throwing premiere parties, and starting an advertising blitz. Campaigns can include publicity stunts such as opening in more than 100 different countries at once, as was done in 2003 with *The Matrix: Revolutions*.

"Opening Big"

Every studio lives by the promotional rule of "opening big." If the movie achieves the number one box office spot on its opening weekend, it becomes an item in news reports. It becomes, by definition, an event. To win its opening weekend, the movie's promotional campaign has to start weeks, maybe even months, in advance. As the marketing chief of Warner Bros.

"Selling movies is like a volcanic eruption. You have to build as much pressure as you can on opening weekend so everyone pours out to see that particular movie."

pointed out: "Selling movies is like a volcanic eruption. You have to build as much pressure as you can on opening weekend so everyone pours out to see that particular movie."[23]

Trailers and Web Sites

The promotional campaign might start with a trailer that appears in theaters months before the movie is slated for release. **Trailers** are the brief (usually two- to three-minute) previews of coming attractions that give the viewers their first impression of the movie. They are especially important because they reach moviegoers as a captive audience, sitting in the theater, unconsciously deciding what films they might see in the near future. They are called trailers because they originally were shown *after* the feature film.

Movie Web sites include clips from the trailer and have become extremely important in movie promotion. The best ones reach teenage audiences effectively and create a buzz before the film is even released. The Web site for *The Blair Witch Project* (1999), for example, was credited with creating the buzz that enabled the $30,000 film to earn $140 million at the box office. That site featured faked police reports and newsreel-style interviews to create the illusion that everything in the movie was real.

Posters, Pull Quotes, and Reviews

The movie posters displayed in theater lobbies are another important form of promotion. These are designed to appeal to regular theatergoers and are distributed long before the movie is released. In fact, throughout movie history, so much care has gone into making the posters that many are now treated as works of art. One original poster for *The Mummy* (1932), starring Boris Karloff, sold at auction for more than $450,000.

The brief quotations printed on posters and ads are designed to relay the impression that critics think the movie is worth seeing. Critics are invited to advance screenings in the hope that they will write positive comments that can be extracted as blurbs. These blurbs are referred to in the industry as pull quotes, and are often selectively edited. Studios have been known to take a quotation like "This movie is a phenomenal waste of time"[24] and edit it down to "Phenomenal!" Sony Studios, at one point, actually made up a critic, identifying him as "David Manning of the Ridgefield Press." When the deception was discovered, Sony was forced to apologize.[25]

Tie-ins

In the movie industry, tie-ins are forms of promotion as well as revenue streams in their own right. **Tie-ins** consist of consumer products—toys, clothes, music, cereals, video games, and so on—that are built around movie characters, especially animated ones. Twelve companies, promoting more than 40 products, were official sponsors of the live-action version of Dr. Seuss's *The Cat in the Hat* (2003). Thirty other retailers featured *Cat* activities in their stores, and 75 companies produced *Cat* products. *The Passion of the Christ* (2004) had a best-selling tie-in book, a sound track album, and a line of tie-in jewelry, including pewter crucifixion nails. Some studios produce items like these and sell them in their own retail stores and theme parks, and all the studios license their characters to outside manufacturers and receive a fee of 10 percent of what those manufacturers make worldwide. The fee can be higher for blockbuster characters.

trailers
Brief previews of coming movies shown in theaters.

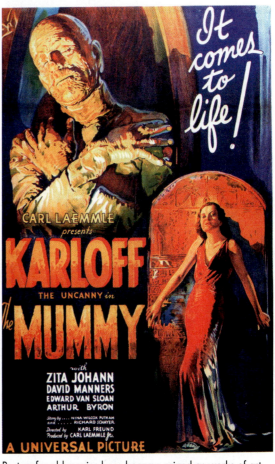

Posters for old movies have become prized as works of art. This poster for *The Mummy* sold for more than $450,000.

tie-ins
Consumer products built around movie characters.

SELF QUIZ What techniques are used to promote movies?

The Spider-Man films also created blockbuster tie-ins, especially at the toy store.

Tie-ins are a form of promotion because tie-in partners agree to buy advertising before and during a film's run that supplements the studio's own advertising.

The practice of creating tie-ins is often thought of as a recent development, but it is as old as moviemaking. Music was the first. Silent films came with musical scores that were played by orchestras in the pits of the movie palaces. Those scores were sold as sheet music and then later as recordings. Movie music continues to be a major revenue generator today.

Product Placement

In recent years, consumer goods companies have made wide use of **product placement**—the inclusion of a product in a movie for marketing purposes. Product placement (also known as *brand integration*) serves as a type of promotional tie-in as well as an additional source of revenue for the movie studio. Advertisers sometimes pay the studios outright for product placement, but often they merely arrange to promote the movie. For example, in the 2001 movie *Crocodile Dundee in Los Angeles,* the title character takes a friend to a Wendy's fast-food outlet, telling him it's "someplace really special." Wendy's did not pay for the placement but instead agreed to promote the film on its tray liners and in radio commercials.[26]

In *Talladega Nights: The Ballad of Ricky Bobby* product placement was written into the script to poke fun at over-the-top corporate sponsorship in Nascar races. The result was a film with unprecedented amounts of brand integration.

EXHIBITION

Exhibition—the showing of films in theaters—is the third rung of the movie industry, after production and distribution. This section of the chapter looks at two aspects of the exhibition segment of the movie industry: that of the theater and that of the audience.

The Theater

The chapter opener referred to some of the problems facing theaters today. Different types of theaters are devoted to the business of showing movies. Art theaters show experimental, avant-garde, and foreign films; second-run theaters show movies that have finished their initial run elsewhere; and specialty theaters show novelties such as large-screen IMAX films. The vast majority of movies, however, are shown in multiplexes, which are theaters with multiple screening rooms. Most multiplexes are owned by chains, such as Regal Cinema (6,273 screens), Loews Cineplex Entertainment (5,700 screens), and Carmike Cinemas (2,450 screens). Theater owners like multiplexes because they enable the owners to offer a variety of films while the costs—for projectionists, ushers, insurance, and so on—are spread out among the many screens.

The largest multiplexes are known as megatheaters. Megatheaters are multiplexes with 16 or more screens and deluxe accommodations such as

FACT FILE 6.3

All-Time Worldwide Blockbusters

This list of the top-grossing movies of all time proves the worldwide power of the teenage audience.

Rank	Total Gross	Title, Year Released
1	$1,835,300,000	*Titanic,* 1997
2	$1,129,219,252	*The Lord of the Rings: The Return of the King,* 2003
3	$1,058,692,843	*Pirates of the Caribbean: Dead Man's Chest,* 2006
4	$968,657,891	*Harry Potter and the Sorcerer's Stone,* 2001
5	$922,379,000	*Star Wars: Episode I—The Phantom Menace,* 1999
6	$921,600,000	*The Lord of the Rings: The Two Towers,* 2002
7	$919,700,000	*Jurassic Park,* 1993
8	$892,194,397	*Harry Potter and the Goblet of Fire,* 2005
9	$880,871,036	*Shrek 2,* 2004
10	$866,300,000	*Harry Potter and the Chamber of Secrets,* 2002

Source: Internet Movie Database, www.imdb.com, "All-Time Worldwide Boxoffice"; accessed November 2006.

high-fidelity sound systems and stadium-style seats with cup holders. Megatheaters are the new movie palaces. A 16-screen theater has around 5,000 seats, and some of the new megatheaters have as many as 30 screens.

Concession sales have always been profitable, and theater owners do not have to share these profits with studios (as they do with ticket sales). Popcorn, for example, yields more than 90 cents of profit on every dollar of popcorn sold. It also serves to make customers thirsty for sodas, another high-margin product. One theater chain executive went so far as to describe the cup holder mounted on each seat, which allows customers to park their soda while returning to the concession stand for more popcorn, as "the most important technological innovation since sound."[27] He also credited the extra salt added into the buttery topping on popcorn as the "secret" to extending the popcorn-soda-popcorn cycle throughout the movie.[28]

As discussed earlier in this chapter, the wave of the future for movie theaters will be digital projection.

The Audience

The mass movie attendance of the 1930s and the 1940s, in which most of the family would go to the theater together to see the same movie, doesn't exist anymore. Now there are multiple audiences—young, old, male, female— and the young are the largest of these. A quick glance at the all-time box office champions reveals the teenage appeal of most of these movies (see Fact File 6.3). The box office champions of the 1940s were far more family-oriented. The top five (in order of revenues) were *Bambi* (1942), *Pinocchio* (1940), *Fantasia* (1941), *Cinderella* (1949), and *Song of the South* (1946), all of which were full-length Disney features.[29]

"I thought it had a lot to say about evil villains who want to take over the world."

© The New Yorker Collection 2000 Bruce Eric Kaplan from cartoonbank.com. All Rights Reserved.

How have movie audiences changed since the golden age?

SELF QUIZ

Marketing research shows that young men usually select the film for a date and that 75 percent of the typical movie audience is white. Studios therefore tend to target a young, white, male audience by including action scenes and female nudity in their films. One studio executive described this audience as one that is "not concerned with the quality of film, or even whether it is in focus, as long as there is action and popcorn."[30] Because of the teenage audience, ticket sales are greatest during the summer, when every day is a school vacation day. The holiday season between Thanksgiving and early January provides the next largest audience.

Studios are thrilled by the fact that teens have a tendency to see certain movies repeatedly. Much of the success of the *Pirates of the Caribbean* movies was attributed to teens who went to see each of the movies two or three times.

Part of the power of the movie audience can be attributed to word of mouth. Some of the best evidence of this power is the way movies earn box office after the opening weekend. Some films open big but die off. *Godzilla* (1998) made $56 million in its opening weekend, but negative word of mouth caused a 60 percent falloff the next week. The much smaller production *My Big Fat Greek Wedding* (2001) made just $600,000 in its opening weekend. Attendance built slowly, but by the end of its first year the movie had earned more than $357 million, compared with *Godzilla*'s total of $136 million. When a film has that kind of staying power, the industry refers to it as "having legs."

Audiences also influence—or at least try to influence—the content of movies through lobbying and public interest groups. Every studio has been picketed or boycotted by one or more groups at one time or another.

Controversies

In terms of the controversies they engender, movies are victims of their own success. Critics say that people go to the movies for entertainment and escape without realizing the real-life impact of the experience. The make-believe world on the screen, they feel, promotes violence and social stereotypes in real life. Controversies about the effects of movies lead, in turn, to controversies about attempts to censor them.

EFFECTS OF MOVIE VIEWING

Movies have been blamed for a wide range of societal trends and individual effects, including the distortion of reality, violence, and stereotyping.

Distortions of Reality

docudramas
Fictional movies that dramatize real-life events.

Many critics worry that **docudramas,** fictional movies that dramatize real-life events, mislead audiences about historic facts. One film, *JFK* (1991), advanced an unproven theory about a conspiracy in the assassination of President John F. Kennedy. Another movie, *Capricorn One* (1978), seemed to suggest that the 1969 U.S. landing on the moon was a hoax. Today there are groups of people who believe the movie-inspired versions of both of these events.

Worries about the distortion of reality extend to even supposedly nonfictional movies. For example, a 1958 Walt Disney documentary, *White Wilderness,* "proved" that the northern rodents, lemmings, commit mass suicide by throwing themselves into the sea. This confirmed what was considered the conventional wisdom of the common metaphor for self-destructive behavior: "like lemmings into the sea." However, scientists now know that lemmings exhibit no such behavior, and critics assert that the producers of *White Wilderness* faked the filmed footage of that event by actually herding a group of pet lemmings over a cliff into the water.[31]

Violence

As we saw in Chapter 2, researchers have known since the 1920s that some viewers imitate what they see in movies. For many, the movie-viewing experience is an intense one. As mentioned earlier, movies are experienced in a darkened theater where most other stimuli are kept to a minimum. The viewer enters an almost dreamlike state as larger-than-life fantasies explode on the screen. It is no wonder that such a viewing experience can lead to imitation (see the Close-Up on Controversy box), especially in young people or troubled people of any age. This is especially worrisome when it comes to movie violence, which has always been controversial, from the first gunshot in Edwin Porter's *The Great Train Robbery* (1903) to the most recent action-adventure movie with a high body count such as the Kill Bill movies.

Anecdotal evidence is often used to demonstrate that the imitation of movie behavior does, in fact, take place. *Taxi Driver,* Martin Scorsese's 1976 film about a New York City cab driver stalking a political candidate, was cited by prosecutors as the inspiration for John W. Hinckley Jr.'s attack on President Ronald Reagan in 1981. A teenager in Los Angeles said that the movie *Scream* (1996) inspired him to kill his mother; in fact, he wanted to wear the "grim reaper" mask and use the voice-distorting box featured in the film, but he could not afford to buy them.

Anecdotal evidence is notoriously unreliable, however. For each story about a person imitating an evil behavior from the movies, there is another about movies being blamed for something they had nothing to do with. For example, the 1995 film *Money Train* was blamed for instigating a copycat murder in the New York City subway. Just as in the movie, two robbers squirted flammable liquid into a token booth and ignited it, burning the clerk to death while he begged for his life. Later, however, the prosecutor in the case announced that the similarity in crimes was just a coincidence. Neither of the criminals had even heard of the movie.[32]

Many of these cases wind up in the courts when families sue the studios. The studios generally win in court, but the cases can take years, and hundreds of thousands of dollars, to adjudicate. To avoid such costs and bad publicity, studios will sometimes cut an offending scene. Disney studios, for example, recalled all 1,300 prints of its 1993 movie *The Program* and deleted a scene from it. One teenager had been killed and two others critically injured while apparently imitating the scene, in which drunken college football players lie down in the middle of a busy highway to prove how tough they are.

 SELF QUIZ What is the anecdotal evidence that movie violence causes violence in real life? How reliable is that evidence?

Stereotyping

Stereotyping of women and minorities has always been a problem in the movies. In her book *From Reverence to Rape: The Treatment of Women in*

Smoking in the Movies

Concerns about the imitation of movie behavior are not limited to violence. There is a long list of health concerns about movie behavior, and smoking is at the top of the list. Sometime in the 1980s movie characters seemed to stop smoking, but in the 1990s they took it up again, this time with a vengeance. Half the movies released between 1990 and 2002 featured a major character who smoked, and three-quarters of all movies contained scenes that involved smoking.[1] Critics claimed that the glamorous image of smoking played a key role in the upsurge in cigarette use by teens during those same years.

Some critics have gone so far as to suggest banning any payments for tobacco product placement in movies.[2] In some municipalities, health departments negotiated with theater owners to play antismoking ads before the feature attraction. But at least one critic suggested that antismoking campaigns and attempts at censorship only make the problem worse:

> Films are merely exploiting the climate of repression and censorship surrounding tobacco, an atmosphere that those well-meaning efforts against smoking have brewed. . . . As the preaching becomes more intense, tobacco use is eroticized and surrounded by the odor of what is reckless and tabooed, intensifying pleasure. . . . In the end, the censor always incites aggressive curiosity about the very thing it aims to keep from view.[3]

Smoking is so much a part of movies that many already addicted stars make their characters smokers so that they can smoke during the filming. Several movie stars have also admitted that they became addicted to smoking because of film roles. Actor Kirk

In *Clerks II* (2006), director-writer-actor Kevin Smith (as Silent Bob, shown here with Jason Mewes) plays a character who smokes.

Douglas never smoked while he was growing up or in college or while he served in the navy. But after one role that required him to smoke, he was soon consuming three packs a day.[4] With that kind of addictive power, it's no mystery why critics become upset when movies encourage young people to try cigarettes.

[1]See, for example, Eric Lindblom, "Impact of Smoking in Movies on Youth Smoking Levels," *National Center for Tobacco-Free Kids Factsheet*, November 22, 2002. Available online at www.tobaccofreekids.org.
[2]Lance Donaldson-Evans, "From Silver Screen to Smoke Screen," letter to the editor, *New York Times*, July 21, 1997, p. A16.
[3]Richard Klein, "After the Preaching, the Lure of the Taboo," *The New York Times*, August 24, 1997, Sec. 2, pp. 1, 31.
[4]Kirk Douglas, "My First Cigarette, and My Last," *New York Times* online, May 16, 2003.

the Movies, Molly Haskell chronicled the ways women have been stereotypically depicted and the ways those stereotypes have changed over the years. For example, Haskell says, films made under the studio system during the 1930s and 1940s treated a large number of female characters as bubbleheaded. However, these films accorded their heroines more respect than films made in the supposedly liberated 1960s and 1970s, when movies started treating women as sex objects and victims of violence.[33]

Others insist that the treatment of women in the movies in the old days was nothing to be proud of. Feminists, for example, have pointed out that Rhett Butler essentially raped Scarlett O'Hara in the famous staircase scene in *Gone with the Wind,* and that movies have long been guilty of portraying women as "happy to have their own sexual choices and refusals crushed by such men."[34]

Some stereotypes of women can be especially eye-opening. Several critics pointed out that the movie *Fatal Attraction* (1987) depicted an extramarital affair as one in which a single career woman seduced and nearly destroyed a happily married man. According to these critics, the popularity of that film said something meaningful about the way Americans perceived career women. One critic claimed that the movie was part of a media backlash against feminism. The thesis of this backlash was that "American women were unhappy because they were too free; their liberation had denied them marriage and motherhood."[35]

The small number of women directors further fuels stereotyping concerns. Women have made great strides in the executive ranks of studios—there are dozens of successful women producers and top studio executives, and a

The point of view of women will be hard to find in American films until more women are allowed to direct movies.

handful of women directors, such as Patty Jenkins (*Monster*, 2003), and Sofia Coppola (*Lost in Translation*, 2003), have experienced success. But according to the Directors Guild of America, female directors work fewer than 5 percent of the total days guild members spend on theatrical films.[36] Because the director supplies the vision for the film, many believe that a woman's point of view is hard to find in American movies. They fear that the stereotyping of women will continue until women direct more mainstream movies.

Native Americans have been one of the most negatively stereotyped ethnic groups in American films. According to one critic, "The Indians are always going to slaughter somebody or they're running by a wagon train full of women and children and the women and children knock them off their horses. Every time they pull a trigger an Indian dies."[37] Most critics agree that the depiction of Native Americans has improved since the 1950s, when European American actors darkened their skins to play American Indians. Still, with the exception of occasional small independent films like *Smoke Signals* (1998), authentic presentations of the Native American experience have been nonexistent.

Critics say that portrayals of people of color (as well as groups marginalized on the basis of gender, ethnicity, class, or sexual orientation), by virtue of their rarity, have the potential to be more influential than depictions of whites. Those portrayals that do exist end up being read by some as strongly representative of the group. These depictions encourage viewers to stereotype members of the group in real life, at the same time that minority children form their images of identity partially through these representations. Sherman Alexie, a Native American author, says, "[As a child,] I watched the movies and saw the kind of Indian I was supposed to be."[38]

Italian Americans have long been stereotyped as Mafiosi in films such as *The Godfather* (1972) and *GoodFellas* (1990). Hispanics receive much the same treatment in movies like *Scarface* (1983), and American Muslims are routinely depicted as terrorists in movies such as *The Siege* (1998). Asians are stereotyped as intellectuals and martial arts experts. And stereotyped treatments go beyond race and gender. Businessmen have protested their depiction as crooked and insensitive, and religious people protested that clergy are often presented as flimflammers, as in *Elmer Gantry* (1960).

Movie producers respond to much of the criticism about stereotyping by pointing out that stereotypes are a time-honored ingredient in storytelling. The cute, scatterbrained blond secretary, the awkward computer geek with tape on his eyeglasses, and the gruff-but-benign boss are efficient shortcuts to establishing character. It is basically unfair, they say, that every group wants a positive image in films, especially when there is controversy about what a positive image is. For example, they say, films that depict blacks as inner-city criminals and welfare recipients are attacked as perpetuating stereotypes. Black organizations sued to block the filming of *Fort Apache, the Bronx* (1981) for that reason. When blacks are portrayed in clean middle-class neighborhoods, the films are attacked as lacking authenticity and for suggesting that social problems no longer exist for African Americans. Some independent studios have tried to combat the problem of stereotyping by encouraging women and minority members to make films. The Sundance Institute sponsors an annual Native Screenwriting Workshop, one of which produced the script for *Smoke Signals*.

Why is stereotyping a problem, and how do producers explain their use of it?

SELF QUIZ

CENSORSHIP

Film censorship may occur when individuals, groups, or governments feel that a particular movie is immoral or is not in the public interest. Some of the harshest forms of movie censorship occur overseas. In Afghanistan, when religious fundamentalists took control of the government in the 1990s, one of the first things they did was close all the movie theaters and burn all the movies. They then ordered the destruction of all videocassette recorders and videotapes, as well as all TVs and satellite dishes. According to these fundamentalists, movies were the primary cause of corruption in society. (Movies and other forms of media have returned to Afghanistan in recent years.) Other countries have milder forms of official censorship. England has its Board of Film Classification, which rates and censors film, requiring studios to cut any scenes it considers objectionable.

In the United States, most attempts at governmental censorship of films are eventually overturned in the courts on First Amendment grounds. In 1988, some municipalities banned *The Last Temptation of Christ* because they found it sacrilegious. They objected to the film's humanizing of Christ, particularly in terms of his sexual fantasy involving Mary Magdalene. A judge overturned the ban.[39] In 1997, police in Oklahoma raided video stores, seizing copies of *The Tin Drum* (1979), an Academy Award winner for Best Foreign Picture. They believed a scene suggesting sex between children violated child pornography laws. That case was also overturned.

The First Amendment only protects against government censorship, and in the United States, as in other countries, censorship is often initiated by private citizens. Several groups have picketed theaters and boycotted studios. The Southern Baptist Convention, for example, charged in 1998 that Disney was "pushing a Christian bashing, family bashing, pro-homosexual agenda" in its films.[40] The convention's leadership urged its members to boycott all Disney films and products. Not long afterward, a committee of the Texas Board of Education voted to sell its $45 million in Disney stock. Ironically, Disney itself was accused of censorship when it refused to distribute Michael Moore's film *Farenheit 9/11* in 2004.

How does film censorship in the U.S. compare with censorship in other countries?

SELF QUIZ

Movie Ratings

Movie ratings were established by the industry to avoid government censorship. The controversy began in 1922, following the Fatty Arbuckle scandal. Arbuckle, a star of silent films, had been accused and tried three times of murdering a young woman following a drunken party. Twice the trial ended in a hung jury, and the third time the star was acquitted. The scandal rocked Hollywood and brought unwanted attention from the halls of Congress. Congress was considering cleaning up the industry by censoring movies before the rest of the country became decadent from Hollywood's example.

In response, the film industry formed a trade group to make such official censorship unnecessary by overseeing movie production and keeping it wholesome. Will Hays, an elder in the Presbyterian Church and a former U.S. postmaster general, headed the group. The industry authorized Hays to prevent the release of films until producers complied with his demands. He proceeded to remove any references to sex, including any mention of breastfeeding or the pain of childbirth.

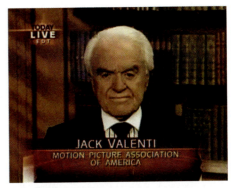

Jack Valenti is the creator of the Motion Picture Association of America rating system. On the *Media World* DVD that accompanies this book (track 12), he discusses the effectiveness of movie ratings.

The Motion Picture Production Code was put in place in 1930, formalizing the kind of rules that Hays had been making up as he went along. For example, if a single bed appeared in a scene with a man and a woman, both actors had to have one foot on the floor. This is the reason that films of this era nearly always depicted the marital bedroom as having two beds. The Hays rules limited not just sex but also violence and activities such as disrespecting the U.S. government or allowing criminals to go unpunished.

The power of the Motion Picture Production Code was diminished when the director Otto Preminger released *The Moon Is Blue* (1953) without the code's seal of approval. The film was both a financial and critical success. Preminger repeated his success with *The Man with the Golden Arm* (1955), also released without the seal, and the code died out altogether. It was eventually replaced with the movie rating system we have today.

The current movie rating system, established in 1968, switched the industry's control from censoring content to simply notifying the audience, especially parents, about that content. This code was revised in 1984 to include the PG-13 rating, and again in 1990 to change the X rating, which had become a form of advertising for pornographic movies, to NC-17. The current ratings are as follows:

NC-17: No children under age 17 should be admitted.

R: Restricted for anyone under age 17 unless accompanied by an adult.

PG-13: Parental guidance suggested for children under 13.

PG: Parental guidance—may be unsuitable for preteens.

G: Suitable for general audiences and all ages.

While some producers still see them as a form of censorship, the ratings (which are strictly voluntary) remain controversial mostly because of lax enforcement that enables many underage kids to see R movies without being accompanied by an adult.

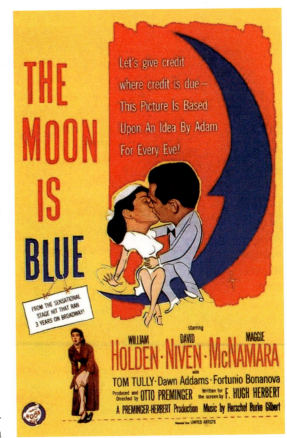

The power of the Motion Picture Production Code was diminished when the director Otto Preminger released *The Moon Is Blue* (1953) without the code's seal of approval.

Summing Up

Movies are both a form of entertainment and an intriguing business. They began as simple peep shows and developed into increasingly sophisticated and complex presentations as viewer demand caught up with technological advances. Thomas Edison developed some of the first motion picture cameras and projectors and created the Motion Picture Patents Company (known as the Trust), which monopolized the New York–based industry. To escape the control of this company, filmmakers moved to Los Angeles, where the first great studios and the star system began. In Hollywood, the studios were run like factories and the star system guaranteed success at the box office.

Tiny nickelodeons showed silent films, and later movie palaces showed the first sound movies to crowds of thousands. Movie admissions peaked in the 1940s and then declined with the advent of television. To compete with television, many movies became wide-screen spectaculars and dealt with adult topics. Today, the age of the movie palace is returning with luxurious multiplexes that give moviegoers their choice of dozens of screens.

Movies are produced with many marketing windows in mind. After the theatrical release there is the international market, DVDs and other types of home media, including downloads for computers and cell phones, and the various types of television sales, including pay-per-view, cable, broadcast network, and syndication. Retail merchandise, theme park attractions, promotional tie-ins, and product placements also generate revenue for the studios. Huge sums of money are generated in the production, distribution, and promotion of films, but the industry as a whole is one of the least profitable media enterprises. Investors routinely lose money in films, and theater owners rely on concession sales for profits.

Of the hundreds of names that scroll by in the final credits, the most important are the producer, who raises the money to make the film; the director, who provides the creative vision, and the editor, who assembles the film and gives it its rhythm and pace. The finished movies are promoted to become events in the mind of the audience. All forms of media are used to advertise them, including some that are unique to the industry, such as trailers and lobby posters.

The primary controversies are of two types: Movies seem to promote violence, stereotyping, and unhealthy habits such as smoking; and they are often censored, which upsets those who view them as art and free speech forms of expression. Movie ratings were established by the industry to avoid government censorship.

Key Terms

These terms are defined and indexed in the Glossary of key terms at the back of the book.

HISTORY

Web Excursion

1. What is your all-time favorite film? Choose one, and search the Web for references to it. Prepare a brief history of this film, based solely on information found on the Web.

INDUSTRY

Web Excursion

2. Can you tell when a movie uses digital effects? Special effects are not always as obvious as you might think. Directors often make changes to a movie in postproduction, after the cameras have stopped rolling. Go to the Web site of Custom Film Effects at http://customfilmeffects.com/.* Click the Demos link and view some "before" and "after" shots of subtle changes made to motion pictures that you might not have noticed. How does this capability change the planning and process that goes into making a film?

CONTROVERSIES

Web Excursion

3. Do movie critics take violence and stereotyping into consideration when reviewing a film? Search the Web for reviews of recent movies you have seen or go directly to a site specializing in reviews such as Roger Ebert's Reviews at www.suntimes.com/ebert. Prepare a statement discussing how these controversies do or do not affect the review.

Media World DVD Excursion

4. View track 12, *Are Movie Ratings Effective?* (from NBC's *Today* show).

Jack Valenti, creator of the movie rating system, and Matthew Felling, director of the Center for Media and Public Relations, discuss the merit of film ratings. Do you think ratings should change as society's tolerance for sex and violence changes? In regard to keeping inappropriate content away from minors, how much responsibility should lie in the hands of the MPAA and how much with parents? Why do you think parents and conservative groups are more sensitive to sexual content than violence? Do you believe ratings and box office revenue are mutually exclusive?

ONLINE LEARNING CENTER WWW.MHHE.COM/RODMAN2

You may access these and additional Web excursions at the Online Learning Center for the book (www.mhhe.com/rodman2). Visit the student portion of this Web site to also access the *Interactive Timeline of Mass Media Milestones,* chapter highlights, self quizzes, and recommended readings, movies, and documentaries for this chapter.

*Some Web site addresses may change. When they do, please search for the Web site by name or topic on your favorite search engine.

Recordings and the Music Industry

Copyright Battles, Format Wars

7

Chapter Highlights

HISTORY: Both copyright laws and recording formats have evolved over the years to make the music business an intensely profitable one—in spite of its current problems with digital file sharing.

INDUSTRY: The recording industry is made up of four major corporate labels and hundreds of independent labels that act as talent scouts for innovative groups and musical styles.

CONTROVERSIES: The primary controversies that concern critics of the recording industry are of two types: the effects of music and its censorship. The two are related—those who are worried about the negative effects of music are often the ones who call for some type of censorship.

The iPod Revolution

The introduction and immediate acceptance of the iPod has been called a media revolution. The brainchild of Steve Jobs, who was the cofounder of Apple Computer Inc. and one of the pioneers of the computer age, the iPod was designed to be used in conjunction with Apple's iTunes, a legal downloading site. Both have been hugely successful. In fact, the iPod has made Apple the leader in worldwide portable digital audio players (also known as MP3 players) and is revolutionizing the online music business.

So many people are plugged into the easy-to-spot white earbuds that some pundits are

The iPod revolutionized the online music industry, and has been culturally influential in a number of ways.

"Please select hymn number 637 on your i-pods."

referring to them as the "iPod Nation." Every age group seems drawn to the device, including young children, teenagers, soccer moms, and grandparents. President Bush has an iPod. His personal assistant downloads songs into it. A cottage industry has even sprung up to serve those iPod owners who don't have enough time to download their favorite CDs to the device themselves.

The iPod's success has made it a cultural phenomenon. It has changed the way people listen to music. People download all their favorite songs and hit the "shuffle" function and get a whole new appreciation of how their musical choices fit together. Radio stations are becoming concerned; parents are suddenly finding that the kids aren't arguing any more over which station to play in the car. Family trips are a lot quieter with each family member plugged into his or her own pod. Perhaps in response, radio stations have come up with new formats, "Bob" and "Jack," that shuffle a mix of well-known hits for different age groups.

The pricey iPod ($150 to $450) has even started a small crime wave of thefts and muggings.

Often, the victims say the worst part of the loss is their missing music—sometimes thousands of songs at a time.

The iPods' popularity has created a huge market for accessories, including everything from mounting devices and protective cases to devices that help iPods take on new chores. Many users have come to depend on their iPods for these secondary uses. For example, the iTalk makes the iPod a digital voice recorder; with its 40-gigabyte hard drive, that allows journalists to store multiple interviews and access them easily to meet deadlines. Other iPod owners use them as personal organizers, for audio-books, and for games. Video iPods are used to view movies and TV programs, and some mobile phone models are now equipped for iTunes. By 2007, several major automakers were offering iPod-ready sound systems.

Perhaps most significantly, the iPod has introduced the idea of *podcasting*, which lets consumers listen to audio content at their convenience on their iPods or another MP3-enabled audio players. Users find audio content on the Web—it could be music, talk, or a combination—and download

it to their pods. They can, in fact, set up a regular feed and have the podcasts delivered automatically to their computers.

The iPod has also revolutionized the concept of legal downloading, causing the music industry to breathe a loud sigh of relief. The ad campaign that features supercool 20-somethings gyrating to their favorite tunes made it cool to buy music instead of stealing it, and the iTunes music store made those purchases economical. Of course, in its fight against illegal downloading, the pod had help from a 2005 Supreme Court decision that allowed copyright holders to sue peer-to-peer (P2P) services such as Grokster and Kazaa as well as from a music industry that was pursuing hundreds of lawsuits against illegal downloaders, including college students. Some users were also afraid of picking up viruses in unauthorized downloads. By 2006, there were almost as many legal downloads as illegal ones, and experts assured the industry that legal downloads would soon be in the majority. The music industry might erect a monument to Steve Jobs some day soon.

How will the recording industry adapt to the new media such as the iPod and the Internet? To answer that question, this chapter examines both the history and the current practices of the music business, as well as some other controversies this industry has generated over the years.

The recording industry is a diverse one. By far the biggest and most influential part of the industry is popular music. Although this chapter focuses primarily on music, we should also note that the recording industry includes everything from books on tape (which we discussed in Chapter 3) to movies on video (which we looked at in Chapter 6) to the recycling of television programs on DVD (which we examine in Chapter 9).

A Brief History *of Recording*

The history of recording can be viewed as a series of copyright battles and format wars. A **copyright,** which we will discuss in more depth in Chapter 14, is a legal right that grants to the owner of a work protection against unauthorized copying. With every new recording technology, from printed sheet music to Internet downloads, the music industry has faced a new set of copyright battles.

Format wars occur when companies selling specific types of recording and playback devices try to put competing companies with competing formats out of business. Such wars began with the earliest recording technology, but the history of the music on which the industry is based started much earlier.

copyright
A legal right that grants to the owner of a work protection against unauthorized copying.

format wars
Rivalries in which companies selling specific types of recording and playback devices try to put competing formats out of business.

MUSIC IN AN ORAL CULTURE

Music has been with us for a long time. The most ancient works of art depict musicians, and some of the oldest artifacts preserved in museums are

Before the popularity of recordings, music was distributed by sheet music. Some popular songs could sell as many as one million copies as sheet music.

musical instruments. Early performers of music included religious choirs, court musicians, and military bands. Some early civilizations, especially the Chinese, believed that music had magical powers.

Before the printing era (which is to say, in the time of oral culture), musicians composed, played, and sang songs for their own enjoyment or for whatever payment they might receive for live performances. When a method of writing music was finally invented around the year AD 1000, it was used to preserve church music. No one bothered to write down secular music, although some lyrics were preserved and are considered great poetry today.[1]

During the European Renaissance, which began in the 14th century, composers began to create, and to write down, what we now call classical music. Even the classical composers, however, wrote only as a sideline. Johann Sebastian Bach (1685–1750), one of the most famous composers of all time, was paid only as an organist and choirmaster, not as a composer, though part of his job was to write the music he played.

During the 1700s, there was a frenzied demand for classical music. The public eagerly attended performances of new works with all the fervor of

The lute, an ancestor of the guitar, was already an ancient musical instrument when this painting was created in the 15th century.

How did ownership of music differ in an oral culture from in a print culture?

SELF QUIZ

phonograph
Thomas Edison's name for his first recording device.

analog recording
A recording technique in which representation of the sound wave is stored directly onto the recording medium.

digital recording
A recording technique in which sound is broken down electronically into a numerical code.

nickelodeons
Early jukeboxes set up in amusement arcades.

fans seeking out new rap music today. In fact, Joseph Haydn produced some 100 symphonies and Wolfgang Amadeus Mozart produced an incredible 600 works before he died at the age of 35. With all their success, however, Haydn and Mozart depended on wealthy patrons who were interested in art, rather than on the listening public.

In the 1800s some serious classical musicians started to study folk music, and when the Industrial Revolution ushered in high-speed printing, printed music became big business. People would buy music to play on their pianos and other instruments at home, while family and friends sang along. In 1831, because of pressure from music publishers, music was included in U.S. copyright law for the first time. A best-selling song could sell more than a million copies as sheet music. Music publishers jealously guarded their copyrights, but the real copyright battles began with the advent of recording technology.

EARLY RECORDING TECHNOLOGY

The recording industry, like the movie industry, began with Thomas Edison. In 1877 Edison made the first recording of a human voice, using a device he called a **phonograph,** which was basically a metal cylinder, a horn, and a hand crank.[2] (Originally a trademark, the name eventually became generic for all home record players.) The cylinder had grooves cut into it and was wrapped with a thin sheet of tinfoil. In his first successful recording, Edison slowly turned the crank by hand to make the cylinder rotate and spoke the words "Mary had a little lamb" into the wide part of the horn.[3] The concentrated sound waves at the narrow end of the horn caused a needle to vibrate. The needle "wrote" the sound vibrations into the foil. The same apparatus played back the recording, using the larger horn to amplify the weak vibrations picked up by the needle.

Edison's phonograph used the basic principles of **analog recording,** a technique that survives to this day. In analog recording, a representation of the sound wave is stored directly into the recording medium. In contrast, **digital recording,** such as that used in today's Internet downloads and CDs, breaks the sound down electronically and assigns each note a numerical code based on a series of 1s and 0s.

The initial sound from the phonograph was of such poor quality that Edison planned to market it only as a dictating machine; he imagined that business executives would use it to record letters and memos to be typed later. The sound improved in 1888 when Edison switched to wax cylinders, and he began to realize that the device might have some entertainment potential. He set up several "phonograph parlors," where amazed customers could listen to recorded sound for a nickel per play. Several other entrepreneurs set up similar machines in amusement arcades. Like the early movie theaters that would come later, these were called **nickelodeons.** They were popular attractions, which led Edison to realize that the phonograph might have promise as home entertainment.

AN INDUSTRY DEVELOPS

Several other entrepreneurs and inventors were experimenting with recorded sound around the same time as Edison. In 1888 an engineer in Alexander

Graham Bell's telephone laboratories, Emile Berliner, patented a device he called the **gramophone.** The gramophone was similar to Edison's phonograph, but it played a flat disc with lateral grooves cut on one side. These discs were easier to mass-produce and were less expensive than the cylinders, although the early cylinders did have a better sound quality. Berliner helped set up the Victor Talking Machine Company in 1901. Its ads featured a cute little dog, Nipper, listening intently to a gramophone horn with the slogan "His Master's Voice" underneath the picture.

gramophone
Early playback device using a flat disc with lateral grooves cut on one side.

Cylinders versus Discs

Soon both Victor's gramophone and Edison's phonographs were selling well, as were the cylinders and discs people played on them. This was the beginning of the first format war. People were either disc people or cylinder people, and (as in the PC and Macintosh rivalry of today) owners extolled the virtues of their choice and denigrated the competition. Collectors began to build libraries of recorded music, mostly classical pieces and Tin Pan Alley favorites such as "Alexander's Ragtime Band." **Tin Pan Alley** was the district in New York City where songs were written "on order" for Broadway shows; its name was shared with pop music that was supposedly of short-lived appeal. (*Tin pan* was slang for a cheap, tinny piano.) **Ragtime** also became popular at this time, with hit songs such as Scott Joplin's "Maple Leaf Rag." At first performed primarily by blacks, ragtime was instrumental music that had a steady, syncopated beat. (In syncopation, the accents are placed on beats that are normally unaccented.)

Tin Pan Alley
District in New York City where songs were written "on order" for Broadway shows.

ragtime
Instrumental music with a steady, syncopated beat.

The first format war was between Edison's phonograph, which used a cylinder, and Victor's Victrola, which used a disk.

Victrola
Early hand-cranked record player introduced by the Victor Company.

Recording technology continued to improve as other companies entered the business. New models hitting the market made prized household appliances obsolete in just a few years—an unheard-of amount of time for obsolescence. What was to become the best-selling model of record player, the **Victrola,** was introduced by the Victor Company in 1906. The first Victrolas were hand-cranked, but they were affordable and they were designed as presentable pieces of hardwood parlor furniture. They quickly became so popular that the trademarked name nearly became a generic word because people called all phonograph players designed as household furniture Victrolas.

Edison began to produce his own cabinet-model phonographs, and then he added an improved spring-driven motor. The Victor Company countered with an electric motor. Early radio tubes were adapted for amplification. Alexander Graham Bell's microphone, developed from his telephone transmitter, was modified to improve the recorded music. Seventy-eight revolutions per minute (78 rpm) became the industry standard speed. Disc and cylinder materials became more durable and produced better sound when soft wax was replaced with harder wax and then shellac. Hit music of the time ranged from John Philip Sousa's marches to such popular tunes as "Meet Me in St. Louis, Louis."

Tin Pan Alley publishers joined forces to form the American Society of Composers, Authors and Publishers (ASCAP) in 1914, to fight for strong copyright laws. In these early days, however, the piracy of recorded music wasn't much of an issue, because recording technology was expensive and controlled by patents. In fact, when U.S. copyright law was revised in 1909, the industry's main concern was that the law would cover rolls for player pianos. These perforated sheets for self-playing pianos had become a popular form of "published" music.

The Victory of the Disc

Victrola discs were easier to mass-produce and were less expensive than cylinders. As the technology improved, the discs also produced sound that was equal in quality to that produced by cylinders. Edison finally switched to discs in 1913. He called them Diamond Discs because they were played with a diamond stylus needle that improved on the earlier sound quality.

Who were the opponents in the first format war?

SELF QUIZ

Edison continued to market cylinders until 1929 for those who had bought his earlier machines, but the disc had already won the first format war. There would be many others.

ENTER RADIO

After World War I ended in 1918, records became a popular form of home entertainment. The birth of commercial radio in the 1920s, however, caused some major changes in the recording industry. At first it spurred sales, because people wanted to hear the records at home that they were hearing on the radio. Jazz recordings became hot, and then big bands and country music. Dance crazes, then as now, would sell records. Composers wrote music specifically for new dances such as the Charleston and the Black Bottom. People bought the records and practiced the dances at home. The Radio Corporation of America (RCA) entered the industry in 1929 by buying out the Victor Company and forming a division called RCA Victor. The new company manufactured records and players. RCA Victor kept the Nipper mascot, which soon became one of the most famous trademarks of all time.

RCA was soon converting most of its phonograph factories to radio factories, as live radio caused a big dip in record sales during the 1930s. With the financial problems encountered during the Great Depression, people had little money to buy records. Those who could afford a phonograph or a radio usually had to choose one or the other. Most chose the latter, since in addition to music, radio also provided comedy, drama, and up-to-the minute news reports.

The recording industry suffered during the 1930s. Still, music continued to be an important part of American culture. Jukeboxes made swing music and jitterbug dances such as the Lindy Hop popular, as did recording stars such as Bing Crosby, who was also being seen in movies. In fact, there was a considerable amount of synergy between the recording industry and talking pictures, as people bought records made by celebrities they saw and heard at the movies.

The 1940s saw several Latin American dance crazes, including the rumba, the conga, the samba, the mambo, and the cha-cha. Production of consumer phonographs was halted during World War II, however, as factories and engineers alike turned to the war effort. The Japanese invasion of Southeast Asia cut off the supply of shellac, the base material that was used for disc records. Record manufacturers switched to vinyl, a plastic resin derived from petroleum. Vinyl turned out to be a vastly superior material, more durable and with less surface noise. It would eventually make possible the long-playing (LP) record, an essential part of the stereo and high-fidelity movement that would take shape after the war.

SELF QUIZ What effects did radio have on the recording industry?

STEREO AND HIGH FIDELITY

The technology of recording entered a new phase after World War II. Times were prosperous and people felt like celebrating—and music has always been an integral part of human festivities. People were now able to take advantage of some of the technology that had been developed during the war. Some of this technology had been around for a while but had not been commercially successful during the leaner years. The **jukebox,** or coin-operated phonograph, for example, had been introduced by the Automatic Music Instrument Company (AMI) in 1927. It had replaced a few coin-operated pianos during the 1930s, but sales were slow until the postwar years, when every tavern and soda shop in America acquired one of Wurlitzer's or Rock-Ola's ornate, classic machines. Frank Sinatra and Patti Page records became huge jukebox hits.[4]

Most of the technical advances in sound recording of the 1930s had been produced in laboratories such as Bell Labs and developed by the motion picture industry as movie sound. Speaker systems were developed with separate **woofers,** which were large speakers used to reproduce low frequencies, and **tweeters,** which were small speakers used to reproduce high sounds. High-quality electric recording had replaced the more primitive method that Edison had used. With the older method, just one sound was recorded, essentially using just one **track,** or recorded sound source. Electric recording made it possible to separate the sections of entire orchestras, with each section given its own microphone and audio circuit. This multitrack recording made **stereophonic sound** possible, allowing tracks to be placed in the right or left speaker, or in "the center" by being played equally on the right and left speakers. This enhanced the realism of the recorded sound by reproducing the directional and spatial impressions of the concert hall.

By 1958, world standards for stereo records had been established, and the first stereo LPs were sold. LPs ran at the speed of 33⅓ rpm, which allowed much more music to be put on each record. Acceptance of LPs was slow at first because it required the purchase of a new record player, but the

jukebox
A coin-operated phonograph.

woofers
Large speakers that reproduce low sounds.

tweeters
Small speakers that reproduce high sounds.

track
A single recorded sound source, used in multitrack recording.

stereophonic sound
Recording technique in which tracks are placed individually in the right or left speaker.

new format could offer an entire symphony or Broadway musical on one disc. RCA Victor had introduced the seven-inch, 45 rpm single a few years earlier, and most people still had a stack of old 78s. Because of this, most phonographs produced during the 1950s operated (with the flip of a switch) on all three speeds: 78, 33⅓, and 45. Production of 78s, however, had stopped.

Vinyl LPs, electronic recording, and stereo sound ushered in the high-fidelity era of the 1950s. **High-fidelity (hi-fi) sound** was recorded "true" to the original. Enthusiasts began to buy separate components to achieve the best possible sound, and the comparisons of amplifiers (amps), speaker power, and tuning capacity were every bit as intense as today's conversations about random-access memory, processor chips, and hard drive size.

Magazines and books were published for the home audio hobbyist, and newspapers began to publish hi-fi columns. Most of the enthusiasm was initially about the technology, but a new form of programming, rock and roll, was right around the corner.

ROCK AND ROLL

By 1947, the popular music industry had come under the control of six large record companies: Columbia, Victor, Decca, Capitol, MGM, and Mercury. The big labels pushed a mainstream music style that was epitomized by the crooning of Bing Crosby and the happy ditties of Perry Como and Doris Day. A big hit song of 1947 was "All I Want for Christmas Is My Two Front Teeth." The hits of the early 1950s were at the same level of sentimental simplicity, with songs such as "How Much Is That Doggy in the Window?" In fact, the most popular song of the 1950s, "Tennessee Waltz," sung by Patti Page, would be considered too low-key for most country-and-western radio stations today.

Teenagers, however, rejected the mainstream sound. A minor label, Essex, released the first national rock hit, Bill Haley's "Crazy Man Crazy," in 1953. Haley soon signed with the major label Decca, with which he recorded two of his greatest hits in 1954: "Shake, Rattle and Roll," and "Rock

Around the Clock." Those two hits brought rock music into the mainstream. Rock and roll combined elements of rhythm and blues, gospel, and country. It was, from the beginning, teenage music. It spoke to teenagers. It defined them. It was sexy. The very term *rock and roll* was said to describe the movements of sexual intercourse. Whether it was used for that or just for dancing, it had a beat that could not be ignored.

Many attribute the invention of rock and roll to a Memphis disc jockey named Sam Phillips. In 1952, Phillips had started a record label to record the new strains of rhythm and blues he was hearing from the black community. Phillips discovered a young singer named Elvis Presley and recorded his first single, "That's All Right" (see the Close-Up on History box). Like Bill Haley before him, Elvis moved on to a major label, RCA, where he recorded several hits in 1956, including "Don't Be Cruel" and "Hound Dog." He became immensely popular and defined rock music until the 1960s when the Beatles and other British groups, such as the Rolling Stones, entered the picture.

Elvis borrowed many of his songs from the black community. He adapted the black musical style, borrowing from rhythm and blues and gospel and adding it to the white hillbilly sound of the day. He proved how successful black music could be with a white artist on the album cover, a practice known as covering. Covering became an accepted industry practice as white singers like Pat Boone began releasing traditionally black tunes that had been toned down and cleaned up a bit. The practice enabled major

high-fidelity (hi-fi) sound
Recorded sound true to the original.

What were the technological advances that helped create the high-fidelity era of the 1950s?

What was the impact of rock and roll on the recording industry?

Elvis Lives

One of the services that Sam Phillips's little Memphis recording studio offered was make-your-own vanity records. The studio charged $3.98 (plus tax) per record as a way of making ends meet. In the summer of 1953, a shy 18-year-old named Elvis Presley became a customer. Shuffling his feet and mumbling "Yes, sir" and "No, ma'am," Presley explained that he wanted to make a record as a surprise for his mother. Phillips would later discover that the Presleys didn't own a record player.

Elvis and his parents had moved to Memphis from Tupelo, Mississippi, when he was 13. He was always interested in music, and Memphis radio stations played black blues singers, white hillbilly singers, and gospel singers of both races. A full year after Elvis cut his vanity record, Phillips was looking for a singer for a band he was putting together. He called Elvis and asked him if he would like to audition. Elvis said, "Yeah, I guess so."

The next day Elvis showed up at the studio, with his name spelled out on his guitar in little stick-on letters. The recording session was uninspired. Then, during a break, as one of the other group members describes it, "Elvis all of a sudden jumped up—nervous energy is what it was—and started frailin' guitar and singin' 'That's All Right, Mama.'"[1] The other group members joined in, and Phillips heard them. "Y'all figure out what you're doin' and let's put it on tape," he said. Phillips gave the song to a local disc jockey, and within 24 hours Elvis had a local hit. He went on the road with his group, driving all night to nickel-and-dime gigs with a box of the records in the trunk. If they passed a radio station, they would go in and give the DJ a copy.

RCA bought Elvis's contract from Phillips, paying him $40,000, the most any label had ever paid for a singer. By 1955, Elvis was appearing on network television, photographed from the waist up because his gyrations were considered too lewd for the great American audience at home. The girls in the audience screamed so loudly that they drowned out the music. Elvis was drafted in 1958, and his induction into the army started a slump in the music business that didn't end until the Beatles arrived in 1963.

By the time Elvis died in 1977, he had sold 41 million albums, recorded 107 Top 40 hits, and made 33 movies. Bing Crosby died that same year. By comparison, Crosby had sold 500 million records, recorded 1,600 hit songs, and made 61 movies, but his influence on today's music and today's industry was minimal compared with Elvis's. Elvis was the original alternative rocker. To snobs, his very name is a joke. To fans, he still lives, more than a quarter century after his death.

[1]Scotty Moore, quoted in "Elvis Lives," *Newsweek,* August 18, 1997, p. 55.

When Elvis was drafted into the army in 1958, it started a slump in the music business. Here, not long after his induction, Elvis visits Bill Haley, who had sung the first national rock hit five years earlier.

Where did rap music originate? What's the difference between rap and hip-hop?

SELF QUIZ

rap
Music composed of rhymed speech over drumbeats.

hip-hop
The backing music for rap; also refers to the culture of rap.

The 1996 murder of Tupac Shakur, shown here with Death Row Records Chairman Marion Suge Knight, was believed to be caused by the rivalry between East Coast and West Coast factions of rap music culture.

labels to take advantage of the vibrancy and originality of black music without threatening their primarily white listeners. Two African Americans who did manage to break through with their own acts were Chuck Berry and Little Richard. Disc jockeys who contributed to the growth of rock and roll by playing this music include Alan Freed in New York and Wolfman Jack in southern California.

By 1959, rock music had hit a lull. On a day that has been memorialized as "the day the music died,"[5] three of rock and roll's biggest stars, Buddy Holly, Richie Valens, and the Big Bopper, were killed in a plane crash. During the same time, Elvis was in the army, Little Richard was in a seminary, and Chuck Berry and several others were having legal problems and had dropped out of sight. Rock went into a type of doldrums, and once again heavily promoted, clean-cut stars like Rickie Nelson and Brenda Lee were singing saccharine songs like "Bye Bye Love."

Rock was revived in 1963 with the Beatles. This British group was made up of four singer–songwriters who were innovative in their lyrics and song styles. They played their own instruments at a time when many pop stars were just singers, and they constantly reinvented themselves with different sounds in a series of hit albums that are still popular today. Their arrival in the United States in 1964 to appear on *The Ed Sullivan Show* is considered the start of the British invasion of American music.

With rock, the music industry became big business. Teens the world over bought into the sound. Since the late 1950s, at least 60 percent of record sales have been in some form of rock, whose family tree has many branches. What was called rockabilly (combining rock and hillbilly music) gave way to folk rock and protest songs. The Motown sound became popular with a softer style that featured romantic lyrics. Hard rock splintered into acid rock, punk, and heavy metal. Probably the biggest development coming out of rock, however, was rap music.

RAP AND HIP-HOP

Rap is defined as speaking in rhyme over drumbeats. **Hip-hop** refers to the backing music for rap, which is often composed of a collage of excerpts, or samples, from other songs; hip-hop also refers to the culture of rap. The two terms are nearly, but not completely, interchangeable.[6]

Rap originated in the early 1970s in the outer boroughs of New York City, especially the Bronx. The Universal Zulu Nation poetry-to-music group was especially influential in bringing what were originally street-corner venting sessions to the attention of the wider public.[7]

The first commercial rap record, "Rapper's Delight," was recorded by the Sugar Hill Gang in 1979. The Beastie Boys, the first white rap group, was formed in 1981. Salt-N-Pepa became the first female rap group to make it big, in 1985. As rap grew more popular in the 1980s, different factions developed on the East and West coasts. The rivalry reached a flash point in the mid-1990s, culminating in the murders of Tupac Shakur in 1996 and Notorious B.I.G. in 1997.

In 1998 West Coast rapper–producer Dr. Dre discovered Marshall Mathers III, also known as Eminem (discussed later in this chapter). The next year, Eminem's *Slim Shady LP* was a huge hit. Rap, which became a Grammy category only in the late 1980s, seemed to have taken over the award ceremony by 2004.[8] Rappers Jay-Z, OutKast, and Pharrell Williams of the Neptunes received more nominations (six each) than any other artists.

THE FORMAT WARS INTENSIFY

To survive in the marketplace, a recording format had to be affordable, durable, and of good quality; moreover, it had to feature a wide range of recordings that people wanted to hear. Since the 1950s, copyright battles and format wars have been fought on two fronts: audio and video.

Audio Formats

The format wars seemed to quiet down in the 1950s: Singles were 45s, albums were 33⅓, and records were vinyl. Then tapes entered the battle, followed by compact discs and eventually digital music files people could download from the Internet.

Tapes

Magnetic recording, in which the sound information is encoded in metal particles on a strip of film, had been around since the earliest days of sound recording. The German company BASF was building magnetic tape recorders before World War II, but the technology was not used for popular music until the 1950s, when RCA Victor marketed prerecorded tapes on open reels. These tapes were much loved by stereo enthusiasts but never caught on with the wider public. In 1963, Philips Electronics demonstrated the first compact audiocassette using ⅛-inch tape, similar to the microcassettes found in some telephone answering machines today. In 1966, some U.S. cars came equipped with larger eight-track stereo cartridge tape players developed by William Lear (who founded the Learjet aviation company and had developed the first practical car radio in the 1920s). The eight-track was a dead format by the early 1980s, replaced by the smaller and more reliable eight-millimeter cassette. Sony's Walkman portable audiocassette player, introduced in 1979, became wildly successful, and assured the popularity of the standard eight-millimeter cassette. Music became more portable than ever, and joggers and commuters strapped on their Walkmans to listen to their favorite audiotapes as they moved about.

The Sony Walkman, introduced in 1979, became wildly successful and made music more portable than ever. It was shown here next to a "crush-proof" pack of cigarettes to show how small it was, although it was huge by today's iPod standard.

When cassette tapes became popular, the Recording Industry Association of America, or RIAA, began lobbying for a royalty on blank tape as compensation for the sales music producers believed they lost to unauthorized copying. It was unsuccessful in this fight until 1992, when the digital audiotape (DAT) format was introduced. The

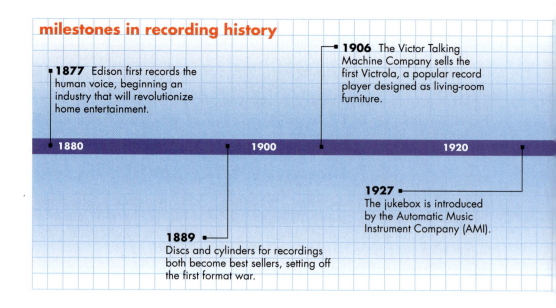

milestones in recording history

1877 Edison first records the human voice, beginning an industry that will revolutionize home entertainment.

1906 The Victor Talking Machine Company sells the first Victrola, a popular record player designed as living-room furniture.

1880   1900   1920

1927 The jukebox is introduced by the Automatic Music Instrument Company (AMI).

1889 Discs and cylinders for recordings both become best sellers, setting off the first format war.

industry then argued that the digital format could be used to make master-quality recordings, and Congress passed the Audio Home Recording Act, which levied a 2 percent royalty on the wholesale price of digital recorders and a 3 percent royalty on blank digital tapes and discs. Even with those royalties, the recording companies refused to release prerecorded tapes in the DAT format, which is one of the reasons DAT failed with consumers. The other reason it failed was that CDs had become popular.

Who were the winners and losers of the audio format wars?

Compact Discs

compact discs (CDs)
Plastic discs with digitally encoded music read by lasers.

In 1983 the first **compact discs (CDs)** were introduced. CDs are plastic discs with digitally encoded music read by lasers. This format revitalized the industry as many music lovers replaced their collections of analog vinyl discs and cassette tapes with the better sound quality and greater durability of the new high-tech medium.[9] The minidisc, a smaller version of the CD, appeared in the late 1990s and continued to battle for market share with CDs and digital download players such as the Rio.

Music Downloading

MP3
The name for compressed digital audio files that enable music to be downloaded from the Internet.

The recording industry welcomed the arrival of the CD at first, in part at least because it was a read-only format. Unlike tapes, CDs could only play back songs, not record them. This view of CDs turned out to be fairly short-sighted, however. In the 1990s listeners began making copies of their CDs on computers, and in 1999 a college student named Shawn Fanning developed Napster, the first successful free file-sharing program. Fanning's Web site made use of **MP3** technology, which consists of compressed digital audio files that enable music to be downloaded from the Internet.

Napster became hugely successful and CD sales dropped precipitously, but the industry still had plenty of money to fight back. The RIAA, shut Napster down through legal action. Several new downloading services sprang up, and the RIAA battled the file-sharing threat on several fronts. First, the industry group went directly after colleges, sending "take down" notices to administrators on several campuses where high-speed Internet connections

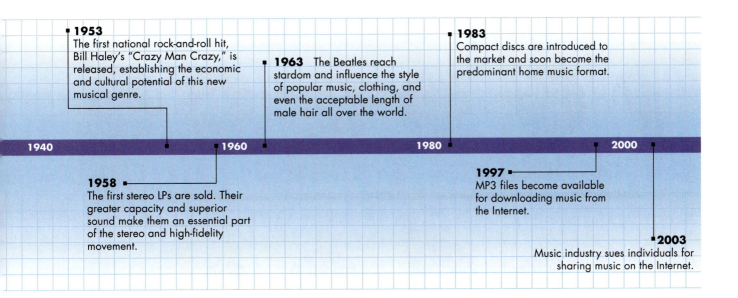

1953
The first national rock-and-roll hit, Bill Haley's "Crazy Man Crazy," is released, establishing the economic and cultural potential of this new musical genre.

1963 The Beatles reach stardom and influence the style of popular music, clothing, and even the acceptable length of male hair all over the world.

1983
Compact discs are introduced to the market and soon become the predominant home music format.

1940   1960   1980   2000

1958
The first stereo LPs are sold. Their greater capacity and superior sound make them an essential part of the stereo and high-fidelity movement.

1997
MP3 files become available for downloading music from the Internet.

2003
Music industry sues individuals for sharing music on the Internet.

were being used by what the RIAA called music pirates.[10] Second, it fought to stop the manufacture and sale of handheld digital recorders, such as the Rio, but lost that battle when the courts declared that the devices could be sold. Third, it fought to close down unauthorized Web sites that distributed copyrighted music. After the Supreme Court ruled that the services could be liable for piracy by their users, the RIAA sent cease-and-desist letters to several firms. Most—including BearShare, WinMX, and Grokster—shut down. Others, including Napster, said they would switch to a licensed, paid model. Some that shut down left software behind that some file sharers continued to use. The RIAA continues to sue select file sharers in this group. As of mid-2006, the RIAA had sued more than 18,000 individuals for sharing songs online, with 4,500 settling for about $4,000 per case.[11] The International Federation for the Phonographic Industry (IFPI), the RIAA's international counterpart, has brought legal actions against more than 3,800 file sharers in 16 countries outside the United States. Both the U.S. and the international campaigns continue to target users of all the major unauthorized P2P networks, including FastTrack (Kazaa), Gnutella (BearShare), eDonkey, DirectConnect, BitTorrent, WinMX, and SoulSeek. The industry knows it cannot sue every single infringer. But it figures that if it makes enough waves in enough countries, its legal actions could have a serious deterrent effect.

"I swear I wasn't looking at smut—I was just stealing music."

The music industry simultaneously embarked on an education campaign to inform file sharers that illegal downloading affects not only music executives and pop stars but also writers, engineers, musicians, roadies, and everyone else involved in making music. Meanwhile, the legal music Web sites such as iTunes had begun allowing users to download a single song for 99 cents, and kids were downloading ringtones for their cell phones for $2 to $5 each.

In 2006 the head of the Recording Industry Association of America declared that unauthorized song swapping had been "contained." "The problem

FIGURE 7.1 Battles in the Audio Format Wars The history of the recording industry could be viewed as a series of format wars. Some of the major conflicts between formats are depicted here.

has not been eliminated," he said, "but we believe [legal] digital downloads have emerged into a growing, thriving business, and file-trading is flat."[12]

Winners and Losers

The great lesson of the history of copyright battles is that the music industry will fight new technologies but eventually adapt to them. In the same way, the recording industry will adapt to new formats, and the market will determine winners of technology battles within the hardware (players and recorders) and software (music) industries (see Figure 7.1). There will be new video forms, musical styles, and dance crazes—and many, many new media formats on which to record them and play them back. Digital technology will continue to create cheaper equipment for producing and distributing recordings, allowing new entrants into the industry. This, in turn, will encourage the continuing fragmentation of audience tastes as it makes it easy for new splinter genres to form.

Understanding Today's Recording *Industry*

In spite of its worry about pirated downloads, the recording industry remains a profitable one. The major labels rarely lose money. Compare the basic economics of the recording industry with its movie cousin: Like the movie industry, the majority of records aren't blockbusters, but the records that lose money don't lose nearly as much as failed movies. To begin with, albums cost a lot less to produce than movies do. Only a tiny percentage of recording artists can command multimillion-dollar contracts, and those are spread over a number of albums. A major album costs a few hundred thousand dollars to produce, compared with the tens of millions it takes to produce a major movie. Profits from an album can start rolling in two or three months after the company decides to make the recording, rather than the two years it takes to produce and release a movie. Each major studio puts out a few hundred albums a year, spreading its risks widely. The movie studios put out a few dozen pictures, so each project represents more of a risk.

All of this means that the recording industry is more profitable, and more consistently profitable, than most other industries, including the film industry. There are ups and downs, but the industry tends to recover quickly. A serious post-disco crash in 1979, for example, was counteracted by the introduction of compact discs and MTV in the early 1980s. To explain why the recording industry is so profitable, we will focus on a handful of components: major labels, independents, industry personnel, promotion, sales, and, of course, the audience.

THE MAJOR LABELS: GLOBAL GOLIATHS

Four major corporations collect around 80 percent of recording industry revenues each year. The business is constantly undergoing mergers, but the four major corporate players as of this writing are Warner, EMI, Sony BMG, and Universal[13] (see Fact File 7.1). A large amount of industry globalization occurred during the 1980s, when CBS was bought by Sony of Japan, and RCA Records, the current version of RCA Victor, was sold to Bertelsmann of Germany. Although they are all international, the major recording companies receive most of their revenues from big-name American performers.

Four major corporations collect around 80 percent of recording industry revenues each year.

Local groups continue to sell well in their own countries, but the majority of the music sold around the world is in English (see Fact File 7.2).[14]

Until the 1980s, part of a major label's business was to develop new talent. To help a performer or group develop, the label would stick with them through several early albums that were barely profitable. Bruce Springsteen was signed to CBS Records (now Columbia) in 1973, but it took him until his third album (*Born to Run*) to be considered a success. In the meantime, he

FACT FILE 7.1

Major Music Labels

Corporate Parent	Labels	
EMI	Angel	EMI CMG
	Astralworks	EMI Televisa
	Blue Note	Mute
	Capitol	Narada
	Capitol Nashville	Parlorphone
	EMI	Virgin
	EMI Classics	
Sony BMG	Arista Records	Legacy Recordings
	Bluebird Jazz	RCA Records
	BMG Heritage	RCA Victor Group
	Burgundy Records	RLG—Nashville
	Columbia Records	Sony BMG Masterworks
	Epic Records	Sony Music Nashville
	J Records	Sony Wonder
	Jive Records	Sony Urban Music
	LaFace Records	Verity Records
Universal	Geffen Records	UNI Records
	Interscope Geffen A&M	Universal Music Classics Group
	Island Def Jam Music Group	Universal Music Enterprises
	Lost Highway Records	Universal Music Latino
	MCA Nashville	Universal Records
	Mercury Nashville	Universal South
	Motown Records	Verve Music Group
Warner	Asylum	Rhino
	Atlantic	Rykodisc
	Bad Boy	Sire
	Cordless	Squint
	East West	Warner Bros.
	Elektra	Warner Music International
	Lava	WBR Nashville
	Maverick	WEA
	Nonesuch	Word
	Reprise	

Source: Corporate Web sites, accessed October 2006.

CONSIDER THIS

Which artist or group do you think will be the next to make the list of all-time best-selling albums? Why?

was heavily promoted as "the new Bob Dylan." Today, an artist like Springsteen would be dropped by one of the majors, or at least be considered not worth promoting because of his lack of instant success.

The blockbuster syndrome that affects the book and movie industries is also alive and well in the recording industry. Once artists have produced a huge hit, the label will advance them millions in search of their next blockbuster. It doesn't always work out. In the 1990s the majors signed multi-million-dollar deals with many superstars, including Michael Jackson, Mariah Carey, Mötley Crüe, and Prince. Most of these projects were disap-

FACT FILE 7.2

Top-Selling Albums of All Time

The Recording Industry Association of America (RIAA) has awarded gold and platinum record awards since 1958. Gold records are awarded for album sales of over 500,000 and singles sales of over one million. A platinum record is for one million albums or two million singles. In 1999, the RIAA began to award diamond record awards for certified sales of 10 million albums.

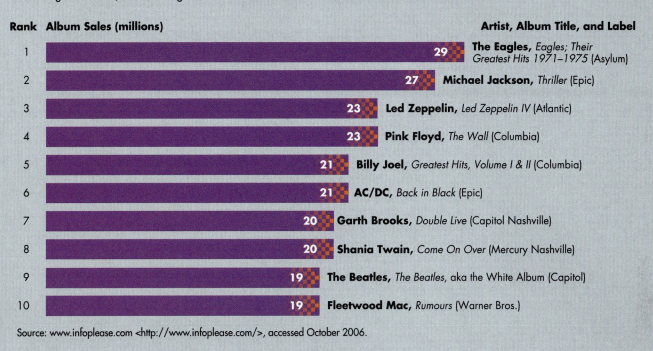

Rank	Album Sales (millions)	Artist, Album Title, and Label
1	29	**The Eagles,** *Eagles; Their Greatest Hits 1971–1975* (Asylum)
2	27	**Michael Jackson,** *Thriller* (Epic)
3	23	**Led Zeppelin,** *Led Zeppelin IV* (Atlantic)
4	23	**Pink Floyd,** *The Wall* (Columbia)
5	21	**Billy Joel,** *Greatest Hits, Volume I & II* (Columbia)
6	21	**AC/DC,** *Back in Black* (Epic)
7	20	**Garth Brooks,** *Double Live* (Capitol Nashville)
8	20	**Shania Twain,** *Come On Over* (Mercury Nashville)
9	19	**The Beatles,** *The Beatles,* aka the White Album (Capitol)
10	19	**Fleetwood Mac,** *Rumours* (Warner Bros.)

Source: www.infoplease.com <http://www.infoplease.com/>, accessed October 2006.

pointments, artistically as well as financially. While these groups laughed all the way to the bank, many garage bands with talent never got a chance. There simply wasn't enough money left over to support them.

The lack of support for developing acts is sometimes blamed on corporate ownership. The head of one major label said, "The corporations don't want you to tell them that you can break an act in two years. They want results in six months. So you stop thinking about developing artists as your main business."[15] Because of this, many of today's promising original groups are coming out on independent labels rather than on one of the majors.

Some observers believe that online music downloads could help alleviate the problems of the blockbuster syndrome. Groups that can't get the attention of a major label might be able to get the attention of fans directly by offering free downloads of their music.

INDEPENDENTS: DEVELOPING TALENT

An **independent label** is any recording industry company not owned by one of the majors. The industry practice is for the majors to acquire any independents that become successful. These independents then continue to produce their own records, which are then distributed by the parent corporation. In effect, former independents become not only laboratories for new ideas but also talent scouts for the corporate owner.

Many independents become successful by handling specialized genres—jazz, classical, religious—that are not profitable for bigger companies. Early hip-hop groups in particular tended to start out on independent labels. In fact, many rappers started one-act independent labels that released what

independent label
Any recording industry company not owned by one of the major labels.

amounted to demo CDs. Wu-Tang Clan, a group of nine cousins and friends from Staten Island, New York, started their own label when they couldn't get a contract with a major. Once their album attracted attention, they signed with a Bertelsmann label.

Several independent labels have become successful by handling material that major labels won't touch because of its controversial nature. Priority Records became the largest independent in the United States in the mid-1990s by distributing rap albums that large corporations shied away from. Priority distributed N.W.A.'s first album, a record so obscene it prompted a letter of complaint from the Federal Bureau of Investigation. Priority also became Ice-T's label when the rapper left Warner Bros. after police groups and the company's shareholders objected to the song "Cop Killer." And Priority signed Suge Knight, who went on to found his own independent label, Death Row Records.

Death Row Records was an extreme example of an independent label. Suge Knight had eight criminal convictions and five contracts on his life in the six years he headed the label. According to industry insiders, Death Row Records "upped the ante of music-industry corruption from a sleazy world of payola and sexual harassment to a dangerous battleground where enemies were pistol whipped or mysteriously disappeared, the label's own artists were beaten at company meetings and contract negotiations were made with baseball bats instead of pens."[16]

But not all rap labels are known for outrageous behavior. Russell Simmons, the hip-hop magnate who founded Def Jam Records, spends a large amount of time on social causes that are important to the hip-hop community. He founded the Hip-Hop Summit Action Network to spotlight issues such as budget cuts at inner-city schools and Rockefeller-era laws that impose long mandatory minimum sentences for drug offenses, even for first-time, nonviolent, and low-level offenders.

In addition to small labels that have sold out to the majors, hundreds of true independents exist without corporate ownership. Together, they collect the 20 percent of the market share left over from the big four labels. Some of them stay independent because they feel that corporate ownership would be corrupting (see the Close-Up on Industry box).

THE PLAYERS

The music industry congregates around several major U.S. cities, each focusing on different forms of music. Los Angeles and New York are centers of both mainstream and emerging forms of music; Nashville is the center for country music; Detroit, the birthplace of Motown, is known for rhythm and

What are independent labels, and how do they differ from major labels?

SELF QUIZ

blues (R&B); and Seattle houses some of the newer sounds, like grunge and alternative. Recording industry personnel have a tendency to gravitate to the center of their preferred style of music. Many of these people operate behind the scenes.

A&R Executives

artist and repertoire (A&R) executives
Specialists in the music industry who discover and develop the groups and performers.

Artist and repertoire (A&R) executives are the talent scouts of the music business; they discover and develop the groups and performers. The name *A&R* comes from the early days of the business, when the company executive would find an appealing singer (the artist) and match that performer with songs that had potential to become hits (the repertoire). A singer like Brenda Lee would come into the studio on an appointed day and record songs she had never seen before—she was simply expected to sing what she was told to sing.

Ani DiFranco and Righteous Babe Records

Ani DiFranco's independence started early. She began singing in public at the age of 9; she was living on her own at the age of 15; and she put out her first album, *Ani DiFranco*, at 20. To do so, she started her own independent label, Righteous Babe Records.

DiFranco describes her company as "a people-friendly, sub-corporate, woman-informed, queer-happy small business that puts music before rock stardom and ideology before profit."[1] Righteous Babe Records is headquartered in Buffalo, New York, DiFranco's hometown. The label hires small local companies to press CDs and print album liners, posters, and T-shirts, although DiFranco could have the work done more cheaply elsewhere. In fact, she has been described as a one-woman urban renewal project for Buffalo.

DiFranco's music is part folk and part punk with an angry-woman attitude. Her concerts contain pure, revival-like energy, with a portion of the proceeds going to various social causes. It is a style that defies easy classification, which is one reason that DiFranco has refused to sign with a major label, despite years of aggressive wooing. She says, "I don't think the music

> **"I don't think the music industry is conducive to artistic and social change and growth. It does a lot to exploit and homogenize art and artists. In order to challenge the corporate music industry, I feel it necessary to remain outside it." —Ani DiFranco**

industry is conducive to artistic and social change and growth. It does a lot to exploit and homogenize art and artists. In order to challenge the corporate music industry, I feel it necessary to remain outside it."[2]

DiFranco's label seems to be doing fine on its own. By 2004, Righteous Babe Records had sold several million copies of the singer's 22 albums and was producing records by nine other artists, all of which were available over the Internet. In fact, to a large degree, digital technology has made DiFranco's success possible. She bought a computer in 1989 that enabled her to prepare a mailing list in minutes. Recording on tiny digital tape cost a quarter of the price of 24-track analog tape. Her fans on the Internet handle much of her publicity. The first site was put up by "a guy called Megazone, a computer geek from Worcester, Mass."[3] There were around 70 different sites by 2007. All indications are that Ani DiFranco will maintain her independence from corporate labels for some time to come.

[1] Andrew C. Revkin, "Righteous Babe Saves Hometown," *New York Times*, February 16, 1998, p. B1.
[2] Janine Jaquet, "Indies' Reservations," *The Nation*, August 25, September 1, 1997, p. 10.
[3] Scot Fisher, quoted in "A Note of Fear," *Economist*, October 31, 1998, p. 68.

DiFranco has a style that defies easy classification, which is one reason that she has refused to sign with a major label.

It was only in the later days of rock and roll that performers began to sing their own songs, or at least songs that they themselves decided to sing. One exception is country music, in which a considerable amount of A&R matchmaking is still done. An A&R executive today spends a lot of time listening to demonstration recordings, or **demos,** sent in by artists' agents, mana-

demos
Demonstration recordings sent in to record companies by artists' agents, managers, or by the artists themselves.

gers, or artists themselves. The executives then have to choose groups who have the right look, sound, and performance abilities.

Producers

producer
In the music industry, the person who oversees the making of a master recording.

In the recording industry, a **producer** is the person who oversees the making of a master recording from start to finish, including mixing and editing. Producers manage a team of engineers and technicians who set up and monitor equipment, mix the various tracks, and remix sounds in postproduction. They are usually in charge during taping sessions and decide when a song will be used, when the takes are good enough, and so on. Producers are often musicians themselves and have creative input in the recording. One of the Beatles' producers, for example, suggested that they include orchestral instruments in songs like "Eleanor Rigby." That suggestion had a significant impact, not just on the Beatles but also on dozens of bands they influenced, including the Moody Blues ("Nights in White Satin") and The Who (*Tommy*).

Recording Artists

The most prominent members of the team, of course, are the recording artists. Most spend years attempting to get recognized, first in local clubs and then by traveling, eventually becoming opening acts for better-known groups on tour. Most artists, including those that manage to make a demo, never get a chance to record for a label. Today, a few unknowns rise to international fame practically overnight courtesy of television programs such as *American Idol* and *Making the Band*. In spite of these sensational exceptions, most recording artists face a long, steep climb.

Most recording artists spend years attempting to get recognized, but today television programs have allowed a few to beat the odds. Taylor Hicks (shown here with Paula Abdul), rose to instant fame by winning the *American Idol* crown in 2006.

Artists who do become successful have to be careful about their dealings with the industry. The history of the business is one of exploitation of talent. Early rock artists such as Chuck Berry and Bo Diddley were robbed by their managers and promoters. Elvis Presley's manager, "Colonel" Tom Parker, kept half of everything Presley made from 1955 until several years after his death.[17] Because today's recording artists are often their own songwriters and lyricists, they have to be knowledgeable about copyright, contracts, and several of the other legal issues that we will discuss in more depth in Chapter 14. In recent years several artists, including Courtney Love, have complained that both major and independent labels have cheated them out of their rightful royalty payments. Love points out that record labels often charge the artist for all production and promotion costs, deducting these costs from royalties. She contends that this practice often leaves the recording artist with no royalties.[18]

Of course, artists who reach the top can become very wealthy. Successful rap artists, for example, routinely have enough money to start their own record labels and clothing lines, and many, such as Jay-Z, Eminem, and Sean "P. Diddy" Combs, have been extremely successful in these sideline enterprises.

Recording artists, even the most successful ones, also have to carefully guard their rights to be creative. New acts that break through are often pressured never to stray from their "promotable" sound. Several industry forces work against a group's ability to change and grow once they become successful. For one thing, groups have to devote one or two years to the promotion of a major album. This includes going on tour and playing the same songs over and over, which can stifle creativity.

Other Members of the Production Team

The production process also involves musicians who specialize in studio work and **arrangers** who adapt the original song for parts for the instruments, background vocals, and other musical elements. A **lyricist,** a professional who specializes in the words of the song, might also be on hand.

ROYALTIES AND PERFORMANCE RIGHTS ORGANIZATIONS

There are two types of royalties: (1) recording artist royalties and (2) songwriter and publisher royalties.

Recording artists earn royalties from the sale of their recordings on CDs, tapes, vinyl, and legal downloads. As mentioned earlier, many performers have complained of being cheated out of these royalties by unethical recording labels. Recording artists don't earn royalties when their recordings are played on radio or TV. This is a long-standing practice that's based on copyright law and the fact that when radio stations play the songs, more CDs and tapes are sold. Songwriters and publishers, however, do earn royalties on radio play and other public performances, as well as on recording sales.

The only place artists earn royalties for performances of their recordings is in a digital arena, such as a webcast or satellite radio. This came about with the Digital Performance Rights in Sound Recordings Act of 1995. This act gave performers of music their first performance royalties for recordings; it also meant that online radio stations had to pay a royalty that on-air stations did not.

Performance royalties for songwriters and publishers are calculated and paid out by performance rights organizations, or PROs. The three main PROs are ASCAP (American Society of Composers, Artists and Publishers), BMI (Broadcast Music, Inc.), and SESAC (Society of European Stage Authors and Composers). The copyright owner registers a song with one of the PROs, who then sells users either a blanket license to use any song in the PRO's catalog, or a per-program license that charges them for only the music they actually use. (This is good for users who don't use much music.) Users include virtually anyone who plays music in a public place, including television networks, cable television stations, radio stations, background music services like MUZAK, colleges, concert presenters, symphony orchestras, Web sites, bars, restaurants, hotels, theme parks, skating rinks, bowling alleys, circuses, and even businesses that play "hold" music on their phone systems. The PROs do sample surveys of all these venues to determine how much a song's copyright owner earns.

PROMOTION

Major labels succeed by spending huge sums on promoting acts, most of which are flops. Only a very few turn into the megastars whose success covers the cost of the failures. Each act has to be marketed carefully. That includes everything from the packaging of the album to the atmosphere of the concert performances.

Radio Play

Promotion begins with getting a record on the charts, the most influential of which are those published weekly in *Billboard* magazine. Radio play and

arrangers
Those who adapt a song for specific singers and other musical elements.

lyricist
A professional who specializes in writing the words of a song.

sales determine placement on the charts, so the promoter's first job is to get a cut from the album played on radio stations. Promoters concentrate on **reporting stations,** which are the 200 to 300 radio stations whose playlists are tracked weekly by Broadcast Data Systems, an independent company. Record promoters visit these stations' music directors, program directors, and programming consultants as often as they can. They play them any of their newest releases that fit in with the station's format. Payola (discussed in detail in Chapter 8), is against the law, but promoters shower stations with copious giveaways, including albums, T-shirts, and concert tickets.

Store Sales

Along with radio play, the charts are also determined through record store sales. For many years, this part of the process was notoriously unreliable. Promoters would pay off record store managers with free albums, concert tickets, and outright bribes. The managers would then report higher sales to *Billboard*. In 1991, however, the system became computerized with the introduction of **Soundscan,** a point-of-sale computer system that records the bar codes scanned at the cash registers of thousands of stores.

The Soundscan system is much more reliable than the old-style reporting, but promoters still try to manipulate the system. They might persuade a local radio station to play a cut before the record is available in the stores, building up demand so that heavy sales in the first week of release get the album on the charts quickly. Promoters also send plenty of free copies of high-priority releases to Soundscan stores, which allows the stores to discount those releases. Field representatives ask the store to display the record prominently and to play it on the in-house sound system. Field reps have even come into stores as customers and bought a key album in small quantities to get their sales figures up. Using the album's regional popularity ratings according to Soundscan, the label then urges local radio stations to put the artist's songs on their playlist. If the record becomes a hit in one influential market, other stations around the country usually start playing it.

Promotional tricks like these can help the song get exposure, but people really have to respond to it before it can become a hit. As one industry insider pointed out: "You can fake it some of the way up the chart but you can't fake it all the way."[19]

Press Coverage and Publicity

Record promoters make extraordinary efforts to get press coverage for new albums (see Figure 7.2). Such efforts might include a press party to celebrate the album's release or an interview in a magazine such as *Rolling Stone* or *Spin*. When Ruffhouse Records wanted to promote Cypress Hill, a Los Angeles group that championed marijuana, promoters arranged for the group to appear on the cover of *High Times* magazine. Promoters will also lobby for awards. There are dozens of such awards, given by media outlets from *Rolling Stone* to MTV. A Grammy Award, in particular, can add millions to an album's sales.

Promoters also feed the hundreds of Web sites that are hungry for industry gossip with such tidbits as "Sheryl Crow was very friendly with Jakob Dylan of the Wallflowers backstage after a concert."[20] These sites, such as Starmagazine.com, have their own daily news services that compile faxes and newsletters with items about pop stars. The faxes go out to DJs and radio-show hosts, providing a constant stream of industry chatter that is considered essential to promotion.

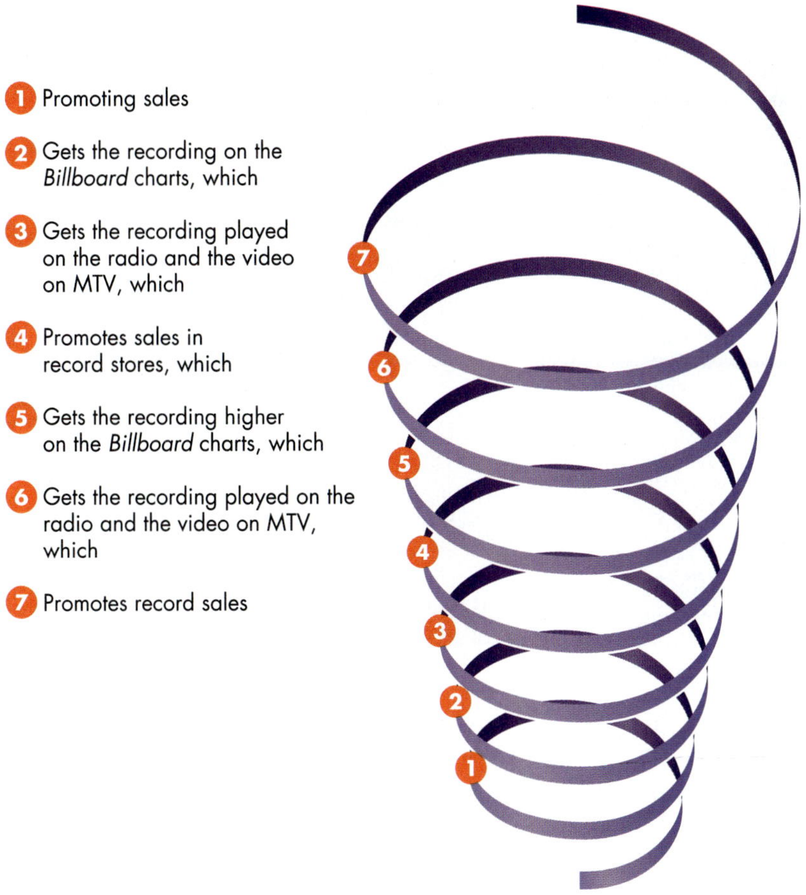

FIGURE 7.2 The Record Promotion Spiral Promotion begins with getting a record on the charts, but radio play and sales determine placement on those charts.

1. Promoting sales
2. Gets the recording on the *Billboard* charts, which
3. Gets the recording played on the radio and the video on MTV, which
4. Promotes sales in record stores, which
5. Gets the recording higher on the *Billboard* charts, which
6. Gets the recording played on the radio and the video on MTV, which
7. Promotes record sales

Music Videos and Other Forms of Buzz

Another facet of the promotional game is to get a record's music video on TV. Videos are now sold in most music stores, but they account for 1 percent or less of the industry's income. Their purpose is mostly promotional, and their main outlets are such cable networks as MTV, VH1, Country Music Television (CMT), and Black Entertainment Television (BET), which are more likely to put a video into rotation if it has noteworthy sales and air play. This is a good example of the way sales, radio play, and other forms of promotion all work hand in hand. Radio stations are influenced by sales figures and by the buzz about the video when determining their playlists, and record stores will display a record more prominently if it is hot on MTV and radio.

The record label also uses movie and television soundtracks to promote its music. These placements are extremely valuable as cross-promotions, especially when the parent corporation owns film and television as well as music divisions, as Time Warner and Universal do. The best soundtracks reflect a film's atmosphere; examples include those for *The Graduate* (1967), *Saturday Night Fever* (1977), and *Titanic* (1997).

Ads, both for the music and as music in ads for other products, are important promotional tools. Music fees in television commercials for nonmusic products are significant revenue generators in their own right. Janis Joplin's 1960s song "Mercedes Benz" has earned large sums in advertisements for the car that is part of the lifestyle the song originally satirized. Those ads have also helped boost sales of the deceased star's work.

A Grammy Award can add millions to an album's sales. Here Mike Dirnt, left, Billie Joe Armstrong and Tre Cool, right, of the group Green Day, pose with their award for record of the year at the 2006 ceremony.

What are the different forms of music promotion, and how are they interrelated?

SELF QUIZ

Record promoters work closely with concert promoters as well. They might try to arrange for corporate sponsorship from Coke or American Express to make sure the tour is cross-promoted. They might also arrange to sell albums, T-shirts, videotapes, and programs featuring the group at the concerts.

DISTRIBUTION AND SALES

Recordings are distributed and sold through a variety of retailers, including traditional and online outlets. Traditional brick-and-mortar stores still sell the most recordings, but online stores are catching up fast. Traditional stores include music specialty stores such as Sam Goody, as well as discount stores (Wal-Mart, Best Buy, Target), electronics stores (Circuit City), and bookstores (Borders, Barnes & Noble). One of the top specialty stores, Tower Records, declared bankruptcy in 2006.

Online stores include Web sites where you can buy traditional CDs, such as Amazon.com, and sites where you can order custom CDs, such as Mixonics and Rhapsody.com. Online stores also include those that specialize in downloads, such as Apples iTunes, as discussed in the beginning of this chapter. Online stores offer pages devoted to genres and individual artists, allow songs to be previewed before purchased, and have tools to help users find music they like by showing them the choices of other people who have similar tastes.

Both iTunes and the new, legal Napster offer over 500,000 licensed songs from all the major labels and most independents, usually for around 99 cents per song. Online distribution has the potential to produce a much higher profit margin than traditional retailing. The labels save the cost of packaging and never have to worry about having unsold overstocks or losing sales because a title is sold out. As the labels continue to fight illegal downloading, they hope that these legitimate sites will benefit sales in the future. The goal, ultimately, is to make it easier for the customer to buy music than to steal it.

THE AUDIENCE

The audience for recorded music is changing. For one thing, consumers are becoming more technologically sophisticated. In the early days, listeners were thrilled to hear a barely recognizable human voice reproduced. Later, many were delighted to hear different tracks from left and right speakers. But music today has to move the listener, to become part of that listener's identity; otherwise, it just gets lost in the noise of everyday living, most of which comes from other forms of media.

Even though music is important to the average consumer, fans tend to be less loyal than they were in the past. Teenagers of the 1950s would buy every album produced by their favorite group. Today's teens are more fickle. Some critics say that the proliferation of choice is the culprit. Up until the 1960s, around 45 albums were released a week; by 2002, that number had grown to more than 500.[21] Other critics say the cause is deeper. They say that fans are less loyal because so many albums contain one slickly produced single aimed at getting airplay, and a dozen or so other songs that are not only bad but completely unlike the single.[22] Having bought an hour-long CD solely for the sake of a four-minute song, the customer does not buy the next album by that group. Individual songs downloaded from the Internet may eventually alleviate that problem for the consumer.

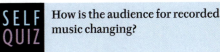

SELF QUIZ How is the audience for recorded music changing?

Other critics suggest that the major labels encourage the fickleness of today's young audiences because they can make more money that way. The labels sign young bands to cheap contracts and make big profits with a single album. Industry executives say that this is one reason rock music is changing from a genre that supported career artists such as the Beatles and the Rolling Stones to one that gives rise to a succession of young, transient acts. At an MTV Video Music Awards ceremony the comedian Chris Rock summed up the situation as follows: "Here today, gone today."[23]

Other critics blame technology for the fans' lack of loyalty. An LP, they say, was "placed gently on a turntable and left alone to spin."[24] Cassettes were also played in their entirety. FM radio stations of the 1960s would play new albums from start to finish. In fact, on June 1, 1967, the day the Beatles' *Sgt. Pepper's Lonely Hearts Club Band* was released, it seemed that stations were all playing the album at the same time. CDs and downloads, on the other hand, encourage tune surfing because they can be so easily scanned and reprogrammed. Albums are seen as shopping malls of selections for different tastes rather than as museums of integrated works of art that have to be appreciated as unified statements. Today's fans want to create their own albums, not the one that the label or even the recording artist planned for them.

Controversies

Copyright battles and format wars might be controversial within the industry, but they are not the controversies that media critics worry about. The primary controversies that concern critics of the recording industry involve cultural effects. These controversies are of two types: the effects of music and music censorship. The two are related: Those who are worried about the negative effects of music are often the ones who call for some type of censorship.

The Shady World of Eminem

The rapper known today as Eminem was born Marshall Mathers in St. Joseph, Missouri, in 1972. He grew up poor and hard, shuttling between his hometown and Detroit. He began performing raps at the age of 14, but it wasn't until 10 years later that he released his first record with a small independent label. That got him into the 1997 Rap Olympics in Los Angeles, where he took second place. From there he became the protégé of Dr. Dre, a legendary rapper who was once a member of the seminal group N.W.A.

Eminem's first album with Dre, *The Slim Shady LP,* went triple platinum (3 million copies) and included the massive hit single "My Name Is." His second album, *The Marshall Mathers LP,* was one of the fastest-selling rap albums of all time, selling close to 2 million copies in its first week of release. His third, *The Eminem Show,* was the world's number-one-selling album in 2002.

The rapper Eminem, whose lyrics tend to be violent and offensive, is one of the most controversial celebrities of all time.

He was no less successful in his other endeavors. His movie *8 Mile* (2002) made more than $54 million in its opening weekend, the biggest debut ever for a first-time leading actor. He won an Oscar for his song "Lose Yourself" from that film. He has won several Grammys, and he has established his own music label, Shady Records, which has a hit artist with 50 Cent. He has his own clothing line, also called Shady.

To those for whom rap is an African American art, Eminem's success with the genre is a form of cultural theft.

And he has done all this while being one of the most controversial celebrities ever. His lyrics, for example, are violent and offensive. In one rap, he fantasizes about raping his mother and murdering his wife. He has deeply offended the gay community with such lyrics as "My words are like a dagger with a jagged edge / That'll stab you in the head / Whether you're a fag or les."

Famous for taking his grudges out in his raps, Eminem has been sued for slander several times, including, most famously, by his mother. In one rap he accused the pop star Christina Aguilera of sexual promiscuity, and in another he asked if Britney Spears was "retarded."

Eminem is also controversial for general bad behavior, having been arrested several times for club brawls. But perhaps what is most controversial about this successful rapper is his race. In the hip-hop world, where inner-city authenticity is everything, a white rapper is an anomaly. To those for whom rap is an African American art, Eminem's success with the genre is a form of cultural theft. Eminem seems to acknowledge this in a rap: "Let's do the math," he chants. "If I was black I wouldn't have sold half."

THE EFFECTS

Because teens identify so strongly with their music, some song lyrics worry parents, educators, and citizens groups who fear their adverse effects. Throughout the 1990s sadomasochistic lyrics, gangsta rap, and shock rock were linked to youthful crime and decadence. Even industry proponents had to admit that hard-core artists like Eminem (see the Close-Up on Controversy

> ### Even industry proponents admit that hard-core artists like Eminem can attract troubled youth who may be prone to act out the images the music evokes.

box) tend to attract, amid their wide and varied fan base, troubled youth who may be prone to act out the images the music evokes. On the Senate floor in the late 1990s, one normally reserved senator apologized for having to recite the lyrics before he said,

> Consider a song like "Slap-a-hoe" by the group Dove Shack, distributed by a large and respected company like Polygram, which touted the virtues of a machine that automatically smacks a wife or girlfriend in line. Or the vile work of the death metal band Cannibal Corpse, distributed through a Sony subsidiary, which recorded one song describing the rape of a woman with a knife and another describing the act of masturbating with a dead woman's head. This is extreme, awful, disgusting stuff that kids are listening to.[25]

The implication is that teens would be influenced by what they heard.

While industry spokespeople insist that such fears are groundless, there is evidence that would suggest otherwise. In several documented cases, teens have committed suicide after listening to recordings such as Ozzy Osbourne's "Suicide Solution" and Judas Priest's *Stained Class* album, although no court of law has ever found an artist responsible.[26] There is also evidence that fans copy the outrageous behavior of their favorite artists. The extreme example of this is those who have killed themselves because their rock idols did so. After Kurt Cobain of the Seattle grunge group Nirvana killed himself in 1994, teen suicides were being inspired by his death three years later in places as far away as France.[27]

If teens are willing to imitate behavior as extreme as suicide, the argument goes, it seems likely that they would be influenced by the casual sex and violence advocated by some musicians. It's not quite that simple, of course, as explained in Chapter 2. The evidence has been impressive enough, however, to result in continuing calls for the censorship of music.

SELF QUIZ What evidence suggests that rock and rap music have negative effects?

CONSIDER THIS *Is outrageous behavior necessary for an artist or group to capture the public's attention? Supply examples to back up your answer.*

CENSORSHIP

Popular music has experienced a long and contentious history of criticism and censorship. In the 1950s conservative ministers sponsored bonfires in which rock records were burned. Even some DJs, unhappy with the new music and its apparent effect on teenagers, joined them. Citizens' groups were formed solely to fight the menace of rock music. Over the years, rock music became a political football as well. Members of Congress spoke out against the sexual suggestiveness of early rock music and derided the Beatles for describing themselves as more popular than Jesus. As discussed in Chapter 1, the word *censorship* means different things to different people. In the music industry, what observers call censorship has taken the form of music labeling, governmental criticism, chain store restrictions, and radio play restrictions.

Album Labeling

During the late 1980s, the Parents' Music Resource Center (PMRC), led by activists Tipper Gore and Susan Baker (whose husbands were both senators at the time), campaigned against obscene lyrics and for parental warning labels. The industry's 1990 decision to include these labels (such as "Explicit Lyrics" and "Explicit Content") was largely attributed to the pressure put on them by the PMRC. Today, some critics believe that the labels should be even more specific, identifying music as violent or misogynist. Other groups are now calling for parental advisory rating labels for concerts.[28] Many in the industry, however, feel that these labels are all a form of censorship and therefore resist them on First Amendment grounds.

Government Criticism

Government criticism seems to pop up during election campaigns and during slow sessions when other items on the agenda fail to excite the popular press. One such drive, in 1995, was directed at Time Warner. A number of senators accused the giant corporation of supporting rap and rock music with degrading lyrics, targeting specifically rapper Ice-T for romanticizing cop killing. Citizen groups joined in by releasing radio ads that accused Warner and other major labels of profiting from "the pollution of our culture and poisoning the minds of our children."[29] These groups also wrote to board members of Time Inc., leading Time Warner to sell its stake in Ice-T's label.

Despite public outcries, gangsta rap and other forms of rough music continue to be some of the industry's most popular and profitable genres. In fact, negative attention often, ironically, increases sales. The rap groups Public Enemy, N.W.A., and 2 Live Crew have all benefited from adverse publicity in this way.

In response to censorship attempts they faced because they spoke out in opposition to George W. Bush and the war in Iraq, the Dixie Chicks posed on the cover of *Entertainment Weekly* wearing only contradictory slogans that had been said about them and to them.

Chain-Store Restrictions

Other forms of censorship have been initiated by large chain stores. The discount chain Wal-Mart, with 2,300 stores around the country, is the nation's single largest seller of pop music. Wal-Mart stores are often the only places at which people in rural areas can buy records without traveling 50 to 150 miles.[30] But Wal-Mart will not carry CDs with parental advisories on them and will often refuse to carry albums for other reasons as well. When the soundtrack for the movie *Beavis and Butthead Do America* was released in 1996, Wal-Mart refused to carry it because the company had a chain-wide ban on all products associated with the vulgar, badly behaved duo.

To avoid such outright bans, most labels are willing to change the albums that are delivered to Wal-Mart.

Obscene words in the lyrics and even entire songs have been deleted. Covers have been changed, for example, by airbrushing bathing suits onto nudes. The most well-known example of Wal-Mart censorship involved the 1996 album *Sheryl Crow*. The chain rejected the album because one of the songs mentioned Wal-Mart by name in the lyrics: "Watch out sister, watch out brother. Watch our children as they kill each other, with a gun they bought at Wal-Mart Discount stores." Crow refused to change the lyric for Wal-Mart. This decision cost her at least 10 percent of her sales.[31]

Wal-Mart is not alone; other retailers, such as Kmart and Blockbuster, make similar decisions. For many in the industry, the worst part of chain-store restrictions is that record producers will force recording artists to censor themselves. In fact, record labels and bands have designed different covers, changed lyrics, and even omitted songs from their albums in anticipation of retailers' objections. The problem, say those who fear censorship, is that artists who want to challenge the status quo by writing controversial songs about race, religion, politics, or sex will be hesitant to do so in fear of being banned from large retail stores.

Sheryl Crow refused to change her song lyrics for Wal-Mart, and paid for it in reduced album sales.

Radio Play Restrictions

Many critics insist that labeling, governmental criticism, and chain-store restrictions aren't really censorship. Many, however, feel that restrictions placed on radio play by the Federal Communications Commission (FCC) are censorship in the classical sense because they represent prior restraint by a government authority. Thus there was an outcry in 2002 when the FCC fined two stations for playing Eminem's "The Real Slim Shady." WZEE in Madison, Wisconsin, was fined for airing the original (unedited) version, which included rough language, but KKMG in Colorado was fined for playing a profanity-free radio edit.

The corporate owners of radio stations have put other radio-play restrictions in place. For example, Clear Channel Communications, the largest owner of radio stations in the United States, released a list of more than 150 "lyrically questionable" songs following the September 11, 2001, terrorist attacks. Clear Channel suggested that each station should pull the songs from their rotations. None of the songs were unpatriotic; they simply had themes that were too reminiscent of the tragedy. The list included Sugar Ray's "Fly," Steve Miller's "Jet Airliner," AC/DC's "Shoot to Thrill," Pat Benatar's "Hit Me with Your Best Shot," Jerry Lee Lewis's "Great Balls of Fire," and the Dave Matthews Band's "Crash into Me."

Clear Channel was also involved in an incident in 2003 in which its stations stopped playing the music of the Dixie Chicks after a member of that group criticized President George W. Bush. Some stations organized events in which Dixie Chicks CDs were stomped to splinters. To those who criticized this action, it was the worst form of censorship.

SELF QUIZ Who attempts to censor popular music, and why?

Summing Up

In early oral cultures, music was something that people created for free, or as sidelines to the jobs they were paid to do. That began to change as music was written down and later published. With the invention of recording technology, however, music became valuable property.

The early technology of recording was built by inventor/entrepreneurs, such as Thomas Edison and Emile Berliner, whose cylinders and discs were the soldiers in the first format wars. These wars have continued to this day, as hundreds of new means of recording have been developed, presented to the public, and allowed to live or die in the marketplace. Copyright battles to enable the music industry to profit from sales of music began before recordings were invented, in the era of printed music.

Edison and Berliner proved that recordings could be an important form of home entertainment, and an industry was built around that idea. Many of the early companies grew into the components of today's industry. Berliner's Victor Talking Machine Company, for example, became RCA Victor and eventually Japan's JVC. Today, RCA Records is part of the huge German global conglomerate Bertelsmann.

Broadcast radio initially increased record sales, but the Great Depression saw consumers choosing radio over the phonograph. The industry revived after World War II and was helped out by the stereo and high-fidelity craze, and especially by the advent of rock and roll.

Today's industry is global and highly concentrated. It is a profitable industry as compared with others, although four major corporations—Universal, Time Warner, Sony BMG, and EMI—together take in 80 percent of the revenue. Independent labels act as talent scouts and testing grounds for the majors. Corporate labels acquire many of the successful independents.

Music industry personnel include artist and repertoire (A&R) executives, producers, arrangers, lyricists, studio musicians, and engineers. Promoters use any available means to push the record's sales, with most of their efforts directed to getting the record on the charts. Since the charts are determined by both radio play and sales, promoters attempt to manipulate those figures in several ways. Music is promoted through movie soundtracks, in ads (both for the music and as music in ads for other products), and in publicity in all types of media. Distribution of recordings takes place through record stores, discount chains, record clubs, and the Internet. The audience determines which records will be hits, although today's audience tends to be less loyal to particular groups and artists than earlier audiences were.

The primary controversies within the recording industry revolve around the effects of music and attempts at censorship. Critics believe song lyrics encourage antisocial behavior and that the stars of popular music act as negative role models. Many artists and industry personnel, however, feel that government and citizen group actions against the recording industry are in fact dangerous and unnecessary infringements of free speech.

Key Terms

These terms are defined and indexed in the Glossary of key terms at the back of the book.

artist and repertoire
  (A&R) executives *230*
analog recording *216*
arrangers *233*
compact discs (CDs) *224*
copyright *215*
demos *231*
digital recording *216*
format wars *215*
gramophone *217*

high-fidelity (hi-fi)
  sound *220*
hip-hop *222*
independent label *229*
jukebox *219*
lyricist *233*
MP3 *224*
nickelodeons *216*
phonograph *216*
producer *232*

ragtime *217*
rap *222*
reporting stations *234*
Soundscan *234*
stereophonic sound *219*
Tin Pan Alley *217*
track *219*
tweeters *219*
Victrola *218*
woofers *219*

HISTORY

Web Excursion

1. The history of the recording industry is incredibly diverse, including more groups and types of music than could be covered in this chapter. If you were to add to this history, what group or type of music would you include? Trace the history of either one on the Web, and prepare a brief report defending your choice. Use your own search techniques, or go directly to a site such as www.heathenworld.com/heathen.html* for the origins of band names or to the All Music guide at www.allmusic.com* to search for the roots of genres (East Coast rap, psychobilly) or any group.

INDUSTRY

Web Excursion

2. What is it that enables an artist or group to become commercially successful? Search the Web for new, undiscovered groups at sites such as www.napster.com* and www.GarageBand.com.* Write a brief statement explaining why this group could or could not become successful.

CONTROVERSIES

Web Excursion

3. As discussed in Chapter 1 (pages 30–31), there are several different interpretations of the term *censorship*. Search the Web for examples of music censorship, or go directly to a site such as Rock Out Censorship at www.theroc.org.* Choose one example and answer the following questions: (a) Do you believe that this is truly censorship? (b) It is dangerous? If so, why?

ONLINE LEARNING CENTER WWW.MHHE.COM/RODMAN2

You may access these and additional Web excursions at the Online Learning Center for the book (www.mhhe.com/rodman2). Visit the student portion of this Web site to also access the *Interactive Timeline of Mass Media Milestones,* chapter highlights, self quizzes, and recommended readings, movies, and documentaries for this chapter.

*Some Web site addresses may change. When they do, please search for the Web site by name or topic on your favorite search engine.

Radio

The Hits Keep Coming

8

Chapter Highlights

HISTORY: The invention of radio created a technology that seemed like science fiction at the time but soon produced a booming industry.

INDUSTRY: The radio business developed around local stations, groups, networks, syndicates, and National Public Radio, a network for noncommercial stations.

CONTROVERSIES: Radio controversies revolve around the phrase "public interest, convenience and necessity," and include the concentration of ownership, the quality of programming, and censorship.

Satellite Wars

If someone asked you to invest $2 billion in a business that was based on charging people around $150 a year for something that they had been receiving free for the last 80 years, would you do it? It sounds like you'd have to be crazy, but that's exactly what the two major satellite radio companies, XM and Sirius, have done. XM launched two satellites (nicknamed "Rock" and "Roll"), and Sirius launched three. They both set up elaborate studios—Sirius in New York and XM in Washington, DC. And they both invested in a stable of high-priced talent—most noticeably Sirius's acquisition of Howard Stern for $500 million over five years.

XM Satellite Radio uses Boeing 702 satellites like the one shown here.

Subscribers seem to be happy with the service. There are no commercials and no static on the music channels. Satellite radio receivers continuously display the artist's name and the song title. It's uncensored, in an age in which government crackdowns have made broadcast radio tamer

Satellite radio is one of the fastest-growing media technologies ever.

than ever. XM Comedy, a channel that features the often raunchy routines of Chris Rock and others, is among the company's 10 most popular.

Each of the services offers more than 100 channels of programming—around half of them commercial-free. There are dedicated channels for rock, pop, rap, hip-hop, show tunes, opera, classical, country and western, jazz, electronic, dance, folk music, blues, latin, and world music, as well as right- and left-leaning talk-show channels, sports, and real-time local traffic and weather service. Because the business model is based on subscriptions rather than ratings, genres that commercial radio shies away from, such as reggae, bluegrass, or talk devoted to African American affairs, get their own channels on satellite radio.

XM and Sirius receivers aren't compatible, so each company had to make separate deals with carmakers to offer satellite as original equipment. XM landed Honda, Toyota, General Motors, and Nissan. Sirius signed Mercedes-Benz, BMW, Volkswagen, and Ford. Both started with auto units only, then moved to home devices, and finally, to handheld units that make satellite radio available anywhere.

Now, it seems that the gamble is paying off. After fewer than five years of operation, the two companies have signed on more than 12 million paying customers. That makes satellite radio one of the fastest-growing media technologies ever—faster, for example, than cell phones. So far, though, neither company has turned a profit.

Will satellite radio be successful? It might depend on the competition—and not just the competition between XM and Sirius. As competitive as these two companies have been, their real competition might be other technologies. Broadcast radio still has 270 million listeners, and stations are promising fewer commercials. Drivers also have local radio, tapes, CDs, and adapters that allow iPods and other personal media players to play on car speakers. And the biggest competition might be in the near future, when the entire Internet will be available via onboard broadband connections. Stay tuned.

XM and Sirius Radio compete as satellite radio broadcasters.

The huge investment that XM and Sirius were willing to put into satellite services reminds us how important radio is throughout the world. It continues to be a prime source of entertainment and information. It is a personal medium, one that people often listen to alone and for which they feel a special affinity. In the United States, there are 675 million radio receivers in use, between 2 and 3 for every man, woman, and child in the country. Americans spend, on average, 3 hours every weekday and five hours on weekends listening.[1] Clock radios wake them up, and car radios keep them company as they travel. For many teens, the radio is like a friend. For devotees of political talk shows, radio is a primary means of information. It is obvious that radio will remain essential even as its technology changes.

A Brief History *of Radio*

Radio is a resilient industry, staying profitable for decades by playing whatever it is—whether songs or other types of programming—that people want to hear. The industry's resilience has been necessary, because radio has always been a changing technology. It was essentially a hobbyist's toy in its early days, became the backbone of national entertainment in its golden years, and finally, evolved to the important local medium it is today.

EARLY DEVELOPMENT

The era of electronic communications media began in 1842 with Samuel Morse's invention of the telegraph (see Chapter 1), which was an important precursor to radio. By 1861 telegraph lines ran from coast to coast in the United States, and by 1866 the first transatlantic cable connected North America to Europe. The telegraph transformed the world of communications, but it had certain limitations. For one thing, it could not reach everywhere. It could not connect ships at sea, and it could not send messages to the rural regions of the world where it was not economically feasible to run wires. The telegraph also could not carry human voices, although that limitation ended in 1876 when Alexander Graham Bell invented the telephone.

Hertz Discovers Radio Waves

It was both the successes and the limitations of the telegraph and the telephone that inspired many inventors to look for a way to free these media from wires. One such inventor was the German physicist Heinrich Hertz. Hertz built on the theories of scientists who had studied electricity since the Renaissance and used the word *radio,* which has the same root as *radius,* to denote the rays that supposedly emanated in a circular pattern from an electrical source.

Although earlier scientists had theorized about these waves,[2] Hertz was the first to demonstrate, in 1887, that they actually exist. He constructed two separate coils of wire and placed them several feet apart. When he ran an electric current through one coil, it produced a current in the other. When the coils were moved across the room from each other, the effect was the same, proving that electricity was moving through the airwaves. If electricity could be sent through the airwaves in the same way that it could be sent through wires, then it stood to reason that these waves could be used to transmit messages. For years after this demonstration, radio waves were called Hertzian waves, and today we measure electrical frequency in hertz (such as kilohertz and megahertz) in the inventor's honor.

The Electrical Revolution

As scientists experimented with radio waves, changes in technology, many of which had to do with electrical power, were turning the world upside down. The electrical revolution, in fact, was similar in many ways to today's digital revolution. By the 1880s Thomas Edison's company, Consolidated Edison, was wiring the streets of New York City. Another one of his companies, the Edison Electric Light Company (which would later become General Electric), was manufacturing lightbulbs for people to use with their new household current.

In the midst of all this progress, scientists were improving their methods of sending electrical energy through the air. They determined that there was an **electromagnetic spectrum,** a range of frequencies that could be used

electromagnetic spectrum
The range of frequencies that can be used for transmitting radio waves with electricity.

Guglielmo (William) Marconi developed his wireless telegraph system when he was 20 years old.

Morse code
Telegraph code of dots and dashes invented by Samuel Morse.

for transmitting radio waves with electricity. Waves could be sent out slowly, at low frequencies, or more quickly, at higher frequencies. The transmission of radio waves remained little more than a laboratory trick, however, until a 22-year-old Italian inventor, Guglielmo Marconi, had the vision to put together several existing components.

Marconi Develops Wireless Telegraphy

Marconi combined Edison's electric power, Hertz's metal coil, and Morse's telegraph key with several of his own improvements, including a grounding system and an antenna of his own design. The result was a wireless telegraph system. Marconi actually developed this invention at his father's estate in Italy in 1896, when he was 20 years old. The Italian government, however, refused to patent the invention, so later that year Marconi took it to England, where he was able to register his patent for radio as a means of communication.

Marconi, like Edison, was both a scientist and an entrepreneur. He set up an international corporation and began to manufacture radio equipment to allow ships at sea to keep in touch through messages in **Morse code,** a telegraph code invented by Samuel Morse in which each letter of the alphabet is represented by a series of short and long impulses (dots and dashes). Marconi recognized that the new radio technology also had applications in land-based communications, especially in the huge geography of America, because it could allow people to send messages to places where no telegraph wires existed. Marconi brought his technology to the United States and set up American Marconi in 1899.

David Sarnoff's Vision

One of Marconi's early employees was a young Russian immigrant named David Sarnoff. Years later, Sarnoff would go on to build the Radio Corporation of America (RCA), after it had bought out American Marconi. Sarnoff had emigrated from Russia at the age of 10. When his father died, he quit school at age 15 to work full-time as an office boy.

At 21 Sarnoff was one of Marconi's wireless operators, and he found himself on duty when the *Titanic* went down in 1912. Sarnoff later claimed

Broadcasting technology had previously been imagined only in scientific conjecture and science fiction.

broadcasting
Using wireless technology to instantaneously reach a wide audience.

wireless telegraphy
Name for early radio transmissions, before human voices could be carried on the airwaves.

that he remained at his post for three days, constantly taking messages giving the names of survivors.[3] He also claimed that in 1915 he wrote a memo to the management of American Marconi, proposing a plan to bring "music into the home by wireless."[4] The plan, he said, was ignored. What Sarnoff had envisioned was **broadcasting,** using technology to instantaneously reach a wide audience. Broadcasting technology had previously been imagined only in scientific conjecture and science fiction. The term came from farming, where it meant to cast seeds over a broad area.

Fessenden Adds Voice to Radio

Throughout all its early development, radio was a form of **wireless telegraphy.** As such, it shared the telegraph's most serious limitation: It could not carry the human voice. It carried only the dots and dashes of Morse code. That code was meaningful only to those who were trained to use it, and even they had to translate it laboriously, one letter at a time, into messages. Reginald Fessenden, an electrical engineering professor at the University of Pittsburgh, was the first to overcome this limitation. Fessenden made the first wireless voice transmission in 1906 with a special high-frequency generator that he had designed. Radio operators at sea, accustomed to hearing only dots and dashes, were amazed at what they heard. The more superstitious ones thought they heard ghosts.

De Forest and the Audion Tube

While Marconi was setting up his American operations, a scientist named Lee De Forest, who had written his PhD dissertation on wireless technology, invented a tube to pick up and amplify radio signals in 1907. He called it an **Audion,** although it is better known today as the vacuum tube, and it became the basic component of all early radios. De Forest called himself the father of radio, but his story stands as proof that not all inventors are good businesspeople. He was arrested and charged with fraud in the sale of stock to start a company to produce radio equipment. He was acquitted, but the legal fight bankrupted him, forcing him to sell his Audion patent to the American Telephone and Telegraph Company (AT&T) for $50,000. De Forest might not have been successful as a businessman, but his Audion tube was the ancestor of the transistor that ran the first portables, and of the integrated circuit that was the forebear of today's computer chip. Many consider him the father of modern electronics.

Audion
A tube invented by Lee De Forest that was designed to pick up and amplify radio signals; also known as a vacuum tube.

SELF QUIZ

Name five people who made significant contributions to the development of the technology of radio, and explain what they did.

The Navy's Patent Pool

Radio technology continued to improve, and several companies fought over various patents. When the United States entered World War I in 1917, the U.S. Navy took over the radio industry to use it strictly for military purposes. The navy pooled all the patents and declared a moratorium on patent lawsuits. This encouraged holders of radio patents to band together and work cooperatively. The navy also trained 10,000 service personnel in the new technology, and after the war ended in 1918 those same people became the amateur enthusiasts and early professionals who developed the radio industry.

The Radio Consortium

When World War I ended, Marconi wanted to renew his American business, but the U.S. government was concerned about such an important technology being under the control of a foreign company. To make it difficult for Marconi to operate in the United States, the government awarded contracts to his American competition. Eventually, the navy's America-first policy was made into a law that forbid any foreign company from owning more than 25 percent of an American broadcasting concern. Two years after the war ended, a few large American companies formed a consortium to take over the radio business in America. Those companies included AT&T (the telephone company), Westinghouse (a manufacturer of electric appliances and equipment), General Electric (GE), and RCA, a subsidiary that GE created specifically for radio. These companies set about to build the radio industry by simultaneously manufacturing radio receivers for the home market and setting up stations to broadcast to those receivers. Although they started out in the spirit of cooperation, the radio pioneers would soon compete as vigorously as XM and Sirius are competing today.

THE FIRST BROADCASTERS

There were many amateur radio enthusiasts in the years after World War I, but the most important was Frank Conrad, who was the first to become a commercial broadcaster.

Frank Conrad of Westinghouse

Frank Conrad proved that radio could be both a business and a form of entertainment. Conrad was an engineer for Westinghouse in Pittsburgh. Radio was his hobby, and he had built a small transmitting station in his garage. When he started broadcasting phonograph records from his home equipment, residents wrote to him to request specific songs. Soon Conrad was broadcasting twice a week from 7:30 to 9:30 P.M. The local newspapers reported on the radio concerts, and a Pittsburgh department store stocked up on receivers. The store took out newspaper ads telling readers that they could come in to listen to the Conrad broadcasts, and if they liked them, they could buy receivers at the store.

Conrad's boss at Westinghouse noticed the ad and realized that broadcasting had marketing potential for the radio equipment that Westinghouse manufactured. He asked Conrad to construct a 100-watt broadcast station on top of the company's nine-story factory. He wanted it ready in time to transmit the results of the 1920 presidential election, which was only 33 days away. Conrad worked furiously, building the station and arranging with the local newspaper to feed him the election results from their telegraph service. He applied for a license and received the call letters KDKA. He finished just in time, and on November 2, 1920, Conrad announced to Pittsburgh that Warren G. Harding had defeated James Cox for president of the United States.[5] Afterward, Conrad broadcast his concerts from the new station for an hour every evening, 8:30 to 9:30 PM.

Frank Conrad, shown here with the transmitter he set up in his garage, was the first commercial broadcaster.

Now, to Make a Profit . . .

Many historians consider KDKA the first commercial radio station, but as Conrad was going on the air, the same kinds of broadcasting experiments were being conducted in other places around the United States. No one is sure which commercial station was actually first on the air. KCBS in San Francisco; WHA in Madison, Wisconsin; and WWJ in Detroit all debuted around the same time. Most radio stations began as promotional vehicles for companies like Westinghouse and for local stores that wanted to sell radio receivers. Newspapers and colleges ran stations also, but they had no means of support and many of them soon gave up.

The companies involved in radio had different philosophies about how to make money with it. AT&T, as you might expect, believed that radio should be a type of telephone service. This was the concept of **toll broadcasting:** Instead of one person talking to one other person, radio would allow one per-

toll broadcasting
Early plan for radio revenue in which access to radio time would be by fee.

son or organization to talk to the masses. Anyone who wanted to broadcast could do so by paying a fee to the telephone company and using its facilities. In 1922, AT&T's radio station WEAF in New York City started to sell time to anyone who wanted to purchase it. WEAF soon saw the problem in its plan: For people to want to broadcast, an audience would have to be there. For an audience to be there, the station would have to stay on the air for regular hours so people would know where to find it. WEAF would have to provide regular programming, whether anyone showed up to pay the toll or not. This type of scheduling became known as **sustaining programming.** Unsponsored programming is still known by that name—and is still something that radio stations seek to avoid, as they would rather have sponsors for all broadcast time. Selling advertising space on regular programming soon became the accepted means of supporting the medium.

Meanwhile, there was a frenzy in radio-related stocks on Wall Street that was rivaled only by the Internet boom of the 1990s. Shares of RCA went from $5 to more than $500 in the 1920s, and investors bought shares of anything involved with radio. The majority of popular radio manufacturers of the 1920s failed, and even RCA would lose most of its value in the stock market crash of 1929.

sustaining programming
Regular unsponsored broadcast shows designed to maintain audience contact until advertising can be sold for that time.

THE RISE OF THE NETWORKS

A broadcast **network** is a group of interconnected stations that share programming. The term is also used to mean a parent company that supplies that programming to stations. **Owned and operated stations (O&Os)** usually carry everything the network provides. Most of the stations in a network, however, are affiliates. A **network affiliate** is a local station that is not owned by the network but does have a contractual relationship with the network. The development of networks would prove to be essential to the growth of radio.

network
A group of interconnected broadcast stations that share programming; also, the parent company that supplies that programming.

owned and operated stations (O&Os)
Broadcast stations possessed by and run by the network; they usually carry everything the network provides.

network affiliate
A local station that has a contractual relationship to air a network's programming.

The First Network: AT&T

The first radio network was born in 1923 when AT&T connected its station in New York to its station in Boston. AT&T created this network to make money, but its most important effect was cultural rather than economic. Eventually, network radio helped unify the country by providing a type of common experience from coast to coast. People all over the country were listening to the same programs at more or less the same time, and these programs were becoming part of the national identity. People would talk about the concert the famous opera singer gave the night before or the sermon of a well-known minister.

Network radio helped unify the country by providing a type of common experience from coast to coast.

National Networks: RCA

AT&T's network operated only regionally, in Boston and New York. Several other small and regional networks formed around the country, but there were only two national networks at first, both owned by RCA, and both formed in 1926 as part of the National Broadcasting Company (NBC). The NBC executives were not terribly creative about naming the two networks, which were called NBC Red and NBC Blue after the colored pushpins used to mark stations on the company's maps. At that point, NBC was truly the Google of its day, controlling the lion's share of an evolving industry.

William Paley and CBS

In 1927, William Paley, the son of a cigar manufacturer, bought a struggling network called the Columbia Broadcasting System (CBS). The network had been an experiment by the Columbia Record Company but had been dropped when it lost too much money. Paley originally bought the network to promote his father's cigar company, but he soon adopted it as his primary business. He built up the network by offering local stations a better deal than NBC was giving them to link up. Later, he raided NBC's on-air talent, stealing away performers such as Jack Benny and Groucho Marx with more lucrative contracts. Paley ran the network for 50 years. He especially built up the network's news divisions, and by World War II CBS was the acknowledged leader of radio news.

Mutual and ABC

A coalition of independent stations, the Mutual Broadcasting System, was begun in 1934. Mutual served smaller stations that were not affiliated with the major networks until 1998, when it went out of business as part of a corporate merger. The American Broadcasting Company (ABC) was created in the mid-1940s when the government forced RCA to sell one of its networks. The government was concerned that RCA would exert too much control over the public airwaves with two networks. RCA sold NBC Blue, the weaker of its two networks, to a group of businesspeople led by Edward Noble, the owner of Lifesavers Candy Company. The resulting network became ABC.

Until the 1950s the "Big Four" radio networks—NBC, CBS, ABC, and Mutual—had an oligopoly (market control by a small number of companies); the largest radio stations were owned by, and the majority of other radio stations were affiliated with, these networks. Network affiliates were originally linked to network headquarters through telephone lines. Since the 1970s, they have been linked by satellite.

SELF QUIZ Who were the main players in the development of network radio?

In the early days of radio, families would gather together for prime-time programming.

EARLY PROGRAMMING

Radio networks invented all the programming genres we have in television today, including formula dramas, situation comedies, soap operas, game shows, musical variety shows, talk shows, and broadcast news and sports. Most radio programs lasted 15, 30, or 60 minutes. When their favorite programs came on, family members would gather in the living room and "watch" the radio—which was often the size of a modern wide-screen TV.

Regulation

With radio came the most direct regulation of American media since colonial days. The First Amendment had created a hands-off government policy for the print media, but the broadcast spectrum created a new problem. That

The Radio Act of 1912 was passed largely in reaction to the Titanic disaster.

problem was **spectrum scarcity,** the fact that there were far more people who wanted to broadcast over the radio waves than there were frequencies to carry them. Radio receivers were emitting a jumble of static as broadcasters, both amateurs and professionals, interfered with one another. National legislation was needed to impose order, although it would take a number of laws to accomplish this.

The Radio Act of 1912

The first of these laws was the Radio Act of 1912, passed largely in reaction to the *Titanic* disaster. When that ship went down, killing 1,500 people, the radio operators of other ships in the area had already shut down their equipment for the night. Lives might have been saved if the ships had realized the *Titanic* needed help. The 1912 law required ships at sea to leave their radios on 24 hours a day. Almost as an afterthought, it also required federal licensing of all radio transmitters. Everyone who wanted a license was granted one, but no government agency was given the power to require a station to broadcast on a specific frequency.

The Radio Act of 1927

By 1927 radio sales were declining sharply because of all the interference caused by broadcasters operating on close frequencies. To solve the interference problem, Congress enacted the Radio Act of 1927, which established the Federal Radio Commission (FRC), with powers to enforce the law and limit the number of broadcasters. With this act, the federal government became the traffic cop of the airwaves. The law gave the FRC the right to assign a frequency and power for each broadcaster and to revoke the license of any broadcaster who did not comply with the rules. This allowed the FRC to organize the radio spectrum into a coherent system.

The 1927 act also required broadcasters to operate in the **"public interest, convenience, and necessity"**—a broad phrase that would cover a wide range of behaviors. What it meant, in effect, was that radio broadcasting had to be good for the community and for society in general. If the FRC believed that a station's actions were not in the public interest, it could revoke that station's license to broadcast.

"public interest, convenience, and necessity"
A phrase from the Radio Act of 1927 requiring that broadcasting be good for the community.

Major Radio Legislation

Legislation	Major Provisions	Significance	Shortcomings
Radio Act of 1912	Required a license to operate a radio transmitter.	Put radio clearly under government control.	Held no provision for assigning specific frequencies or for revoking licenses.
Radio Act of 1927	Gave the Federal Radio Commission (FRC) the power to enforce frequency assignments, and established the requirement of operating in "the public interest, convenience, and necessity."	Cut down on broadcast interference.	Covered only wireless communication.
Communications Act of 1934	Changed the FRC to the FCC and placed interstate wire communication, as well as wireless, under its control.	Allowed for adaptation to new media like television and cable, but placed restrictions on station ownership.	By the 1990s, the act's limits on ownership were seen as inappropriate for the digital age.
Telecommunications Act of 1996	Deregulated most ownership limitations, along with several other provisions.	Led to a huge consolidation of ownership, especially in radio, as chains and conglomerates bought up hundreds of stations.	Critics believe that this act allowed a small number of companies to become too powerful, cutting down on the diversity of opinions that are necessary in a democracy.

The Communications Act of 1934

Federal Communications Commission (FCC)
Government agency in charge of regulating all means of interstate telephone and radio communication.

With the Communications Act of 1934, the FRC became the **Federal Communications Commission (FCC)** and was given the power to regulate all means of interstate telephone, telegraph, and radio communication. With various amendments (to cope with new technology such as television, cable, and the Internet), the act remains in force today to govern electronic media and telephone communications. Some of the amendments concerned station ownership rules, for example, lifting limits over the years on the number of stations a company could own from 7 to 12 to 20. A major overhaul to the 1934 act was the Telecommunications Act of 1996, which dropped most limits on station ownership and led to a huge consolidation in the industry in the late 1990s. A thumbnail comparison of the laws regulating radio is provided in Fact File 8.1.

Why did radio, unlike the print media, need to be regulated by the government?

SELF QUIZ

Call Letters for Station Identification

call letters
Broadcast station identifications assigned by the FCC.

Call letters to identify stations were established with the Radio Act of 1912, and in 1927 it was decided that a station's call sign would begin with a *W* if it was east of the Mississippi River and with a *K* if it was west of that point. The 30 or so stations established before this rule (e.g., KDKA in Pittsburgh, KYW in Philadelphia, and WHO in Des Moines) were allowed to keep their call signs. Several owners made up call letters as a quick way to define the station's character. A station in the farm community of Salinas, California, chose KSBW to stand for "Salad Bowl of the World," and WZPR in Meadville, Pennsylvania, announced that town as the birthplace of the zipper.[6] Call letters generally have to be in good taste and significantly different from others in their service area. The government did allow an Arlington Heights, Illinois, station to use the call letters WSEX, but other variations on that term have been rejected over the years.

Edwin Armstrong and the Birth of FM

In the early days all radio used **amplitude modulation (AM),** which tended to have static and a poor sound quality for music. A scientist named Edwin Armstrong believed that he could improve broadcasting by changing the basic way that radio waves worked. AM radio creates its signal by changing (modulating) the power (amplitude) of the carrier wave. Armstrong believed that wave changes based on frequency would be of higher quality. A **frequency modulation (FM)** wave creates its signal by modulating the speed (frequency) at which the wave travels (see Figure 8.1). Armstrong demonstrated FM for the first time in 1936.

The development of FM radio encountered resistance from RCA, which wanted to protect its AM empire. RCA chief David Sarnoff initially supported Armstrong's work but lost interest in order to pursue the development of television. Armstrong continued without RCA and soon sold 400,000 superior-sounding FM receivers. All those receivers became useless in 1949 when the FCC, at the urging of RCA, moved FM to a new band. Meanwhile, RCA and others were using FM circuitry for television and their own receivers without paying the licensing fees that Armstrong demanded. Armstrong sued everyone who had, he felt, infringed on his patents. Exhausted after years of lawsuits, the scientist committed suicide in 1954. After his death, his estate won every one of the major lawsuits he had brought against RCA and the other companies that were using FM.

Edwin Armstrong, shown at the beach with his first portable radio.

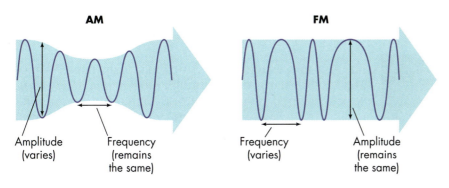

AM

Amplitude (varies)

Frequency (remains the same)

FM

Frequency (varies)

Amplitude (remains the same)

FIGURE 8.1 AM and FM Waves AM broadcasting works by controlling the power of the wave. FM broadcasting controls the frequency.

THE GOLDEN AGE OF RADIO

The golden age of radio lasted from the 1930s until just after World War II, when television began to replace radio as the primary medium of mass communication. During its golden age, radio boasted the nation's best and most popular entertainment and each week's programming became part of a countrywide conversation. Talk shows were broadcast in the morning, soap operas in the afternoon, and a full range of programming in the evening prime time. Musical shows featured big bands, often live, with such singers as Bing Crosby and Frank Sinatra. Comedy shows featured Jack Benny, George Burns and Gracie Allen, Bud Abbott and Lou Costello, Bob Hope,

The War of the Worlds and the Power of Radio

If there was a defining moment that demonstrated the enormous power of broadcast radio in its golden age, it might have been the Halloween night 1938 broadcast of *The War of the Worlds*. Six million people listened to this nationwide radio network adaptation of H. G. Wells's novel. It is estimated that one million of them actually believed that Martians were invading the Earth.[1]

ers tuned in to hear Bergen's opening monologue—which posed as a dialogue with his ventriloquist's dummy, Charlie McCarthy.[2] If they were not interested in the guests for that evening, listeners would start dial spinning—the 1930s version of channel surfing. The introduction to *The War of the Worlds* explained that the play would include make-believe news flashes.

Within a span of 45 minutes, the Martians had blasted off from their planet, landed in New Jersey, defeated the Earth's armies, and occupied whole sections of the country.

Looking back, it seems strange that anyone could be fooled by the radio play. Within a span of 45 minutes, the Martians had blasted off from their planet, landed in New Jersey, defeated the Earth's armies, and occupied whole sections of the country.

Part of the reason people were fooled, however, was that many had missed the play's introduction. They had tuned in to the first few minutes of Edgar Bergen's comedy show on another network. Much like today's viewers of David Letterman or Jay Leno, listen-

Unfortunately, people who tuned in late thought the program's mock news format was real.

The fictional invasion took place in Grovers Mills, New Jersey. Soon, real-life residents there were running for cover with wet towels wrapped around their heads to protect their brains from Martian heat rays. Across the nation, police switchboards were jammed with calls from people who believed the invasion was real. Young men reported for military duty to fight the invaders.

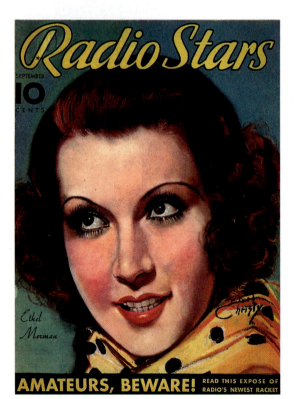

During radio's golden age, several popular magazines covered radio entertainment. Besides *Radio Stars*, shown here with Ethel Merman on the cover, there was *Radio Mirror, Broadcast Weekly,* and *Radioland.*

and the misadventures of a fictional team named Amos and Andy. Many critics thought that *Amos and Andy,* which featured two white actors mimicking blacks, was racist, but the show was hugely popular. (When it moved to television in the 1950s, it featured an all-black cast.) Radio dramas included *The Shadow, The Lone Ranger,* and *The Green Hornet.* Original plays such as *The War of the Worlds* (see the Close-Up on History box) were broadcast regularly. Popular game shows included *Truth or Consequences* and *The $64 Question.*

The day after the Japanese attacked Pearl Harbor in 1941, 60 million people tuned their radios to President Franklin D. Roosevelt's address to Congress, which is still the largest audience ever for any radio talk. The American public stayed glued to their receivers for the remainder of the war. Roosevelt used his frequent "fireside chats" to broadcast encouragement to the American people during the war years. He knew how to take advantage of the in-

The play was directed and narrated by Orson Welles, a 23-year-old boy wonder who was the leader of the Mercury Theater of the Air. Welles was already well known by radio fans as the original voice of the Shadow. The further fame that he garnered from *The War of the Worlds* panic enabled him to launch his film career in Hollywood, where he produced and directed *Citizen Kane,* which the American Film Institute considers the best American film of all time.

In the aftermath of the panic there were a series of Congressional hearings in which politicians decried this use of the airwaves as irresponsible. The FCC declared new rules requiring disclaimers both before and during radio plays that imitated newscasts. Major research studies were commissioned into the effect the broadcast had on the audience, and the incident helped establish a "powerful effects" perspective of media impact (see Chapter 2). The incident certainly demonstrated the way in which radio takes advantage of human imagination. But perhaps the most significant effect of the panic caused by the radio program was that the American public lost some of its

Orson Welles, the 23-year-old leader of the Mercury Theater of the Air, was the director and narrator of the 1938 "War of the Worlds" panic broadcast.

trust in the broadcast media. That effect continues to this day.

[1]The facts of this panic are documented in Hadley Cantril's landmark study, "The Invasion from Mars: A Study in the Psychology of Panic," in Shearon Lowery and Melvin DeFleur, *Milestones in Mass Communication Research,* 2nd ed. (New York: Longman, 1988), pp. 55–78.

[2]Edgar Bergen was the father of Candace Bergen, TV's Murphy Brown. The fact that so many people tuned in to a ventriloquist's radio show is a testament to the way radio inspires the imagination—usually the audience's enjoyment of this type of act is watching the ventriloquist's lips to make sure they don't move.

timate nature of the new medium. People who listened to those broadcasts said that they felt as if the president were in the room with them, like a friend or neighbor.

SELF QUIZ When was radio's golden age, and what was golden about it?

REACTING TO TV

The rise of television in the 1950s caused a decline in the radio networks' usefulness as distributors of a full range of programming to stations. Drama, comedy, and game shows moved to television. Three things helped radio survive in the face of the onslaught of television's popularity: the rise of FM, the development of the transistor, and format programming.

The Rise of FM

As mentioned earlier, Edwin Armstrong didn't enjoy the success of FM radio before his death, but by 1958 the radio industry was using the superior sound of FM to compete with television. By the mid-1970s there were more FM than AM listeners. Today, FM is three times as popular as AM. Many AM stations have adapted to the prominence of FM by moving to all-talk and all-news formats. Sound quality is less important with talk than it is with music, and the greater reach of the AM signal is an advantage for news. People have always turned to radio for late-breaking news, and they will probably continue to do so.

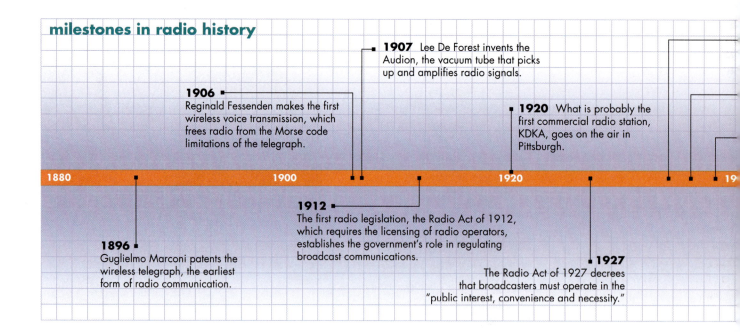

milestones in radio history

1907 Lee De Forest invents the Audion, the vacuum tube that picks up and amplifies radio signals.

1906 Reginald Fessenden makes the first wireless voice transmission, which frees radio from the Morse code limitations of the telegraph.

1920 What is probably the first commercial radio station, KDKA, goes on the air in Pittsburgh.

1880   1900   1920   19

1912 The first radio legislation, the Radio Act of 1912, which requires the licensing of radio operators, establishes the government's role in regulating broadcast communications.

1896 Guglielmo Marconi patents the wireless telegraph, the earliest form of radio communication.

1927 The Radio Act of 1927 decrees that broadcasters must operate in the "public interest, convenience and necessity."

The portable radio became a virtual outgrowth of the American teenager's ear in the 1950s.

transistor
A durable, solid-state, miniature version of the large and fragile vacuum tubes used in early radios.

format
Consistent programming formula with a recognizable sound and personality.

The Transistor Portable

A second development that helped radio compete with television was the transistor, which made radio portable. The **transistor** was a miniature version of the vacuum tube that Lee De Forest had invented earlier. Vacuum tubes made radios big, bulky, and fragile. They also needed a lot of power. The transistor, invented in 1948, was not only a fraction of the size of the vacuum tube but also more durable and less draining on power sources. The first portable transistor radios were introduced in 1954, and by the 1960s they were cheaper than conventional vacuum tube radios. Suddenly radio could be taken anywhere: to the beach, the corner hangout, the park. The portable radio became a virtual outgrowth of the American teenager's ear.

Format Radio

The third development that allowed radio to survive television's popularity was format radio. A **format** is a consistent programming formula that creates a recognizable sound and personality for a station. Music formats, for example, place a small number of similar types of records in rotation for multiple plays throughout the day. Station owners like formats because they encourage listener loyalty. Advertisers like them because they enable ads to target audiences with specific needs and buying habits.

Format programming was originated by Todd Storz, a station owner in Omaha, Nebraska, and Gordon McLendon, the owner of KLIF, Dallas, at around the same time in 1949. Both of these innovators noticed that patrons in local taverns played the same songs over and over on the jukebox, without noticeable complaint from other customers. Storz and McLendon wanted to instill the same kind of loyalty in their radio listeners. **Top 40,** the name of one of the most popular formats, came from the number of records stored in the typical jukebox of the day.

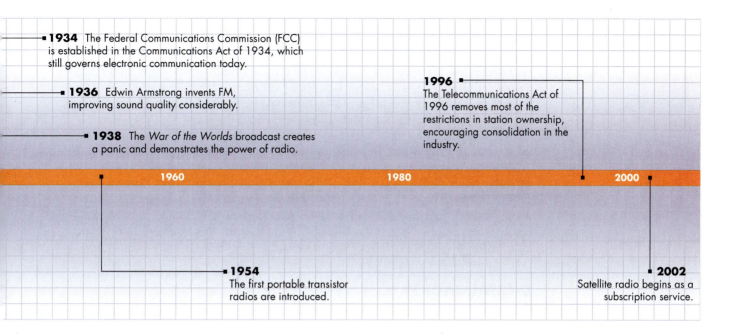

1934 The Federal Communications Commission (FCC) is established in the Communications Act of 1934, which still governs electronic communication today.

1936 Edwin Armstrong invents FM, improving sound quality considerably.

1938 The *War of the Worlds* broadcast creates a panic and demonstrates the power of radio.

1996 The Telecommunications Act of 1996 removes most of the restrictions in station ownership, encouraging consolidation in the industry.

1960   1980   2000

1954 The first portable transistor radios are introduced.

2002 Satellite radio begins as a subscription service.

Payola, Round 1

Format programming led to the payola scandals of the 1950s. During that time disc jockeys (DJs) selected the limited number of records that would be played. The DJs were much sought out by record companies, because airplay was the primary form of promotion for recordings. When record promoters began to pay DJs to play certain records, the practice became known as **payola.** When the practice became public knowledge, a major scandal ensued. Many DJs were fired, including the famous Alan Freed. Congressional hearings were held, and the Communications Act of 1934 was amended to make the practice illegal. As a result, record selection responsibility was taken away from the DJ and given to the program director of the station.

Formats and Diversity

Format radio also led to opportunities for women and ethnic minorities, although problems still exist in this area (these will be discussed later in this chapter). In Memphis, Tennessee, Sam Phillips, the legendary record producer who had discovered Elvis Presley (see Chapter 7), started an all-woman radio station in 1955. Prior to this, there had been a bias against female voices in radio, with male management insisting that women didn't sound credible on the air. Philips started WHER in a Holiday Inn in Memphis, with women as producers, DJs, technicians, advertising salespeople, and so on. The station

Format radio led to opportunities for women and ethnic minorities.

was successful in that format for 16 years and paved the way for a new generation of women in broadcasting.

CONCENTRATION AND FRAGMENTATION

The radio industry today is becoming concentrated in terms of ownership at the same time that it is becoming more segmented in terms of audience. Of

Top 40
Radio format in which the current 40 best-selling songs are played in rotation.

payola
A practice in which record companies paid radio station personnel to play certain records.

CONSIDER THIS

The move from national networks to local stations is sometimes referred to as a move from broadcasting to narrowcasting. How does radio's evolution in this way compare with the evolution of other forms of media, such as magazines? Use specific examples.

 SELF QUIZ How did radio react to the growth of television?

the 13,750 stations on the air today, more than 10,000 are commercial. Giant corporations own most of the largest and most profitable stations, especially since the Telecommunications Act of 1996 removed most of the restrictions on ownership. Between 1996 and 2000, chains bought more than 2,000 radio stations.[7] One company, Clear Channel Communications, owns 1,200 of the largest and most powerful radio stations in the United States. Several other companies own hundreds of stations (See Fact File 8.2).

Despite the fact that radio station ownership is becoming more and more concentrated, audiences are becoming more fragmented. Around 1,000 radio stations were on the air during the golden age of radio, and most of those were full-service network stations that provided the range of programming we see on TV stations today. Today's 10,000 commercial stations are defining themselves with narrower and narrower formats. We will examine the trends of concentration and fragmentation more closely later in this chapter.

DIGITAL RADIO

analog radio
Radio transmissions in which an electronic waveform represents the sound on a carrier wave.

digital radio
Signal transmissions by assigned numbers rather than analog waves.

Until the 1990s, radio still worked mostly on the AM technology of the 1920s and the FM technology of the 1960s. In traditional **analog radio,** an electronic waveform represents the sound on a carrier wave. Such a waveform carries static and is easily corrupted. In **digital radio,** transmitted sounds are assigned numbers (digits) that result in a crisp, clear signal. Most observers insist that the difference between traditional analog broadcasting and digital broadcasting is like the difference between AM and FM in terms of quality. Digital radio is also able to display information on a small screen of the receiver, information such as the channel number, the format, and the title and performer of each piece of music. Digital radio signals can radiate from satellites, as discussed in the vignette that began this chapter, but they can also originate from the Internet and from local stations.

Webcasting

As of 2007, around 10,000 Web radio stations were in operation. Around 4,000 of these were broadcast radio stations from 150 countries that stream online.[8] The rest were personal Internet channels that emanate from bedrooms and basements around the world. Web radio stations therefore include everything from the highly official, such as China Radio International (en.chinabroadcast.cn), to the highly eccentric, such as the all–"Ave Maria" channel (www.avemariaradio.tv), which plays that song 24 hours a day. Some webcasters offer podcasts and other types of programs "on demand," presenting their customers with a handy library of prerecorded shows they can hear whenever they care to download them. Each of the big online service providers—such as AOL's Radio Network, Yahoo's LAUNCHcast, and Microsoft's MSN Radio and WindowsMedia.com—offers a vast range of stations, each webcasting niche music to satisfy diverse musical tastes.

Web radio is so unique that many observers wonder if it can still be called radio. For example, on the large commercial sites listeners can pause or skip songs they don't like. When they come across one they enjoy, they can read its details, pay to download it, order the CD, or buy the ringtone. Some online music stations, such as Last FM (named by its founders as the last radio station a listener will ever need), have the ability to adapt themselves to suit each listener's tastes. Information about any music you play on your computer or buy online is fed into the site. Eventually, the system builds a detailed picture of your musical tastes, which enables it to play new music it thinks you'll enjoy. It also provides you with links to like-minded people so that you can share music ideas. One of the founders of Last FM has proclaimed: "Maybe one day, when you have a high-speed Internet connection in your car or on your iPod, this type of radio station will take over."[9]

Local Digital: HD Radio

Local radio stations are also beginning to change to digital technology, in preparation for the day when digital, high-definition (HD) radio becomes popular. According to equipment manufacturers, HD radio, which requires an HD receiver, brings FM-quality sound to AM stations and CD-quality sound to FM broadcasts. It also enables stations to send advertising messages over the HD receiver's text display screen. Stations have used this method to promote concerts and movies during songs by the appropriate bands; others flash the advertiser's telephone number with the message "CALL NOW." (Consumer advocates have objected to this additional distraction as a safety hazard for drivers.) Most importantly, digital radio will provide for extra signals, so radio stations can offer four or five programming choices on one channel, providing more diverse programming in the style of today's satellite radio.

M4Radio.com, which originates from Kissemmee, Florida, broadcasts only online. Many webcasters have stopped broadcasting because of required royalty payments to music labels. M4, however, surviving over eight years (one of the oldest net only stations), accepts only music that is unsigned or signed to true indie labels, making it royalty free. Reprinted by permission of M4Radio.

SELF QUIZ What forms does digital radio take?

Understanding Today's Radio *Industry*

While radio evolved from a form of at-home, family-style entertainment to a mobile, personal companion, one thing remained constant: Radio professionals have always had as their primary objective to keep the listener listening. They do this by using every technique they can find, from playing the music people want to hear to constantly giving teasers regarding news, weather, and upcoming contests. Their desire to keep the listener from switching stations provides an object lesson in what media practitioners can do to control consumer behavior. To understand why today's radio industry does what it does, you need to familiarize yourself with the roles played by formats, ratings, industry structure, station personnel, and the audience.

FORMATS

Nearly all of today's commercial radio stations are formatted, aiming to dispense a consistent sound day and night. They may play classical music, rhythm and blues, jazz, or alternative rock, but they play it without exception (see Fact File 8.2). They announce their formats continually with slogans like "Young country!" "No rap, no metal!" and "All the hits!"

Dayparts

Although they don't change the type of music they present, many stations change their formats slightly for various dayparts. **Dayparts** are the time

dayparts
Time divisions that radio stations make in the day in order to determine programming.

Top Formats by Audience Listening Preference

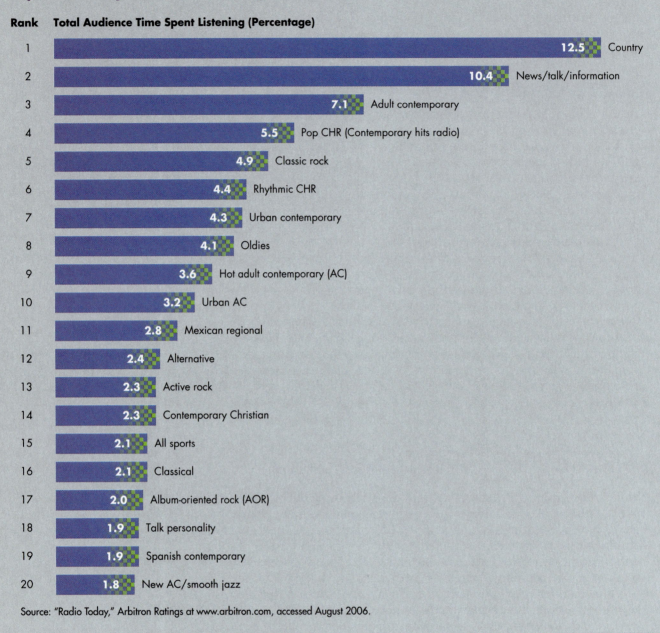

Rank	Total Audience Time Spent Listening (Percentage)		
1	12.5		Country
2	10.4		News/talk/information
3	7.1		Adult contemporary
4	5.5		Pop CHR (Contemporary hits radio)
5	4.9		Classic rock
6	4.4		Rhythmic CHR
7	4.3		Urban contemporary
8	4.1		Oldies
9	3.6		Hot adult contemporary (AC)
10	3.2		Urban AC
11	2.8		Mexican regional
12	2.4		Alternative
13	2.3		Active rock
14	2.3		Contemporary Christian
15	2.1		All sports
16	2.1		Classical
17	2.0		Album-oriented rock (AOR)
18	1.9		Talk personality
19	1.9		Spanish contemporary
20	1.8		New AC/smooth jazz

Source: "Radio Today," Arbitron Ratings at www.arbitron.com, accessed August 2006.

divisions radio stations make in the day in order to determine programming. The following is a typical breakdown of dayparts:

Morning drive time	6:00 AM to 10:00 AM
Midday	10:00 AM to 3:00 PM
Afternoon drive time	3:00 PM to 7:00 PM
Evening	7:00 PM to midnight
Overnight	Midnight to 6:00 AM

Drive times are the prime time of radio programming, so that is when shows hosted by the station's top on-air personalities, such as Howard Stern or Don Imus, might run. Morning drive time is especially important, because programmers believe that if they can get you to tune in to a personality in the morning, you'll be more likely to stay loyal to that station during the day. During drive time, programming is also adapted to commuters who listen to the radio in their cars. This audience might be given more traffic and weather reports, as well as more news. During the overnight hours the typical listener might be lonely or bored, so more call-in shows might be scheduled.

Talk/News Formats

Talk radio has become extremely popular since the 1980s; the number of stations featuring talk radio grew from around 170 in 1987 to more than 1,300 by 2007. Talk radio appeals especially to working-class and middle-class adults over 35, many of whom appreciate the outspoken opinions of the shows' hosts. In fact, in the last few presidential elections, conservative talk shows, such as Rush Limbaugh's, have been extremely influential. Many critics believe these shows helped elect Republicans.

News formats attract a somewhat more upscale audience by providing a formula that listeners can rely on for information they are interested in. For example, WINS, a popular all-news station in New York City, adheres to the following blueprint 24 hours a day:

Complete news update every 22 minutes.

Time every 3 minutes.

Weather every 5 minutes.

Traffic every 10 minutes.

Sports at 15 minutes before, and 15 minutes after, every hour.

The Format Clock

Radio programmers lay out their broadcast hour in a formula that can be drawn as a **format clock,** which looks like a pie chart, with every aspect of the programming hour shown (see Figure 8.2). Some of the aspects of the clock are givens. The FCC requires station identification at the top of every hour, and the station's business office will require that a certain number of commercials air. Also, the ratings services measure audience in 15-minute segments, so programmers generally shy away from commercials and other talk around the 15-minute mark in the hopes of "sweeping" the audience from one 15-minute segment to another. Contests and other types of promotions designed to get audiences to listen at key rating times of day have also become staples of most format clocks. The arrangement of all other aspects of the format clock are as various as the number of stations who use them.

As mentioned earlier, foremost in the mind of radio programmers is to keep the listener listening. Programmers assume that people will occasionally tune to the station through random channel surfing, so their main strategy is to schedule every broadcast minute so that people stay tuned in once they land on the station. Each segment of the programming hour will be part of an overall strategy. In the format clock shown in Figure 8.2, network news, local headlines, and weather are given at the top of the hour because that is when people tend to look for them. Then a catchy jingle reminds the listeners what station they are listening to (encouraging the all-important listener loyalty). An oldie is then played, on the assumption that someone who tuned in just for news might stick around to hear an old favorite. The next song introduction overlaps the

format clock
Graphic used by radio programmers showing each feature of the programming hour.

SELF
QUIZ   What is format radio?

FIGURE 8.2 Sample Format Clock

Radio programmers map out every minute of the broadcast day, with the sole objective of keeping the listener listening.

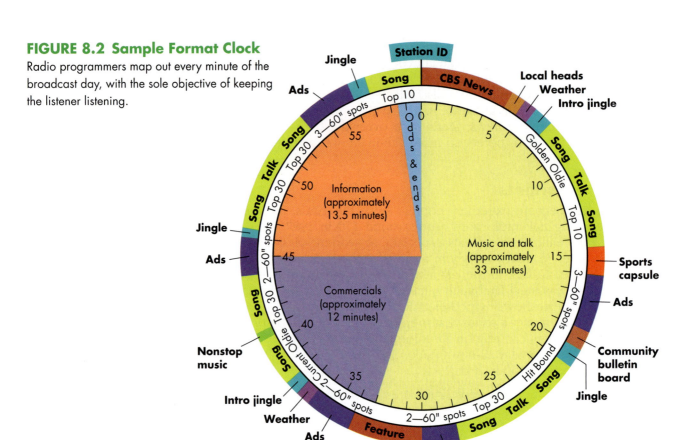

end of the oldie with a song-talk-song sequence. That is, the DJ introduces a top-10 hit over the last few bars of the oldie, so there is little or no talk space between the songs. Again, the strategy is that people who stayed tuned for an oldie might now be in the mood for a contemporary hit.

RATINGS

Ratings are all-important to radio station managers. Poor ratings necessitate changes, sometimes in format, sometimes in personnel. Radio stations have to prove to their advertisers how many and what types of people are listening. Whereas the print media can actually count the number of newspapers and magazines sold, the broadcast media have to rely on **sampling** in the form of ratings. In sampling, a small percentage of the audience is chosen to represent the behavior of the rest. If the sample is big enough and if it is randomly chosen, the ratings numbers should be accurate to within just a few percentage points. Each ratings point represents 1 percent of the audience. In most markets, because there are so many competing stations, the ratings numbers are extremely small. A rating of 4 or 5 could mean a big success.

Ratings in the radio industry are measured by several independent research firms, the largest of which is Arbitron (www.arbitron.com). Arbitron sends out diaries to a sample of the audience. They ask those in the sample to fill out the diary by recording all their radio listening for a week and then to send it back. Members of the sample are paid a few dollars for their compliance. Other firms, such as Scarborough Research, conduct telephone interviews to collect the same kinds of information. (We'll have more to say about ratings in Chapter 9, on television.)

sampling
Measurements taken from a small percentage of the audience, chosen to represent the behavior of the rest of the audience; broadcast ratings are a form of sampling.

INDUSTRY STRUCTURE

The structure of today's radio industry is best described in terms of five entities: local stations, station groups, networks, public radio, and syndicators.

Local Stations

In spite of inroads in national programming made on the Internet, today's radio is still very much a local medium. Local stations might be AM or FM, commercial or noncommercial, and they might serve small, medium, or large markets. Commercial stations earn their revenue mostly from advertising booked by area merchants. In a typical year, U.S. radio stations will collect around $19 billion in advertising. Of that, more than $13 billion will be for local spots. The rest comes from various forms of national advertising, some of which is provided by networks or group owners.

Groups

Group owners are those with two or more radio stations. The advantages of group ownership include (1) a centralized management that oversees all the stations at once and (2) great savings in the production and bulk purchase of program materials, including shows with popular but expensive on-air personalities. Many functions—such as the sale of national advertising—can be centralized at great savings also.

In earlier years groups were restricted by the FCC to owning no more than 7 stations; the number was subsequently increased to 12, then to 20. Today, there are few limits to the number of stations one group can own. The Telecommunications Act of 1996 limits only the number of stations a group can own in one geographical area. The act allows a group to own eight stations in larger cities and up to five in smaller markets, with no limit on the total number. Because of this, today several groups own more than 100 radio stations each (see Fact File 8.3).

Even with the per-market restrictions, group owners can develop a significant presence in a community. In New York City, for example, CBS Radio owns six stations, including the two largest all-news stations, WCBS-AM and WINS-AM. All told, CBS's New York stations receive 37 percent of the advertising dollars spent on radio in the New York market.[10] CBS Radio, with about 180 stations, is the nation's fourth-largest chain. Clear Channel Broadcasting is the largest chain, with 1,200 stations.

Program Providers

As mentioned earlier in this chapter, the classic definition of a broadcast network is a group of interconnected stations that share programming. Today, however, most program providers call themselves radio networks. For example, Premiere Radio Networks, a subsidiary of the Clear Channel radio group, is a large program provider. Premiere syndicates 70 radio programs and services to more than 7,800 radio affiliates and reaches over 180 million listeners weekly. Premiere features personalities such as Rush Limbaugh, Dr. Laura Schlessinger, Jim Rome, Rick Dees, Casey Kasem, Dr. Dean Edell, Bob (Kevoian) & Tom (Griswold), Phil Hendrie, Leeza Gibbons, George Noory, Blair Garner, Carson Daly, John Boy and Billy, Matt Drudge, Kidd Kraddick, Glenn Beck, and Art Bell.

The station that carries a network's programs might do so in return for compensation from the network. In that case the network inserts its own

The *Media World* DVD that accompanies this book (track 3, *Radio: Inside WKNE-FM*) features a visit to a radio station in Keene, New Hampshire, where Steve Hamel is a DJ and also in charge of programming and operations.

Slogans and logos like this one for KCGQ in Cape Girardeau, Missouri, help promote local stations.

SELF QUIZ How has the definition of *radio network* changed since the golden age of radio?

FACT FILE 8.3

Largest Radio Group Owners

Group Owner	Corporate Parent	Number of Stations
Clear Channel	Clear Channel Communications, Inc.	1,200
Cumulus	Cumulus Media	306
Citadel	Citadel Communications	213
CBS Radio	Viacom/CBS	179
Entercom	Entercom Communications	119
Cox Radio	Cox Communications	80

Source: Company Web sites and telephone inquiries, October 2006.

Premiere Radio Networks, a subsidiary of the Clear Channel radio group, reaches over 180 million listeners weekly. Premiere Radio Networks, Inc. Used with permission.

national advertising into the programming. Spots are also left blank for local advertising, the income from which the local station can keep. Other networks provide programming on a straight-payment basis, in which the local station buys the programming and inserts all the advertising itself.

turnkey networks
Companies that provide fully automated around-the-clock programming for radio stations.

Turnkey networks provide around-the-clock music coverage. They allow local stations to be fully automated, sometimes staffing just one engineer who inserts the station ID, local ads, and occasional announcements. Turnkey networks allow a small local station to offer up a professional big-city sound, but they lose a lot in local flavor.

Public Radio

Public radio, also known as noncommercial radio, consists of broadcast outlets that derive their income from sources other than the sale of advertising time, such as through listener memberships and corporate underwriting. Noncommercial stations, many of which are housed on college campuses, have their own networks, the most important of which is National Public Radio (NPR). Noncommercial radio began in the 1920s as educational radio, but most of the original AM stations died out because of a lack of funding. In 1945, when the FCC was allocating FM channels, it reserved the lower portion of the FM band—88 to 92 megahertz—for educational use. Most public stations broadcast on that part of the spectrum today.

Congress set up National Public Radio in 1970 to connect noncommercial stations and produce programs for them to use. Today, NPR provides its member stations with about 22 percent of their daily schedules, including morning and afternoon news, and musical and cultural programs. *All Things Considered* and *Morning Edition* are two of NPR's most popular programs.

NPR requires its stations to be on the air at least 12 hours a day. Member stations must have program schedules that consist of more than in-school educational instruction, and they are not allowed to advocate a religious or political philosophy. By 2007, more than 800 stations were NPR members. NPR's member stations pay $6,000 in annual dues, plus programming fees based on audience size that can run into millions of dollars. Other organizations that produce or distribute programming for public radio stations include Minnesota Public Radio, a 37-member station group, which produces *A Prairie Home Companion*.

NPR relies on its member stations for funding, but money is a constant problem for those stations. Government funding was reduced drastically during the budget cutting of the 1980s, and today it is minimal. NPR stations have to appeal to their listeners and to corporations for donations. Most observers consider examination of government and business entities to be one of the primary responsibilities of noncommercial stations. Critics therefore fear that the stations that accept corporate underwriting will not offer programming that critically examines their donor corporations. (See the Close-Up on Industry box.)

SELF QUIZ How does NPR differ from commercial radio?

Public Radio around the World

The United States is one of the few countries in the world in which public radio is much smaller than its commercial cousin. In most other countries,

The United States is one of the few countries in the world in which public radio is much smaller than its commercial cousin.

public radio stations are owned and operated by the government, and are more dominant than the commercial stations. In England, for example, the British Broadcasting Corporation (BBC) had higher ratings than the commercial stations until 1995. Even today, commercial radio's lead is so small there that the BBC often regains the advantage.

Japan has a similar system, with both public and commercial stations, but twice as many stations are public. In both England and Japan, the public stations are supported through mandatory user fees that consumers pay on each radio they own. The United States also has one of the few

Has Public Radio Gone Commercial?

Public radio has always had to struggle for its financial survival, and in recent years the federal government has made things worse. Today, public radio stations receive only 11 percent of their support from the federal government, compared with more than 30 percent in 1980.[1]

As conservative legislators threatened to cut off even more funding in recent years, public radio stations and their program providers, such as NPR, scrambled to look for other forms of support. Station executives knew from extensive surveys that listeners found on-air fund drives to be annoying, but those same listeners said they weren't bothered by corporate underwriting messages. Public stations decided to move in the direction of increased underwriting.

They found many willing takers. Corporate sponsors are interested in noncommercial radio's relatively wealthy and educated audience. This audience has an annual median household income 26 percent higher than that of the population as a whole. These listeners also tend to travel, dine out, and own financial securities.[2]

But now many of these listeners feel that noncommercial radio has gone commercial. They worry about underwriting announcements that sound like ads.

NPR's *A Priarie Home Companion* is popular with listeners even though it features old-style ads for imaginary products. Those same listeners are less enthusiastic about today's underwriting messages that sound like ads. Shown here are Garrison Keillor, the host of *A Prairie Home Companion*, with actors Meryl Streep and Lindsay Lohan in the 2006 film that was inspired by the program.

After all, most of these listeners tune to public radio to avoid ads. These listeners are questioning whether their local stations can still be called commercial-free. Some feel that even on-air pledge drives amount to advertising because so many products are offered as an incentive to give.

public radio systems in which the national government does not control content. In China, for example, until very recently all radio stations were government-owned public stations. China has recently allowed a few privately owned commercial stations to open, but all content at those stations is regulated by the Propaganda Bureau of the Chinese Communist Party Central Committee.

STATION PERSONNEL

Radio station personnel rosters vary according to the size of the station and the size of the market it serves (see Fact File 8.4). For many stations, the most important personnel are the on-air talent and the program directors, both of whom work to keep the listener listening.

Listeners also worry about corporate influence on programming. Will *NPR News,* for example, take on commercial interests that it relies on for income?

Public radio stations are extremely sensitive to their listeners, who supply them with more than a third of their support through direct donations. Station executives know that these listeners don't like commercials, which is one reason that public radio calls them underwriting messages. Until a few years ago, the FCC refused to let corporate sponsors reveal much more than their name and location in these announcements. The FCC now allows underwriters to describe products and give out their telephone numbers. They can't, however, mention prices, ask listeners to buy their product, or use comparative or qualitative descriptions such as "best." Still, the underwriting announcements have become much more adlike, and there are more of them. They are even weaved into programming breaks like traditional commercials, rather than lumped at the end of each show.

So public radio execs try to be careful in the way they present underwriting announcements. "There are ways to do them that are consistent to the values of public radio," says Ken Stern, NPR's chief operating officer. "People are turned off by length. People expect them to be informational, not salesmanlike."[3]

So NPR inserts only about a minute and a half of sponsorship announcements into each hour of its programming, and limits the announcements to 10 seconds each. An NPR employee reads them in a neutral voice that is supposed to blend in with the programming. That should make them considerably more palatable than ads on commercial stations, which take up 15 minutes of every hour and are more intrusive.

Along with public radio's listeners, commercial broadcasters are concerned about the stations going commercial. The ad revenue for commercial stations has remained flat in recent years, and commercial broadcasters are already dealing with competition from Internet radio, satellite radio, and iPods. The last thing they want to see is public radio emerging as one more competitor.

"What you're seeing is public broadcasting moving toward commercialization, and that is troubling," says one industry executive. "As they become the equal of commercial stations, they should be treated the same."[4] This executive, like many others in commercial broadcasting, believes public radio has an unfair advantage: It is nonprofit and tax exempt.

[1] Sarah McBride, "As Sponsorship Sales Blossom, Public Radio Walks a Fine Line," *Wall Street Journal,* online, March 17, 2006.
[2] Sarah McBride, "As Sponsorship Sales Blossom."
[3] Quoted in Sarah McBride, "As Sponsorship Sales Blossom."
[4] Saul Levine, owner of Los Angeles–based Mount Wilson FM Broadcasters Inc., quoted in Sarah McBride, "As Sponsorship Sales Blossom."

On-Air Talent

A radio station's on-air talent might include a morning or an afternoon talk-show host, the most popular of whom will be syndicated to other stations. The conservative political commentator Rush Limbaugh, for example, is syndicated to more than 600 stations. Other players include features, sports, and news reporters. The most numerous radio personalities today, however, are disc jockeys (DJs).

The role of the DJ has changed considerably since the payola scandals of the 1950s. Most current DJs don't expect to choose music; their job is to disguise the mechanical nature of the format. As they play a preordained list of hits, they try to add some personality to the 100th spin this week of a song in heavy rotation. Most work a 4- or 5-hour shift, but with preparation and promotional responsibilities these often amount to 12-hour days. On

FACT FILE 8.4

Radio Station Jobs

The following are standard employment positions for radio stations.

Position	Job Description
Managerial Positions General Manager	Operates a station overall.
General Sales Manager	Hires and supervises the sales staff, develops sales plans and goals. (Some larger stations may have separate national, regional, and local sales managers.)
Program Director	Controls production, talent, program schedules, and other on-air aspects of the station.
Business Manager	Manages all financial transactions.
News Director	Runs the news department, assigns stories to reporters, identifies news issues within the community.
Promotions Director	Promotes the station's image and programming through contests, events, and other activities.
Chief Engineer	Manages all technical operations at the station.
On-Air Positions Announcers/Disc Jockeys	Depending on a station's format, hosts and produces programs, reads commercial copy, and/or presents public service announcements.
Sales Positions Account Executive	Makes calls on potential advertisers to sell time on the station.
Administrative Positions Sales Assistant	Offers administrative support to the sales staff and the managers; may also draft sales proposals.
Traffic Director	Links the programming and sales departments by collecting data to prepare a daily broadcast schedule, keeps up-to-the-minute track of commercial time availabilities.
Promotions Assistant	Offers administrative support to the programming and promotions staff.
Receptionist	Carries out entry-level duties that vary by station.

Source: CBS Radio Web site at www.cbsradio.com, accessed November 2006.

CONSIDER THIS

Talk radio is filled with commentators, such as Rush Limbaugh, who are said to be politically powerful. In your opinion, does talk radio affect the outcome of U.S. elections?

small stations, on-air talent might also sell advertising, produce commercials, and work other jobs. Most successful large-market DJs started out at either a college radio station or a small-market station.

The Program Director

In radio, the program director (sometimes called the music director) determines the playlist for the station. The typical rock playlist includes about three dozen new singles, or "currents." A "hot" current will be placed in heavy rotation, airing four or five times a day.[11] Often, the program director will use computer software to make programming decisions. With software known as Selector, a day's worth of songs can be scheduled in a minute or so. That schedule will be based strictly on numbers, including the local sales figures for individual records.

The program director will often hire a programming consultant to help determine both the playlist and the overall format of the station. Programming consultants will conduct various types of research. They might run focus groups in which they have sample listeners sit in rooms and rate records. They might also conduct polls on the telephone to rate current hits. As one critic of today's radio has pointed out, "Gut reactions to music from disc jockeys have been all but replaced by chart analyses and surveys."[12]

The services of a program consultant can be expensive. Because of this, consultants' clients tend to be station groups, especially those with stations in major markets. Format successes in large markets will be heavily copied nationwide, which means that program consultants are extremely influential across the industry. More than anyone else, they determine the sound of today's radio.

THE AUDIENCE

Listeners invented radio as it exists today. They did this first by asking pioneers like Frank Conrad to program music for them to listen to, and later by responding to format programming in a big way, as measured by the all-important ratings. Changing audience habits change the structure of the industry. When radio was entertainment for the home, prime time was in the evening, after dinner. Today, radio is portable, most listeners are commuters, and prime time consists of the morning and afternoon drive times.

Most listeners today don't want to pay attention to the radio; they want a station to be a dependable accompaniment to other activities. Most listeners are loyal to just two or three stations, and different demographic groups have different musical tastes. Around every 10 years a new musical generation is created, for example, and 20-somethings will probably not be listening to the same music as teens or 30-somethings. The majority of listeners to hip-hop stations will be African Americans, the majority of listeners to Latin stations will be Hispanics, and the majority of listeners to both country and classical stations will be white. It is also true, however, that radio has allowed many listeners to develop musical tastes outside their ethnic and regional origins. DJs like Alan Freed, for example, made the "Negro music" of rock and roll popular with most teens in the 1950s. Today, people of all ethnic backgrounds enjoy rap, bluegrass, and gospel music. The unlimited possibilities of satellite and Web radio may well expand this cultural sharing.

"Starting Monday, this radio station will switch from classical music to hard-core rap."
© The New Yorker Collection 2002 Robert Armstrong from cartoonbank.com. All Rights Reserved.

Controversies

Many of the controversies surrounding the radio industry today revolve around a seemingly simple phrase: "the public interest, convenience, and necessity."

This phrase is a key part of the law governing radio today. It was the standard, or rationale, by which the U.S. government decided not to charge broadcasters for the use of the airwaves. In effect, broadcasters paid for this use by providing a public service. This standard has led to a number of controversies. Critics ask, for example, if concentration of ownership, homogenized programming, and the use of shock jocks are truly in the public interest. Others debate whether the public interest calls for a degree of censorship.

THE EFFECTS OF CONCENTRATION

Critics have always been concerned about the power of radio being placed in the hands of a few owners. Such concentration of ownership has the potential (1) to cut down on the number of different voices that are heard in the important debates of the day and (2) to open the way for the abuse of power by large conglomerates and networks. In the early days, the U.S. government tried to regulate the power of networks by limiting the number of stations they could own. When listening choices began to multiply because of an increase in the number of independent stations, as well as competition from television and cable, those rules were relaxed.

As noted earlier in this chapter, the Telecommunications Act of 1996 essentially did away with such restrictions on station ownership, and now more radio outlets are being placed into fewer hands. This leads to some potential conflicts of interest. Disney owns the ABC radio networks, for example, and those networks report on the cultural and entertainment news of that giant corporation. At one point, Disney was roundly criticized for refusing to air news reports critical of its theme parks. Conglomerates like Disney own book publishers; magazine publishers; film studios; and cable, satellite, and broadcast television properties as well as radio networks. That means that they can present their point of view to consumers via a number of media, making it difficult for people ever to hear a differing point of view.

HOMOGENIZED PROGRAMMING

Critics often complain about the quality of radio programming, including the blandness and uniformity of station formats. Although there are more formats than ever before, many of them sound the same, except for their particular style of music. Successful formats tend to be copied, leading to a homogeneity that has been magnified by concentration of ownership. Broadcasting chains have spent huge sums to buy new stations, and they have incurred heavy debts in doing so. This has forced them to press program directors to deliver ratings and advertising dollars quickly. They are too deeply in debt to take chances.

The result has been the encouragement of risk-free, generic formats, each with a numbing predictability. Across the United States and, increasingly, the world, you'll hear the same DJ style and even the same slogans on country,

Successful formats tend to be copied, leading to a homogeneity that has been magnified by concentration of ownership.

rock, and hip-hop stations: "More music, less talk" or "10 in a row." And the musical selections on each type of station tend to be the same. The idea is not to play something listeners might be thrilled to discover; it's to play what they won't dislike so that they won't tune out. As one observer pointed out, "Commercial radio has never seemed more organized and less invigorating."[13]

The one place where programming tends to not be homogenized today is on college stations. According to one music promoter, "Even on a national level, these stations have really strong reputations for being experimental, forward-thinking alternatives. They're the places where people go to hear the obscure, out-there tracks that you're otherwise never going to hear."[14]

SHOCK RADIO

Another problem related to the quality of radio programming is the obscene and sometimes pornographic nature of shock radio. **Shock jocks** like Howard Stern derive humor and ratings from lewd and tasteless comments (see the Close-Up on Controversy box). The idea behind shock radio is to see what jocks can get away with on the air. Vulgarity, racism, sexism, cynicism, and anything else that will attract amazed listeners—all are fair game. Critics complain that this type of broadcasting airs during the day, when children are likely to be listening in, and the FCC has levied fines against several stations that air shock radio. The fines became so heavy by 2007 that shock radio moved mostly to satellite radio.

shock jocks
Radio personalities who derive humor and ratings from lewd and tasteless comments, using tactics such as vulgarity, racism, sexism, and cynicism.

HATE RADIO

A close cousin of shock radio is hate radio, a format in which the on-air personalities appeal to the worst in their listeners—their ignorance, their economic insecurity, their fear of anything different or new—to encourage them to despise a particular class of people. The concept of hate radio is not new: A priest named Father Charles Coughlin was famous for it in the 1930s. Every Sunday afternoon, Coughlin's broadcasts were heard by millions. In a beautiful clear voice he exhorted his audience to hate socialists, communists, "international banksters," and especially Jews. He identified Jews with communism and claimed that they were themselves responsible for Hitler's persecution of them. Despite Coughlin's anti-Semitism, he had considerable political clout. At his command, hundreds of thousands of telegrams would arrive at a congressional representative's office, demanding that Congress back Father Coughlin's political agenda. Looking back, it is easy to see that Coughlin was both irresponsible and dangerous.

The effects of hate radio have been demonstrated gruesomely overseas. During 1994's ethnic massacre of Rwanda's Tutsi by the dominant Hutu, the Hutu pop music radio station would encourage its listeners to "finish off the Tutsi cockroaches." The names of prominent Tutsi, who were then killed, were read over the air. By the time the bloodletting was done, hate radio was blamed for promoting the massacres of 800,000 Tutsi and moderate Hutu in Rwanda.[15] In 2003 the executives of the station were convicted of genocide by an international tribunal, and sentenced to life in prison.[16]

Since much of the commentary on hate radio is directed at minorities, many critics believe that the problem would be at least partially alleviated by more minority ownership of radio stations. Critics and governmental experts believe that minority-oriented programming would be a natural offshoot of minority ownership, which would also give minorities a chance to succeed in a profitable and influential business. Fewer than 3 percent of U.S. commercial broadcasting stations are minority owned.[17]

The concept of hate radio is not new. Father Charles Coughlin was famous for it in the 1930s.

SELF QUIZ What is hate radio, and what are its effects?

DIVERSITY AND CENSORSHIP

Because of the local nature of radio, and the diversity of voices possible in the great number of stations, radio has been the medium of choice for a

Howard Stern's Public Parts

When Howard Stern moved to Sirius Satellite Radio in 2006, the deal cost Sirius $100 million a year for five years. Executives at the satellite service thought it was money well spent. Stern was just what Sirius needed to get listeners to pay for their programming. And Stern would finally escape the government scrutiny that had dogged him for years. The FCC had fined the radio stations that carried Stern millions of dollars over the years. The FCC doesn't regulate satellite, because it is received only by subscribers.

Howard Stern, shown here in his Sirius Satellite Radio studio, says, "The premise of the show is to split open my head and let out the unadulterated id."

Most critics condemn Stern for being lewd and tasteless. His own children are not allowed to listen to his show. "They think I'm a Harvard professor," he says with a straight face. But Stern has legions of loyal fans, and ratings have improved for his time slot in every market that picks up his show. He brings in a young male audience that would not be listening to radio at that hour without him. In fact, Stern proclaims himself the "king of all media." His multimedia empire in-

cludes his books *Private Parts* and *Miss America;* television programs, audiotapes, videocassettes, and compact discs; and the movie *Private Parts* (1997, based loosely on the book), which was well received by both the critics and the viewing public.

All of this from a man who claims to be a sex fiend whose development was arrested in adolescence. Stern invites female guests to disrobe, interviews Ku Klux Klan members, and makes fun of retarded and mentally ill visitors. According to Stern, it is the basic idea of his show that makes it so successful: "The premise of the show is to split open my head and let out the unadulterated id."[1] Over the years Stern has discussed every minute detail of his personal life, including his wife Allison's miscarriage and their eventual divorce.

The id that Stern refers to might help explain some of the appeal of shock radio. According to psychologists, the id is the part of the unconscious mind that seeks satisfaction in impulsive pleasures. Stern believes that people need to give their id some exercise—and some critics agree. One such critic said, "In some societies, when people want to open themselves to the voice of the unconscious, they build a bonfire and carve a model of a gigantic erect penis, and then they dance around it until they loosen up. In our society, the voice is on the radio, writes best-selling books and stars in a movie about his life."[2]

[1] Howard Stern, quoted in David Remnick, "The Accidental Anarchist," *The New Yorker,* March 10, 1997, p. 56.
[2] Jamie Malanowski, "Brace Yourself for Howieland," *Playboy,* April 1997, p. 76.

wide range of commentators with minority, radical, and artistic points of view. Talk shows feature the opinions of everyone from white supremacists to radical Hispanic feminists to militant vegetarians. These speakers rely on the same right of free speech on which shock jocks and hate radio commentators rely. When their points of view appear to be censored, controversy is almost automatic.

pirate radio stations
Low power, unlicensed, illegal stations.

Pirate Radio

Some radical groups have tried to avoid the censorship of their views by creating **pirate radio stations,** which are unlicensed, illegal, low-power outlets. Some pirates use portable equipment and move it from location to location to keep from being closed down by the FCC. Others broadcast from ships. Most pirate stations are now moving to the Web, out of FCC jurisdiction. Radio 4 All (www.radio4all.org) maintains a directory of these stations.

Low-Power FM

For years, the FCC debated whether to license low-power stations to increase the diversity of broadcast voices. The goal was to allow such stations to fill in small blank spots on the spectrum where they would not interfere with established stations. The FCC licensed 590 low-power stations between 2000 and 2007. Existing stations and their trade group, the National Association of Broadcasters, fought bitterly against this proposal, and managed to block any more stations.

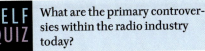

SELF QUIZ What are the primary controversies within the radio industry today?

Payola, Round 2

Payola didn't end in the 1950s; its target merely changed from disc jockeys to program directors. Some program directors began to use a legal form of payola called pay-for-play, which is done in the open. The record company would pay the station to play a song, and the station would make an appropriate announcement ("This record was brought to you by . . .").

Still, independent record promoters seemed to prefer the illegal version of payola, in which the payment was made secretly. With consolidation in the music and radio industries, it became much easier for deals to be struck behind the scenes. By 2006 the practice was so common that New York State Attorney General Eliot Spitzer uncovered clear-cut evidence that high-ranking executives had secretly traded cash for airplay of songs by such artists as Avril Lavigne, Liz Phair, and Jessica Simpson. These deals included payments for songs that became major hits, including Jennifer Lopez's "I'm Real" and John Mayer's "Daughters."[18]

Spitzer forced major music companies to pay fines of $10 million each. He then turned his attention to the other end of the scandal—the radio stations—and turned his evidence over to the FCC. The FCC goes into action only on the basis of complaints, so there had been no recent action on payola before Spitzer acted. The FCC was impressed with his evidence. "I can't believe that radio stations are putting their licenses at risk," said FCC Commissioner Jonathan Adelstein. "It seems to me they thought the FCC was asleep and they shot someone in front of the policemen. The policeman is obligated to act when evidence is so clear."[19]

Stations guilty of payola can be fined or have their licenses revoked. The current investigation, the biggest since the 1950s, is ongoing. It serves as a good example of how history is destined to repeat itself as long as airplay remains an integral part of record sales. Christopher Sterling, a George Washington University professor who has extensively studied the payola phenomenon, stresses the importance of radio in this process:

> Radio has lots of competition, which it did not have before—including satellite radio. But it's still incredibly important—despite the changes, despite the additions of lots of services, despite the sort of digitalization of life, radio is incredibly important—because it is really the first way that most people hear songs. They may then download [a song] to their iPod—they may, and this is what the record industry would like, they may actually go to the store and buy the bloody record. That's happening less and less, and that's what's driving all this.[20]

Summing Up

The telegraph started the electronic communications revolution, but that revolution made its most giant strides in radio. Radio waves were first demonstrated by Heinrich Hertz. Working from the findings of Hertz and other scientists, Guglielmo Marconi developed the first practical radio telegraph. Lee De Forest invented a tube to pick up and amplify radio signals, and Reginald Fessenden made the first wireless voice transmission, using a high-frequency generator he had designed.

The U.S. Navy took over radio technology during World War I, and after the war several companies divided up the field. These companies included American Telephone and Telegraph (AT&T), General Electric (GE), Westinghouse, and the Radio Corporation of America (RCA).

One early broadcaster was Frank Conrad, who set up what some believe was the first commercial station, KDKA in Pittsburgh. The first radio network was born when AT&T connected its station in New York to its station in Boston. Soon there were three national networks, two owned by NBC and one by CBS. NBC eventually sold one of its networks, which became ABC.

Regulation became necessary because stations had to be assigned frequencies and rules for broadcasting. There were four primary pieces of legislation regulating radio. The Radio Act of 1912 required transmitters to be licensed. The Radio Act of 1927 required stations to operate in "the public interest, convenience, and necessity." The Communications Act of 1934 created the FCC, which continues to regulate all forms of electronic interstate communications, including telephone and television as well as radio. The Telecommunications Act of 1996 provided for sweeping deregulation of ownership rules.

Radio programming enjoyed a golden age in the 1930s and 1940s. National, network radio was the country's primary form of at-home entertainment during those years. Radio networks invented every form of prime time entertainment that now appears on television.

Three things helped radio survive the arrival of television: FM, which gave radio a superior audio signal for music; the transistor, which made radio portable; and format radio, in which the programming was tailored to a particular type of listener. Current trends include the consolidation of ownership, audience fragmentation, and digital broadcasting.

The industry structure includes local stations, groups, program providers (now often called networks), and National Public Radio, a network for noncommercial stations. The audience essentially invented radio programming and continues to exert a powerful influence on it.

Radio controversies revolve around the phrase "public interest, convenience, and necessity," and include the concentration of ownership, the quality of programming, and censorship.

Key Terms

These terms are defined and indexed in the Glossary of key terms at the back of the book.

amplitude modulation (AM) 255

analog radio 260

Audion 249

broadcasting 248

call letters 254

dayparts 260

digital radio 260

electromagnetic spectrum 248

Federal Communications Commission (FCC) 254

format 258

format clock 263

frequency modulation (FM) 255

Morse code 248

network 251

network affiliate 251

owned and operated stations (O&Os) 251

payola 259

pirate radio stations 274

"public interest, convenience, and necessity" 253

public radio 267

sampling 264

HISTORY

Web Excursion

1. This chapter discusses a number of technological advances that led to radio broadcasting as we know it today. Search the Web for radio history sites, or go directly to a site such as the Radio History Project at www.radiohistory.org.* Find at least three early innovations that were not mentioned in this chapter. Defend or attack their importance to the development of radio.

Media World DVD Excursion

2. View track 3, *Radio: Inside WKNE-FM*. This track introduces you to the daily operations of a small-market radio station. List two advantages and two disadvantages to small-market radio. According to the video, what are the two main reasons people listen to the radio?

INDUSTRY

Web Excursion

3. What's your favorite radio station? Who owns it? Is it part of a group, network, conglomerate, or NPR? Trace its ownership on the Web by searching under its call letters or going directly to www.cjr.org/owners.* Analyze any conflicts of interest that might exist, such as the station's reporting on other properties that the parent corporation owns. Prepare a brief report on your findings.

Media World DVD Excursion

4. View track 3.3, *Issues: Getting a Job*. This track explains what it takes to work in radio broadcasting. If you were to pursue a career in radio broadcasting, would you rather work for a small- or a large-market station? Explain why.

5. View track 13, *Radio of the Future May Be on the Internet* (from NBC News Archives). Internet radio webcasters and members of the recording industry debate licensing and royalty fees for Internet radio. Do you believe webcasters should pay as much as traditional radio stations do for the use of music? What are the advantages of Internet radio? Do independent artists suffer when larger, established artists demand fees and royalties? Is there a common solution?

CONTROVERSIES

Web Excursion

6. Are critics justified in their complaints about the homogeneity of radio programming? Go to one of the directories of radio stations on the Web, such as Web Radio at www.webradio.com* or Radio Tower at www.radiotower.com.* Access rock (or your chosen format) stations from at least three different

sections of the United States and at least one from overseas. Defend or attack the charge that radio formats are homogenized.

Media World DVD Excursion

7. View track 3.2, *Issues: Competition and the Future*. This track discusses the future of radio broadcasting. In the near future, if radio went strictly Internet-based, would you miss over-the-air radio? Explain how radio contributes to the way you receive music and information.

ONLINE LEARNING CENTER WWW.MHHE.COM/RODMAN2

You may access these and additional Web excursions at the Online Learning Center for the book (www.mhhe.com/rodman2). Visit the student portion of this Web site to also access the *Interactive Timeline of Mass Media Milestones,* chapter highlights, self quizzes, and recommended readings, movies, and documentaries for this chapter.

*Some Web site addresses may change. When they do, please search for the Web site by name or topic on your favorite search engine.

Television

Reflecting and Affecting Society

9

Chapter Highlights

HISTORY: Many technical and economic problems had to be solved for television to evolve into the powerful industry and cultural force we have today.

INDUSTRY: An understanding of today's television industry includes understanding its delivery systems, which consist of cable, satellite, over-the-air broadcast, and new media alternatives such as cell phones and iPods.

CONTROVERSIES: Television is our most controversial medium, with the largest concern focusing on what it does to us as individuals and as a society.

Humiliation TV

South Park, Comedy Central's cartoon for adults, features a group of foul-mouthed fourth graders named Cartman, Kyle, and Stan. In a recent season premiere, an alien disguised as a giant talking taco informs the boys that Earth is actually a reality television show that has been set up for the amusement of beings from another planet.

The taco explains the concept: "Asians, bears, ducks, Jews, deers, and Hispanics, all trying to live side by side together on the same planet. Great TV, right?"

Kyle is shocked. "Dude, that's messed up," he says.

"Why?" asks the Taco.

Watching less talented performers humiliate themselves is part of the appeal of *American Idol.*

"You're playing with people's lives," says Stan. "You're turning people's problems into entertainment."

"Yeah," says Cartman. "We'd never do that on Earth."

Of course, Cartman was being naive. American TV has made a staple of turning people's problems into entertainment. One of the most successful early television programs was *Queen for a Day,* in which housewives competed to see who had the most heartbreaking problems. The winner was showered with new appliances. One of today's hit programs, *Extreme Makeover,* showers the lucky contestant with plastic surgery and cosmetic dentistry.

Many of today's reality programs, however, have added something to the equation: They actually create the problems for the participants. Consider the following recent hit shows:

● *American Idol,* which submits its less-talented contestants to Simon Cowell's abuse: "Dreadful.... There are only so many words I can drag out of my vocabulary to say how awful that was.... You will never, never, never have a career in the music business.... Listen to these words: you are not a singer.... You should sue your music teacher."

● *The Apprentice,* in which Donald Trump gets to fire a job applicant each week, after telling that applicant why he or she is unworthy of working with him.

● *Fear Factor,* which has ordinary people tackling death-defying or merely disgusting stunts, such as being placed in a pit with hundreds of rats.

● *Joe Millionaire,* a program in which attractive women get duped into thinking that Joe Millionaire's bank assets are as good as his abs.

Reality programming is a global phenomenon. *Wife Swap,* in which two women switch husbands and families, was a hit in England before being imported to the United States. *Shattered,* in which contestants try to stay awake for a week, experiencing hallucinations and paranoia, was popular in Canada.

And yet there is no shortage of contestants willing to trade their dignity for their minute or two of fame. That deafening howl you hear is the critics' reactions to these shows. Many of them ask, What are these programs doing to us? The more important question for our purposes here might be, What do they say about us?

What do reality shows say about us?

The world loves television. Over the years audiences' viewing pleasure has been enhanced with devices such as remote controls, VCRs, DVRs, and HDTV. People have enjoyed watching television over the airwaves, via cable and satellite, online and on iPods. Each new feature has changed the way people watch, but none has quelled their passion for watching. Television remains Americans' most time-consuming activity, next to sleeping, and it is the world's main source of news and information. It is the medium through which politics is conducted, and it is humanity's main form of entertainment. It is also the world's most powerful sales tool.

In spite of all the competition from other media, people are watching more television than ever before. The average American home has two television sets, which are on for eight hours a day.[1] The average person watches four and a half hours a day in the United States,[2] and the rest of the world is catching up. In Japan, average viewing time is even a few minutes more than in the United States.

Television has also substantially changed all the media discussed in the preceding chapters of this book. Books, magazines, and newspapers have all become more like television, while the radio, film, and recording industries exist at least partially as adjuncts to the huge business of television. In many ways, television is the epitome of the American media.

A Brief History *of Television*

Radio paved the way for the development of television. It was through radio that people learned to turn to a piece of furniture in their homes for news and entertainment. It was radio that proved that advertising could make an electronic communications medium profitable. It was radio that developed the various types of programs. In fact, many early television programs, such as Milton Berle's *Texaco Star Theater,* moved over directly from radio.

EARLY TECHNOLOGY

Theoretical work into the idea of adding a visual component to radio began in the early 1900s. Many scientists were involved in this work, but two inventors are best remembered for making television a reality. In 1927, Vladimir Zworykin, a Russian immigrant working for Westinghouse Corporation, developed a circuit for transforming a visual image into an electronic signal. Around the same time, a 24-year-old maverick inventor in California named Philo T. Farnsworth developed a similar system. Both of them believed that they had invented the basis of electronic television (see the Close-Up on History box).

SELF QUIZ Who invented television, and when was it invented?

Apparently, television was an idea whose time had come. Inventors in several countries, including England, Japan, and Russia, claim to have come up with the idea contemporaneously with Farnsworth. In the United States, David Sarnoff of RCA spent $1 million promoting the new medium. He built one of the first commercial television stations in 1932, with transmitting facilities in the Empire State Building. Early TV sets, like today's HDTV sets, were extremely expensive, and they were owned by only a few people, such as industry insiders, hobbyists, and wealthy people who felt that they were the ultimate status symbol.

Sarnoff decided that the formal initiation of commercial television would begin in 1939, at the World's Fair in New York, whose theme was "The World of Tomorrow." Franklin Roosevelt became the first president to appear on television when he formally opened the fair. Not many people rushed out to buy televisions, though. There wasn't much programming, and there were no set technical standards. A similar situation had happened with FM radio, and in that case the people who bought early sets were stuck with expensive doorstops when the standards changed—much like the computers from a few years ago that many people now have in their basements.

DEVELOPMENT OF TECHNICAL STANDARDS

The U.S. government and industry players fought for years over national standards for television technology. Each manufacturer had its own patents, and each wanted to reap the big profits that would follow if its patents became the required broadcast standards. Some wanted their black-and-white technology to be the standard,

SELF QUIZ What were the technical standards that had to be set for television manufacturing?

Philo T. Farnsworth: The Unknown Father of Television

Not many people know the name Philo T. Farnsworth, but most media historians believe he was the true inventor of television. Farnsworth was a self-taught genius from a small farming community in Idaho. It is said that his great idea came to him as he was plowing a potato field at the age of 14. The hundreds of parallel lines that the plow left in the field gave him the idea for how an image could be electronically scanned along parallel lines inside a picture tube. He drew up rudimentary plans and presented them to his science teacher, but his ideas were so advanced his teacher didn't know what to make of them. Farnsworth continued to work on the concept of television, and to develop the knowledge and skills that he would need to complete the project. Part of his plan was a college education, but in his freshman year his father died and he had to drop out.

Philo Farnsworth with one of the television cameras he developed to send pictures to his early television sets.

In 1926, 19 years old and newly married, Farnsworth talked two friends into investing $6,000 in his plan to patent the first television. To get the patent, Farnsworth would need a working model. He moved to California, where he and his wife, Elma, with the investors as helpers, set about making a prototype television. As there were no stock electronic parts for him to use, Farnsworth had to fashion all his materials from scratch. He worked with a glassblower, for example, to develop his first picture tubes. He was so secretive about his work that his neighbors thought he was bootlegging liquor, and the police raided him.

Farnsworth completed his working model and applied for his patent in 1927. Top brass at Westinghouse and the Radio Corporation of America (RCA), where Vladimir Zworykin had been working on a similar project for years, were not amused. They had put hundreds of thousands of dollars into their system and were just getting ready to patent it themselves. They sued Farnsworth, who in turn sued them. In the end, Farnsworth won. RCA proceeded to pay the young man $1 million—the equivalent of $20 million today—for the rights to his patent. Combined with the work that Zworykin and his team of professional engineers had done, the makings of the first electronic television system were in place.

lines of resolution
Rows of lighted dots, or pixels, that make up a television picture image.

pixels
Lighted dots that create a television picture image.

while others were working on color and wanted government to wait for it to be perfected. Other patents involved different **lines of resolution,** those rows of lighted dots, or **pixels,** that make up the picture image. Standards were finally established in 1941, when government and industry agreed that television would present black-and-white pictures with 525 lines of resolution moving at a speed of 30 frames per second.

A Wartime Freeze

Everything needed for the explosive growth of television was now in place: consumer demand, industry backing, and technological standards. World War II intervened, however, effectively freezing the development of television from 1940 through 1945. Electronic technology was needed for the war effort, and most of the engineers in television joined the military, where they were put to work developing radar, sonar, radio-guided missiles, and battlefield communications devices. Elec-

In what ways did World War II affect the growth of television?

SELF QUIZ

tronics manufacturers stopped producing televisions and concentrated on the war effort.

Postwar Development

When the war ended in 1945, television did not develop as quickly as some had hoped. Broadcasting companies were making good money with radio, and they saw little incentive to get into the higher-priced medium of television. Consumer demand, however, pushed them into it. More and more consumers were becoming enthralled with television, although there were few shows to watch. In the first two years after the war, broadcasters spent all their money on expensive equipment and had little left over for programs. They put just about anything on camera that was available: talentless talent, live shots of a sunset, even test patterns. Because the medium was so new, and it was so exciting for the audience to see any transmitted picture, viewers were content to put up with this nonprogramming. Soon, though, that would change. By 1948, set sales had increased by 500 percent over the previous year, and viewership had risen by 4,000 percent.

Channel Allocation

In spite of the consumer demand, there was still one impediment to television's growth as an industry: channel allocation. **Channel allocation** is the placement of a station's frequency on the electromagnetic spectrum, that range of frequencies that is used for transmitting electronic signals. The Federal Communications Commission (FCC) was not sure where to put all the stations. There was obviously going to be a huge demand for stations, but if you put them on frequencies that were too close together, they would interfere with one another. To complicate matters even more, most broadcasters wanted to broadcast to the wealthy urban areas where advertising revenue would be the highest, and the FCC wanted to make sure that the poorer and more rural markets would also have at least some television coverage. (Even in those years, policymakers were concerned about the gap between the information haves and the information have-nots.)

It was a huge, complex engineering task to make sure that every community in America would be supplied with at least one television channel, with no overlapping or interfering channels. The FCC placed a four-year freeze on all license applications, from 1948 until 1952, to give itself time to work out the problem. At the time, there were only 108 stations in the entire United States. Still, during that period, the number of sets purchased rose from 250,000 to more than 17 million. When the licensing freeze was lifted in 1952, the number of stations tripled.

THE RISE OF NETWORK TELEVISION

At first there were four television networks: the National Broadcasting Company (NBC), the Columbia Broadcasting System (CBS), the American Broadcasting Company (ABC), and DuMont. The first three had come over from radio, and the DuMont network was founded by Allen B. DuMont, a manufacturer of television equipment who got into production to increase demand for his sets. DuMont's network existed from 1946 to 1955, until the industry got too large and the network could no longer compete.

During its brief life the DuMont network carried mostly low-budget programming—quiz, variety, and sports shows—but it did offer some memorable milestones. It was DuMont, for example, that brought Jackie Gleason

channel allocation
The placement of assigned spots on the electromagnetic spectrum to individual broadcast stations.

to television, with a show called *Cavalcade of Stars*. Within it, Gleason introduced a running sketch called *The Honeymooners,* which became its own program on CBS. Today, *The Honeymooners* is recognized as a television classic.

ABC and DuMont were both weak networks, and for years it looked as if either one could fail. The DuMont network lacked the radio station relationships that ABC had, so it was not able to line up enough **affiliates,** those stations that would agree to show its programs, to be attractive to advertisers. Because of that, it couldn't afford a full slate of competitive programming. (Gleason, for example, left the network for CBS in 1952.) In 1955, when Du-Mont dropped out, ABC experienced an immediate 68 percent rise in advertising revenue. The stations that DuMont owned went on to become the nucleus of a major independent station group, Metromedia Television, which eventually became the Fox Network.

It took a while for the networks to hook up with all their affiliates coast to coast. Coaxial cable, much like that used for cable television today, had to be strung across the country to connect the affiliated stations to each network headquarters in New York. Stations that were not connected by cable had to run kinescopes of network programming. **Kinescopes,** the forerunners of videotape recording, were poor-quality films taken directly from television monitors in the network studios.[3] When they were broadcast over early transmitting equipment, many of them were barely visible. Most of the affiliates preferred to run old theatrical films or local programming instead. AT&T completed hooking up the networks to its affiliates in 1951.

affiliates
Local stations that have a contractual relationship with the network but are not owned by the network.

kinescopes
Poor-quality films taken directly from television monitors in the network studios; they were forerunners of videotapes.

Jackie Gleason with the cast of *The Honeymooners*. This classic program began as a sketch on Gleason's *Cavalcade of Stars,* which aired on the DuMont network.

Television's Golden Age

Network television's golden age (1948–1958) was a time of unusually good dramatic programming. Many factors came together that encouraged original, high-quality drama to be produced live during this period. First, quality dramas were needed to attract wealthy, educated viewers who could afford to purchase television sets. Second, the networks had to hire playwrights to write original works, since the major motion picture studios refused to allow the plays they owned to be aired by potential competitors. Third, since network programming originated in New York City, producers had access to up-and-coming Broadway writers, actors, and directors. And fourth, most of the television dramas were performed live because videotape recording hadn't been invented yet, and filming was too expensive. The majority of the golden age dramas were one-hour and even half-hour plays, shown in dozens of anthology series with names that included the name of their sponsors, such as *Kraft Television Theatre, Philco Playhouse, Alcoa Theatre,* and *The U.S. Steel Hour.*

Even though the live dramas produced during this time were mainly of high quality, many critics feel that *golden age* is a misnomer. They point out that then, as now, there were more trivial, lowest-common-denominator shows than there were quality programs on TV. Shows with titles like *Fire-*

ball Fun for All and *Treasury Men in Action* were some of the typical mind-numbing programs. The hugely popular *I Love Lucy,* with its depiction of the hapless housewife who was always foiled in her attempts to work outside the house, was especially despised by many critics when it debuted on CBS in 1951.

Other critics point out that the golden age wasn't golden for everyone. Lucy wasn't the only woman who was portrayed as incompetent outside of her traditional gender role. Programs such as *Father Knows Best* and *Ozzie and Harriet* portrayed women as stereotypical housewives whose husbands made all the important decisions. Even when female characters ventured out of the home, as Lois Lane did in *Superman,* they were usually subordinate to men.

Furthermore, virtually all the playwrights, producers, actors, and directors of the live dramas were white. African Americans, Asians, Latinos, and Native Americans were systematically excluded from production jobs and only rarely permitted to appear in programs. In their infrequent appearances in TV shows, they were presented as subservient, secondary characters such as maids, butlers, chauffeurs, and cooks—examples include Jack Benny's personal servant, Rochester, and the main character of the show titled *Beulah.*

Television's golden age wasn't golden for everyone. Women were portrayed as stereotypical housewives. African Americans, Asians, Latinos, and Native Americans rarely appeared in programs, and then only as subservient characters such as maids, butlers, chauffeurs, and cooks.

Even the first show to feature a nearly all-black cast, *Amos and Andy,* depicted blacks as ignorant and clownish. These problems in representation and hiring practices were slow to change. As late as 1977, in *Roots,* the blockbuster miniseries about slavery, there were no black producers, writers, or directors, and two white actors earned more money for their performances than did all of the black cast combined.[4] The success of the *Cosby Show* in the 1980s, however, led to an increase in black-oriented programs, including some, such as *A Different World, In Living Color,* and *Fresh Prince of Bel-Air,* with black staffs.

The Entrance of the Movie Studios

One of the last obstacles to the entertainment dominance of television programming was the resistance of the movie studios. As we discussed in Chapter 6, the movie studios considered television a competitive threat. People sitting home watching television were less likely to get up and go to a theater, they reasoned—and

Roots, the 1977 blockbuster miniseries about slavery, remains one of television's landmark programs. It was the first great ratings success for a program with black heroes and white villains. Still, there were no black producers, writers, or directors involved with the program.

they were right. Most of the studios tried to obstruct the growth of the new medium in any way they could. They would not, for example, allow recent feature films to be shown on television. Walt Disney was the first of the studio leaders to associate his name with a television program. In 1954, when his company's original theme park in California was about to open, Disney agreed to produce a series of programs for ABC. In an early example of horizontal integration (see Chapter 1), Disney saw the possibilities of TV for promoting his park and his feature films as well as for generating the income from the program itself. The result was a program called *Disneyland,* which ran under various names (*Walt Disney's Wonderful World of Color, The Magical World of Disney*) for many years.

When was television's golden age, and why was it golden?

SELF QUIZ

After Warner Bros. began to produce the western *Cheyenne* for ABC in 1955, all the major film studios made it their business to produce television programming as well as feature films. Both NBC and CBS had established production studios in southern California by 1955, moving west just as the film industry had 40 years before. The business end of TV stayed in New York City.

CONSIDER THIS

Many early television programs came over directly from radio. As these programs became visual, how would the family viewing experience differ? What kind of effects might this have had on family life?

Television Changes Family Life

With all the changes going on in the television business, the biggest changes were occurring in American society, especially in terms of family life. Television continued the social trends that radio had started: bringing the American family indoors to experience programming together, but actually interacting less in the time they spent together. Families didn't talk during hit prime-time programs. They talked later, among themselves and among outsiders, about what they had seen on television the night before.

Different types of programs affected society in different ways. News programs made people more aware of political issues, and set up the wide-ranging involvement in civil rights and antiwar activities in the years to come. But they also confused people with *too much* information on conflicting sides of important issues, and were blamed for the audience's political apathy in later years. *Camel Cavalcade of News* with John Cameron Swayze, which ran from 1948 until 1956, is considered the father of network television news. Newsmagazines started in 1968 with *60 Minutes,* which continues to be a ratings leader today. (We'll have more to say about classic news programs in Chapter 11.) Classic children's shows, such as *Bozo the Clown, Romper Room,* and *Sesame Street,* prepared kids for school and made their parents more aware of their roles in children's education. But they also taught kids that education should be fun, fast-paced, and entertaining, and therefore were blamed for the kids' short attention spans when they got to school. Televised sports programs such as *Wide World of Sports* and televised events such as the Super Bowl slowly created an obsession with sports among American males, changing again what they talked about among friends. At the same time, after-

I Love Lucy, with its depiction of the hapless housewife who wasn't allowed to work outside the home, was a hugely popular situation comedy in the 1950s.

FACT FILE 9.1

Classic Prime-Time Programs

We can describe classic television programs as those that have had a large degree of cultural significance over time. They have resulted in societal changes, sometimes in the way people talk and sometimes in the way people look at things. Everyone has her or his favorite classic prime-time programs, but most critics would cite the following 10 programs as especially important:

1. *I Love Lucy* (1951–1957), the classic situation comedy (sitcom), featured a Cuban bandleader, his ditzy but determined wife, and their nosy but benign neighbors. The entire country waited for the episode featuring the birth of Lucy's baby, which aired on the same day that Lucille Ball gave birth to her real-life son, Desi Arnaz Jr.

2. *Gunsmoke* (1955–1975) was television's longest-running prime-time series with continuing characters, which included Marshal Matt Dillon; his deputy, Chester; his unrequited love interest, Miss Kitty; and his friend Doc. Dodge City and the local graveyard, Boot Hill, became part of the American vocabulary.

3. *Bonanza* (1959–1973) told of the adventures of Ben Cartwright and his three sons, Adam, Hoss, and Little Joe, on their huge Nevada ranch, the Ponderosa. The Cartwrights spent little time running their ranch, which they apparently did with just one employee, their cook Hop Sing. Most of their time was spent helping neighbors and fighting for truth and justice. Little Joe was played by Michael Landon, who went on to write, direct, and star in *Little House on the Prairie* and *Highway to Heaven*.

4. *Laugh-In* (1968–1973) was a fast-moving hour of sight gags, one-liners, short skits, and blackouts. This show changed the pace of television comedy and brought such phrases as "Sock it to me," "You bet your bippy," and "Look that up in your Funk & Wagnall's" into common usage. Regulars included Ruth Buzzi, Henry Gibson, and Goldie Hawn.

5. *All in the Family* (1971–1983) was the first sitcom to deal successfully with bigotry, prejudice, and hot issues such as abortion, birth control, and homosexuality. Along with a number of taboo racial terms that had never been heard on television before, the show is remembered for Archie Bunkerisms such as "Dingbat," "Meathead," and "Stifle yourself!" Meathead was Rob Reiner, who went on to a successful career as a movie director.

6. *Happy Days* (1974–1984) was a nostalgia piece set in the 1950s starring Ron Howard, who also went on to direct movies. The Fonz, a leather-jacketed, ultracool biker, was one of the most popular characters. Two minor characters were spun off into *Laverne and Shirley* (1976–1983), another successful show.

7. *Dallas* (1978–1991) was a prime-time soap opera about two generations of the oil-rich Ewing family, especially the good son Bobby (Patrick Duffy) and the roguish J.R. (Larry Hagman). The "Who Shot J.R.?" cliffhanger was a national obsession during the summer of 1980. The show was a runaway hit overseas also.

8. *The Cosby Show* (1984–1992) appeared at a time when most critics insisted that the age of the sitcom had passed. Bill Cosby played the doctor dad, and Felicia Rashad the lawyer mom. The show spearheaded last-place NBC's drive to first place, which it held for several years. Cosby had earlier made television history by becoming the first black performer to star in a network dramatic series (*I Spy*, 1965–1968).

9. *Roseanne* (1988–1995) featured "domestic goddess" Roseanne Barr as the head of a working-class family that turned Cosby's family values on their ear. The kids had problems, their overweight parents seldom had the answers, and America thought it was looking at real life.

10. *Seinfeld* (1990–1998), a self-described "show about nothing," was actually about the mundane aspects of the everyday life of four self-absorbed New Yorkers: Jerry Seinfeld (playing himself) and his friends George, Elaine, and Kramer. Plot lines revolved around such issues as finding a parking space, waiting to be seated at a restaurant, and "double dipping" a chip into the party dip.

---

noon soap operas changed the pace of housework, as women followed their stories while performing household chores.

Some of the most striking societal effects were attributed to regularly scheduled, long-running, prime-time entertainment programs. Several of these ratings champions captured the imagination of a wide public in unique ways: They changed not only what friends talked about over coffee the next day, but also how people talked, with popular phrases from the series entering the national lexicon.

Fact File 9.1. lists some of the classic prime-time entertainment programs that have had significant social effects. Critics continue to worry about the effects of today's prime-time entertainment. The editors of the *New York Times*, for example, looked at the humiliation TV programs discussed at the beginning of this chapter and observed, "It seems peculiar that a nation so torn apart over what message gay marriage

CONSIDER THIS

What program or programs would you add to the list of classic television shows? Why?

or prayer in school will send to impressionable youth is so unified in giving a pass to a program that teaches young people that it's extremely cool to be mean."[5]

Television's Economic Golden Age

The networks were broadcasting all their prime-time shows in color by 1966, and people were rushing out to replace their old black-and-white sets—just as they are changing over to HDTV receivers today. Public television was established in 1967, so even highbrow viewers had an excuse to buy a set. If television's creative golden age was 1948 to 1958, its economic golden age was 1960 to 1980, when the big three networks had few competitors, within the industry or outside it. With little competition, being a network affiliate was virtually a license to print money during the 1960s and 1970s. Independent stations began to compete a little, but the real challenger to network television would be cable.

ENTER CABLE

community antenna television (CATV)
The first cable television systems, designed to give viewers in hard-to-reach areas satisfactory reception from their nearest broadcast television stations.

Cable television began in the 1950s as **community antenna television (CATV).** CATV was designed to give viewers in hard-to-reach areas satisfactory reception from their nearest broadcast television stations. These systems sprang up in valleys, on hillsides, and in remote rural areas—any location that would make it difficult to receive an over-the-air signal. The earliest CATV pioneers were appliance dealers who hoped to sell TV sets in their communities. They would install a large antenna on a nearby hilltop, amplify the signals that were received, and distribute them to the local community by means of a cable. Program services of early CATV systems were limited to the delivery of local stations. CATV became cable television in the 1970s when it began to offer additional signals from distant stations, a service called **importation.**

importation
In cable television, the bringing in of additional signals from distant stations.

At first, there was little friction between CATV systems and the broadcast industry. After all, cable operators were just extending the reach of broadcast stations, bringing their signals into homes that would not have otherwise been able to receive them. With importation, however, cable came to be seen as a competitor by the broadcast industry. Local stations suddenly found themselves being challenged by other affiliates from their own network from different cities, and their ratings began to suffer. Broadcasters complained, and the FCC had to step in.

must-carry rules
FCC regulations that require cable systems to carry all local television stations within the system's area of coverage.

One of the first FCC rules for cable television was that cable systems could not duplicate network programs on the same day that the network aired them. Another important regulation came to be known as **must-carry rules,** which said that cable systems had to carry all local television stations within each system's area of coverage. This was an important rule for local broadcasters, because when some of them had adverse dealings with the local cable company, the cable company would simply threaten not to carry the local station at all. The threat of being blacked out would make it very difficult for the local station to negotiate with the cable company.

Cable's big period of growth was between 1970 (at which point, 10 percent of U.S. homes were wired) and 1990 (by then, 60 percent of the homes

Cable was built on a simple premise: Most Americans want more TV channels, and they are willing to pay for them.

were wired). Of great significance was Time Inc.'s successful launching of Home Box Office (HBO), the first pay cable channel, which proved that people would be willing to pay extra for premium channels. Today, around 60 percent of American homes receive TV through cable.

Cable was built on a simple premise: Most Americans want more TV channels, and they are willing to pay for them. Cable television's major improvement over standard television was its large channel capacity. The airwaves were inherently limited, as only a half dozen or so channels could be broadcast before the allotted frequencies were full. Early cable systems were designed to carry at least 12 channels, while today's systems can carry hundreds. (We'll look at today's cable industry in the next section of this chapter.)

SELF QUIZ

What were must-carry rules, and why were they enforced?

EMERGING NETWORKS

Following the death of the DuMont network in 1955, the conventional wisdom held that there was room for only three television networks. NBC, CBS, and ABC were just too big and too powerful to compete with. With the rise of cable, that same conventional wisdom saw a future in which fewer, not more, over-the-air networks would be needed. In the early 1980s, however, independent stations became increasingly profitable. Their success caught the attention of press baron Rupert Murdoch, who came up with the previously unthinkable idea of starting a new network. In 1985, Murdoch purchased 20th Century Fox studios and the Metromedia chain of independent TV stations. The next year, Fox began its national programming.

Ten years later, Fox was earning more money per program than CBS or ABC, and was quickly catching up to NBC.[6] Fox's ratings were particularly strong among viewers between the ages of 18 and 49, a demographic group that advertisers cherish, and it had outbid CBS for the right to broadcast National Football League (NFL) games. Although Murdoch paid an incredibly high sum for the NFL contract—twice what it was worth, by most estimates—it soon became apparent what he had in mind. Many of the best CBS station affiliates defected soon after the NFL joined Fox. From that point on, the Fox network was competitive with the big three.

Despite Fox's success, other new networks were slow to develop. By 1995, however, deregulation had made it possible for the established networks to produce their own prime-time programs. This had once been forbidden, to make sure that the networks would not monopolize program production. When the restrictions were lifted, at least two of the studios that produced programming for the networks under the old rules wanted to make sure they would continue to have a market for the shows they created.

Warner Bros. (The WB) and United Paramount Network (UPN) started within a week of each other in January 1995. UPN was started by Paramount Television Group with other industry backers.[7] The WB's partner was Tribune Broadcasting, which owned a group of stations. There were not enough broadcast stations left to affiliate with, however, and The WB had to rely on over-the-air stations in only the top 100 cities. For the other markets, the company signed up cable operators to run its programming. In 2006, The WB and UPN merged into a new network, The CW (for CBS–Warner). The new network merged the most successful programming and stations from the old ones.

Video Recording

videotape recorder (VTR)
A device for recording sounds and images on reels of magnetic tape.

The Germans developed videotape during World War II, and Ampex Corporation introduced the first **videotape recorder (VTR)** in 1956. Early VTRs were expensive (around $75,000) reel-to-reel models that were used only by

Popular programs like *Grey's Anatomy,* starring Patrick Dempsey, are now available as downloads for home computers, cell phones, and other types of digital media.

videocassette recorder (VCR)
An improvement on the videotape recorder (VTR) that uses cassette tapes instead of reels.

time shifting
Recording of a television program for playback at some later time.

zapping
Avoiding commercials by using the Pause button while videotaping or by fast-forwarding through them during playback.

digital video recorders (DVRs)
Specialized computers with oversized hard disks on which video signals are saved.

television stations and production companies. It wasn't until 1975, when Sony introduced the Betamax in the United States, that the home market became viable. The Betamax was the first **videocassette recorder (VCR),** which used cassette tapes instead of reels. When JVC introduced the Video Home System (VHS) format less than a year later, a major format war began, which VHS eventually won. Movie studios tried to make VCRs illegal, but they lost, and by the early 1990s nearly 90 percent of U.S. homes had a VCR.

VCR Effects

The cultural effects of the VCR were many. **Time shifting** released consumers from the television station's schedule and allowed them to watch programming at their convenience. **Zapping,** when the user pressed the Pause button to cut out commercials while taping or fast-forwarded through commercials during playback, made it easier for consumers to avoid advertising.

Digital Recording

Digital video discs (DVDs) reached the market in 1996, combining the quality and durability of CDs with the popularity of videotapes. DVDs provided a huge capacity for multiple versions of movies, as well as crystal-clear searches and freeze frames. **Digital video recorders (DVRs),** which are actually specialized computers with oversized hard discs on which video signals are saved, were introduced in 1999. DVRs, such as TiVo and the generic models used by cable TV companies, can record and play back at the same time, allowing the viewer essentially to rewind live television. They can also record two programs at once and can allow the user, with one command, to tape

DILBERT © Scott Adams/Dist. by United Features Syndicate, Inc.
DILBERT reprinted by permission of United Features Syndicate, Inc.

an entire season of a program, even if the program changes time or day. Digital video recorders have automated the process of zapping commercials. To fight this technology, advertisers first tried to make commercials in which the product or its name could still be seen in a high-speed scan, and then moved toward Web-style banner ads and product placement as their preferred style of advertising.

ADAPTING TO NEW TECHNOLOGIES

Although DVRs have been a significant annoyance to the TV industry, broadcast television networks are also in a fight for survival with other competing technologies, including cable, satellite, on-demand video, video games, and the Internet. Each year the original networks lose more of their total audience to these competitors: From their 1960s audience-share peak of 90 percent, they now fight over less than 40 percent.

High-Definition Television

While dealing with these competing technologies, the broadcast television industry is also preparing for its changeover to digital, high-definition broadcasting. In **high-definition television (HDTV)**, the scanning lines are more than double the standard—1,125 lines instead of the 525 lines of conventional TV, creating a sharp, clear picture. In addition, the HDTV screen is wider (allowing movies to be shown without their size having to be adapted for TV) and the sets feature high-quality digital sound, interactivity, and various other advanced digital services. HDTV became standard in cable TV in 2006, while over-the-air broadcasters have until 2009 to convert from analog to digital broadcasts.

Three dozen stations around the country began digital broadcasts in 1998, but hardly anyone noticed because very few people had digital televisions yet. Like all other broadcast innovations (such as FM radio and color television), HDTV caused a standoff: Stations didn't want to convert because so few people had sets capable of receiving HDTV signals, and viewers don't want to buy new sets because the stations weren't broadcasting HDTV. The first sets that came on the market cost around $10,000 each. Prices have since gone down, but before the conversion is complete, as many as 230 million new sets will be purchased, at a cost to consumers of $150 billion.[8]

high-definition television (HDTV)
Digital technology for transmitting television programs using more than double the standard number of scanning lines, creating a clearer, larger picture.

SELF QUIZ What is HDTV, and how does it differ from traditional TV?

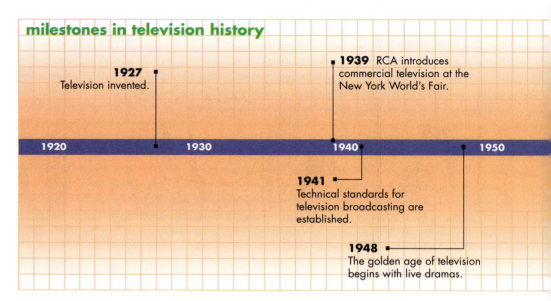

milestones in television history

1927 Television invented.

1939 RCA introduces commercial television at the New York World's Fair.

1941 Technical standards for television broadcasting are established.

1948 The golden age of television begins with live dramas.

1920 · 1930 · 1940 · 1950

The Video iPod, shown here in a leather case, is one of the new media that could change the way we watch television—or not, if we decide the picture is too small.

On the *Media World* DVD that accompanies this book (track 17, *Future Television*), media professionals explain to Matt Lauer that television programs soon will be delivered over the Internet. As one of them explains, "Your computer and your TV will be one."

 video on demand (VOD) Services that allow subscribers to order recent feature films, sporting events, concerts, news items, and special events at any time.

multiple system operators (MSOs) Companies that own several local cable service providers, usually in different areas of the country.

Online TV

Today television networks and program suppliers are experimenting with ways to offer programming downloaded from the Internet to home computers, cell phones, and other digital media, including gaming platforms such as Microsoft's X-Box. Some experts believe that **video on demand (VOD)** through these types of downloads will be the wave of the future, and the success of sites such as YouTube.com suggest these experts might be right.

An alternate convergence of the Internet and television occurred with Current TV, a cable network in which all the programming is user-generated and presented first online, where users vote on whether it will appear on cable.

Understanding Today's Television *Industry*

Television both reflects and affects its viewers like no other medium does. The television industry affects everyone. To explain this industry, we have organized this section of the chapter according to television's primary delivery systems, its program providers, and its ratings services.

DELIVERY SYSTEMS

Television's delivery systems—that is, the way people receive the television signal into their homes—include cable, satellite, and over-the-air broadcast. Currently, around 60 percent of Americans receive their television via cable, 25 percent by satellite, and 15 percent by over-the-air broadcast. A small but growing percentage is watching TV online and via new media.

The Cable Industry

In the early days of cable, many small, mom-and-pop operations in the United States served only the customers in their local community. Cable television today is a huge global industry. Today's cable operations are run almost exclusively by large **multiple system operators (MSOs),** which are

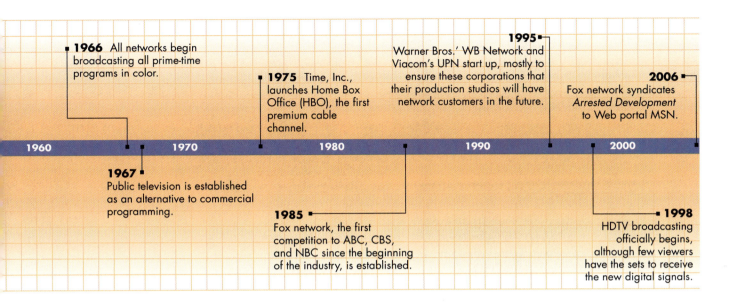

1966 All networks begin broadcasting all prime-time programs in color.

1967 Public television is established as an alternative to commercial programming.

1975 Time, Inc., launches Home Box Office (HBO), the first premium cable channel.

1985 Fox network, the first competition to ABC, CBS, and NBC since the beginning of the industry, is established.

1995 Warner Bros.' WB Network and Viacom's UPN start up, mostly to ensure these corporations that their production studios will have network customers in the future.

2006 Fox network syndicates *Arrested Development* to Web portal MSN.

1998 HDTV broadcasting officially begins, although few viewers have the sets to receive the new digital signals.

| 1960 | 1970 | 1980 | 1990 | 2000 |

companies that own several local cable service providers, usually in different areas of the country. Most MSOs are owned by giant communications corporations such as Time Warner or Comcast. Although there are nearly 200 MSOs in the United States, the top 10 systems operators have enrolled more than 50 percent of the country's subscribers.

To establish itself, an MSO must first reach a franchise agreement with the local government. Generally, the local government receives a small percentage of the operator's gross revenues. Most municipalities also require the cable company to provide access channels (which are open to the general public on a first-come, first-served basis) and channels for local schools. Often cable systems also set up their own local stations to provide local news and advertising.

Basic Cable

Basic cable is made up of those channels that are supplied with the least expensive program package the cable provider offers (see Fact File 9.2). These channels, such as Music Television (MTV) and Cable News Network (CNN), supplement their ad revenue by charging the system operator for each subscriber that carries their signal—usually 20 to 50 cents per subscriber, per month. The most popular channels, such as MTV, can charge significantly more; less popular ones, especially those that are trying to get a foothold in the business, offer themselves for free or even pay for the privilege of being included on the system. On average, the basic channels get about 30 percent of their revenue from subscriber fees and 70 percent from ad revenues.

The earliest basic cable channels adopted 24-hour formats similar to those used by radio stations. The Entertainment and Sports Programming Network (ESPN) broadcast 24-hour sports, CNN had 24-hour news, MTV provided 24-hour music videos, and the Cable-Satellite Public Affairs Network (C-SPAN) aired 24-hour government affairs. This programming proved successful and has allowed many specialized channels to flourish. Today, these specialized channels include the Fishing Channel, the Golf Channel,

Lost is presented by ABC, an over-the-air network that is seen on cable by most Americans.

basic cable
Those channels that are supplied with the least expensive program package the cable provider offers.

FACT FILE 9.2

Top Basic Cable Channels

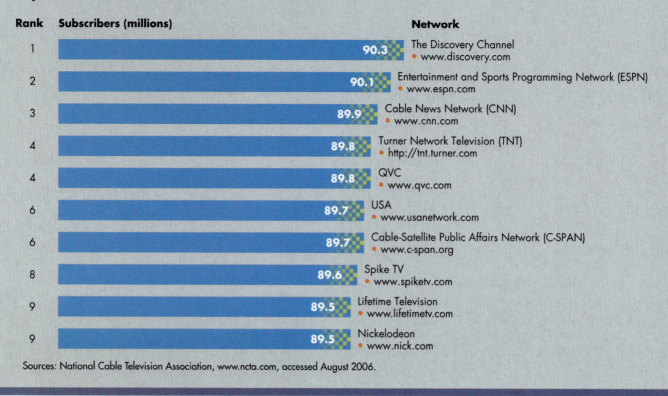

Rank	Subscribers (millions)	Network
1	90.3	The Discovery Channel • www.discovery.com
2	90.1	Entertainment and Sports Programming Network (ESPN) • www.espn.com
3	89.9	Cable News Network (CNN) • www.cnn.com
4	89.8	Turner Network Television (TNT) • http://tnt.turner.com
4	89.8	QVC • www.qvc.com
6	89.7	USA • www.usanetwork.com
6	89.7	Cable-Satellite Public Affairs Network (C-SPAN) • www.c-span.org
8	89.6	Spike TV • www.spiketv.com
9	89.5	Lifetime Television • www.lifetimetv.com
9	89.5	Nickelodeon • www.nick.com

Sources: National Cable Television Association, www.ncta.com, accessed August 2006.

a la carte pricing
Charging customers only for those cable channels they choose to receive.

Ted Turner invented the superstation. Later, he would go on to found CNN. Here he expresses his opinion of a rival, Rupert Murdoch.

 superstation
A local station whose signal is delivered to cable systems via satellite.

Home & Garden Television, the Travel Channel, the Weather Channel, and the Food Network.

By 2007 the average cable subscriber received 96 channels, but actually watched only 15 of them.[9] Cable companies generally charge for tiers, or packages of programming that include many channels that individual subscribers don't use, and that some subscribers complain about because they feel they are inappropriate for children. Because of this, several legislators and media critics have asked cable companies to offer **a la carte pricing,** which will allow people to receive just the channels they want. So far, the cable industry has resisted this idea, saying that it would put the smaller, less popular channels out of business.

Superstations

Superstations are a type of basic cable channel. A **superstation** is a local station that is delivered to cable systems via satellite. The first superstation was created in 1976 when Ted Turner sent the signals of his Atlanta UHF station, WTBS, up to a satellite for distribution throughout the country. (The station, which Turner had bought in 1970, was a low-powered, low-rated channel.) Cable operators all over the country could pick up the Atlanta station and deliver the signal to subscribing homes. By making his station a superstation Turner was able to raise his advertising rates and turn the lowest-rated station in Atlanta into a financial success. As of 2007 there were seven superstations: KTLA-Los Angeles, KWGN-Denver, WGN-Chicago, WPIX-New York, WSBK-Boston, WWOR-New York, and WTBS-Atlanta.[10] Their programming is very similar to that of other independent stations, although their greater advertising revenue allows them to offer more expensive movies, news, sporting events, and so on.

Premium Cable

Premium cable channels such as Home Box Office (HBO), Showtime, and Cinemax, sometimes called pay cable, are those that provide programming to cable subscribers for an additional fee, over and above their basic cable subscription fee. A converter, or cable box, in the subscriber's home unscrambles the signals for premium cable. Some premium programming has the advantage of being free of commercial interruptions as well as offering unedited program material. Other types of premium services include **pay-per-view channels,** allowing customers to order recent feature films, sporting events, concerts, and other special events on a set schedule, and video on demand, which provides the same type of programming at any time.

Just as movies competed against television in the 1950s by dealing with more adult themes, premium cable competed with broadcast and basic cable channels by offering explicit sex and language. Programs such as *The Sopranos* and *Sex in the City* have been part of HBO's claim that "It's not TV, it's HBO." Broadcasters and basic cable, however, in turn increased their use of explicit sex and language, in programs such as *NYPD Blue* and *Desperate Housewives,* to compete with premium cable.

premium cable channels
Cable channels that provide programming to subscribers for an additional fee, over and above their basic cable subscription fee; sometimes called pay cable.

pay-per-view channels
Systems that allow cable TV subscribers to order recent feature films, sporting events, concerts, and other special events when scheduled.

SELF
QUIZ
What is the difference between basic and premium cable?

Public Access Channels

Public access channels are provided by cable systems as part of their community franchise agreements. They are of three types, known as PEG, for public, educational, and government channels. They are all nonprofit and commercial-free, and cover everything from school board meetings to Little League games. The public type of public access channel is open to anyone who pays a small fee and takes an orientation course in studio operation. These channels feature programs that range from religious discussion to live music by local garage bands to the sort of offbeat basement talk show made famous in the movie *Wayne's World.* On public channels, 30 percent of the programming is religious; 30 percent or so is civic; at least 20 percent is creative, including, for example, teleplays and children's fashion shows; and another 15 percent is dedicated to sports.[11]

Across the United States, 3,000 public access channels operate out of more than 1,000 stations set up by cable companies. Although described by one critic as

The energy and amateurism of public access channels were celebrated in the movie *Wayne's World* (1992), which began as a sketch on *Saturday Night Live.*

"mere speed bumps on the dial between ABC and HBO,"[12] these channels are extremely important to the people who use them. They mirror community interests and needs, and serve as a public square for a form of electronic soapbox oratory. As one expert in this area explains, "The whole concept is a somewhat radical, democratic vision—giving ordinary citizens access to the most persuasive communications medium that exists."[13]

Satellite TV

Satellites were an integral part of the success of cable television. Satellites enabled services like HBO and TBS to become established cable channels,

FIGURE 9.1 Satellites in Geostationary Orbit

A geostationary satellite orbits the earth at the same speed that the earth rotates on its axis, making it essentially parked in space. In orbit at 22,300 miles, three satellites can cover almost the entire earth.

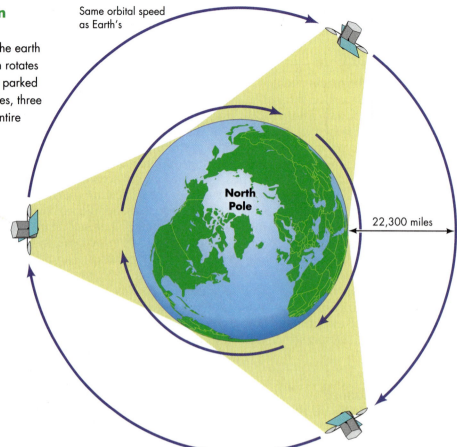

Same orbital speed as Earth's

North Pole

22,300 miles

geostationary
A term describing the placement of satellites so that they orbit the earth at the same speed that the earth rotates, effectively parking the satellites in one spot.

direct broadcast satellite (DBS)
Systems that deliver television programming to individual homes via satellite.

How does a satellite become geostationary?

SELF QUIZ

and today virtually all cable channels are sent from their headquarters to local cable systems in this manner.

Satellites had been used for point-to-point communications since the 1960s. These early spacecraft moved across the sky while orbiting the earth and were available for only part of the day before they moved out of range. Satellites couldn't be used for widespread mass communication until the 1970s, when they were made **geostationary,** or essentially parked in space, above one section of the earth, 24 hours a day (see Figure 9.1). This rather amazing feat is accomplished by putting the satellite in orbit 22,300 miles above the surface of the earth. At this altitude, a satellite will orbit the earth at the same speed that the earth rotates, so it will essentially stay in one place in relation to the earth. Three orbiting satellites can cover the entire earth, with the exception of the North and South Poles.

Direct broadcast satellite (DBS) systems deliver television programming to individual homes. The first attempts at making DBS profitable in the early 1980s were not successful. The systems were costly for corporations to set up and required each home to purchase a large, expensive satellite dish to receive the signals. DBS began to succeed in the United States in 1994, when improved technology allowed companies like DirecTV and the Dish Network the use of much smaller dishes that were able to deliver even more programs—sometimes three or four times more than cable systems. DBS's most serious drawback at that time was that, because of legal restrictions, it could not deliver local stations, but legislation resolved that problem in 1999. Satellite companies claimed more than 27 million subscribers (almost one-quarter of all television homes) by 2007, making DBS a serious competitor with cable.

Broadcast Television

Broadcast television, which is also known as over-the-air television to distinguish it from cable (although it is mostly seen on cable systems), is made up of a variety of entities. These entities include local stations, networks, independent stations, and station groups.

Local Stations

Technically, all broadcast television stations are local stations. As with radio, signals that emanate from a television station's transmitter reach only to the line-of-sight horizon, so unless they are picked up by some other form of distribution (cable, satellite, Internet), they will be seen only up to 50 miles from their transmission point. There are almost 1,600 local television stations across the United States today. About 1,200 of the local stations are commercial, and around 400 are public stations.

Three factors determine the size and profitability of a commercial broadcast television station:

1. *The channel.* A **channel** is a spot on the electromagnetic spectrum that the FCC licenses to a specific station. About half of the 1,600 stations on the air are **very high frequency (VHF)** stations—main-channel stations that operate on channels 2 through 13. The other half are **ultra high frequency (UHF)** stations—they transmit on channels 14 and up. While many UHF stations, especially those in major markets, are making money today, they are generally not as profitable as VHF stations, which have stronger signals and greater over-the-air reach. As cable has increasingly penetrated large urban markets, the VHF/UHF distinction in those markets has become less relevant, because all channels are equally accessible on cable. UHF is left at a disadvantage in homes without cable, however.

2. *The market.* A **market** is all the surrounding areas from which business tends to flow to a central point, usually a major city. Stations are licensed to a city, but their overall market is the important thing to the advertisers that support them. For example, NBC affiliate KCRA-TV on channel 3 is licensed to operate from the city of Sacramento, where there are 343,502 television homes. But the Sacramento market area, which includes surrounding suburbs, contains 903,700 television homes, ranking it 20th in size among all markets in the country. There are 211 television markets nationwide (see Figure 9.2).

3. *Network affiliation.* Stations that are affiliated with a network tend to be more valuable than independent stations (these will be discussed later in this section).

Networks

Television networks, like the radio networks discussed in Chapter 8, are corporations that provide programs to local stations, a few of which they own and operate. Most of the owned and operated stations (O&Os) are located in major markets, which means that their signals can reach a fair share of the national audience, making these stations both large and profitable. In fact, they are usually the most profitable part of the network. The O&Os usually carry everything the network provides. They usually operate on different channels in different markets—the NBC O&O in

The *Media World* DVD that accompanies this book includes a tour of a television station, WSEE–TV 35 in Erie, Pennsylvania (track 4). The main studio of the station is shown here.

channel
A spot on the electromagnetic spectrum that the FCC licenses to a specific station.

very high frequency (VHF)
Term used to describe the main-channel television stations that operate on channels 2 through 13.

ultra high frequency (UHF)
Term used to describe stations transmitting on channels 14 and up.

market
All the surrounding areas from which business tends to flow to a central point, usually a major city.

SELF QUIZ What three factors determine the value of a local station?

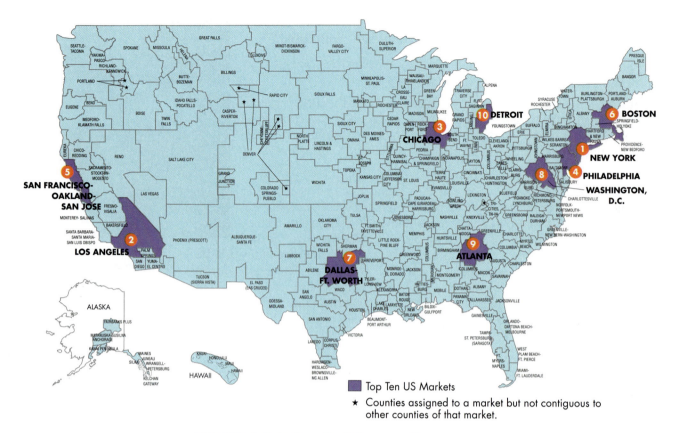

FIGURE 9.2 U.S. Television Markets There are 210 television markets nationwide.

Source: Nielsen Media Research, at www.nielsenmedia.com, accessed November 2006.

Los Angeles broadcasts on channel 4, for example, but their O&O in Chicago is on channel 5.

The majority of today's broadcast television stations are network affiliates. An affiliate is a local station that has a contractual relationship with the network but is not owned by it. Generally, a TV network affiliate agrees to carry network programs in return for compensation from the network.[14] The network provides the programming with its own national advertising inserted, with other spots available for local advertising. Local advertising profits belong entirely to the affiliate. The network provides the average affiliate with about 60 percent of its programs, including the most popular programs that will attract large audiences. Network affiliates, therefore, like O&Os, tend to be among the largest and most profitable stations in their markets. Also like O&Os, they often air on different channels in different cities.

What is the relationship between a television network and its affiliate?

SELF QUIZ

Independent Stations

In television, an independent station is one that is not affiliated with or owned by a network. For many years, a station was seldom independent by choice; usually, it was independent because it could not get an affiliation. In the days of three networks, only three local stations could be affiliates. Since an independent did not have the popular network programs, its programming tended to consist of old movies and syndicated network reruns. It generally attracted a smaller audience and was less profitable than the network affiliates in its community. During the 1980s, however, major-market independent stations became increasingly competitive by scheduling local professional sports, and first-run syndicated series that had never aired on the networks. Although these independent stations were free of all network ties, they were sometimes owned by a station group.

Station Groups

Nearly all television licensees today are group owners with properties in two or more markets. As in radio, groups once were restricted by the FCC to owning no more than 7 television stations, but the restriction was later bumped to 12, then 20. Today, there is no limit to the number of stations one group can own, although, because of FCC worries about a company or mogul having the power to influence politics and public opinion, one group cannot own stations that together reach more than 35 percent of the U.S. population.[15]

Most station groups own affiliates with different networks. Gannett Broadcasting, for example, owns 22 television stations: 10 are affiliated with NBC, 2 are affiliated with ABC, 6 are affiliated with CBS, and 1 is affiliated with The CW.

As in radio, the advantages of group ownership include a centralized management that oversees all the stations at once and great savings in the production and bulk purchase of program materials. Many functions—such as the sale of national advertising—can be centralized at great savings also.

PROGRAM PROVIDERS

No matter which delivery system is used to bring television programming into the home, it all originates from one of three places: the stations or cable channels themselves, networks, or syndicators. Local stations, whether they are network affiliates or independents, are likely to produce their own local newscasts and local public affairs programs. Some of the cable channels, such as CNN and MTV, produce most of their own programming. Others, such as TNT and Lifetime, rely on syndication.

Network Programming

Networks provide programming to their affiliates for a large part of the broadcast day: There are network morning shows (such as ABC's *Good Morning America*) late-night programs (such as NBC's *The Tonight Show*), and a full prime-time schedule. Although networks have begun to produce their own prime-time programs, many of the dramas and comedies are still produced by the major film studios. The network usually retains the rights to show these programs only twice: once during the regular season, and once as a rerun. After that, the ownership of the program returns to the producing company. At that time, the producing company can either syndicate the program itself or sell the syndication rights to another company.

Program Syndication

Program syndication is the sale of television programs directly to stations, cable channels, and online venues. In other words, syndicated programs are those that are not sold to one of the networks. Because producing most entertainment programming is out of their budget range, independent stations need syndicated shows for most of their broadcast day. Network affiliates

program syndication
The sale of programs directly to stations or cable channels.

The Fox program *Arrested Development* is now being syndicated online.

off-network programs
Syndicated programs that were shown earlier on one of the television networks and are now being licensed on a station-by-station basis.

strip programming
A system of showing a program in the same time period five times a week.

original syndication
The station-by-station licensing of new television programs that were not earlier shown on a network.

How does syndication differ from network programming?

SELF QUIZ

need syndicated programming for those parts of their broadcast day that the networks do not cover.

Syndication deals usually allow a station sole use of the program in the station's market for a specified period, during which the station may broadcast the program a limited number of times (usually two, but sometimes as many as six times). Syndication of a popular show can be extremely lucrative. The marketplace is international, and popular shows can be sold for many years.

Today, programs can also be syndicated online. When Fox put *Arrested Development* into syndication in 2006, it sold the online syndication rights to all 53 episodes to the Web portal MSN. It also syndicates 16 programs, including *24* and *Prison Break,* to iTunes, where the shows sell for $1.99 an episode as downloads.

Syndicated programs are either off-network or original. **Off-network programs** are those that were shown earlier on one of the networks. The network on which the program was first seen has no bearing on the affiliation status of the station or channel that shows the program as a syndicated rerun. Reruns of *Seinfeld,* for example, a program originally shown on NBC, are shown on the affiliates of the other networks as well as on independent stations and cable channels throughout the country.

Normally, a program provider will want to build up a package of around 100 episodes before offering an off-network series in syndication. This is because most stations like to use **strip programming,** a system of showing a program in the same time period five times a week. This uses as many episodes in one season as were originally shown in five.

Original syndication involves the sale of new programs that were not earlier shown on a network. Many relatively inexpensive programs such as talk shows and game shows are produced for original syndication. *Wheel of Fortune, Jeopardy,* and *Oprah* are all highly profitable in original syndication.

Public Television

So far, our discussion of broadcast television has focused on commercial television. Public television, which began as educational TV (ETV), operates somewhat differently from its commercial cousin. In 1952, 10 percent of all U.S. channels were reserved for ETV. From the beginning, educators, legislators and industry leaders all agreed that television would be a wonderful medium for education. But there was very little agreement about how educational TV should operate, and how much responsibility government should have to support it.

At first, ETV was seen mostly as an improved audiovisual service for schools and colleges, and many educational institutions rushed to become licensees. There wasn't much money available for programming, however, and what was aired consisted mostly of lectures and panel discussions. It soon became apparent that practically no one was watching this low-budget, locally produced programming. In 1959 a group of stations formed National Educational Television (NET), a cooperative service designed to help educational stations share quality programming. Through NET, stations were able to distribute a few hours per week of moderately successful shows. The programs were delivered to stations by mail. After showing a program, one station would send it on to the next station. This distribution system meant that the programs were shown on different days throughout the country.

The Carnegie Foundation, a nonprofit organization, decided in 1967 to look into the problems and potential of educational television. The foundation formed a commission, known as the Carnegie Commission, which found that ETV was essentially a wasted national resource. The commission recommended that Congress establish a "corporation for public television." A key term in the commission's report was the word *public*. Using *public* rather than *educational* implied that the noncommercial stations should be more than an addition to the local school's audiovisual room. Rather, these stations should provide a broad cultural and informational service for the general public. In effect, the commission was suggesting that public television stations should provide alternative programming that would not be available on commercial television. Public television would provide programs that were intellectually challenging, as well as programs for groups that weren't being served adequately by commercial stations, including minorities, children, and the poor. The public stations would also be more dedicated to meeting local needs than the commercial stations were.

PBS is known for the quality of its nature documentaries, such as *Nature: The Dolphin Defender.*

In one of the most powerful examples of the good that can be done by a nonpartisan, nonpolitical, nonprofit foundation, the Carnegie Commission's recommendations were enacted into law six months after the report came out. The Public Broadcasting Act of 1967 created the **Corporation for Public Broadcasting (CPB),** the words having been changed by Congress at the last minute from *public television* to *public broadcasting* to include radio. The CPB, in turn, created the **Public Broadcasting Service (PBS),** an organization made up of public stations. The CPB's main responsibility was to act as a buffer between the government and PBS so that there could be no political interference in programming decisions. The Public Broadcasting Act did not set up a permanent level of funding, however, and PBS stations have to make up the difference with donations from corporations and viewers.

PBS acts like a network, but it is different from the commercial networks in one major way: It doesn't produce programming. Instead, PBS helps member stations share programs. (They are called member stations rather than affiliates, to accentuate how PBS is different from a commercial network.) Much of the programming is produced by major stations, such as WETA in Washington, DC, KQED in San Francisco, KCET in Los Angeles, and WGBH in Boston. WGBH alone produces about a third of PBS's prime-time schedule. The Children's Television Workshop, which produces *Sesame Street,* is headquartered at WNET in New York. Many of the major stations import programming from England's BBC, causing some critics to complain that PBS will run anything with a British accent.

Today's public broadcasting stations are owned by four groups: States and municipalities own around 40 percent of the stations, colleges and universities own around 25 percent, community nonprofit foundations own 33 percent, and public school boards own

Corporation for Public Broadcasting (CPB)
The government entity whose main responsibility is to act as a buffer between the government and PBS, to prevent political interference in programming decisions.

Public Broadcasting Service (PBS)
Government-sponsored association of public television stations designed to facilitate the sharing of programs.

 SELF QUIZ How does PBS differ from the commercial networks?

FIGURE 9.3 PBS ownership

Today's public broadcasting stations are owned by four groups.

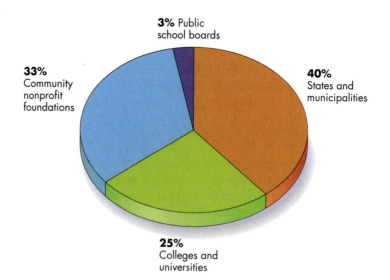

3% Public school boards

33% Community nonprofit foundations

40% States and municipalities

25% Colleges and universities

less than 3 percent (see Figure 9.3). The small current ownership by public schools demonstrates how far PBS has moved away from its ETV beginnings.

THE RATINGS

Because advertising profits depend on the size of the audience, the ratings that measure that audience are extremely important to the television industry. The word *ratings* actually includes two separate aspects—ratings and shares—that are sometimes confused. The **rating** is the percentage of all homes equipped with televisions that are tuned to a particular station at a particular time. The rating therefore includes in its calculation homes in which the TV is not turned on. The **share** is the percentage of homes in which the television is in use and tuned to a particular station. Because ratings take into consideration all television homes, whether the set is in use or not, the rating number is always smaller than the share number. A top-rated program today might have a 20 rating and a 33 share. If we round off today's 110 million homes with television to 100 million for the sake of simplicity, a 20 rating and a 33 share for a program (we'll call it program *X*) would both work out to 20 million viewing households. The formulas look like this:

Rating = 20 million households watching program ÷ 100 million homes with TV, whether they are on or not = a 20 rating

Share = 20 million households watching program ÷ 60 million households watching TV at that time = a 33 share

When we're discussing ratings, it is important to recognize that we speak in terms of households. The difference between "households viewing" and "people viewing" leads to a commonly misquoted statistic. The average U.S. household has a TV set turned on around eight hours a day. The average

The power of the ratings demonstrates just how important the audience is to the television industry.

person, however, watches around four and a half hours a day. Different people in the household tend to watch at different times.

The typical prime-time broadcast network program has a rating of around 15; the typical broadcast daytime program and top-rated cable programs aver-

rating
The percentage of all homes equipped with televisions that are tuned to a particular station at a particular time.

share
The percentage of homes in which the television is in use and tuned to a particular station.

FACT FILE 9.3

Top-Rated Television Programs of All Time

The top-rated television programs were all presented by traditional networks, most of them in the 1970s and 1980s before increased competition led to audience fragmentation. (Earlier ratings had a smaller audience because of the smaller number of homes with television.)

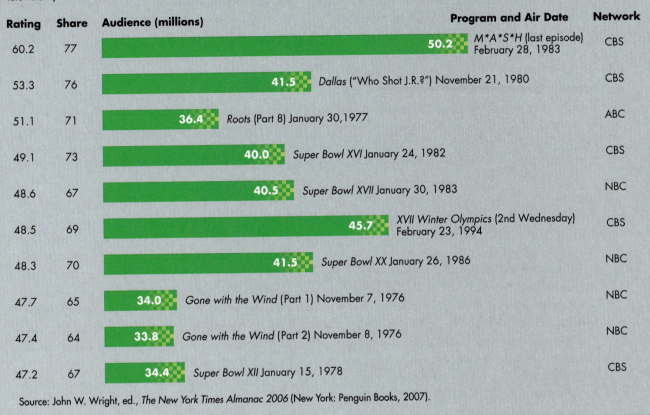

Rating	Share	Audience (millions)	Program and Air Date	Network
60.2	77	50.2	M*A*S*H (last episode) February 28, 1983	CBS
53.3	76	41.5	Dallas ("Who Shot J.R.?") November 21, 1980	CBS
51.1	71	36.4	Roots (Part 8) January 30, 1977	ABC
49.1	73	40.0	Super Bowl XVI January 24, 1982	CBS
48.6	67	40.5	Super Bowl XVII January 30, 1983	NBC
48.5	69	45.7	XVII Winter Olympics (2nd Wednesday) February 23, 1994	CBS
48.3	70	41.5	Super Bowl XX January 26, 1986	NBC
47.7	65	34.0	Gone with the Wind (Part 1) November 7, 1976	NBC
47.4	64	33.8	Gone with the Wind (Part 2) November 8, 1976	NBC
47.2	67	34.4	Super Bowl XII January 15, 1978	CBS

Source: John W. Wright, ed., *The New York Times Almanac 2006* (New York: Penguin Books, 2007).

age around a 6. The final episode of *M*A*S*H* in 1983 had the highest entertainment rating to date, with a rating of 60.2 (see Fact File 9.3). Super Bowls are the top-rated sports programs. The most popular Super Bowls have achieved ratings of more than 40.

The best-known television rating service is Nielsen Media Research. Nielsen collects ratings for network and local stations, syndicated programs, cable channels, and World Wide Web sites. Nielsen's national ratings are constantly cited to prove the success or failure of prime-time shows. Nielsen sells its findings to the networks, to individual stations, to advertising agencies, and to anyone else (such as large advertisers or program producers) who is willing to pay for them.

SELF QUIZ What is the difference between a rating and a share?

Nielsen relies on a national sample of around 10,000 families. This sample has increased in size steadily over the years in the search for ever-more-precise figures. Viewers are selected randomly to become Nielsen families (you cannot apply for the honor). Nielsen installs meters directly to the TV sets in the homes of its national sample. For years, the Nielsen device (called an audimeter) recorded only which station the set was tuned to, but many Nielsen clients complained that this provided no information on who was actually watching a given program. In one highly publicized case, a woman admitted that she turned on her set only to keep her cat amused. In that case, the cat represented the viewing habits of tens of thousands of human beings.

Gays on TV

Until recently, the subject of homosexuality was nearly taboo on television, but gay characters and gay-themed programs have experienced a surge in popularity in the past few years. By 2004, prime time included 20 sitcoms, dramas, and reality shows that featured gay and lesbian life, and in 2005, Logo, a 24/7 all-gay cable channel was created by MTV networks. Some critics found this distressing, while

the news that she was gay. (At the same time the star of that program, Ellen DeGeneres, revealed that she was a lesbian.)

Other activists say the turnaround point was in 1998, with the debut of *Will and Grace,* a sitcom about a gay man and a straight woman who are roommates. *Will and Grace* featured a lead character who was subtly gay and supporting characters who

"TV is really leading the way for America to talk about gay and lesbian issues."

gay activists felt the change was long overdue. Either way, the manner is which television has dealt with the issue of homosexuality provides an interesting view into the way the industry works.

Before the 1970s, gay characters were invisible on network television. Then in 1972, ABC presented *That Certain Summer,* a made-for-television movie starring Hal Holbrook as a divorced gay man who has to explain his lover (Martin Sheen) to his son. Several advertisers withdrew their support because of the controversial subject, but this movie opened the door for other rare exceptions that dealt with homosexuality in an open way. Billy Crystal played a supporting character who was gay in the sitcom *Soap* from 1977 until 1981. In the 1980s it became avant-garde to include gay supporting characters in ensemble casts, a trend that continued well into the 21st century in programs such as *ER* and *NYPD Blue.*

The 1990s saw several milestones in the depiction of gays and lesbians. In 1991, two women characters on *L.A. Law* shared the first same-sex romantic kiss on prime time. (The first gay-male romantic kiss on prime time occurred nine years later, on *Dawson's Creek.*) Some gay activists say that the truly groundbreaking moment on network television occurred in 1997, when the main character in the sitcom *Ellen* went public with

were wildly flamboyant. Its popularity led the way for a crop of new shows with gay lead characters. One of the most popular of the new shows was *Queer Eye for the Straight Guy,* which debuted on the basic cable network Bravo in 2003. *Queer Eye* was a reality program that featured five gay cast members with an innate sense of style making over straight men who were fashion-challenged. Its huge popularity turned all the cast members into stars. NBC, Bravo's owner, also showed some episodes of this program.

The broadcast and basic cable networks, however, were cautious about presenting the sexual aspects of homosexuality. As one expert in the area pointed out, "A lot of the concerns or the discomfort that people feel about what they identify as gay is often associated with gay sex. So whenever any sort of intimacy is shown of gay people, it makes people uncomfortable."[1] Broadcasters also worried that programs depicting gay and lesbian sex might invite FCC fines, so only subscription-based pay cable would take a chance on them. (The FCC does not control pay cable for indecency—it reasons that if consumers are offended, they can simply stop their subscription.)

Pay cable's breakthrough program was Showtime's *Queer as Folk,* which debuted in 2000. This

Today, Nielsen uses a device it calls a people meter that allows each individual within the family to "punch in" when viewing begins and "punch out" when it is completed. This enables Nielsen to more precisely tell who is viewing, especially for those all-important overnight ratings that let the

sexually explicit drama dealt with provocative issues such as AIDS, promiscuous sex, drug use, and gay bashing. Showtime also debuted a series in 2004 called *The L Word,* about a group of lesbians in Los Angeles, and HBO featured the explicit behavior of a bi-racial gay couple in *Six Feet Under.*

The industry had solid economic reasons to portray more gays. An estimated 6 to 7 percent of the U.S. adult population identifies itself as gay, lesbian, bisexual, or transgender. The purchasing power of this market segment is huge, accounting for nearly $500 billion in annual sales. The average income is about 8 percent higher in gay households than straight ones.[2]

Social scientists see this proliferation of gay-and-lesbian-themed television as reflective of society's wider acceptance of homosexuality, but research suggests the programs affect, as well as reflect, audience attitudes. A Kansas State University researcher studied about 200 relatively sheltered rural Kansas college students and found that popular TV shows dramatically improved their attitudes toward and increased their acceptance of gays and lesbians.[3] Perhaps most important, this programming is affecting conversations about sexuality in American homes. As one expert pointed out, "TV is really leading the way for America to talk about gay and lesbian issues."[4]

Logo is a cable network devoted to programming with gay, lesbian, and transgendered themes. Screen shot used by permission of Logo Network.

[1]Wes Combs, president of Witeck-Combs, a public relations and advertising firm that tracks gay and lesbian trends, quoted in "Gays on TV," *NewsHour* online, November 19, 2003.

[2]"Viacom Plans to Start Gay TV Channel," CNN online, March 29, 2004.

[3]The study was conducted by psychology professor Richard Harris, and cited in Kristen Philipkoski, "Change Channels, Change Minds?" *Wired* online, September 2, 2003.

[4]Scott Seomin, entertainment media director for the Gay and Lesbian Alliance Against Defamation, quoted in Kim Campbell, "Gays on Prime Time," *Christian Science Monitor* online, April 6, 2001.

networks know how their programs are doing. Arbitron, the other major ratings company, is currently developing a wireless people meter that individuals simply carry around with them during the day while it automatically records all their media use. When fully developed, this prototype will pick up an inaudible signal from any TV, radio, or billboard that they encounter. At night the meter is simply inserted into a docking station and the day's data is downloaded to Arbitron as the unit recharges.

Although the overnight ratings are most important to the networks, for local stations the important statistics are generated during the **sweeps months:** November, February, May, and July. During the sweeps, local stations use the ratings to set their basic advertising rates for the next three-month period. November sweeps tend to be most important, because they supply information on the success or failure of the season's new shows. The July sweeps are probably least important, because so many people are on vacation and the new season hasn't started anyway. Networks try to help out the local stations by offering their most attractive programming, and local news organizations suddenly find a lot of sex and violence in the news during these periods. The sweeps periods also result in "stunt" programming, such as contests, guest stars, and special episodes.[16] The sweeps also lead to a general change in the quality of the programs. For example, during the sweeps periods you are likely to find three great movies all being aired at the same time, after two months of nothing that you wanted to see.

There are many criticisms of the Nielsen television ratings. Some critics point out that the ratings don't measure all people. They measure homes only, not bars, airports, college dorms, or hotels where TV viewing also takes place. Some critics are more concerned that shows live and die by the small samples of viewers that are used for ratings, although the ratings services say their samples are statistically valid. A more widespread criticism is that programmers take too much stock in ratings, using them to cancel programming regardless of its quality.

Arbitron's wireless people meter is carried by the viewer and automatically recognizes choices when that viewer is in a room with a television.

Controversies

Television is a victim of its own success. It is controversial because practically every home in the United States has at least one set, and children usually have virtually unlimited access to it. Content that other media might get away with, including some forms of sex and violence, meets with controversy in a medium that is also a standard piece of household furniture. Most of the controversies related to television revolve around the nature of programming; the parental advisory ratings established by the industry; and, perhaps at the root of it all, excessive viewing.

THE NATURE OF PROGRAMMING

To reach the greatest possible audience, most television programs are designed to make limited intellectual and aesthetic demands on their viewers. People spend a lot of time entertaining themselves watching television, however, so critics are concerned that the poor quality of lowest-common-denominator programming damages viewers intellectually and emotionally. New York University professor Neil Postman expressed this point of view in his book *Amusing Ourselves to Death* (1985), and it is also expressed in the names that critics have traditionally assigned to television—names such as boob tube, idiot box, and plug-in drug. As far back as the 1960s, FCC commissioner Newton Minnow called TV programming a "vast wasteland."

Two areas in which entertainment programming comes under particularly heavy attack are in its perpetuation of violence and its reinforcement of stereotypes. Another large concern is television's overall lack of educational programming.

Perpetuating Violence

Most critics agree that television entertainment is too violent. One comprehensive study found that premium cable channels like HBO and Showtime are the most violent, with 85 percent of their programming including some violence, followed by basic cable channels with 59 percent, and programming on independent stations with 55 percent.[17] Network television had the lowest violence level, 44 percent, which is still far too high for most critics.[18]

Other critics point out that not all violence is equal. On television, the context of the violence—how it is shown and why it is shown—is important (see the Close-Up on Controversy box). When children are watching, they say, it can be dangerous to present violence as the way to solve problems. When the detectives on *CSI* or even one of the Teen Titans beats up a bad guy to resolve the basic conflict of the story, it teaches children to use violence instead of alternate forms of problem solving. Critics also contend that violence is especially dangerous when its depiction ignores the real-life consequences of violent action. People who are grievously injured in a scene are shown in the next scene as healed and healthy, without a bandage or a limp, when in real life they would be permanently disabled.

Television violence is also considered particularly dangerous when it goes unpunished. In the same study mentioned earlier, in 73 percent of the

On the *Media World* DVD that accompanies this book (track 16, *Violence On the Media and Its Effects on Children*) Robert Peters (right), president of Morality in Media, says that children learn violence from popular culture. Dick Wolfe (left), producer of *Law and Order, Miami Vice,* and other crime-oriented television programming, insists that the real cause of violence in society is the lack of gun control and parental responsibility.

Drama is real life with the boring bits taken out, and those boring bits include lessons about the consequences of mayhem.

cases, characters who committed violent acts were not punished in the same scene. By the end of the show only 62 percent of the "bad characters" had been punished, and a mere 15 percent of the "good characters" were punished for acting violently. Television producers, however, insist that pleasing the critics would severely impede storytelling. Drama, they say, is real life with the boring bits taken out,[19] and those boring bits include the pro-social lessons about the proper uses and consequences of mayhem.

SELF QUIZ Why is television the most controversial of all media?

Reinforcing Stereotypes

Extensive research into television entertainment indicates that television programs contain ethnic, racial, and sexual stereotypes, and that exposure to televised material increases the acceptance of these stereotypes.[20] Because of its power and popularity, television has traditionally worried those groups who do not want stereotypes to be accepted by the general public. In the 1950s, protests by civil rights groups against *Amos and Andy,* the first television program with an all-black cast, led to the show's cancelation by CBS. Other groups have launched similar protests over the years. The National Organization for Women (NOW) has objected to demeaning depictions of

Wrestling, Kids, and Televised Sports

Professional wrestling is one of the oldest—and most controversial—genres of television programming. In its early days in the 1950s, the big controversy was whether or not the matches were fixed. Today's more sophisticated kids realize that the matches are not just predetermined—they are scripted. There is always a good guy, known in wrestling jargon as the babyface, and a bad guy, the heel—and these two opposing forces of good and evil are supplemented by what one critic calls "a Greek chorus of morally ambiguous characters."[1]

The fake nature of today's wrestling, however, is part of the problem. "It's not real, they don't get hurt," kids say, "and we're not going to get hurt either." Unfortunately, neither statement is always true. In spite of their superb conditioning and careful choreography, the pros get hurt all the time, and occasionally they get killed. Wrestler Owen Hart, for example, died in a 50-foot fall while entering the ring in a failed stunt in 1999.

Children mimic the moves they see on TV, and sometimes the results can be equally deadly. In Texas, a seven-year-old boy killed his three-year-old brother with a move called the clothesline. Asked by detectives to demonstrate what he had done, the boy backed up about 10 feet and ran toward a doll about the same size as the three-year-old. He thrust one arm out at shoulder level and struck the doll at its neck, knocking it backward. In 2000 Court TV produced a film, *Wrestling with Death,* that documented dozens of such incidents and included footage of older kids putting on backyard wrestling exhibitions in which they jumped off roofs onto their opponents in the ring and hit each other with steel chairs.

Some critics insist that the World Wrestling Federation, whose programs run on UPN and USA Network, and World Championship Wrestling, which is shown on Turner Network Television, encourage this behavior, and therefore bear responsibility for the casualties, because of the way their programming glamorizes violence. Others point out that a wealth of other antisocial behaviors are glamorized on the programming as well. One of wrestling's brightest stars, Stone Cold Steve Austin, swills beer, spouts profanity, and salutes other wrestlers with obscene gestures. Still other critics insist that the way wrestling is presented has encouraged all sports to become more violent. One of them says:

> This popular entertainment may be a glimpse of a future toward which most of sports is inexorably slouching. It is getting harder to figure out where "over the edge" begins, and how soon that dangerous territory on the

women. In one action it objected to the use of the word *girls* for grown women and got most producers to use the word only for female persons under the age of 18. The National Gay and Lesbian Task Force asks producers to avoid stereotypical depictions of limp-wristed, lisping gays and truck-driving lesbians. Several groups protested against Jerry Lewis's muscular dystrophy telethon, claiming that it featured helpless children rather than self-sufficient adults, and that Lewis's approach implied that the disabled cannot be successful without outside help.

One form of stereotyping that critics find especially annoying is making an ethnic minority invisible. During recent television seasons, the National Association for the Advancement of Colored People (NAACP) noticed a lack of minority actors on ABC, CBS, NBC, and Fox programs, as well as a dearth of minority employment behind the scenes. The group threatened a national protest, including demonstrations at network headquarters and a massive boycott by as much as 20 percent of the viewing audience. The networks responded by pledging to establish minority recruitment programs, add mi-

other side will become our home field. One season's coach-choker becomes another season's sentimental star. Why doesn't my heart jump anymore when a hockey goon slams an opponent's face into the Plexiglas? Do I need teeth spilling out like Chiclets? When the racing car spins into the crowd, will they show replays? How soon will Mike Tyson be ready to bite someone's head off?[2]

In response to the controversy, several advertisers, including Coca-Cola and Wrigley's Gum, have withdrawn from wrestling programs, but others have rushed in to fill the gaps. Wrestling is extremely popular with males ages 12 to 34, a highly coveted demographic for advertisers.

[1]Alex Kuczynski, "Cue the Music, Roll the Mayhem," *New York Times* online, November 22, 1999.
[2]Robert Lipsyte, "Going Over the Edge to Death and Applause," *New York Times* online, May 30, 1999.

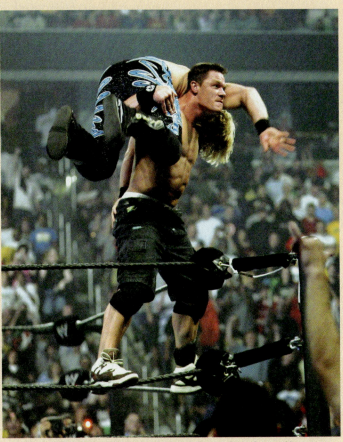

John Cena vs. Chris Jericho on WWE Raw Smackdown. If imitated by a non-professional, a move like this could cause a serious injury.

nority writing slots to successful shows, and do more business with minority suppliers.

During their negotiations with the NAACP, the networks pointed out that much of their minority audience had moved to explicitly black and Hispanic cable channels, such as BET and the Spanish-language Univision, which is now the nation's fifth-largest and fastest-growing network. Furthermore, just as in the movie industry, producers who feel besieged by all the protests like to point out that stereotyping is important in story-telling because it allows writers to establish characters quickly and get on with the plot. Still, the best producers realize that this is an ethical issue that they have to consider. Stereotypes on TV can deprive young people of appropriate role models, and when those stereotypes become accepted by portions of society, they can lead to racial and ethnic discrimination.

Most critics agree, however, that television has made impressive progress in recent years in terms of the depiction of homosexuals.

 SELF QUIZ What aspects of television entertainment cause the most controversy?

CONSIDER THIS

What is your all-time favorite television program? How would it rate in terms of violence and stereotyping?

As noted earlier in this chapter, popular programs such as *Will and Grace* and *Queer Eye for the Straight Guy* have increased tolerance toward gays in the general public.

Lack of Educational Programming

It was not until 1996 that the FCC passed a regulation requiring television stations to show three hours of children's educational programming each week.[21] Before this, Congress had passed the Children's Television Act of 1990, which required stations to serve the educational or informational needs of children. The 1990 act did not define what it meant by *educational*, however, and many stations either counted shows like the sitcom cartoon *The Jetsons* as educational (because it taught children about the possibilities of life in the future), or ran 30-second educational spots, or showed some traditional educational show at 5:30 AM, when few people were watching.

It took six years for the FCC to stipulate that the requirement was for three hours a week of programs that were at least 30 minutes long and aired between 7:00 AM and 10:00 PM. At least some broadcasters complied by offering high-quality educational programs such as *Beakman's World* or *Bill Nye, The Science Guy* at reasonable hours. Most critics, however, insist that there is still too little educational programming on TV.

PARENTAL ADVISORY RATINGS

Some critics are less concerned with the lack of educational programming than with what television does seem to teach effectively—violence, sex, and unacceptable language. That's where parental advisory ratings come in. Although they have been established as a solution to a problem, they have turned out to be controversial in themselves. For years, when people spoke of TV ratings, what came to mind was Nielsen, not parental advisories. In 1996, however, Congress warned the industry to devise a voluntary rating system for shows, or the U.S. government would do it for them. These ratings would be shown in television listings and on air before the shows run. They would also enable parents to block out programming with the use of a **V-chip,** an electronic device that can be set to recognize and block programs with a particular rating. The Telecommunications Act of 1996 required that new television sets be required to contain V-chips beginning in 1998.

Jack Valenti, then president of the Motion Picture Association of America, headed the industry panel that came up with the parental advisory ratings. Valenti had previously helped design the largely successful voluntary ratings system for movie theaters. He and the industry panel came up with the following ratings for television, to be assigned by the show's producers or networks:

TV-Y (for all children).

TV-Y7 (inappropriate for children under 7).

TV-G (for general audiences, not specifically children).

TV-PG (parental guidance urged).

TV-14 (not for children under 14).

TV-M (adults over 17 only).

Not everyone approved of these ratings categories. Parent groups believed that the categories were too vague to be of much help to television viewers. They wanted more explicit information about nudity, sex, violence, and profanity. Program executives said they worried that if the ratings system got too elaborate, viewers would find them too difficult to understand

V-chip
An electronic device that can be set to recognize and block programs with a particular rating.

and simply not use them. Executives also feared that pressure groups would start demanding labels for controversial subjects (e.g., abortion) and then organize boycotts against any advertisers on those shows. This, they said, would cut down on the variety of political opinion that is so important in a democracy. After a protracted battle, industry and consumer groups agreed to add V ratings (for violence), S ratings (for sexual situations), L ratings (for language), D ratings (for suggestive dialogue) and, on children's programs, FV ratings (for fantasy violence).

EXCESSIVE VIEWING

Television can be a serious time thief when used indiscriminately. In fact, the outcry against "media addiction" has been stronger against television than against any other medium. One science writer summarizes the argument as follows: "The proposition that television can be addictive is proving to be more than a glib metaphor. The most intensive scientific studies of people's viewing habits are finding that for the most frequent viewers, watching television has many of the marks of a dependency like alcoholism or other addictions."[22]

Researchers say that compulsive television viewers have several traits.[23] First, they watch a lot of television. College students who consider themselves addicted watch twice as much as other students: 21 hours a week instead of 10. Adults in general who describe themselves as addicts watch an average of 56 hours a week, as compared with around 30 hours a week for the average grown-up. In extreme cases, compulsive television viewers rarely go out for entertainment. Aside from work and necessary errands, they stay home and watch TV. They are also not very selective in what they view. They will stay glued to anything, even if they don't enjoy it. Often they will complain about programs while they watch them.

Second, compulsive viewers use television as a distraction, an escape from unhappy lives or unhappy parts of otherwise tolerable lives. They watch TV to make themselves feel better when sad, upset, or worried. Critics say spending too much time in front of the television keeps viewers from dealing with their problems productively. It also keeps them from exercising, from spending time with their kids, and from taking up various forms of self-improvement. Defenders of television, however, insist that it is no more addicting than any other form of pleasurable activity.

SELF QUIZ Why is time management a television issue?

CONSIDER THIS
How many hours per day do you watch television? Would you consider yourself a light, moderate, or heavy viewer? What effects does this viewing have on your life?

Summing Up

From its beginning, television has both reflected and affected the lives of its viewers. It has been the most popular medium, and its popularity has pushed greater and greater technology into existence. The picture got larger, clearer, and more colorful, while the technology moved from airwaves to cable to satellites.

The early history of television was a race first for its invention, and then for the development of technical standards that would allow everyone in the United States to use one system and to receive at least one over-the-air channel. The early networks created what many remember as a golden age of television between 1948 and 1958, when many original dramas were performed live. This golden age wasn't golden for everyone, however, as women and minorities were often depicted in stereotyped ways.

The big three networks had few competitors during the 1960s and 1970s. Other programming delivery systems such as cable, satellite, and recording devices have created the highly fragmented universe of copious viewing choices we have today. Understanding today's television industry requires an understanding of the way broadcast, cable, and newer delivery systems differ. Program providers and ratings services are essential to all these types of delivery.

Television is the most controversial of all media, with the largest concern focusing on what it does to us as individuals and as a society. In entertainment programming, controversies swirl around such issues as violence and stereotyping. Among the many controversies involving children's programming are the lack of educational programming and the use of parental advisory ratings. A final controversy involves the fact that people simply watch too much television.

Key Terms

These terms are defined and indexed in the Glossary of key terms at the back of the book.

a la carte pricing 296

affiliates 286

basic cable 295

channel 299

channel allocation 285

community antenna television (CATV) 290

Corporation for Public Broadcasting (CPB) 303

digital video recorders (DVRs) 293

direct broadcast satellite (DBS) 298

geostationary 298

high-definition television (HDTV) 292

importation 290

kinescopes 286

lines of resolution 284

market 299

multiple system operators (MSOs) 294

must-carry rules 290

off-network programs 302

original syndication 302

pay-per-view channels 297

pixels 284

premium cable channels 297

program syndication 301

Public Broadcasting Service (PBS) 303

rating 304

share 304

strip programming 302

superstation 296

sweeps months 308

time shifting 293

ultra high frequency (UHF) 299

V-chip 312

very high frequency (VHF) 299

video on demand (VOD) 293

videocassette recorder (VCR) 293

videotape recorder (VTR) 293

zapping 293

Electronic Excursions

HISTORY

Web Excursion

1. The invention of television is controversial; many people and nations claim credit for it. Search the Web for evidence of this controversy. See if you can find an alternative version of the invention of television; then report on it. (Hint: Try "John Logie Baird" or "Paul Nipkow" as search terms.)

Media World DVD Excursion

2. View track 4.2, *Issues: The Ratings Battle*. This track takes you inside a midsize commercial television station in Erie, Pennsylvania. Do you believe that the statement "If it bleeds, it leads" accurately represents trends in TV news viewership? What factors do you consider when choosing a station for watching your news?

INDUSTRY

Web Excursion

3. Do you believe that public television fulfills its mandate of providing high-quality programming that would not be shown on commercial TV? Search the Web for the home pages of your local public television stations, or go directly to PBS at www.pbs.org.* Prepare a brief statement criticizing or defending the programming choices of these stations.

Media World DVD Excursions

4. View track 4.6, *Issues: Sports Journalism*. Why do you think sports segments are shown at the end of a newscast? Do you consider the typical lineup of the day's sporting highlights to be journalism?

5. View track 17, *Future Television* (from NBC's *Today* show). *TV Guide* editors Max Robins and Doug McCray discuss the changes this medium has in store. With the vast options available on the Internet, do you think interactive television will be successful? Is there a danger of dissuading viewers by offering too many channels, too many options? Do you think network TV should go the route of HBO and Showtime (i.e. airing shows of a much more graphic nature)?

CONTROVERSIES

Web Excursion

6. Some critics find television news too liberal, some too conservative, some too centrist. Search the Web for criticism of television news programming, or go directly to media bias sites such as AIM at www.aim.org* and FAIR at www.fair.org.* Prepare a brief statement supporting your point of view about bias, if any, in the direction of television news.

Media World DVD Excursion

7. View track 8, *Author James Steyer Discusses His Book* The Other Parent (from NBC's *Today* show). The author discusses the harmful effects of children's overexposure to media. Do you think new technologies, such as the V-chip, and TV ratings provide adequate limits for child viewers? Are these restrictions bordering on censorship?

ONLINE LEARNING CENTER WWW.MHHE.COM/RODMAN2

You may access these and additional Web excursions at the Online Learning Center for the book (www.mhhe.com/rodman2). Visit the student portion of this Web site to also access the *Interactive Timeline of Mass Media Milestones*, chapter highlights, self quizzes, and recommended readings, movies, and documentaries for this chapter.

*Some Web site addresses may change. When they do, please search for the Web site by name or topic on your favorite search engine.

The Internet

Convergence in a Networked World

Chapter Highlights

HISTORY: The Internet began as a military application and has rapidly become a convergence of all the media that preceded it.

INDUSTRY: To truly understand the Internet, you have to look at its architecture, which includes service providers, browsers, search engines, and various channels of communication.

CONTROVERSIES: The freedom and lack of regulation that make the Internet unique also make it an unreliable and dangerous place.

Is MySpace the New Mall?

How do you account for the huge popularity of social networking sites such as MySpace and Facebook? Within two years, MySpace went from virtual obscurity to a property that was eagerly acquired by Rupert Murdoch's News Corporation for $580 million. By 2007 MySpace had approximately 100 million registered users. As one teenager said, "If you're not on MySpace, you don't exist."[1] And Facebook, which caters to college students, had enrolled more than 85 percent of college students on campuses where it exists.

Both sites, as well as other social networking sites such as Xanga and hi5, allow individuals to create profiles and link to others ("friends")

Children use social networking sites like MySpace to experiment with and establish their online identities.

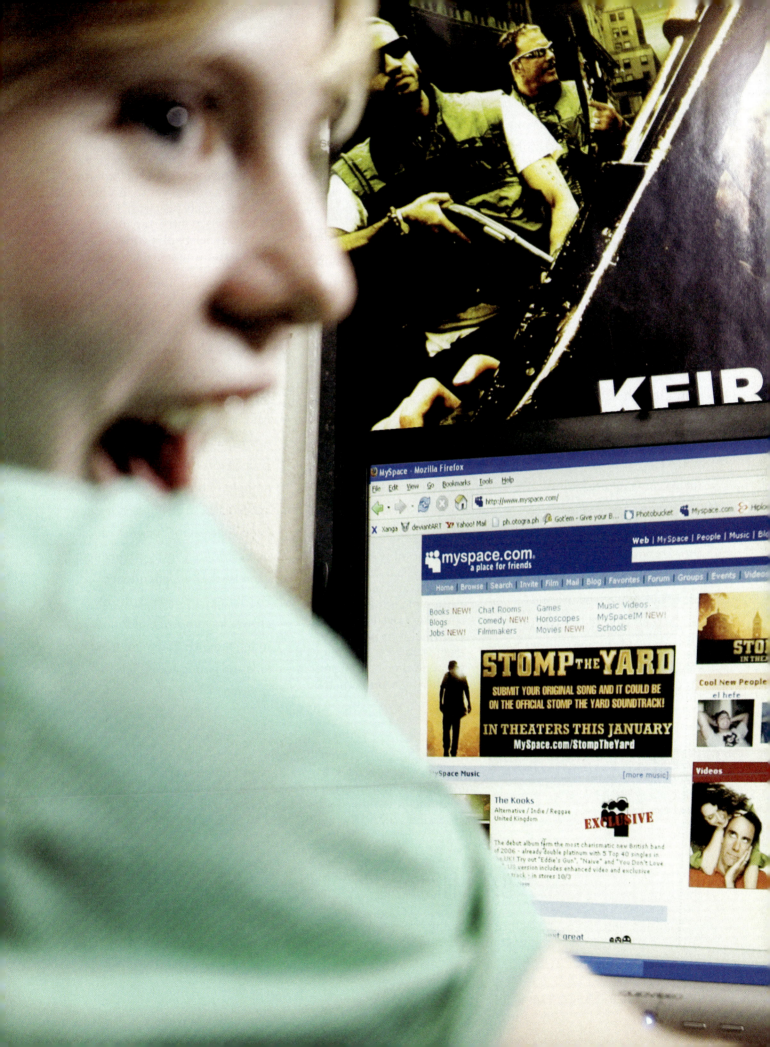

within the system. These sites let young people use their familiar digital tools—cell phone cameras, iPods, laptops, and user-friendly Web editing software—to experiment with and establish their online identities. Kids still use regular e-mail to communicate with adults, but many of them now use their networking sites as their primary form of communication with friends about such formative issues as body image, peer pressure, drugs, and relationships. The sites have been described as "a cross between a yearbook and a community Web site."[2] They are the very latest in media convergence.

Young people tend to treat social networking sites as though they are youth-only worlds—and of course, they are not. Parents have read about drug use and sex on their childrens' pages on MySpace, and at some colleges, campus police have raided parties that they have read about on Facebook. In other cases, graduating seniors have lost jobs when their prospective employers accessed their profiles and didn't like what they read. The biggest controversy—one that we'll look at in more depth in this chapter—has been the use of these networks by sexual predators.

In spite of the dangers, critics believe that the sites are popular because they give kids substitutes for the types of places that most adults took for granted growing up—places like neighborhood parks, basketball courts, and even street corners. These were places where kids could hang out without adult supervision, but are now inaccessible for many young people. As one expert explains:

> Their mobility and control over physical space is heavily curtailed and monitored. Although youth are able to socialize privately with one another in the homes of friends, most are not allowed to spend time hanging out in public, unaccompanied by parents or adults. They view social networking sites as places where they can be who they are, joke around with friends and make certain to stay in the loop about everything that is going on around them. Just as youth in a hunting society play with bows and arrows, youth in an information society play with information and social networks.[3]

Stephanie Olsen, a writer for CNET News, points out that today's kids have even fewer places to hang out than kids of just a few years ago. "For their Gen X predecessors, malls and cafes were among the few sanctuaries away from home. But many proprietors have restricted the amount of time teenagers can spend at these businesses, leaving cyberspace as the hangout of choice where youths can begin to exercise their independence. . . . For their grandparents, the bicycle was a symbol of childhood independence. Today, for many kids and young adults, it is the Internet."[4]

The huge success of social networking sites, and the impact they have on young peoples' lives, offers striking testimony to the global impact of today's Internet (see Fact File 10.1). Some treat this new medium as a danger, and others treat it as the road to utopia. As with earlier media, the truth is somewhere in between.

A Brief History *of the Net*

Before discussing the Internet itself, we begin with a look at the history of the computer and how it became a medium of mass communication.

FACT FILE 10.1

Top Five Internet Nations by Penetration (percentage of population)

There are more Internet users in the United States than in any other country, but heavy Web use is far from an American phenomenon.

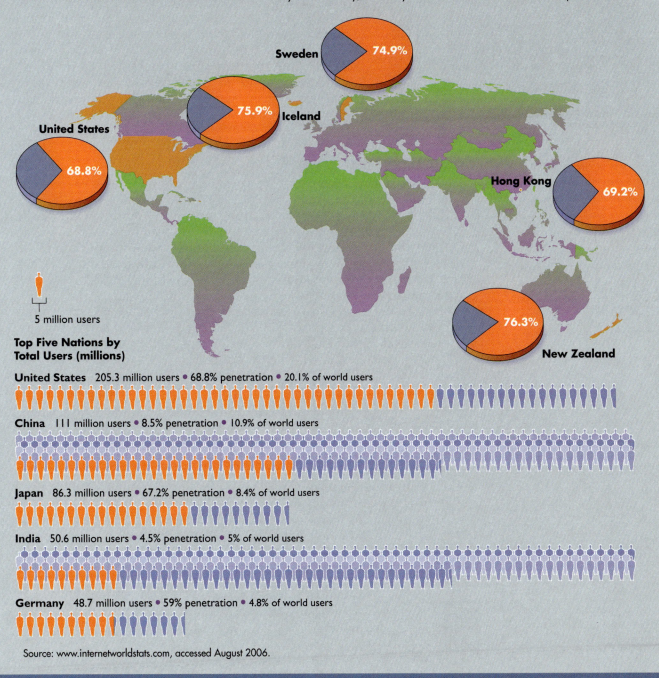

Sweden 74.9%

Iceland 75.9%

United States 68.8%

Hong Kong 69.2%

New Zealand 76.3%

5 million users

Top Five Nations by Total Users (millions)

United States 205.3 million users • 68.8% penetration • 20.1% of world users

China 111 million users • 8.5% penetration • 10.9% of world users

Japan 86.3 million users • 67.2% penetration • 8.4% of world users

India 50.6 million users • 4.5% penetration • 5% of world users

Germany 48.7 million users • 59% penetration • 4.8% of world users

Source: www.internetworldstats.com, accessed August 2006.

THE COMPUTER

Like the radio and the television before it, the computer would eventually become a home appliance that many people look at as an indispensable medium of communication. The device now familiar to us as a personal computer actually got its beginnings thousands of years ago as a calculator, or counting machine.

A small, early Roman abacus, made of bronze. It probably served as the pocket calculator of an ancient merchant.

The Abacus

Although we think of the computer as a modern invention, the first rudimentary computer was the abacus, a simple counting aid invented around 3000 BC in Babylonia, the area that is now Iraq. The abacus used movable beads to represent the Arabic system of numbers, which introduced to the world the concepts of the zero and fixed places for tens, hundreds, thousands, and so on. When Arabic numbers replaced Roman numerals around AD 700, mathematical calculations were greatly simplified.[5]

Going Electronic: From Tubes to Chips

Electronics enabled computers to be programmable, so a series of formulas, or algorithms, could be stored and activated automatically. Both Germans and Americans developed early electronic computers during World War II, first for the accurate placement of artillery fire and then for code breaking so that enemy messages could be read when intercepted. The early computers were enormous machines that relied on vacuum tubes. When Bell Telephone laboratories replaced bulky tubes with transistors in 1947, computers became more powerful, but they were still huge. Computers with a fraction of today's power took up space in several large rooms. Computers like the Universal Automatic Computer (UNIVAC) amazed people in the 1950s, making them wonder how much further technology could possibly take them.

The integrated circuit, which enabled electronic components to be manufactured in a solid block without connecting wires, became available in 1959. Once again, this allowed computers to become more powerful yet smaller. A computer the size of a small refrigerator could do rudimentary word processing by 1968. It cost $20,000. Like today's computers, these early models were basically made up of three components: (1) the central processing unit (CPU), which processes the algorithms that crunch the numbers; (2) random-access memory (RAM), which holds the data currently being worked with; and (3) storage (in the form of a hard drive or another device), which holds data, including programs and documents.

IBM became the first large, successful computer manufacturer in the 1960s. During the 1970s integrated circuits, now produced on small slices of silicon called chips, were becoming smaller, more powerful, and less expensive. Young computer enthusiasts such as Bill Gates and Steve Jobs were busy writing programming language to run the new machines. Apple Computer was selling a small personal computer for a little more than $1,000 by 1977. The personal computer revolution had begun, and it was about to intersect with military activity that had begun some years before.

What were the technological advancements that led to today's personal computer?

SELF QUIZ

THE MILITARY ROOTS OF THE NET

President Dwight D. Eisenhower had U.S. military interests in mind when he started a scientific research agency called the Advanced Research Projects Agency (ARPA).[6] When ARPA began to hook computers together into networks in response to the Cuban missile crisis (see the Close-Up on History box), it meant that the early Internet, like early radio, would be developed with military funds. Also like radio, the Internet was put to civilian use after

The Internet's Cold War Genesis

Most experts agree that the Internet's year of birth is 1969, the year the U.S. Department of Defense set up a computer network called ARPANET. But the foundation of the digital network was actually laid in 1962, during what came to be called the Cuban missile crisis. At the time, John F. Kennedy was president of the United States and Fidel Castro was the communist dictator of Cuba. During the height of the cold war, Castro invited the Soviet Union to set up military bases on the island, 90 miles south of Florida. The Soviets, recognizing a strategic location when they saw one, brought in a battery of nuclear missiles and aimed them at the United States. In response, President Kennedy announced that if the missiles were not removed, their placement would be considered an act of war—and the United States might strike first with its nuclear missiles. For the first time in history, the world was on the brink of a nuclear war.

After a tense standoff, the Soviets finally removed their missiles, but the Cuban missile crisis had exposed a fatal weakness in U.S. military capabilities: A first strike by the Soviet Union with even just one bomb could have wiped out America's entire military communications. The United States needed a computer network with no central control point, a network with a "redundancy of connectivity," meaning that if one or even several lines of communication were broken, the fail-safe network would continue to work.

To develop this supernetwork, the government set aside a significant amount of money both in the budgets for its own labs and in the form of grants to university computer scientists. The university professors who were the primary creators of the Net were mostly uninterested in Defense Department concerns, but that was where the Internet project originated nonetheless.[1]

President John F. Kennedy proclaims in a televised speech on October 22, 1962, that Cuba has become an offensive Soviet base. The Cuban missile crisis eventually led to the formation of the Internet.

[1]See, for example, Katie Hafner and Matthew Lyon, *Where Wizards Stay Up Late: The Origins of the Internet* (New York: Simon & Schuster, 1996).

the government helped develop it. As with all previous media technology, the Internet's popularity with civilians depended on its becoming inexpensive and easy to use.

GOING DIGITAL

Before scientists could complete the ARPA computer network, they first had to sell the military on a digital form of communication. Computers at this time were used for crunching numbers in long mathematical equations, not for communication. Military personnel communicated by voice or by analog-generated code. As you will recall from earlier chapters, analog communication is the way telephone,

SELF QUIZ

What were the technological steps that had to be taken before the first military computer network became functional?

radio, and television worked for most of their history. A person's voice or a symbolic code was converted into an electronic analog, or likeness, which was then sent over a cable or the airwaves. ARPA researchers eventually convinced the senior military officials in the Defense Department that digital communication would be more accurate and reliable than analog, because a message converted into digits could be sent without distortion. As long as the full set of digits arrived at the destination, the message received would be an exact copy of the message sent.

Protocols

The second step in building the Internet was to overcome the obstacles that made it impossible for computers to talk to one another. Early computers, like early record players, had been developed by different companies and were not compatible. To achieve the goal of compatibility, programmers developed **protocols,** or codes that allow one machine to communicate with another.

protocols
Software codes that enable one computer to communicate with another.

From the Military to the Civilian Net

The U.S. Department of Defense completed its national system of computers, the Advanced Research Project Agency Network (ARPANET), in 1969. Within a few years ARPANET had joined with other networks operated by U.S. allies overseas and was eventually joined by networks supported by the Department of Energy, the National Aeronautics and Space Administration, and the National Science Foundation. By the late 1970s, however, the Net would begin its conversion to civilian use.

Usenet

Know for the quiz

Usenet
An application used to support newsgroups on the Internet.

newsgroups
Online bulletin boards, organized according to topic.

World Wide Web
A simplified means of navigating the Internet based on hypertext links and graphical user interfaces.

hypertext links (hyperlinks)
Highlighted words and images within a Web page that allow the user to move to another site by pointing and clicking a mouse button.

In 1979, civilian researchers who had been excluded from ARPANET decided that they needed their own Internet. Drawing on the technology developed by the Department of Defense, they invented **Usenet.** Usenet did everything that ARPANET did, but it also included the ability to support discussion groups that could carry on conversations in real time and disseminate information in the form of online bulletin boards, what are now called **newsgroups.** In a few years, this network and other governmental, university, and commercial networks joined ARPANET. At this point, the basic idea of the Internet was pretty much in place, but only people with access to sophisticated computers at universities, corporate research centers, and military installations could use it.

The First Commercial Online Services

Right after Usenet emerged in 1979, CompuServe, the first successful general interest online service, began.[7] The service was at first limited to e-mail and technical support for contacting Internet sites, and users had to master complex codes and commands to retrieve the simplest information. Meanwhile, the revolution in personal computers was occurring, led by Bill Gates, who had now founded Microsoft, and Steve Jobs, the cofounder of Apple Computer.[8] Many businesses and educational institutions equipped themselves with personal computers (PCs), and people who used PCs at work began to purchase units for the home. America Online appeared in 1989, with software that was much easier to use than that of CompuServe. The true simplification for users, however, would come with the advent of the World Wide Web.

What were the first two commercial, general interest online services? How were they different?

SELF QUIZ

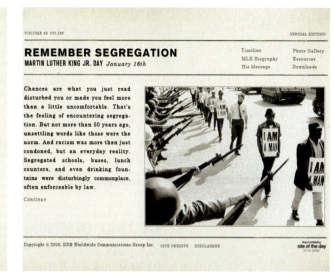

The World Wide Web has become a powerful conduit of social ideas. The Remember Segregation site asks visitors to recall the life of Dr. Martin Luther King, Jr. Web site used with permission of DDB Worldwide Communications Group. Photo © Corbis-Bettmann.

THE WORLD WIDE WEB

The Internet is a vast interconnected hardware system made up of different types of computers. The World Wide Web, in contrast, is a software system that simplifies Internet navigation. Tim Berners-Lee invented the **World Wide Web** in 1989 and made his invention public in 1993. Among the Web's innovations are **hypertext links,** also known as **hyperlinks,** which are highlighted words and images within a Web page that allow the user to move from one site to another by simply pointing and clicking a mouse button.

Berners-Lee made no money on his invention. He didn't patent it, and he released it for free. "I was mostly interested in making the technology work," he said later.[9] The World Wide Web greatly increased the popularity of the Internet. This popularity was further enhanced in 1993 when Marc Andreessen, a student at the University of Illinois at Urbana-Champaign, created the first Web browser, Mosaic, which used icons, pull-down menus, and colorful links to display hypertext documents. Andreessen became one of the founders of Netscape, the hugely successful commercial Web browser company, and eventually the chief technology officer for America Online (AOL) when AOL took over Netscape.

By 1995, so many people were online that the Internet was no longer useful for national security purposes and the military turned it over to the public sector.

Tim Berners-Lee is the inventor of the World Wide Web and the director of the World Wide Web Consortium, which oversees the Web's continued development.

 SELF QUIZ Who invented the World Wide Web, and how much did this originator make from this invention?

THE YouTube PHENOMENON

Advances in the technology of the Web led to great increases in computing power, storage capacity, and communication technology. By the late 1990s, the outcome of all these advances was a usable form of streaming technology, which enabled video to be delivered via the Web and viewed on a computer screen. The streaming process involved buffering, meaning that the file was being downloaded and saved on a hard drive at the same time that it was being viewed, so that enough digital information was buffered on the drive to keep the video going when the downloaded packets were not coming in. The technology resulted in YouTube in 2005, which became the epitome of user-generated content in 2006, with 100 million videos to air and users uploading an additional 70,000 each day. Users shared their homemade videos along with favorite movie clips, TV program clips, and commercials. This user-generated content distinguished the Web from any previous form of mass media.

Current TV, a cable television network in which the programming originated from user generated content on their Web site, was another example of the new power of user-generated content, as are MySpace, Wikipedia, Flickr, and Digg. Google bought YouTube for $1.65 billion in 2006, less than a year after its launch.

GLOBAL DIMENSIONS

In a way, the Internet has truly made the world a *global village,* a term coined by early media theorist Marshall McLuhan (whom we discussed at length in Chapter 2). Web surfers connect on a personal level with other Web surfers in other countries every day (see Figure 10.1). Such global connections are made possible by a worldwide infrastructure of satellites, telephone circuits, and undersea coaxial and fiber-optic cables that provide a physical interconnection among 160 countries of the world.

However, governments sometimes throw up obstacles. In Iran, Jordan, Saudi Arabia, Syria, China, North Korea, and Myanmar (formerly Burma), governments allow people limited Internet access. In China, for example, regulations specifically forbid the posting and dissemination of *state secrets,* a vaguely defined term that has been applied by the government to cover any information whose release it has not sanctioned.[10] And yet even these countries are in better shape than many of the developing countries of Africa and Asia, most of which have little or no access.

Many countries, including the United States, worry about a digital divide or technology gap between those who have an understanding of computer

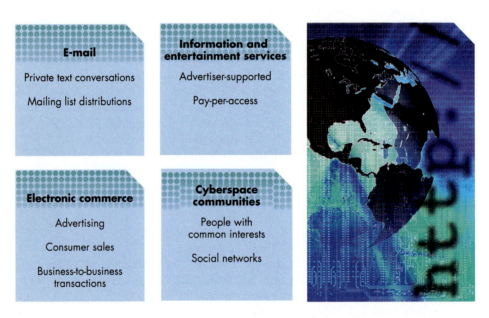

FIGURE 10.1 Internet Components The Internet has evolved into a system with these four basic components: e-mail, information and entertainment services, electronic commerce, and cyberspace communities.

Arab Culture and Civilization
A Collaborative Web Project Sponsored by the National Institute for Technology and Liberal Education

Introduction

The Al-Musharaka Initiative of the National Institute for Technology and Liberal Education has developed this site, with funds from the Andrew W. Mellon Foundation. It is intended to serve as a resource for all who would develop a better understanding of the Arab world. While our principal audience is the students, faculty, staff and alumni of the liberal arts colleges served by NITLE, the site is open to all visitors.

The materials comprising the site are organized thematically into a set of ten modules, each of which contains a variety of original texts, video clips and audio files from online and print sources.

Please note that these materials are not in the public domain, and may not be used without the permission of their respective copyright holders. For more information about citing and requesting permission for copyrighted work on our site, please refer to our copyright policy.

This website represents a collaborative effort between many scholars, technologists, and institutions. You can find a full history of the project on our about page, or see a complete list of contributors on the credits page.

Faculty members and librarians from colleges affiliated with NITLE are invited to participate in the broader Al-Musharaka initiative of which this site is one project. This initiative includes seminars, collaborative teaching projects, opportunities for computer-mediated dialogue, and the creation of materials to support teaching and research.

Introduction

About the Site

Main Menu

Acknowledgements

Copyright

Contact

The World Wide Web, being by far the most diversified communications medium, has something for every cultural group, and for those who would like to develop an understanding of those groups. One example of such sites is the Arab Culture and Civilization site, http://arabworld.nitle.org/, hosted by the National Institute for Technology and Liberal Education. Used with permission from the National Institute for Technology and Liberal Education.

technology and those who do not. In today's world, an inability to use the Internet puts an individual at a distinct disadvantage. In the United States the digital divide is much less of a problem than it was a few years ago, and programs exist to address it in poor and underserved communities.

CULTURAL DIVERSITY ON THE WEB

The World Wide Web, being by far the most diversified communications medium, has something for every cultural group. Women, for example, have their own **portals,** which are gateways to the rest of the Net, the sites from which people begin their Web surfing. The largest of these portals include Women.com Networks (www.women.com), iVillage (www.ivillage.com), and Oxygen Media (www.oxygen.com). Portals for African Americans include the Black Web Portal (www.blackwebportal.com) and The Black World Today (www.tbwt.org).

Hispanic portals include Hispanic Online (www.hispaniconline.com), which is run by *Hispanic* magazine; Hispanic Surf (www.hispanicsurf.com); and Hispanic dot com (www.hispanic.com), which has as its mission "the creation of a cyber-barrio where we can meet and help each other through the Internet to improve the quality of family life and achieve economic success and political empowerment." There are more than 500 sites devoted to Native American culture, including the cultures of different indigenous nations of Canada, Mexico, and the United States. These include portals such as NativeWeb (www.nativeweb.org), and media sites such as that for the *Navajo Times* (www.thenavajotimes.com) and the Native American Public Telecommunications Network (www.nativetelecom.org), producers/distributors of educational Indian radio and television programming. There is also a Native American Journalists Association (www.naja.com), which provides

portals
Sites from which people begin their Web surfing; they act as gateways to the rest of the Internet.

milestones in internet history

1969 U.S. Department of Defense sets up a computer network called the Advanced Research Project Agency Network (ARPANET), connecting university, military, and defense contractor computers. This is considered the birth of the Internet.

| 1965 | 1970 | 1975 | 1980 |

1979 Civilian researchers who had been excluded from ARPANET invent Usenet, which features discussion groups.

1979 CompuServe, the first successful general interest online service, begins operating.

CONSIDER THIS

Choose a culture of an acquaintance or classmate. Perform a Google search on that culture and follow as many leads as you can in 10 minutes. What were you able to discover?

news and links about jobs and education programs of interest to Native Americans.

Portals for gay and lesbian culture include PlanetOut (www .planetout.com). Web sites for people with disabilities include Disabilityinfo.gov, a gateway to the federal government's disability-related information and resources. There are sites for all religious denominations, and many that provide information on a wide variety of religions. These include www.holidays.net, which explains the meaning of religious celebrations.

Understanding Today's Internet *Industry*

Convergence or competition? The *Media World* DVD that accompanies this book (track 5) looks at the challenges that the Internet is presenting to established media such as newspapers, magazines, radio, and television.

hosts
Internet computers that contain actual Web sites.

The Internet is changing the way people communicate around the world, and it is changing the way the world does business. When you consider further that digital convergence is making the Internet a conduit for all other media—books, magazines, newspapers, movies, radio, recordings, and television—it is clear that the cultural significance of the Internet in our lives will be ever more pervasive. To understand the Internet is to understand the media of the future. To explain this industry, we'll focus separately on its architecture (the components that make it up) and its economics (how money is made on it).

THE ARCHITECTURE OF THE NET

The Internet, a huge network of computer networks, allows each computer on each network to communicate with other computers through multiple pathways. These pathways resemble, conceptually, the lines of a fishnet. The main computers, the ones that house the actual Web sites, are called **hosts.** These hosts might be at university computer centers, or they might be in the data processing department of a major corporation, a small business, or a government agency anywhere in the world.

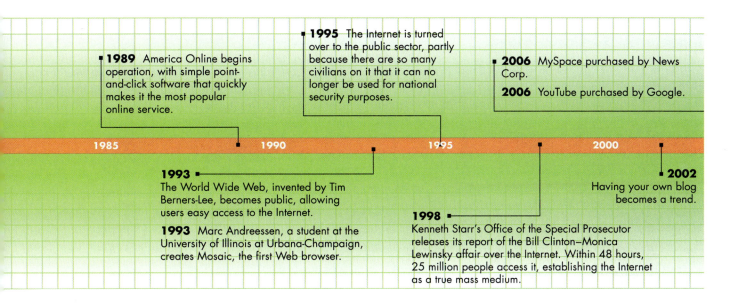

1989 America Online begins operation, with simple point-and-click software that quickly makes it the most popular online service.

1995 The Internet is turned over to the public sector, partly because there are so many civilians on it that it can no longer be used for national security purposes.

2006 MySpace purchased by News Corp.

2006 YouTube purchased by Google.

1985   1990   1995   2000

1993 The World Wide Web, invented by Tim Berners-Lee, becomes public, allowing users easy access to the Internet.

1993 Marc Andreessen, a student at the University of Illinois at Urbana-Champaign, creates Mosaic, the first Web browser.

2002 Having your own blog becomes a trend.

1998 Kenneth Starr's Office of the Special Prosecutor releases its report of the Bill Clinton–Monica Lewinsky affair over the Internet. Within 48 hours, 25 million people access it, establishing the Internet as a true mass medium.

Access Providers

Users connect to the Internet via the host computers belonging to Internet service providers (ISPs). ISPs include the broadband services provided by cable television coaxial and fiber optic lines, telephone companies' digital subscriber line (DSL) technology, and dial-up services such as AOL. The vast majority of users now have some form of broadband service. In fact, in 2006 Nielsen/NetRatings reported that 72 percent of home-based Internet users had high-speed connections, compared with 57 percent in 2005.[11]

Most major ISPs have their own proprietary, self-contained content: They have their own e-mail services, chat rooms, forums on everything from astrology to zoology, and stock portfolio managers that allow you to follow your personal investments. There are several thousand ISPs (see Fact File 10.2 for the top 10), although some of them serve only limited geographic areas.

Internet Addresses

Internet addresses are strings of words and symbols that take users from place to place on the Net. Internet addresses follow the same kind of specific-to-general pattern that street addresses do. For example, the snail-mail (U.S. Postal Service) address for the president of the United States is written as follows:

The President of the United States

The White House

1600 Pennsylvania Avenue NW

Washington, D.C. 20500

The president's e-mail address moves from specific to general in the same way:

President@whitehouse.gov

The first part of the address is the type of protocol, which tells the host computer the type of language that a network uses. A **user ID** (e.g., President) followed by the "at" sign (@) lets the host know that you're using the "mail" protocol. The next portion of the address is the **domain,** which identifies the

user ID
The first part of an e-mail address.

domain
The portion of an Internet address that identifies the network that handles the account.

FACT FILE 10.2

Top Internet Service Providers

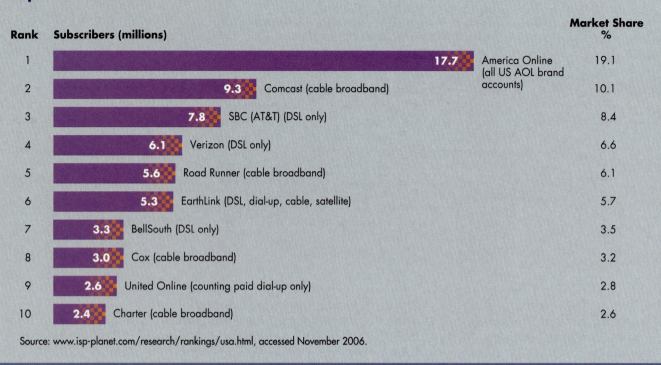

Rank	Subscribers (millions)		Market Share %
1	17.7	America Online (all US AOL brand accounts)	19.1
2	9.3	Comcast (cable broadband)	10.1
3	7.8	SBC (AT&T) (DSL only)	8.4
4	6.1	Verizon (DSL only)	6.6
5	5.6	Road Runner (cable broadband)	6.1
6	5.3	EarthLink (DSL, dial-up, cable, satellite)	5.7
7	3.3	BellSouth (DSL only)	3.5
8	3.0	Cox (cable broadband)	3.2
9	2.6	United Online (counting paid dial-up only)	2.8
10	2.4	Charter (cable broadband)	2.6

Source: www.isp-planet.com/research/rankings/usa.html, accessed November 2006.

uniform resource locator (URL)
An Internet address that connects the user to a Web site on a particular computer.

hypertext transfer protocol (http)
The protocol that enables computers to recognize links on the World Wide Web.

hypertext markup language (HTML)
The basic computer language used to write hypertext transfer protocol (http).

Java
An advanced programming language used for animated images and advanced sound applications.

network that handles the account, with periods between each level of that network. The domain name in the e-mail address consists of the organization (whitehouse) and the type of organization (.gov, or U.S. government entity).

The networks attached to the Internet are organized into a limited number of categories. The main categories, or top-level domains, include .com (pronounced "dot com," for commercial entities), .edu (educational), .gov (U.S. government), .org (nonprofit organizations), and .net (network access providers).[12] Domain signifiers such as these generally make up the farthest-right part of the Internet address, unless a two-letter country designation such as .jp (Japan) or .mx (Mexico) is appended. It is assumed that if there is no geographic code, the domain is located within the United States.

A Web site address, in contrast to an e-mail address, is known as a **uniform resource locator,** or **URL** (often pronounced "Earl"). The URL for the White House's Web site is:

http://www.whitehouse.gov

In a URL, the protocol is indicated by **http.** This stands for **hypertext transfer protocol,** the most common Internet protocol besides that used for e-mail; it is the protocol that enables computers to recognize links on the World Wide Web.[13] The basic computer language used to write http is known as **hypertext markup language (HTML).** A more advanced programming language, **Java,** is used for animated images and advanced sound applications.[14]

In URLs, there can be many different levels to the domain name, and domain names can be followed by file names. For example, the archives (stored copies) of the comic strip *Dilbert* are found at the following address:

http://www.unitedmedia.com/comics/dilbert/archive
(protocol) (domain name)   (files at that site)

Most Popular Web Sites

1. Yahoo
2. Google
3. MySpace
4. MSN (Microsoft Network)
5. eBay
6. Amazon.com
7. YouTube
8. Craigslist.org
9. Wikipedia
10. CNN (Cable News Network)

Source: Alexa, http://alexa.com, accessed November 2006.

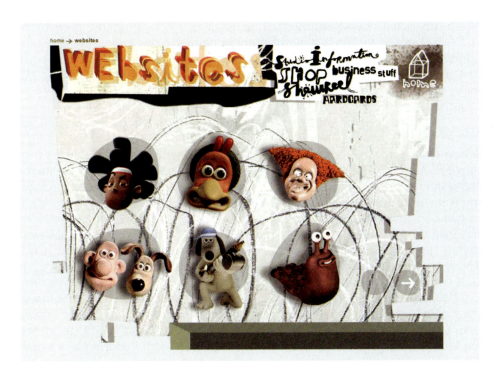

Aardman Animation, the home of the Wallace and Gromit films, uses Java applications on its Web site. Copyright © 2006 Aardman Animations Ltd. All Rights Reserved.

Here, the domain name (unitedmedia.com) is that of the company that syndicates *Dilbert*. The file name (comics/dilbert/archive) takes you directly to the pages on United Media's Web site that house the *Dilbert* archives.

Domain Names

United Media, like most other large companies, has secured a domain name for its URL that matches the company name. There was a brisk trade in domain names in the early days of the Web, when it cost only $70 to register a name with InterNIC, the organization set up for that purpose. Some speculators bought dozens of promising names for future resale. The domain name drugs.com, for example, sold for $823,000 in 1999. That was hardly the record, however. Compaq Computer paid $3.5 million for Altavista.com, and business.com was sold to a Los Angeles company for $7.5 million.[15] One of the more interesting transactions was made by a Houston entrepreneur who bought the name eflowers.com in 1997. Two years later, he sold the name to Flowers Direct for $25,000, a 50-cent commission from each order placed through www.eflowers.com, and a bouquet of flowers to be delivered to his wife, every month, for life.[16]

A browser such as Netscape Navigator decodes the HTML used in Web documents, allowing Net surfers to click and jump through dense data fields.

cybersquatting
The practice of registering trademarked domain names with hopes of reselling them to those who own the trademarks.

cyber-
As a prefix, a metaphor for anything pertaining to the Internet.

browser
A software program that enables a user to move around the Internet.

graphical user interface (GUI)
A set of browser features such as icons and hot spots that allow users to navigate Web sites easily.

What are the major components of the Internet's architecture?

bots
Short for robots which are software programs capable of carrying out automated searches over the Web.

directory
A type of search engine in which sites are arranged into categories by human editors.

hybrid search engines
Search engines that use both robots and human editors.

metacrawler
A type of search engine that combines results from a number of other search engines.

The market in domain names encouraged some speculators to begin **cybersquatting,** the practice of registering trademarked domain names with hopes of reselling them to the companies that own the trademarks. (**Cyber-,** as a prefix, is a metaphor that has come to mean anything pertaining to the online world, or cyberspace.)[17] A California speculator, for example, bought the domain name porschecar.com and tried to sell it to Porsche Cars of North America. Cybersquatting became illegal in 1999. Some free speech advocates opposed the regulation of domain names, citing cases like that of a young boy nicknamed Pokey who almost lost pokey.org to the toy company that owned the rights to the Gumby and Pokey characters, and a young girl named Veronica whose Web site was sought by Archie Comics.[18]

Browsers

A **browser** is a software program that acts as the vehicle that enables you to move around the Internet. A browser such as Netscape Navigator or Microsoft's Internet Explorer decodes the HTML used in Web documents, allowing Net surfers to click and jump through dense data fields. Instead of typing in cumbersome URLs every time you want to see a new Web page, you can navigate through sites by using hyperlinks, icons (small symbols), pull-down menus, and hot spots, which turn your cursor arrow into a pointing hand. These features are part of what is called the **graphical user interface,** or **GUI** (pronounced "gooey").

You visit a site by downloading a page of information into the memory of your computer. Once you visit a site, it is held in your computer's memory until you quit the browser. This makes it quicker to "revisit" a site (using the back arrow, for example) that you have already visited during a session.

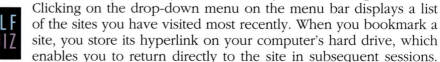

Clicking on the drop-down menu on the menu bar displays a list of the sites you have visited most recently. When you bookmark a site, you store its hyperlink on your computer's hard drive, which enables you to return directly to the site in subsequent sessions.

Search Engines

One of the first Web sites that most users visit is a search engine, an electronic index of Web sites. Search engines enable the user to make sense of the amorphous mass of the Web. There are several types of search engines. The traditional type sends out automated software robots, or **bots,** called spiders or crawlers, to discover new sites and to categorize them according to the information that is contained on their home page.

A second type of search engine is the **directory,** in which sites are arranged into categories by human editors. With directories, site owners submit their home page information to the search engine; then the editors, acting as gatekeepers, assign it to an appropriate category. Directories won't return as many results as the typical search engine, but they are often more accurate. All the major search engines (see Fact File 10.4) are **hybrid search engines,** which have both robots and human editors. Another type of search engine, the **metacrawler,** combines results from more than one search engine at a time. Dogpile and Hotbot are metacrawlers.

FACT FILE 10.4

Top Search Engines

The following are the top choices for search engines according to Search Engine Watch.

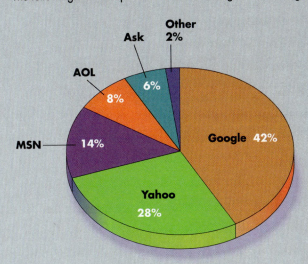

Source: Search Engine Watch, www.searchenginewatch.com, accessed August 2006.

Search engines receive most of their revenue from selling advertising, although some receive revenue from online services that feature them. Each of them sells ads that appear as you perform your search. Some of those ads are keyed to what you are searching for. Type in "automobiles," for example, and your search results will include an ad for cars. Several search engines also offer "paid inclusion," which means that the advertiser's Web site is guaranteed to come up in a search for that product.

The top search engines, such as Google and Yahoo, have become portals by adding proprietary features like those that were once the province of the online services, features such as news, e-mail, and "channels" of entertainment. Portals are valuable cyber–real estate, because they can influence the direction of the user's search for information, entertainment, and commerce. They increase the chances that users will move in the direction of the ads they run.

Channel Convergence

The Internet has allowed the convergence of mass communication channels such as Web sites with interpersonal channels such as e-mail, chat rooms, and instant messages. **Chat,** which was originally called Internet Relay Chat (IRC), is an application that allows users to take part in live, real-time conversations. Instant Messenger, a program originated by America Online, allows for chats with a standard group of friends from a "buddies list" that is set up in advance. It has become one of the most popular Internet functions for teenagers.

chat
An application that allows Internet users to be part of live, real-time text conversations.

Netiquette

Because the Internet allows interpersonal communication, a form of etiquette for the Net, called **netiquette,** is part of online culture. For example, when you don't know the person with whom you are communicating, netiquette

netiquette
A form of etiquette, or rules of acceptable behavior, for the Internet.

The Internet extends the channels of earlier media, making content such as these editorial cartoons accessible to a wider audience. Time.com screen shot used with permission of Time.com. Cartoon from Copley News Service and Steve Breen, used by permission.

flaming
Sending vicious personal attacks over the Internet.

requires that you refrain from **flaming**—sending vicious personal attacks—and from responding if that person flames you.[19] It is also considered polite to stay on topic in a newsgroup, and typing in all capital letters is considered shouting.

Along with its own brand of etiquette, Internet communication is also generating its own language style. To save time and space, people writing instant messages, e-mail, and so on use a shorthand that includes numerous acronyms, that is, words formed from the first, or first few, letters of a series of words.[20] Common acronyms include AKA for "also known as," BTW for "by the way," and IMHO for "in my humble opinion." Emoticons (AKA smileys), which are formed from keyboard symbols such as colons, dashes, and parentheses, are also used as a form of abbreviation (see Fact File 10.5). Emoticons are viewed sideways, such as :-) for "happy," :(for "sad" and :-V for "shouting." These symbols are designed to compensate for the absence of nonverbal cues when communicating on the Internet, and some e-mail and instant messaging applications will insert a graphic smiley when the appropriate keystrokes are entered. Some elaborate emoticons have been invented, such as *<:-) for "happy birthday." The humorist Dave Barry had suggested the use of :-D for "person laughing," and :-D* for "person laughing so hard that he or she does not notice that a five-legged spider is hanging from his or her lip."[21]

Newsgroups

An interesting convergence of interpersonal and mass communication can be found in newsgroups, the Usenet features that are like online bulletin boards or message boards that can be accessed from a Web site at any time. Newsgroups create a type of discussion forum in which all participants can read all the messages and the replies sent by members of the group. Unlike real-time chat, in which all users are actually sitting at their computer keyboards at the same time, newsgroups allow participants to post and access questions and answers at any time. When one user responds to another's posting, it creates a **thread,** or a connected series of messages.

thread
A connected series of messages in newsgroup or online discussion group postings.

FACT FILE 10.5

Emoticons and Acronyms

Emoticons are facial expressions made by a certain series of keystrokes, usually producing an image of a face sideways.

:-)	Classic smiley	;-D	Winking and laughing	(8(I)	Homer
:-(	Frown	>:)	Little devil	O+	Female
:-*	Kiss	>:->	Very mischievous devil	O->	Male
:-o	Surprised look, or yawn	>:-<	Angry	0:-)	Angel
:-P	Sticking out tongue	>:-(	Annoyed	]:->	Devil
:-V	Shouting	<:-)	Innocently asking dumb question	]:-)	Happy devil
:-}	Mischievous smile			`:-)	Raised eyebrow
;-)	Wink	<:-I	Dunce	{{ }}	Hug: the one whose name is in the brackets is being hugged

Acronyms, or e-mail shorthand, are formed from the first letters of the words in a common expression.

BFN	Bye for now	IOW	In other words	TIA	Thanks in advance
BTW	By the way	IRL	In real life	TMI	Too much information
FAQ	Frequently asked questions	LOL	Laughing out loud	TTFN	Ta-ta for now
FWIW	For what it's worth	LTNS	Long time no see	TYVM	Thank you very much
FYI	For your information	MHOTY	My hat's off to you	WDYMBT?	What do you mean by that?
HTH	Hope this (that) helps	MTFBWY	May the force be with you		
IAE	In any event	NRN	No reply necessary	WYSIWYG	What you see is what you get (pronounced "wizzy-wig")
IJWTK	I just want to know	OIC	Oh, I see		
IJWTS	I just want to say	OTOH	On the other hand	WTG	Way to go
IMO	In my opinion	ROTFL	Rolling on the floor laughing	YGBK	You gotta be kiddin'
IMHO	In my humble/honest opinion			YMMV	Your mileage may vary
IMNSHO	In my not so humble opinion	RSN	Real soon now		
		RTM	Read the manual (When impatient, RTFM)		

Sources: High-Tech Dictionary, www.computeruser.com/resources/dictionary/emoticons.html; Internet Dictionary, www.netlingo.com/emailsh.cfm; and the author's various instant-messaging correspondents.

Users can also read the messages without responding, a practice known as **lurking.** There are newsgroups on practically any topic, and anyone can start one. An integral part of online communities, they serve to advise, inform, and support people with similar interests.[22] Newsgroups are broken down into categories, such as alt. (alternative topics, from the mundane to the bizarre); rec. (recreational, sports, and arts-oriented topics); and soc. (social issues and socializing). You can search for newsgroups on any search engine—use the keyword "newsgroups" on AOL, or use the Groups tab on the Google home page.

List Servers
List servers (also known as mailing lists, Listservs, e-groups, and online discussion groups) are much like newsgroups, but rather than being accessed

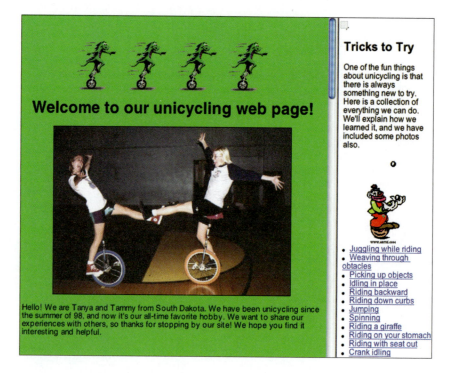

Tricks to Try

One of the fun things about unicycling is that there is always something new to try. Here is a collection of everything we can do. We'll explain how we learned it, and we have included some photos also.

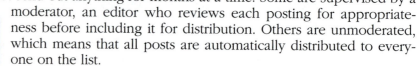

www.artie.com

- Juggling while riding
- Weaving through obtacles
- Picking up objects
- Idling in place
- Riding backward
- Riding down curbs
- Jumping
- Spinning
- Riding a giraffe
- Riding on your stomach
- Riding with seat out
- Crank idling

Welcome to our unicycling web page!

Hello! We are Tanya and Tammy from South Dakota. We have been unicycling since the summer of 98, and now it's our all-time favorite hobby. We want to share our experiences with others, so thanks for stopping by our site! We hope you find it interesting and helpful.

Personal Web pages such as this are an interesting convergence of interpersonal and mass communication. Unicycling web page by Tamara Kula and Tanya Marsh. Reprinted with permission. "Juggling Clown on Unicycle" is copyright © 2004 ARG! Cartoon Animation, www.artie.com. Reprinted with permission.

on the Web, everything posted to the list server is sent out to each member's e-mail address, often several times a day. Some lists are very active and will stuff your electronic mailbox with 20 or more messages a day. Other lists might not send out anything for months at a time. Some are supervised by a moderator, an editor who reviews each posting for appropriateness before including it for distribution. Others are unmoderated, which means that all posts are automatically distributed to everyone on the list.

What's the difference between a newsgroup and a listserver?

SELF QUIZ

Personal Web Pages

Personal Web pages (also called personal home pages and personal main pages) enable Internet users to tell the world about themselves or about topics of interest to them. Personal Web pages might include a simple listing of a person's identifying information, likes and dislikes, and hobbies and interests, as well as images, audio files, video clips, and links to other sites. Grandparents use personal Web pages to post pictures of their grandchildren, entrepreneurs use them to publicize home businesses, and activists use them to organize community groups.

In the early days of the Web (which is to say, those dark ages of the 1990s), you needed a fairly advanced set of programming skills to set up a professional-looking Web page. Current Web-page-building tools are based on the principle of what you see is what you get (WYSIWYG), which means that when you are building your Web page, you can see on the screen exactly what the Web page will look like when someone else views it. All of today's major Internet service providers supply free Web pages for their users, as well as tools for creating them.

At first, people created Web pages because they wanted to conquer the new technology and tools of the Internet. As sites became less of a challenge to build, they became more like directories, a means of being found, and even a way to obtain a small version of the media spotlight. But as they became more popular, personal Web pages became a forum to present personal ideas and even confessions.[23] At that point Web pages became Weblogs.

Blogs

Weblogs, or **blogs** for short, are essentially online journals. Some sites, such as LiveJournal, Blogger, and Xanga, are set up specifically to provide users with free blogs. The major ISPs also offer this service, such as AOL Journals. When building a blog on AOL, the user starts by giving it a name, entering a description, and picking a community, such as Family, Dating and Relationships, or My Thoughts. WYSIWYG tools enable the user to create a custom layout.

Blogging became a cool thing to do in 2002, and by 2004 there were some 10 million blogs online. Political blogs were seen as an important force

More than half of those with blogs are between 13 and 19 years old.

in the 2004 presidential election. Other notable bloggers include journalists and university professors, but most bloggers are teens and young adults. In fact, 90 percent of those with blogs are between 13 and 29 years old, and more than half are between 13 and 19.[24]

It is interesting how much privacy some people are willing to give up in their blogs, especially when you consider that reading a teenager's diary was once considered the ultimate invasion of privacy. Research suggests, however, that most bloggers have a specific audience in mind.[25] For example, teenage bloggers might be thinking of their school friends or online acquaintances as their readers, and they are sometimes embarrassed when members of a different group (such as parents or teachers) gain access to their blogs.

Technology is rapidly changing the way people go about blogging. Bloggers with cell phones, for example, can post news as it is happening or invite others to come see an event in progress. When enough people respond to these invitations to form a crowd, they are called **smart mobs.**[26] Camera cell phones allow bloggers to instantly post photos to the Web; this practice is now called **moblogging,** short for mobile blogging.

Online Games

Electronic games include video games played on consoles like Sony's PlayStation, Nintendo's Game Cube, and Microsoft's XBox, and single-player computer games. By far the fastest-growing segment of the industry, however, is multiplayer online games such as the Sims, EverQuest, and World of Warfare. These are known as **massively multiplayer online role-playing games (MMORPGs).** In MMORPGs (sometimes pronounced "morpegs"), the players are almost always strangers.

Players generally have to purchase the software and then pay a monthly subscription fee. The online version of the Sims, for example, costs $50 for the software, and a $10 a month fee to play after the first month. Some games, such as Planeshift, are advertiser-supported and can be played for free.

The games permit players to create their own simulated person, choosing a variety of personality and physical traits. Interestingly, many gamers choose to play characters of the opposite gender. (Male gamers often say they find that female characters generally get treated better in male-dominated virtual worlds.) The players then have adventures in a fantasy world (such as in EverQuest) or are nurtured through various life experiences (as in the

weblogs
Online journals or diaries; called blogs for short.

blogs
See *weblogs.*

smart mobs
Crowds formed in response to cell phone postings.

moblogging
Posting photos from a cell phone directly onto the Web.

massively multiplayer online role-playing games (MMORPGs)
Games such as EverQuest that allow many players to join in over the Internet.

The fastest-growing segment of the electronic game industry is multiplayer online games such as EverQuest®. Screen shot of EverQuest® used with permission of Sony Online Entertainment. EverQuest is a registered trademark of Sony Online Entertainment LLC in the U.S. and/or other countries. © 2006 Sony Online Entertainment LLC. All rights reserved.

Sims, in which players earn popularity credits for how many other people come to visit their homes or parties). The games are played with or against other players around the world, in real time.

Online games have become so popular that the virtual items, character profiles, and currency that exist only in cyberspace have become hot commodities on eBay. Virtual characters, in fact, are now sometimes worth thousands of dollars.

Critics worry that MMORPGs have an addictive quality. Like all other commercial media, online games are designed to keep the user interested. Several critics have pointed out that the escapism inherent in the game fantasy is the main reason for their addictive quality. But there are other reasons. The reward structure of the games, for example, is designed strategically so that rewards are given very quickly in the beginning of the game. The player can, for example, kill a creature with two or three hits and gain a new level in 5 to 10 minutes. But then the intervals between these rewards grow significantly, and soon it takes 5 hours and then 20 hours of game time before the player can gain a level.

Also, the player builds a network of relationships with other players, some of which might be romantic. Players then have to continue playing to remain at the same level as their virtual friends. In some ways, the online relationships seem particularly strong. The anonymity of the computer-mediated chat environment encourages self-disclosure, and many players find themselves telling personal secrets to online friends that they have never told their real-life friends or family.

THE ECONOMICS OF THE NET

The Internet is changing the ways the world does business. To get an overall picture of how these changes are taking place, we will look at employment patterns, revenue, and costs associated with the Internet.

Employment Patterns

Like the various media that preceded them, Internet properties have two types of owners: entrepreneurs and corporations. Because of its open access, the Internet is considered to have great potential for entrepreneurs. Some early Internet entrepreneurs started out with a dream and little financial backing. Jerry Yang and Dave Filo, the founders of Yahoo, started it in a tiny office in a trailer at Stanford University, while they were students. Google founders Sergey Brin and Larry Page also met at Stanford, and developed Google's technology out of Page's dormitory room. Both Google and Yahoo are worth billions today.

Employment in the early years of the Internet was concentrated in Silicon Valley, the area outside San Francisco where most high-tech firms were located. Today, the people who work for these entrepreneurs and corporations might be located anywhere, as both firms and individuals take advantage of their ability to work from any location. Workers within the new medium are making up entirely new employment categories, such as the following:

network engineers
The people who design and build the systems that make up the Internet.

1. **Network engineers** are the people who design and build the systems that make up the Internet. Most work for large telecommunications compa-

nies, large network service providers, and information technology consulting firms, although some are independent and work as consultants.

2. **Network managers** provide the day-to-day maintenance of local systems, also called intranets or local area networks (LANs). Most corporations and organizations rely on their network managers to keep everyone's computer running and communicating.

3. **Webmasters** are the people who maintain either content or systems for large Web sites. Systems-oriented webmasters have computer science and programming skills, and they understand the networking protocols and software involved in running a Web site. Content-oriented webmasters have backgrounds in media, editing, graphic design, desktop publishing, and art. They are often called Web site producers.

4. **Knowledge workers** are the people who use the Net and other information sources in their work. These people might be content providers who post information on the Net, such as online journalists, or they might be workers who use information provided on the Net, such as print and broadcast journalists, researchers, library professionals, business analysts, consultants, financial professionals, or marketing specialists.

network managers
Those who provide the day-to-day maintenance of local systems and intranets.

webmasters
Those who maintain either content or systems for large Web sites.

knowledge workers
Employees such as journalists, library professionals, and business analysts who use the Internet for research as part of their jobs.

Revenue Sources

There are three primary revenue sources on the Internet: online product sales (e-commerce), online advertising sales, and online sales of information (paid content).

E-Commerce

E-commerce is, simply, the selling of goods and services online. So far, the Web sites that are making the most money are the ones that take orders online for real-life products. Almost anything can be sold over the Net, and it is a very inexpensive way for most businesses to bring their goods and services to market. It is less expensive to maintain a Web site than a chain of stores that could serve the same population. Companies that are successful with e-commerce are usually those that take advantage of the Net's unique capabilities: its interactivity, its ability to allow businesses to target very specific customers, and its ability to offer inventories that couldn't exist in physical space. Walmart.com, for example, carries six times as many items as the largest Wal-Mart store; Amazon.com offers its customers millions of choices in books, music, electronics, and other merchandise, far more than could exist in any retail establishment; and eBay provides a trading environment for tens of millions of members.

Some companies increase their profits by using the Web to save money, such as by providing information that would otherwise tie up their phone lines and their personnel. Using the Internet, a customer can get full information on a company's product before making a purchase. After buying the product, the customer can consult the Web site for warranty information. The company can handle both sets of information without having a paid employee sitting in a cubicle with a telephone. Even a toll-free telephone number with a recorded message would be considerably more expensive.

Finally, some Web site operators generate sales prospects for other Web sites, and are paid a fee for each lead. This arrangement, called revenue partnering, involves links to related products.[27] For example, if a Web site sells car parts, it might have links to an auto dealer and an auto insurance

The Internet has created a wide diversity of knowledge-worker careers. Trish McDermott is vice president of romance at Match.com, an Internet dating service.

At Youthink (http://youthink .worldbank.org/) the World Bank uses striking visual effects to teach children about world issues. Used with permission from The World Bank.

company, each of which pays the original Web site for visitors who come to it from that site.

Advertising

A variety of ads appear on popular Web pages (see Chapter 13) and allow users to access the advertiser's Web site with one click of a mouse button. Advertisers find this an important form of customer communication because only people who are interested in their product will ask for more facts about it, and once they visit the Web site, those customers can get a potentially unlimited amount of information. Generally, advertisers pay a flat rate to get their ad on the Web, and once the ads are established, they are charged per hit, meaning each time the ad is accessed by a user.

Advertising on the Web has been controversial. Pop-up ads, animated ads, and online commercial spots are all seen as intrusions that clutter up the memory of the user's computer. An especially controversial tactic of on-line advertisers involves **spyware,** or programs that track the user's activities and report them back to advertisers. When users accept free software programs such as those used to download music and movies, they also accept the spyware that comes with them. Advertisers say that spyware simply allows them to provide users with the ads they will be most interested in, as seen by their preferences in Web sites. Critics, however, warn that spyware is a potential invasion of privacy, an issue we will explore more fully later in this chapter.

spyware
Programs that track Internet users' activities and report them back to advertisers.

By far the most controversial type of advertising has been the unsolicited e-mail known as spam, which will be discussed later in this chapter.

Paid Content

The third way to make money online, and so far the least successful, is to provide content that people will pay for. Although few are flourishing today, online information services were actually the first companies to make a profit from the Internet, preceding the World Wide Web by several years. As early as 1973, a personal computer could be used for subscribers to connect to the databases of Mead Data Central's Lexis, which supplied a full legal library. The same company started Nexis, a full-text newspaper database, in 1978. Today, Web-based information services such as Lexis/Nexis, Proquest, Infotrac, and Newsbank are used by schools, libraries, and professional journalists.

The *Wall Street Journal* (www.wsj.com) was still charging for full access to its Web pages in 2006, but many other brand-name information providers have been forced to switch to a different revenue model. The *Encyclopaedia Britannica* (www.eb.com) attempted to charge for access but changed to advertiser support in 1999. Some information services, such as the Electric Library (www.elibrary.com), give some information for free but charge a small fee for unlimited use of their research facilities. Some newspapers, such as the *New York Times* (www.nytimes.com), provide mostly free information but charge for full-text downloads of articles from their archives.

distance learning
Taking classes away from a school facility, especially online.

One industry that makes money by providing content is the online pornography industry, which has been financially successful. Another service that people seem willing to pay for is online education, or **distance learning.**[28] Students who can't make it to a traditional classroom—for example, those who live in remote places, those whose disabilities prevent travel, or those who are just too busy with family and careers—can take advantage of courses offered on the Internet. The Internet, like the older media that came before it, can be a powerful teacher.[29] Professors have found e-mail, list servers, and online chats to be a good way to keep in touch with students.

One of the more interesting content services has been online matchmaking. Millions of Americans visit at least one online dating site, such as Yahoo Personals, Match.com, eHarmony.com, or Friendster, every month. There are small specialty sites for every ethnic and interest preference. There is even Vanitydate.com, whose motto is "Survival of the Prettiest," which bills itself as the world's largest database of good-looking, rich, superficial people.

"I loved your E-mail, but I thought you'd be older."
© The New Yorker Collection 1998 Robert Weber from cartoonbank.com. All Rights Reserved.

Online Dangers: Hacker Attacks

At one point, the word *hacker* meant simply one who is proficient at using or programming a computer. In recent years, **hacker** has more commonly meant one who uses programming skills to gain illegal access to a computer network or file.

hacker
One who uses programming skills to gain illegal access to computer networks or files.

Why do hackers hack? When attacks are used to steal financial data (and thereby to steal money), the motive is clearly that of financial gain. Spammers

To Google

The name Google originated from an intentional mis-spelling of *googol,* which refers to a 1 followed by 100 zeros. In 2006, however, the word officially became a verb when it was listed in major American dictionaries, with the meaning "to use the Google search engine to obtain information on the Internet."

Google began as a research project at Stanford University in January 1996, the work of two graduate students named Larry Page and Sergey Brin. At that time, search engines found Web sites according to how many times the search term appeared on the site. Page and Brin thought it would work better to use a formula that analyzed a site's importance by counting how many other pages linked to it.

The resulting search engine attracted a loyal fol-lowing among Web surfers who were impressed by Google's speed, efficiency, and simple, clean design. The company was founded with borrowed money in 1998, headquartered in a friend's garage in Menlo Park, California. Page and Brin used hundreds of low-end computers to keep Google running, and by 2000 it had achieved the reputation as the Web's best search engine. It was only then that the com-pany started selling ads referenced to the search key-words. To maintain an uncluttered page design and to maximize page-loading speed, the ads were text-based only. Advertisers bid competitively on the most desired keywords, with bidding starting at $.05 per click.

The company was soon very successful and con-tinually put its money back into new-product develop-ment: Google News, Google Images, Gmail, Google Maps, Froogle, Google Earth, Google Talk, Google Scholar and Google Video all appeared in quick succession. In 2006, the company purchased YouTube, the video sharing site, for $1.65 billion.

One of Google's company mottos is, "You can make money without doing evil." In spite of that phi-losophy, Google has found itself at the heart of several controversies. With Gmail, for example, Google dis-plays ads referenced to the content of the e-mail mes-sage. Privacy advocates insisted that the company was, in effect, reading individual e-mails. Google, however, insists that the process is fully automated and that no humans read the content of users' mes-sages. Google Print ran into copyright battles with the Authors Guild over Google's effort to digitize millions of books and make the full text searchable. Google's cooperation with the governments of China, France, and Germany to filter search results accord-ing to the laws of those countries led to claims of censorship. And a number of governments have

hoping to harvest e-mail addresses and hijack innocent computers to relay their messages have perpetrated several recent attacks. But by far the major-ity of attacks offer no monetary rewards.

Some attacks seem to be motivated by hackers' desires to impress peers with their technical prowess. Most online vandals, however, have turned out to be teenagers using relatively simple programming skills. This caused one computer expert to write,

> Should we blame the teenager? Sure, we can point the finger at him and say, "Bad boy!" and slap him for it. Will that actually fix anything? No. The next geeky kid frustrated about not getting a date on Saturday night will come along and do the same thing without really understanding the consequences. So either we should make it a law that all geeks have dates—I'd have sup-ported such a law when I was a teenager—or the blame is really on the com-panies who sell and install the systems that are quite that fragile.[30]

Sometimes hackers assert that they are demonstrating the vulnerability of the system, as a type of perverse public-spirited warning. At other times, the hacker just wants to make a statement, perhaps as a protest against the

"I can't explain it—it's just a funny feeling that I'm being Googled."

Larry Page (left) and Sergey Brin invented Google, which beecame both a huge corporation and a verb. Cartoon © The New Yorker Collection 2002 Charles Barsotti from cartoonbank.com. All rights reserved.

raised concerns about security risks posed by the geographic details provided by Google Earth's satellite imaging.

In 2006, when *Forbes* magazine listed the world's richest people, Sergey Brin was number 26 with a net worth of $12.9 billion, and Larry Page was number 27, with a net worth of $12.8 billion. The original Google search engine continues to service around a billion requests per day.

Sources: Google corporate Web site, www.google.com/about.html, and Wikipedia, the free encyclopedia, http://wikipedia.org, accessed November 2006

commercialization of the Net. Hackers in these cases object to the fact that the medium inherently perfect for communication suddenly became just another way for big businesses to sell and advertise the same old things.

The main types of hacker assaults have been viruses, worms, and Trojan horses. Each of these is explained in the following paragraphs.

Viruses

A **virus** is a computer program designed to reproduce by copying itself into other programs stored in a computer. Some viruses can be relatively harmless, perhaps causing one or two documents to come up with implanted messages. (One said, "Billy Gates why do you make this possible? Stop making money and fix your software!"[31] Another just showed a picture of a raised middle finger.) Other viruses can be extremely destructive, causing programs to operate incorrectly, corrupting the computer's memory, or deleting key files needed to operate the computer. Some viruses have caused millions of dollars in damages by simply replacing 3s with 2s in corporate financial documents.

virus
A program designed specifically to damage other software, and to propagate itself to other computers.

What are the primary ways to protect against viruses?

SELF QUIZ

There are three primary methods of avoiding viruses. The first is never to open an e-mail attachment or download a file unless you are absolutely sure where it came from and what it is. The second is to install antivirus software, such as that sold by McAfee and Symantec, that is automatically updated daily. Antivirus software will both detect and eliminate viruses. The third method is to install a **firewall,** which is a program that prevents unauthorized access to a computer or a network.

Virus has become a generic term to signify any type of malignant attack. In fact, however, many of the attacks called viruses are actually worms or Trojan horses.

firewall
A program that prevents unauthorized access to a computer or network.

Worms

Worms are programs that take over e-mail systems and send themselves to other computers from the infected computer's address book. Worms can drain computer resources by reproducing on a large scale and clogging in-boxes and memory. They sometimes also delete data from the computers they infect. Worms are generally transmitted in attached files. Many e-mail users now routinely ask their friends to cut and paste files directly into the body of their e-mail messages so that they do not need to send them as attachments.

What are the differences among viruses, worms, and Trojan horses?

SELF QUIZ

Trojan Horses

Trojan horses are named after the large, hollow wooden horse in which the soldiers of ancient Greece hid during the Trojan War. The Greeks left the horse outside the Trojan city's fortified gates, and the Trojans brought the horse in, thinking it was a gift. That night the Greeks sneaked out and opened the city gates to their army. Trojan horses sneak into infected computers and open them up in the same way. One Trojan horse came disguised as an animated St. Patrick's Day card. As leprechauns danced on the screen, the Trojan Horse infected financial software and sent bank account records to the Philippines, where money from each account was transferred to an account in a Philippines bank.

Some of the worst Trojan horses have been set lose by spammers trying to harvest e-mail addresses. As well as plundering address books for new victims, the Trojans also implant background programs that turn infected machines into a relay for spam sent by the virus's creator.

Phishing

Phishing is the practice of sending out official-looking fake e-mails that use stolen brand names and trademarks of legitimate banks and Internet merchants, with the intent of luring the victim into revealing sensitive information, such as passwords, account IDs, or credit card details. Typically, phishing attacks will direct the victim to a counterfeit Web site. The site then tricks the victim into supplying the desired information, which can be used to access bank accounts and open fake credit cards.

Trojan Horses are named after the one Virgil wrote about in his epic poem, *The Aeneid*. This is the movie version from *Troy* (2004).

Spam has seriously disrupted the efficiency of e-mail.

View: **All** | Unopened

Select item(s) to: **Delete** | Remove from Junk | Move selected item(s) to... ▼ | Mark Message as... ▼

Select All | Clear All

Messages 1-25 of 69| First| Previous| Next(25)| Last

		From	Subject	↓ Date / Time	Size
✉	☐	months	UsGet Involved Sound	10/26/06 02:21 AM	16K
✉	☐	US Immigration	Become a citizen of the United States.	10/25/06 07:26 PM	6K
✉	☐	Matthew Franks	jury	10/25/06 05:53 AM	18K
✉	☐	summer Youre	sent	10/25/06 05:44 AM	16K
✉	☐	"Cheap ViagraCialisValium_y[1-3	(No Subject)	10/24/06 11:30 PM	1K
✉	☐	Drug Rehab	Best Drug Rehab	10/24/06 07:19 PM	7K
✉	☐	Reg Walls	c/o cerebral	10/24/06 07:06 AM	18K
✉	☐	Jennie Thurman	vegan carol	10/24/06 04:23 AM	16K
✉	☐	When You Really Have To Go	No toilets around?	10/23/06 09:02 PM	6K
✉	☐	US Immigration	Find United States immigration help.	10/22/06 07:32 PM	7K
✉	☐	Human Resources Training	Human resources training. Learn how to handle any issue.	10/22/06 01:43 AM	7K
✉	☐	Hubert Odell	unspeakable healthful	10/21/06 10:54 PM	16K
✉	☐	comment closedcopy	when first	10/21/06 09:02 PM	20K
✉	☐	Raymond Gunter	stream	10/21/06 09:38 AM	19K
✉	☐	VA Loans	Veteran loans	10/20/06 07:34 PM	6K

Experts suggest that users exercise great care with any type of Internet transaction. They point out that it's not difficult to fake a professional-looking e-mail or Web page, but there are usually suspicious clues if you look closely: obvious grammatical mistakes, strange return addresses, or telephone numbers with an incorrect area code.

Spam

Spam, or unsolicited e-mail messages,[32] has seriously disrupted the efficiency of e-mail. Relatively unknown in the 1990s, by 2000, spam was clogging most people's in-boxes, often with messages that the recipients considered offensive. While some spam comes from legitimate merchants, much of it does not. Unethical spammers use phony e-mail addresses and subject lines. The messages they send are usually equipped with a fake "unsubscribe" option. Recipients who think they are opting out of the spammer's mailing list are in fact simply confirming that their e-mail address is active. The spammer then sends more messages and includes that address on a list that is sold to other spammers.

Spam has made people less trusting of e-mail. It has also caused them to delete mail they actually wanted to read. Spam filters are used to block messages that look or act like spam, but these filters sometimes block wanted mail as well.

The first federal law to address the spam problem took effect in January 2004.[33] The act required unsolicited commercial e-mail messages to be labeled (though not by a standard method) and to include opt-out instructions and the sender's physical address. It prohibited the use of deceptive subject lines and false headers. It authorized (but did not require) the Federal Communication Commission (FCC) to establish a "do-not-e-mail" list similar to the "do not call" list that allows people to opt out of telemarketing calls.

spam
Unsolicited e-mail messages.

SELF QUIZ What are some of the proposals to fight spam?

CONSIDER THIS
What would you do to fight spam?

Controversies

The answer to "Who controls the Internet?" is both "no one" and "everyone." The answer is "no one" because there is no central authority, and "everyone" because every country, corporation, and content provider (and that's everyone) has partial control. The primary controversies dealing with the Internet today revolve instead around this central issue: Who *should* control the Internet?

Defenders of the Internet like to point out its positive effects: how it provides access to huge amounts of information from around the world, how it engages users in interactive—rather than passive—entertainment, and how it encourages the development of reading and writing skills in young people. Other proponents like to extol the fact that this is an unrestricted, truly democratic medium in which the masses can say whatever they want. To critics, however, these exact same characteristics are troubling rather than encouraging. The following sections explore controversies regarding control versus freedom, commercialism versus public service, censorship, privacy, and reliability of information.

CONTROL VERSUS FREEDOM

The unlimited freedom of the Internet has caused a number of problems, many of which we have touched on in this and other chapters. Leading the list are propagation of viruses, fraud, spam, copyright infringement, child pornography, malicious hacker attacks, and identity theft. Most users are understandably upset about these types of problems, and many yearn for an era of more control. In fact, China and many other countries exert control over the Internet by holding their ISPs responsible for the content that is sent over them. The government orders the ISPs to block any sites that the government doesn't like. Of course, in a country led by a dictator or in an otherwise authoritarian regime, political dissent will be stifled unless the dissenters have the technical skills and the daring to evade the ISP blocks.

There have been many proposals for methods of controlling the Internet. Some pundits have suggested that all users should have Internet driver's licenses and all computers should have registrations, making driving on the information highway more like driving on the road. Other theorists have proposed systems that would electronically watermark every computer, program, and file. Critics of such plans point out that they could be used to ensure that no one could post anything without permission. Such proposals will continue to be debated for years to come.

COMMERCIALISM VERSUS PUBLIC SERVICE

Another continuing debate about the Internet is whether it should be dedicated to commercial or public service uses. This issue creates controversies about issues such as Net neutrality and municipal Wi-Fi.

Net Neutrality

The basic question of Net neutrality is whether there should be centralized commercial control over the Internet. Right now, the Net is neutral, meaning no one controls it. Broadband suppliers like Comcast and AT&T, however, point out that new applications such as online television programming require that new networks be built. They contend that it is only fair that they should be able to charge extra to those who use the most bandwith. These large ISPs have asked the government to allow them to charge different rates to users, both senders and receivers, who use the most bandwith. Critics of the ISPs and proponents of Net neutrality say that this will make the Internet into a form of cable television in which the ISPs can control who has access to which sites. An ISP could make it slower and harder to reach Gmail, for example, than

Yahoo mail, if Yahoo paid more. Comparing the Internet to the Interstate Highway System, proponents of Net neutrality say that ISPs' establishing varying rates would be like Interstate 95's announcing an exclusive deal with General Motors to provide a special "rush-hour" lane for GM cars only. The critics would prefer that the big ISPs (which are, in most communities, a duopoly of one cable TV company and one telephone company) not have that power.

Municipal Wi-Fi

Wi-Fi stands for "wireless fidelity," or high-speed wireless Internet access. Municipal Wi-Fi (or Mu-Fi) is the idea of providing free or low-cost wireless coverage to all homes, schools, and virtually everyplace else in a municipal area. Commercial ISPs are understandably threatened by this concept and fight against it, but successful experiments have been carried out in Philadelphia and San Francisco, and Boston and Chicago have systems in the works.

CENSORSHIP

In the United States, several controversies swirl around what information, if any, should be censored on the Internet. This issue brings up all sorts of interesting problems regarding the First Amendment and jurisdiction. The Communications Decency Act of 1996, for example, made it illegal to make "indecent communication" available to anyone under 18. The indecency provision of the act was found unconstitutional and overturned by the Supreme Court the following year. Although it sounded like a noble piece of protection, the act was too broad. Because it covered the entire Internet, private e-mail exchanges could have come under scrutiny. Censoring e-mail would be like censoring traditional mail, a policy that most Americans would oppose. There is also an analogy to print media: The providers of pornographic Web sites claim that their sites are like newspapers or magazines sent out only to subscribers. The analogy to print media is especially troubling to First Amendment purists, because print media are protected by the First Amendment against government censorship.

The Internet is offering the First Amendment its biggest challenge ever, and pornography is just the tip of the iceberg. The rantings of hate groups and racist organizations can be found on the Web, along with bomb-making instructions and advice on how to procure stolen credit cards. There are sites that provide gambling services in communities where gambling is illegal, sites that provide the addresses of doctors who perform abortions, and sites that provide instructions on how to kill those doctors. There are sites that distribute term papers for students to plagiarize, and others that distribute unauthorized copyrighted material such as books, recordings, and movies. Even legitimate sites such as MySpace can be controversial when they are used for illegitimate purposes (see the Close-Up on Controversy box).

 SELF QUIZ What are the arguments for and against censorship on the Internet?

PRIVACY

Personal privacy becomes a problem on the Internet because all manner of information is online, from the pattern of credit card purchases to the secrets friends send each other by e-mail. When private information becomes digital information, it can easily be bought and sold, the way mailing lists are today. Most people believe that individuals have the right to keep secrets when using computers and other forms of electronic communications, just as they do when using telephones and traditional mail.

As mentioned earlier, spyware that tracks the user's activities and reports them back to advertisers is often attached to free software programs. Some Web sites also track their visitors' Web use. When a Web surfer enters a site for the first time, an identifying number is placed on the user's hard drive in a file known as a cookie. The cookie then allows the company to track the surfer's movements through other sites. The sites say tracking enables their advertisers to focus on exactly the right customers and personalize their appeals. This, they say, assures that people will see only those ads that interest them and are relevant to their needs. If they surf to many alternative music sites, they will see ads for exactly that kind of music. If their surfing pattern shows that they are interested in automobiles, they will see ads for cars and related products.

Many users willingly give up information. Registering at a restricted site, for example, enables surfers to reenter the site whenever they want to. The site recognizes the cookie and allows them in. This type of registration allows the sites to perform extra services also. For example, 1-800-flowers.com will remind you to buy a bouquet for your spouse if you register your anniversary date at the site.

Privacy advocates are concerned that few consumers realize they are being monitored, and when they do realize it, they often find it difficult to opt out. Advertisers, for their part, routinely pledge that they will not collect data on medical, financial, or sexual behavior or on children's surfing habits. Privacy advocates do not accept such pledges because advertisers are under no legal obligation to live by them.

So far, the U.S. government has favored self-regulation of Web sites to avoid the stigma of government censorship. Critics, however, say that Web

Web site operators interpret self-regulation as "Do whatever you want or do as little as you want."

PRIVACY
BBBONLINE

reviewed by
TRUST·e
site privacy statement

The Better Business Bureau Online is an independent organization that certifies sites as having trustworthy privacy policies.

site operators interpret self-regulation as "Do whatever you want or do as little as you want."[34] Several independent organizations now certify sites as trustworthy in terms of their privacy policy. These organizations include the Better Business Bureau Online (www.bbbonline.com) and TrustE (www.truste.com), both of which will allow certified sites to display their logos.

RELIABILITY OF INFORMATION

The Internet is a party to which everyone is invited. Anyone can post a Web site. This allows an undifferentiated mass of information to appear online: Authoritative information provided by authors with excellent credentials sits side-by-side, in the same format, with nonsense and fraud. In fact, a common metaphor for the Internet is that it forms the world's largest hard drive by connecting thousands of smaller ones. It's important to remember that anyone who wants to can put information on that hard drive. The apparent disregard for reliability exists even in some Web searches. On any keyword search, some entries are essentially fake because proprietors of Web sites that want extra traffic, such as pornography sites, will include all sorts of terms in their home page description that have nothing to do with what they offer.

Reliability of information is especially important to college students, who are graded on the validity of their research. Library experts suggest the following four criteria to evaluate Web pages used for research:

1. *Attribution.* Does your page list the author and institution that published it? Is there a way to contact the author or institution, such as an e-mail ad-

dress or telephone number? Can the URL be traced to the name of the institution publishing the document? If the source is anonymous or masked in any way, assume the information is biased.

2. *Authority.* Is this person or institution qualified to write this document? What credentials are listed for the author? Is there a way to check on the facts presented—either in the form of footnotes or links to other sites? If no means to check is presented, assume the author is not qualified and seek out a second source of any information you need to use.

3. *Objectivity.* What are the apparent goals and objectives of the author? What opinions are expressed? Is the page a mask for advertising or some other form of persuasive message? If it is, assume the information is biased.

SELF QUIZ What are the criteria used to evaluate the reliability of information in a Web page?

4. *Currency.* How up-to-date is the information presented? When was it written? When was it last updated? If it doesn't tell you, assume that it is out of date.

As a general rule, information that sounds like it should have been a news report, but wasn't, could be checked out on the urban legends site at www.snopes.com. Verifying information of an inflammatory political nature is especially important. For example, one e-mail campaign that circulated widely made a number of accusations against the Target Corporation—that it does not contribute to veterans' causes, that it provides corporate grants only for gay and lesbian causes, that it does not contribute to the U.S. Marines' Toys for Tots program, that it does not allow reservists called to active duty to continue their health benefits. The e-mail campaign even insisted that the Target Corporation is French-owned. The Snopes site proved

The Urban Legends home page at www.snopes.com is a good place to verify the accuracy of suspicious e-mail messages. Urban Legends Reference Pages © 1995–2006. Used with permission.

Online Predators

Dateline NBC rented a house and wired it with hidden cameras. Meanwhile, volunteers posed as teens in chat rooms and on social networking sites, saying they were home alone and interested in sex. Within hours, unsuspecting males were at the door. These men ranged from college students to firefighters to ministers. A young child's voice told them to enter, and as they crossed the threshold, *Dateline NBC* correspondent Chris Hansen confronted them and reread their X-rated Internet conversations. He tells the offenders, one at a time, that they are on camera and are free to leave. As they exit, the police arrest them.

Dateline has done a number of these specials. In one two-week period, Hansen and his team caught 129 adult men soliciting sex with children online and showing up to meet them. These specials fed a growing panic among parents, teachers, and law enforcement officials. Web sites such as protectkids.com cite a 2001 article in the *Journal of the American Medical Association* (JAMA) that showed that 19% of kids who used the Internet regularly—nearly 1 in 5 aged 10 to 17—had been sexually solicited online.[1]

To help fight the problem, federal legislators proposed the Deleting Online Predators Act, which would require schools and libraries "to protect minors from commercial social networking websites and chat rooms." The proposed law would require schools and libraries to deploy Internet filters to deny access to any site that allows users to create a profile and communicate with strangers.

Not everyone thinks such a law would be a good idea. Many educators believe that online networking is an important educational experience for kids. Danah Boyd, a researcher whose specialty is how kids negotiate identity formation through digital publics such as MySpace, adds: "The media coverage of predators on MySpace implies that (1) all youth are at risk of being stalked and molested because of MySpace; [and] (2) prohibiting youth from participating on MySpace will stop predators from attacking kids. Both are misleading; neither is true."[2]

Reacting to the JAMA report, Boyd points out:

A careful reading of this report shows that 76% of the unwanted solicitations came from fellow children. This includes unwanted date requests and sexual taunts from fellow teens. Of the adult solicitations, 96% are from people 18–25; wanted and unwanted solicitations are both included. In other words, if an 18-year-old asks out a 17-year-old and both consent, this would still be seen as a sexual solicitation. . . .

Unfortunately, predators lurk wherever youth hang out. Since youth are on MySpace, there are bound to be predators on MySpace. Yet, predators do not use online information to abduct children; children face a much higher risk of abduction or molestation from people they already know—members of their own family or friends of the family. Statistically speaking, kids are more at risk at a church picnic or a Boy Scout outing than they are when they go on MySpace. . . .

Just as most teens know to say no to strange men who approach them on the street, most know to ignore strange men who approach them online. When teenagers receive solicitations from adults

that all these accusations are false. The site established that the message had been started by a member of local Vietnam Veterans organization in Indiana, who had written it after failing to secure a $100 sponsorship for a Vietnam Veterans Memorial from his local Target store. He had been rebuffed because Target does not give out cash donations through local stores; it donates money only at the corporate level.[35]

Another important method for checking the credibility of information from the Web is to check it on library databases, which are noncommercial and edited for accuracy.

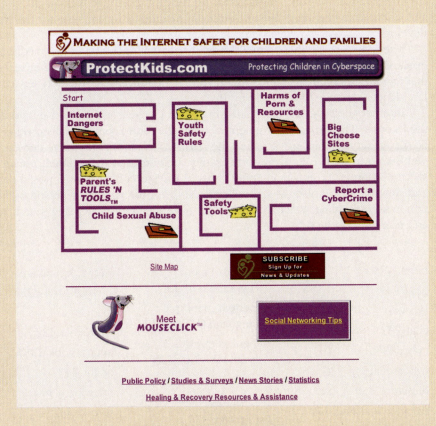

Web sites such as ProtectKids.com warn about online sexual predators. © 2001 Donna Rice Hughes at protectkids.com.

on MySpace, most report deleting them without question. Those who report responding often talk about looking for attention or seeking a risk. Of those who begin conversations, few report meeting these strangers.[3]

For Boyd and other researchers, the key is educating kids about how to conduct themselves online. As another scholar who studies the effects of social networking sites says: "Historically, we taught children what to do when a stranger telephoned them when their parents are away; surely, we should be helping to teach them how to manage the presentation of their selves in digital spaces."[4]

[1] Kimberly J. Mitchell, David Finkelhor, and Janis Wolak, "Risk Factors for and Impact of Online Sexual Solicitation of Youth," *Journal of the American Medical Association*, June 20, 2001, pp. 3011–14.

[2] Danah Boyd, quoted in an interview with Sarah Wright, "Discussion: MySpace and Deleting Online Predators Act," MIT News Office, May 24, 2006, available at www.danah.org/papers/MySpaceDOPA.html.

[3] Danah Boyd, quoted in Wright, "Discussion: MySpace."

[4] Henry Jenkins, codirector of the MIT Comparative Media Studies program, quoted in Wright, "Discussion: MySpace."

Summing Up

The Internet began with an investment made by the U.S. Department of Defense in the 1960s. The Net soared in popularity in the 1990s with the development of the World Wide Web, which included the transmission of advanced graphics and sound, and allowed easy access to Web sites through hyperlinks.

The architecture of the Net includes standardized addresses, including e-mail addresses and URLs; access providers that supply the hookups, and hosts that house the Web sites. Software programs such as browsers and search engines enable users to move quickly around the Net and find what they are looking for. Other components include converged channels that combine aspects of both interpersonal and mass communication, such as newsgroups, list servers, personal Web pages, weblogs, and online role-playing games. A system of netiquette, or etiquette for the Net, has developed.

The Internet's business model—how money will be made in this medium—has evolved, much as it did in the broadcast media, from subscription to a mixed model that includes e-commerce, advertising, and pay-for-access information services. Online dangers include viruses and fraud.

Internet controversies are related mainly to the question of who should control the Internet. The issues involve control versus freedom, commercialism versus public service, censorship, privacy, and the reliability of information. The censorship of Web-based information, even pornography, bothers First Amendment purists, who see the Internet as similar in some ways to private conversations, postal services, and newspapers. Privacy is a problem because of the wealth of personal information available online. Reliability problems have included misleading search results, and outright fraud.

Key Terms

These terms are defined and indexed in the Glossary of key terms at the back of the book.

blogs *335*

bots *330*

browser *330*

chat *331*

cyber- *330*

cybersquatting *330*

directory *330*

distance learning *339*

domain *327*

firewall *342*

flaming *332*

graphical user interface (GUI) *330*

hacker *339*

hosts *326*

hybrid search engines *330*

hypertext links (hyperlinks) *322*

hypertext markup language (HTML) *328*

hypertext transfer protocol (http) *328*

Java *328*

knowledge workers *337*

list servers *333*

lurking *333*

massively multiplayer online role-playing games (MMORPGs) *335*

metacrawler *330*

moblogging *335*

netiquette *331*

network engineers *336*

network managers *337*

newsgroups *322*

portals *325*

protocols *322*

smart mobs *335*

spam *343*

spyware *338*

thread *332*

Usenet *322*

user ID *327*

uniform resource locator (URL) *328*

virus *341*

weblogs *335*

webmasters *337*

World Wide Web *322*

Electronic Excursions

HISTORY

Web Excursion

1. Now that the historical importance of the Internet is clear, many people are stepping up to claim credit. This leads to an interesting question about alternate versions of history. How do different eyewitnesses interpret how the Net began? Search the Web for different versions, or go directly to the Internet Society's History of the Internet link at www.isoc.org/internet/history/.*

Media World DVD Excursion

2. View track 5, *The Challenge of the Internet*. Members of the magazine, newspaper, television and radio industries discuss the threats and benefits of the Internet. What shared benefits does the Internet provide to each industry? Which medium is most vulnerable to Internet competition?

INDUSTRY

Web Excursion

3. The Internet is growing so quickly that statistics change by the minute. If you had to guess, how many people would you say used the Net in the last 30 days? How many now have access to an ISP at home? What is the total number of URLs worldwide? How many of these are .com domain names? Search the Web for these statistics or go directly to a site dedicated to them such as www.mediamark.com* or http://www.whois.sc/internet-statistics/.* Report on your findings.

Media World DVD Excursions

4. View track 5.2, Issues: Reaching an Audience. Which age group uses the Internet most? How do the various media lure this audience to their product? Describe how each medium uniquely uses the Internet to their advantage.

CONTROVERSIES

Web Excursion

5. What are your thoughts about censorship on the Internet? Should pornography be censored? How about hate sites or instructions on how to build bombs? Search the Web for Internet censorship issues, or go directly to the UCLA Online Institute for Cyberspace Law and Policy at www.gseis.ucla.edu/iclp/hp.html.* Find the links for the latest developments in cyberlaw. In your opinion, do these developments represent too much censorship or are they steps in the right direction? Explain.

Media World DVD Excursion

6. View track 21, *The Drudge Report* (from NBC's *Today* show). *Today's* Matt Lauer and Matt Drudge, creator and author of *The Drudge Report,* discuss the validity and reputation of the Web site. While largely considered a gossip page, do you think the Drudge Report has a valid place in the media? Is it journalism or gossip? Drudge was the first to report the affair between President Bill Clinton and White House intern Monica Lewinsky even though *Newsweek* had leads on the story. The newsmagazine held off to do more reporting, thereby losing its scoop. For a story with such an obvious public interest, which approach is better?

ONLINE LEARNING CENTER WWW.MHHE.COM/RODMAN2

You may access these and additional Web excursions at the Online Learning Center for the book (www.mhhe.com/rodman2). Visit the student portion of this Web site to also access the *Interactive Timeline of Mass Media Milestones,* chapter highlights, self quizzes, and recommended readings, movies, and documentaries for this chapter.

*Some Web site addresses may change. When they do, please search for the Web site by name or topic on your favorite search engine.

PART FOUR

Information and Persuasion Industries

This part of *Mass Media in a Changing World* provides separate chapters on the electronic news, public relations, and advertising industries. Because of their informative and persuasive objectives, these tend to be the most controversial of media businesses. We will look at them here from both critical and industry points of view.

Electronic News

Information as Entertainment

11

Chapter Highlights

HISTORY: Much has happened to the shape the definition of news as it moved from print into the electronic media. Each medium changed the ways news was defined and presented.

INDUSTRY: This section explains how today's news industry works, with special attention given to how news stories are chosen in electronic media.

CONTROVERSIES: The news industry is a powerful opinion shaper. Its power can be greatly influenced by various gatekeepers, including giant global corporations and individual news professionals. Most of the controversies involving news can fit into two problems in gatekeeping: political bias and news as entertainment.

Inside Katie Couric

Is it the end of television news as we know it? Or is it just a recognition that the news has already changed and is no longer the all-boys club that it used to be?

When Katie Couric announced that she was leaving NBC's morning show to become the first female solo anchor for a broadcast network newscast, she became the big story of the day. The war in Iraq was all but forgotten and immigration reform was pushed to the background as the news covered Couric's hairdos, wardrobe, and new salary—$60 million over four years. The normally staid *Times* of London looked at

Katie Couric left NBC's *Today Show* for CBS to become the first female solo anchor for a broadcast network newscast.

all the fuss and wondered, "Why do they care so much?"[1]

Couric was the longest-serving anchor—15 years—in the 54-year history of the *Today* show, and many critics genuinely doubted her credentials as a serious journalist. Now she would become the anchor and managing editor of *CBS Evening News,* the hallowed beacon of television journalism that Walter Cronkite and Dan Rather had built. Her critics pointed out that Katie was best known as the girl with the perfect look and the perky smile who had done more on-air weddings and cooking in the studio kitchen than hard-hitting interviews with world leaders.

And was she objective? Conservatives said Couric's work on *Today* revealed a liberal bias. They insisted she was soft on Democrats and hard on Republicans, soft on abortion and hard on the war in Iraq.[2] But liberals said her bias was shown in the opposite direction. They said she often failed to challenge guests who asserted conservative falsehoods and doubted liberals even when they were telling the truth.[3]

Both Couric's fans and detractors point out that she is the first network anchor who has had a nationally televised, on-camera colonoscopy, which she had after her husband died of colon cancer at the age of 42. Critics said it was an outlandish publicity stunt, but her fans declared it an act of incredible courage. She won a Peabody award for that program. She has also won six Emmys and several other awards for her journalistic and humanitarian work. She has brought so much attention and money to colon cancer research that a University of Michigan study attributed a national surge in colonoscopies to the "Couric effect."[4]

One thing that most observers seem to agree on: Couric is coming to this job at a time when news at all the networks is in a state of turmoil. Viewership is being drained away by cable, the Internet, and new media. To make matters worse, the average age for viewers of *CBS Evening News* is around 60, which does not bode well for the future.

Can Couric—or any other anchor—save network news? As one veteran journalist pointed out:

> The technological changes—the Internet, iPod, on-demand video on multiple formats and things we've probably yet to see—are changing the nature of news in more profound ways than a new anchor ever could. It's a changing landscape and everyone seems to be scrambling to figure it out and keep up. If Couric and a newer version of the "Evening News" fit into this new world, CBS will naturally benefit. In the end, the real test may well be the number of cell phone screens she appears on, not TV screens.[5]

A Brief History *of Electronic News*

Chapter 3 covered the early history of news. It showed how the concept and definition of *news* has developed over the years. A close reading of that chapter also showed that news as entertainment didn't begin with Katie Couric or even with television. It just reached its zenith there, to the point where critics are concerned that today's viewers might not receive enough meaningful news to be productive participants in a democracy. This chapter will focus on news in the electronic media, especially radio, television, and the Internet. The earliest example of electronic news, however, was newsreels.

NEWSREELS

From World War I until television became popular in the 1950s, movie theaters showed newsreels with their feature attractions. **Newsreels** were short films, usually around 10 minutes long, containing five or six items of current news, human interest features, and sports events. The first newsreel shown in a theater was presented in Paris by Charles Pathé, in 1909. The next year newsreels were introduced in U.S. and British theaters, where they became hugely popular. They were the first sound films, and their popularity helped convince movie theater operators to equip themselves with sound in 1927.

In the early days the typical newsreel company provided one new installment each week, but by the 1930s the demand was so high that some companies were producing four installments a week. Because it was expensive and time-consuming to set up a film crew, newsreels mostly covered expected events, such as parades and beauty contests, and **residual news,** or stories about events that are recurrent or long-lasting, such as floods. Fox Movietone News produced some of the most popular newsreels, and one of the most critically acclaimed series was *The March of Time,* produced by Time, Inc., which combined filmed news with interpretive interviews and dramatizations.

During World War II the U.S. government supervised most newsreels, which were highly propagandistic. Most of the combat footage shown in documentary films about that era comes from newsreels. Newsreels were replaced by television news in the 1950s, but they had an abiding influence on the format of television news. As explained later in this chapter, many of the newsreel producers went to work for television news companies, and television news eventually styled itself on the newsreel format. But before television entered the picture, radio became the dominant news medium.

newsreels
Short films dealing with current events, shown in movie theaters prior to the advent of television.

residual news
Stories about events that are recurrent or long-lasting.

Americans witnessed the battles of World War II through movie newsreels. Here Don Senick, Fox Movietone newsreel cameraman, takes shots of combat action in the Philippines in 1944.

RADIO NEWS

Radio was a natural for news. The first amateur broadcasters and experimenters enjoyed chatting about both local and national stories they had read in the newspapers. Lee De Forest, for example, in experiments testing his Audion tube, broadcast the results of the 1916 presidential election. Because the newspaper he was reading from got the results wrong, De Forest announced that Charles Evans Hughes, not Woodrow Wilson, had been elected president. It made little difference, for De Forest's audience consisted of only a few amateur scientists who cared little about the election.

The first radio newscast with a significant audience, as discussed in Chapter 8, was Frank Conrad's broadcast of the 1920 presidential election. Unlike De Forest, Conrad announced the correct winner (Warren G. Harding).

The Press–Radio War

At first, newspapers weren't concerned about radio announcers reading their news over the air. But when radio began to swell in popularity, the newspaper industry began to see it as serious competition. When that happened, the first thing the newspapers did was cut down their coverage of radio. There were suddenly no more feature stories about exciting broadcasts. Most newspapers also stopped printing radio schedules unless the stations paid them to do so.

By 1928 the wire services such as the Associated Press were providing two reports daily to radio stations. Newspaper executives put pressure on the wire services to stop servicing radio. Executives from the Columbia Broadcasting System (CBS) and the National Broadcasting Corporation (NBC), which owned the only networks of that time, agreed to sit down with the publishers and hammer out an agreement. They met at the Biltmore Hotel in New York City in 1933 and established what came to be known as the Biltmore Agreement.

According to the Biltmore Agreement, the radio networks would air only two five-minute newscasts each day. These newscasts would not air in the morning before 9:30 AM or in the evening before 9:00 PM, so as not to interfere with newspaper sales. The networks would offer no bulletins of breaking news from the wire services, and the newscasts would not be sponsored because that might interfere with the newspapers' advertising revenues. The fact that the networks agreed to such restrictions speaks volumes about how much more powerful the newspaper industry was than the radio industry in 1933.

The Biltmore Agreement, however, lasted less than one year and failed to rein in radio news. Before the ink was dry on the agreement, radio broadcasters had found a loophole: The agreement did not forbid **commentaries,** which were discussions about the news. Commentators would make it a point to discuss the implications of fires, floods, crimes, and any other newsworthy events in their locality. By discussing the implications of the news, though, commentators were in effect presenting the news. CBS's and NBC's commentators began to compete, and both networks began to hire people to find and write news items for them.

Also, nonnetwork stations were not a party to the Biltmore Agreement, and several independent radio news services sprang up to service these stations. Before long, the Biltmore Agreement was meaningless. Top newscasters such as Lowell Thomas at NBC and H. V. Kaltenborn at CBS became radio stars. Radio also showed a propensity for soft news as gossip columnists like Walter Winchell took to the air and became hugely popular.

We know now, however, that the newspaper executives of the 1930s had worried over nothing. Radio news didn't interfere with newspaper sales. In fact, it aided them by whetting the audience's appetite for in-depth reports on the events they had heard about on the radio.

Radio quickly showed its aptitude for providing eyewitness reporting of breaking news. One particularly compelling set of on-the-spot bulletins involved the explosion of the German dirigible the *Hindenburg* in 1937 (see the Close-Up on History box). People got used to the idea of turning to their radios for news. This was one of the factors that helped cause the panic following the *War of the Worlds* broadcast of 1938 (see Chapter 8), which was widely seen as a demonstration of the power of radio news.

Live Reports

Radio news became increasingly popular as fascism began to take hold in Europe. The networks set up live overseas broadcasts from Europe, relayed by shortwave radio to network headquarters in New York. Radio audiences heard live reports of Hitler's annexation of Austria in 1938, the invasion of Poland a year later, and the attack on Pearl Harbor in 1941. CBS was becom-

commentaries
On-air discussions about the news.

The *Hindenburg* Story

Historians have identified several big radio news stories as milestones. Perhaps the most important was the explosion of the *Hindenburg* in 1937, because that event marked the beginning of eyewitness news accounts of catastrophic events that were reported while they were happening.

The *Hindenburg* was a zeppelin, a type of blimp designed to fly luxury passengers across the Atlantic in a fraction of the time it took ships to make the journey. It was nearly as large and luxurious as the legendary passenger ship *Titanic*, with which it would share a fate.

The *Hindenburg*, which had been featured in German propaganda films, was financed by the Nazi party and displayed swastikas on its fins. It had come to represent the power and technical achievements of Adolf Hitler's government. In fact, it was the military implications of the craft that discouraged the United States, the sole source of helium at that time, from selling that nonflammable gas for use in the blimp. The United States priced the helium the *Hindenburg* needed at $600,000, an enormous sum at the time. The frustrated Germans filled the ship with highly flammable hydrogen gas instead.

The *Hindenburg* was on its 11th round-trip voyage in its first year of existence when it approached its mooring mast in Lakehurst, New Jersey. Seeing this ship land, 10 stories high and nearly as long as three football fields, was an unforgettable sight, and several journalists were there to cover the event. One of them was 31-year-old Herb Morrison, who was reporting live for Chicago's radio station WLS. As the ship neared the ground, a spark, perhaps caused by static electricity, ignited it. Morrison, in tears, reported what he was seeing: "It's burning, bursting into flames . . . this is one of the worst catastrophes in the world! Oh, the humanity . . . !"[1] Thirty-five passengers and crew members, along with one victim on the ground, died in the explosion.

Radio news coverage of the explosion of the *Hindenburg* was the first eyewitness account of a catastrophe to reach a mass audience as it was happening. This shot shows the airship exploding in a ball of fire as it lands in Lakehurst, New Jersey.

[1] Joe Garner, *We Interrupt This Broadcast* (Naperville, IL: Sourcebooks, 2002), pp. 3–4.

ing the leader in broadcast news, presenting a daily half hour devoted to a foreign news roundup originating live from key points such as London, Paris, and Berlin.

Audio Recording

Live radio reports helped make radio the dominant medium of its day, but it is interesting to note that there was another economic reason that live reports were used: Audio recording had not yet been perfected. Recording on discs, which required a studio setup, was time-consuming and expensive. The only other kind of audio recording device known to Americans prior to World War II was the wire recorder, a device able to capture sound on a thin wire. Because editing wire recordings was a cumbersome and unreliable process—it involved tying a knot in the wire and fusing it with heat—they were not useful in broadcasting.

During the war, American troops storming German radio stations found them unoccupied, with programming emanating from machines playing back recordings on a thin plastic tape. This tape had a much higher fidelity than the American wire recordings, and the editing process was more workable: The tape could be cut with a razor blade and spliced with adhesive. The edits were precise and unnoticeable in playback. The German recorders were sent back to America, where they became the basis for future generations of audio and video recording.

World War II

Radio news expanded greatly during World War II. The networks cut into their regularly scheduled programming to announce the bombing of the U.S. fleet at Pearl Harbor just hours after the attack had begun. They then scrambled to assemble features on the significance of the event. The next day, 62 million people listened to President Franklin Delano Roosevelt's "Day of Infamy" declaration of war.

Journalist Edward R. Murrow's wartime newscasts from London, often heard in the midst of a bombing raid, became hugely popular. CBS built a corps of correspondents, led by Murrow, who became the voice of the war for American listeners. In 1945, when the United States dropped atomic bombs on Hiroshima and Nagasaki, Japan, radio announcers gave detailed reports.

The Postwar Period

After World War II, radio was the dominant source of news for most Americans. A poll taken in 1946 indicated that 63 percent of Americans cited radio as their primary source of news.[6] This continued until television took over a decade later.

In 1948, radio news was able to dramatically demonstrate its advantages over the slower-moving print media. In the presidential election of that year, the Democratic incumbent, Harry Truman, defeated the popular Republican governor of New York, Thomas Dewey. This outcome was one of the biggest surprises in American political history. Since all the polls had predicted a Republican landslide, newspapers put out early editions stating that Truman had lost. While these papers were on the streets, network radio was able to instantly broadcast the news that Truman had actually won.

The All-News Format

As television became more popular, radio began to rely more on all-music formats with only brief news reports, often at the top of the hour. But in 1960 executives at a San Francisco–area radio station had the idea that a station providing all news, all the time, could also have appeal. The station adopted the call letters KFAX (K-Facts) and began to present a "newspaper of the air" 24 hours a day in 1960. By doing so, KFAX became the first all-news radio station.

KFAX invented the "newspaper of the air" format—listening to it was like hearing an entire newspaper read over the air from front to back, including a sports section, cooking features, and a "comics page," which consisted of comedy recordings. The broadcast industry watched this innovation with great interest, but the station failed financially. Some analysts assumed that

Unlike some newspapers of the time, radio news got the results of the 1948 election right. Here, Harry Truman, the newly re-elected president, holds an early edition of the *Chicago Tribune* that got it wrong.

both listeners and advertisers weren't ready for the innovation, but others pointed out that the format wasn't suited to radio. A revived KFAX adopted a religious format a few months later and continues to broadcast successfully today.

In 1964, a few years after KFAX's failure, a Chicago station, WNUS (W-News), also adopted an all-news format but provided a schedule more attuned to the radio listener, with top stories repeated regularly and sports and features in regular rotation. WNUS was a success, and similar all-news stations began to appear in the major markets. Today all-news is one of AM radio's most popular formats.

In the 1980s, radio news began to decline on regular stations. The Federal Communications Commission (FCC) had relaxed its standards requiring stations to present news, and since music was more profitable, that's what most stations presented. All-news stations became the place where radio listeners turned for news.

SELF QUIZ When was the first all-news radio station established?

BROADCAST TELEVISION NEWS

Television news started slowly. After World War II many television executives believed that people would continue to rely on radio for news, and that TV would be used as an entertainment medium. They did not believe that TV news would be profitable, and they hesitated to invest any money in it. However, a few visionaries, such as Edward R. Murrow at CBS, believed that television should move forward.

At first, because of the difficulty in obtaining film of breaking news events, TV news mostly showed newscasters sitting at a desk and discussing the day's events, as if merely reading radio news in front of a camera. Then the networks made deals with the newsreel companies and began to show film with their newscasts.

Mobile Units

The first regularly scheduled television news programs, which were 15 minutes long, began in 1940. Mobile units, however, were set up

SELF QUIZ When did regular television newscasts begin?

One of the two trucks composing the first mobile television station in the United States shown as it was delivered to NBC at Radio City, New York City, December 12, 1937. David Sarnoff, chairman of NBC, chose the 1939 World's Fair for the first commercial use of this unit.

three years before that to experiment with using pictures for newscasts. The mobile units consisted of two huge buses, one with a studio crammed with equipment for field use, the other a mobile transmitter to send the signal to the Empire State Building for broadcast over the network. David Sarnoff, chairman of NBC, chose the 1939 World's Fair for the first commercial use of this mobile unit.

Sponsored Newscasts

By 1947 the network newscasts had regular sponsors. The CBS newscast, sponsored by Camel cigarettes and starring John Cameron Swayze, was called *Camel News Caravan*. Swayze had an enthusiastic style and a famous motto for the world news summary part of his program. "And now," he would say, "let's go hopscotching the world for headlines!" Often this brief portion of the program covered the truly important news, each story mentioned only briefly because there was no film footage to make it interesting.

The sponsor of this newscast had a few strict rules. Since Camel sold cigarettes but not cigars, no news subjects could be shown smoking a cigar. The one exception to that rule was Winston Churchill, who was an important newsmaker who always seemed to have a cigar in his mouth. Also, camera operators and editors were instructed to make sure that no NO SMOKING signs would be seen on-screen.

Film Units

stringers
Independent journalists who are paid only for material used.

By the early 1950s the networks began to develop their own film units, hiring mostly former newsreel employees as that industry withered. The networks maintained film crews in important locations and in other places relied on **stringers,** which are independent, self-employed journalists. In this case, stringers also included freelance camera people who got paid only when their footage was used.

TV's reliance on newsreel-type film footage meant that news events that could not be filmed simply would not be covered. This included almost anything that happened in Africa. Later, this tradition would continue, but the networks would compete furiously for footage of predictable events that had caught the public's interest, such as the coronation of Elizabeth II of England in 1953. NBC, to get film of the event on the air before CBS, commissioned the invention of a portable film developer and installed it at an airport in England. Its reporters then filmed the British Broadcasting Company (BBC) coverage of the event off a television set, developed the film on the spot, and put it on a chartered airliner from which the seats had been removed to make room for editing equipment. The film was then edited as the plane flew toward Boston, where the network broadcast it. NBC did indeed beat CBS with this film but, ironically, lost out by a few minutes to the upstart American Broadcasting Company (ABC), which acquired the BBC feed from Canada, where it had arrived via transatlantic cable.

Because television news favored events that could be planned for in advance, networks came to depend on the public relations people who planned events such as press conferences, meetings, and even some protests. The public relations people were usually working with a business or governmental organization and had their own points of view to get across. Critics pointed out that public relations management of the news created a further distortion of news values. These planned events came to be called **pseudo events**,[7] because they would not have occurred had the media not been there to cover them. Television executives responded that TV brought a new (meaning visual) dimension to the news, but critics insisted that television was actually reducing the scope of the news to stories that had film to support them.

pseudo events
Happenings that would not have occurred if media were not there to record them.

Videotape, which would require no processing, would eventually help free television news from its reliance on film, but it didn't appear until the mid-1970s. Even with videotape, however, television news would continue to rely heavily on planned events and visual images.

Murrow and the Television Documentary

Radio journalist Edward R. Murrow moved to television in the early 1950s. After becoming the CBS vice president for news and public affairs, he continued his leadership role by helping to bring quality to television news. Working with Fred Friendly, a young collaborator who would eventually become president of CBS News, Murrow started a television news documentary unit that was styled after one he had developed for radio. A **documentary** is a long-form filmed examination of a social problem or historical subject. Murrow and Friendly produced such classic documentaries as *Harvest of Shame,* about the mistreatment of migrant farm workers. Murrow documentaries are still studied by journalism students today as examples of excellence.

documentary
A long-form filmed examination of a social problem or historical subject.

Murrow believed strongly in social causes and had the courage to act on his beliefs. He was one of the few people in the media industry to stand up to Senator Joseph McCarthy during the blacklisting era of the 1950s. McCarthy used rumor and innuendo in Senate hearings to suggest that communists and communist sympathizers were acting as agents from within the U.S. government and the entertainment industries. He ruined many lives in his quest for political gain and became very powerful. Murrow did a documentary titled *The Case Against Milo Radulovich A0589829,* which defended an airman who had been discharged from the Air Force because his father and sister had read "radical papers." This documentary was an examination of the true motives and techniques of McCarthyism. Murrow and Friendly had to use their own money to advertise the program because CBS refused, and McCarthy did attack Murrow afterward as a communist sympathizer. The Air Force later reinstated

Edward R. Murrow moved his radio documentary series, *Hear It Now,* to television, where it was called *See It Now.*

What was Edward R. Murrow's contribution to both radio and television news?

SELF QUIZ

Lieutenant Radulovich, on camera, as part of its response to Murrow's program. Later, Murrow devoted an entire episode of his program to McCarthy's tactics, using mostly film footage of the Senator conducting his various hearings, which showed how he used rumor, innuendo, and false evidence. At the end of the program Murrow delivered a now-famous speech:

> As a nation we have come into our full inheritance at a tender age. We proclaim ourselves—as indeed we are—the defenders of freedom, what's left of it, but we cannot defend freedom abroad by deserting it at home. The actions

"We cannot defend freedom abroad by deserting it at home."—Edward R. Murrow

> of the junior Senator from Wisconsin have caused alarm and dismay amongst our allies abroad and given considerable comfort to our enemies, and whose fault is that? Not really his. He didn't create this situation of fear; he merely exploited it, and rather successfully. Cassius was right: "The fault, dear Brutus, is not in our stars but in ourselves. . . ." Good night, and good luck.[8]

Murrow's programs became the model for today's TV newsmagazine programs such as *60 Minutes* and *20/20*.

Lee Harvey Oswald, in police custody, speaks to reporters in Dallas, November 23, 1963, one day after the assassination of President Kennedy. Oswald, who had just been formally charged with murder, denied any involvement in the assassination. The following day, the murder of Oswald by Jack Ruby became America's first see-it-as-it-happens national news event.

Coverage of Assassinations and Civil Unrest

Following the assassination of President John F. Kennedy in 1963, TV news brought a divided people together in a time of national mourning. Kennedy had charmed the nation with the way he handled questions, and reporters, at his news conferences. His on-camera charisma was one of the things that made him an immensely popular president.

On November 22, 1963, Kennedy's visit to Dallas included a trip by motorcade through the downtown area that his advisers hoped would demonstrate the president's popularity in a city he had lost in the 1960 election. No live cameras were there to record the assassination, but for the next four days the three television networks broadcast without interruption. Coverage of Kennedy's funeral brought a shocked nation together in sorrow. It was a rare moment of national unity.

An hour after Kennedy was shot, police had arrested their prime suspect. Lee Harvey Oswald was an ex-Marine and a trained marksman who worked in the building that the fatal shots had come from. Two days later, as he was about to be transferred from the city jail to the Dallas County jail, hundreds of reporters pressed forward to interview Oswald. Part of the throng was a live camera crew for NBC. In the pandemonium a reporter stepped forward and asked, "Do you have anything to say in your defense?" At the same time, Jack Ruby, a Dallas nightclub owner, moved forward and shot Oswald. Stunned, America witnessed its first see-it-as-it-happens national news event. For many critics, it was also an event that the media had helped cause, first by its sensational coverage of the event and then by interfering with the work of the Dallas police.

The Kennedy assassination marked the beginning of a turbulent decade that would include the assassinations of Kennedy's brother, Robert, and of Martin Luther King, both in 1968, as well as a number of urban riots that were sparked by protests against racial discrimination and the war in Vietnam.

Coverage of Vietnam

Network television coverage of the Vietnam War was extensive and had a profound effect on viewers. In the early years the networks refused to be critical of administration policies—for example, no television newscaster ever whispered that the United States had blocked free elections in Vietnam because it knew that 80 percent of the population would have voted for Ho Chi Min, the communist leader.[9] Reporting on such matters was considered unpatriotic and against the national interest. When the Senate began a hearing on Vietnam in 1966, CBS started covering it but abruptly switched to reruns of *I Love Lucy* and *The Real McCoys*. Fred Friendly, by then president of CBS News, resigned in protest.[10]

Even as television was eventually forced to cover the antiwar protests that were flaring up around the country, President Lyndon Johnson and members of his administration did all they could to manage the news. It was not uncommon for the anchors and reporters of television newscasts to get angry phone calls from government officials and from the president himself. At one hostile press conference, Johnson turned to a reporter and said, "Why do you come and ask me, the leader of the free world, a chicken-shit question like that?"[11]

One of the things that made it difficult for Johnson to control the news was the depth of on-the-scene reporting coming back from the battlefield. The networks had sent teams of reporters, many of whom went with a strong belief in the American cause, only to be disillusioned by what they saw there. The people the United States was supposed to be liberating were not supporting U.S. policies. At the same time, the bloody footage of young U.S. soldiers being killed and maimed on the battlefield brought the horrors of the war into the living rooms of America. Soon, the term **credibility gap** was being used to define the difference between what the Johnson administration was saying and what the public believed to be true. When Johnson heard Walter Cronkite criticize his administration's policies on the evening news, he is reported to have said, "If I've lost Cronkite, I've lost the American People." He announced soon afterward that he would not run for a second term.

credibility gap
The difference between what a government says and what the public believes to be true.

CABLE NEWS

In the 1970s, 60 percent of America watched one of the big three network news programs—CBS, NBC, or ABC—every day. That dominance was soon to be challenged by cable news.

CNN

In 1980, Ted Turner launched Cable News Network (CNN), the first live, 24-hour-a-day, all-news cable network. Turner's idea was to take the format of all-news radio and adapt it to television, and in doing so provide a news format that was not available on the broadcast networks. Broadcast news had already shown the power of 24-hour news stories, from the assassinations of

CNN's biggest ratings to date came with its nonstop coverage of the September 11, 2001, terrorist attacks.

John F. Kennedy and later his brother Robert, in 1968, to the seizure of the American Embassy in Iran in 1979. Turner had already turned his local Atlanta station, WTBS-TV, into a superstation by linking it to cable systems via satellite, and he believed that satellite distribution to cable systems was the future of TV.

CNN started slowly. In the beginning, Turner worked with a budget of less than $2 million a week to produce 24 hours of news. In comparison, the networks spent around $15 million each to produce just an hour or two of news. In the early years, many network executives referred to CNN as the "Chicken Noodle Network" because of its cut-rate budget. Yet even at that budget, Turner barely kept the network alive, constantly mortgaging his other properties to make the next week's payroll. CNN finally became profitable in 1985, after an investment of $185 million.

In the mid to late 1980s, several 24-hour-a-day news stories hit, including the explosion of the space shuttle *Challenger* in 1986 and the fall of the Berlin Wall in 1989. Suddenly CNN was a true competitor with the networks and would often beat them in the ratings. CNN's greatest success was in covering the Gulf War in 1991. CNN sent a large contingent to report on the action, although access to the battlefield was carefully controlled and the "action" consisted mostly of official briefings showing how well the latest American armaments worked. Still, this was America's first war to be televised in real time, and studies showed that half the viewers felt unable to leave their sets.

CNN's ratings also spiked with the coverage of the O. J. Simpson trial in 1995. When the verdict was handed down, 150 million people were watching. CNN's biggest ratings to date, however, came with the nonstop coverage of the September 11, 2001, terrorist attacks.

Fox News

If the idea behind CNN was to bring the all-news radio format to television, then the idea behind Fox News was to bring the feistiness of talk radio to television. Launched in 1997, Fox News was started by Roger Ailes, a former Republican media consultant and producer of Rush Limbaugh's television show. He had originated a cable channel for NBC called America's Talking, which he envisioned as an all-talk channel. When his superiors decided to join forces with Microsoft and convert that channel to MSNBC, Ailes quit. He then met with Rupert Murdoch, and together they decided that it was time for Fox Television to develop its own 24-hour news network. Ailes felt that CNN was too liberal and that there was a market for a more conservative point of view. Ailes chose "Fair and balanced" and "We report. You decide" as his promotional mottos, but most critics agreed that Fox news had a conservative bias.

Fox's big 24-hour story came with the Bill Clinton–Monica Lewinsky affair and President Clinton's subsequent impeachment trial. The competition did not devote as much attention to the story, and people started to turn to Fox for another one of those stories that they couldn't tear themselves away from. By 2005, viewers were turning to Fox News for other 24-hour stories, such as the Asian tsumamis, the death of Pope John Paul II, and the devastation of New Orleans.

ONLINE NEWS

There were several early attempts to use new television technology to deliver **news on demand,** providing information that users could access whenever they wanted to. **Videotext,** an experimental system for delivering electronic newspapers to homes via television sets, was attempted in the 1980s but never caught on with the public.[12] But the computer, with its built-in capacity for the storage and transmission of data, seemed to hold more promise than television for news on demand.

news on demand
Information that users can access whenever they want it.

videotext
An experimental system for delivering electronic newspapers to homes via television sets.

The Early Days

Online news preceded the World Wide Web by more than a decade. In these early days, database companies allowed users to access newspapers online. Mead Data Central, for example, started Nexis, a full-text newspaper database, in 1978. Within a few years, it was offering subscribers a full-text retrieval service of more than 100 newspapers. Subscribers connected directly to the Nexis database via the early modems on their home computers. Between the slow modem time and the slow processing power of early PCs, it would take about 10 minutes to download a typical newspaper article—that is, if the connection stayed up and all the commands were entered correctly. The newspapers were several weeks old by the time they could be accessed, and the monthly subscription fee was around $40. Newspapers and libraries were the main subscribers. DataTime, Newspapers Online, and Dialog Retrieval Service were the other main newspaper database services.

In the 1980s a few innovative newspapers began to offer their content to online subscribers. These were local **bulletin board services (BBSs)** that usually consisted of one PC at the newspaper's offices with off-the-shelf BBS software and a few extra telephone lines. The *Fort Worth Star-Telegram* was the first to go online this way, having started its modem service in 1983. It wasn't fast or easy to use, but at least users were accessing the same day's paper.

bulletin board services (BBSs)
Early online news services.

The rise of online services such as CompuServe and America Online paved the way for more newspapers to go online. Two of the first major papers to go online this way were the *San Jose Mercury News* and the *Chicago Tribune,* both of which were available on AOL in 1993. These early services were all text, with no photos, comics, or crossword puzzles.

Newspapers Take to the Web

The release of the World Wide Web in 1993 made navigation on the Internet easier and encouraged many more newspapers to establish online editions. As the software became more sophisticated, the new media employees that the newspapers had hired to design their Web sites began to learn how to add search functions, information from outside sources, feedback from readers, archives, and linked articles, along with "all the news that didn't fit" in the paper version. By 1995, some 150 newspapers were online. Today there are thousands.

Early Bloggers

In the mid-1990s a few individuals were setting up weblogs, or blogs, that provided news and comment online. Some of these, such as the Drudge Report (see the Close-Up on Industry box), dealt in hearsay, rumor, and speculation. Today, weblogs have become an increasingly important source of

Matt Drudge, Pioneer Blogger

Matt Drudge was a D– student in high school and barely graduated. By the time he was 27, in 1995, he was managing a CBS gift shop in Hollywood. That was the year Drudge became convinced that people would be willing to pay to hear the kind of gossip that he was hearing in and around the gift shop. He wrote the Drudge Report on an inexpensive Packard Bell computer that his father had purchased for him at Circuit City. His business plan was simple: He would e-mail his report out to anyone who would pay him $10 a year for it. Eventually, he also established a Web site (www.drudgereport.com) where he would post the news every few days. The term "blogger" hadn't been coined yet, but that's what Drudge was.

Working from his $600-a-month apartment, where three TVs were within sight of the computer,

In the *Media Talks* DVD that accompanies this book, Matt Lauer of NBC interviews Matt Drudge about his blogging style. Drudge tells him, "I go where the stink is."

Drudge got most of his tips by phone or e-mail. Often the tips came from subscribers, who numbered more than 5,000 after the Drudge Report's first year, and 50,000 after its second. Many of the tips were wrong, but some of them proved to be both correct and highly interesting to Drudge's clientele. Drudge broke stories about the salary demands of movie and television stars and about high-level firings (he broke the story about Connie Chung getting fired from her co-anchor job at CBS before Chung knew herself). He often had advance word about which movies would be hits and which would be bombs.

Drudge's online comments showed him to be a political conservative—a liberal basher, in fact—and his tips soon became political. His most famous scoop came when he broke the Bill Clinton–Monica Lewinsky scandal before his print competition. The conservative talk-show host Rush Limbaugh, noting Drudge's penchant for Clinton bashing, dubbed him "the Rush Limbaugh of the Internet."

The Drudge Report is currently advertiser-supported. Industry sources estimate that Drudge makes some $800,000 a year from the Web site,[1] and more from his syndicated radio program, which can be heard Sunday nights in 203 markets. His Web site now mostly links to other news sources, with occasional bits of rumor, gossip, and liberal bashing.

[1] Geoff Keighley, "The Secrets of Drudge Inc.," *Business 2.0* online, April 2003.

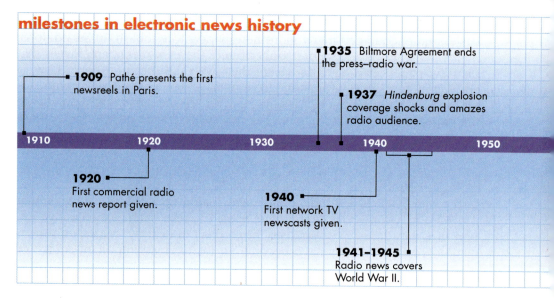

milestones in electronic news history

1909 Pathé presents the first newsreels in Paris.

1935 Biltmore Agreement ends the press–radio war.

1937 *Hindenburg* explosion coverage shocks and amazes radio audience.

1910   1920   1930   1940   1950

1920 First commercial radio news report given.

1940 First network TV newscasts given.

1941–1945 Radio news covers World War II.

news. All the major online news sites now have these online diaries where their journalists can record their thoughts, and there are thousands of sites where in-house, freelance, and amateur journalists can post their observations and analyses of world events. Every point of view is represented in what is now referred to as the blogosphere, and many of these come from a one-sided political point of view.

SELF QUIZ How did radio, television, and the Internet each affect the way news is presented?

Linking Services

Several of the original online news services were strictly **linking services;** that is, they provided links to wire services, newspapers, and other news sites. At first, there were some legal problems with this type of site. Total-News, for example, got into trouble for "framing" the news content of other sites (framing it around its own logos and ads, that is). The company was sued by the news sites and settled out of court by stopping the practice.

linking services
Online sites that connect the user to other news sites.

Personalized News Services

Almost from the start, online news services began to offer **personalized news services.** The idea behind this was that computer technology made it fairly simple for a news service to seek out stories on a particular subject and either deliver them by e-mail or provide them on a separate Web page that the user could access. Promoted as a means to tame the information monster, these services used a type of artificial intelligence called intelligent agents or bots (short for *robots*) to seek out the news of interest to the user.

personalized news services
News services that collect only information identified as being of interest to a client.

Personalized news services were like an electronic version of **clippings services,** which had been in existence for a hundred years. These services, part of the public relations industry, would collect newspaper clippings from around the country or around the world on topics of interest to their clients. Today' personalized news services, such as Google's News Alerts, extend the idea of a clippings service to online sources. An up-and-coming movie actor, for example, could use Google's free service to see how often his or her name was being mentioned in the press. Many online news sources provide headlines and summaries directly to a subscriber's desktop through RSS (Really Simple Syndication) feeds.

clippings services
Businesses that collect newspaper articles of interest to a client.

Headlines are now delivered to cell phones and handheld computers through RSS (really simple syndication) feeds, each of which contains a description and link to the related Web page.

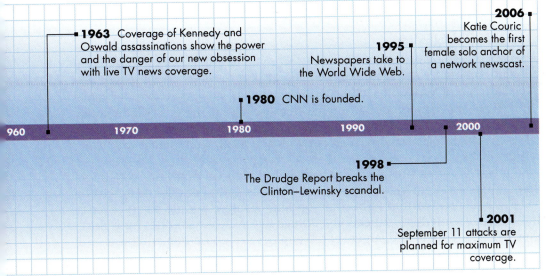

1963 Coverage of Kennedy and Oswald assassinations show the power and the danger of our new obsession with live TV news coverage.

1995 Newspapers take to the World Wide Web.

2006 Katie Couric becomes the first female solo anchor of a network newscast.

1980 CNN is founded.

960   1970   1980   1990   2000

1998 The Drudge Report breaks the Clinton–Lewinsky scandal.

2001 September 11 attacks are planned for maximum TV coverage.

FACT FILE 11.1

Top Online News Sites

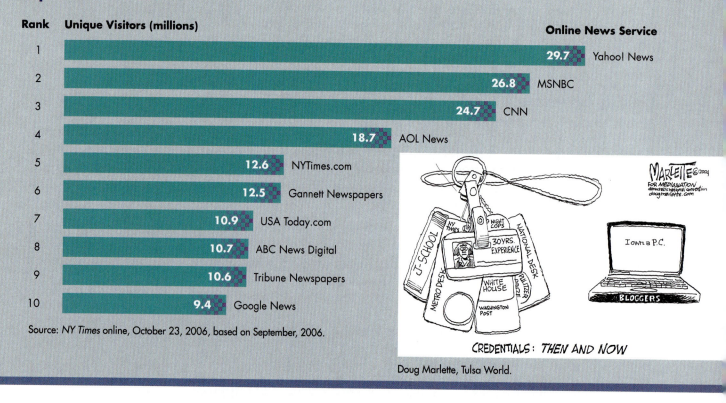

Rank	Unique Visitors (millions)	Online News Service
1	29.7	Yahoo! News
2	26.8	MSNBC
3	24.7	CNN
4	18.7	AOL News
5	12.6	NYTimes.com
6	12.5	Gannett Newspapers
7	10.9	USA Today.com
8	10.7	ABC News Digital
9	10.6	Tribune Newspapers
10	9.4	Google News

Source: *NY Times* online, October 23, 2006, based on September, 2006.

CREDENTIALS: *THEN AND NOW*

Doug Marlette, Tulsa World.

News Tickers

Another innovation of online news was a scrolling **news ticker** that appeared on the user's desktop. Once the user had downloaded and installed the software, headlines would scroll by whenever the ticker was activated. For example, ENewsBar (www.enewsbar.com) offers a ticker that provides both headlines and their source so that the user is aware of where the news comes from. Services developed for specialized news include Weatherbug (www.weatherbug.com) for the weather and QuoteTracker (http:// quotetracker.com) for stock quotes. Most of these services are advertiser-supported, so their users receive advertising messages such as pop-ups as a result of subscribing to them.

news ticker
Scrolling headlines on a screen.

ONLINE TV NEWS

List at least three different types of news sites that have been developed on the Internet.

SELF QUIZ

Next online, in the mid-1990s, were television news sites (see Fact File 11.1). CNN.com went online in 1995, and MSNBC, the partnership of Microsoft and NBC, simultaneously launched a 24-hour cable news channel and an online news service in 1996. ABCnews.com followed in 1997 with a number of local stations close behind. By 2000 most television news organizations, both network and local, were online with well-designed sites.

video on demand
Television clips that users can access whenever they want to.

Online TV news sites were the leaders in **video on demand,** which enabled users to call up video clips of news events, both current and archived. Video on demand started to become popular as more people gained access to high-speed Internet connections. Portals like AOL began offering it next, then the newspapers and larger search engines. Video on demand became a

ENewsBar (the green strip on top) is a news ticker that scrolls information on a user's desktop. ENewsBar ticker. Used by permission of Media Tru Inc.

mainstream service in 2003 during the war in Iraq, when people connected to news sites from workplaces where TVs were not available.

Understanding Today's News *Industry*

This section will look at today's news industry, paying special attention to how news stories are chosen and who does the choosing. Basically, news professionals choose stories according to a set of criteria known as news values.

NEWS VALUES

News is such a basic concept that we haven't bothered to define it yet in this chapter. Most critics would say that the most important news deals with public affairs, government activities, and politics. These are the topics, at least, that are required to keep an audience informed about the democracy they are expected to take part in. And yet different people define news in different ways. For a sports enthusiast, news might be the latest team scores; a businessperson might define news as the latest financial information. There are dozens of specialized cable networks and thousands of specialized Web sites. So we need to begin our analysis of the news industry with a general definition: **News** is the presentation of information that is timely, important, and interesting to its audience. This is a simple, well-accepted definition of news, yet if we look at each of these characteristics (known as **news values**) we begin to see the complexity of the task of the various gatekeepers who decide what should be included in each day's news—and what should not. A look at the traditional defining characteristics of news will also show how the definition of news is changing over time.

news
The presentation of information that is timely, important, and interesting to its audience.

news values
Characteristics that define news, including timeliness, importance, and interest.

Timeliness

News is information about events that are currently happening or that have happened so recently that most people haven't heard about them yet. The industry's obsession with being first with breaking news is all the evidence we need of this defining characteristic. In colonial days it took months for news to arrive from Europe, and weeks for it to come in from other colonies. But as technology allowed news to be more current, the audience began to expect news to be up-to-date and eventually up-to-the-minute. The timely nature of news means that in today's 24-hour news environment, news has to be kept fresh. When an act of terrorism is reported on the 6:00 PM news, we don't want to see the same report at 11:00 PM or on the next morning's news. New information needs to be found for each new report on the event, perhaps about the victims, the perpetrators, or the significance of the act. The pressure to make news "new" often results in the reporting of rumors and incomplete information, a trend explored later in this chapter. It also creates some rigid deadline pressures on journalists.

Importance

News has to have an impact on its audience, or at least on a large proportion of its intended audience. The more people who are affected, the greater the chance that the item will be included in a news report. News might be important to audience members because it will have some consequence on them, such as a storm heading their way. It might be important because it is useful in some way, such as a report about the possible disruption of transit services.

Interest

News has to grab the attention of the audience, if only because people can't receive the message if they aren't paying attention. There are many ways to make information interesting, and a professional with a good nose for news will find a **peg,** or angle, to make important, timely information interesting to the audience. For example, a reporter might use the peg of proximity, which means that the news has something to do with where audience members work or live. A far-off conflict might be given the peg of proximity if a nearby military base houses personnel that might be sent into that conflict. Another peg is prominence, which means that the news relates in some way to someone well known to the audience, perhaps a celebrity in the realm of entertainment, sports, or politics. Yet another peg is known as human interest, which means that the story has elements that are typically interesting to human beings, such as conflict (between one person and another, between two or more different ideas, or between people and nature); novelty; or uniqueness. A legendary editor once pointed out, "When a dog bites a man, that is not news. When a man bites a dog, that is news."[13]

What are the characteristics that cause editors and producers to pick one story over another for inclusion in a news medium?

SELF QUIZ

CONSIDER THIS

Which is the most essential news value—audience interest, importance, or timeliness of the story? Why?

THE PLAYERS

Chapter 3 discussed the staff positions at a newspaper, and indeed, most news organizations will have employees doing the jobs of reporters, editors, and publishers, although they might go by different names in different media. A big difference between newspapers and electronic news media, however, is that jobs are easier to find at newspapers—there are more of them. Still, many students think of television when they say they want to become journalists, perhaps because even though TV jobs are scarce, those at the top of the field tend to be glamorous and well paid.

Lisa Zompa is an anchor–producer at WSEE in Erie, Pennsylvania. The *Media World* DVD that accompanies this book (track 4) includes a tour of the station's newsroom.

Anchors

The most prominent position in broadcast news, whether on the local or network level, is that of **anchor,** the newsreader who occupies the seat in the studio. Industry research proves that viewers pick their newscasts according to their favorite anchor, which makes this media personality a highly paid, much-sought-after star. Although they are paid mostly to be a presence on the screen—a job that looks like anyone could do it—anchors have generally spent decades working their way up the ranks as field reporters and correspondents. They are usually smart, experienced, and driven.

Often, on the network level, anchors will be hired to do one or two magazine-type shows in addition to the evening newscast, as well as promotions and specials. Dan Rather, for example, when he was the anchor and managing editor of *CBS Evening News,* hosted *48 Hours,* and served as a correspondent on *60 Minutes II.* Tom Brokaw, when he was the anchor and managing editor of *NBC Nightly News,* also hosted *Dateline NBC* and MSNBC specials. Anchors are not forced to do these extra duties. Often they will demand this kind of guaranteed on-screen time in their contracts. In smaller markets, local news anchors might get less on-screen time and work behind the screen writing their own newscasts.

Before Katie Couric's rise in 2006, the anchors of prime-time evening network newscasts had generally been men. In fact, in the days of the dominance of the Big Three networks, the anchors were often referred to as "three white guys in suits." In 1976 ABC tried pairing Barbara Walters and Harry Reasoner; CBS tried co-anchoring Connie Chung with Dan Rather 17 years later. In both cases, the pairing didn't improve ratings, and the women got fired. As Connie Chung pointed out: "I thought it was the dream job. I loved having it for those two years. Barbara only had it for two years, too. I just didn't know there were term limits."[14]

While many critics feel that Couric's rise is a big step forward for women on the network level, others feel that the real changes are needed in the back office. As one reporter pointed out: "None of the network chiefs are female and until one of their suits is worn by a woman it will be hard to say that women have really achieved equal clout in television news."[15]

One area where women seem to have prevailed is as anchors on local news. Although men once anchored virtually every local newscast in America, there are now more women than men in that position. One of the reasons for this change is that stations want young anchors, and it is difficult for most young men to enter the profession—simply because of the way they look. According to one researcher, "If you dress up the average woman coming out of college and put on makeup, she looks like an adult. The average man coming out of college looks like he's going through puberty. . . . Sure, he'll get a job in a smaller market, but it will take longer for him to move forward."[16] Young broadcast reporters also have to put up with low salaries, averaging about $20,000 a year. Women anchors have also achieved equal numbers with men in radio news.

Two reporters from different stations interview a widow attending a memorial service at Ford Hood, Texas for US soldiers killed in Operation Iraqi Freedom.

Correspondents

In television news, the on-camera reporters in the field are known as correspondents. These are the reporters who do on-location stand-ups—segments in which the reporter faces the camera, with the news scene in the background. Often, a correspondent will work with another person who serves as driver, cameraperson, and videotape technician. For **satellite news gathering (SNG)**, they go together in a van with a prominent antenna on its roof to the site of the news event. While the reporter conducts interviews and does other types of research, the driver–technician sets up the satellite dish and makes sure that the team has good contact with the station.

Then the correspondent completes the on-camera interviews and other story elements as the cameraperson videotapes them with portable equipment for **electronic news gathering (ENG).** Together, the team then edits

satellite news gathering (SNG)
Reporting the news with equipment that enables transmission via satellite.

electronic news gathering (ENG)
Reporting that uses portable field equipment.

that tape, which will become the main part of the story package. During the newscast the correspondent will go live, at the scene, to introduce the tape. Taping the main part of the story in this way allows for a smooth presentation, while the correspondent's stand-up still gives the story a sense of on-the-scene immediacy.

What are reporters called in radio and television news?

For radio news, the correspondent performs a similar function with an audio package. Usually, the radio correspondent works alone and often brings an edited tape into the station by hand.

Producers

For large stories, television (and radio) correspondents are backed up by field producers, who are essentially behind-the-scenes, off-screen reporters who do the interviews, research, and writing for the on-screen correspondent. Field producers make the ethics of broadcast news different from that of newspaper news. In 2003 the *New York Times* fired Rick Bragg, one of its top reporters, because a freelance stringer had reported and written some of a news story that appeared under Bragg's byline. In contrast to newspapers, one critic has pointed out, "In TV news—which lives and dies by a star system—[crediting a report to the on-screen correspondent alone] not only happens routinely, it's encouraged and rewarded."[17] TV newsmagazines such as *60 Minutes* do list the names of their field producers. For the nightly news, however, the field producers' names rarely even scroll by quickly at the end of the newscast—news programs have eliminated most credit rolls because audiences have a tendency to switch channels during them.

Consultants

Broadcast news consultants are ratings specialists. They are brought in by radio and television (mostly television) news organizations to increase the audience appeal of a newscast. Consultants carefully research a station's market and then suggest changes in any number of areas, including but not limited to length of stories (seldom more than a minute), type of stories, popularity of newscaster, graphics, music, and even set design. The fast-paced local formats known as Eyewitness News or Action News were originally designed by consultants.

Technical Specialists

Broadcast news has always required technical specialists, and today's radio, television, and online news organizations continue that tradition. Most technical specialists today are computer experts. Radio networks have audio technicians who are skilled in the latest software, which can seamlessly splice out a sound imperfection (an "uh" or an entire sentence) in a few seconds. Television operations have technical specialists who keep the ENG and SNG equipment running smoothly. They also have videotape editors to work with the producers.

Online news operations have software specialists who are constantly debugging their Web sites. Google News, for example, has a staff of 10 that

Google News automates most of what the news site does, presenting information from 4,500 news sources worldwide.

manages to automate most of what the site does, which is to present information culled from approximately 4,500 news sources worldwide and to arrange that information to present the most relevant news first. This is accomplished solely through the use of computer algorithms (a type of multistage formula) based on many factors, including how often and on what sites a story appears on the Web. The editing process is accomplished without human intervention. The stories are constantly updated and included without regard for political viewpoint or ideology.

In addition to technical specialists, however, today's newsroom requires everyone to have some type of computer skills. Computerized news operations now allow the copywriter's word processing to go directly to a teleprompter, the machine that displays the prepared text that the anchor reads over the air. The computer also times the story, telling the producer exactly how many minutes or seconds are left in a newscast so that adjustments can be made. In earlier days these adjustments were made by hand and often resulted in some frantic moments in the control room. Computers generate visual elements—graphs, charts, logos and so on—for stories that might otherwise be boring. Computers also provide a systematic filing system in which all stories, graphics, research, and footage can be stored and easily retrieved. Reporters also use in-depth audiovisual databases that allow access to file footage that can be used to make breaking news visual.

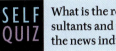

SELF QUIZ — What is the role of program consultants and technical experts in the news industry?

Experts and Pundits

All news organizations maintain a stable of experts who can be called on at short notice to speak expertly on the topic at hand. News organizations are often criticized for their reliance on the same experts every time they need someone to analyze a certain type of story. These experts also come in for criticism when they spin theories that are counterproductive to law enforcement or national security. During the 2002 sniper shootings in the Washington, DC, area that left 10 people dead in a period of three weeks, news organizations called on their usual consultants, former Federal Bureau of Investigation profilers and forensic psychologists, to describe a likely suspect. They surmised that the sniper was probably a resident of Montgomery County, Maryland, a young white man from a violent family who was married and who returned to his wife and children on weekends. The pair of gunmen turned out to be opposite of that description in almost every respect, and critics pointed out that media coverage of the expert's ideas might have taken attention away from a more general and possibly open-minded search for the perpetrators.

Another problem is that news organizations' hired experts often have a point of view that is less than objective. For example, critics believe that the military consultants (mostly ex-generals) hired by the networks to analyze the conduct of operations in the Iraq war simply echoed statements coming from the Pentagon and acted as cheerleaders for the war.

The Audience

The audience for news differs greatly by generation and gender. In periodic surveys, we learn that men follow the news more than women, and that older people (those over 30) follow it more than younger people.[18] In fact, research suggests that people under 30 read fewer newspapers, read less news online, and even watch television news less than older people. More than half of the population gets most of its news from television, and about a quarter gets most of its news from newspapers and other print media. The rest is divided between radio and online sources. Just over half the population believes

Al-Jazeera, the Web site of the Arab television news channel, presents news in English from an Arab perspective. Al-Jazeera home page in English. Used with permission.

Young people get news from late-night comics. Here, Conan O'Brien tells his audience: "Last week, the United States eliminated Iraq's No. 1 terrorist, Abu Musab al-Zarqawi. This week, Al Qaeda announced his successor: Abu Ayyub al-Masri. When asked why, an Al Qaeda spokesperson said: 'We have a lot of leftover stationary that says: "From the desk of Abu."'" ("Week in Review," *New York Times* online, June 8, 2006.)

it is important to keep up with the news, but younger people are less likely to express this view and more likely to say they do not have time to keep up with the news. Around 60 percent of those surveyed say they trust television news more than other news outlets when they encounter conflicting versions of a story.[19] Young people are more likely than older people to get their news online.

Within each medium, consumers can get their news from a wide variety of sources. Many young viewers report getting their news from satirical comedy sources, such as Jon Stewart, Jay Leno, or David Letterman (see Fact File 11.2), and about a fifth of all consumers report that they get at least some of their news from radio talk shows, a source that is far from objective.[20] Within cable television and the Internet, there is also a wide variety of viewpoints. In recent turmoil in the Mideast, for example, news consumers could access the points of view expressed by friend and foe alike. One critic pointed out that this variety of viewpoints makes today's news consumers something like "the reader of a novel with several unreliable narrators."[21]

Many news organizations, concerned that younger people are not interested in news, have tried a variety of methods to get younger people involved. They have designed flashier graphics, hired anchors who seem young and hip, and increased entertainment coverage. The thing that works best, however, is a big news story. Following hurricane Katrina in 2005, for example, there was a big spike in news consumption, much of it attributed to younger people. The challenge for news organizations is to turn these one-time consumers into loyal audiences or subscribers.

One other concern about today's news audience is that there are so many sources of news that people no longer feel the sense of community that they used to feel when news was more commonly shared. Especially online, people can select only the news that interests them or that expresses

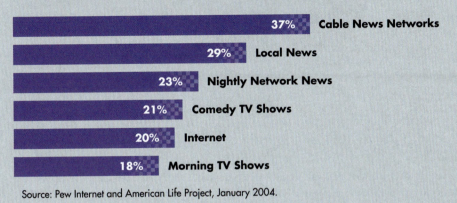

FACT FILE 11.2

Where Young People Get Their News

Based on a sample of Americans ages 18–29 during the early stages of the 2004 presidential election campaign. Survey subjects were asked from which news outlets they "regularly learn something about the election." Note that because some respondents indicated more than one source, the total exceeds 100 percent for the entire group.

37%	Cable News Networks
29%	Local News
23%	Nightly Network News
21%	Comedy TV Shows
20%	Internet
18%	Morning TV Shows

Source: Pew Internet and American Life Project, January 2004.

views, no matter how radical, in which they already believe. The final product of what they receive has been labeled the "daily me." Many critics believe that this narrow perspective increases intolerance and bigotry.

Controversies

The news industry is a powerful opinion shaper. This power can be greatly influenced by various gatekeepers, including giant global corporations and individual news professionals. The power of these gatekeepers is the basis of the controversial nature of the news business. Most of the controversies involving news can fit into two distinct but interrelated categories: political bias and news as entertainment.[22] The public's reaction to perceived political bias and entertainment values in the news has helped to contribute to the decline in credibility discussed at the beginning of this chapter.

"Actually, I work for a newspaper, but people won't talk to me without it."

POLITICAL BIAS

Much of the controversy about bias in the news revolves around politics. Conservatives, through organizations such as Accuracy in Media (AIM; www.aim.org), and liberals, through organizations such as Fairness and Accuracy in Reporting (FAIR; www.fair.org), both argue that the media are unfair and show partiality. AIM says journalists have a **liberal bias** because they are anti–big business, pro–big government, antifamily, antireligion, and anti-Republican. AIM claims, for example, that "all the major media surveys for the past 20 years have shown that 80 to 90 percent of the mainstream media [practitioners] consistently vote for Democrats."[23] Liberal organizations such as FAIR say

liberal bias
Point of view that is generally purported to be anti–big business, pro–big government, pro social programs, pro–diversity, and anti-Republican.

Conservatives, through organizations such as Accuracy in Media (AIM; www.aim.org), and liberals, through organizations such as Fairness and Accuracy in Reporting (FAIR; www.fair.org), both argue that the media are unfair and show partiality. Accuracy in Media home page, used with permission; FAIR, Fairness & Accuracy in Reporting, used with permission.

conservative bias
A point of view that is generally purported to be pro–big business, anti–big government, profamily, proreligion, and pro-Republican.

that the media often have a **conservative bias,** mainly because they are big businesses and big business is inherently conservative. FAIR has also run surveys of reporters that show most of them actually hold conservative views on specific issues, such as affirmative action.

Conservatives versus Liberals

There are a number of prominent conservative media voices and outlets, including Rush Limbaugh's radio talk show, the *New York Post*'s editorial page, the Drudge Report, and some commentators on the Fox News Channel. They are quick to point out what they see as liberal bias. Much of the information for their critiques comes from a conservative media watchdog organization called the Media Research Center, which hires full-time monitors to analyze the network newscasts. They are particularly watchful of any behavior

> **"Just getting the facts straight is monumentally difficult. We don't want to have to wonder if we are saluting properly."**

that seems unpatriotic, and news executives are aware of this monitoring. Erik Sorenson, the president of MSNBC, expressed the executives' collective frustration when he said, "These are hard jobs. Just getting the facts straight is monumentally difficult. We don't want to have to wonder if we are saluting properly."[24]

Still, the networks make news decisions with possible criticism in mind. CNN, for example, required

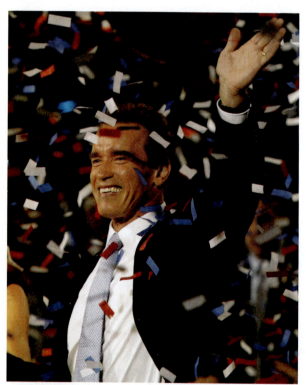

In California, the local press reported accusations of inappropriate sexual behavior against Arnold Schwarzenegger right before the 2003 gubernatorial election. The press said this was timely news; critics said it was political bias. Schwarzenegger won the election.

that reports of civilian casualties in Afghanistan be balanced with reminders of the September 11 toll.[25] The result is a type of self-censorship that worries some critics, who feel that news media should be watchdogs, not cheerleaders, of government policy. The watchdog function becomes difficult during wartime, however (see the Close-Up on Controversy box).

Centrist Bias

Not all critics, however, accuse the media of being too liberal or conservative. There are some who insist that the media have a **centrist bias,** because mainstream mass media simply will not report on radical points of view from either extremely liberal or extremely conservative sides.[26]

centrist bias
Failure of the news media to report on radical points of view.

Creeping Bias

According to both liberals and conservatives, bias is often not blatant. **Creeping bias** is a subtle form of slanting that manifests itself in understated ways, such as the placement of stories, the choice of photos and the captions that go with them, and even what might be subconscious language choices. For example, in the months building up to the war in Iraq in 2003, some critics believed that the use of the term *impending war* was a form of creeping bias. As one critic said, "Used by politicians, [the phrase] may be part of the political negotiation that goes on. But when journalists do it, accepting it as a given, it creates the impression that, in fact, neutral or objective people are concluding that war is inevitable."[27]

creeping bias
A subtle form of slanting that manifests itself in understated ways.

Some critics point out that with electronic media, there are many ways for bias to creep into the news. Glitzy graphics and special effects, for example, can change the tone and atmosphere of the news. Critics have even pointed out that the use of music can be a form of bias. One critic pointed out that, during the buildup to the U.S. war with Iraq, network music introducing stories about the war was "overtly warlike, a surging electronic wall of sound that seems to use the beating rotors of attack helicopters as its rhythmic inspiration."[28] One composer hired by a network said that his music was specifically meant to inspire a "climate of fear."[29]

Some conservatives believe that since the Vietnam War, reporters have tended to be antimilitary. The military has attempted to deal with this attitude in a variety of ways. In the Gulf War of 1990–91, reporters were kept from the battlefield and limited to official briefings about the action. Some

In most surveys, people will say that the news media are biased. Respondents will also see the direction of that bias according to their own liberal or conservative mindset.

supporters of this method of news control said that it kept journalists out of the way of dangerous battles, protecting both them and the troops. Other proponents of these restrictions pointed out, perhaps more honestly, that it was necessary to keep the grim realities of war away from the public to maintain support for the war at home and the morale of the soldiers in the field. Those who objected to the restriction of journalists insisted that it was a denial of the public's right to know and that it would be impossible for voters to decide whether they should support the war if they didn't know what was happening there.

In the war in Iraq that began in 2003, nonmilitary reporters were embedded with military units. These **embedded journalists** were given equipment

embedded journalists
Nonmilitary reporters attached to a military unit.

Mr. Murdoch's War[1]

Rupert Murdoch is the chairman of News Corporation, an international media conglomerate that owns, among many other media properties, major newspapers around the world (the *New York Post*, the *Times of London*); influential magazines (the *Weekly Standard*); and all-news cable and satellite networks in India, China, Italy, England, Australia, and the United States. Believing that the BBC in England and CNN in the United States had a liberal bias, Murdoch sought to correct that bias with Fox News, which was the top-rated all-news channel in the United States in 2003 as the debate raged over whether or not to invade Iraq. At that same time at least one of his publications, the *Weekly Standard*, was closely read by the Bush White House.

According to his critics, Murdoch actively influenced the conservative bias of each of his news properties through phone calls and personal visits to his editors. Murdoch, however, plays down his active involvement in shaping editorial policy: "Unfortunately, I have a very big company to run," he says. "Twenty years ago I used to enjoy spending a couple of hours in a newsroom. But now I am not in any one place long enough to do much direct managing of anything."[2]

Whether he demands it or not, all of his 175 editors around the world seem to agree with his conservative point of view. This was seen most powerfully in his influence in encouraging the war against Iraq. Critics say Murdoch doesn't have to demand a particular stance. His employees know how he feels, and they make sure they agree with him.

Believing that other media had a liberal bias, Murdoch sought to correct that bias with Fox News.

Each of Murdoch's papers took a pro-war editorial stance. Each attacked antiwar demonstrators. His papers even attacked France for not supporting the U.S. plans for war. The *New York Post* called France part of the "axis of weasels" (a pun on Bush's declaration of North Korea, Iran, and Iraq as an "axis of evil"). A picture of World War II graves in Normandy was headlined "Sacrifice: They Died for France but France Has Forgotten."[3]

Murdoch made no secret of his opinion about going to war. As the war debate raged, Murdoch told an Australian magazine, "We can't back down now, where you hand over the whole of the Middle East to Saddam. Bush is acting very morally, very correctly. . . . The greatest thing to come of this for the world economy, if you could put it that way, would be $20 a barrel for oil. That's bigger than any tax cut in any country." At a business conference he added, "There is going to be collateral damage. And if you really want to be brutal about it, better we get it done now than spread it over months." When the war with

---

What types of political bias are news organizations often accused of?

SELF QUIZ

CONSIDER THIS

Should reporters give up political involvement, including party registration and voting? What would be the benefits and detriments of such a policy?

and minimal training and were considered a semiofficial part of the military. Those who supported this procedure believed that it provided the public with accurate information about the war without unduly jeopardizing the lives of either journalists or U.S. soldiers. Those who opposed the embedding of journalists felt that news people who were part of a military unit would identify with that unit and slant the news from the military's point of view. There was some evidence that embedded journalists did, indeed, identify strongly with their units. One journalist admitted that he acted as a spotter of enemy troops, pointing out their locations so that they could be fired on.[30]

Most news professionals insist that what looks like bias is really unintentional and the result of the pressures of the newsroom that include dead-

Iraq finally began, according to one report, "Rupert Murdoch watched the explosions over Baghdad on a panel of seven television screens mounted in the wall of his Los Angeles office, telling friends and colleagues over the phone of his satisfaction that after weeks of hand-wringing the battle had finally begun."[4]

His critics contend that Murdoch wields his influence as mightily as the press barons of old, such as William Randolph Hearst, who has been credited with helping to start the Spanish-American war (see Chapter 4). One critic said of Mr. Murdoch: "He has extended the most blatant editorializing in the entire world through his media properties, and that is exactly the example of what we need to worry about when any one entrepreneur owns and controls too many media outlets."[5]

[1] The title of this box comes from David D. Kirkpatrick, "Mr. Murdoch's War," *New York Times* online, April 7, 2003.
[2] Quoted in Kirkpatrick, "Mr. Murdoch's War."
[3] Roy Greenslade, "Their Master's Voice," *The Guardian* online, February 17, 2003.
[4] Kirkpatrick, "Mr. Murdoch's War."
[5] Gene Kimmelman, a director of the Consumers Union, quoted in Kirkpatrick, "Mr. Murdoch's War."

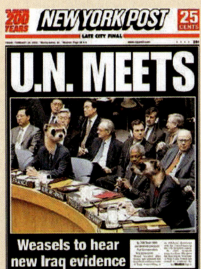

His critics contend that Rupert Murdoch, shown here with his son Lachlan, also an executive in News Corporation, wields his influence as mightily as the press barons of old. In the *New York Post* cover at right, countries that don't support the U.S. invasion of Iraq are referred to as "weasels."

lines, budget restrictions, reader expectations, editorial conventions, and self-serving sources. Still, in most surveys, most people will say that the news media are biased. Interestingly enough, however, most respondents will see the direction of that bias according to their own liberal or conservative mindset. Many reporters cite that as evidence that they are probably doing their job correctly.

NEWS AS ENTERTAINMENT

Whereas the charge of political bias is a serious one, some critics point out that the more serious media bias is one toward show business and entertainment values and against serious and important news. When former ABC executive producer Av Westin said, "TV News is show business, but it uses show business techniques to convey information rather than distort it,"[31] critics responded that Westin understated the danger of mixing entertainment and news. The arguments over whether and to what degree TV news should entertain have been around since the first feature story and have been greatly enlivened by the visual nature of television news.

Entertainment Values

Critics contend that the mixing of news and entertainment is obvious in several ways. It can be seen in the way television news promotes its newscasts, such as when promotional announcements promise that a particular story is "coming up next" (when in fact, it is coming up last), or in the titillating way announcers sell the newscast with a fearsome teaser. For example, "Is your water poisoning your children?" the 9:00 PM teaser says. "Our report at 11."

According to critics, in what ways have entertainment values damaged the news?

SELF QUIZ

Then, one of the last stories on the 11:00 report mentions that one legislator was concerned about water quality, but it turns out the water is OK.

Television news has also been guilty of creating news stories whose sole purpose is to promote entertainment programs elsewhere on the schedule. The CBS morning news program, for example, extensively covered the events on the network's own program *Survivor*.

Mostly, though, critics say that news stories, especially those chosen for inclusion on the magazine programs, are almost always chosen just for their entertainment value. They point to examples such as the sudden proliferation of stories about pop star Michael Jackson in 2003. First, *Dateline NBC* loudly announced that it would devote a whole hour to the evolution of Michael Jackson's face. Then ABC's *20/20* presented a two-hour documentary on Jackson's bizarre parenting practices, followed by an hour-long interview with the reporter who had interviewed Jackson. *Dateline* then expanded its program to two hours. Jackson, upset by the ABC program, put together his own response, which was presented by Fox. ABC then scheduled a second showing of the original two-hour documentary. Altogether, more than a dozen network prime-time news hours were devoted to this one entertainment subject—and this was *before* Jackson was charged with child molestation.

The media's obsession with celebrities such as Brad Pitt and Angelina Jolie demonstrates how the line between news and entertainment has become blurred.

Polls as Entertainment

The influence of entertainment values on news can be seen in the way news organizations now use audience polls. To professional pollsters, polls are highly scientific tools that lead to reliable findings. Electronic news organizations, however, often use them for entertainment. These polls often ask frivolous questions. One Fox News Channel poll, for example, asked, "While it is a highly unlikely situation, if you had the opportunity, would you personally kill Osama bin Laden?" Other questions concern things audience members could not possibly know, such as whether Iraq had nuclear weapons or whether Osama bin Laden is dead or alive. Sometimes the questions are just inappropriate, as when CNN and *Time* asked, on September 13, 2001, whether Congress should declare war. Sixty-two percent of the respondents said yes. When the audience was then asked against whom war should be declared, 61 percent of the respondents said they didn't know.

One of the problems with polls as entertainment is that, having invested the time and money in running the poll, the news organization feels obligated to use the results as part of the news, giving them significance that they simply do not warrant. CNN's Garrick Utley, for example, reported the results of the poll about declaring war and said, "That uncertainty gives President Bush flexibility and time to determine what kind of a war he intends to wage."[32]

Often the news organization will include disclaimers saying that the results are not scientifically accurate and only represent the views of the people who choose to respond, but professional pollsters feel that people don't pay much attention to this kind of warning.

Naked News

Gimmicks and stunts have always been a part of trying to sell the news, but news organizations sometimes go overboard in their quest to make news entertaining. One extreme example of this trend is the use of naked newscasters.

The first naked newscast appeared in Russia in 2000. This was really just a soft-core pornography program that had strippers who happened to read the news, generally without much skill or enthusiasm. But a year later a cable news program in Bulgaria, *The Naked Truth,* went nude, and its producers insisted that they were producing serious news and simply using the new format to make it more entertaining to the audience. Within the first week that it was on the air, the program beat the usual favorite—the state television's late-evening news program—in the ratings. It was the first time in Bulgaria that a cable program had beaten state television.

In Canada another program, *Naked News,* is presented both on pay-per-view cable and on the Internet. As the executive producer of that program explains: "The news right now is somber and morbid; there is a lot of stress and tension in the world and this makes the news a little more carefree."[33] To critics of the trend of news as entertainment, the last thing the world needs is news that is more carefree.

Summing Up

Journalism is recorded in all types of media, and the development of each medium changes how news is presented. Newsreels made news visual, and radio made it aural and immediate. Television news combined the visual nature of newsreels with the immediacy of radio and slowly continued the evolution of mixing entertainment values with news. Online news allowed all the earlier forms to converge and made it possible for both professionals and amateurs to generate news items. Online news includes newspaper sites, original content sites, linking sites, and television news sites.

The radio and newspaper industries had a long-standing war over radio's right to broadcast the news. In the end, the newspaper industry need not have worried, because radio only stimulated the audience's interest for in-depth newspaper news. Television news was influenced by newsreels and came to rely on filmed coverage of planned events. Cable news channels brought the format of all-news radio to television. Online news services fulfilled the promise of news on demand that had been attempted with other media and also brought new technology such as personalized news and news tickers to the users of home computers.

Today, news is chosen by professional gatekeepers according to a set of criteria known as news values; according to these basic values, news is information that is timely, important, and interesting to the audience. The industry gatekeepers go by different names in different media, but they still fulfill the roles of reporters, editors, and technical specialists.

Controversies in the news industry derive from its power as an opinion shaper. This power can be greatly influenced by various gatekeepers, including giant global corporations and individual news professionals. Most of the controversies involving news can fit into two problems in gatekeeping: political bias and news as entertainment. Different critics see political bias in the news as favoring liberalism, or conservatism, or centrism. For some, the worst bias is one toward entertainment, which causes amusing distractions to replace serious and important information.

Key Terms

These terms are defined and indexed in the Glossary of key terms at the back of the book.

anchor *372*

bulletin board services (BBSs) *367*

centrist bias *379*

clippings services *369*

commentaries *358*

conservative bias *378*

credibility gap *365*

creeping bias *379*

documentary *363*

electronic news gathering (ENG) *373*

embedded journalists *379*

liberal bias *377*

linking services *369*

news *371*

news on demand *367*

newsreels *357*

news ticker *370*

news values *371*

peg *372*

personalized news services *369*

pseudo events *363*

residual news *357*

satellite news gathering (SNG) *373*

stringers *362*

video on demand *371*

videotext *367*

Electronic Excursions

HISTORY

Web Excursion

1. Much has happened to the shape and definition of news as it moved from print into the electronic media. Search the Web for history timelines of the news industry, or go directly to the Center for History and New Media, http://chnm.gmu.edu.* Select a news event that occurred at least 20 years ago and compare how the impact of that story would change if it happened today. Identify the major differences and similarities of how news was perceived in the past compared with today.

INDUSTRY

Web Excursion

2. Whether through satire, partisan rhetoric, or sheer entertainment value, media personalities have increasing influence on how consumers receive and perceive the news. Visit the Web pages of Howard Stern, www.howardstern .com,* Rush Limbaugh, www.rushlimbaugh.com* and Jon Stewart, www .comedycentral.com/tv_shows/ds/,* and compare how each personality delivers today's top stories. Then visit a general news site such as www.cnn.com or www.latimes.com and search for the same stories. How does the presentation differ? Compile a brief report on your findings.

CONTROVERSIES

Web Excursion

3. The legal cases of O.J. Simpson, Kobe Bryant, and Michael Jackson turned into entertainment events rather than news stories. Pick a current news event based on a legal case and search sites such as www.accesshollywood.com, www.nightline.com, www.extra.com, www.mtv.com, www.cnn.com and www.latimes.com.* Compare and contrast how these news outlets present the story. If you were a news director at a newsmagazine such as *Nightline* or an entertainment show such as *Access Hollywood,* how would you decide to handle the story? Explain when and why a story should be considered news or entertainment.

Media World DVD Excursions

4. View track 10, *Journalism Students Free Wrongly Accused Death Row Inmate* (from NBC News Archive). Northwestern University students practice civic journalism each semester in Professor David Protess's class by looking into actual—and often controversial—death-row cases. Using this story as an example, answer the following questions: What is civic journalism? What other ways could a journalism class practice civic journalism?

5. View track 4.4, *Issues: A Pretty Face.* This segment explores gender politics in the world of broadcast news. Do you believe most people are more likely to watch a station with a young, attractive anchor team as opposed to a graying-yet-credible cast? How does this contribute to the entertainment trend of television news?

ONLINE LEARNING CENTER WWW.MHHE.COM/RODMAN2

You may access these and additional Web excursions at the Online Learning Center for the book (www.mhhe.com/rodman2). Visit the student portion of this Web site to also access the *Interactive Timeline of Mass Media Milestones,* chapter highlights, self quizzes, and recommended readings, movies, and documentaries for this chapter.

*Some Web site addresses may change. When they do, please search for the Web site by name or topic on your favorite search engine.

Public Relations
The Image Industry

12

Chapter Highlights

HISTORY: The history of public relations extends far into antiquity, long before the practice was called public relations.

INDUSTRY: Public relations has a profound influence on the news you read, the products you buy, and the laws that govern your behavior. In this chapter we look at some of the activities, functions, and tools of this industry.

CONTROVERSIES: Disagreements between public relations practitioners and their critics include concerns about the ethics of certain tactics; the lack of attribution for public relations materials in some news reports; and accountability, the question of who polices the industry and guards against ethical abuses.

Virtue or Villainy?

It started with a speech by President George W. Bush, in which he said that immigration laws needed to be reformed, and that he thought some temporary workers should be allowed to apply for citizenship. Although he never said the word *amnesty*, that's what immigration opponents heard, and forgiveness for illegal aliens is an idea that sets them into action.

Conservative talk-show hosts were suddenly railing against what they called the invasion of illegal workers across the border. John Kobylt of *The John and Ken Show* on KFI–AM in Los Angeles explained: "That speech, where the president announced he was for amnesty, really

Hundreds of thousands of marchers gathered in Los Angeles because of the public relations tactics of local disc jockeys.

set us off. Our listeners savaged their congressmen with calls and e-mails, and it was running 1,000 to 1 against Bush's proposal."[1]

Hearings were called in both the House and the Senate to examine the issue, and reporters observed that those hearings had "no actual purpose except to promote visions of the immigrants as action figures of either incredible virtue or inestimable villainy."[2] The Senate came up with a proposed law that would allow illegal immigrants to obtain legal status, and eventually citizenship, by working for six years, paying a fine, undergoing a background check, and learning English. Opponents immediately denounced the idea as amnesty, and a citizen army known as the Minutemen staged a "border action" near Tucson, drawing a few hundred volunteers in pickups and RVs, armed chiefly with lawn chairs and binoculars. They were trailed by hundreds of reporters from around the world who were drawn to a story of Wild West cowboys and aliens.

In the House, Representative James Sensenbrenner, a longtime advocate for stricter immigration controls, proposed a law that would turn all illegal immigrants into felons and criminalize aid to them by welfare or church workers. Immigrants and their sup-

porters sprang into action. Web sites such as Immigrant Solidarity called for protest action, but the real action came from ethnic radio. Spanish-language disc jockeys took a page from their conservative colleagues and rallied their audiences. In Los Angeles, Eduardo Sotelo, who goes by the name El Piolín (Tweety Bird), and Ricardo Sánchez, known as El Mandril (the Baboon), met with other disc jockeys and protest organizers to figure out how to help the movement. Their subsequent broadcasts help turn out 500,000 immigrants and their supporters at a Los Angeles rally in March 2006.

Organizers then called for a national protest for May 1. They called it "A Day without Immigrants," and asked those opposed to tighter restrictions on immigration, including the immigrants themselves, to flex their economic muscle by boycotting all aspects of commerce, including work and school. The DJs urged their audience members to remain nonviolent. They told them to carry American flags and dress in white to symbolize peace.

In Chicago, the protesters marched through the streets carrying signs that read, "We're not terrorists" and "We build your homes." In New York, marchers formed a human chain at exactly

12:16 PM to mark the exact time that the Sensenbrenner bill passed the House. In Los Angeles, 200,000 marched to City Hall on Monday morning, and 400,000 marched along the city's Wilshire Corridor on Monday evening. In San Francisco, 55,000 people banged on drums and chanted in Spanish, "We are united." Similar demonstrations occurred in Washington, Las Vegas, Miami, Atlanta, Denver, Phoenix, New Orleans, Milwaukee, and dozens of other cities. In total, there were millions of participants.

But organizers on the other side of the issue were not done. An online forum, the Send-a-Brick Project, organized its followers to send some 10,000 bricks to Congress as a way to emphasize the benefits of building a wall along the border with Mexico. As one congressional staffer noted: "Given the approval ratings of Congress these days, I guess we should all be grateful the bricks are coming through the mail, not the window."[3]

The immigration issue has always polarized America. It will probably continue to do so in the future. As it does, those who fight on either side probably won't recognize their actions as public relations strategies, but that is what they are.

Defining Public Relations

Public relations, commonly called PR (although some practitioners object to the shortened label as undignified), is a controversial profession. It is often referred to as the image industry, because its professionals try to improve how their clients are viewed by the public. Critics feel that public relations works to make an unworthy client (or politician) palatable to the public, but practitioners insist that public relations tactics are used every day for honest and worthwhile purposes.

Public relations is defined as the art or science of establishing and promoting a favorable relationship with the public. Public relations is different from advertising, which consists only of paid messages from an identified sponsor. Public relations and advertising are both persuasive endeavors, however, and they work together in what is known as **integrated marketing.** A professional in the field would add that public relations includes all of a client's activities that help that client maintain a beneficial relationship with its various publics. *Publics,* as a plural, is also an important distinction for public relations practitioners.

There are many publics, generally categorized as either internal or external. **Internal publics** are those within the client's organization; they might include employees, stockholders, and members. Public relations people often handle employee newsletters, annual reports for stockholders, or mem-

CONSIDER THIS

If you wanted to protest something on your campus, how would you go about it?

public relations
All the activities that maintain a beneficial relationship between an organization and its various publics.

integrated marketing
Public relations and advertising working together.

internal publics
Public relations term for groups inside the client's organization.

Public relations has a profound influence on the news you read and the products you buy.

ber benefits. **External publics** are those outside the client's organization, including the community, the news media, customers, voters, and legislators. Public relations professionals handle news releases, special events, and lobbying efforts for these publics. This chapter looks at how public relations activities seek to influence the opinions of one or more of these publics. As you will see, public relations has a profound influence on the news you read, the products you buy, the public officials who are elected, and even the laws that are passed. The first place to go for an understanding of this field is its history.

external publics
Public relations term for groups outside the client's organization.

A Brief History *of Public Relations*

Public relations has played a part in every historical epoch, including those of the American Revolution, the Industrial Revolution, and two World Wars. During its history, public relations grew from being rather crude attempts to aggrandize a ruler's accomplishments to being the full-service communication industry it is today. Now, new media and globalization are again changing the face of public relations. The story of this industry begins, however, long before the term *public relations* was coined.

American patriots used a variety of slogans and symbols to gain public support for the American Revolutionary War. Both are evident in this "Don't Tread on Me" flag of 1775.

PRECURSORS OF PUBLIC RELATIONS

People have always had opinions, and other people have always tried to influence those opinions. The ancient Greeks hired teachers of rhetoric called Sophists to help fight their verbal battles in public forums. Sophists were trained to argue on any side of an issue, and were paid well to do so, acting as the lobbyists of their day.[4] Roman emperors hired writers to publish news reports that were thinly disguised promotions of their achievements and qualifications to lead. Ancient rulers all over the world employed spies whose job it was to keep in touch with public opinion and to spread rumors favorable to the sovereign.

Public Relations Activities in Early America

Since the term had not yet been coined, Sir Walter Raleigh didn't know he was using public relations techniques in 1584 when he persuaded settlers to come to Roanoke Island, Virginia. The island was mostly swampland, but Raleigh's descriptions of it, sent back to England and published in early newsletters, made it sound like a paradise. In fact, many of the early settlers to America came as the result of a campaign by the Virginia Company that offered 50 acres of free land to those who brought groups to the new colony.

Public relations activities were a major part of the American Revolution. Loyalist groups vehemently opposed independence, and the great majority of the people were indifferent to the cause. The patriots used a variety of public relations techniques to gain public support for the war. The Boston Tea Party of 1773 was a staged event that, like the sensationalized reports of the Boston Massacre, was designed to garner publicity and crystallize public opinion. The patriots also used easily recognizable symbols, such as the liberty tree flag, and emotion-arousing slogans, such as "Taxation without representation is tyranny," to get their points across.

After the revolution, the people of the newly minted United States had to be convinced that they should adopt a constitutional democracy as their form of government. Alexander Hamilton, James Madison, and John Jay's series of articles, known as the Federalist Papers (see Chapter 4), were successful in persuading Americans to ratify the Constitution. Today scholars call the Federalist Papers "history's finest public relations job."[5]

> **What was the role of public relations in the American Revolution and the ratification of the U.S. Constitution?**

SELF QUIZ

Press Agentry

In the new democracy, freedom of speech and free enterprise combined to encourage quick-witted people, from sideshow barkers to Broadway press agents, to come up with original, creative, and sometimes outrageous ways to publicize their livelihoods. **Press agents** worked to generate publicity for their clients, with the main objective of having their clients featured (in a positive way) in newspapers. The dramatic and impressive means they used to generate publicity was known as **hype.**

press agents
People who work to generate publicity for a client.

hype
Dramatic publicity techniques.

Barnum and the Art of Hype

Hype reached a zenith with the work of Phineas T. Barnum, who began his career as a showman in 1835, at the age of 25. One of his first exploits was to promote an elderly African American woman as the former nurse of George Washington. He planted stories in the press claiming that the woman was 161 years old (she was actually about half that old). To increase attendance at his show in Boston, Barnum wrote an anonymous letter to the editor of a local paper, claiming that the woman was a fraud. She was a fraud, the letter said, not because she was too young to have worked for the Washingtons, but because she was actually a robot, animated through springs and pulleys. Attendance soared as people came to see the technological wonder of an automated person.

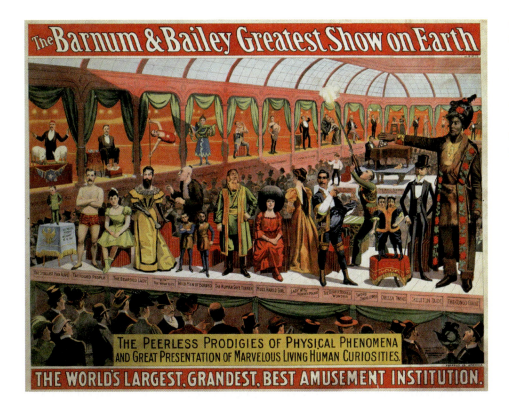

Everything P. T. Barnum did was hyped, as exemplified in the slogan for the circus that still bears his name: "The Greatest Show on Earth." The Barnum Circus was absorbed by James A. Bailey, and then the Ringling Brothers, after Barnum's death. This poster is from 1898.

Barnum promoted the marriage of one of his attractions, the midget Tom Thumb, as one of the events of the century. He sold people on the concerts of Jenny Lind, the "Swedish Nightingale," by making her opening nights around the country charity events. Everything he did was hyped, as exemplified in the slogan for his circus: "The Greatest Show on Earth."

Public Relations and the Frontier

Land speculators helped build the American West by using public relations techniques. These speculators enticed people west in the 1800s with glowing reports of how fertile the land was and how cooperative the natives were with newcomers. Railroads especially encouraged westward migration to generate customers for their services.

Throughout the 1800s, press agents publicized many of the commercial and political figures of their day. Some of these figures are legends today, such as Buffalo Bill, who had touring shows featuring the Sioux medicine man Sitting Bull and sharpshooter Annie Oakley.

Andrew Jackson and Political Public Relations

Another frontier hero, Andrew Jackson, won the presidential election of 1828 by appealing to the common man through public relations tactics. Known as "Old Hickory" from his military days,[6] Jackson had an aide who essentially served as a press secretary, although no such title existed at the time. The aide sampled public opinion, advised Jackson about it, and wrote his speeches so that the candidate's rough-hewn ideas would make sense to the public at large. After the election the aide also acted as an advance agent on Jackson's trips, giving local newspaper editors prewritten, complimentary articles about the president. He would then purchase reprints of these articles and circulate them to other editors. Jackson eventually built up a

Henry Ford standing beside his famous racer 999 with Barney Oldfield at the tiller. Both Ford and Oldfield made headlines by driving this four-cylinder, 80 horsepower racer to world speed records in 1904.

public relations machine. At one point, he had 60 full-time journalists from around the country on the White House payroll.

Publicity Agencies

The first publicity agency, the Boston Publicity Bureau, was formed in 1900, establishing press agentry as a separate business enterprise. Evidence of the fact that business leaders accepted the importance of publicity was seen in 1903, when automaker Henry Ford began entering his cars in races. Ford hired Barney Oldfield, the most famous racer of his day, to drive a Ford car at the incredible speed of more than 90 miles an hour, a feat that landed the Ford name on the front pages of every newspaper in the country. Around the same time, President Theodore Roosevelt was garnering publicity through news conferences, interviews, and presidential tours. Roosevelt viewed the White House as a bully pulpit for his views on social reform, antitrust actions, and the concept of national parks, and was said to rule the country from the headlines of its newspapers.

When was the first publicity agency founded?

PUBLIC RELATIONS AS A PROFESSION

Public relations emerged as a profession at the beginning of the 20th century, when businesses began to recognize the benefits of aligning themselves with the public interest. During much of the 19th century, business attitudes were best summarized by the railroad magnate William Henry Vanderbilt: "Let the public be damned." Business secrecy was the norm. The founders of huge American industries, who were becoming known as robber barons, did not want to publicize their exploitation of both labor and natural resources. Their secrecy was foiled, however, by the muckrakers, the turn-of-the-century reporters who conducted investigative journalism for social reform (see Chapter 5). Newspaper and magazine stories about strikes and about possibly dangerous products, such as spoiled meat, began to interfere with business, and business leaders looked for a solution to their tarnished images.

How and when did public relations emerge as a profession?

Ivy Lee

The solution that business leaders found was Ivy Ledbetter Lee, who is widely recognized as the father of the modern public relations industry and the first public relations adviser. Like most early public relations practitioners, Lee was a newspaper person, a business reporter for Joseph Pulitzer's *New York World*. Lee quit his reporting job to run election campaigns, then opened a public relations firm. In 1906, Lee was hired by U.S. coal mine owners during a major strike.[7] His first advice to the coal owners was to talk to the press. The workers were already talking to reporters, and they were receiving more favorable press coverage as a result. Before Lee began advising them, the mine owners were so arrogant that they even refused to talk to President Theodore Roosevelt, who was seeking to arbitrate the dispute. The most arrogant of the owners was John D. Rockefeller Jr., for whom Lee went to work in 1914 (see the Close-Up on History box).

Working with the Rockefeller family, Lee followed certain principles that he would espouse for the rest of his career. He was against corporate secrecy. He believed in being open with reporters and not trying to suppress the news. As he stated:

> In brief, our plan is, frankly and openly, on behalf of business concerns and public institutions, to supply the press and the public of the United States prompt and accurate information concerning subjects which it is of value and interest to the public to know about.[8]

Many contemporary scholars believe that the information that Ivy Lee distributed about the Rockefellers was purposely exaggerated. Nevertheless, Lee's principles changed public relations. Because of Lee, the goal of public relations was no longer to fool the public, as P. T. Barnum and the early press agents had, or to ignore it, as the robber barons had. Lee believed that businesses should align themselves with the public interest rather than insisting that the public interest align itself with business. While he believed in image building, he also believed that corporations' performance should fit the image that their public relations professionals built.

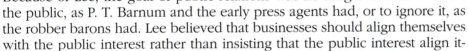

SELF QUIZ What tactics did Ivy Lee use to rehabilitate the Rockefeller image?

Public Relations Goes to War

World War I brought the U.S. government into the public relations business in a very big way. President Woodrow Wilson authorized the formation of the Committee on Public Information (CPI) in 1917 and charged it with promoting the war as "the war to end all wars," and one that would "make the world safe for democracy." The CPI was headed by George Creel, a former journalist who was known as a muckraker because he had written an exposé of Rockefeller and Ivy Lee's role in the Ludlow Massacre. Muckraker or not, Creel proved to be the consummate public relations professional, throwing himself into a national campaign to mobilize public support for the war, to encourage enlistment in the armed forces, and to promote the sale of Liberty Bonds.

Creel built up a huge organization and used a variety of techniques. The CPI held rallies featuring film stars such as Charlie Chaplin and Mary Pickford.[9] It commissioned America's foremost commercial artists to paint posters. It sent out the weekly *Bulletin for Cartoonists*, suggesting ideas and captions for patriotic editorial cartoons. The CPI's Division of Films set up a scenario department, which drafted story outlines that

Douglas Fairbanks, Mary Pickford, and Charles Chaplin promoting Liberty Bonds during WWI.

Rebuilding the Rockefeller Image

Ivy Ledbetter Lee, the father of modern public relations, faced his greatest challenge in rebuilding the Rockefeller image. In the early 1900s, following several exposés, such as Ida Tarbell's *History of the Standard Oil Company*, the Rockefeller name was much despised. The Rockefellers, like most of the other industrialists of the period, believed that business and social responsibility were two separate and unrelated things.[1] Business was cutthroat; social responsibility involved charity. Thus, they would give millions to institutions such as orphanages and churches but still squeeze every penny out of their labor force, allowing their workers to toil in dangerous conditions for little pay. Most coal miners were forced to live in company towns and shop in company stores. They were paid so little that miners with families often had to spend all their pay at the company store. Their hard work was doing little more than keeping their families alive.

In response to these conditions, 9,000 mine workers at Rockefeller's Ludlow, Colorado, mines went on strike in 1913. They demanded recognition for their union as well as higher wages and improved working conditions. The strike went on for several months, and the miners were evicted from their company-owned housing. They lived in tents as they continued their fight. Company guards attacked the miners' camp on April 20, 1914. The guards fired repeatedly into the tents and then, while the miners and their families huddled inside, the guards doused the tents with kerosene and set them on fire. In the attack, 21 people were killed and 100 were wounded.[2] The dead included 11 children and two women. A 10-day civil war ensued, and 19 more people were killed before federal troops were called in to restore order.

With what came to be known as the Ludlow Massacre, public respect for the Rockefellers reached a new low. John D. Rockefeller Jr., the son of the man who founded the Standard Oil empire, had been in charge of the mines. Rockefeller denied having anything to do with the killings, but reporters found evidence that he was at least aware of the company's tactics. Crowds gathered outside Rockefeller's man-

The Committee on Public Information promoted World War I to the American people. This poster advertised a film produced by the CPI's Division of Film in 1918.

were sent to the studios to become films. Community leaders were enlisted to become Four-Minute Men, volunteers who presented brief speeches at local gatherings and movie theaters. It was the first time that a public relations campaign had as its objective to saturate the entire fabric of public perception, and it worked.

THE INDUSTRY MATURES

Largely because of the success of the CPI, public relations as a profession grew significantly in the years following World War I. One business analyst of the day stated: "The war taught us the power of propaganda. Now when we have anything to sell the American people, we know how to sell it."[10]

Colorado State Militia machine gunners and hired strike breakers overlook the tent camp of the miners and their families at Ludlow, Colorado, in 1914. When the militia attacked, 21 people, including 11 children, died.

sion, screaming that he should be lynched. It was into this harrowing situation that Ivy Lee was called for damage control.

Corporate arrogance made Lee's work extremely difficult. Rockefeller and his business associates simply refused to meet the miners' demands. Once tempers had cooled, Lee did manage to persuade Rockefeller to visit the miners and their families. He had the mogul eat in the miners' dining hall, swing a pickax in their mines, have a beer with them after work, and even dance with their wives—all in front of the news photographers Lee had invited. The positive articles that resulted from these visits made Rockefeller more popular with both the miners and the public. In the end, Rockefeller even granted the workers a raise and some increased benefits, although a union was still out of the question.

Lee's success with John D. Rockefeller Jr. led the family to hire him to improve the image of other Rockefellers as well. Lee publicized their charitable contributions, which were substantial and had been given without any public notice. Lee is also credited with suggesting to John D. Rockefeller Sr. that he hand out dimes to children he encountered on the street. Lee himself said that this was a long-standing practice of the old man, and he simply alerted newspaper reporters and photographers to it.

[1] See, for example, Ron Chernow, *Titan: The Life of John D. Rockefeller, Sr.* (New York: Random House, 1998).

[2] The many accounts of this massacre include several different numbers of those killed. This number is cited in Vincent Tompkins, *American Decades 1910–1919* (Detroit: Gale Research, 1996), p. 229.

Edward and Doris Bernays

After World War I, one couple, working together, helped build the field of public relations by proving how effective its tactics could be. Edward Bernays was a former press agent and one of the chairmen of the CPI. His wife, Doris Fleischman Bernays, was a well-known writer. The Bernayses had a genius for getting their clients' interpretations of things across to the public. They helped the brewing industry establish beer as "the beverage of moderation." For Dixie cups, they founded the Committee for the Study and Promotion of the Sanitary Dispensing of Food and Drink, which prompted people to dispose of cups after one use. They extolled the virtues of a hearty breakfast for a bacon processor, and they connected smoking and slimness for women with the invitation "Reach for a Lucky instead of a sweet."

Although historians are beginning to appreciate Doris's contributions today, at the time Edward received most of the credit. He coined the term *public relations counsel* in his landmark book, *Crystallizing Public Opinion*, published in 1923. He also taught the first university course in public relations, at New York University, that year.

SELF QUIZ **What techniques did the CPI use to promote World War I?**

Getting Women to Smoke

Perhaps because Edward was a nephew of the famed psychoanalyst Sigmund Freud, he and Doris based their work on psychology, especially on

The Torches of Freedom parade was a scandal, but it led to the kind of publicity that Edward and Doris Bernays wanted.

the concept of the unconscious mind. Hired by the American Tobacco Company to increase the sales of Lucky Strike cigarettes, the Bernayses reasoned that smoking, which was considered strictly a man's privilege at the time, especially in public, might be seen as a symbol of liberation by women. This gave them the idea for a "Torches of Freedom March." They hired 10 attractive debutantes and instructed them to light up Lucky Strikes at a dramatic moment in New York City's Easter parade in 1929. They hired photographers to take pictures of the event, which they then distributed to newspapers nationwide. The next day the event made front-page headlines across the country and prompted a debate over whether women should be allowed to smoke in public. According to some critics, this one event helped change the social context of tobacco use.

Making Coolidge Cool

President Calvin Coolidge was another one of the Bernayses' clients. Coolidge was perceived by Americans to be a bit of a grump. To soften this image, the Bernayses allowed a select group of photographers to take pictures of the dour president with various celebrities, provided they would use the Bernayses' headlines to go with the pictures. A photo of Coolidge with star entertainer Al Jolson read, "Jolson Makes President Laugh for the First Time in Public."[11]

Light's Golden Jubilee

The Bernayses' masterpiece was the 1929 event called Light's Golden Jubilee. Hired by General Electric to make a big splash out of the 50th anniversary of Thomas Edison's invention of the electric lightbulb, Edward and Doris Bernays made sure that the event drew worldwide attention. The event was to take place in Dearborn, Michigan, and the Bernayses publicized it nationally for months in advance. As a result, groups of people across the country prepared to take part. Mayors and governors issued proclamations; universities offered special lectures; schools, libraries, and museums put on special exhibitions. Most magazines and newspapers ran stories and pictures. George M. Cohan, the most famous of the Tin Pan Alley composers, wrote a song, "Edison—Miracle Man," and the sheet music was distributed around the world. The U.S. Post Office even issued a commemorative stamp honoring Edison.

The big night arrived October 21. Many of the world's utilities shut off their power for one minute. Then, in Dearborn, in a replica of his first laboratory, accompanied by dignitaries including President Herbert Hoover, Henry Ford, John D. Rockefeller Jr., and Adolph Ochs of the *New York Times,* a frail 82-year-old Thomas Edison switched on a replica of his first incandescent lightbulb. At this signal, people all over the world turned on a single light at the same time. The resulting publicity for General Electric was as huge as the event.

The Great Depression

The Roaring Twenties gave way to the stock market crash of 1929 and the Great Depression. Public relations played a role in this period also. Large corporations, seen as part of the cause of the country's economic problems, hired public relations counselors to improve their image. They began community programs that included sponsoring scholarships; repairing schools; and building new parks and playgrounds, as well as cleaning up old ones.

The biggest role for public relations during this period, however, was selling President Franklin D. Roosevelt's New Deal programs as a way to lift the U.S. economy out of the depression. The government combined CPI-style posters and local speeches with radio ads and Roosevelt's own fireside chats to drum up support for federal tax-supported programs such as the Works Progress Administration (WPA), which put unemployed people to work building roads, maintaining parks, and completing other government projects.

SELF QUIZ What role did Edward and Doris Bernays play in public relations' becoming a profession?

World War II

World War II brought the U.S. government even further into the public relations business. To promote the war effort, Roosevelt established the Office of War Information (OWI) in 1942 and appointed Elmer Davis to head it. Davis was a radio news commentator and had been a *New York Times* reporter and a novelist. He was extremely successful at government public relations, as the OWI went on to promote war bonds, victory gardens, work productivity, and the rationing of food, clothing, and gasoline. Central to the OWI's work was warning the public to keep quiet about weapons development in the factories they worked in and information about troop movements that they might get from family members in the military. This campaign featured the slogan "Loose lips sink ships." The OWI's film division enlisted directors such as Frank Capra to produce documentaries and feature films about the army and the U.S. cause. Davis also established the Voice of America, the government shortwave radio service that was to carry news of the war around the world.

After the war the government's public relations operation was not shut down as it had been after World War I. President Dwight Eisenhower converted the OWI into the United States Information Agency (USIA), whose mission was to "tell America's story abroad." The USIA took over the Voice of America and all the government's international public relations efforts, including films and printed material to be distributed at American embassies overseas. This effort was seen as essential because the Soviet Union, one of America's most important allies in the war, was now seen as a serious threat to democracy.

The Birth of the PRSA

Although the USIA was popular with the American public, many critics began to take a closer look at the work of public relations professionals in U.S. businesses in the postwar years. Most of these critics were troubled by practices they considered unethical, such as the planting of anonymous information in news reports. To combat the negative impression of the industry, a group of practitioners got together in 1947 and founded the Public Relations Society of America (PRSA). The goals of the PRSA were to promote professional standards and to put forth a positive image. To that end, society members adopted the industry's first code of ethics in 1950. This code includes guidelines such as these: "A member shall conduct his or her professional life in accord with the public interest," and "A member shall exemplify high standards of honesty and integrity while carrying out dual obligations to a client or employer and to the democratic process." The complete current code can be found at the PRSA Web site (www.prsa.org/profstd.html). Although the PRSA helped improve the industry's image, problems still persist; these are discussed in the Controversies section of this chapter.

SELF QUIZ What was the goal of the founding of the PRSA?

The FBI's Ten Most Wanted Fugitives program is a classic public relations success.

Postwar Era

Public relations expanded during the postwar boom of the 1950s and 1960s. One classic success of the era began when a reporter asked the FBI to name the toughest of their most wanted fugitives. After the story generated a huge amount of positive publicity, the FBI started its Ten Most Wanted Fugitives program. Of the 458 names that have appeared on the list since its inception, 429 have been apprehended, including 137 nabbed as a direct result of tips from the public. The list was immortalized in numerous movies, the popular *Dick Tracy* comic strip, the ABC radio network program *FBI, This Week,* and the Fox network TV show *America's Most Wanted: America Fights Back.*

The rest of the 1960s was a time of great social divisions and unrest, an era of protest that saw many demonstrators using public relations tactics. Protestors against the war in Vietnam, for example, would make sure that media representatives were in attendance at their rallies, often timing their demonstrations to ensure their appearance on the evening TV news. A common chant at these rallies was "The whole world is watching."

THE CHANGING FACE OF PUBLIC RELATIONS

The character of the public relations industry began to change during the postwar years. Some people used public relations techniques to promote racial and ethnic equality. The industry itself expanded worldwide and began to embrace new technologies.

Public Relations and Diversity

In the late 1950s and early 1960s, organizations such as the National Association for the Advancement of Colored People (NAACP) and the Congress of Racial Equality (CORE) fought to secure constitutional rights that were being denied to minorities by local governments, including voting rights, access to public accommodations, and education.[12] Many people resist using the term

Civil rights organizations had a public relations problem: They had to consider how two publics—blacks and whites—would interpret their actions.

public relations to describe the activities of these groups, because the groups followed the Indian nationalist and spiritual leader Mahatma Gandhi's principles of passive resistance and nonviolent confrontation more than the Bernayses' strategies for gaining publicity. Still, the problems and the solutions that civil rights groups found were very much in the realm of public relations. These groups had image problems. Many whites viewed them as radical troublemakers, while some blacks viewed them with suspicion because they worked within the "white" court system. Because of this, the groups had to consider how two publics—blacks and whites—would interpret their actions. This was one reason that civil rights organizations stressed nonviolent forms of protest such as marches, picket lines, and sit-ins. Organizations trained their members to endure all manner of physical and verbal abuse without counterattack. The composure of these demonstrators in the face of violence against them won much sympathy and admiration for the movement.

Public Relations' Global Expansion

Nations have increasingly begun to use public relations to improve their image in other countries. Often this is done for business purposes. Countries with expanding economies, such as South Korea and some of the new democracies of the former Soviet Union, have hired public relations firms to improve their status in the eyes of international investors. Companies have also hired public relations firms to teach their personnel about foreign cultures and business practices to avoid committing embarrassing cross-cultural gaffes.

Often, though, international public relations is a matter of national security. The terrorist attacks of September 11, 2001, awakened many Americans to the fact that they had a bad image in countries that were predominantly Arab and Islamic. The home-grown media in those countries would portray the United States in extremely negative terms, and even satellite television services such as Aljazeera, which prided itself on its objectivity, seemed to find it difficult to present the U.S. side of any story.

American officials recognized the need to address anti-U.S. sentiment in the Arab media. In 2004 the United States built Alhurra, a slickly produced Arab-language news and entertainment cable television network that is beamed by satellite from the United States to the Middle East. Alhurra, whose name translates to English as "The Free One," was designed to be a fair and objective competitor to Aljazeera. Two years earlier the United States had established an Arabic-language radio service known as Radio Sawa, and the Farsi-language Radio Farda, both of which are youth-oriented stations that mix Western and Eastern pop with considerable success, building an audience of 15 million listeners throughout the Middle East.

The U.S. government also uses public relations in print media in the Middle East. It sponsors *Hi,* a lifestyle magazine geared toward Iraqi elites, to "build bridges of communication" between Arabs and Americans. *Hi* has a target audience of Arab men and women ages 18 to 35, and has been generally well received by its intended readership. Other attempts have been less successful. An Arabic video produced in 2003 by the State Department highlighting Muslims living prosperously in the United States was met with skepticism by Arab viewers. Critics felt that all these forms of governmental public relations lost credibility by stressing the similarities between Arabs and Americans while ignoring the real policy issues that divide them.

The problems faced by civil rights groups were very much in the realm of public relations, and their solutions involved nonviolent protest. Here, the Reverend Martin Luther King Jr. waves to participants in the March on Washington, August 28, 1963.

SELF QUIZ What public relations tactics were used during the civil rights movement?

CONSIDER THIS

Most critics contend that U.S. public relations efforts in Arab and Islamic countries have been largely unsuccessful. If you were an adviser to the president, what would you suggest doing to improve these results?

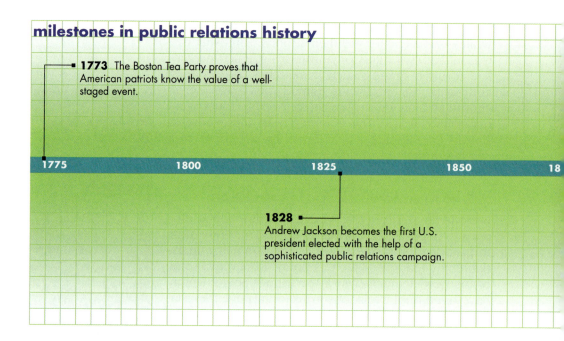

milestones in public relations history

1773 The Boston Tea Party proves that American patriots know the value of a well-staged event.

1775   1800   1825   1850   18

1828 Andrew Jackson becomes the first U.S. president elected with the help of a sophisticated public relations campaign.

The U.S. government sponsors *Hi* magazine to improve its image in the Middle East.

Embracing New Technology

Historically, public relations practitioners have always been brought in to help companies harness the potential of new technology to improve their relationship with their publics. This was true with specialized magazines, radio, and television, and is especially true with today's technology. Satellite communications, for example, have been a staple of public relations practitioners practically from the moment they became commercially available. When someone poisoned Tylenol capsules in 1982, for example, the president and other officials of the drug's manufacturer, Johnson & Johnson, were able to sit down for a satellite teleconference, a news conference in which newsmakers and reporters in different locations are joined by a satellite hookup.

A **teleconference**—also known within the public relations industry as a videoconference or a satellite media tour (SMT)—allows a business executive to be interviewed by dozens of reporters in different parts of the country, all from one studio that the executive's company controls. Tylenol's teleconference involved 600 reporters in 30 cities. Company officials were able to explain to the reporters the extraordinary precautions that Johnson & Johnson was taking to protect consumers. This satellite feed was downloaded to TV stations nationwide, and the Tylenol brand was brought back from the brink of ruin.

The industry has embraced the Internet just as passionately. Politicians routinely use the Internet now for raising funds and mobilizing supporters. In fact, a savvy use of the Internet was believed to be the reason candidate Howard Dean enjoyed an early surge in the race for the 2004 Democratic presidential nomination. A wide variety of businesses are becoming increas-

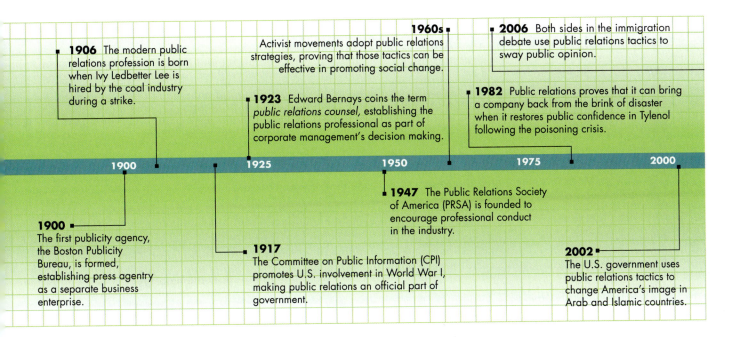

1906 The modern public relations profession is born when Ivy Ledbetter Lee is hired by the coal industry during a strike.

1960s Activist movements adopt public relations strategies, proving that those tactics can be effective in promoting social change.

1923 Edward Bernays coins the term *public relations counsel,* establishing the public relations professional as part of corporate management's decision making.

2006 Both sides in the immigration debate use public relations tactics to sway public opinion.

1982 Public relations proves that it can bring a company back from the brink of disaster when it restores public confidence in Tylenol following the poisoning crisis.

| 1900 | 1925 | 1950 | 1975 | 2000 |

1900 The first publicity agency, the Boston Publicity Bureau, is formed, establishing press agentry as a separate business enterprise.

1917 The Committee on Public Information (CPI) promotes U.S. involvement in World War I, making public relations an official part of government.

1947 The Public Relations Society of America (PRSA) is founded to encourage professional conduct in the industry.

2002 The U.S. government uses public relations tactics to change America's image in Arab and Islamic countries.

ingly concerned with their online reputations, or what some public relations professionals call word of mouse. The box office success of the movie *My Big Fat Greek Wedding,* for example, was attributed to multiple favorable reviews on Web sites, which may have helped the film compensate for a small advertising budget. There are now several sites designed entirely for online press release distribution. The most well-known are Business Wire (www.businesswire.com), and PR Newswire (www.prnewswire.com). Interested journalists, students, and consumers can consult the sites and sign up for e-mail alerts.

New technologies, especially those associated with the Internet, have been a mixed blessing for the field of public relations. On the one hand, a company can go directly to the public with information it wants it to have. On the other hand, the company's critics have the same kind of access. The fashion designer Tommy Hilfiger had to respond to rumors on the Web that he had made racist remarks about blacks and Asians. Several sites on the Web take aim at companies from Ford to Microsoft, complaining about their products and services. As one industry insider points out, this provides "obscure organizations and even disgruntled individuals with the ability to publish whatever they please, without even the limited accountability of the mainstream media."[13]

teleconference
A news conference in which newsmakers and reporters in various locations are joined by a satellite or an Internet hookup; also called a videoconference or a satellite media tour (SMT).

Understanding Today's Public Relations *Industry*

The public relations industry has a profound influence on the news you read, the products you buy, and even the laws that govern your behavior. It is also an industry in which those with top-notch communication skills and training can make their fortunes. Sometimes, those fortunes can even be made while doing some good for society. To help you understand this industry, we first look at the scope of public relations as it is practiced today. We then cover the industry's activities, strategies, and tools.

Featured Campaign

The *Media World* DVD that accompanies this book (track 6) takes a look at the way a combined public relations–advertising agency develops its various campaigns.

FACT FILE 12.1

Top Public Relations Agencies by Number of Employees

Rank	Number of Employees		
1		3000	**Weber Shandwick** • New York • www.webershandwick.com
2		2000	**Fleishman-Hillard** • St. Louis, MO • www.fleishman.com
3		1500	**Ketchum** • New York • www.ketchum.com
4		1096	**Hill & Knowlton** • New York • www.hillandknowlton.com
5		978	**Ogilvy Public Relations Worldwide** • New York • www.ogilvypr.com
6		950	**Manning Selvage & Lee** • New York • www.mslpr.com
7		577	**Waggener Edstrom** • Bellevue, WA • www.wagged.com
8		450	**Golin/Harris** • Chicago • www.golinharris.com
9		400	**APCO Worldwide** • Washington, DC • www.apcoworldwide.com

= 100 employees

Other top agencies include **Porter Novelli** • New York • www.porternovelli.com and **Burson-Marsteller** • New York • www.burson-marsteller.com, but neither firm discloses their number of employees. Both firms explain that they retain this data because of the Sarbanes-Oxley Act of 2002, which makes Chief Executive Officers responsible for the accuracy of the financial information they disclose. Source: Council of Public Relations firms at www.prfirms.org, company Web sites, as listed, and interviews with company executives, October 2006.

THE SCOPE OF PUBLIC RELATIONS

At the beginning of this chapter, we defined *public relations* as all of a client's activities that maintain a beneficial relationship with several publics. As that definition suggests, public relations encompasses a wide scope. Public relations practitioners work as individual consultants, as part of large independent agencies, and as part of in-house shops for corporations like AT&T and McDonald's. The in-house shop might be given a title such as Office of Corporate Communications, Community Affairs, Public Information, or Publicity and Promotion. The largest independent agencies are listed in Fact File 12.1.

There are more than 6,000 public relations firms in the United States, and four out of five large companies and trade organizations have their own public relations departments.[14] This represents impressive growth in recent decades. Around 35,000 people worked in the field in 1960; that number had grown to 500,000 by the year 2007. In 1986, for the first time, more than half of all public relations practitioners were women, although most of those women did not hold upper management positions; their place in the profession has been referred to as the "velvet ghetto." The industry is also overwhelmingly white, with African Americans, Hispanics, and other minorities seriously underrepresented, especially in management positions.

The client might be an individual, such as a celebrity or a politician, but it is more likely to be an organization in business, government, or nonprofit public service. A small business might have a budget for advertising only until it hits a snag that needs a public relations solution. Then the business hires a consultant. A medium-sized business might use a public relations agency; a large corporation will have its own public relations division but will hire an agency for special projects.

FIGURE 12.1 Public Relations Activities

Research	Counseling	Communication
Define problems. Identify publics. Test concepts. Monitor the progress of campaigns. Evaluate campaign effectiveness.	Advise management in decision making. Suggest policies for internal and external communication. Train personnel to promote a positive corporate image.	With internal publics: those within organizations, including employees and stockholders. With external publics: those outside organizations, including the community, news, media, customers, and legislators.

FIGURE 12.1 Public Relations Activities

Public relations is a broad field that includes a wide range of activities. Research, counseling, and communication, however, are the three primary activities of the industry.

As history makes clear, governments use public relations all the time. Nonprofit agencies such as educational institutions, public hospitals, charities, professional associations, and labor unions also need to use public relations. Often a nonprofit agency uses public relations for its fund-raising efforts. It might also use it to fulfill its mission, as when a school uses public relations techniques to convince parents that its new program in sex education is worthwhile.

PUBLIC RELATIONS ACTIVITIES

Public relations is a broad field that includes a wide range of activities. The primary activities of public relations practitioners can be divided into the categories of research, counseling, and communication (see Figure 12.1).

Research: Finding Answers to the Client's Questions

Research occurs throughout the public relations process. It is used to define problems, to identify publics, to test concepts, to monitor the progress of a campaign, and to evaluate its effectiveness when it is over.

Edward Bernays was adamant about public relations being a science as well as an art. He defined a public relations practitioner as "an applied social scientist who advises a client or employer on the social attitudes and actions to take to win the support of the publics upon whom his or her or its viability depends."[15] When Bernays stressed applied social science in this way, he meant that public relations practitioners should use the most up-to-date scientific methods possible, including attitude testing, focus groups, and statistical analysis. In fact, most public relations agencies today employ social scientists, although much of their research is less than scientific. Nike, for example, hires "cool-hunters" to ask teenagers what the next hot sneaker will be. Others use observational research to discreetly watch prospective customers where they shop. In a car dealership, they will note what questions consumers ask and whether buyers appear timid or confident. When one study found that customers saw cars as art objects, Lexus and Mercedes made that a major point in their public relations campaigns. When another study found that people think of their mail carriers as friends, the U.S. Postal Service worked that theme into its campaign to improve its image.

Often, public relations practitioners will make their research public. This makes the research itself a public relations tactic. Several colleges and universities have increased their visibility by conducting polls that get the college's name into newspapers and onto television news reports. Marist College in Poughkeepsie, New York, has developed a name for itself with its wide variety of polls, asking such questions as "Which president do Americans most admire?" (Answer: John F. Kennedy, with Abraham Lincoln as number two.) Schools like Marist have found that polling people for views on topics like political candidates, abortion, and race relations is helping them stand out among the 5,500 U.S. colleges seeking top applicants.

Counseling: Giving the Client Advice

Public relations practitioners pride themselves as being counselors. In the business world, public relations professionals like to make the distinction that public relations is a management function rather than a marketing function. By this they mean that they serve as counselors to the top management of the company and therefore are involved in basic decision making and organizational policymaking. Public relations practitioners like to make their role proactive instead of reactive. In other words, they like management to review all policies with them before problems arise, rather than being called in to solve problems that management has already created.

For example, the American Society of Composers, Authors and Publishers (ASCAP) decided on a policy in 1997 to stop camping organizations from making free use of copyrighted songs around the campfire. When these organizations, which included the Girl Scouts and Boy Scouts of America, heard that they would now be charged a fee to sing "God Bless America" and "Happy Birthday" around the campfire, they went straight to the media, and the result was a huge amount of negative publicity for ASCAP. An ASCAP official, trying to explain the policy, told the *Wall Street Journal* that the scouts "buy paper, twine and glue for their crafts—they can pay for the music, too."[16] Public relations consultants all over the country read those words and thought, "He should have asked me first before saying that." They would have advised the official to be sensitive to how the public might perceive his statements.

Public relations practitioners like to deal with problems before they arise. When they heard the way Martha Stewart reacted to accusations of security fraud, for example, they wished she had consulted them first. Here, Stewart heads to court, where she was eventually convicted of obstruction of justice and lying to investigators.

Public relations professionals felt the same way about other public relations disasters: the Texas cattlemen's lawsuit against Oprah Winfrey for criticizing hamburger; Martha Stewart's lying to federal investigators about her stock trades, and Scope mouthwash's declaration that Rosie O'Donnell was one of the "least kissable" television talk-show hosts. In the Rosie O'Donnell case, Listerine jumped right in and told O'Donnell that it would donate $1,000 to charity for every celebrity she kissed. O'Donnell took the company up on the offer. The bit went on for weeks, with Listerine getting priceless publicity with every kiss and Scope getting more and more egg on its face.

Sometimes public relations counseling involves media training. For example, chefs who are becoming public figures because of cooking shows and best-selling books train with public relations experts to improve their image. The experts coach them in how to behave during on-camera interviews, offer grooming advice, and even arrange for voice lessons. Media trainers also teach politicians how to recite the party line and avoid direct answers to questions in on-camera interviews. For critics, media training creates what one television newsman called "an orchestrated dance where no-body gets at the truth."[17] Public relations professionals, however, say that media training is necessary if public people are to present themselves effectively when their lives are on continual media display.

Communication: Getting the Client's Message Out

The most visible part of the public relations process is communication, which is defined in the industry as the creation and distribution of messages designed to meet goals and objectives. This aspect of the public relations profession is practiced with regard to both internal and external publics. Arthur Page, who became the first public relations executive at AT&T in 1927, was a champion of strong internal public relations. For Page, good external public relations began with good word of mouth from employees. Page knew that if a reporter was looking for dirt on a company, there would be no surer place to find it than by asking a disgruntled employee. He set up a system of internal communications that enabled questions and criticisms from employees and the public to travel back up the company hierarchy to management, where they would be dealt with. News of the solutions would then travel back down the hierarchy to the employees and the public. Page also made sure that contact employees (those having direct dealings with the public) were trained in how to be helpful and polite, and he instituted several programs to enhance employee morale.

SELF QUIZ What are the general activities of public relations professionals?

As important as internal communications are, however, public relations' largest preoccupation by far is gaining the goodwill of the public through favorable publicity (see the Close-Up on Industry box). The best way to explain the various forms of external public relations communication is to look at the strategies that are used in these communications.

PUBLIC RELATIONS STRATEGIES

Public relations professionals use many different strategies, including news management, community relations, crisis management, and lobbying (see Figure 12.2).

News Management

Create and distribute messages to generate favorable publicity.

Develop and maintain contact with reporters (media relations).

Community Relations

Maintain good relations with government and community groups.

Use corporate aid and sponsorship.

Make charitable contributions on both local and national levels.

Crisis Management

Repair a client's public image following an error or accident.

Guide corporate response to an emergency.

Rehabilitate public image following a scandal.

Lobbying

Monitor government activities.

Maintain relationships with legislators.

Disseminate information to legislators supporting laws favorable to clients.

Influence legislator voting through personal contacts.

FIGURE 12.2 Public Relations Strategies These are the primary strategic functions that public relations professionals perform for their clients.

Public Relations Jobs

The Public Relations Society of America (PRSA) maintains a Web site dealing with public relations careers. Two parts of this site are of particular interest to students considering a career in public relations. The first part describes a typical day at work:

• Public relations offices are busy places; work schedules are irregular and frequently interrupted. The junior employee may answer calls for information from the press and public, work on invitation lists and details for a press conference, escort visitors and clients, help with research, write brochures, deliver releases to editorial offices, and compile media distribution lists.

• Employees will brief their management on upcoming meetings; help write reports, speeches, presentations and letters; research case histories; help produce displays and other audiovisual materials; proofread copy; select photographs for publication, arrange for holiday and other remembrances; conduct surveys and tabulate questionnaires; and work with letter shops and printers.

• Public relations programs operate against deadlines. Under such high-pressure conditions, nine-to-five schedules go out the window. Public relations executives are not tied to their desks for long periods. Meetings, community functions, business lunches, travel assignments, special speaking and writing commitments, and unscheduled work on "crisis" situations often mean long hours.

The second part of the Web site describes personal qualifications and preparation students will need for a career in public relations:

• Because public relations covers many kinds of tasks, there is no single set of "ideal" qualifications. Most people think of public relations executives as highly articulate and imaginative individuals. Yet, public relations executives themselves stress judgment

as the most important single qualification needed in their field.

• The public relations practitioner is a counselor whose advice and services are often sought when an organization faces the prospect of trouble. Therefore, it is important to develop the capacity to think analytically under pressure, to draw out necessary information, and to express persuasive practical solutions. Other qualities needed by the public relations work include:

• Imagination, for coping with present problems and anticipating future ones.

• Communication skills, with demonstrable competence in writing.

• Personal confidence, for successful face-to-face contacts with individuals and groups.

• Sensitivity to other people (simply to "like people" will not help a candidate get a job).

• Both diplomacy and a more-than-ordinary ability to place oneself in the shoes of another.

• Organizing and planning ability, applied to oneself and others.

As with many other occupations, managerial skills are invaluable for successfully climbing the public relations ladder.

Source: "Careers in Public Relations: An Overview," PRSA Web site, www.prsa.org, accessed November 2006.

Young people work in public relations around the world. Here, a young woman in Mumbai, India, gives out free samples of soy milk in an event shared by Soya Products and PETA (People for the Ethical Treatment of Animals). PETA backs soy milk as a cruelty-free drink. The green mascot is a giant "Soy Pod."

News Management: The Heart of Publicity

News management includes all the activities that public relations professionals do to get desired information about their clients into the news, and to keep undesirable information out of the news. News management techniques include publicity stunts, news hooks, media relations, government news management, leaks and trial balloons, and exclusives.

Publicity Stunts

Effective news management makes a product newsworthy. This has always been the idea behind the publicity stunt. A **publicity stunt** is any action designed to create a human interest story; many publicity stunts are outlandish or outrageous. When Justin Timberlake ripped Janet Jackson's costume during the 2004 Super Bowl halftime show, leaving her partially topless, every news organization in the country carried the story for days. The incident occurred just before Jackson released a new album.

publicity stunt
Any action designed to create a human interest story; many are outlandish or outrageous.

News Hooks

A **news hook** is the angle or approach that makes an organization's activities newsworthy. In other words, it is the viewpoint that will interest media gatekeepers in the information that the client wants to publicize. One way to give an activity an automatic news hook is to get a celebrity involved.

news hook
The angle or approach that makes information newsworthy.

Nonprofit organizations are quick to solicit the services of celebrity spokespersons: Elizabeth Taylor and Elton John for AIDS research, Daryl Hannah for environmental concerns, Kim Basinger to fight the use of animals in research.

Corporations, of course, are old hands at this game, such as when Bob Dole, the 1996 Republican presidential candidate, was chosen as the spokesperson for the anti-impotence drug Viagra. Dole's enlistment was considered such a coup that one journalist observed, "Pfizer has refined the art of publicizing a blockbuster drug . . . not unlike the way Hollywood releases a summertime action flick."[18] Top sports stars such as Michael Jordan and Tiger Woods can make tens of millions of dollars annually endorsing a single product.

The actress Daryl Hannah sat in a walnut tree at an urban farm to protect it from developers. She was eventually arrested, but her involvement brought the issue to the attention of the media.

Media Relations

Part of the art of news management is **media relations** (also called press relations, particularly when referring to the print media), the practice of developing and maintaining contact with reporters. When a public relations practitioner needs to get a press release to a news outlet, it helps if that practitioner knows a reporter personally. Reporters, for their part, have deadlines that limit their time, so they tend to appreciate help with their stories. Public relations practitioners do all they can to act as resources for reporters. That way, when reporters don't know where else to go, they will turn to the public relations agency and ask, "Do you have an expert in this area?"

media relations
The practice of developing and maintaining contact with media gatekeepers; also called press relations.

Government News Management

Governments try to manage their news coverage by controlling the flow of information to the press. In the 1990–91 Gulf War, for example, the U.S. government carefully controlled what journalists could see and report on. In the invasion of Iraq that began in 2003, the government embedded journalists with military units, hoping that they would bond with the soldiers and accept their common objectives. And the U.S. government has done only what every other country attempts to do in times of conflict—it is an inevitable truth that public relations is an integral part of every war effort. During the 1999 bombing campaign against Yugoslavia by the North Atlantic Treaty

Public relations is an integral part of every war effort.

Organization (NATO), for example, Yugoslav authorities at first kept reporters out of the Serbian province of Kosovo and away from the physical evidence of the Serbs' atrocities against civilians. But when NATO planes accidentally killed civilians, suddenly reporters were being given tours of the carnage.

Leaks and Trial Balloons

leaks
Unauthorized disclosures to the press.

Governments and corporations both try to control news through methods such as leaks. Technically, **leaks** are unauthorized disclosures to the press. In reality, leaks are often planned to publicize information without attribution to a source, as when a politician wants to throw mud at an opponent without getting himself or herself dirty. Leaks are also used to publicize information that the source is not legally permitted to make public. In 2003, for example, when a former U.S. ambassador spoke out against President George W. Bush's Iraq policies, White House officials leaked to a journalist that the ambassador's wife was an undercover agent for the Central Intelligence Agency (CIA). Exposing the identity of a CIA agent is a federal crime.[19]

trial balloons
Leaks in which the source reveals that some action is being considered, in order to test public feeling about the action before going ahead with it.

Trial balloons are a specific type of leak in which the source reveals that some major policy is being considered. Perhaps a corporation is considering a merger, or the president is considering sending ground troops into a foreign country. The source can then test the public reaction to the leak before going ahead with the action. If the stock price goes down, the merger might be canceled. If a veterans organization protests, the president might deny ever having considered military action.

Exclusives

exclusive
A story granted to just one news outlet.

An **exclusive,** a story granted to just one news outlet, can be used to increase the impact of publicity. According to Howard Kurtz, in his book *Spin Cycle,* President Bill Clinton would have his press secretary grant exclusive stories to carefully chosen news outlets. *USA Today* got an exclusive on a $5 billion proposal to renovate schools, the *New York Times* got one on tracking illegal gun sales by computer, and ABC's Peter Jennings got one on kids and cigarettes. According to Kurtz, "Marginal stories that would barely rate a mention on television were pumped up by virtue of being exclusive."[20] This would create a "two-day bounce" for the story, forcing everyone else to cover it the day after the exclusive.

There is risk involved with exclusives, however. The media outlets that did not get the exclusive might be less helpful the next time the public relations practitioner wants coverage of an event. A recent trend in politics is giving exclusives to entertainment, rather than news, outlets. Arnold Schwarzenegger, for example, announced his candidacy for governor of California on Jay Leno's *Tonight Show*.

Community Relations: Doing Good and Getting Credit

Community relations involves aiding groups of people within society. These groups might be local, national, or global. On the local level, public relations seeks to maintain a good relationship with government and community groups in those places where the company maintains an office, store, or manufacturing facility. That relationship might come in handy if the company needs to gain official or public support for such projects as building or expanding a factory; it might also mean the recruitment of better employees. Perhaps most important, community relations provides an example of organizational citizenship that the company can brag about anywhere. Today, multinational corporations truly have to think globally and act locally, because both good and bad publicity travel quickly around the world. To that end, businesses have adopted the practice of **corporate aid.** This form of large-scale community relations can involve anything from adopting schools (which usually involves supplying everything from computer equipment to volunteer teacher's aides) to adopting highways (by being responsible for their cleanup).

community relations
Public relations activities designed to aid and to maintain a beneficial image with groups on the local, national, or global level.

corporate aid
Community relations activity in which a company helps society on a large scale.

With community relations, public relations can truly be what its proudest practitioners claim it is: the practice of doing good and getting credit for it. Of course, corporate aid is often cleverly strategic. For example, Panasonic Oxyride batteries declared June 14, 2006, to be Neuter Your Bunny Day. That is the time of year, Panasonic explained, when thousands of bunnies given as pets on Easter wind up abandoned. So Panasonic treated pet owners in New York City to free neutering of their pet rabbits in "an educational effort to build awareness for the health benefits of neutering bunnies and the performance benefits of using Oxyride batteries."[21] Panasonic also donated $10,000 to the House Rabbit Society to support the cause. Panasonic didn't even have to mention that the Energizer Bunny was their main competitor.

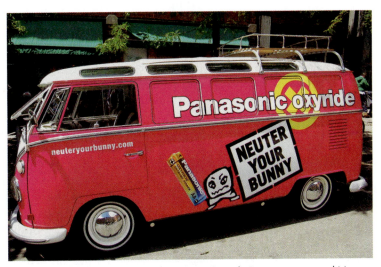

In Manhattan, on June 14, 2006, Panasonic Oxyride Batteries sponsored Neuter Your Bunny Day as a public service that also made fun of the Energizer Bunny.

Crisis Management: Dealing with Emergencies

Crisis management is the action used to repair a client's public image following an emergency such as a major error, accident, or sabotage. Perhaps a manufacturer has to recall a product or an airline has to explain a crash. Part of the public relations function in crisis management is getting clients to take action during a period when the disaster might otherwise have them paralyzed. Thus, in the Tylenol poisoning case mentioned earlier in this chapter, crisis management had to be used twice. First, public relations counselors helped the company manage its response by recalling all of its capsules and reintroducing newly manufactured capsules in tamper-resistant packaging. After more deaths occurred in a second round of tampering, the company

crisis management
Public relations activity used to repair a client's public image following an emergency.

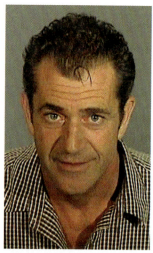

When Mel Gibson (shown here in his mug shot) was arrested for drunk driving and an anti-Semitic tirade, he responded with Hollywood-style crisis management. He gave an abject apology and checked himself into rehab.

lobbying
Any attempt to influence the voting of legislators.

What are some of the strategies that public relations professionals use?

SELF QUIZ

CONSIDER THIS

Critics of lobbying say that it allows special interest groups with money to influence legislation, thereby giving those groups advantages that individuals don't have. Defenders of lobbying say it is a First Amendment right. Should there be laws limiting the amount of lobbying public relations professionals can do?

press release
Brief document containing the information needed to write a news story; also called a news release.

then pulled the capsules for good and came out with caplets, which are more difficult to alter.

The Dell Computer Corporation found itself in a crisis situation when one of its notebook computers burst into flames at a conference in Osaka, Japan, in 2006. Pictures of the event were posted on several Web sites, and they were picked up by newswires and appeared in several newspapers and television programs. Dell felt the incident got more publicity than such incidents usually do because several bloggers were upset about Dell's decision the year before to cut service at its call centers. In response to the incident, Dell publicized its new program to spend more than $100 million to improve service.

Lobbying: Influencing Government Action

The term **lobbying** refers to any attempt to influence the voting of legislators. This form of persuasion gets its name from the traditional practice of public relations representatives speaking to lawmakers in the lobbies outside their hearing rooms. U.S. corporations spend hundreds of millions of dollars in their lobbying efforts annually. Some people are shocked to hear that this practice is even legal, but in fact multimillion-dollar industry associations are set up purely for the purpose of influencing how laws are written. (The Controversies section of this chapter discusses this issue more fully.) Companies that try to rise above lobbying, however, soon see the error of their ways. Microsoft, for example, was a powerful innovator in software but not very active in lobbying—that is, until the government brought against it an antitrust suit for which Microsoft's competitors had lobbied. Those competitors, who had hired powerful public relations firms to lobby for them, had testified at Senate Judiciary Committee hearings leading up to the suit—hearings from which Microsoft was barred.

Microsoft fought back. "They're using the government to compete against us rather than competing in the marketplace," a Microsoft spokesperson complained. "We have to respond to that campaign."[22] Microsoft proceeded to hire its own high-pressure lobbyists, including two former congressional representatives, one of whom was a Democrat and the other a Republican. When former senator Bob Dole sent out letters to businesses, trade associations, and consumers urging them to join the anti-Microsoft movement, Microsoft quickly distributed a floor speech Dole had made a few years earlier, in which he stated that it was un-American for the government to dictate how Microsoft did business.[23]

Microsoft continues to battle with the government on antitrust issues, but its lobbying efforts have helped minimize the impact of these battles on the company's bottom line.

SOME PUBLIC RELATIONS TOOLS

Public relations practitioners perform their functions using a variety of tools. Some of these—such as brochures, newsletters, and company memos—are fairly traditional. Here we will look at some specialized tools, especially those used to reach out to external publics: press releases, video news releases, press kits, special events, and corporate sponsorships.

Press Releases

A **press release,** also known as a news release, is a short document, written in standard news form, that contains the information needed to write a news report. Press releases are often written by a public relations firm on

**FIGURE 12.3
Sample Press
Release Format**

A press release should be
written in standard news
form, and contain all the
information needed to write
an article.

FOR IMMEDIATE RELEASE

Begin with this heading, which announces that no permission is required to publish
the following information.

BRIEF CONTACT INFORMATION

Person for media to contact, phone number, e-mail address.

HEADLINE

Create an active and descriptive headline that will capture the reader's attention. The
headline should appeal to journalists as newsworthy. Make the news hook clear,
if possible.

SUMMARY

Write a summary of your story that helps clarify the headline and describes what the
press release is about.

BODY

Here you will answer the *where, when, who, what, why* and *how* in typical news
story form.

Lead Paragraph

Dateline: City, State—Month, Day, Year—Answer the *what* in the rest of this
paragraph. Avoid excessive adjectives and complicated language. Present only
facts, not opinions or a sales pitch.

Include Quotes

Include quotations that add interest to the press release. Add credibility by identifying the people you quote using their title and organization name in addition to
their name.

Answer the *Why* and the *How*

The second paragraph of the body should connect the first paragraph to more
detailed information about the *why* and the *how* of the news event.

Additional paragraphs should contain supporting information and industry
statistics. Make the writer's or reporter's job as easy as possible by providing
accurate and complete information.

Call to Action

The last paragraph is where you can make a call to action. This is your opportunity
to prompt your target audience to do something.

###

Use three number signs—centered, with space between, on the second line below
the last line of the text—to denote where the press release ends.

ORGANIZATION SUMMARY

Include a short summary about your organization.

COMPLETE CONTACT INFORMATION

Provide comprehensive contact information for one or two people with whom the media
can follow up.

Person's name, organization name, mailing address, phone numbers, fax number, e-mail
and Web addresses.

client letterhead. Their sole purpose is to place favorable information about
the client or product in a news report. (See Figure 12.3.)

Today, much of the news we receive from any medium consists of information supplied by press releases. Newspapers especially rely on them, although any press release faces stiff competition at the editor's desk, where
so many are received that most of them are immediately discarded.

Press releases that arrive as a digital file to be inserted into newspaper feature or editorial sections with no change are known as **canned news.** Local newspapers with small budgets for news gathering are eager to use canned news. An **audio news release** is recorded material ready for insertion into broadcast news reports. Usually sent to radio stations, audio news releases typically include interviews and sound bites. **Sound bites** are short, carefully crafted phrases that repeat a major idea that the speaker wants to emphasize. One executive, for example, when interviewed about his company's concern about the environment, repeated the sound bite "We want to be part of the solution, not the problem."[24]

Video News Releases

A **video news release (VNR)** is a ready-to-broadcast recording designed for use in television news programs. Created by professionals, these videos feature good production values. Most VNRs include not only a preproduced news story, complete with reporter and voiceover, but also the same footage without the reporter—to allow stations to use their own reporters to package the story.

The *Media World* DVD that accompanies this book (track 22, *Fit to Print*), compares the way Republicans and Democrats provide prepackaged news, in the form of VNRs, to news organizations.

VNRs have become an integral part of crisis management. Several years ago, a man in Tacoma, Washington, claimed to have found a hypodermic syringe in a can of Diet Pepsi. As the story broke, several other people across the country came forward with similar reports, claiming to have found a broken sewing needle, a screw, a bullet, and a narcotics vial in Pepsi products. Company officials announced that the insertion of such objects in their bottling lines was impossible, but no one seemed to be listening. The story was too compelling, the evidence was mounting, and people still remembered the Tylenol poisoning incident that had cost seven people their lives. Pepsi sent out VNRs showing how their high-speed canning lines actually worked, with cans moving by at 2,000 a minute, far too fast for any tampering to occur. This helped, but the real crisis was averted when a surveillance camera at a local convenience store caught a customer inserting an object into a Pepsi can after she opened it. She then went to the cashier and complained. Pepsi acquired the tape and included it with its other evidence in a VNR sent to every television station in the country. The tape included a reassuring statement by Pepsi's chief executive officer, Craig Weatherup. The crisis was over within 24 hours.

Fake News: Criticism of VNRs

VNRs have become increasingly controversial in recent years and have come to be called fake news when they are used without attribution. In fact, a 2006 study by the Center for Media and Democracy found 36 VNRs that had aired on 77 stations. The center posted these broadcast segments on its Web site and proved that not only did the stations fail to report the true source of the tapes, but some stations also altered screen graphics to include the station's logo and inserted voice-overs to make it seem that they had done the reporting themselves.[25] Congress and the FCC took up the issue of fake news in 2006 after the *New York Times* reported that the federal government had produced hundreds of video news releases, many of which were broadcast without a disclaimer of the government's role. Congress passed legislation temporarily requiring videos from federal agencies to clearly disclose the government's authorship.

Press Kits

Whereas a press release is a simple document, usually no longer than two or three typewritten pages, a **press kit** is an elaborate collection of publicity photos, color slides, product samples, and fact sheets. Many press kits also contain **backgrounders,** which are articles going into depth on such matters as company history, the management team, the product or market. All these items are usually contained in a large, specially designed folder that features the company logo, arresting graphics, and pockets for the various contents. The folders are either sent directly to media outlets or given out at news conferences. Often, press kits are used for the kickoff of a new product or the announcement of a major special event.[26] Many organizations now also provide press kits online.

Press kits are more expensive than press releases, but they are still cost-effective. Levi Strauss & Company sent out a press kit to publicize a survey it had conducted on the lifestyles of college students. Results of the survey, called the Levi's 501 report, were sent to fashion editors at the top 500 U.S. newspapers, and within three months, 345 articles appeared.[27] The total cost of preparing and sending the press kit was $20,000, a mere fraction of what that much newspaper advertising space would cost. Moreover, the news articles, having more credibility than ads, had a value to the company far beyond what any advertising would have had.

press kit
A collection of publicity items given out to media gatekeepers.

backgrounders
In-depth articles contained in press kits.

The International Space Station is the largest and most complex international scientific project in history. And when it is complete just after the turn of the century, the the station will represent a move of unprecedented scale off the home planet. Led by the United States, the International Space Station draws upon the scientific and technological resources of 16 nations: Canada, Japan, Russia, 11 nations of the European Space Agency and Brazil.

Many press kits, such as this one for the International Space Station, are now online. Web site courtesy of NASA, Houston.

Special Events

In the 1980s, Coca-Cola made a classic marketing blunder. It changed the formula for Coke. Consumers rejected New Coke, and the company had to return to the earlier formula, renaming it Coke Classic. Coke's image had been shaken, though, so the company needed a special event to brighten it up. The answer was a celebration of its 100th anniversary. The planning for this event took several years and cost the company more than $23 million. Publicity began several months in advance and included press releases, press kits, VNRs, interviews, and ads. The day of the celebration included a parade in Atlanta, home of the company's headquarters, with 30 floats and marching bands, and 300 clowns. The crowd of 300,000 included 12,500 Coca-Cola employees from 120 countries.

Some special events, like the Coke anniversary, are planned from the start, whereas others take advantage of unforeseen circumstances. For example, in 1998 Cornell University experienced a phenomenon that came to be known as the Great Pumpkin Mystery. Around Halloween a huge orange object was impaled on a lightning rod atop a 173-foot campus bell tower. There was no access to the steep roof of the bell tower. This event caused five months of speculation as the object stayed there through harsh winter weather. Was it real? Who put it there? How did the prankster get up to the impossible perch? A Web site created about the mystery drew 700,000 hits.

The university's public relations office decided to make a special event out of the Great Pumpkin Mystery. Members of the office placed an orange fence around the bell tower and put up BEWARE OF FALLING PUMPKIN signs. They announced a date on which the object would be formally retrieved and identified. Members of the news media were invited to watch as the university provost was hoisted by crane to bring it down. Pumpkin ice cream and commemorative T-shirts were sold to hundreds of spectators. An ambulance was standing by to take the thing to a laboratory, where horticultural experts would analyze it. The event had an unexpected twist when the crane bumped into the lightning rod, knocking off both the rod and the object impaled on it. The provost still retrieved it, the ambulance rushed it away, and the event was written up across the country (it was a real hollowed-out pumpkin, preserved by the cold weather). The write-ups made Cornell seem like a place with a sense of humor, a college that would be fun to attend.

When someone mysteriously placed a 50-pound pumpkin atop a 173-foot tower at Cornell University in October and it stayed there most of the winter, the administration made a public relations event out of it.

Corporate Sponsorship

Another tool used by public relations practitioners to polish the image of their clients is sponsorship of someone else's special event, such as a sports contest. Miller Brewing Company, for example, sponsors almost 90 events, from the Kentucky Derby Festival in Louisville to the Official Shrimporee of Texas in Aransas Pass, Texas. Many such events now have multiple sponsors—a typical plug might go as follows: "Texaco/Havoline Presents the Budweiser/G. I. Joe's 200, a FedEx Championship Series Event." Event titles like that have caused one reporter to comment, "Corporate sponsorship of special events is not a new phenomenon. But these days, you can barely find the event for the sponsors."[28]

Corporations also purchase naming rights for stadiums, such as Busch Stadium, where the St. Louis Cardinals play, and the Washington Redskins' FedEx Field. A rarer sponsorship strategy involves the naming rights for the team itself. A common occurrence in youth sports such as Little League, the practice moved up to the minor leagues in the 1990s when Coors Brewery purchased the naming rights for the Colorado Silver Bullets, a women's baseball team that played in the men's leagues. In 2006, Red Bull paid $100 million to change the name of the MetroStars soccer team to the New York Red Bulls. In both cases, the teams went along with the plans—for the money and because the company names translated into appropriate team names. As one industry professional pointed out, "No one's going to want to see the Coca-Cola Cowboys or the Kraft Singles."[29]

What are the main tools used by public relations professionals?

SELF QUIZ

Controversies

It's ironic that the public relations profession, which is devoted to the formation of positive images, has such a negative image itself. Probably no facet of media communications divides observers so clearly. On one side are

For an industry devoted to the formation of positive images, public relations has some image problems of its own.

critics who believe that the profession is basically untrustworthy. On the other side are practitioners who believe they are criticized unfairly while the good they do is ignored. Whichever side you happen to be on, there is no doubt that critics look for ethical lapses in many of the industry's practices—

and often find them. The use of public relations tactics in an issue as serious as whether or not a nation goes to war worries many critics, who fear that countries might enter into bloody wars based on false information (see the Close-Up on Controversy box). Other current controversies involve ethics, lack of attribution, and accountability.

THE ETHICS OF PUBLIC RELATIONS TACTICS

Study after study confirms that journalists, who have come to rely on public relations organizations for most of their information, still have a negative view of public relations tactics.[30] This attitude is seen in the terms journalists use for public relations people, terms such as *spin doctors* and **flacks.** One explanation of the word *flack* holds that it derives from the term for World War II antiaircraft fire, suggesting that public relations damages journalism the same way those munitions damaged planes. In fact, many public relations professionals and reporters have a love–hate relationship—neither respects the job the other is doing, yet they are mutually dependent, and it's not unusual for an individual to move between the two careers.

Criticism of public relations is as old as the industry itself. The poet Carl Sandburg once called Ivy Lee a "hired slanderer" and "paid liar."[31] Stanley Walker, a long-ago city editor of the *New York Herald Tribune,* said of Edward Bernays, "The more thoughtful newspaper editors, who have their own moments of worry about the mass mind and commercialism, regard Bernays as a possible menace, and warn their colleagues of his machinations."[32] Tactics that especially catch the eye of today's critic include spinning, the big lie, greenwashing, lobbying, and freebies.

Spinning

The definition of *spin* probably depends on whether you are a public relations practitioner or a critic of the industry. To some, the word has become synonymous with the practice of public relations. Stuart Ewen, a well-known media critic, titled his 1996 book on public relations *PR! The Social History of Spin.* To Ewen, spinning is the practice of twisting the truth so that the speaker is not lying, just putting the best possible face on the facts. Spinning attempts to supplant the public relations version of reality over other versions that might be less beneficial to the spinner, such as when a politician claims credit for economic or social gains he or she had nothing to do with.

Other critics contend that most spinning is a type of lying, or at best the telling of a half-truth. Such critics are word lovers and do not like to see language abused, and they believe that public relations people do commit abuses. Sometimes they do it using euphemisms, or substitute words that soften a harsh truth. One annual report referred to a plane crash as the "involuntary conversion of a 707," which caused one pundit to point out,

One report referred to a plane crash as the "involuntary conversion of a 707."

"Perhaps they would have fooled more people if they had just called the disaster a layover in Cleveland."[33] Other critics are angered by euphemisms like *early retirement* for firing; *rightsizing*

"Hi, hon. Guess who's going to be on national television apologizing to the American public."
© The New Yorker Collection 2000 Charles Barsotti from cartoonbank.com. All Rights Reserved.

flacks
Derogatory term for public relations professionals.

CONSIDER THIS
Is it ethical for a nation to use public relations to support its war effort? Why or why not?

 SELF QUIZ What is spin? How is it viewed differently by public relations practitioners and critics?

Media War Making

The Bush administration's campaign to convince the public that war with Iraq was necessary in 2003 was extremely controversial. Members of the administration implied in a long series of tightly coordinated media appearances that Saddam Hussein, the dictator of Iraq, had weapons of mass destruction and was willing and able to use them at short notice. They also implied that intelligence reports linked Hussein to the terrorist group responsible for the September 11, 2001, attacks against the United States. The United Nations and many of the United States' allies refused to accept the need for an invasion and felt justified when no weapons of mass destruction, or link to Osama bin Laden's terrorists, were found. Critics insisted that it was a sustained public relations campaign, rather than a real threat to U.S. security, that led to the invasion. The Bush administration disagreed, saying that it truly believed that Iraq had been a threat and that the campaign to convince America about the rightness of the war was a common duty for a wartime administration.

The Gulf War of 1990–91 had its controversial public relations aspects also. In 1990, when the United States was deciding whether to respond to Iraq's invasion of Kuwait, every network television news program carried the story of Nayirah, a 15-year-old Kuwaiti girl who had testified before Congress. Nayirah, who was identified as a hospital worker, told the hearing,

"I saw the Iraqi soldiers come into the hospital with guns. They took the babies out of the incubators . . . and left the children to die on the cold floor." Her evidence was mentioned often in the debates that led to the war. With each telling, the number of incubator deaths seemed to increase, reaching 312 at one point.

Critics insisted that it was a sustained public relations campaign by the Bush administration, rather than a real threat to U.S. security, that led to the invasion of Iraq in 2003.

After the war it was revealed that Nayirah's testimony was the centerpiece of an $11.5 million campaign by the Hill and Knowlton public relations firm, paid for by the Kuwaiti government. The coverage of the hearings was supplied to television stations as a video news release that was part of the campaign. It was also revealed that Nayirah was not a simple hospital worker but rather the daughter of Kuwait's ambassador to the United States.[1]

[1] Arthur E. Rowse, "How to Build Support for War," *Columbia Journalism Review*, September/October 1992.

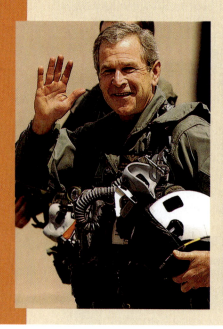

President George W. Bush was criticized when he flew in on a fighter jet in May 2003 to declare major combat in Iraq at an end. Later he made a surprise Thanksgiving visit to soldiers in Baghdad and posed for the picture on the right.

for firing an entire department, *restructuring* for putting a whole town out of work and *unlocking shareholder value* for dismembering an entire company.

Robert L. Dilenschneider, chairman and founder of the New York public relations firm the Dilenschneider Group, Inc., believes that the critics have it wrong. In a 1999 speech, he defined *spin* as "mankind's attempt to put its best foot forward" and went on to say, "Lovers are master spinners. So are job applicants. Ditto for kids around Christmas. Spin is happening every minute of every day in every city and town around the world." In short, he said, to spin is to persuade others to your point of view. Dilenschneider maintained that critics confuse "good spin" with "bad spin":

> In spinning we try to give ourselves, our cause or our point of view the advantage. We can get that advantage ethically or unethically. In good taste or bad. With a pure heart or with malice. And that's the difference between good spin and bad spin. Good spin is being smart but also being on the level. Good spin sticks with reality. Bad spin is to be mean-spirited, opportunistic, sleazy. Bad spin crosses the line from reality to fiction.[34]

The *Media World* DVD that accompanies this book (track 18, *Pentagon Planning to Plant Misinformation in Foreign News Sources*) discusses the ethics of using the big lie to help win a war.

The Big Lie

The big lie occurs when a prominent person states something he or she knows to be untrue and sticks to it no matter what evidence refutes it, hoping that the press and the public will eventually become confused by the issue and forget about it. Those who have been accused of this tactic include cigarette industry executives, who swore under oath for years that tobacco is not addictive, in spite of medical evidence that suggested otherwise. Later, they explained that it depended on what was meant by "addictive." Critics also accused President Bill Clinton of resorting to the big lie when he wagged his finger at television cameras and intoned, "I did not have sex with that woman." (The truth of his statement depended, of course, on the meaning of *sex.*) Professionals respond that tactics like the big lie might be seen by critics as forms of public relations, but they are seldom if ever recommended by public relations counselors. They are more often perpetrated by clients who have either deceived their counselors as well as the public or have stubbornly insisted on using the tactic against the advice of those counselors.

Bill Clinton used the big lie technique when he announced, "I did not have sex with that woman."

Greenwashing

A standard public relations tactic that goes by the name **whitewashing** consists of using public relations messages to cover up problems without correcting them. A more recent version of this practice is **greenwashing,** the covering up of environmental problems caused by a client by associating that client with beneficial environmental actions. Critics say that major polluters are co-opting environmentalism through this practice. Gasoline companies, for example, have distributed materials suggesting that the way to save the environment is to ride a bike—or drive on radial tires. Arco printed a series of such suggestions on tree-shaped air fresheners, during a year when critics said Arco was one of the nation's worst industrial polluters.[35]

Some public relations campaigns brag about company actions that are actually required by law, as when lumber corporations who make it a practice to clear-cut ancient redwoods brag about replanting forests, a practice that environmental laws force them to do. Public relations practitioners respond that for whatever reason, companies are becoming more aware of environmental issues, and they do a public service when they make their customers aware of it.

whitewashing
The practice of using public relations messages to cover up problems without correcting them.

greenwashing
The public relations practice of covering up environmental problems by associating a client with beneficial environmental actions.

Lobbying against the Public Interest

Lobbying, as mentioned earlier, is an integral part of public relations, but critics become incensed when the objectives of lobbying seem counter to the public interest. The tobacco industry, which spends tens of millions of dollars annually on lobbying, comes in for a fair share of this criticism, but other industries are also singled out. In 1999, for example, the government announced that it would let the wine industry use labels on its bottles that mention the "health effects of wine consumption." The wine industry's lobbying association, the Wine Institute, had convinced lawmakers to allow this move in spite of the fact that the labels were opposed by several health organizations, including the American Cancer Society, the American Medical Association, the American Heart Association and the Center for Science in the Public Interest.[36]

Freebies

Many critics believe that public relations practitioners' offers of **freebies**—which include everything from trips, meals, and gifts to research help on a big story to finding an agent for a journalist's screenplay—amount to bribes for journalists. These critics ask how journalists can be expected to be objective about a news source that provides them with such favors. Public relations practitioners, however, insist that offering freebies is a legitimate technique to arouse journalistic interest in their products and that the items are neither intended nor perceived as bribes.

Extremely common in many areas, freebies seem to be especially prevalent with high-tech items. When Iomega wanted to introduce a hardware/software package for editing home movies on a personal computer, the company threw a party for journalists who write about consumer electronics. Each invitation noted that the party would include a sample of the product, "a $199 value."[37] Journalists who are loaned consumer electronics items like VCRs, TVs, and computers to review usually find that the public relations firm that arranged for them to receive those products is not concerned about getting them back.

LACK OF ATTRIBUTION

Attribution is the act of providing the source for information that appears in news reports. One of the things that makes public relations controversial is that so much of it operates behind the scenes, without attribution, as though the messages come from an unseen hand. Critics blame both public relations professionals and reporters for this practice; they believe that journalists should make it clear when information comes from a press release or another public relations source. These critics are particularly convinced that VNRs are fake news, especially when a company sends out a VNR showing several satisfied customers (and no dissenters) extolling the virtues of the company's new product. One survey revealed that almost half of TV station news directors admitted that they did not identify the source of VNRs on their news programs.[38] Many stations even imply that certain VNRs are the work of their own staffs. Critics say the design of the VNRs encourages the practice; as noted earlier in this chapter, the tapes are often set up so that the local correspondent can sit in as the interviewer or anchor of a report.

The lack of attribution for public relations messages is seen as particularly insidious when it implies that the message comes from some place that it doesn't. In a practice called Astroturf lobbying, named after the artificial turf used on football fields, a public relations organization sets up a fake grassroots movement. (A genuine grassroots movement arises when members of the public form a group to battle some problem that truly concerns them.) The bogus organization then gets people to join it through mailing-list solicitations. Some Astroturf organizations have confusing names that imply the exact opposite of their true purpose. Northwesterners for More Fish was actually an Astroturf coalition of utilities and other companies in the Northwest under attack by environmental groups for depleting the fish population. A pro-hunting group called itself the Abundant Wildlife Society of North America and built up a mailing list of people who believed the group's main purpose was to protect wildlife. According to one critic, Astroturf groups specialize in "seizing on unformed public sentiment, marshalling local interest groups and raining faxes, phone calls and letters on Congress or the White House on a few days' notice."[39] Most critics agree that Astroturf lobbying makes it difficult to tell the difference between manufactured public opinion and genuine explosions of popular sentiment.

Blurring the distinction between news and advertising through public relations tactics can imperil media's function of providing consumers with accurate, unbiased information.

Blurring the distinction between news and advertising through public relations tactics like VNRs and Astroturf lobbying can imperil media's function of providing consumers with accurate, unbiased information about the marketplace. Disguising ads as news reports casts doubt on everything presented as news. The public relations industry responds that the press itself is part of the secrecy conspiracy, because it doesn't want to admit how many public relations materials it uses. As one reporter pointed out, "No writer is going to walk into his editor's office and say, 'This public relations guy called with a great idea for a story.'"[40]

SELF QUIZ What are some of the public relations tactics that critics consider to be of questionable ethics?

ACCOUNTABILITY

A final controversial issue revolves around the question of to whom public relations practitioners should be accountable. Who, for example, should punish them for ethical infractions? Should a practitioner who has been guilty of repeated ethical lapses still be allowed to continue to practice? Questions such as these have led to the suggestion that public relations practitioners should be licensed by their professional associations, in the manner of doctors, lawyers, and accountants. The Public Relations Society of America (PRSA), however, is against licensing as a clear infringement of the First Amendment's guarantee of freedom of speech.

However, the PRSA does believe in **accreditation,** in which members who are trained and have good records are given a credential and allowed to use the designation APR (Accredited in Public Relations) after their name. The PRSA uses its accreditation program, which has been in existence since 1965, to encourage public relations professionals to conduct their affairs in an ethical manner. To become accredited, a member must have at least five years' experience, must have a sponsor who is an accredited PRSA member who will testify as to the applicant's integrity and ability, and must pass an extensive written and oral examination. By 1999, nearly a quarter of PRSA's members were accredited.

accreditation
Certification by an industry association.

The Board of Ethical and Professional Standards of the PRSA reviews complaints about members and member organizations. Board members will gather evidence and negotiate a solution to the grievance. The board can also reprimand, censure, suspend, or expel a member. Expulsion, the most severe punishment, simply means the person or company is no longer a member. The PRSA board has no power to keep the expelled party from practicing public relations. It does have the power of public announcement, however, which is a relatively strong incentive. As far as critics are concerned, accreditation is a step in the right direction, but since the PRSA has little real power, the issue of accountability is still very much alive.

What is public relations accreditation, and how does it work?

SELF
QUIZ

Summing Up

Public relations includes all of a client's activities that maintain a beneficial relationship with its internal and external publics. Public relations is practiced in businesses large and small, in government, and in nonprofit organizations.

Long before the term *public relations* was coined, public relations tactics were used to bring settlers to the New World, to galvanize support for the American Revolution and the ratification of the Constitution, and to build the western territories. Industrialization brought corporate abuses, and muckrakers exposed those abuses. Captains of industry hired counselors to help them improve their public image. Ivy Ledbetter Lee established the principles of openness with the press and honesty with the public; he encouraged corporations to make sure that their performance fit the image that their public relations professionals had built. Later, Edward and Doris Bernays went on to build the field with their effective public relations work.

The greatest developments in public relations in government have come in periods of crisis, eras marked by two world wars, the Great Depression, and the cold war. Today, globalization and new technology such as the World Wide Web make public relations a complex undertaking. Public relations professionals perform many different strategic functions for their clients, including news management, community relations, crisis management, and lobbying. Their major tools include press releases, press kits, video news releases, special events, and corporate sponsorships.

The public relations industry depends on media to get its message out, and media depend on public relations practitioners for much of their content. In spite of—and because of—this interdependence, public relations remains a controversial field. Primary controversies revolve around the ethics of such tactics as spinning, the big lie, greenwashing, lobbying, and freebies, as well as the lack of attribution for public relations materials in some news reports and accountability, the question of who polices the industry and guards against ethical abuses.

Key Terms

These terms are defined and indexed in the Glossary of key terms at the back of the book.

Electronic Excursions

HISTORY

Web Excursion

1. The history of public relations is closely related to the history of social, political and economic affairs. If you were adding to the brief history of public relations found in this chapter, what events would you add? Search the Web for "history timelines" of the country or issue of your choice, or go directly to sites such as the Smithsonian Institute's History of the U.S. timeline at www.si.edu/resource/faq/nmah/timeline.htm* or the Environmental History timeline at www.radford.edu/~wkovarik/hist1/timeline.new.html.* Choose one event and justify its inclusion in your expanded history.

INDUSTRY

Web Excursion

2. Imagine if you were to become an independent public relations counselor. Find a product or service that needs a public relations solution. This "product" could be a consumer product, your school, even one of your friends. Search the Web for "public relations services" or go directly to PR Newswire at www.prnewswire.com and access the "services" hyperlink. Which of these services would you take advantage of for your product or service?

Media World DVD Excursion

3. View track 6.3, *Issues: Serve the Client or Public?* This track explains how public relations agencies straddle the line between public service and private profit. Public relations is a client-driven business—does that affect its concern for public service? Explain how public relations firms such as Ogilvie attempt to avoid ethical dilemmas.

CONTROVERSIES

Web Excursion

4. Search the Web for "current public relations issues" by searching for that key term, or other terms such as "public relations accountability," or "public relations ethics," or go directly to the Center for Media and Democracy's PR Watch

at www.prwatch.org. Choose one issue that you find important, and prepare a brief report on it.

Media World DVD Excursion

5. View track 19, *Why Is the United States Viewed So Poorly in the Arab World?* (from NBC News Archive). Has the United States fallen too far behind in the propaganda war? America is trying to get its message out to hundreds of millions of Muslims around the world, but it doesn't seem to be working. Is it possible to improve a company's or nation's image without actually changing or improving the company or nation?

ONLINE LEARNING CENTER WWW.MHHE.COM/RODMAN2

You may access these and additional Web excursions at the Online Learning Center for the book (www.mhhe.com/rodman2). Visit the student portion of this Web site to also access the *Interactive Timeline of Mass Media Milestones,* chapter highlights, self quizzes, and recommended readings, movies, and documentaries for this chapter.

*Some Web site addresses may change. When they do, please search for the Web site by name or topic on your favorite search engine.

Advertising

The Media Support Industry

Chapter Highlights

HISTORY: Advertising has a long and varied history, during which it has affected the development of various media.

INDUSTRY: Advertising is a big business, one that is best understood through an analysis of the client, the agency, the objectives of the advertising, and the type of media that are used to fulfill those objectives.

CONTROVERSIES: Controversies in advertising tend to revolve around freedom of speech, which is a complex topic when it includes ads that are potentially misleading; ads directed at children; and the influence that advertisers have on media content.

The Subservient Chicken

Millions of people found out about the subservient chicken from their friends by e-mail. When they accessed the Web site, they saw first the Burger King logo and then a giant chicken in garters. Or rather, they saw a person in a chicken suit wearing a garter belt in a nondescript living room.

In fact, the room had all the ambiance of a voyeuristic webcam site, windowless with cheap furniture. When the visitor typed in commands (Wreck the room, Lay an egg, Do Pilates), the chicken complied. Subserviently. Unless it was asked to do something pornographic, in which case it approached the camera and shook a

Millions of people found out about the subservient chicken from their friends by e-mail.

forbidding wing feather at the viewer. The responses of the chicken were cleverly achieved using an archive of canned video clips. The video clips were so seamlessly presented and the commands that the chicken could follow were so numerous that many visitors believed, at least at first, that the chicken character was live.

The chicken's compliance was meant to reinforce Burger King's "Have It Your Way" trademark for 20- to 30-year-olds who are media savvy and do not respond to more mainstream advertising. A link on the site labeled "BK TenderCrisp" took visitors to the fast-food chain's home page. There were also links for a chicken mask to print out and wear and, most important as far as the ad's creators were concerned, a "Tell a friend" button that allowed viewers to pass on the following message: "Finally, somebody in a chicken costume who will do whatever

you want. Check it out: http://www.subservientchicken.com."

The subservient chicken Web site is an example of a process called viral marketing, which relies on word of mouth rather than mainstream mass media. Advertisers have discovered that sufficiently offbeat ads will "go viral" and can reach large numbers of people as they are passed from friend to friend by email (or "word of mouse").

The viral marketing seemed to work. When Burger King's ad agency launched the subservient chicken site, only 20 people were told about it—all friends of people who worked at the agency. In its first week, more than 400,000 people visited the site. Within two months, 20 million people had seen it, and a search for the phrase "subservient chicken" on the Internet search engine Google produced more than 40,000 results, including several that cataloged

more than 300 commands that the chicken could obey.

The Web site was a phenomenon, but many experts questioned whether it was effective advertising. Some said it was ineffective because they didn't think that it was actually selling any Burger King TenderCrisp Chicken sandwiches. But the site's creators thought otherwise. After all, the chicken site was drawing willing consumers away from other advertising on the Web. Anytime you can persuade the public to pay attention voluntarily to an advertising campaign, you have scored a coup. One of the creators explained that the whole idea was to get site visitors to like the Burger King brand. "If consumers like your brand, they're more likely to go experience your brand," he says. "So it's no different than a charming television commercial—except that, on average, people spend seven minutes with it."[1]

From what you read about the subservient chicken Web site, do you think it fulfilled its objectives? Why or why not?

The approach used in the subservient chicken Web site demonstrates how eager advertising professionals are to get their messages noticed. According to a study conducted in 2004 by a major marketing research firm, 61 percent of consumers believe that advertising is "out of control." In addition, 60 percent said they feel "much more" negative about advertising than they did a few years ago.[2]

The main reason that consumers feel negatively about advertising is that there is just so much of it. About 65 percent of an average newspaper is advertising, and newspapers get around 75 percent of their income from ads. Half of an average magazine is advertising, and magazines pull in 50 percent of their income there. Most of the content and revenue for Web sites now come from advertising. Commercial television and radio stations devote around 25 percent of their broadcast time to advertising (and more than 30 percent during prime time). Broadcast income is derived almost entirely from advertising.

It is becoming increasingly difficult to find spaces where advertising doesn't appear. Ads for milk and movies have appeared on individual apples, bananas, and oranges. Other ads appear on the street (literally on the

It is becoming increasingly difficult to find spaces where advertising doesn't appear.

street, where people looking down can see them), on the floors of stores, on airport baggage carousels, and on the walls above urinals. Ads talk to you from automated teller machines, and commercials appear on the television-like screens of gas pumps as you fill your tank. One company has even offered cash-strapped towns free police cars as long as it can put ads on the hoods and trunks. The offer has been accepted by 20 towns.[3]

Yet in spite of all the intrusiveness, most people would be unhappy without advertising, because it truly is the media support industry: It brings us all the "free" and inexpensive media content we enjoy.

But what is advertising, exactly? When designers put their names and logos in large print on your clothing (and you oblige them by wearing that clothing through the mall), is that advertising? What about when a soft drink company arranges to have its products used by the stars in a hit movie? Is that an ad? Advertising should not be confused with public relations (defined in Chapter 12 as all of an organization's activities that help it maintain a beneficial relationship with its various publics, such as its customers and employees), but it might be part of a public relations campaign, however. Nor should advertising be confused with publicity, the branch of public relations that seeks news coverage for products and services.

The American Marketing Association defines **advertising** as "any paid form of nonpersonal presentation and promotion of ideas, goods, or services by an identified sponsor." Several terms in that definition bear further scrutiny—for example, the word *paid*. Advertisers might own the media in which ads appear, but they are still paying for the ads in the sense that they pay for the paper in the newspaper or the transmitter at the broadcast station. Because ads are paid for, the advertiser has control over what the ad says and where it goes. The word *nonpersonal* distinguishes advertising from in-person selling, which includes the salespeople in stores as well as those annoying telemarketers who always

advertising
According to the American Marketing Association: "any paid form of nonpersonal presentation and promotion of ideas, goods, or services by an identified sponsor."

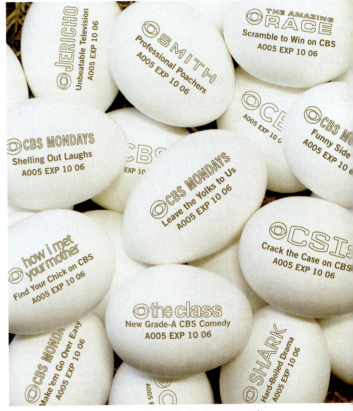

The CBS television network recently advertised its fall lineup on 35 million eggs sold in supermarkets. The network used laser imprints of slogans such as *CSI: Crack the Case on CBS*, *The Amazing Race: Scramble to Win on CBS*, and *Shark: Hard-Boiled Drama*. CBS's copywriters referred to the medium as "egg-vertising."

call at dinnertime. The words *presentation* and *promotion* are used in the definition of advertising to make sure that entertaining messages, as well as informative and persuasive ones, are recognized as ads. The expression *ideas, goods, or services* reminds us that advertising is not limited to commercial products but can also be used to sell ideas, for example, political concepts such as tax cuts or campaign reform. Finally, the term *identified sponsor* reminds us that we generally know who placed the ad and what that person or group is selling. This term also reveals that the American Marketing Association has ethical advertising in mind in its definition. Unethical advertising sometimes attempts to disguise or hide the true sponsor. Some political

SELF
QUIZ

ads, for example, try to make it appear as if the message comes from a public interest group rather than the opposing candidate.

To answer the question we posed earlier, the designer's placement of its name and logo on your clothing might be brilliant marketing, but it isn't advertising according to the definition we're using here. Designers don't pay you to wear their names. In fact, you're paying them.

In this chapter, we'll look at the history of advertising to trace how the industry got to where it is today. Then we'll take a look at the size and shape of that industry, examining the players—the clients and the agencies—and their objectives, the media they use, and the way they do business. Finally, we'll take a look at some of the controversies the ad industry has generated.

A Brief History *of Advertising*

Advertising is an ancient activity, as old as the business of selling. In fact, we can only speculate about when the first ads appeared. We know that the ancient Egyptians had roadside billboards carved in stone, that gladiator shows were advertised on the walls of ancient Rome, and that the ancient Greeks had town criers who shouted ads in the streets. These town criers proved that some of the basic principles of today's advertising have actually been with us from the beginning. The criers were hired for the quality of their voices, much like today's radio and television announcers. Musicians also sometimes accompanied them. All of this suggests that ancient advertisers understood the value of entertainment in conveying their message.

The first printed advertisements were **handbills,** announcements on single sheets of paper. Handbills were often posted on the doors of churches, where people who were able to read would be likely to see them. The first known printed handbill was distributed by the English printer William Caxton in 1478. It advertised the books he printed. Handbills today are usually called flyers, leaflets, or handouts.

handbills
Announcements on single sheets of paper.

trade advertising
Business-to-business promotions.

consumer advertising
Ads directed to the retail customer.

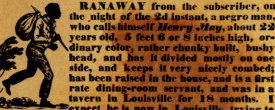

Some of the earliest display ads sought the return of runaway slaves. This ad appeared in 1838.

ADVERTISING COMES TO AMERICA

Advertising was an integral part of early America. In fact, most of the first settlers who came to the New World did so because of advertisements they had read in England, touting free and fertile farmland. The first edition of the *Boston News-Letter,* which appeared in 1704 (see Chapter 4), carried ads that were similar in format to today's classifieds. These early ads were simple notices of wares for sale, usually directed from manufacturers to local merchants, what we now call business-to-business advertising or **trade advertising.** There wasn't much use for **consumer advertising**—ads directed to the retail customer—because most colonists were self-sufficient people who grew their own food and made their own clothing. When they bought something, it was because they needed it, and if they needed it, the small, local general store would have it. Even when the first consumer ads finally began to appear, in the early 1800s, they resembled the simplest classifieds of today. There wasn't much in the ads to attract the attention of an idle reader, as they were designed for customers who were purposefully looking for goods and services such as horses, household goods, land, or transportation.

Display ads—print ads that are larger than classified ads and include artwork, fancy typefaces, and snappy slogans to capture the reader's attention—weren't common until the 1860s, when large department stores such as Macy's and Wanamaker's were founded. Department stores had to lure substantial numbers of customers away from the general stores, and they used display ads to do it. Chain stores such as A&P and mail-order houses such as Sears and Montgomery Ward needed large customer bases also, so they took up the practice of placing display ads in their catalogs as well as in newspapers. As the technology for printing improved, **trade cards** became available at the counter of every store. These illustrated cards usually had a business message on one side and a piece of artwork on the other. They were one more technique businesses were using to establish a large and loyal customer base.

display ads
Print ads that include artwork and fancy typefaces to capture the reader's attention.

trade cards
Illustrated cards with a business message on one side and artwork on the other.

ADS AND THE INDUSTRIAL REVOLUTION

The American Industrial Revolution that began in the 1830s saw vast advances in steam power, transportation, and mass production. It also created a surge in the growth of the advertising industry.

Creation of Mass Demand

Industrialization led to modernization as people started to adopt up-to-date, factory-built innovations such as vacuum cleaners and gas-fired stoves. It also led to urbanization as people left farms to work in city factories. A national system of railroads was completed in 1869, making it possible to distribute products across the entire country. The leaders of the Industrial Revolution, manufacturers such as Andrew Carnegie (whose factories supplied the steel of the late 19th century) and Henry Ford (who built the automobiles of the early 20th century), believed that mass production would not be possible without advertising. Advertising would create mass demand, and with that demand, manufacturers would be able to produce goods in large quantities. Advertising would thus make big business, and big corporations, possible. Early industrialists believed that advertising would pay for itself, because mass-produced goods would be much cheaper for consumers to buy than custom-produced goods.[4]

Diffusion of Innovations

In addition to creating mass demand, advertising led to the diffusion, or spreading out, of almost every type of innovation. Some of these innovations were matters of personal hygiene; for example, advertising encouraged people to bathe more often. It was commonly said that before the Industrial Revolution people worshiped every day and bathed once a week, but advertising encouraged them to reverse that pattern. Advertising also encouraged them to brush their teeth and wash their clothes. It encouraged men to shave daily at home rather than to visit the barber shop every few days. Advertising also encouraged the diffusion of a wide range of household medicines, such as cough drops and pain relievers, and packaged foods, such as breakfast cereals and canned vegetables.

During this period, Americans had to be converted from users of home-made products and unbranded merchandise to consumers of standardized, brand-name, nationally distributed goods. The stage was then set for the

This advertising poster for one of the first washing machines appeared in 1869.

innovations of the early 20th century, including washing machines, automobiles, farm machinery, and agricultural products such as fertilizers and pesticides. Many of these products were created and promoted as solutions to environmental and health problems. The automobile, for example, was advertised as the solution to air pollution—its manufacturers said it would solve the problem of dried horse manure blowing as dust through city streets. Packaged, processed foods were sold as guarantees of good nutrition. Ironically, automobiles and processed foods are now contributing to the environmental and health problems of today.

What effect did the Industrial Revolution have on advertising? What effect did advertising have on the Industrial Revolution?

THE ADVENT OF ADVERTISING AGENCIES

Ever since Benjamin Day ushered in the era of the penny press in 1833 with the publication of the *New York Sun,* advertising was the chief means of support for newspapers. Most newspapers, however, did not want to maintain a full advertising department. Early newspaper publishers believed their job consisted of finding and reporting the news, not chasing down ad accounts. In addition, they often had a difficult time getting paid. Volney Palmer of Philadelphia saw a way to provide a needed service. As an **ad broker,** he would act as a liaison between advertisers and newspapers, buying up ad space from the newspapers at a discount and selling it to advertisers for full price. Volney started the business in 1841, and it soon became widespread. Publishers liked the service because they could now concentrate on the news and still have a steady source of revenue. Advertisers liked brokers because they gave them the ability to advertise in several papers at once. One broker charged a standard fee of $100 for one column inch in 100 newspapers.

ad broker
A liaison between advertisers and newspapers.

From Brokers to Agencies

To make ads attractive for sale, brokers became proficient at designing them. When they did that, they moved from being merely brokers to being advertising agencies. As advertisers became dependent on agencies, the agencies began to hire professional writers and artists. By 1860, 30 major agencies were servicing some 4,000 newspapers and magazines. By this time, however, many manufacturers had become so large that they needed agencies that worked directly for them rather than for the newspaper or magazine. The first of these modern agencies was N. W. Ayer & Son, founded in 1869. Its real founder was the son, Frances Wayland Ayer, who was 21 years old at the time. He knew that the businessmen of the day would have a difficult time accepting someone so young, so he named the business after his father. Ayer was one of the first proponents of advertising ethics. He wouldn't work with a product that was dangerous or place ads that he considered deceptive.

SELF QUIZ

How do modern advertising agencies differ from brokers?

EARLY INDUSTRY CONTROL

Not all advertising agencies were as ethical as N. W. Ayer. In fact, advertisers had always been prone to exaggeration, a practice that came to be known as

If people were fooled by false advertising claims, it was too bad for them.

puffery.[5] By the latter part of the 1800s, the advertising industry was largely out of control. Outrageous claims and outright deception were the order of the day. The free speech and free enterprise foundations of American society encouraged an attitude of *caveat emptor* ("let the buyer beware") about advertising. If people were fooled by false advertising claims, it was too bad for them. The U.S. government maintained a hands-off policy toward advertising, partially because of the constitutional guarantees of free speech, but mostly because of *laissez-faire* ("leave it alone") theories of business designed to encourage the country's growth.

A variety of products carried misleading claims, but the most striking examples came from the patent medicines of the day. These nonprescription drugs were marketed with promises to cure gout, tuberculosis (also called consumption), cancer, heart disease, and anything else that might ail someone. Those who sold the so-called miracle elixirs often backed their outlandish claims with testimonials from satisfied customers. One ad featured a

puffery
Exaggeration in advertising claims.

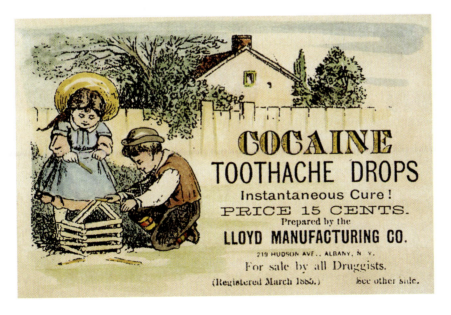

Many patent medicines contained addictive drugs that are illegal today. This ad was obviously intended for young children as well as adults.

farmer who claimed, "My wife was about to die of consumption, but after a few bottles of Dr. Hartman's Peruna, she was able to get up and work again."[6] Many patent medicines, including Dr. Hartman's Peruna, were either useless or harmful. The flavored, colored liquids consisted mostly of alcohol and often contained addictive drugs such as cocaine and morphine.

As Americans became more sophisticated about the products they were using, the attitude of "let the buyer beware" became "let the seller be honest." The Pure Food and Drug Act was passed in 1906 largely as a reaction to patent medicine claims. The Federal Trade Commission was established as a national watchdog of business and advertising in 1914. Eventually, several government agencies began to regulate ads in one way or another. The U.S. Postal Service took responsibility for overseeing ads sent through the mail. The Securities and Exchange Commission was charged with regulating ads about stocks and bonds. The Food and Drug Administration regulated ads about foods, drugs, cosmetics, and health care products.

Many reputable advertisers actually welcomed government regulation. Companies with established brand names that could not afford to make deceitful claims did not want to be forced to compete with fly-by-night products that could. Besides, obviously deceitful advertising weakened the credibility of all advertising.

Despite its early support of government control, however, the industry became nervous when some legislators began to attack all advertisers with great zeal. Self-control by the industry seemed like a better idea, for at least two reasons. First, if the industry controlled itself, the government would not have to be quite so zealous. Second, industry control would show that advertisers wanted to be ethical—they did not need to have ethics forced on them by the government. Self-governed ethical practices would strengthen the credibility of their advertising.

In 1924 the American Association of Advertising Agencies, the industry trade organization, published its code of ethics. Member agencies pledged not to knowingly produce advertising that contained:

1. False or misleading statements or exaggerations, visual or verbal.
2. Testimonials that did not reflect the real choice of a competent witness.
3. Misleading price claims.
4. Comparisons that unfairly disparaged a competitive product or service.
5. Unsupported claims or claims that distorted the true meaning of statements made by professional or scientific authorities.
6. Statements, suggestions, or pictures offensive to public decency.

This code is still in effect (and still voluntary), and the industry has set up a committee, the National Advertising Review Council, to investigate complaints. If necessary, the council pressures the subjects of those complaints to correct their legal or ethical breaches. If an advertiser persists, the council turns the complaint over to the appropriate authorities for prosecution.

ADS TAKE TO THE AIRWAVES

Just as advertising was starting to get its ethical house in order, a new and potentially powerful medium, radio, appeared on the horizon. The potential for advertising abuse within this new medium worried many people, and early amateur broadcasters like John Brinkley, who pushed his own brand of fake

Why were some businesses in favor of government regulation? Why did they eventually prefer self-regulation?

CONSIDER THIS

In your opinion, how well does today's advertising industry follow the American Association of Advertising Agencies' ethics code of 1924?

medicines and surgical procedures over the air, confirmed their worries. As the radio industry developed in the early 20th century, a movement arose to leave broadcasting free of advertising, to run it as a common carrier of mediated interpersonal communication like the telephone. Secretary of Commerce Herbert Hoover insisted that "the quickest way to kill broadcasting would be to use it for direct advertising."[7]

Along with his worries about the power and ethics of radio advertising, Hoover (who would eventually become president) believed that radio was different from print media in that listeners would find it more difficult to avoid advertising that they didn't want or need to listen to. In newspapers they could skip over the ads, but in radio they would have to sit through them or risk missing the programming.

Some countries, in fact, did take an alternate route at this point. Britain, for example, decided in 1926 to fund its state-run broadcasting system, the British Broadcasting Corporation (BBC), by license

Federal regulations were established to guard against false advertising, such as that broadcast by radio quack Dr. John Brinkley, who pushed his own brand of fake medicines and surgical procedures over the air during the 1920s.

fees paid by radio owners, not advertising. British radio and television did not begin to accept advertising until the 1950s. China, the Soviet Union, and other communist countries kept their broadcast media state-owned and commercial-free until the 1990s.

In spite of all the resistance to the idea of using radio to sell products in the United States, government and industry eventually agreed that advertising was the best way to cover the steep costs of setting up and operating radio stations. The first commercial was run in 1922 by AT&T's flagship station, WEAF in New York. The commercial advertised an apartment complex in Queens, and the copy reflected the ambiguity that early broadcasters felt about advertising. The commercial was a very calm 10-minute talk by a company executive, introduced as follows:

> This afternoon the radio audience is to be addressed by Mr. Blackwell of the Queensboro Corporation, who through arrangements made by the Griffin Radio Service, Incorporated, will say a few words concerning Nathaniel Hawthorne and the desirability of fostering the helpful community spirit and healthful, unconfined home life that were Hawthorne's ideals.[8]

By 1926, when network radio began, advertising had become the acceptable means of supporting radio. Network radio changed the ad industry, giving it greater reach and impact than it had known previously. Dial twisting, however, made individual ads much easier to avoid than Hoover had imagined. The consensus among agencies was that radio advertising needed to be entertaining and attention grabbing to keep the listener tuned in. Creative talent was needed more than ever, and ad agencies grew as they hired radio specialists.

Network radio advertising became so profitable that it actually delayed the beginnings of commercial television. Doing well with radio, the broadcast networks were in no hurry to switch to the new, expensive, unproved medium of television. The first television commercial, for Bulova watches, did not run until 1941, and the station was able to charge only $9 for the airtime. Popular demand more or less pushed the radio networks into television. The beginning of network television in 1948, combined with the postwar economic boom, however, created the heyday of American advertising.

Subliminal Fraud

Americans in the 1950s became fearful of what they assumed to be the immense persuasive powers of advertising. Their fears were stoked by Vance Packard, who in his 1957 book *The Hidden Persuaders* warned that advertisers were using their knowledge of Freudian and behavioral psychology to affect the consumer's unconscious mind. Consumers, Packard claimed, were being influenced and manipulated far more than they realized. Packard explained that motivational researchers, those social scientists who specialized in uncovering hidden human motivations, were being used by advertisers to probe people's

Despite all the attention, the idea of subliminal advertising was never anything more than a hoax.

minds. Packard's ideas reflected the general paranoia of the 1950s that was also seen in congressional hearings into communist subversion and in popular science fiction that featured tales of mind control.

Into this atmosphere of paranoia a new controversy arose about subliminal advertising, which supposedly used messages below the threshold of human consciousness. Around the same time that Packard's book was climbing the charts, James Vicary, an unemployed market researcher, claimed that he had run an

experiment in a New Jersey movie theater in which he inserted single frames of ad messages into a film. This resulted, he said, in messages—"Drink Coca-Cola," "Eat popcorn"—that appeared at a speed so fast that the human eye could not perceive them. Vicary explained that because the unconscious mind works like a high-speed tape recorder, filing away far more information than humans can deal with consciously, it was possible for people to be influenced without being aware of it. Vicary claimed that his experiment accounted for a "clear and otherwise unaccountable boost" in movie theater concession-stand sales. This claim started a controversy that continues to this day and led to congressional hearings and local laws (although no national ones) outlawing subliminal advertising. Wilson Bryan Key, a Canadian author, wrote several books, including *Media Sexploitation* and *The Clam Plate Orgy*, supposedly exposing the technique in mainstream advertising.

Despite all this attention, the idea of subliminal advertising was never anything more than a hoax. Vicary made up his findings in order to sell images to major advertisers. When investigators got too close to the truth, Vicary "disappeared, leaving no bank account, no clothes in his closet, and no forwarding address."[1] Although carefully controlled scientific studies have shown that subliminal perception exists—

How did radio and television change the type of work ad agencies did?

Advertisers soon saw the advantages of combining audio and video messages in a piece of popular household furniture. Before long, television was demonstrating its power to make any brand name a household word, as people would discuss the previous night's Timex watch commercial ("Takes a lickin' and keeps on tickin'!") or the Lipton soup commercial that comedian Arthur Godfrey did that morning.

With television, advertising became a specialized art form. Television ads became 30-second entertainments—when cute cartoon characters like Speedy Alka-Seltzer sang catchy jingles like "Plop, plop, fizz, fizz, oh, what a relief it is!" people went around humming them the next day. Other media had to react, usually by putting more creative energy behind their ads. One failed but controversial attempt at a new style of promotion was **subliminal advertising,** which involved images of which the consumer wasn't consciously aware (see the Close-Up on History box).

subliminal advertising
Promotional messages that the consumer is not consciously aware of.

the mind does indeed record more information than it can deal with at any one time—subliminal persuasion has never been proved to work. In fact, research run with scientifically reliable controls has confirmed that it is impossible to use subliminal techniques to produce predictable responses such as the purchase of a specific product.

Although it has been debunked, some people and even some businesses still believe in the power of subliminal persuasion. During the 1990s, consumers spent $50 million annually on subliminal self-help products, including audiotapes that supposedly allow them to learn a foreign language in their sleep. Some retailers go so far as to air messages over their store sound systems that try to discourage customers from shoplifting. Eagle-eyed observers still insist that they can find subliminal messages in ads and animated films, but no one has come forward to admit placing the messages there, so we may never know if such images are jokes or genuine attempts at subliminal persuasion.[2]

[1] James Twitchell, *AdCult USA: The Triumph of Advertising in American Culture* (New York: Columbia University Press, 1996), p. 114.

[2] See, for example, the Urban Legends reference page for Disney's *The Lion King* at www.snopes.com/disney/films/lionking.htm.

Break out the frosty bottle

GILBEYS
LONDON DRY
GIN

and keep your tonics dry!

Wilson Bryan Key, in his first book, *Subliminal Seduction*, insisted that there were hidden sexual messages in this ad for Gilbey's gin. Most experts would agree that the letters "S-E-X" were mischievously airbrushed into the ice cubes by someone in the studio, but research has shown that such a technique would do nothing to improve the ad's effectiveness.

DIVERSITY AND TARGET MARKETING

Today's advertising is distinguished by **target marketing,** the process of breaking up the advertising audience into diverse segments to reach those individuals most likely to purchase a particular product. A manufacturer of ski equipment, for example, can advertise directly in *Skiing* magazine. Target marketing came about because advertisers like to minimize **circulation waste,** that part of advertising received by people whom the advertiser has no interest in reaching. Circulation is wasted on those who can't afford the product and those who live too far away to visit the advertiser's store or take advantage of a particular service. John Wanamaker, the founder of Wanamaker Department Stores, expressed the feelings of most advertisers about circulation waste. "I know that one-half of the money I spend on advertising is wasted," Wanamaker was fond of saying. "The problem is, I don't know which half."

SELF QUIZ
What is subliminal advertising? Does it work?

target marketing
The process of breaking up the advertising audience into diverse segments to reach those individuals most likely to purchase a particular product.

circulation waste
That part of advertising received by people whom the advertiser has no interest in reaching.

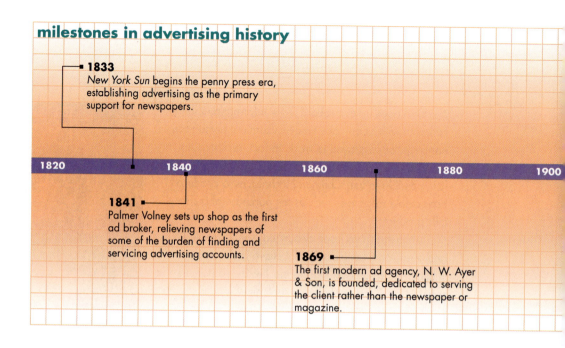

milestones in advertising history

1833
New York Sun begins the penny press era, establishing advertising as the primary support for newspapers.

1820		1840		1860		1880		1900

1841
Palmer Volney sets up shop as the first ad broker, relieving newspapers of some of the burden of finding and servicing advertising accounts.

1869
The first modern ad agency, N. W. Ayer & Son, is founded, dedicated to serving the client rather than the newspaper or magazine.

CONSIDER THIS

Researchers have shown that subliminal persuasion doesn't work, yet some critics insist that the constant barrage of regular advertising keeps certain brand names in the consumer's mind, making it seem natural to subconsciously reach for that brand on the store shelf. Do you agree that this could be considered a form of subliminal advertising? Why or why not?

Aware of the buying power of cultural segments of the population, advertisers use target marketing to reach different groups.

As discussed in Chapter 5, magazines especially felt they could compete with television's impact by reducing circulation waste. After all, television in the mid-20th century was strictly a mass medium; it delivered the message to people of all interests and income levels within the reach of the broadcast station. In response, the magazine industry began to develop specialized magazines to appeal to the specific audiences that advertisers wanted to reach. The same process took place in radio. When network television caused the death of national radio programming, radio became a local medium and fragmented into different formats that appealed to different types of people. Television itself followed the trend of segmentation in the 1980s when the industry developed specialized cable channels. The Internet has been a highly segmented medium from the beginning, allowing people to choose only those sites that interest them. Internet ads began to appear in 1994, and by 2004 they were generating more than $5 billion in annual revenue.

As advertisers became aware of the buying power of cultural segments of the population, they used target marketing as a way of reaching these diverse audiences. Women's products were an early segment, but ad campaigns directed toward ethnic groups such as African Americans and Hispanics have also become prominent. Gays and lesbians are also targeted, and major corporations such as IBM and AOL now place ads in gay media. Target marketing has created job opportunities for minorities and women in the advertising world as agencies have sought out their perspective to make targeted advertising successful. These agencies seek to avoid mistakes such as those

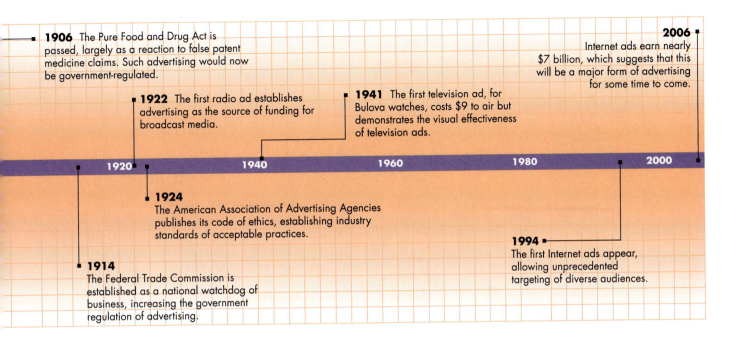

1906 The Pure Food and Drug Act is passed, largely as a reaction to false patent medicine claims. Such advertising would now be government-regulated.

1922 The first radio ad establishes advertising as the source of funding for broadcast media.

1941 The first television ad, for Bulova watches, costs $9 to air but demonstrates the visual effectiveness of television ads.

2006 Internet ads earn nearly $7 billion, which suggests that this will be a major form of advertising for some time to come.

1920   1940   1960   1980   2000

1924 The American Association of Advertising Agencies publishes its code of ethics, establishing industry standards of acceptable practices.

1994 The first Internet ads appear, allowing unprecedented targeting of diverse audiences.

1914 The Federal Trade Commission is established as a national watchdog of business, increasing the government regulation of advertising.

made by Denny's, a restaurant chain successfully sued by African American plaintiffs for racial discrimination. Denny's ran ads featuring affluent African Americans visiting the restaurant where they were greeted with the slogan "Hi, welcome back to Denny's." The plaintiffs pointed out that the ads compounded their sense of injustice by suggesting that only well-off blacks were welcome at Denny's.[9]

 In what ways does advertising pull society apart? In what ways does it bring society together?

As valuable as target marketing is for advertisers, however, not everyone thinks it is beneficial for society. Inner-city communities become enraged when alcohol and tobacco advertisers target their African American and Hispanic populations. Some critics even suggest that segmented advertising is encouraging the fragmentation of American society at a time when greater unity is needed.[10] Narrowly targeted ads, according to these critics, encourage society to fragment along lines of race, class, age, and sex; to separate into ever more splintered groups; and to develop habits that stress the difference between their groups and others. Ad executives, however, like to point out that advertising, segmented or not, is an important part of the glue that holds society together. Americans share very little common knowledge about history or culture, they say, but whistle an ad jingle or recite a slogan, and people will immediately know what you are referring to.

GLOBALIZATION

Since the 1980s, advertising has become an international business, and agencies, especially those in the United States, Japan, and Britain, have been growing and merging into transnational behemoths. Global companies like McDonald's and American Express find it more efficient to deal with one agency that has offices all over the world than to hire different agencies in different countries. Recent

Advertising has become a global business. In Shenzhen, China, this street vendor displays his wares beneath an ad for McDonald's.

years have seen tremendous growth in international marketing, especially in places such as China and the republics of the former Soviet Union, where political reform and the desire to create a free-market economy are creating a significant role for advertising. A current challenge for global advertising agencies is to adapt to the indigenous cultures of new markets.

Understanding Today's Advertising *Industry*

Advertising, a big business in itself, is the engine that allows the rest of the business world to flourish. It is also a constantly changing field, with advertisers continually looking for new techniques and media for selling products and services. The best way to make sense of this gargantuan enterprise is through an analysis of the agency, the objectives of the advertising it produces, and the type of media it uses to fulfill those objectives. First, though, we need to look at where the process begins: with the client.

THE CLIENT

The advertising process begins with the client—the company that provides the product to be sold. It is the client who decides how much of the budget will be devoted to advertising, or whether advertising will be used at all. Usually a company's advertising budget is figured as a percentage of projected sales. Clients, on average, spend about 20 percent of their revenue on advertising.

Until recently, most clients paid agencies on a commission system. The agency would bill the client for the full price of the advertising time or space, which the media would give to the agency at a discount—usually around 15 percent. That 15 percent was the agency's basic compensation. Many advertisers, however, have now moved to alternate forms of payment. Some agencies make their money by charging fees for designing and producing the ads. Some companies use performance-based compensation, an arrangement in which the agency will accept a lower fee but be given a bonus if certain client objectives, such as product sales, are met or exceeded. The gross dollar amount spent by the client is known as the **billings.**

Clients have to consider many things when selecting an agency. They look at each agency's track record, personnel, style of ads, and amount of clout in the industry. They also have to consider the agency's other clients, because agencies usually don't take on competing companies. If an agency picks up a new cosmetics line, for example, it generally drops its old one. Otherwise the client would have to worry about a conflict of interest on the part of the agency. The top 10 ad clients, some of their major products, and the agencies that serve them are presented in Fact File 13.1.

billings
The gross dollar amount that an advertising agency's client spends.

SELF QUIZ

What are the procedures used by an ad agency to bill its clients? How have these procedures changed in recent years?

THE AGENCY

There are more than 13,000 ad agencies based in the United States. Many are huge international mega-agencies created through mergers and acquisitions in the boom days of the 1980s. In recent years, even larger conglomerates have bought up most of the mega-agencies. Today's top advertising organizations are listed in Fact File 13.2.

Today's advertising agency has three basic functions: to create, to produce, and to place the advertising messages that will fulfill the client's objectives.

FACT FILE 13.1

Top Advertising Clients and the Agencies That Serve Them

Primary Agencies Are Color-Coded by Parent Company

1. General Motors Corp.

Buick-Pontiac-GMC
  Buick vehicles
    McCann Erickson Worldwide
  GMC vehicles
    Lowe Worldwide
  Pontiac vehicles
    Leo Burnett Detroit

Cadillac Motor Car Division
  Leo Burnett Detroit
Chevrolet Motor Division
  Campbell-Ewald
GM Service & Parts Operations
  Campbell-Ewald; Leo Burnett Detroit

GMAC
  Campbell-Ewald
Hummer
  Modernista!
OnStar Corp.
  Campbell-Ewald

Saab Cars USA
  Lowe Worldwide
Saturn Corp.
  Goodby, Silverstein & Partners

2. Procter & Gamble Co.

Clairol, Cover Girl, Downy, Fabreze, Hydrience, Joy, Natural Instincts, Nice 'n Easy, Pantene, Pringles, Sure, Torengos, Ultress, Zest
  Grey Worldwide
Aussie, Daily Defense, Dawn, Herbal Essences, Infusium 23, Renewal 5X, Swiffer
  Kaplan Thaler Group

Always, Bounce, Cheer, Gain, Max Factor, Noxzema, Pert Plus, Secret, Tampax
  Leo Burnett Worldwide
Asocol, Intrinsa, Metamucil, oral care franchise, Prilosec OTC, ThermaCare
  Publicis Healthcare Communications Grp.

Asacol, Bounty, Charmin, DayQuil, Metamucil, NyQuil, Pepto-Bismol, Prilosec, Puffs, ThermaCare, Vicks
  Publicis USA
Cascade, Crest, Dreft, Fixodent, Folgers, Head & Shoulders, Iams, Luvs,

Millstone, Olay, Pampers, Plastic Booster, Pur, Safeguard, Scent Expression, Scope, Tide
  Saatchi & Saatchi
Eukanuba, Old Spice
  Wieden & Kennedy

3. Time Warner

America Online
  BBDO Worldwide
Home Box Office
  BBDO Worldwide

Time Inc.
  Fallon Worldwide
Time4 Media
  In-house

Time Warner Cable
  Ogilvy & Mather Worldwide
Turner Broadcasting System
  Assigned on a project basis

Warner Bros. Entertainment
  Grey Entertainment

4. Pfizer

PFIZER CONSUMER HEALTHCARE
Lubriderm, Rogaine
  BBDO Worldwide
Actifed, Anusol, Benadryl, Ben-Gay, Benylin, Cortisone, Desitin, Dramamine, Efferdent, e.p.t., Kaopectate, Listerine, Listerine Essential Care Toothpaste, Listerine Pocket

Paks, Ludens, Neosporin, PediaCare, Purell, Rolaids, Sinutab, Sudacare, Sudafed, Tucks, Unisom, Visine, Zantac
  JWT
Listerine, Zantac75, Rogaine, Nicotrol
  CommonHealth

PFIZER PHARMACEUTICALS GROUP
Relpax
  Arnold Worldwide
Zyrtec
  Berlin Cameron United
Caduet
  Cline Davis & Mann
Bextra, Dostinex, Dynastat, Genotropin, Inspra, Lasofoxifene, Lyrica,

Somavert, Varenicline
  Euro RSCG Life LM&P
Celebrex, Zoloft, Lipitor
  Kaplan Thaler Group
Bextra, Viagra
  McCann Erickson Worldwide
Detrol
  Saatchi & Saatchi Healthcare
Macugen
  Medicus Group International

5. DaimlerChrysler

Chrysler Division
  BBDO Detroit

Dodge Division
  BBDO Detroit

Jeep Division
  BBDO Detroit

Mercedes-Benz USA
  Merkley & Partners

COLOR KEY FOR AGENCY HOLDING COMPANIES	Omnicom Group	Interpublic Group of Cos. / WPP Group	Publicis Groupe / Havas

Source: Fact Pack 2006, Supplement to *Ad Age* magazine, www.adage.com, accessed November 2006.

Agencies are categorized into one of three types: (1) **in-house agencies,** which are organizations built into the product manufacturer's corporate structure; (2) **boutique agencies,** which specialize in creative services but don't cover the technical aspects such as media buying; (3) or **full-service agencies,** which are organizations that supply all the advertising, marketing, and often public relations services that their clients need. All the top international agencies are full-service agencies. They might be involved in creating trademarks and trade characters, redesigning packaging, handling publicity, conducting sales training, designing point-of-sale merchandising displays, and even creating new products. The whole idea of freeze-dried coffee, for example, was the brainstorm of a full-service ad agency.

Most full-service advertising agencies have four basic organizational areas: account management, research, creative, and media (see Figure 13.1).

FACT FILE 13.2

Top Advertising Organizations Worldwide

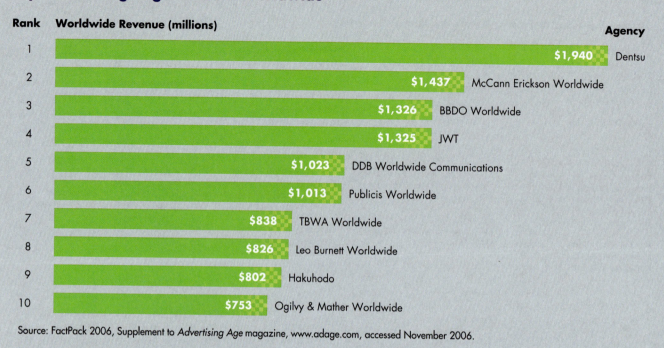

Rank	Worldwide Revenue (millions)	Agency
1	$1,940	Dentsu
2	$1,437	McCann Erickson Worldwide
3	$1,326	BBDO Worldwide
4	$1,325	JWT
5	$1,023	DDB Worldwide Communications
6	$1,013	Publicis Worldwide
7	$838	TBWA Worldwide
8	$826	Leo Burnett Worldwide
9	$802	Hakuhodo
10	$753	Ogilvy & Mather Worldwide

Source: FactPack 2006, Supplement to *Advertising Age* magazine, www.adage.com, accessed November 2006.

Account Management

Coordinates agency services for the client.

Represents the client within the agency.

Puts together teams for ad campaigns.

Coordinates the pitching of new accounts.

Research

Plans, executes, and interprets research.

Audience research: Gathers data about target consumers (demographics and psychographics).

Copy research: Tests the effectiveness of ad content through pretesting and posttesting.

Creative

Designs and produces advertisements.

Creates ad copy.

Designs the visual styles of ads.

Hires and directs freelance illustrators, graphic designers, photographers, and musicians.

Produces and casts radio and television spots.

Media

Allocates advertising budgets among print, broadcast, and other media.

Purchases media space and time.

Oversees and maintains quality.

FIGURE 13.1 Full-Service Advertising Agency Organization The four departments of a full-service agency work together to create, produce, and place the advertising messages that fulfill their client's objectives.

account executive
Employee who coordinates the agency's services for the client.

pitching accounts
Presenting new ideas for ad campaigns to a prospective client.

Account Management

The account management area of a full-service advertising agency is staffed by numerous account executives. An **account executive** represents the client within the agency and coordinates the agency's services for the client. Account executives have to understand the target customer and represent that customer's point of view at every step of the creative process. They are also responsible for bringing in new business. In this capacity, they coordinate the process of **pitching accounts,** which involves preparing and presenting new ideas for ads to a prospective client. The account executive then puts together the team that will work on the actual campaign.

The Research Department

Ad campaigns live and die by the results of research. Because clients spend so much money on their campaigns, they want reassurance in advance that the ads will work. The research department strives to provide this reassurance through the planning, execution, and interpretation of two main types of investigations: audience research and copy research.

Audience research involves the gathering of data about the targeted consumers who are likely to buy the product. The data-gathering methods include interviews and surveys of both satisfied customers and potential new customers. Researchers learn about customers by using both demographics and psychographics. **Demographics** are measurements of audience characteristics that are easily observed and labeled, such as age, gender, income, occupation, and ethnicity. **Psychographics** are measurements of audience characteristics that are difficult to observe and label, such as the psychological (and sometimes hidden) dimensions of attitudes, beliefs, values, interests, and motivations. One of the best-known approaches to psychographics is SRI Consulting Business Intelligence's (SRIC-BI's) VALS™ framework (see Figure 13.2) which divides consumers into types such as "Believers" who are literal, loyal, and moralistic, and "Achievers," who are more upscale, goal oriented and brand conscious.

Both demographics and psychographics help advertisers in terms of **positioning,** the process of finding the product's most specific customer type and creating appeals that will be effective with that type. For example, early research showed that people who loved Volkswagens appreciated their simplicity and economy. The resultant campaign was "Think Small." IBM found out through audience research that its customers were interested not in machines but in solutions to their computing problems, so it came up with the campaign "Solutions for a Small Planet."

Along with positioning existing products, audience research is key in the development of new products. This type of research led to the creation of caffeine-free colas in the 1980s. It also results in new approaches: Research showed that most of the beer sold in the United States is consumed at

audience research
The gathering of data about consumers targeted in an advertising campaign.

demographics
Measurements of audience characteristics that are easily observed and labeled, such as age, gender, income, occupation, and ethnicity.

psychographics
Measurements of audience characteristics that are difficult to observe and label, such as the psychological (and sometimes hidden) dimensions of attitudes, beliefs, values, interests, and motivations.

positioning
The process of finding specific customer types and creating advertising appeals for them.

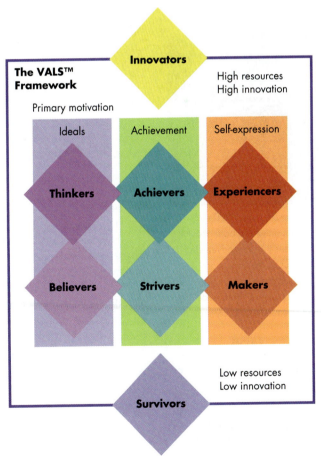

FIGURE 13.2 VALS™ Framework The VALS system divides consumers into eight types based primarily on how much they are motivated by ideals, achievement, and self-expression. VALS was originally an acronym for "Values and Lifestyles." The current VALS system is based on psychological traits instead of social values, so its owners dropped "Values and Lifestyles" but retained the VALS brand.

The VALS™ Framework. Source: *SRI Consulting Business Intelligence* (SRIC-BI); www.sric-bi.com/VALS.

This classic Volkswagen ad from the 1960s was based on research that showed the target audience liked simplicity and economy.

Think small.

18 New York University students have gotten into a sun-roof VW; a tight fit. The Volkswagen is sensibly sized for a family. Mother, father, and three growing kids suit it nicely.

In economy runs, the VW averages close to 50 miles per gallon. You won't do near that; after all, professional drivers have canny trade secrets. (Want to know some? Write VW, Box #65, Englewood, N. J.) Use regular gas and forget about oil between changes.

The VW is 4 feet shorter than a conventional car (yet has as much leg room up front). While other cars are doomed to roam the crowded streets, you park in tiny places.

VW spare parts are inexpensive. A new front fender (at an authorized VW dealer) is $21.75.* A cylinder head, $19.95.* The nice thing is, they're seldom needed.

A new Volkswagen sedan is $1,565.* Other than a radio and side view mirror, that includes everything you'll really need.

In 1959 about 120,000 Americans thought small and bought VWs. Think about it.

The *Media World* DVD that accompanies this book (track 6) discusses the way advertising and public relations work together. Here, a combined team at Ogilvy Worldwide maps out a strategy for a campaign.

copy research
Studies that test the effectiveness of ad content, or copy.

focus groups
Small groups of potential consumers observed by a researcher.

the end of the workday and is perceived as a reward. This finding became the basic idea behind the long-running "Miller Time" campaign.

The second type of investigation conducted in the research department, **copy research,** tests the effectiveness of the actual ad content. Copy research involves both pretesting and posttesting. Pretesting, which is conducted before the ads run, might involve pulling aside consumers at a shopping mall to ask their opinions on various commercials or print layouts.

Sometimes pretests involve **focus groups,** small groups of potential users who sit around and chat about a potential campaign under the guidance of the researcher. Account executives like focus group pretests, but these techniques have their problems. As one creative director complained:

> It is not uncommon for a campaign to be strangled at birth by a few dozen housewives from Queens. The problem is that any genuinely original idea is likely to receive mixed reviews because of its very originality; show those housewives something familiar and they will give you more comforting reactions. In this way, research often perpetuates tame and derivative work.[11]

There have been several famously successful campaigns that originally tested badly in focus groups, including Miller Light's "Tastes Great—Less Filling" and the Absolut vodka bottle ads.

Posttests, which are conducted after the ad campaign has started, are used to test the effectiveness of the campaign. They might take the form of telephone surveys or focus groups, usually centering on whether people remember the ad and the product that was advertised, and how they felt about it.

Both audience research and copy research might be part of an introduction of the product into a test market, to see if a wider rollout would be successful. Minneapolis has been a popular test market over the years. People there have seen ads for ChocoChill, a chocolate-flavored Kool-Aid-type powdered drink mix; a Mr. Coffee filter tea blend, brewed in a coffeemaker; and McDonald's Shanghai McNuggets, which came with chopsticks and oriental dipping sauces—each of which failed in the test market and was not offered nationally.

Creative Departments

The creative department of a full-service advertising agency performs the primary functions of designing and producing ads. Creative directors put together teams that usually include copywriters, who create the words for the ad, and an art director, the staff member responsible for setting the visual style of the advertising. The art director chooses the individual photographers, illustrators, and graphic designers. Other staff members include radio and television producers, musicians, and casting experts.

In today's global marketplace, the creative staff is also often called on to come up with creative solutions to cross-cultural problems (see the Close-Up on Industry box).

The Media Department

The media department of a full-service advertising agency plans how advertising budgets will be allocated among various media and arranges for the purchase of the media space and time. Specialists in this department determine the media mix, that is, which media, and how much space or time in each, will be used for the campaign. Different media have their own advantages and disadvantages in reaching potential customers (see Figure 13.3). Media department professionals consider the uniqueness of each medium in their recommendations to the client. The following list highlights various media as vehicles for advertising and discusses their advantages and disadvantages:

 SELF QUIZ What are the organizational areas of a full-service agency, and what are the responsibilities of each area?

Different media have different advantages for advertisers.

- *Newspapers.* Newspapers provide easy-to-find ads on the most current local sales, and they offer "money off" coupons that the shopper can take to the store. They also have a short lead time, which means that an advertiser can place an ad just a few days before it runs, which allows for the use of the latest information, such as sales prices. Newsprint doesn't allow for glossy artwork, though, so some advertisers shy away from newspapers for image advertising.

- *Television.* With its reach and visual impact, television is perfect for image advertising. Television encourages name recognition better than most

The Tribulations of Global Image Promotion

The rationale behind creating world brands is that global markets are converging by becoming more similar and more Westernized.[1] Still, advertising that works in one country could very well wind up inhibiting sales in another. Sometimes the problem occurs in language translations. When the Coors Brewing Company wanted to translate its slogan "Turn It Loose" into Spanish, the result was read as "Suffer from Diarrhea." Clairol kept the name "Mist Stick" for its curling iron in Germany, but in German *Mist* is slang for manure. The pen maker Parker tried to sell a ballpoint pen in Mexico with the slogan "It won't leak in your pocket and embarrass you." The company assumed that the word *embarazar* meant "to embarrass"; it actually means "to impregnate." So the resulting ad read, "It won't leak in your pocket and make you pregnant."[2]

Sometimes the problem is in the use of a visual image. When Gerber started selling baby food in Africa, it used the same packaging as in the United States, with the beautiful baby on the label. Company executives were puzzled when African consumers reacted with shock and revulsion. Later, Gerber learned that since most Africans can't read English, companies there routinely put pictures on the label of what's inside. In Malaysia, U.S. cigarette firms wanting to stress outdoorsy greenery in their billboards found that the color green represented death and disease to the local citizens. In Arab countries, American ads that use cartoon animals to sell food products ran into trouble because Arabs see animals as unclean.

When cultures differ, advertisers have to find creative solutions. Cigarette maker Philip Morris and its ad agency, Leo Burnett, had difficulty exporting the

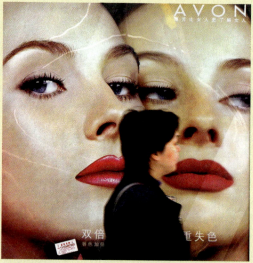

Global corporations like Avon have to be careful when placing ads overseas. Advertising that works in one country could very well wind up inhibiting sales in another.

quintessentially American Marlboro cowboy to Hong Kong, where the cigarette was selling poorly. They discovered that in China, the cowboy was a common laborer—there was little romance attached to his image. A white horse, however, was a symbol of esteem. So the Burnett agency put the Marlboro Man on a white horse, and sales skyrocketed in Hong Kong.[3]

[1]Laurel Wentz, "World Brands," *Advertising Age*, September 9, 1996, p. 121.
[2]David Helin, "When Slogans Go Wrong," *American Demographics* 14 (February 1992). The other examples of translation blunders come from Shelly Reese, "Culture Shock," *Marketing Tools*, May 1998, available online at www.demographics.com.
[3]Cited in Randall Rothenberg, "The Big New Pitch for Old Ads," *New York Times*, October 9, 1988, p. 4.

---

other media. Its biggest disadvantage is that it is extremely expensive. Thirty-second spots for a prime-time network hit like *Grey's Anatomy* cost around $1 million to air, while spots for special events such as the Super Bowl now cost $2.5 million. In fact, the commercials on the Super Bowl have become almost as important as the game itself. Well-known movie directors have done many of these spots.

Another disadvantage of television advertising is called **clutter,** the glut of commercials that compete for the viewer's attention. The average TV viewer sees about 38,000 television commercials a year,[12] and after a while they can blur. Along with **infomercials** (program-length commercials that

clutter
The glut of ads that compete for the public's attention.

infomercials
Program-length television commercials.

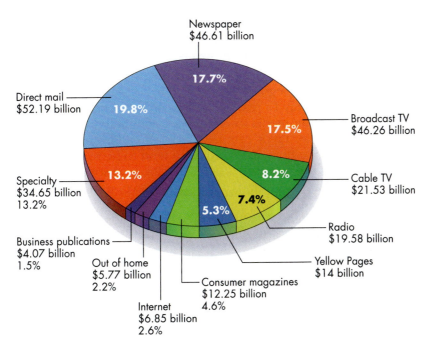

Newspaper
$46.61 billion

17.7%

Direct mail
$52.19 billion

19.8%

Broadcast TV
$46.26 billion

17.5%

Specialty
$34.65 billion
13.2%

13.2%

8.2%

Cable TV
$21.53 billion

7.4%

5.3%

Radio
$19.58 billion

Business publications
$4.07 billion
1.5%

Yellow Pages
$14 billion

Out of home
$5.77 billion
2.2%

Consumer magazines
$12.25 billion
4.6%

Internet
$6.85 billion
2.6%

FIGURE 13.3 Top U.S. Advertising Media by Revenue Total annual U.S. ad revenue is around $264 billion.

Source: FactPack 2006, Supplement to *Advertising Age* magazine, www.adage.com, accessed November 2006.

follow the format of information or talk shows) and the typical 30-second spots, there are now quite a few 15-second spots that allow even more messages to be squeezed into an hour's viewing.

- ***Direct Mail.*** **Direct mail advertising** includes catalogs, flyers, coupon packages, and computer-generated letters that are sent through the postal service. Direct mail is also known as direct marketing to advertisers and as junk mail to the people who receive it. Advertisers like direct mail for a number of reasons. For one thing, the advertiser can choose from a wide range of formats. Catalogs, for example, can have the glossy paper of magazines, which allows for high-quality illustrations and an extended shelf life.

  Another advantage of direct mail is that its results are very measurable. The advertiser knows exactly how many pieces were sent out and how many came back with a positive response, so calculating the cost per thousand (CPM—see Chapter 5) is easy and accurate. That doesn't mean that direct mail is particularly cheap; a 1 or 2 percent response rate is considered fairly successful, so it is not uncommon for each response to cost the advertiser as much as $15.

- ***Specialty Ads.*** Specialty ads consist of everything from matchbook covers to T-shirts, pens, party balloons, and even the inside doors of public toilets. This type of advertising is found

direct mail advertising
Advertising sent by mail.

Specialty ads can appear on anything from pens to paperweights.

on every type of medium, including videotapes and CD-ROMs that car manufacturers send out to potential customers. Until 1998, advertising on the World Wide Web was included in the specialty category also, but it has become lucrative enough since then to be included in its own category.

- **Radio.** Radio's highly segmented formats make it easy to target specific audiences. It is a great way to reach everyone from young people who are difficult to reach via other media to adults who commute to work—political consultants, for example, favor campaign ads on radio news programs to reach adults during drive time. Radio ads also tend to be relatively inexpensive. Production costs are minimal, and often station personnel will produce ads free of charge. Radio airtime is also inexpensive, especially compared with television airtime.

A problem is that listeners use radio ads, like TV ads, as a cue to switch stations. To combat this, radio stations try to blend in advertising with the programming as seamlessly as possible. The ads are often presented by the disc jockey or other on-air personality, so they become part of the general chatter. If the station has a musical format, the same type of music is usually used in the ad.

Neither the name "yellow pages" nor this "walking fingers" logo was ever copyrighted. We now have many different yellow pages, many of which display this logo.

- **Yellow Pages.** Yellow pages advertising is based on the concept that it is a good idea to advertise in the book that people use to find the telephone number of the business they need. The first yellow pages were invented and owned by the Bell Telephone system. When the Bell system broke up into smaller regional companies in the early 1980s, other entrepreneurs began publishing yellow pages, aided by the fact that neither the name "yellow pages" nor the "walking fingers" logo was ever copyrighted by Bell. As a result, we now have a wide variety of yellow pages, many of which have become specialized, including segments for different language groups. In the New York City area alone, there are yellow pages catering to, and in the language of, Russians, Israelis, Portuguese, Cubans, Dominicans, Filipinos, Koreans, and Colombians.[13] The major problem with yellow pages is that they come out only once or twice a year. A lot can change for a business in that amount of time, and those changes can't be reflected in the ads.

- **Magazines.** The advantages of advertising in magazines include their pass-along rate (four to five extra people read each copy besides the purchaser or subscriber) and their shelf life (people keep them for weeks, and sometimes longer). Their glossy paper makes them appropriate for fine artwork. Since the 1950s, magazines have been the medium of choice for special interest advertising. As noted in Chapter 5, there is a magazine for nearly every activity or interest imaginable, from *Abrasive Engineering Society Magazine* to *Zoo Biology,* with very little wasted circulation within each subscription list. Computerized printing technology makes segmentation even easier, allowing regional and local ads to be built into different zip codes and mailing lists. *Newsweek,* to name one example, has more than 150 different versions, printed for different geographic and occupational segments.

The most exotic magazine ads, known in the business as spectaculars, hit their height in the late 1980s—and resulted in some spectacular failures. A 1987 musical Christmas ad for Absolut vodka malfunctioned in scores of magazines, causing them to play "Jingle Bells" endlessly. Another problem was caused by scratch-and-sniff ads, which bothered people with allergies.

- **Outdoor Advertising.** Outdoor ads are big, impressive, and striking—and they can't be turned off like television or thrown away like a newspaper. This category of advertising includes billboards; signs; posters; placards on buses, taxis, trains, and bus shelters; and even the carved figures that once stood outside stores, the most famous of which was the cigar-store

Indian. Outdoor ads have an image of simplicity and directness ("Eat Here—Get Gas") and in fact the messages on them do have to be simple but catchy, because people tend to pass them quickly. But outdoor ads have their own spectaculars, such as the neon and special-effects billboards that can be found in Los Angeles, Las Vegas, and Times Square in New York City. These spectaculars include cigarette ads that exhale puffs of smoke, golfers who actually swing their clubs, and waterfalls of real water. One type of billboard "talks" by directing the motorist to tune to a particular radio frequency; the billboard itself is fitted with a low-power radio transmitter. Another form of outdoor advertising, "coptermedia," features flying electric signs lifted into the skies by helicopter. Other airborne ads are carried on balloons and blimps, towed by planes, or written across the skies with skywriting.

• **Online Advertising.** The World Wide Web is the most rapidly growing medium for advertising. Whereas it generated practically no advertising revenue in 1995, it was earning nearly $7 billion annually by 2007. In many ways, Web ads are a convergence of all former ads. They are both print- and image-oriented. As in newspapers and the yellow pages, ads on the Web are placed precisely where consumers are looking for product information. Online ads compete with magazines in terms of artwork. They involve motion and sound, and therefore have the entertainment advantages of radio and television. They involve and motivate the customer because they are interactive—customers can order merchandise and have their orders confirmed in seconds. A disadvantage of online ads is that some users resent them because they, like TV ads, create clutter. This is especially true of spam, the unsolicited e-mail messages discussed in Chapter 10. Also, not everyone has access to the Web, although users do tend to be in the younger, higher-income groups that advertisers like to reach.

Online ads include standard banner ads, which are strips that run across the top of a Web page; skyscrapers, which run up the side of the page; and buttons, which are small ads of various sizes. Images that move in any way are known as rich media in the online ad business. They include pop-ups, which overlay all or part of the page being viewed, and pop-unders, which appear when the user exits the page. Online ads that include games for children, now called advergames, are an especially effective interactive environment. Kraft's Nabiscoworld.com features advergames for at least 17 brands of snack food.

SELF QUIZ What are some of the advantages and disadvantages of the various media for advertising?

Once the media department experts decide on the media mix, **media buyers,** those who actually purchase the time and space, take over. Media buyers tend to be skilled negotiators and specialists in radio, spot-television, network-television, print, or online buying. They have to interpret the data received from the research department and translate it into the best possible media buys for their clients. The media department is also responsible for the annual analysis of industry developments, such as which television shows are going to be hits and which print media are likely to develop the best demographics for a particular product. They make sure, for example, that advertisements for maternity clothes don't wind up in a magazine read primarily by men.

The media department is also responsible for ad maintenance. This could mean anything from making sure that shrubs don't block the view of a billboard to hiring observers to make sure that purchased TV commercials actually run. If a broadcast commercial doesn't run in the spot it is supposed to, or if there is a technical problem with the spot, the media department makes sure that the client receives a "make good," or replacement spot.

media buyers
Advertising agency personnel who purchase ad time and space.

ADVERTISING OBJECTIVES

One of the first things the agency and client have to determine is the objective of an advertising campaign. A lot of time, effort, and money will be expended in building the campaign, and having a clear objective helps the agency devise a road map to minimize false turns and wasted effort. Advertising professionals help their clients think in terms of traditional and nontraditional objectives.

Traditional Objectives

Traditional objectives for advertising campaigns typically relate to product sales. These include building name recognition, spreading news about the product, promoting an image, and adding value to the product.

Name Recognition

A basic objective of advertising is to make the product familiar to the potential buyer. The recognition of brand names is important in an era in which customers shop in huge megastores. When there is no one to help them, buyers are likely to grab a product with a familiar brand name. Ad agencies therefore work hard to come up with clever brand names and the catchy slogans that go with them, such as "Sunny Delight: The good stuff kids go for"; "M&Ms melt in your mouth, not in your hand"; and "Nobody doesn't like Sara Lee." Advertisers also look for other creative ways to keep the name familiar, such as the Absolut vodka ads that associate the name and the shape of the bottle with well-known objects. A swimming pool in the shape of the bottle becomes "Absolut Hollywood"; "Absolut Brooklyn" features the bottle shape of the Brooklyn Bridge.

Spreading News about a Product

Another traditional objective is to spread news about a product. Does it have new ingredients that will make it even more effective? Is it coming out in a new version, model, or edition? *New* is the most frequently used word in advertising copy, and companies love to tout new uses for their products in ads. In the 1980s Arm & Hammer ran several campaigns promoting new uses for its baking soda. Before these campaigns, people used baking soda only in cooking and sometimes as an emergency replacement toothpaste. Arm & Hammer devised a series of ads that told consumers to use baking soda to deodorize the refrigerator. Simply open a new box every month, they were told, and leave it in the refrigerator to get rid of unpleasant fish and onion smells. The campaign worked—so well in fact that the next campaign instructed consumers to use the product as a cleaner and deodorant for their toilets. Because of the ads, people were buying boxes of this product and throwing them immediately down the toilet.

Promoting an Image

image advertising
The promotion of an idea that becomes associated with a product.

Some ads do not sell a product directly as much as they promote an image indirectly. **Image advertising** is designed to associate a product with an image in the audience's mind. Sometimes advertisers achieve this association by giving their clients' products a personality. The Leo Burnett Agency of Chicago was famous for this. It was Burnett who gave us the Marlboro Man (changing what was once considered a lady's filtered cigarette into a product fit for a macho cowboy) and the Doublemint Twins. Advertisers have also created a wide range of cartoon characters for this purpose, including the Campbell Soup Kids, Tony the Tiger, the Jolly Green Giant, the Pillsbury Doughboy, Charley the Tuna, and the toga-clad Little Caesars pizza man.

Sometimes companies get together to change the image of an entire industry, creating what is known as **institutional ads.** Thus the cotton industry, through its trade group, gave us "Cotton: The fabric of our lives." The milk industry established the image of the celebrity milk mustache, while other industries gave us "Beef is real food," "Pork: The other white meat," and "The incredible edible egg." The Great Lakes Mink Association has produced campaigns promoting the fur coat industry since 1968. Its ads simply show a female celebrity swathed in an opulent mink coat, along with the slogan "What Becomes a Legend Most?".

Adding Value to the Product

When a sexy female model is draped over the hood of a car in an ad, she seems to be promising herself to the male consumer who is the main customer for new cars. Does she really come with the car? In a way, she does, because another traditional objective of advertising is to add value to the product that is not inherent within it. A cake mix is a simple food, but advertising will try to associate it with family happiness and love. That makes the cake more than a simple dessert, so value has been added to it by the advertising. Adding value is also an important consideration in the advertising for children's toys. Children want the toys they see advertised on television, so the advertisement itself makes the toy more valuable to them. This is a controversial technique, as we will see later in this chapter.

Each of the institutional ads for the mink industry show a female celebrity (in this case, Elizabeth Taylor) wrapped in a mink coat, along with the slogan "What Becomes a Legend Most?"

Nontraditional Objectives

Sometimes advertisers have objectives that go beyond or stand instead of merely selling a product. Such nontraditional objectives include advocacy, correction, and public service.

SELF QUIZ What is meant by advertising's adding value to a product?

Advocacy Ads

Advocacy ads are designed to affect public opinion or government policy. These ads are also called editorial ads because, like standard newspaper editorials, they express an opinion. The National Rifle Association is famous for its advocacy ads—often featuring celebrities and the slogan "I'm the NRA"—that protest various forms of gun control.

Corrective Advertising

Corrective ads have the objective of rectifying an inaccurate impression formed by earlier ads. Sometimes these ads are required by a legal settlement, such as the one reached between the Federal Trade Commission (FTC) and the makers of the mouthwash Listerine. Listerine's ads used to claim that the mouthwash could kill the germs that cause colds, when in fact it could not. The FTC made Listerine run $10 million worth of ads that said, "Listerine will not help prevent colds or sore throats or lessen their severity." In another case aspirin maker Bayer was told to spend $1 million to correct

Counteradvertising: The "Shards O' Glass Freeze Pops," commercial is a parody of cigarette advertising. In it, a spokesman explains, "The only proven way to reduce health risks from our glass pops is to not eat them."

counteradvertising
Ads designed to fight an image that is not in the public interest.

guerrilla advertising
Advertising that uses unorthodox tactics.

public service announcements (PSAs)
Ads on public interest issues presented as a service to the community.

What are some of the traditional and nontraditional objectives of advertising?

the impression that people could reduce their chances of heart attack or stroke simply by taking aspirin daily.

Counteradvertising, another type of corrective advertising, isn't run by the company that ran the original ads and isn't required by any type of legal settlement. Counterads are usually run by a nonprofit agency, such as Adbusters (www.adbusters.org), to fight the image created by large-scale campaigns that the agency feels are not in the public interest. Often these ads are parodies that make fun of the original ads. The American Legacy Foundation, which sponsors the "Truth" antismoking campaign, presented a counterad during the 2004 Super Bowl that parodied the corrective advertising that tobacco marketers had been forced to adopt. The commercial featured a spokesman for an imaginary company that made ice pops laced with shards of glass. "At Shards O' Glass Freeze Pops, we now agree there's no such thing as a safe glass freeze pop," the spokesman explains. "The only proven way to reduce health risks from our glass pops is to not eat them." The commercial sent viewers to a satiric Web site, Shardsoglass .com, and ended with this disclaimer: "And remember, Shards O' Glass Freeze Pops are for adults only." Counteradvertising based on parody is a form of **guerrilla advertising,** a technique so named because, like guerrilla warfare, its tactics are unorthodox.[14]

Promoting the Public Interest

Promoting the public interest is yet another nontraditional advertising objective. This is usually accomplished through **public service announcements (PSAs),** which are ads on public interest issues presented at no cost as a service to the community. The Partnership for a Drug-Free America, a nonprofit coalition of media professionals, has sponsored numerous well-known PSAs. Through PSAs, the full creative force of a volunteer ad agency is often put into campaigns to fight social ills such as drunk driving, teenage pregnancy, AIDS, dropping out of school, prejudice, and racism.

Many ad clients like PSAs because they help put all advertising in a more credible and favorable light. The Advertising Council, a nonprofit association supported by ad agencies, conducts dozens of major public service campaigns each year. These campaigns have created many memorable slogans, such as "A mind is a terrible thing to waste" (for the United Negro College Fund), as well as some memorable characters, such as Smokey Bear ("Only you can prevent forest fires") and McGruff the Crime Dog ("Take a bite out of crime").

Controversies

To those who practice the trade, advertising is both an art and a science. Advertisers study the human mind very carefully, and their output shows what they have learned about consumers. Ads also affect consumer behavior in a variety of ways, and that is the basis for most of the controversy about advertising.

American advertising has always been controversial, in part because advertisers wield enormous power. A continuing controversy involves the question of how much freedom of speech advertisers should have. Other issues

Postal Service	**Food and Drug Administration**	**Federal Trade Commission**
Regulates direct-mail advertising since 1895.	Created by the Pure Food and Drug Act in 1906. Regulates ads about foods, cosmetics, drugs, and health care products.	Established in 1914. Protects against false advertising and unfair business practices.

Securities and Exchange Commission	**Federal Communications Commission**
Established in 1934. Regulates advertising of stocks and bonds.	Established in 1934. Regulates political ads on television and radio.

FIGURE 13.4 U.S. Government Advertising Regulations The regulation of advertising began in the United States when the policy of "Let the Buyer Beware" changed to "Let the Seller Be Honest."

that draw criticism are truth in advertising, ads directed at children, and advertiser influence on media content.

ADVERTISING AND FREEDOM OF SPEECH

Advertisers believe that their messages should be treated like any other form of speech, but courts and legislators have in certain cases decided that the paid, persuasive nature of advertising calls for some limits. As mentioned earlier in this chapter, several government agencies, such as the U.S. Postal Service and the Food and Drug Administration, regulate advertising in some way (see Figure 13.4). The Federal Trade Commission (FTC) is the main government watchdog against deceptive advertising. When the FTC receives a complaint, it will often ask an advertiser to substantiate its claims. For example, when oil companies claimed that premium gasoline would give all cars better mileage and help them run cleaner, the FTC stepped in. The oil companies couldn't verify that any car except high-performance sports cars could benefit, so the FTC told them to cease and desist advertising that claim.[15] Most of the companies complied right away. The one that didn't, Exxon, was sued by the FTC and forced into compliance.

If the government doesn't intervene, individual consumers still have access to the courts when they feel advertisers have gone too far. Within those courts, advertising enjoys a certain amount of freedom of speech, but not as much as the news media do. When an Atlanta businessman was murdered in 1986, his business partner and two hit men were convicted of the crime. But the family of the victim went further when they learned that the partner had found the hit men from a Soldier of Fortune magazine ad. The classified ad read as follows:

> GUN FOR HIRE: 37-year-old professional mercenary desires jobs. Vietnam Veteran. Discrete [sic] and very private. Body guard, courier, and other special skills. All jobs considered. Phone . . .

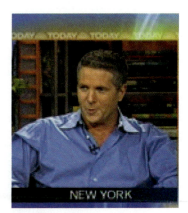

On the *Media World* DVD that accompanies this book (track 28, *The Debate Over Free Speech*) ad executive Donny Deutsch and political commentator Fay Buchanan disagree on the idea of government control of advertising.

The family sued the magazine and won $4.3 million in damages. The court ruled that a publisher can be held liable for damages if an ad "on its face, and without the need for investigation, makes it apparent that there is a substantial danger of harm to the public." If the name and contact information of someone willing to carry out a hit had been printed in a news article, the First Amendment would have protected the newspaper's right to do so, but commercial speech enjoys less protection.

Who regulates advertising, and how is it regulated?

SELF QUIZ

TRUTH IN ADVERTISING

Most people will agree that ads should not lie. Government regulations demand it, as do industry codes. But the line between truth and deception can often be quite thin. There are several problems in determining whether advertisers are telling the truth, or, for that matter, what the word *truth* means in the context of an ad. After all, modern advertising has always been more about human motivation than product virtues. Consumers don't buy the product, they buy the satisfaction that the product offers. As the old saying

Most people will accept deception in entertainment, so why not in entertaining ads?

bait-and-switch advertising
Technique in which a seller provides bait in the form of an advertised bargain and a switch when the customer is talked into a more expensive product.

parity statement
An assertion of equality that sounds like an assertion of superiority.

goes, advertisers sell the sizzle, not the steak. To make matters even more confusing, ads today have converged into a form of entertainment. Most people will accept deception in entertainment, so they are not likely to question it in entertaining ads. Ad professionals ask, "When a TV ad suggests that a pair of sneakers can turn a kid into a superhero, where's the harm?"

Critics insist, however, that some ads push the legal boundaries established to protect consumers from deception. Others may technically be legal yet ethically questionable. **Bait-and-switch advertising,** for example, provides bait in the form of an advertised bargain and a switch when the customer is talked into a more expensive product.

Other forms of deception are often seen in direct mail advertising. According to the U.S. Postal Service, which receives hundreds of thousands of complaints about direct mail advertising every year, the most common deception involves the statement "You're a guaranteed winner." Sometimes it turns out that recipients are "winners" because they are being given the "opportunity" to buy magazine subscriptions. Other times, when the purported prize-winners call the number provided, they are asked to send in a "processing fee," but they never receive a prize.[16]

Critics point out that some wording, such as "part of this complete breakfast," is subtly deceptive.

Some critics assail advertising not for outright dishonesty, but for subtle deception. They accuse copywriters of clever wording that misleads without lying. As the humor columnist Dave Barry points out, an ad saying that a certain cereal is "part of this complete breakfast" usually is referring to "some compressed sugar compound placed on the table next to real food."[17] Another type of deceptive wording is the **parity statement,** defined as an assertion of equality that sounds like an assertion of superiority. An ad using a parity statement is really claiming that the product is just as good as its competition—no better, no worse. "Nothing is proven to work better or last longer than Advil. NOTHING" is a parity statement, in spite of the announcer's dramatic inflection.

ADS DIRECTED AT CHILDREN AND TEENS

Worries about the effects of advertising intensify when critics consider ads directed at children. In fact, many critics feel that ads should not be directed toward very young children at all, and the governments of Denmark and other Scandinavian countries prohibit advertisers from targeting preteens. In the United States, where such ads are common, parents' groups such as the National PTA and watchdog groups such as Action for Children's Television point out that preschoolers do not understand that commercials are there to persuade them—they see ads as just more entertainment. Critics also say that young children are too emotionally susceptible to be exposed to ads. Appeals such as "Make friends with Kool-Aid, make Kool-Aid with friends," they say, are based on deeply felt psychological needs.

Children as Consumer Trainees

Another criticism is that ads treat children as consumer trainees at a time when they should be learning some of the higher values of life. According to this argument, ads mold the character and personality of the child by encouraging greed and by suggesting that people's importance is based on what they own rather than who they are. Worse yet, according to this argument, advertising discourages critical thinking by encouraging children to buy things they don't need and can't afford. Children are also indirect consumers who persuade their parents to make the actual purchases. An ad that makes a child desire a product that the parent does not want to buy ends up adding to family tension.

Junk-Food Ads

Many critics are concerned about unrestricted junk-food ads directed at children. They blame the growing obesity problem in the United States at least partially on these ads. The Center for Science in the Public Interest began legal action in 2006 against the Kellogg Company and the Nickelodeon cable network.[18] The lawsuit aims to prevent these companies from marketing junk foods in venues where 15 percent or more of the audience is under the age of eight. In addition, they seek to stop this marketing through Web sites, contests, or any other practices geared toward that age group. The center was particularly concerned that renowned children's characters such as Tony the Tiger and SpongeBob SquarePants are used to promote these foods.

Alcohol and Cigarette Ads

Critics are especially concerned about the effects of alcohol and cigarette advertising on children (see the Close-Up on Controversy box). During the 1990s the U.S. government began to battle cigarette ads directed to children. Studies of that time showed that one-third of the students in a typical high school either

"I was all set to quit, but when the bastards killed off Joe Camel I swore—never."

Selling Alcohol to Children

Many critics were enraged by the beer ads shown during the 2004 Super Bowl. The humor seemed to be aimed toward a 12-year-old mentality. Perhaps the prime example was the "flatulent horse" ad for Budweiser beer. In it, a young couple is on an idyllic one-horse sleigh ride. The girl happens to be holding a candle, and when the horse breaks wind explosively, Power Rangers, and Kellogg's Frosted Flakes' Tony the Tiger.[1]

That kind of advertising impact is especially troublesome to critics, who point out that young people see nearly 2,000 commercials for beer and wine each year. These critics note that for every public service announcement with a message like

Children see nearly 2,000 commercials for beer and wine each year.

she is badly burned. Her clueless boyfriend asks, "Hey, you smell barbecue?"

Unfortunately, 2004 was not an exception. Super Bowl beer ads, and beer ads in general, have for many years seemed to be directed toward juveniles. Whether or not advertisers do this intentionally, children pick up on them. A few years ago, three animated Budweiser frogs appeared in a Super Bowl commercial, croaking in sequence the syllables "Bud," "wei," and "ser." The commercial was replayed often, and one year later researchers discovered that children ages 9 to 11 were more familiar with what the three frogs croaked than they were with Smokey Bear, the Mighty Morphin'

"Just say no" or "Know when to say when," teens will view 25 to 50 beer and wine commercials that say, essentially, "Drinking is cool."[2]

Meanwhile, underage drinking remains a widespread problem. Many young people are beginning to consume alcohol around the age of 13, a large majority will do their heaviest drinking before their 21st birthday, and 64 percent of high school seniors use alcohol.[3]

Advertisers say that they target their ads only to the over-21 audience, but critics counter that common advertising tactics such as animation, humor, and rock music are extremely attractive to young people, especially children ages 10 to 14. Beer advertisements in

Cigarette ads featuring Joe Camel and other cartoon characters were banned in 1999.

wore or carried items, such as T-shirts, hats, and backpacks, promoting cigarettes, and that teenagers toting these specialty items were four times more likely than other teenagers to be smokers.[19] Such advertising seems particularly inappropriate in a society in which 3,000 children begin smoking each day, and 1,000 of those will eventually die a tobacco-related death.[20] Joe Camel and other cartoon characters that appealed specifically to children were particularly worrisome to critics.

A 1999 settlement between tobacco companies and states attorneys general banned all transit and billboard advertising of tobacco products throughout the United States. It also banned the distribution of apparel and other nontobacco merchandise with brand names or logos; prohibited brand-name sponsorship of concerts and events with a significant youth audience; banned payments for the use of tobacco products in movies, television shows, and theater productions; and restricted the distribution of free samples. The advertising of cigarettes on television had already been prohibited.

particular often glamorize drinking and provide no information about the potential negative effects alcohol has on the body, including nausea, blackouts, and liver problems.

No matter what age group the advertisers are targeting, critics say, ads for alcoholic beverages appeal to the underage market. George A. Hacker, director of the Alcohol Policies Project at the Center for Science in the Public Interest, has said, "It's impossible to construct an advertisement that appeals to a 21-year-old, on his 21st birthday, and doesn't appeal to someone who's 18 years old or maybe even 16." In a televised event like the Super Bowl, he added, "even though the underage audience is a small proportion, it's still the largest audience of kids for any show ever."[4]

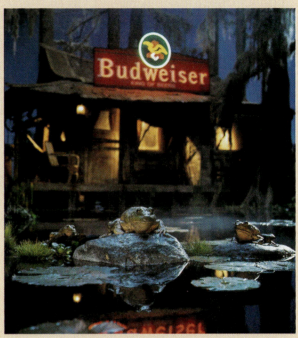

Many critics complain that beer ads seem to be directed toward kids. In this ad three animated frogs croak the syllables "Bud," "wei," "ser" in sequence. Researchers found that children were more familiar with what the three frogs croaked than they were with Smokey Bear, the Mighty Morphin' Power Rangers, and Kellogg's Frosted Flakes' Tony the Tiger.

[1]Mediascope Issue Brief, www.mediascope.org/pubs/ibriefs/yoaa.htm, accessed February 15, 2004.
[2]Alcohol Policies Project, www.cspinet.org/booze/liquor_branded_advertising_FS1.htm, accessed February 15, 2004.
[3]Mediascope Issue Brief.
[4]Quoted in Nat Ives, "Is the Alcohol Industry Pitching Products to Young Audiences?" *New York Times* online, September 10, 2003.

Many in the industry feel that these are unfair restrictions on free speech regarding a product that is, after all, legal. Critics, however, point out that other countries go even further. Cigarette ads are banned outright in Britain, India, and Brazil because of their influence on children. In countries with no restrictions, such as China and Vietnam, tobacco use is very high.

ADVERTISER INFLUENCE ON MEDIA CONTENT

The issue of advertiser influence on media content involves two related controversies. Advertisers influence content both through product placement in entertainment programming and through their economic clout over news media.

Product Placement: Influencing Entertainment Content

Product placement—or, as it is known in the industry, product integration—was defined in Chapter 6, "Movies." This technique is becoming increasingly common in other media as well. Television executives have been concerned about viewers skipping commercials for years. Commercial breaks have always cued viewers to run to the bathroom or get a snack. The avoidance of commercials was heightened by a succession of technological devices, including

CONSIDER THIS

Why are ads directed at children and teens so controversial? Do you believe they should be banned?

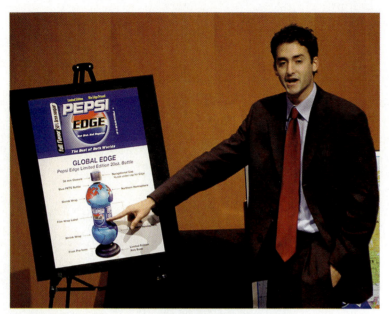

The NBC program *The Apprentice* features product placements in contestant competitions. Here, the task is to come up with an ad campaign for a new Pepsi product.

remote controls, videotape recorders, and most recently, digital devices such as TiVo that can automatically skip ads. Many industry professionals feel that their only recourse is to make commercials part of the programming itself. That's why you will see sitcom characters occasionally stopping to extol the virtues of a breakfast cereal or characters in police dramas stopping to talk in front of large billboards.

On Reality TV

Reality programs have been especially ripe for product placement. Sears, for example, had a product placement deal with ABC for that broadcaster's program *Extreme Makeover: Home Edition.* The show has included not just the use of Sears products but also several scenes of Sears trucks delivering merchandise, plumbers and other workers from Sears home-improvement services making repairs, and visits to Sears stores by the show's makeover team cast. Fact File 13.3 lists the top shows in terms of product placement.

In Books

Other media are also experimenting with product placement. This includes books, one of the few media left that seldom include advertising. The Italian jeweler Bulgari commissioned best-selling novelist Fay Weldon to write a novel with references to the Bulgari name. The novel, *The Bulgari Connection,* was published in 2001. In 2006 Cover Girl Cosmetics signed a marketing partnership with the publisher of the novel *Cover Girl* to have its products mentioned in various parts of the novel.

In the News

Of particular concern to critics have been recent incidents of product placement in the news. Advertisers say they are increasingly being pitched opportunities from local stations to integrate their clients' products into news programming in exchange for buying commercial time or paying integration fees. Most stations are focusing these efforts on morning news shows, where lifestyle segments allow for more integration opportunities without sounding as many alarm bells with viewers as it might if product integration popped up in the hard news portions of their newscasts.

Some stations, however, go further. For example, Univision's KMEX–TV in Los Angeles has an integration partnership with health care provider Kaiser Permanente Southern California as part of what the station calls its "Lead a healthy life, get the facts" public service campaign. Kaiser physicians are interviewed on health topics on Univision's various news programs, news footage is shot at Kaiser facilities, and Kaiser patients and support groups are featured in news segments. As part of the arrangement, Kaiser pays additional fees for the placements, which are not disclosed as such during the news programs.[21]

FACT FILE 13.3

Top Product Placement Programming

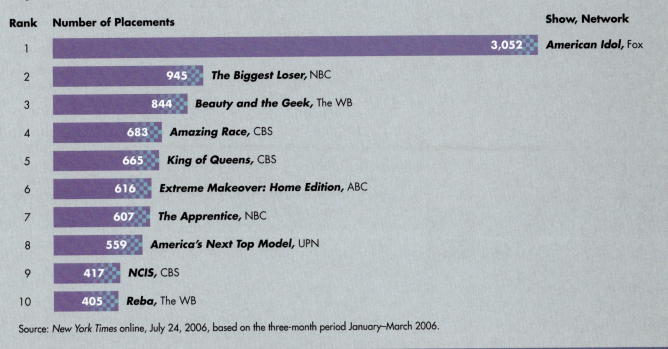

Rank	Number of Placements	Show, Network
1	3,052	**American Idol,** Fox
2	945	**The Biggest Loser,** NBC
3	844	**Beauty and the Geek,** The WB
4	683	**Amazing Race,** CBS
5	665	**King of Queens,** CBS
6	616	**Extreme Makeover: Home Edition,** ABC
7	607	**The Apprentice,** NBC
8	559	**America's Next Top Model,** UPN
9	417	**NCIS,** CBS
10	405	**Reba,** The WB

Source: *New York Times* online, July 24, 2006, based on the three-month period January–March 2006.

Critics of product placement believe that the practice confuses viewers by masking the sponsors' role in determining the content of entertainment programming. One critic called the practice "an affront to basic honesty."[22] Critics also insist that product placement defies the very definition of advertising, which, as mentioned at the beginning of this chapter, includes the idea of an identified sponsor.[23]

Economic Clout: Influencing the News

The revenue generated by advertising in television, newspapers, and other media gives advertisers an extraordinary amount of power. This power becomes controversial when it is used to influence the content of the news or information that the medium carries. For example, Xavier Suarez, the mayor of Miami, Florida, threatened to pull the city's legal advertising from the *Miami Herald* in 1998 unless it became "a lot nicer to me, my people, my citizens and my city."[24] The *Herald* was investigating accusations of voter fraud by Suarez campaign supporters at the time of his threat, which the mayor left on the managing editor's answering machine. The city advertising was worth about $200,000 a year. In response to the mayor's threat, the editor of the paper publicly announced that the news columns and the advertising columns of the paper would remain separate.

Sometimes advertisers try to influence content by canceling ads if they don't agree with ideas expressed in a particular story, episode, or program. When CBS ran a story in 2004 critical of auto dealers on *60 Minutes II*, the Philadelphia Dodge Dealers Group withdrew all its advertising from the local CBS station, costing that station more than $100,000 in revenue. After a Catholic group called for a boycott of *Nothing Sacred*, an ABC television series about a young, hip Catholic priest who questions church doctrine, Sears, Isuzu, and Weight Watchers withdrew their ads.

Advertisers explain that they are concerned about the surrounding environment in which their ads appear. Because of this, airlines ask newspapers and broadcast news programs to pull their ads if they will appear near news stories of air disasters. Grocery stores politely request that their commercials go on after cooking segments and not after famine reports. Many other advertisers ask for advance notice of stories that might create a negative environment for their ads. Critics point out that this practice encourages self-censorship, because the media might avoid those stories so as not to lose ad revenue. For years cigarette companies required "early warnings" of anti-smoking articles that would be run in magazines in which they advertised. The magazines knew that these warnings would enable the companies to pull their ads. To avoid the loss of revenue, some magazines dropped stories about the relationship between smoking and health.[25]

Too often, the media are willing to be influenced by their advertisers. Some local newspapers may entice new advertisers by offering to run news

stories about their businesses. In all media, memos occasionally arrive from the business office reminding the rest of the staff that the medium can't stay in business by constantly offending advertisers.

How do advertisers influence the editorial content of the media in which their ads appear?

Summing Up

Advertising helped create the mass market necessary for mass production, and it allowed for the diffusion of a wide variety of innovations. It enabled the establishment of brand names sold nationally. It also made the establishment of new media possible by supporting them financially. The Industrial Revolution; the penny press; and the advent of radio, television, and the World Wide Web have all been major events in the growth of advertising.

Advertising agencies are categorized as either in-house, boutique, or full-service. They are usually organized into four areas. Account management coordinates all work with the client. Research departments predict audience reaction and measure ad performance. Creative departments actually devise and produce the ads, and media departments determine the media mix and buy the space or time in the various media. Each medium has its own advantages and disadvantages for advertising. Traditional objectives typically include building name recognition, spreading news about the product, promoting an image, and adding value to the product. Some nontraditional objectives are advocacy (changing public opinion or government policy), correction (changing an impression given by earlier advertising), and public service (promoting the public interest).

Advertising has been controversial from the first printed ads to those currently being developed for the World Wide Web. The biggest controversy concerns how much freedom of speech advertising should be given. A related debate revolves around the nature of truth in advertising. Critics contend that some ads lie outright, while others use subtle deception. Other controversies swirl around ads that affect children. Some critics believe that no ads should be directed to small children and that promoting drinking and smoking can be detrimental to teens. Other critics are concerned about the ways advertisers influence the news and information that a medium carries.

Key Terms

These terms are defined and indexed in the Glossary of key terms at the back of the book.

Electronic Excursions

HISTORY

Web Excursion

1. How were ads different in earlier times? What do these differences suggest about changes in consumers? To find out, go to one of the repositories of old ads on the Web. Do a search for "old ads" or "advertising history," or go to http://scriptorium.lib.duke.edu* or a company site such as www.coke.com or www.nike.com and search for advertisements. Choose an old ad that interests you and update the campaign for a contemporary audience.

INDUSTRY

Web Excursion

2. Come up with a list of a half dozen or so of your favorite products, services, stores, fashion designers, and the like. Plug them into your browser with a .com address, such as www.pepsi.com, www.benetton.com, www.clubmed.com, or www.jcrew.com to see if they have a company name Web site. If they don't, key word the company name into any search engine to see if they have one under a different name. When you find your six products, evaluate each Web site as a form of advertising. Is it successful?

CONTROVERSIES

Web Excursion

3. Search the Web for current advertising issues. You might want to go to one of the ad criticism sites such as the BADvertising Institute at www.badvertising.org* or the Center for Commercial Free Education at www.commercialfree.org.* Alternatively, you could access the FTC Consumer Protection site at www.ftc.gov/ftc/consumer.htm* to read about the current advertising issues that the FTC feels the public needs to be warned about. Choose one of these issues and prepare a brief report for the class.

Media World DVD Excursion

4. View track 20, *Your Ad Here: Pizza Hut Places Billboard on Spacecraft* (from NBC News Archive). Are we bombarded with too many ads? If you were offered considerable compensation, would you wear only articles of clothing with a certain company's ads on them? Would you have an ad tattooed on your body? Would you name your first child Hershey Kiss? Where would you draw the line?

ONLINE LEARNING CENTER WWW.MHHE.COM/RODMAN2

You may access these and additional Web excursions at the Online Learning Center for the book (www.mhhe.com/rodman2). Visit the student portion of this Web site to also access the *Interactive Timeline of Mass Media Milestones,* chapter highlights, self quizzes, and recommended readings, movies, and documentaries for this chapter.

*Some Web site addresses may change. When they do, please search for the Web site by name or topic on your favorite search engine.

PART FIVE

Media Law and Ethics

This part of *Mass Media in a Changing World* provides an in-depth examination of two essential areas of media studies: law and ethics. Media law includes a history of media regulation, a discussion of that regulation's current structure, and the controversies surrounding it. Media ethics includes a history of media morality, the philosophy behind that morality, and the controversies it creates.

14 Media Law

15 Media Ethics

Media Law

Understanding Freedom of Expression

14

Chapter Highlights

HISTORY: The history of media law is a history of battles about how free our media should be. Most of these battles have dealt with interpretations of the First Amendment.

TODAY'S MEDIA LAW: Media law is part of a complex legal system that encompasses the areas of personal rights, intellectual property rights, and news-gathering rights.

CONTROVERSIES: Media law controversies include those based on censorship and conflicting rights.

Who Needs the First Amendment?

A survey released in 2005 showed that one in three U.S. high school students say the press ought to be more restricted. The survey of more than 100,000 students, conducted by researchers at the University of Connecticut, found that 36 percent believe newspapers should get "government approval" of stories before publishing, and 32 percent say that the press enjoys "too much freedom." Of students surveyed, 74 percent say people shouldn't be able to burn or deface an American flag as a political statement, and 75 percent mistakenly believe it is illegal.[1] (The U.S. Supreme Court in 1989 ruled that burning or defacing a flag is protected free speech.) Congress has debated

A protestor holds a burning American flag at a demonstration at Amherst College. A majority of young people mistakenly believe that burning a flag is illegal.

flag-burning amendments regularly since then, but none have passed.)

According to the authors of the survey, young people are

Young people are often unaware of the freedoms associated with the First Amendment.

often unaware of the freedoms associated with the First Amendment, which protects free speech, free press, freedom of religion, freedom of assembly, and the right to petition the government. Students do come to appreciate the First Amendment if they are taught about it and given a chance to practice it. Students who take part in school media activities, such as student newspapers or radio stations, are much more likely to support expression of unpopular views. But critics feel that the majority of students are taught to be obedient and compliant rather than to express their views or feel strongly about them. As the editor of one major newspaper warns: "Continue to erode appreciation for the First Amendment, and just maybe that nettlesome provision someday will go away. Life then could be free of conflict and easier to manage. Like it was, say, in Afghanistan under the Taliban, or in Iraq under Saddam Hussein."[2]

The comedian Bill Maher said it a little differently: "In four years, you can teach a gorilla sign language. Is it too much to ask that in the same amount of time a kid be taught what those crazy hippies who founded this country had in mind?"[3]

Surveys that reveal how the public feels about the First Amendment illustrate how confusing media law can be. But the larger question that comes to mind is this: In a free society, just how free do we want our media to be? The answer begins with a brief look at the history of media law and expands into a consideration of today's media law and the controversies surrounding it.

A Brief History *of Media Law*

The history of the media is also a history of legal battles. Many of those battles had to do with adapting to new media technology. In most cases the impact of those battles on the media's growth and development was immense. The first of the legal battles dealt with the development of the philosophy of free speech, a philosophy that would eventually lead to the First Amendment to the U.S. Constitution.

THE DEVELOPMENT OF THE PHILOSOPHY OF FREE SPEECH

Arguments over freedom of speech—or, to include all media, freedom of expression in general—have raged at least since the times of the ancient Greeks, who debated whether anyone other than male landowners should be allowed to express views in public. Similar debates surrounded the new technology of printing in the 17th century, when England's leaders sought to limit free expression with strict licensing laws designed to assure that only those who agreed with the government could be printers.

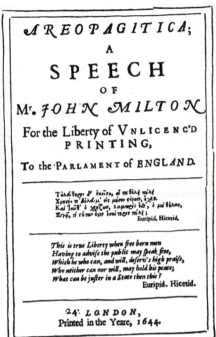

Areopagitica

It was at this time that a religious argument was advanced in favor of freedom of expression. One of the best-known articulations of this argument was put forth by John Milton in 1644, in a pamphlet entitled *Areopagitica*. Milton, one of England's greatest poets and the author of *Paradise Lost,* was a Puritan. Among the Puritans' beliefs was the notion that people were placed on Earth to be tested, to choose for themselves between truth and falsehood. Obviously, you could not make a proper choice without access to both. Without the freedom to think for themselves, people would not be able to prove their goodness and thereby earn their admission into heaven. "Let truth and falsehood grapple," Milton insisted. "Who ever knew truth put to the worse, in a free and open encounter?"[4] The language of *Areopagitica* is still cited by legal scholars today to explain the philosophical importance of free speech and a free press.

SELF QUIZ What was the influence of John Milton's *Areopagitica* in the development of a free speech philosophy?

Licensing

Many of the founders of the American colonies were influenced by the Puritan philosophy that made up much of the intellectual dialogue of the day. The Puritans were also Protestants, as were all the other sects that had broken away from the Roman Catholic Church. The freedom to protest was understandably important to members of these sects. People with Protestant backgrounds chafed under England's licensing laws, which did not allow them to express their religious views. These laws followed settlers to the New World, where the British ruled for more than 100 years.

The colonists were generally allowed to express religious views, but politics was a different story. As noted in Chapter 4, the colonial government shut down Benjamin Harris's *Publick Occurrences* in 1690 after just one issue; the reason given was that Harris wasn't a licensed printer, but that was likely just an excuse given by a government that objected to Harris's views

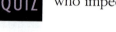

Benjamin Franklin's *Pennsylvania Gazette* for the week of June 3rd, 1731, contained his "Apology for Printers." The front-page editorial was a powerful argument for freedom of speech.

What were some of the tactics that colonial governments used to try to control the press?

SELF QUIZ

seditious libel laws
Laws established in colonial America that made it illegal to criticize government or its representatives.

contempt
Willful disobedience of the rules of a court or legislative body.

What five freedoms were guaranteed by the First Amendment?

SELF QUIZ

on the governor's honesty and the French king's relationship with his daughter-in-law, among other things. More than 30 years later, in 1722, James Franklin was jailed for failing to get government approval to publish the *New England Courant.*

James's brother Benjamin Franklin conveyed the feelings of colonial publishers in a 1731 editorial, which he called "An Apology for Printers." In it, Franklin wrote, "The opinions of men are almost as various as their faces. . . . If all printers were determined not to print anything till they were sure it would offend no body, there would be very little printed."[5]

Seditious Libel and Contempt

As the free speech debate raged among the future founders of the United States, the British colonial government had no doubt about the benefits of censoring the press. The British exerted their control mostly through **seditious libel laws,** which made any criticism of government or political leaders illegal. However, as discussed in Chapter 4, the 1735 acquittal of John Peter Zenger, publisher of the *New York Weekly Journal,* established that a person should not be punished for publishing truthful criticism of the government. There were no more convictions for seditious libel in the colonial courts after Zenger. The case received wide publicity and was important in solidifying the popular view against this type of censorship.

The colonial governments reacted to the Zenger verdict by switching tactics. A new tactic was to find publishers in **contempt,** the legal term for willful disobedience to the rules of a court or legislative body. Contempt power enabled lawmakers to act as prosecutor, judge, and jury to punish those printers who published material they didn't like. Contempt power is still used by judges and lawmakers today to punish those who impede trials or legislative proceedings.

THE FIRST AMENDMENT

The first 10 amendments to the U.S. Constitution, known as the Bill of Rights, were ratified in 1791, two years after the Constitution itself had been accepted by the original 13 states. The First Amendment was the founders' ultimate statement of the importance of freedom of expression in the democracy they were building.[6] Just 46 words long, the amendment guaranteed citizens of the new country essential freedoms in five related areas:

> Congress shall make no law respecting an establishment of [1] religion, or prohibiting the free exercise thereof; or abridging the freedom of [2] speech, or of [3] the press; or of the right of the people peaceably [4] to assemble, and [5] to petition the Government for a redress of grievances.

Far from ending the argument about free expression, however, the First Amendment ignited a long and sometimes bitter debate that continues to this day. Obviously, there had to be limits: Publishers could not be allowed to destroy an honest citizen's reputation or invade his or her privacy. National security issues, such as military secrets, were also a concern. Just how much freedom of expression was good for a country?

The Alien and Sedition Acts

In spite of the new country's experience with the British colonial government, in 1798 the administration of John Adams pushed through a set of four laws known collectively as the Alien and Sedition Acts. The last of these, the Sedition Act, once again made it illegal to criticize the government. This law was aimed at publishers who supported Adams's political opponent, Thomas Jefferson. An unpopular law, the act lasted only two years. Opposition to it helped Jefferson win the presidency in 1800, and the U.S. government did not pass another sedition law for 117 years (in the midst of World War I).

Early Obscenity Laws

The conflict between the people's right to freedom of expression and the government's ability to regulate moral behavior created some interesting battles in the 1800s. The first obscenity law, a customs law forbidding the importation of immoral materials, was passed in 1842. The most well known obscenity legislation, known as the Comstock Law, was passed in 1873. Named after the man who had pushed it through Congress—Anthony Comstock, a self-appointed reformer of all things he considered depraved—the law banned sex education and, among other things, made it illegal to send information about birth control or abortion through the mail. Comstock went on to become the chief enforcer of this law, as the inspector for the U.S. Post Office.

Adapting to Early Technology

During the 1800s media law adapted to the burgeoning print media at the same time that it adapted to other aspects of the Industrial Revolution. Louis Brandeis, a law professor who later became a Supreme Court justice, complained in 1890 of "new mechanical devices" and "instantaneous photographs" that allowed the media to overstep "the obvious bounds of propriety and decency."[7] The practices of the yellow journalists were particularly troubling, and Brandeis objected to their publication of gossip and of such information as "the details of sexual relations."[8]

Some of the new laws that affected the print media were inspired by the work of the muckrakers (see Chapter 5). These investigative journalists influenced the passage of laws such as the Sherman Antitrust Act of 1890, which limited big business monopolies. Many years later that same act would cause the breakup of the early movie studios. The muckrakers also helped pass the Pure Food and Drug Act of 1906, which would lead to restrictions in what and how the media could advertise.

DEFINING LIMITS

As mentioned earlier, seditious libel laws returned with World War I. The Espionage Act, passed in 1917, upheld the censorship of ideas considered injurious to the war effort. The Sedition Act of 1918 went one step further—as one historian has pointed out, it made all criticism of President Woodrow Wilson's administration illegal:

> Under the general terms of the Espionage and Sedition acts, newspapers were continually silenced by orders and prosecutions. Individual critics of the war

and the Wilson program were rounded up by the government, often without warrants of arrest, hustled to jail, held incommunicado without bail, tried in courts where the atmosphere was heavily charged with passion, lectured by irate judges, and sent to prison for long terms—in one case an adolescent girl for twenty years.[9]

The Clear and Present Danger Doctrine

Both the Espionage Act and the Sedition Act were heavy-handed, but they did arouse the U.S. courts to attempt to define the limits of freedom of expression. In 1919, Supreme Court justice Oliver Wendell Holmes set forth an important ruling in which he wrote, "The most stringent protection of free speech would not protect a man in falsely shouting fire in a theater and causing a panic."[10] Holmes went on to formulate what is now called the doctrine of clear and present danger, saying that expression should be punished only when words "are used in such circumstances and are of such a nature as to create a clear and present danger that they will bring about the substantive evils that Congress has a right to prevent."[11]

The Smith Act

If the 19th century was one in which laws adapted to the growing print media, the 20th century became the era of laws adapting to electronic media. Worries about the power of the electronic media even helped bring about the passage of another sedition law. Because soapbox oratory could now reach the multitudes through radio, Congress passed the Smith Act in 1940, making it illegal to advocate the violent overthrow of the U.S. government. The law was softened in 1957 when the Supreme Court ruled that the defendant must advocate specific violent action toward the overthrow of the government, and that the advocated action must be likely to have some effect in terms of producing a clear and present danger.

The Smith Act was aimed at the Communist Party of the United States and led to the imprisonment of several members of that party during the 1950s. It was the basis, in fact, for many of the blacklisting efforts that we will examine in Chapter 15.

> **SELF QUIZ**
>
> Explain how each of the following helped determine the extent and limitations of freedom of speech: Comstock Law, Smith Act, clear and present danger doctrine.

REGULATING BROADCASTING

Radio was destined to be subject to far more regulation than the print media had ever been. The new technology had to be regulated because of spectrum scarcity: There simply were not enough frequencies to go around, and the government had to apportion them. However, the Federal Communications Commission (FCC), created by the Communications Act of 1934, regulated far more than the placement of stations on the frequency spectrum. Part of the argument for strong broadcast regulation was the justification that the public owns the airwaves; hence, the government has the right to intervene on behalf of the public. This spirit of robust government control was evident in many of the FCC's rules.

- *Equal Opportunity Rule.* The Equal Opportunity Rule was part of the Communications Act of 1934. This rule, still in effect, mandates that if a broadcast station permits one legally qualified candidate for any elective public office to use its facilities, it must afford an equal opportunity for all other legally qualified candidates for the same office.

The Equal Opportunity Rule is used mostly to ensure that candidates will be able to buy time for their campaign commercials on stations that do not support them. (There is, however, no guarantee that candidates will be able to afford to buy as much time as their opponents, so the common name for this rule, the "equal time law," is really a misnomer.)

- *The Fairness Doctrine.* Another regulation, the fairness doctrine, which went into effect in 1949 and lasted until 1987, required broadcasters to provide airtime for the discussion of important public issues, and to ensure that all viewpoints on those issues were covered. These were actual restrictions on the content of the media, which were unheard of for print media at that time.

- *Ownership Limitations.* FCC regulations were also established to keep broadcasters from becoming too powerful. Chain broadcasting regulations passed in 1941, for example, limited the power the networks could exert over their affiliates (for example, no affiliate could be forced to air a network program) and the number of local stations the networks could own. The chain broadcasting regulations also resulted in the breakup of NBC Radio's two networks, one of which became the American Broadcasting Company (ABC).

The Spirit of Regulation

The spirit of regulation seen in the FCC beginning in the 1930s was seen in other government agencies, such as the Federal Trade Commission (FTC) and the Justice Department. The FTC controlled advertising messages as never before, stepping in often to stop ads it considered false and misleading. The Justice Department fought business monopolies through antitrust actions. In fact, the last great antitrust action of the regulatory era was against AT&T's Bell System. The government fought AT&T for eight years (1974–1982), accusing it of using its monopoly on local phone service to keep competitors out of the long-distance and telephone equipment markets. AT&T finally settled the case by agreeing to spin off its local telephone companies into separate entities.

Deregulation

The era of strong regulation ended in the 1980s, during the administration of President Ronald Reagan. Legislators began to feel that business regulation crippled the United States in global competition. Slowly the government began a process of **deregulation,** which involved the dismantling of many of its controls. In media businesses, this meant that ownership restrictions and restrictions on programming such as the fairness doctrine were phased out. It meant longer licensing periods and easier renewal applications. Deregula-

deregulation
The repeal of government rules and regulations.

Media conglomerates became bigger than ever because of the Telecommunications Act of 1996.

tion continued with the Telecommunications Act of 1996, which removed many of the restrictions on a wide range of communications industries, allowing cable television, long-distance carriers, local telephone companies, information services, and Internet service providers to merge at will. Media conglomerates became bigger than ever because of this law.

Obscenity and Indecency

The spirit of deregulation did not extend to obscenity laws. These laws stayed on the books, affirming that obscenity was not within the area of

Sam Sheppard's Trial by Media

Coverage of legal cases seems to have become more and more sensational in recent years. The media circuses surrounding the trials of O. J. Simpson, Scott Peterson, and Robert Blake each seemed to be huge. But the most important case of media trial coverage occurred more than a half century ago.

The trial and conviction of Cleveland osteopath Dr. Sam Sheppard was a classic case of detrimental trial publicity. Sheppard's pregnant wife, Marilyn, was brutally murdered on July 4, 1954. It was a sensational case: Sheppard was socially prominent, wealthy, and good-looking. The night Marilyn was killed, he claimed that he had returned home to find a "bushy-haired stranger" running from his home. Sheppard wasn't arrested at first, but the local newspapers covering the investigation found circumstantial evidence suggesting that Sheppard could be the killer. He had argued with his wife, and he was having an affair with another woman. The papers, convinced of his guilt, pushed for his arrest with headlines such as "Getting Away with Murder" and "Why Isn't Sam Sheppard in Jail?"

Largely because of media pressure, Sheppard was arrested and brought to trial. A true media circus erupted around the courthouse. The trial judge was running for reelection, and he did everything he could to accommodate the press, including supplying reporters with a list of the names and addresses of all 75 potential jurors. Nearly every seat in the 26-by-48-foot courtroom was reserved for members of the press, some of them no more than 3 feet from the jury box. Photographers were allowed to take pictures of the jury members in the box at will; more than 40 photos of the jury appeared in Cleveland papers alone during the trial. Jury members went home at night, and almost all of them later admitted reading about the case in the newspapers and listening to radio reports about it.

Sheppard was convicted and sent to prison. When he appealed, he submitted as evidence five scrapbooks full of headlines, photographs, and stories that had been published during his trial. The headlines included straightforward demands for conviction like "Sheppard Must Swing!" The photos included a picture of Marilyn Sheppard's bloodstained pillow, altered to "show more clearly" the outline of "a surgical instrument" like those Dr. Sheppard used in his practice. The stories reported on other scientific "proof" of Sheppard's guilt that was never presented at the trial. One paper ran a story with the headline "Sam Called a 'Jekyll-Hyde' by Marilyn; Cousin to Testify." No such testimony was introduced at the trial, nor was the cousin called as a witness. Sheppard served 12 years in prison before the Supreme Court ruled that his trial was tainted by excessive press attention and the carnival-like atmo-

constitutionally protected speech or press. The courts, however, found it difficult to define what they meant by the word *obscene*. Until 1957, the Comstock Law was the law of the land, and *obscene* meant whatever government officials believed it to be. Many works of literature, such as D. H. Lawrence's *Lady Chatterly's Lover,* were censored under the Comstock Law. In 1957, in *Roth v. United States,* the Supreme Court decreed that a work could be declared obscene if, according to the perceptions of the average person applying contemporary community standards, the dominant theme of the material taken as a whole appealed to the prurient (lustfully depraved) interest of the consumer. That definition tended to confuse rather than clarify—court case after court case proved that various interpretations of the ruling excluded speech that should have been protected, such as works of art or discourses into the politics of sexuality. In 1964 Supreme Court justice Potter Stewart

sphere in the courtroom. He was retried in 1966 and acquitted.

The Sheppard trial had been a national obsession, much as O. J. Simpson's in the 1990s and Scott Peterson's in 2004. In fact, F. Lee Bailey, who would later be one of Simpson's lawyers, was the young attorney who won Sheppard's appeal and retrial. The Sheppard case became the basis for the television program *The Fugitive* (1963–1967), and the 1993 movie with the same title that starred Harrison Ford. A 1999 television movie, *My Father's Shadow: The Sam Sheppard Story,* was based on the younger Sheppard's lifelong quest to clear his father's name.

More than 40 years after Sheppard's conviction, DNA evidence seemed to clear Sheppard and suggest that a "bushy-haired" window washer was indeed the real killer.[1] One of Marilyn Sheppard's rings had been found in this man's house in 1959, but the police had refused to consider him a suspect at the time. The window washer died in prison, where he had been serving time for rape.

As for Sheppard, he never got his life back in order. He died just four years after he was released from prison. During those four years he married and tried to reestablish his medical practice but failed (two patients died as a result of mistakes he made). He divorced; remarried; and, in a somewhat pathetic attempt to capitalize on his notoriety, turned briefly

After serving 12 years in prison, Dr. Sam Sheppard (left) walks into court in Cleveland in 1966, where he was acquitted of the 1954 murder of his wife. Because of the Sheppard case, today's courts insist that a defendant be protected from prejudicial trial publicity.

to professional wrestling (he defiantly called himself Killer Sheppard and appeared in a doctor's white lab coat with a stethoscope around his neck). His case, however, forever changed the way criminal trials are conducted in the United States. Today's courts insist that a defendant be protected from the kind of trial publicity to which Sheppard was subjected. (See pages 490–492 for a discussion of the legal techniques used to provide this protection.)

[1] Fox Butterfield, "DNA Test Absolves Sam Sheppard of Murder, Lawyer Says," *New York Times,* March 5, 1998, p. A14. See also James Neff, *The Wrong Man: The Final Verdict of the Dr. Sam Sheppard Murder Case* (New York: Random House, 2001).

CONSIDER THIS

Name a current crime or trial that has received a lot of publicity. Do you believe that the coverage has interfered with the defendant's right to a fair trial? Why or why not?

expressed his frustration at the difficulties of defining obscenity when he said, "I can't define it, but I know it when I see it."

In a 1973 decision (*Miller v. California*), the Supreme Court reaffirmed its three-part test: If the "average person applying contemporary community standards" would find that, taken as a whole, (1) the material appealed "to the prurient interest in sex," (2) portrayed sexual conduct "in a patently offensive way," and (3) lacked "serious literary, artistic, political or scientific value," then the work was obscene, and obscene works were illegal. A new category, **indecency,** had to be invented for broadcast controls. Indecency, which is legal for the print media, is material that depicts sexual or excretory activities in a patently offensive manner but still arguably has some social value, such as education or even humor. The FCC considers material indecent if it is "offensive to the community standards for broadcasting." Indecency is permitted in broadcasting but restricted to hours when

indecency
Offensive content with possible social value.

children are not expected to be listening or watching. Many of the broadcasts of the shock jock Howard Stern (see Chapter 8) were indecent by FCC standards because they aired in the morning.

NATIONAL SECURITY AND PRIOR RESTRAINT

Another area of regulatory concern was the press's role in national security matters. In covering the Vietnam War, the press was initially given great freedom, but in 1971, in the Pentagon Papers case, the U.S. government for the first time tried to stop the publication of material by major newspapers. In that case, the government restrained the *New York Times* and the *Washington Post* for two weeks from publishing a history of the Vietnam War, claiming that it would undermine the effort to win that ongoing conflict. In the Pentagon Papers case, the Supreme Court came down against the idea of prior restraint of the media. The Court ruled that in all but the most essential national security cases, the media must be allowed to publish; they can be prosecuted after the fact if they break a law, but they must not be prevented in advance from publishing.

Government administrations and reporters have been at odds about government secrecy ever since. In 2006, for example, several newspapers, including the *New York Times,* the *Wall Street Journal,* and the *Los Angeles Times,* disclosed a secret Bush administration program to monitor international banking transactions. The papers published the story in spite of appeals from senior administration officials not to do so. The administration said that the newspapers hampered their abilities to uncover terrorists, while the newspapers said that the program was important for the people to know about.

CURRENT TRENDS IN MEDIA LAW

The evolution of media law continues to this day. Some of the current changes affecting this type of law include globalization, concentration of ownership, and new technology (see Figure 14.1).

Globalization

Media corporations are doing worldwide business today, but very few countries have press freedom laws like the First Amendment. Western European nations and Japan all have some sort of law guaranteeing media freedom, but that freedom is more limited than in the United States. In England, for example, libel laws (which we examine later in this chapter) make it difficult

Globalization	Concentration of Ownership	New Technology
Media need to keep up with laws from many different countries.	Media companies need to be large in order to meet rising legal costs.	Media need to keep up with the legal implications of changing technology.

FIGURE 14.1 Trends in Media Law Media law continually adapts to changes in the media landscape.

to report on public figures.[12] American pop superstar Michael Jackson, for example, won a settlement from Britain's *Mirror* newspaper over claims by the tabloid that his face had been "hideously disfigured" as a result of cosmetic surgery. In the United States, this case would have been quickly thrown out of court. In Germany, it is illegal to write about Nazism. In Japan, journalists must belong to an official association and they must be accredited, meaning that the government decides who can and cannot practice journalism.

Most other countries have no constitutional guarantees of press freedom at all, which means that they can restrict the media when they seem to be getting out of hand. Jordan's parliament, for example, recently passed laws prohibiting publication of any item deemed insulting to the king or royal family, to any of Jordan's religious groups, or to any heads of "Arab, Islamic or friendly states."[13] Under this law the press is barred from publishing any critical discussion of the main issues facing the country, such as the peace process with Israel or the position of Islam in society. Similar laws were passed in Russia, the Philippines, Venezuela, Egypt, Iran, and Indonesia.

Globalization has meant that media organizations need to keep up with the laws of many countries. In some Muslim countries, for example, American movies that are given a PG rating in the United States are outlawed as

Globalization has meant that media organizations need to keep up with the laws of many countries.

obscene. With its global reach, the Internet has made such laws particularly troublesome for media conglomerates.

Concentration of Ownership

On the one hand, the concentration of media ownership has actually been encouraged by large legal settlements. Only large corporations can afford to pay such settlements or even defend against them. A small-town newspaper, for example, faced with an accusation of libel, may have no choice but to merge with a larger corporation to avoid bankruptcy. On the other hand, concentration of ownership has caused many of these large settlements, because lawyers can argue that big judgments are necessary to get the conglomerate's attention and teach it a lesson. The result has been increasingly larger awards, often awarded by juries who see the press as too powerful, too arrogant, and too intrusive. In 1997, a jury awarded $223 million to a brokerage firm that said it had been libeled by the *Wall Street Journal,* which is part of the Dow Jones conglomerate. Many of these large awards have been overturned on appeal, and the amount of the award in many surviving judgments substantially reduced, but the trend still has a chilling effect on the media. A tobacco company that felt it had been wronged by ABC (part of the Disney conglomerate) sued for $10 billion. Many observers say that such cases are part of another national trend: the tendency for lawyers to see civil litigation as less of an equitable righting of wrongs and more as a lottery in which great wealth can be won.

New Technology

Finally, media law attempts to keep up with fast-changing technology. In 1996, for example, Congress passed the Communications Decency Act, which made it a crime to transmit indecent and obscene material over the

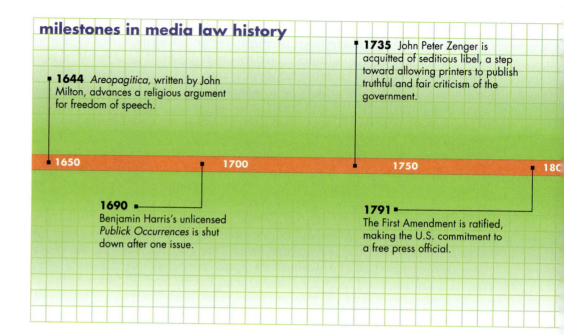

milestones in media law history

1644 *Areopagitica*, written by John Milton, advances a religious argument for freedom of speech.

1735 John Peter Zenger is acquitted of seditious libel, a step toward allowing printers to publish truthful and fair criticism of the government.

1650   1700   1750   18C

1690 Benjamin Harris's unlicensed *Publick Occurrences* is shut down after one issue.

1791 The First Amendment is ratified, making the U.S. commitment to a free press official.

Internet if minors could gain access to that material. The Supreme Court found the indecency provision of this law unconstitutional, however, because the new medium deserved the same kind of protection that print media enjoyed rather than the restrictions imposed on TV and radio.

Other laws have had to be written for crimes that did not exist before the Internet. There were no laws, for example, against computer hacking—breaking into computer networks to cause a wide variety of mischief—before computer networks came into being. Today the U.S. military considers the Internet so unsafe for classified information that it doesn't transmit even low-level secrets there anymore. However, a wealth of government information still resides online. A 1996 law made computer espionage illegal, and an Argentine college student was quickly charged with that crime when he hacked his way into research computers at Harvard University. Those computers contained military research data, including information about satellites, radiation, and engineering.[14]

Some older laws, such as those against the crime of fraud, have had to be applied to the Internet. As more and more commerce is conducted online, and more and more purchases are made by credit card, criminals are seeing new opportunities to fleece the innocent. One of the most infamous cases of Internet fraud to date was perpetrated by a hacker named Kevin Mitnick. In 1995, Mitnick stole some 20,000 credit card numbers online. He was caught and given a lengthy prison sentence. Other types of online fraud seem to be limited only by the imagination of the perpetrator. One hacker was convicted of electronically fixing radio call-in contests. He broke into the radio stations' computers to make sure that his would always be the winning call. Before being caught, he managed to win two sports cars and tens of thousands of dollars.[15]

In the 1990s, federal law made the development and purposeful transmission of computer viruses illegal. Punishments included a jail term of up to five years and a $250,000 fine, plus assessment of damages. The government also set up the Computer Emergency Response Team to investigate attacks on computer networks.

What are some of the ways that media law has adapted to new technology?

SELF QUIZ

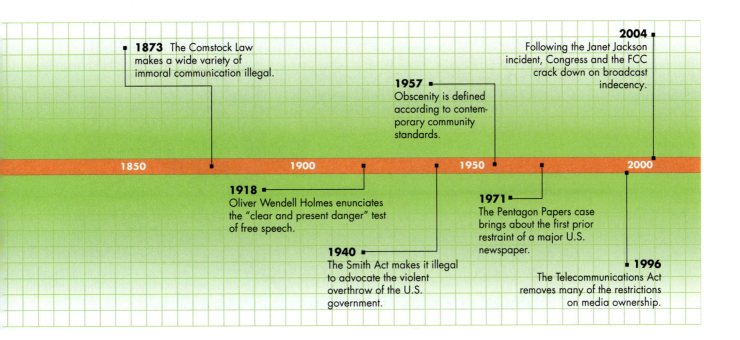

1873 The Comstock Law makes a wide variety of immoral communication illegal.

1957 Obscenity is defined according to contemporary community standards.

2004 Following the Janet Jackson incident, Congress and the FCC crack down on broadcast indecency.

1850   1900   1950   2000

1918 Oliver Wendell Holmes enunciates the "clear and present danger" test of free speech.

1940 The Smith Act makes it illegal to advocate the violent overthrow of the U.S. government.

1971 The Pentagon Papers case brings about the first prior restraint of a major U.S. newspaper.

1996 The Telecommunications Act removes many of the restrictions on media ownership.

Understanding Today's *Media Law*

Today's media law could be looked at as a balancing act: balancing the rights of the individual with the public's right to know, for example, or balancing the rights of business to make money with the rights of people to use their own media as they see fit. To help you understand this balancing act, we first discuss some basics of the U.S. legal system. We then discuss the protection of rights in media law.

THE LEGAL SYSTEM AND TYPES OF LAW

The American legal system is complex. There are 52 different court systems: one for each state; one for Washington, DC; and one for the federal government. In each, there is a trial court system and an appellate, or appeals, division. A jury might interpret the law one way, as when it awards a multimillion-dollar settlement to a public figure who has been libeled in the press, but the appeals court may overturn that ruling. Often the media will report the jury award more loudly than the appeals ruling that overturns it, which can make the final outcome of a case confusing to the public.

In addition to numerous court systems, there are several different types of law. The major distinction is between criminal and civil law. In **criminal law,** the government tries individuals who are accused of illegal acts; in **civil law,** disputes between two private parties are resolved. Other types of law include constitutional law, statutory law, administrative law, and common law.[16] Each of these includes laws dealing with the media (see Figure 14.2).

One aspect of today's media law that makes it confusing is that many cases involve different types of law, with a plaintiff suing for many related things. For example, Fred Rogers, the soft-spoken host of PBS's *Mister Rogers' Neighborhood,* once sued a novelty store chain for selling T-shirts that displayed a picture of him with his well-known sweater and smile—and a silver handgun. Instead of saying, "Won't you be my neighbor?" the T-shirt

criminal law
Public law that deals with crimes and their prosecution.

civil law
Law that considers disputes between private parties.

Constitutional Law	**Administrative Law**
Based on documents written by the founders of governments. For example: the First Amendment.	The rules and regulations of government agencies. For example: FCC restrictions on indecency.
Statutory Law	**Common Law**
Collected laws written by legislative bodies. For example: the Telecommunications Act of 1996.	Judges' rulings that have become precedents. For example: privacy law.

FIGURE 14.2 Types of Media Law Media laws are of these four different types.

Mr. Rogers was saying, "Welcome to my 'hood.'" The lawsuit involved trademark violation, invasion of privacy, and libel, all at one time. That case was settled out of court.

Constitutional Law

constitutional law
Basic laws of a country or state.

Constitutional law derives from the documents written by the founders of a country or state. Constitutions are the supreme source of law because they reflect the basic rules that the founders of the country or state had in mind. Constitutional law is essential to our discussion here because so much of media law hinges on the First Amendment to the U.S. Constitution. The U.S. Constitution prevails over state law, which means that any law, state or local, that contradicts the First Amendment cannot legally be implemented. The Supreme Court is often called on to put an end to such laws. For example, in 1974 the Court declared unconstitutional a Florida law that required newspapers to print replies to published attacks on political candidates.[17]

Statutory Law

statutory law
Collection of laws, or statutes, written by legislative bodies, such as the U.S. Congress.

Statutory law is based on the collection of laws, or statutes, written by legislative bodies, such as the U.S. Congress, the state legislature, county commissions, and city councils. Almost all criminal law, such as the prohibition against mailing obscene materials, is statutory. So are advertising and copyright laws. Judges interpret how statutes apply in specific cases, as when the U.S. Supreme Court ruled in 1984 that the Copyright Act allows homeowners to tape television programs on their VCRs.[18]

Administrative Law

Administrative law is made up of the rules and regulations of government agencies such as the Federal Communications Commission (FCC), the Federal Trade Commission (FTC), and the Federal Election Commission (FEC). These agencies are created by legislatures to supervise legal activities that require more attention than legislators and traditional law enforcement

Personal Rights	Intellectual Property Rights	News-Gathering Rights
Defamation (slander, libel)	Copyright	Sunshine laws
Privacy	Trademark	Freedom of Information Act
	Patents	Shield laws

FIGURE 14.3 Protection of Rights in Media Law Each of these three broad, essential areas of media law deals with a different type of right.

agencies can provide. Under **administrative law,** government agencies can make rules, and they can adjudicate, or pass judgment on, those rules. The FTC, for example, has a rule that requires advertisers to measure the size of television screens diagonally so that screen sizes can be compared by consumers. If the FTC commissioners decide this rule has been broken by a manufacturer, they can determine the size of the fine that the manufacturer must pay.

administrative law
The rules and regulations of governmental agencies.

Common Law

One final type of law, **common law,** is sometimes referred to as "judge-made law." Common law derives from medieval times in England. It is made up of judges' rulings, which become precedents for future cases. If a judge decides that a certain type of news gathering is illegal—trespassing to photograph an individual, for example—and that finding is upheld on appeal, it goes on the books as a precedent that media practitioners must follow in the future. In fact, the laws of privacy were almost all created through common law, as individual judges interpreted just what rights people had to be let alone.[19]

common law
Precedents based on judges' rulings.

Once again, the way media report on new laws tends to make them confusing to the public. Media report on laws in development, for example, by reporting on proposed actions, on bills that are sent down by various committees, and acts that pass each house of congress. All these will likely be different from the final law, if in fact the bill becomes law.

SELF QUIZ: Name the four types of law, and give a media law example of each one.

PROTECTION OF RIGHTS

Three broad, essential areas of media law have to do with the protection of rights: personal rights, intellectual property rights, and news-gathering rights (see Figure 14.3). We will look at these areas in terms of the laws they inspire and how those laws operate.

Personal Rights

Media laws that began as protections of personal rights include privacy and defamation laws.

Privacy

The right of individuals to be let alone, especially in their own homes, has been established through common law. Privacy law is always changing with the times. For example, following the September 11, 2001, terrorist attacks, Congress passed the Uniting and Strengthening America by Providing Appropriate Tools Required to Intercept and Obstruct Terrorism Act (USA

The USA PATRIOT Act permits the government to examine more closely the books Americans buy or check out at the library. Critics call this a threat to the right to privacy.

PATRIOT Act, often called simply the Patriot Act). This act gave the federal government expanded rights to gain access to personal and private communications, among other things. The law also permits the government to examine more closely the books Americans buy or check out at the library. Critics of the Patriot Act consider it a threat to the right to privacy.

In the realm of media law, privacy protection has been extended in three primary areas:[20]

1. *Private Facts.* This area of privacy law protects against the disclosure of embarrassing, sensitive personal information that is not essential to a news story. The classic case in this area is that of *Barber v. Time*. The Missouri Supreme Court ruled in 1942 that *Time* magazine invaded the privacy of a woman named Dorothy Barber when it published her picture as part of a story about an unusual eating disorder, one that causes victims to lose weight even though they eat large amounts of food. The court said that although Barber's disease was newsworthy, the public could have been told of it without revealing her identity.[21] Most plaintiffs, however, lose private fact cases. The classic example of this occurred when a man named Oliver Sipple saved the life of President Gerald Ford in 1975, and the press reported that he was gay. Sipple, an ex-Marine, did not want his sexuality exposed to his family back in the Midwest, but the court ruled that his privacy had not been invaded because he was already a well-known member of San Francisco's gay community. Because Sipple had already made his sexuality public, the court ruled that it was acceptable for the press to report this personal information. Private fact laws are designed to protect both public figures and everyday people, but those who become part of a news event, or are newsworthy for any reason, are accorded less protection.

2. *Intrusion.* This area of law prevents the press from unauthorized entry when gathering news. It is designed to protect the privacy of individuals in their homes and other places where privacy would be expected. Laws against news-gathering intrusions include restrictions on trespassing, and on the use of surveillance equipment, secret recordings, tapped phone lines, telephoto lenses, and other forms of technology that essentially trespass for you. If photographers take pictures in a public place of a newsworthy subject who can be seen with the naked eye, they are generally in the clear. However, if they physically intrude in any way on private areas, they could be in trouble. When *Playgirl* magazine published nude pictures of the actor Brad Pitt in its August 1997 issue, Pitt sued under this area of privacy law, saying that the pictures had been taken by a photographer who trespassed on the grounds of a hotel where he had stayed. The judge agreed with him and not only stopped *Playgirl* from selling any more copies of the offending issue but also ordered a recall of the magazine. That meant that the magazines had to be pulled from newsstands and that subscribers had to be contacted and asked to send their copies back to the publisher (although few did in this case).

3. *Appropriation.* This area of privacy law says that individuals own the right to their own image and name, neither of which can be used (appropriated) without their permission, except in the reporting of news. Thus, if a photographer took your picture and then used that picture in an advertisement or charged people to see it without your permission, your privacy would have been invaded. Dustin Hoffman sued under this area of privacy law when a picture of him from the movie *Tootsie,* in which he plays a man who pretends to be a woman, was used in an ad to sell dresses.[22]

Appropriation as an invasion of privacy has been a particular problem on the Internet. Alyssa Milano, the star of TV series such as *Who's the Boss?, Melrose Place,* and *Charmed,* has successfully sued the owners of several Web sites for posting nude photographs of her. Some of the photos were from movies she had made, and some were electronically altered to place her face on someone else's body. Milano is straightforward about the commercial nature of this privacy action. "I have no problem with the nudity I've done," she says. "I just don't want someone taking it out of context and making $15,000 a month off of it."[23] Milano has formed a company called Cybertrackers that surfs the Web for unauthorized nude photos of celebrities. She started the business after her 12-year-old brother logged on to an "Alyssa" Web site and got an eyeful of his famous older sister.

Several celebrities have won cases against intrusive photographers, known as paparazzi, under areas unrelated to privacy law. One of the first was Jacqueline Kennedy Onassis, who won a harassment case against a particularly pesky photographer, Ron Galella, in 1973. In this case the photographer was given an order stating that he had to stay 300 feet away from Kennedy's home and 150 feet away from her person. More recently, two photographers were given jail terms of 90 and 60 days for pursuing the movie star Arnold Schwarzenegger (before he was governor of California) and his wife, the television correspondent and Kennedy cousin Maria Shriver. The photographers forced the Schwarzeneggers' car to stop and then swarmed around it, taking pictures. They were convicted of false imprisonment and reckless driving.[24]

Dustin Hoffman sued under the appropriation area of privacy law when a picture of him from the movie *Tootsie* was used in an ad to sell dresses.

SELF QUIZ What are the three primary types of privacy actions? Give an example of each.

Defamation

Defamation is any type of false communication that injures the reputation of an individual. Claiming that an innocent person is guilty of criminal or unethical behavior, for example, would be defamation. There are two types of defamation: **Slander** is defamation that appears in a transitory form, such as speech, whereas **libel** is published or broadcast defamation. The distinction between the two is important because in many states libel is dealt with more harshly than slander. The reasoning behind this difference is that slander is more likely than libel to be accidental or spoken in the heat of anger. Spoken defamation on TV and radio, however, is usually treated as libel. For the most part, so is chatting on the Internet. Even though it feels like speech to the participants, the test is whether the comments appear in a fixed form that can be recorded for others to have access to.

The rap star Eminem, for example, has been sued repeatedly for both slander and libel. When he mentions someone negatively in the lyrics of a song, the suit is usually for libel. When he makes an offhand comment that is picked up by a reporter, he is sued for slander. The most highly publicized slander suit against Eminem was brought by his mother, who sued him for $10 million when he referred to her as "the epitome of white trash" during a magazine interview. (The suit dragged on for years, with Eminem's mom finally settling for $25,000 in 2006.)

defamation
Communication that is false and injures a reputation.

slander
Defamation that occurs in a transitory form, such as speech.

libel
Published or broadcast defamation.

There are four primary defenses against a charge of libel:

1. **_Truth._** In most cases, truth is the absolute defense against a charge of libel.[25] Demi Moore and Bruce Willis, for example, sued the tabloid newspaper *Star* for reporting that they were on the verge of divorce. The couple were forced to drop the suit when they announced that they were, in fact, going to be divorced.

Many media outlets have tried to stay within the limits of the truth test by simply publishing what someone else said. Louis Farrakhan, the Nation of Islam leader, sued the *New York Post* for libel in 1997 for a column implicating him in the 1965 assassination of Malcolm X. The column had directly quoted Malcolm X's widow, Betty Shabazz, saying in an NBC interview that Farrakhan was responsible for the murder.[26] Although the allegation was untrue, Farrakhan lost the case because the court accepted the newspaper's defense that it was just repeating what had occurred in the interview. Other courts have made clear, however, that reporters cannot knowingly or recklessly repeat a falsehood, even if it is a direct quotation from a source.

actual malice
Reckless disregard for the truth of published, defamatory information.

2. **_The_ Times _Rule._** The *Times* rule makes it extremely difficult for a public figure to claim that he or she has been libeled. The rule states that a public figure must prove **actual malice,** which is a legal term for reckless disregard for the truth of published, defamatory information. A court may rule that a defendant exhibited actual malice by failing to check on facts that were readily obtainable. The rule is based on the case of *New York Times v. Sullivan* (1964), which began when a group of Alabama ministers placed an ad in the *New York Times* asking for donations for a civil rights organization. Within the ad, the ministers described an "unprecedented wave of terror" that civil rights protestors were subjected to by the police. One police commissioner, L. B. Sullivan, sued the ministers and the paper, saying that although he had not been mentioned by name, he had been indirectly libeled. He won in the Alabama courts. The U.S. Supreme Court, however, unanimously overturned the ruling of the Alabama courts, saying that the *Times* had not exhibited actual malice in running the ad. Democracy is best served, the judges said, by robust debate about public issues, and public figures cannot be separated from the issues of which they are a part.[27] The *Times* rule therefore gives news media greater latitude in criticizing public figures than in criticizing private citizens.

privilege
Exemption given public officials to speak without fear of being sued for libel.

3. **_Privilege._** Statements made by public officials acting in their official capacity are privileged. **Privilege,** in this sense, means that these officials have a special right to speak freely. The defense of privilege was established to allow judges, lawmakers, and witnesses in a trial to be free to call a defendant a murderer, or anything else that is alleged in the case, without worrying that they will be sued. Lawmakers and other public officials enjoy the same privilege in both public meetings and public records.

By extension, journalists enjoy what is known as a qualified privilege, in that they are allowed to repeat the charge and to report what goes on in courts and legislatures, even if the statements made there are libelous. This privilege includes a broadcaster's right to air the false defamatory speech of political candidates. Journalists' rights are qualified only by the requirement that the reports be fair and accurate. To be fair and accurate, however, a member of the news media must make a reasonable effort to determine the truth of what is said in a legal proceeding. One trick that people have used to libel their enemies and get away with it is to file a lawsuit filled with false accusations, then mail a copy of the filings to a reporter, hoping that the reporter will publish whatever is in the complaint. To discourage this practice, several states have ruled that they do not consider copies of complaints that reporters receive from lawyers to be official court documents.

4. *Fair Comment.* **Fair comment** includes any honest opinion or criticism, such as that expressed by a movie or book reviewer. You must be sure, however, that you are expressing an opinion and not making a statement of fact. If you are reviewing a play and you say that the star of that play *acted as if* he were under the influence of drugs, that's opinion. If you said the actor *actually* was under the influence of drugs, that is a potentially libelous statement of fact. Satire and comedy, however, are protected as forms of fair comment. The players on *Saturday Night Live,* for example, can put on a skit suggesting that a public figure is guilty of all types of illegal and immoral activity yet still be protected against a libel conviction.

Another part of fair comment concerns a small group of people whose reputations are so shaky that they are considered libel-proof. You can pretty much say what you like about convicted mobsters, for example. The movie *Donnie Brasco* (1997) was based on the experiences of an FBI agent who had infiltrated an organized crime family. While there, the agent testified, he had seen a mobster named John Cerasani aid in the murders of three mob leaders. By the time the movie came out, however, Cerasani had been acquitted of the killings depicted in the movie and therefore felt that he had been libeled. The judge pointed out that Cerasani was still a convicted racketeer, Mafia associate, bank robber, and drug dealer; thus, his reputation was already so "badly tarnished" that it could not be further harmed. The judge said that Cerasani was "the exceptional, libel-proof plaintiff."[28]

- ***Libel Verdicts.*** Libel is the most common type of legal problem faced by media practitioners. Media organizations have, in fact, been subjected to a large number of highly publicized, high-award cases in recent years. There is a consistent pattern to these cases: In three out of every four, the claim is dismissed without a trial, usually because of one of the four defenses listed above. In the remaining cases, the plaintiff will win on the trial level. Juries often side with the individual rather than the media, which they see as large, arrogant, and in need of punishment. Awards tend to be substantial. In the last decade, the average jury award has been more than $1 million.[29] If the verdict is appealed, however, it is usually reversed on First Amendment grounds. In fact, 70 percent of libel verdicts are overturned or at least reduced on appeal.[30]

- ***The Chilling Effect.*** Few libel prosecutions are successful in the long run, but they still have a chilling effect on the media because some reporters will self-censor under the threat of libel. The average cost of defending a libel suit, even though most don't even go to trial, is $100,000.[31] On the flip side, companies bringing a libel suit have to consider the public relations costs of their action. When McDonald's decided to bring a libel suit against two British protesters who had distributed leaflets titled "What's Wrong with McDonald's—Everything They Don't Want You to Know," the resulting trial turned into the longest in British history (2½ years). McDonald's "won" the case, but lost significantly in terms of public relations.[32]

fair comment
Defense against a charge of libel based on opinion or criticism.

SELF QUIZ

What are the defenses against a charge of libel?

Oprah Winfrey during her beef defamation trial.

- **Trade Libel.** Libel law began as a protection of a personal right, but it has expanded to include protections of institutions, companies, and products. Defamation of a company or its products is referred to as product disparagement or trade libel. The most famous product disparagement case was the 1998 suit against Oprah Winfrey by Texas cattlemen, who claimed that the talk-show host had disparaged beef in an episode of her program about mad cow disease. Winfrey won, although the cattlemen, apparently gluttons for public relations punishment, immediately announced that they intended to appeal the verdict. They lost, and the verdict stood.

Intellectual Property Rights

Federal law covers three types of intellectual property: trademarks, patents, and a diverse category of creative work known as writings. Writings include printed works, artworks, photographs, sound recordings, movies, and videos, all of which are protected under copyright law.

The FBI initiated this antipiracy warning text, to be displayed on digital and software intellectual property, in 2004.

Copyright

The basic idea of copyright is embedded in the term itself: it is a "right to copy." **Copyright law** grants to the author of a work the right to make and distribute copies of that work for a specified period. Copyrights can also be sold or assigned to another party, who then becomes the owner of the copyright. The pop star Michael Jackson, for example, has purchased the copyright to many of the songs of the British group the Beatles.

There was a major rewriting of the U.S. law in the Copyright Act of 1976, which became effective in 1978, so the law differs somewhat for works created before and after 1978. For example, for works created after 1978, the term of protection for copyrighted material is the life of the author, plus 70 years. For works created before 1978, the copyright lasts a total of 95 years, no matter how long the author lives.[33]

copyright law
Law that entitles the owner of a work to make and distribute reproductions of it.

first-sale doctrine
The doctrine that allows purchasers of a copyrighted work to resell it or rent it out.

- **First-Sale Doctrine.** It is important to distinguish between owning a copyright in a work and owning a copy of that work. Under the **first-sale doctrine,** anyone who purchases a copy, or facsimile, of copyrighted work owns that facsimile, including the right to resell it or rent it out. This allows college bookstores to buy back and resell used textbooks without paying further royalties to book authors. It also allows video stores to rent out tapes without paying royalties to the studios. The buyers of the facsimile do not, however, have the right to make copies and sell or rent them.

- **Copyright and Ideas.** Copyright does not protect ideas; it protects only the expression of those ideas, such as a novel or screenplay. Copyright law specifies that the work of expression must be "fixed" in a tangible medium such as paper or a recording medium. If you were to tell your ideas for a great story to your friend the scriptwriter or your other friend the novelist, either writer could take those ideas and develop them any way he or she chose, without your permission and without paying you for them. If you handed the writer a first-draft script or an outline for a novel, however, it would be protected.

SELF QUIZ

What does copyright law protect, and how long does the protection last?

- **The Copyright Sign.** One misconception that people have about this area of law is that a work needs to carry the copyright sign (©) to be protected. In truth, any work, published or unpublished, is automatically protected. The reclusive novelist J. D. Salinger won a copyright case against a biographer who quoted and paraphrased from Salinger's unpublished letters, which were stored in a research collection in a library and carried no copyright.

A copyright notice does, however, serve as a formal warning to potential infringers. Registration with the U.S. Copyright Office in Washington, DC, is used as proof of ownership in the case of a lawsuit. Sending a completed application form, two copies of the work, and a $30 fee to the Copyright Office will register any work.[34] An international treaty, signed by every major developed country except China, standardized copyright law globally.[35] Enforcement of that treaty has been a problem, however, as evidenced by the pirated music and movies that appear on the streets (and in file-sharing programs) around the world.

Fair Use

The rights to control a work given to copyright holders have a number of exceptions. The best known of those exceptions is a doctrine called **fair use.** Fair use allows the copying of a work for a noncommercial use, as long as that copying does not interfere with sales or other exploitation of the work by the copyright holder. The writers of the Copyright Act wanted to make sure that people would be free to comment on and criticize ideas, to ensure the robust debate that is so important to the idea behind the First Amendment. Because of this, the authors of the act made sure that copyright holders could not block news reports and commentary about their work, and that educators and researchers would be given reasonable access to it.

The main element of fair use is the noncommercial nature of the copying. Piracy, the practice of misappropriating recordings and movies, which was discussed in earlier chapters, is a clear-cut copyright infringement under this criterion. Courts accept without argument that pirating is a commercial enterprise. Online file-sharing of music and movies has also been a problem because of its effect on industry profits. Yet the noncommercial nature of home copying was important in the 1983 Sony Betamax case, in which the courts ruled that video recording for private use was not an infringement of copyright, but only "time shifting" for the user's convenience. The court made clear in this ruling that it would not protect a homeowner who went on to sell the recording or to show it for commercial profit.[36]

Copyright, Music, and Video Clips

Music properties have a long history of copyright problems. Songwriters have always tended to pick up pieces of melody and harmony from earlier songs. In one interesting case, former Beatle George Harrison was found to have infringed the copyright of the earlier Chiffons' song "He's So Fine" (1963) with his 1970 hit "My Sweet Lord." The judge in that case said Harrison was guilty of "unconscious plagiarism." He believed that Harrison had not meant to copy the song, but the two tunes were so much alike that the melody had somehow stuck in Harrison's head without his realizing it.

Rap artists, in a technique known as sampling, have used digital technology to actually transfer sections of an earlier recording to their own. In one case, a judge ruled that musician Biz Markie violated the copyright of the song "Alone Again (Naturally)" when he digitally copied and repeated a 10-second phrase without permission.[37] Borrowing from an earlier work is different, however, if parody is involved. Fair comment and criticism are considered specially privileged in copyright law, and parody is considered

fair use
Doctrine that allows the copying of a work for a noncommercial use.

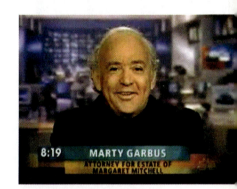

On the *Media World* DVD that accompanies this book (track 9), copyright lawyer Marty Garbus insists that the book *The Wind Done Gone* is piracy, not a parody of *Gone With the Wind*.

These logos are all trademarks.

trademark
A word, symbol, or device that identifies a seller's goods.

a form of criticism. To be fair use, however, a parody must do more than merely copy. It must transform the original work. In 1989 Luther Campbell, lead singer for the rap group 2 Live Crew, wrote and performed a parody of Roy Orbison's 1964 hit "Oh, Pretty Woman." Campbell's version made fun of the original song's sentimentality with lyrics like "Oh, hairy woman. You better shave that stuff." Although musically the two songs were very similar, Campbell's parody was considered fair use by the courts.

Copyright law needs to be reconsidered with each new technology. Videotape, CDs, photocopy machines, and commercial copy centers such as Kinko's have all caused reexamination of the law. In a case involving Kinko's, for example, the courts made clear that these outlets may not knowingly participate in copyright infringement, and also are liable for violations that they have the right and ability to prevent.[38]

The Internet is causing the largest reexamination of copyright law ever (see the Close-Up on Media Law box). The basic question is, How can you extend copyright principles to this new medium?[39] This question is an important one, because many corporations are interested in the speed and economy of distributing books, music, software, and even movies online, but they worry about how these properties can be protected against theft and unauthorized use. In one attempt at this kind of protection, Congress passed the Digital Millennium Copyright Act in 1998. This law makes it a crime to subvert or break through any technology such as a firewall intended to secure digital copies of software, literary works, videos, and music. The law also states that, while they are not strictly liable for content, Internet service providers and Web site owners are required to remove infringing material if they are made aware that it has been posted. The burden to find the infringer, however, is on the owners of the copyrighted material. Thus, when Comedy Central decided it didn't want its clips of *The Daily Show With Jon Stewart* and *South Park* shown on YouTube in 2006, it contacted Google, the new owner of YouTube, and requested that the clips be removed. Other owners of copyrighted material allowed their material to stay on the site for publicity and promotional purposes. NBC-Universal, for example, did not request the removal of clips from *Saturday Night Live* and *The Office* that users had posted on YouTube.

Trademarks

A **trademark** is any word, symbol, or device—or combination of the three—that identifies one seller's goods and distinguishes them from goods sold by others. Names like Jell-O, Walkman, and Xerox, and symbols such as Microsoft's Windows logo, McDonald's golden arches, and the Energizer bunny are registered trademarks. Packaging can also be trademarked; the hourglass shape of the classic Coca-Cola bottle, for example, is registered. Slogans such as the *New York Times*' "All the News That's Fit to Print" can also be protected by trademark law.

The U.S. Patent and Trademark Office registers trademarks through a process similar to that used by the Copyright Office. Registration must be renewed every 10 years, and renewals can continue for as long as the mark is used. A registered trademark is denoted with the symbol ®. Companies often print a ™ next to a trademark whose registration is pending. Trademarks must be registered in other countries to have international protection, although a new international organization, the World International Property Organization (WIPO) was created as part of the United Nations in 1999 to protect intellectual property, including trademarks, worldwide.

Although the U.S. Patent and Trademark Office registers trademarks, it does not police their use. That is the trademark holder's responsibility.

The Paris Hilton Video

The sex video surfaced on the Internet late in 2003 and circulated quickly. Within days anyone who wanted a copy had downloaded it from one of the Web's many file-sharing services. The video had been made more than two years earlier, in France. It featured hotel heiress Paris Hilton and her then-boyfriend Rick Salomon. The tape scandalized the Hilton family, but it made Hilton a household name and helped assure the success of her new reality television program, *The Simple Life.*

The release of the tape brought up many questions about media law. The first involved privacy. Hilton insisted that the release of the tape was an invasion of her privacy. The tape had been made for her own, and Rick Salomon's, private enjoyment. She had never intended for it to be made public. Her family therefore threatened to sue Salomon for invasion of

privacy. But Salomon insisted that he had not been the person who released the tape. Legal experts suggested that Hilton would have a difficult time proving invasion of privacy anyway, since she had been establishing herself as a public figure and sex symbol, had knowingly allowed the tape to be made, and had entrusted it to Salomon's care after they had broken up. And even if she could prove "a reasonable expectation of privacy," a court action would do little good. The video had already been made public, and the Web being what it is, there was no way to stop its distribution. According to one lawyer, trying to hold it back would be like "trying to catch a rainstorm in a paper cup."[1] No matter how many people the Hilton family sued, the sex tape would be available forever online.

A second area of media law that the tape highlighted was libel law. When the Hilton family accused Salomon of making the videotape public, he sued them for $10 million, claiming they had slandered him. Legal experts didn't give that suit much hope of success, because of Salomon's reputation.

The issue then entered the realm of copyright law. The Digital Millennium Copyright Act makes it illegal to put copyrighted material online without the copyright holder's permission. The law says that the tape didn't need to be officially registered with the copyright office; ownership comes into existence upon creation of a work in tangible form. So Salomon sued several porn sites that were selling the tape, claiming that he was the copyright holder. But the courts invalidated his claim, saying that Hilton had also directed the tape and therefore shared copyright with him. Salomon countered by selling the tape on his own Web site, charging $50 for five plays.

[1]From the Web log of Parry Aftab, Esq., www.aftab.com/hiltonvideo.htm, accessed March 13, 2004.

A private sex video made by Paris Hilton and her then-boyfriend Rick Salomon became an example of several different types of media law cases when it was released on the Internet.

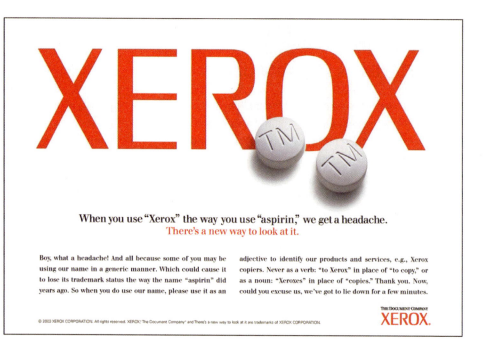

When Microsoft decided on Internet Explorer as the name for its World Wide Web browser, it failed to notice that a defunct software company had a pending application to register that trademark. The company sued, and Microsoft was forced to pay it $5 million for the right to continue using the name.

• *Trademarks as Generic Terms.* Trademarks can be lost if they become generic terms for a product. Companies spend large sums every year on ads in trade magazines reminding journalists not to use trademarks like Xerox for all photocopying or Kleenex for all tissues. Under trademark law, if a trademark loses its ability to distinguish one company's goods from another's, its owner cannot prevent other companies from using it. Xerox Corporation, for example, does not want you to make "xeroxes"; it wants you to make photocopies on Xerox® machines.

• *Fair Use of Trademarks.* Fair use of others' registered trademarks includes comparative advertising, news reporting, and commentary. Companies have a tendency to fight all but the most obvious fair use cases, however. One controversy in this matter centers on the Internet fan sites set up by and for people who admire a particular music group, TV program, or movie. In one of these sites, a fan might post copyrighted material such as images of a star, script material, or studio logos. Although most of these sites exist only to praise and promote the products, studios and networks have threatened legal action and forced their removal. Some professionals don't want amateur promotion, and they don't want their trademarks associated with messages they can't control. Ironically, fan sites have fewer defenses under current law than do Web sites set up to criticize and parody.

• *Expressions as Trademarks.* In recent years the trademark office has allowed companies and individuals to make trademarks out of fairly common expressions. For example, Fox News was allowed to trademark the expression "Fair and Balanced" for its news program, but when the company sought an injunction to prohibit distribution of satirist Al Franken's book *Lies and the Lying Liars Who Tell Them: A Fair and Balanced Look at the Right* (2003), the courts ruled in favor of Franken, saying that the book's subtitle was not an infringement of Fox's trademark because the phrase was being used for a different purpose. (If Franken had started a cable news channel and used the phrase, it might have been a different story.) Donald Trump sought to trademark the expression "You're Fired," from his television program *The Apprentice,* but he was careful to ask for the trademark only in terms of games, playthings, and casino services.[40]

Patents

A **patent** is an exclusive right given to an inventor to manufacture, use, or sell an invention for a specified number of years. Federal copyright law gives inventors 17 years in which to enjoy exclusive commercial exploitation of the machines, processes, manufactured products, and designs they create. Thomas Edison had this period to manufacture his phonographs and movie projectors; Bill Gates has the same amount of time to sell each of his Windows products before they enter the public domain (not that anyone today is likely to want to manufacture the operating system for a 1980s vintage computer).

Software programs are patented inventions, and the problem of patent violation has cost the software industry billions of dollars, both domestically and overseas. One company claimed that its program was one of China's hottest computer products, even though the company had sold only one official copy in the country.[41] Industry groups estimate that almost half of the programs in use have been pirated rather than purchased.[42] The FBI and the U.S. Justice Department have teams of detectives to investigate patent infringement, but the problem is too large for them to cover alone. In fact, the pirating problem has spawned a new cottage industry: Internet private detectives, hired by a variety of companies trying to protect their copyrights, trademarks, and patents. The Software Publishers Association, among others, has hired teams of recently graduated computer science majors to surf the Net and find those who would illegally distribute patented software.

patent
An exclusive right granted an inventor to manufacture, use, or sell an invention.

SELF QUIZ
How does patent law pertain to mass media?

News-Gathering Rights

A third area of media law consists of laws that help news gatherers in their jobs. Three types of laws seek to ensure that meetings, documents, and news sources will be made available to news reporters: sunshine laws, the Freedom of Information Act, and shield laws.

Sunshine Laws

Sunshine laws, or open-meeting laws, ensure that public meetings are conducted in open sessions that reporters are allowed to attend. Each state has such a law, although restrictions vary. A typical sunshine law will cover such legislative units as city councils, school boards, and state commissions as well as state and national legislatures. It will require those legislative units to meet at regular times and places, and to announce meetings to the public, including those members of the public who happen to be journalists. Only specifically listed actions, such as a collective bargaining session with a union or personnel actions, can be closed.

sunshine laws
Laws that ensure that public meetings are conducted in the open.

The Freedom of Information Act

The Freedom of Information Act (FOIA) was passed in 1966 to ensure open documents. This law requires federal agencies to list all their documents and provide them for news agencies on request. Requests must be disposed of within 10 working days, and no justification is needed for the application. Certain documents are excluded from the FOIA requirement, including those classified as top secret or whose release would violate privacy laws. The law has been used to reveal how the FBI harassed Dr. Martin Luther King Jr. and how the Central Intelligence Agency (CIA) illegally monitored domestic political groups and experimented on prisoners with mind-control drugs. It has also been used to uncover unsafe conditions at nuclear power plants and the presence of poisonous wastes in drinking water. Several governmental agencies have resisted FOIA actions, however, making it difficult for journalists and citizens to get the information they request.[43] The American Civil Liberties Union provides a step-by-step guide to using the Freedom of Information Act at www.aclu.org/library/foia.html.

Shield Laws

Shield laws are designed to ensure confidentiality of news sources. Some sources want to remain anonymous; for example, a local small-business owner who is being extorted by gangsters might want to provide the story to the local investigative reporter without worrying about mob retaliation.

Such news sources would not come forward with their information if they believed their identity would later be revealed. Judges, however, often want those sources to testify, and they will use their contempt power to jail journalists who refuse to identify them (see Close-Up on Controversy, pages 490–491). Some judges have also permitted the search and seizure of the notes of reporters who refuse to reveal their sources. Today, most states have established shield laws to help protect such sources. Reporters can still be required to testify about their sources, however, if the court can prove a compelling need.

SELF QUIZ

What do sunshine laws, the Freedom of Information Act, and shield laws protect? Give specific examples.

CONSIDER THIS

Should reporters be required to testify about their sources? Why or why not?

Controversies

All law is controversial. If there were not at least two sides to every issue the law addresses, there would be little need for the court system. Primary controversies in media law include those related to censorship and conflicting rights. Central to all these controversies are questions about the First Amendment. Is the First Amendment supreme, or was its placement at the top of

If censorship is the mother of all media controversies, then conflicting rights is the father.

the bill of rights random? Was it meant to be considered over other rights, or was it only listed first among equals? These questions, though essentially unanswerable, will continue to create controversies in the future.

CENSORSHIP

We have looked at the idea of censorship in earlier chapters of this book, beginning with the Close-Up on Controversy box in Chapter 1. It was mentioned there that the word *censorship* has been used to describe restrictions of communications activity by nongovernmental organizations and individuals, and even mere criticism of communication. In the legal sense, however, censorship consists of either prior restraint or prosecutions after the fact by government organizations. Free-speech advocates worry about any type of government censorship. Even when the government tries to prevent hate sites from operating on the Internet, free-speech groups such as People for the American Way and the American Civil Liberties Union rise up to fight. Although they abhor the ideas these sites contain, they want to defend the site sponsors' right to free expression.

The editors of the *New York Times* summed up the problem with fights over censorship this way: "The push to create safeguards is understandable, but it should not be allowed to diminish the fundamental right to free expression or the equally basic right of consenting adults to decide for themselves what to watch or read."[44] According to one point of view, the correct way to restrict materials disseminated electronically is to use technology to let people decide what they want to see in their own homes. Devices like V-chips and filter programs for home computers are examples of this type of technology.

Many forms of expression are protected, but some forms are more protected than others.

Part of the reinterpretation of the First Amendment that has occurred over the years is the accepted idea that many forms of expression are protected, but some forms are more protected than others (see Figure 14.4). One criterion for the level of protection is the type of speech. **Political speech**—which includes all the ideas, and the facts that back up the ideas, about the meaning and correct course of government—is the most protected. Next to that is **artistic speech,** which includes creative work such as painting, dance, and literature. Then there is **commercial speech,** which includes advertising, and finally there is indecent speech, or indecency, as discussed earlier in this chapter. Indecent speech enjoys the least protection.

Another criterion for the level of First Amendment protection is the type of medium. Throughout U.S. history, print media have enjoyed the highest level of protection. Movies, however, were not given First Amendment protection until 1952. Before that time, they were considered a novelty rather than a significant medium for the communication of ideas. Radio and television also enjoy less protection than print because they need to be government-regulated and operate under license. Even within the print media, there are different levels of protection. Magazines and books, for example, have less protection than newspapers in libel cases. It is assumed that newspapers operate under more stringent deadline pressure, while magazine and book writers have more time to check their facts.

Controversies arise when laws targeted at a type of speech with lesser protection—say, indecency—are used to censor speech about political ideas such as whether abortion should be legal. This, in fact, was one of the reasons the indecency provisions of the Communications Decency Act (discussed earlier in this chapter) were found to be unconstitutional in 1997—these provisions in effect prohibited both political and indecent speech. Other controversies arise when laws that apply to one type of medium are extended to another with greater protection, such as the Florida law that required newspapers to print replies to published attacks on political candidates (*Miami Herald v. Tornillo,* 1974). Television and radio stations at that time were required to broadcast replies, but the Supreme Court found the law unconstitutional for newspapers.

FIGURE 14.4 Levels of Free Speech Protection Some types of communication enjoy more First Amendment protection than others.

political speech
Messages about the meaning and correct course of government.

artistic speech
Creative work, such as painting, dance, and literature.

commercial speech
Advertising.

Jailing Judith Miller

Nowhere is the battle over free press/fair trial more pointed than in the fight over confidentiality of sources. Today, most states have some form of shield law to help journalists protect the identity of their sources (see page 488). The federal government, however, has no such law. So when two journalists refused a federal prosecutor's demand to reveal their sources about a story they had investigated, a federal judge threatened to send the reporters to jail for contempt of court.

The investigation concerned the source of a leak to the press that revealed the identity of an undercover CIA operative. For reasons of national security, it is against the law to publicly reveal the name of covert CIA agents. Making the matter more politically charged was the fact that the agent's husband, U.S. ambassador Joe Wilson, had publicly refuted some of the government's reasons for going to war in Iraq.

Traditionally, the news media had resisted efforts to force reporters to testify. Reporters had gone to jail for months and news organizations had paid hundreds of thousands of dollars in fines to protect sources. In fact, the 1970s are looked upon as a golden era in American journalism because major stories such as Watergate and the Pentagon Papers case were made possible through the use of confidential sources that were protected by both reporters and the companies they worked for.

The CIA case went all the way to the Supreme Court, which refused to protect the journalists in 2005. One of the reporters, Matthew Cooper of *Time* magazine, was saved from jail when his publisher agreed to hand over his notes and his source agreed to release him from his pledge of secrecy. The other reporter, Judith Miller of the *New York Times*, refused to reveal her source and was jailed for three months.

At her sentencing, Miller, a Pulitzer Prize–winning journalist, told the judge, "I do not make confidential pledges lightly but when I do, I keep them. In this case, I cannot break my word just to stay out of jail."[1]

Just a few weeks before Miller went to jail, the anonymous source of Carl Bernstein and Bob Woodward's Watergate secrets came forth of his

"Since you have already been convicted by the media, I imagine we can wrap this up pretty quickly."
© The New Yorker Collection 1991 Misha Richter from cartoonbank.com. All Rights Reserved.

CONFLICTING RIGHTS

If censorship is the mother of all media controversies, then conflict of rights is the father. All the laws mentioned so far have an inherent conflict of rights. Privacy, libel, and copyright laws, for example, often conflict with the public's right to know. One of the clearest conflicts exists between the rights of a free press and the rights of a defendant for a fair trial.

Free Press/Fair Trial

The defendant has the right to a public trial and the public has a right to know about the actions of its legal system. The Sixth Amendment to the U.S. Constitution requires that a trial be public, that members of the community be allowed to monitor the proceedings for fairness. News stories about criminal defendants and trial proceedings create what many see as an inherent conflict between the First and the Sixth Amendments. Since the Sam Sheppard trial (see the Close-Up on History box earlier in this chapter), the courts have tried

own accord. He was Mark Felt, a former FBI official identified previously only as "Deep Throat." Many observers said it was ironic that Felt came forward around the same time that Cooper's employers gave up his notes and Miller went to jail; if Woodward and Bernstein had been given as little protection as Cooper and Miller, the Watergate story would have never come to light 30 years earlier.

Journalists lamented that times had changed for the worse. As one First Amendment specialist said: At stake is the American people's right to know about the uses and misuses of power in high places. Where the impact will be greatest will be in reporting about organized crime, reporting about public or corporate corruption and, finally, national security. All of these are subjects for which confidential sources are not merely desirable but indispensable."[2]

Judith Miller, accompanied by her lawyer, arrives at court to be sentenced for contempt.

[1]Miller, speaking before Chief U.S. District Judge Thomas F. Hogan, quoted in "Miller Jailed for Refusing to Reveal Source," Associated Press online, July 6, 2005.

[2]Peter Scheer, executive director of the California First Amendment Coalition, quoted in Elizabeth Fernandez, "Reporters Handcuffed in New Era; They Fear Jailing of Journalist Will Prompt Sources to Clam Up," *San Francisco Chronicle,* July 7, 2005.

to work out methods to avoid this conflict. At first they tried the **gag order**— ordering the press not to report on the trial—but the Supreme Court soon found such orders unconstitutional. The court suggested several alternatives, each of which has its own set of advantages and disadvantages:

- In a **continuance,** the trial is postponed until the publicity about it dies down. In some cases, such as particularly ghoulish murder cases, this method has been successful. Other news comes up, so people (and therefore media practitioners) have less interest in the trial when it is finally held. In other cases, however, the publicity merely reignites when the trial finally begins. Another problem is that the defendant has a right to a speedy trial, which is essentially lost with a lengthy continuance.

- In **sequestering,** members of the jury are isolated, either during deliberations or during the entire trial, to shield them from the influences of the press. Members of the O. J. Simpson jury were sequestered for more than six months. During that entire time they were housed in a hotel at state expense and were not permitted to visit with friends and relatives. Their phone calls were screened, and they could read only after their newspapers, magazines, or books had objectionable material deleted by court officers. Sequestering is controversial because it is expensive, and it is difficult on the jurors.

- Another way to minimize the effects of trial publicity is a **change of venue,** the moving of a trial to a different location. A change of venue takes the trial to another community where the issues involved in the trial are less

gag order
Judicial command not to speak about trial proceedings.

continuance
Postponement of a trial.

sequestering
Isolating members of a jury.

change of venue
The moving of a trial to a different location.

inflammatory. The highly publicized trial of Scott Peterson, for example, was moved away from Modesto, California—where prosecutors said he killed his wife, Laci, and their unborn son—to Redwood City, California, early in 2004. Change of venue, like sequestering, is costly. Court officers such as the judge and the various attorneys, as well as the defendant and witnesses, all have to be moved and housed at state expense. Another problem is that publicity about a trial of national interest will follow it wherever it goes.

admonition

A judge's warning to jurors to consider only evidence presented in the courtroom.

• The easiest and least costly solution to prejudicial publicity is **admonition,** in which a judge warns jurors not to read, watch or listen to news reports, and to consider only the evidence that is presented in the courtroom. The main problem with admonition is that it is extremely difficult, in the age of the cable network Court TV and 24-hour news coverage, to expect jurors and even witnesses to avoid the news. In fact, Court TV has caused at least one mistrial, when a witness could not resist watching her mother testify when the judge had ordered her not to.[45]

What techniques do the courts use to protect a defendant against prejudicial trial publicity?

SELF QUIZ

The coverage of today's most sensational trials is so intense that it is difficult to see how any of these alternatives can now work. Every minute of the 1999 impeachment trial of President Bill Clinton, for example, was covered on 24-hour cable news programs. The rest of the day's broadcast schedule was crowded with talk shows, where every facet of the trial was repeatedly analyzed from various points of view.

Price $3.00 THE Mar. 8, 1999
NEW YORKER
SHOOTING GALLERY
41 SHOTS 10¢

When four New York City policemen were accused of shooting and killing an unarmed civilian, this magazine cover was cited by the judge as part of the prejudicial publicity that required the trial to be moved to another location, away from New York.

Cameras in Court

Nowhere is the controversy of free press/fair trial more noticeable than in the continuing debate about cameras in court. Cameras are of course commonplace in court today, but this use has occurred slowly and has been controversial from the beginning. In 1935, Bruno Richard Hauptmann was tried (and eventually convicted and executed) for the kidnapping murder of aviator hero Charles Lindbergh's infant son. During the trial, film companies installed a hidden camera in the balcony of the courtroom. Before the trial was over, newsreels of the courtroom action were being shown to audiences in movie theaters, contributing to the overwhelming popular opinion that Hauptmann was guilty. Hauptmann's jury could not help being influenced by this kind of coverage, and after the trial the American Bar Association banned cameras in courtrooms for more than 30 years.

By the 1960s the cameras were for television footage, and those in favor of their use in court were saying that the practice would enhance public accountability of the justice system without sacrificing the rights of trial participants. Arguing on the other side of the issue, the chief justice of the Supreme Court, Earl Warren, warned in 1965 that if television cameras became normal in the courtroom, the medium would begin to hire "persons with legal backgrounds to anticipate possible trial strategy, as the football expert anticipates plays for his audience."[46] He also predicted that certain trials would be unfairly singled out for prejudicial, televised attention. Television, he said, would concentrate on trials involving "a sensational murder," a "fallen idol," or a celebrity. Warren's fears seemed to have been realized. As one critic later pointed out, O. J. Simpson was a "three-time loser" by Warren's standard.[47] Today, cameras are allowed in at least some courtrooms in all 50 states, under certain conditions, but they are banned in federal courts, including the Supreme Court.[48]

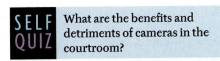

SELF QUIZ What are the benefits and detriments of cameras in the courtroom?

CONSIDER THIS

Should cameras be allowed in court? Why or why not?

Summing Up

The philosophy of free expression on which the First Amendment is based developed over many years, beginning with the ancient Greeks and leading to the Puritan and Protestant thought that influenced the people of the colonial era. When the colonists won their independence, the First Amendment became their statement of the importance of freedom of expression to American democracy.

Over the years, the courts have sought to define the limits of press freedom. The laws of the 19th century, which were based on print media, had to adapt to electronic media in the 20th century, just as they are currently adapting to the converging digital media of the 21st century. One of the questions that has been constantly examined is the degree to which the government should play a role in regulating media. An era of heavy regulation began during radio's heyday in the 1930s and an era of deregulation began in the 1980s.

Media law is currently adapting to major trends such as globalization, which means that the media of one country can be affected by the laws of another. The rise of media conglomerates has led to heavier jury awards, and new technology has led to new legal problems, such as those created by hacking into computer networks.

Media law operates within a complex system that involves the trial and appellate courts of every state and the federal system, all of which deal with criminal, civil, constitutional, statutory, administrative, and common law. Laws that were designed to protect personal rights include privacy and libel laws. Privacy laws include those based on private facts, intrusion, and appropriation. Defenses against libel include truth, privilege, fair comment, and the *Times* rule. Laws based on intellectual property rights include protection for copyright, trademarks, and patented inventions such as software.

Some laws have been established to protect news gatherers. Sunshine laws provide for open public meetings; the Freedom of Information Act (FOIA) allows for open government documents; and shield laws help protect a journalist's confidential sources.

Media law controversies include those based on censorship and conflicting rights. Censorship, from a constitutional point of view, consists of prior restraint and prosecutions after the fact by government. Conflicting rights are exemplified in free press/fair trial issues such as cameras in court. Controversies such as these will recur as the First Amendment continues to be examined and reinterpreted.

Key Terms

These terms are defined and indexed in the Glossary of key terms at the back of the book.

actual malice 480	copyright law 482	political speech 489
administrative law 477	criminal law 475	privilege 480
admonition 492	defamation 479	seditious libel laws 466
artistic speech 489	deregulation 469	sequestering 491
change of venue 491	fair comment 481	shield laws 488
civil law 475	fair use 483	slander 479
commercial speech 489	first-sale doctrine 482	statutory law 476
common law 477	gag order 491	sunshine laws 487
constitutional law 476	indecency 471	trademark 484
contempt 466	libel 479	
continuance 491	patent 487	

Electronic Excursions

HISTORY

Web Excursion

1. More incidents have been involved in the development of free speech philosophy than could be discussed in this chapter. Search the Web for sites related to the First Amendment or freedom of speech, or go directly to the timelines at the Media History Project at www.mediahistory.umn.edu/.* Identify at least three events, besides those discussed in this chapter, that have contributed to the idea of freedom of speech. Explain your choices.

INDUSTRY

Web Excursion

2. What kind of legal problems do the student media such as those on your campus encounter? Search the Web for "student media law," or go to the Student Press Law Center at www.splc.org. Find one example of a legal problem that might be relevant to the media on your campus and explain why.

CONTROVERSIES

Web Excursion

3. Since its ratification, the First Amendment has been subject to conflicting interpretations that have outraged individuals and institutions alike. Go to the Freedom forum site at www.freedomforum.org and follow the links to the "State of the First Amendment Report." Briefly review the page and explain how you would answer the questions presented on the annual survey on freedom of speech issues.

ONLINE LEARNING CENTER WWW.MHHE.COM/RODMAN2

You may access these and additional Web excursions at the Online Learning Center for the book (www.mhhe.com/rodman2). Visit the student portion of this Web site to also access the *Interactive Timeline of Mass Media Milestones,* chapter highlights, self quizzes, and recommended readings, movies, and documentaries for this chapter.

*Some Web site addresses may change. When they do, please search for the Web site by name or topic on your favorite search engine.

Media Ethics

Understanding Media Morality

15

Chapter Highlights

HISTORY: The history of media is replete with scandals, controversies, and various interpretations of ethical standards.

ETHICAL PRINCIPLES: The two primary types of ethical guidelines are absolutist and situation. Both areas have been explored and expanded upon by philosophers who help us interpret today's media actions.

CONTROVERSIES: Many ethical considerations within media have the potential to be controversial, because there is often a conflict between ethics in theory and what media practitioners face in the real world.

The Danish Cartoons

The editor of a conservative Danish newspaper asked a group of cartoonists to draw cartoons depicting the prophet Muhammad. He knew that this would be a provocation, because many Muslims believe that any depiction of the prophet is blasphemous, and that all references to him should be respectful.

The editor stated that he wanted to start a dialogue to "differentiate between radical and moderate Muslims," that is, between Muslims who accept the rule of secular law and those who insist that all nations follow Islamic law.

Twelve cartoons were published in the paper, including one depicting Muhammad wearing a bomb as a turban, and another with the prophet

This protest in Pakistan against Danish cartoons depicting the prophet Muhammad was one of many that eventually left 139 people dead.

shown at the gates of heaven, arms raised, saying to men who look like suicide bombers, "Stop, stop, we have run out of virgins!" (an allusion to the reward of 72 virgins that some Islamic fundamentalists believe are promised to martyrs).

The reaction, when it finally hit several months later, was hardly the type of dialogue the editor was expecting. Some fundamentalist Islamic leaders demanded execution or amputations for the cartoonists and their publishers. Muslim protesters burned the Danish and Norwegian missions in Syria. In Lebanon, rioters set fire to the Danish mission and vandalized a church. Fatal riots occurred in Nigeria, Indonesia, and a dozen other countries. At least 139 people lost their lives in these riots.

Very few media outlets in the United States published the cartoons. The editors of the *New York Times* said that they chose not to run them at least in part because the cartoons were so easy to describe in words.

Moderate Muslim Americans tried to explain why they objected to the publication of the cartoons. One stated that is was "not because they offend my prophet or my religion, but because they fly in the face of the tireless efforts of so many civic and religious leaders—both Muslim and non-Muslim—to promote unity and assimilation rather than hatred and discord; because they play into the hands of those who preach extremism; because they are fodder for the clash-of-civilizations mentality that pits East against West."[1]

The Danish editor sought to explain his actions. "I commissioned the cartoons in response to several incidents of self-censorship in Europe caused by widening fears and feelings of intimidation in dealing with issues related to Islam,"[2] he explained. For example, a Danish children's author wanted to write a book about Muhammad, but he could find no one to illustrate it; everyone he asked said they were afraid. A Dutch filmmaker had been killed and several authors had been threatened with death sentences for dealing with Islam in a critical manner.

The editor added, "One cartoon—depicting the prophet with a bomb in his turban—has drawn the harshest criticism. Angry voices claim the cartoon is saying that the prophet is a terrorist or that every Muslim is a terrorist. I read it differently: Some individuals have taken the religion of Islam hostage by committing terrorist acts in the name of the prophet. They are the ones who have given the religion a bad name."[3]

The editor felt that his publication of the cartoons was an ethical act. Many would disagree with him.

CONSIDER THIS

Was the publication of the cartoons depicting Muhammad an ethical act? Why or why not?

ethics
The study of guidelines that help people determine right from wrong in their voluntary conduct.

Ethics is the study of guidelines that help people determine right from wrong. Unlike law, the topic of Chapter 14, ethics deals primarily with self-determined, voluntary conduct. The two fields are related, however, because some moral issues have been codified into legal statutes and others perhaps should be. As everyone involved in the Danish cartoon incident learned, ethics is also related to media impact (Chapter 2), because mass communication messages can have a powerful effect.

Because media ethics deals with voluntary rather than required conduct, freedom of speech actually increases controversies in this area. There is very little debate about the nature of media ethics in countries such as Cuba or China, where press guidelines are dictated by law.

We considered ethics at various points in earlier chapters. We looked at some codes of ethics that several media industries maintain, and we considered how well the industries conform to those codes. We discussed the effects of concentration of ownership on media's responsibility to their communities, advertiser influence on the news, the impact of images in magazines and movies, the reliability of information on the Internet, truth in advertising, and credibility in public relations. It should be obvious at this point that ethics is a thorny area. There are different perceptions of what is right or wrong, and there are often gray areas.

Ethical guidelines derive from various sources. One source is the professional field. In the case of media ethics, the field is where journalists have to make immediate judgments under deadline pressure, where advertising executives have to sell a product, and where entertainment moguls have to worry more about how to make people laugh or cry than about how to make them better people. We will examine the professional field from a historical perspective in the first part of this chapter.

The second source of ethical guidelines is the realm of the philosopher, the thinker who has time to look at history and theory, to think about those bodies of knowledge, and to make some careful distinctions. Philosophers come up with their ideas about ethics over centuries of writing, publication, and discussion. They refer to that extensive material when they examine the complicated world of today's media ethics. We will summarize some of their findings in the second section of this chapter, on understanding today's media ethics.

The third source of ethical guidelines is the controversies that erupt around them. After a controversial use of media power, for example, both practitioners and regulators will begin to look at the controversial actions and propose guidelines to reduce the controversy the next time around. We'll take a look at some current controversies in the final section of this chapter.

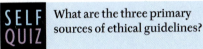

SELF QUIZ   What are the three primary sources of ethical guidelines?

A Brief History *of Media Ethics*

Many people think that violations of media ethics are currently more widespread than ever before. If you are one of them, a brief look at the history of media ethics might change your perception. This history includes a series of scandals, controversies, and various interpretations of the concept of ethics itself. Many of these controversies seemed to repeat themselves during three time periods: the print era, the electronics era, and the current, digital, era. The fact that they repeat themselves suggests that ethics has more to do with human nature than with any particular technology.

THE PRINT ERA

Controversies over media ethics are as old as the media. Following the invention of the printing press in the 15th century, for example, many church leaders objected to the printing of Bibles. To put the word of God into a form in which common people could access it and derive their own interpretations, independent of the official church teachings, seemed to border on the blasphemous. Later, royal rulers defined ethical publishing as that which included only information that supported their rule. Anything printed that was seen to threaten the sovereign's power was unethical by decree.

Early America

Some early media behavior wasn't controversial in its own day, but we look back on it today and discuss it in ethical terms. This would be true, for example, of the early advertisements that brought settlers to the New World, perhaps promising them more than the advertisers knew to be possible. An ethical analysis of the first newspaper published in America, Benjamin Harris's *Publick Occurrences,* would characterize it as a scandal sheet of rumor and innuendo by today's standards. A look back at the press of the American Revolution would find sensationalistic reporting of the Boston Massacre and staged public relations events such as the Boston Tea Party.

In the days of the early republic, people's view of ethics probably depended on their political orientation. The press was truly partisan, and the advancement of one's political point of view was often more important than a search for truth. The founders of the Constitution were philosophers as well as politicians, however, and many of them wondered out loud whether the print media could do more for the public good. Some proposed that journalistic standards should be based on the idea of **objectivity,** the practice of describing something according to the characteristics of the thing being described rather than the feelings of the one describing it (subjectivity). Objectivity, however, became a widely accepted journalistic guideline only when technology and commerce imposed it on the media in the 19th century. Technology, in the form of the telegraph and the Associated Press of New York, allowed news to be shared by papers with different views. Commerce, in the form of the needs of the penny press for a large audience of people with a wide range of political views, also demanded that objectivity be used.

objectivity
Description according to the characteristics of the thing being described rather than the feelings of the one describing it.

Press Hoaxes

Objectivity in journalism did not automatically establish ethical standards, however. Political partisanship was toned down, but the demands of the penny press in the 1830s were for readership and advertising revenues more than the good of humankind. Many critics debated the ethics of newspaper and magazine reporting at this time. These critics, for example, were upset that **hoaxes,** or purposeful deceptions of the reading public, were often used to sell newspapers. In 1835 the *New York Sun* perpetrated what has come to be known as the Great Moon Hoax. It published a series of stories purported to have been published earlier in the *Edinburgh Journal of Science* and written in a precise language and tone that unsuspecting readers took to be that of a scientific journal. The series told the story of an astronomer who had discovered life on the moon, describing lakes with amphibious creatures, grassy plains with herds of brown quadrupeds, and forests of strange trees and goatlike blue monsters. Even some scientists were taken in by the hoax. Other newspapers picked up the stories, causing a national sensation that died down only when the reporter admitted one night in a bar that he had made it all up. Hoaxes were so commonplace, in fact, that when reports of the invention of the telegraph in 1844 claimed that messages could be sent between Washington and New York in a few seconds, many readers thought it was just another media prank.

hoaxes
Purposeful deceptions of the public.

Other Excesses of the Penny Press

As the penny press changed the way journalism was conducted, many criticized its excesses. Horace Greeley, publisher of the *New York Tribune,* spoke

The original caption for this *New York Sun* lithograph read, "Voyage to the moon. Lunar animals and other objects discovered by Sir John Herschel in his observatory at the Cape of Good Hope and copied from sketches in the *Edinburgh Journal of Science*."

out against crude sensationalism in a now-famous editorial about "satanic" newspapers. He warned that "steamships, railroads, electric telegraphs, [and] power-presses, render communication so rapid that ideas circulate from mind to mind like lightning, and are received in all the vivid energy of their fresh conception." This made the press even more dangerous, as the "perverted product of a diseased civilization wherein debauched and prurient appetites gloat upon the unripe and poisonous fruit of the Tree of Knowledge." The satanic press, Greeley said, had only one goal: "To achieve notoriety and coin gold for its director by pandering to whatever is vile and bestial in a corrupted and sensual populace."[4]

Greeley, for all his righteousness, had his own ethical problems by today's standards. He was very willing, for example, to throw his political weight around. He was a staunch supporter of Abraham Lincoln and helped him get elected, but he then exerted his power in front-page open letters to the president, demanding action on the battlefield ("Forward to Richmond!") and in the legislature ("EXECUTE THE LAWS"). He was also ruthless in the promotion of the causes he believed in, never letting objectivity get in the way of a good denunciation of alcohol, capital punishment, or slavery, all of which he opposed.

The Yellow Press

Many of the techniques of 19th-century yellow journalism were ethically questionable. The sensational slant on the news, the lurid headlines, and especially, William Randolph Hearst's incitement for the United States' entry into the Spanish American War in 1895 (see Chapter 4) caused many to decry the state of journalistic ethics. The yellow press was also accused of contributing to the assassination of a U.S. president. Five days after the September 6, 1901, assassination of President William McKinley by a self-described anarchist, the *Brooklyn Eagle* published an editorial, entitled "Yellow Journalism and Anarchy" that read, in part:

DICTATOR GREELEY dismisses the Cabinet, and Warns Lincoln that he will stand no more Nonsense.

"A decimated and indignant people demand the immediate retirement of the present Cabinet from the high places of power, which, for one reason or another, they have shown themselves incompetent to fill. The people insist upon new heads of Executive Departments."—*New York Tribune, July 23.*

Horace Greeley, publisher of the *New York Tribune,* used his position in journalism to exert political power, as seen in this editorial cartoon from a competing paper. He was also a tonsorial innovator: What looks like a fur collar in this portrait is actually his beard.

The journalism of anarchy shares responsibility for the attack on President McKinley. It did not mean that he should be shot. It only wished to sell more papers by commenting on and cartooning him as "a tyrant reddening his hands in the blood of the poor and filling his pockets and those of others with dollars coined out of the sweat and tears and hunger of helpless strikers, their wan wives, and their starving children."[5]

The publishers of the yellow press period believed that in spite of their tactics, they were taking an ethical course of action.

The publishers of the yellow press period believed that in spite of their tactics, they were taking an ethical course of action. Joseph Pulitzer, in a 1907 editorial, said that his newspapers would

. . . always fight for progress and reform, never tolerate injustice or corruption, always fight demagogues of all parties, never belong to any party, always oppose privileged classes and public plunderers, never lack sympathy with the poor, always remain devoted to the public welfare, never be satisfied with merely printing news, always be drastically independent, never be afraid to attack wrong, whether by predatory plutocracy or predatory poverty.[6]

How did the penny press and the yellow press eras affect media ethics?

Muckraking

When Theodore Roosevelt gave the investigative reporters of his day the name muckrakers, they wore it with pride, believing it was ethical to un-

The yellow press was harsh in its treatment of President William McKinley, as seen in this 1896 editorial cartoon, in which he divides the spoils of the election with one of his wealthy supporters. Critics believe that this press treatment helped lead to McKinley's assassination by a self-described anarchist.

cover corruption. Roosevelt, however, had meant the term to be a pejorative; he believed the muckrakers went too far in their criticism, while ignoring the good things that government accomplished. In a speech at the laying of the cornerstone of the House of Representatives office building in Washington, Roosevelt stated:

> In [John] Bunyan's *Pilgrim's Progress* you may recall the description of the Man with the Muckrake. . . . There is filth on the floor, and it must be scraped up with the muckrake; and there are times and places where this service is the most needed of all the services that can be performed. But the man who never does anything else, who never thinks or speaks or writes save of his feats with the muckrake, speedily becomes, not a help to society, not an incitement to good, but one of the most potent forces of evil.[7]

SELF QUIZ What were some of the major scandals of the print era that highlighted problems in media ethics?

Ethical Codes

Worries about the power of media led to the development of a variety of **ethical codes,** the lists of guidelines issued by professional associations. An influential code, the Canons of Journalism, which outlined the need for fair and impartial reporting, was published by the American Society of Newspaper Editors (ASNE) in 1923 (see Chapter 4). The American Association of Advertising Agencies followed suit in 1924 with a code that established false and misleading advertising as unethical (see Chapter 13). The Public Relations Society of America established a code in 1950 to remind its practitioners to operate in the public interest (see Chapter 12). These self-imposed guidelines helped curb ethical breaches, although abuses continued to occur.

ethical codes
Lists of guidelines issued by professional associations.

THE ELECTRONIC ERA

The power of the electronic media to reach huge audiences ushered in a new realm of ethical controversy. The depiction of sex and violence in the movies,

General Francisco "Pancho" Villa (1878–1923) signed a contract with a Hollywood studio, allowing it to film his battles.

for example, was seen as a problem immediately and eventually resulted in the harsh Motion Picture Production Code of 1930, which specifically limited the sex and violence that could be portrayed in movies and led to the movie rating system we have today. Hollywood producers also became notorious for ethical lapses beyond the mere depiction of sex and violence. Around 1916, for example, the charismatic Mexican bandit and guerrilla leader Pancho Villa signed a contract with a Hollywood studio letting it film his battles. The $25,000 contract with the Mutual Film Corporation stipulated that Villa had to fight his battles during the daylight so that they could be filmed.[8] Later, Villa led brutal attacks on U.S. citizens in Mexico and the American Southwest, including one in which 16 North Americans were executed. Many critics felt that Hollywood money had helped finance those attacks.

The technology of radio also created some new ethical quandaries. Dr. John Brinkley, a famous radio "doctor" of the 1920s, had no license or medical degree. This did not stop him from answering health questions on the air at $2 an inquiry. He would also promote his surgical practice in his programs—he was well known for performing an operation to implant goat glands in a man's scrotum as a cure for impotence. In a practice that online pharmacies are emulating today, Brinkley would send out medicines without ever seeing the patient. When his broadcasting license was revoked in 1930, he took advantage of radio's wireless technology and moved his show to Mexico, where he could continue to broadcast into the United States.

Reacting to broadcasting abuses such as those of Brinkley, the National Association of Broadcasters (NAB) established a powerful code of ethics in 1929. It set standards for both programs (limiting sex and violence) and commercials (banning, for example, appeals directed at children). The NAB code survived through many revisions as technology changed, but the courts found it to be in violation of antitrust laws and it was abandoned in 1983. It is ironic that government action should have ended the NAB code, because the purpose of the code was to appease the government and head off regulation. When Congress, the Federal Communications Commission (FCC), or the Federal Trade Commission (FTC) would propose any kind of new rule for broadcasters, the NAB would adapt its code to head off formal regulation. When the FCC complained about stations airing too many commercials, for example, the NAB adjusted its code to reduce advertising time. The Justice Department, however, charged that the TV code's limitations on advertising restricted the amount of television advertising time available and thereby kept TV commercial rates artificially high. This amounted to a conspiracy among the networks, an antitrust violation.

The 1950s saw many ethical controversies. Ed Sullivan, for example, had to decide whether or not to allow Elvis Presley's gyrations to appear on his show. (He decided to shoot the singer from the waist up. He thought it was unethical to inflame the passions of his teenage audience.) Payola, record promoters' payments to DJs to play their songs, was both an ethical and legal scandal in the radio and recording industries. Probably the biggest scandal, however, was the one associated with early television quiz shows (see the Close-Up on History box).

SELF QUIZ

What was the purpose of the NAB code? Why was it eliminated?

blacklisting
The practice of keeping a particular type of person from working in media and other industries.

Politics and Media Ethics

Another ethically questionable practice in media history was **blacklisting,** or keeping a particular type of person from working in media and other in-

The Quiz Show Scandals

Television quiz shows of the 1950s gave rise to one of the most famous media ethics scandals in history when the producers of these shows were found to

and winning $129,000. Van Doren be-came a celebrity and was hired by NBC to be a member of the *Today* show cast. He was celebrated as a role

The quiz show scandal ended advertisers' control of television content.

Contestant Charles Van Doren is shown in an isolation booth "concen-trating" as he tries to remember the correct answer on the quiz show *Twenty-One.*

have blatantly lied to their audience. Shows like CBS's *The $64,000 Question* and NBC's *Twenty-One* were the first two success stories in the mid-1950s. Almost immediately, the networks put dozens of similar quiz shows on the air. Advertisers sponsoring the shows were in charge of production, and they decided who the contestants would be.

In 1958 contestant Charles Van Doren, a likable young Columbia University instructor, was a runaway success on *Twenty-One*, staying on the program for 15 weeks

model for American youth, a quiet, unassuming young man who proved that you could be successful using your brain. But then several disgruntled losers brought forth claims that the shows had been fixed. Van Doren testified before a grand jury, denying that he had been given the answers in advance on any of the shows in which he had appeared.

Later, the jury was given evidence proving that Van Doren had lied. Not only had he been given the answers, but he had been coached on how to appear as if he was straining to think of them: the concerned look, wiping his brow with a handkerchief when things got tough. To his great shame, Van Doren was indicted for perjury. He received a suspended sentence, but he lost his jobs at Columbia University and NBC, withdrew altogether from the public, and became a lifelong recluse. Federal laws were passed against fixing game shows, and networks took back control of their programs from the advertisers. The quiz show scandal ended advertisers' control of television content. From then on, the networks would have that job.

dustries. In the 1950s, media executives caved in to the demands of Senator Joseph McCarthy and others who were fanning the national fear that communists had infiltrated the U.S. government, military, universities, and media. The United States was involved in a cold war with the Soviet Union, and many conservative political groups claimed that a Soviet communist take-over was under way, led by spies working secretly within the film and broadcasting industries. Zealous members of self-described "citizen-patriot" groups compiled blacklists of so-called communist sympathizers.[9] Actors, directors, writers, and producers who had joined study groups about communism in the 1930s, when it was an elite and fashionable thing to do, suddenly saw their pasts come back to haunt them. Others were placed on the lists for supporting "radical" organizations such as labor unions, or for participating in war rallies in which the Soviet Union—an important U.S. ally in World War II—was praised.

Blacklisted writers: Seven members of the Hollywood 10 arrive at court in 1950, at the height of the blacklisting era. Left to right: Samuel Ornitz; Ring Lardner, Jr.; Albert Maltz; Alvah Bessie; Lester Cole; Herbert Bieberman, and Edward Dmytryk.

Movie studios and broadcasting networks fired the blacklisted individuals, including a group of screenwriters who came to be known as the Hollywood Ten. Finding it impossible to work in the industry, some of those on the lists even committed suicide. Many people fought against blacklisting. One of its most famous opponents was Edward R. Murrow, who had become famous as a World War II correspondent for CBS and had a popular television program, *See It Now*. Murrow took on McCarthy in his program in 1954, showing footage of the senator using rumor and innuendo to smear innocent people. Another media professional who helped bring the blacklist to an end was John Henry Faulk. A popular radio personality who had been fired, Faulk took on the blacklisters in a 1956 libel lawsuit and won.

Once the blacklisters were exposed as opportunists who were purposely creating a "red scare" for their own political purposes, broadcast executives stopped paying attention to them and they faded from public consciousness. The ethical stance of not giving in to power groups making unjustified demands, however, has been a sore point for media professionals ever since. It helps explain why many of them refuse to give in to demands for "political correctness" today, such as when pressure groups ask for positive images. We'll explore this tendency further in the controversies section of this chapter.

What was blacklisting, and how did it work?

Politics and media ethics again converged in the 1960s, this time in the public statements of Spiro Agnew, who was Richard Nixon's vice president until forced to resign because of bribery and tax evasion he had committed earlier in his political career. Agnew's attacks on the press are remembered mostly for alliterative but insulting epithets for newspeople, such as "nattering nabobs of negativism." Agnew was reviled by most members of the press, but his comments raised questions regarding credibility, fairness, and bias that are interesting to look at today—in fact, some of his pronouncements now ring true. Agnew pointed out that the television networks were the sole source of national and world news for millions of Americans, and that newscasters sometimes abused their power:

> A raised eyebrow, an inflection of the voice, a caustic remark dropped in the middle of a broadcast can raise doubts in a million minds about the veracity of a public official or the wisdom of a government policy. The American people would rightly not tolerate this kind of concentration of power in government.

Is it not fair and relevant to question its concentration in the hands of a tiny and closed fraternity of privileged men, elected by no one, and enjoying a monopoly sanctioned and licensed by government?[10]

Agnew also warned about the power of pseudo events, defined in Chapter 11 as news incidents that would not have happened if journalists were not there to record them. "How many marches and demonstrations would we have," Agnew asked, "if the marchers did not know that the ever-faithful TV cameras would be there to record their antics for the next news show?"[11]

In one address Agnew protested the practice of instant analysis of political speeches. After one Nixon speech he fumed, "When the President completed his address—an address that he spent weeks in preparing—his words and policies were subjected to instant analysis and querulous criticism. The audience of seventy million Americans—gathered to hear the President of the United States—was inherited by a small band of network commentators and self-appointed analysts, the majority of whom expressed, in one way or another, their hostility to what he had to say."[12]

 SELF QUIZ How did the politics of the 1950s and 1960s affect media ethics?

More Media Hoaxes and Deceptions

If politics is a continuing thread in the evolving interpretation of media ethics, so are large-scale media hoaxes and other deceptions. A few of these have been mentioned earlier, including Stephen Glass's fabrications in *The New Republic* (see Chapter 5). There have been many others.

Janet Cooke

A young reporter named Janet Cooke pulled off an infamous hoax at the *Washington Post* in 1980. Cooke won a Pulitzer Prize for a series of stories, entitled "Jimmy's World," featuring an eight-year-old heroin addict. Many people, however, insisted that the story had to be fake. Others, including the mayor and police chief of Washington, demanded to know where Jimmy was so he could be found and helped. Cooke told her editors that if she disclosed the real names of the characters in her story, her life would be in jeopardy. At age 26, Cooke was one of the paper's rising stars, but she

Janet Cooke, shown in a 1982 photo, returned the Pulitzer Prize for feature writing after admitting she made up the story "Jimmy's World."

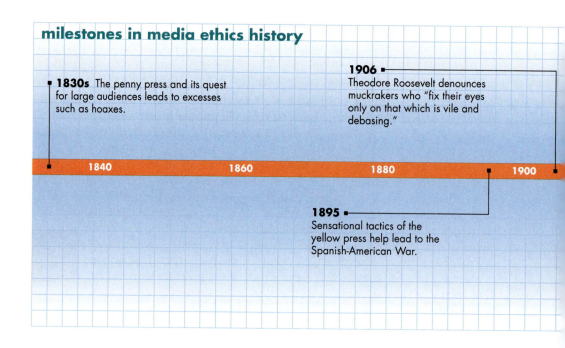

1830s The penny press and its quest for large audiences leads to excesses such as hoaxes.

1906 Theodore Roosevelt denounces muckrakers who "fix their eyes only on that which is vile and debasing."

1840   1860   1880   1900

1895 Sensational tactics of the yellow press help lead to the Spanish-American War.

finally had to admit that Jimmy did not exist. The Pulitzer had to be returned, and Cooke lost her job.

The Hitler Diaries

In 1983, another hoax occurred when the German magazine *Stern* acquired the rights to what its editors believed were the authentic diaries of Adolf Hitler. There were 62 volumes of the diaries, purportedly pulled from the wreckage of a cargo plane nine days before Hitler's suicide in 1945. *Stern* described the miraculous discovery of the diaries as "the journalistic scoop of the post World War II period." Evidence soon appeared that the diaries might not be genuine, however. Experts said the handwriting was not even close to Hitler's. Chemical analysis of the books' binding showed that it contained polyester threads, which were not produced until after World War II. The glue contained postwar chemicals too. The physical appearance of the diaries alone should have set off alarms. All 62 volumes, supposedly written over a 13-year period, were precisely alike and all their pages were miraculously unstained and unworn. In the United States, *Newsweek* decided to purchase rights to publish the diaries anyway. Its May 2, 1983, cover story mentioned the possibility of fraud, but dismissed it, saying, "Genuine or not, it almost doesn't matter in the end." One critic said of that line, "This is believed to be first time a major news organization informed readers that it didn't much matter whether the news they were getting was true."[13]

Jayson Blair

At the age of 23, fresh from the University of Maryland, Jayson Blair began a meteoric career at the *New York Times*. He moved quickly from intern to cub reporter to full-time staffer to national reporter. In less than three years he had published 600 articles. His stories even began to receive front-page placement when the *Times* management assigned him to cover the Washington sniper case in the fall of 2002.

What were the ethical problems associated with Janet Cooke, the Hitler diaries, and Jayson Blair?

SELF QUIZ

But then the editor of a Texas paper contacted the editor of the *Times,* complaining that Blair had plagiarized one of his reporter's stories about the family of a soldier missing in Iraq. When the *Times* editor looked into this

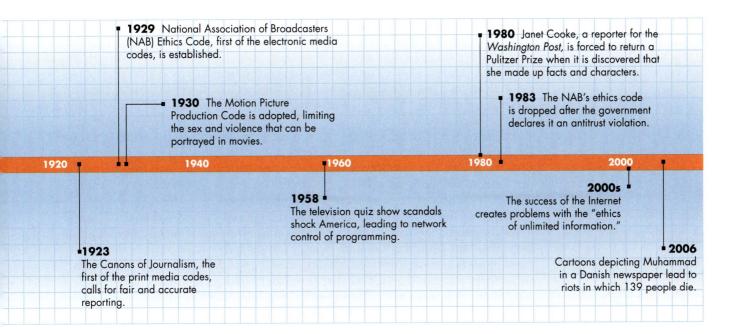

1929 National Association of Broadcasters (NAB) Ethics Code, first of the electronic media codes, is established.

1930 The Motion Picture Production Code is adopted, limiting the sex and violence that can be portrayed in movies.

1980 Janet Cooke, a reporter for the *Washington Post*, is forced to return a Pulitzer Prize when it is discovered that she made up facts and characters.

1983 The NAB's ethics code is dropped after the government declares it an antitrust violation.

| 1920 | 1940 | 1960 | 1980 | 2000 |

1958 The television quiz show scandals shock America, leading to network control of programming.

2000s The success of the Internet creates problems with the "ethics of unlimited information."

1923 The Canons of Journalism, the first of the print media codes, calls for fair and accurate reporting.

2006 Cartoons depicting Muhammad in a Danish newspaper lead to riots in which 139 people die.

allegation, he found not only that that article had indeed been plagiarized but also that 36 of the 73 articles Blair had submitted in the previous few months contained similar types of plagiarism, factual errors, and fabrications.

One of Blair's favorite forms of deception was to not reveal his whereabouts when he was reporting. He had been using his cell phone and laptop to make it seem as if he was jetting around the country on assignment while he was actually not traveling at all. He wrote some stories from the *Times* newsroom when he was supposed to be on the road.

When confronted by the editor, Jayson Blair resigned immediately, but the *Times* investigation proceeded. In May 2003 the results of that inquiry appeared as a 14,000-word story, which is approximately the same length as a full chapter of the book you are now reading. It was the kind of coverage that the *Times* usually reserves for cataclysmic events of global importance. The editors of the paper called the incident "a low point in the 152-year history of the newspaper." The publisher called it "a huge black eye."[14]

THE DIGITAL ERA

The digital era has ushered in a rethinking of media responsibility that might be called "the ethics of un-

On the *Media World* DVD that accompanies this text (Track 26, "Jayson Blair: Burning Down My Masters' House"), Blair explains his actions to Matt Lauer of the *Today* show.

limited information." Pornography and hate sites flourish on the Web, and several 24-hour cable news services have shown that no contemporary information, no matter how lurid or embarrassing, can be hidden from children. The 1998 Bill Clinton–Monica Lewinsky affair, for example, created daily ethical quandaries. Should legitimate news organizations publish rumors generated on the Internet? Should information about the affair, in all its graphic detail, be placed on the Net for all to access?

New information served up on the Internet continually raises ethical questions. For example, does DeathNet, which helps terminally ill people find sources of self-euthanasia, encourage people to kill themselves? How about the Heaven's Gate suicide cult, which recruited members on the Internet before its mass suicide?[15] What about the ethics of posting term papers online? Are those who sell such papers "research companies" or "term paper mills"? When one university tried to sue the term-paper sites, the courts refused to hear the case, saying that the matter was an ethical rather than a legal issue.[16] Online medical prescriptions have become a legal problem for doctors whose prescriptions cross state lines (doctors are licensed to practice only within certain states); the American Medical Association, though, says in-state online prescriptions are unethical, not illegal.[17]

The new media have led to a reexamination of various established practices. Amazon.com, for example, adopted the bookstore practice of charging publishers for prominent display space. On its Web site, that practice meant placing books on its "Destined for Greatness" and "What We're Reading" lists. Customers were not informed that publishers had paid to have their books placed on these lists, and critics pointed out that Amazon was, in effect, selling its recommendations. Responding to the criticism, Amazon said it would offer full refunds for any recommended book and would tell customers which displays had been paid for from that point on.[18] In another case, it was discovered that several authors were supplying the "anonymous" reviews of their own books on Amazon.

New media have made the continuing controversies over media ethics even more confusing than they were before. The following section will explore some of the ways both practitioners and critics have tried to make sense of this confusion.

How has the digital era affected media ethics?

SELF QUIZ

Understanding Today's *Media Ethics*

Media history shows us how some ethical controversies and guidelines have evolved out of real-world, high-pressure media practices. As mentioned earlier, the second source of ethical guidelines is the realm of the philosopher, who considers the basic orientations, philosophical backgrounds, and conflicting loyalties involved in ethical choices. This philosophical realm can be used to help today's media practitioners determine which choices are ethical. They can also help us consider the complications of truth telling.

BASIC ETHICAL ORIENTATIONS

At the most basic level, there are two primary ethical orientations: absolutist ethics and situation ethics (see Figure 15.1).

Absolutist Ethics

The term **absolutist ethics** describes the position of those who believe there is a clear-cut right or wrong response to every ethical dilemma. This black-and-white per-

Absolutist Ethics

A perspective calling for codes of professional ethics that hold true regardless of situation or consequence.

Prescriptive codes stipulate specific behaviors to follow.

Proscriptive codes stress what should not be done.

Situational Ethics

A perspective calling for making rational ethical choices without adhering to a rigid set of rules.

Actions are good or bad depending on the given situation.

Followers think in terms of "more" or "less" ethical choices, rather than ethical vs. unethical.

FIGURE 15.1 Basic Ethical Orientations At the most fundamental level, these are the two primary ethical orientations.

spective holds true regardless of background, situation, or consequence. The absolutist's guidelines, often based on religious ideals and rigidly enforced, allow for codes of professional ethics to be written. **Prescriptive codes** stipulate specific behaviors to be followed (such as the ASNE Canons of Journalism), and **proscriptive codes** stress the things that should not be done (such as the early motion picture code's ban on sexual content).

There is a tradition of absolutism in journalism, probably resulting from the feeling some journalists have that they are fulfilling a moral duty in a world that is set against them. This point of view was expressed as early as 1903 by Samuel Sidney McClure, the publisher of *McClure's Magazine* and one of the founders of muckraking:

> Capitalists, workingmen, politicians, citizens—all breaking the law, or letting it be broken. Who is left to uphold it? The lawyers? Some of the best lawyers in this country are hired, not to go into court to defend cases, but to advise corporations and business firms how they can get around the law without too great a risk of punishment. The judges? Too many of them so respect the laws that for some "error" or quibble they restore to office and liberty men convicted on evidence overwhelmingly convincing to common sense. The churches? We know of one, an ancient and wealthy establishment, which had to be compelled by a health office to put its tenements in sanitary condition. The colleges? They do not understand.
>
> There is no one left; none but all of us.[19]

Many newspapers develop absolutist rules to this day. Some papers, fearing the threat to a reporter's objectivity, absolutely forbid the acceptance of gifts (freebies) or trips (junkets) from news sources. Most have rules against fabrications, plagiarism, and the intentional slanting of the news. Other papers hold hard and fast to a **two-source rule,** which states that nothing will be published as fact unless a second, independent source confirms it. This rule was championed by the *Washington Post* in the Watergate era.

A newspaper's rule against deception is often absolutist in nature. A Kentucky reporter wrote a series of newspaper columns describing her imminent death from what she described to her readers as "terminal brain cancer." She was fired when her publisher found out that she actually had AIDS. It didn't matter that she actually was dying, that the specific disease was only peripheral to the story, or that she had lied because of the stigma associated with AIDS. The publisher would not waver from his hard-and-fast rule against deception.[20]

The philosophical background of absolutist ethics is based on the work of both classical and modern philosophers (see Figure 15.2). The most important of the classical philosophers was Immanuel Kant; the best-known modern adherent is John Rawls.

Kant's Categorical Imperative

In the 1700s, German philosopher Immanuel Kant developed the idea of the **categorical imperative.** In this sense, *categorical* means unconditional. The primary ethical guideline is to look for rules that will apply in every similar situation, without exception. Kant's ideas have been extremely influential in the development of media ethics; each profession has searched for universal principles that can be set down in the form of ethical codes. Some practitioners also develop personal codes based on categorical imperatives. Many journalists, for example, consider freedom of the press and the public's right to know to be universal principles. Anything that interferes with these ideals, no matter what the consequences, is to be discounted.

absolutist ethics
Position from which there is a clear-cut right or wrong response for every ethical decision.

prescriptive codes
Guidelines that stipulate specific behaviors to be followed.

proscriptive codes
Guidelines that stress the things that should not be done.

PROVIDENCE, RI   CRANSTON, RI

On the *Media World* DVD that accompanies this book (track 11), Brooks King (left), editor in chief of Brown University's *Daily Herald,* and Shaun Joseph, a student coalition leader, discuss the ethical implications of publishing an allegedly racist ad. As they do so, they also divulge their basic ethical orientations.

two-source rule
Common newspaper rule stating that nothing should be published as fact unless at least two sources confirm it.

categorical imperative
The ethical guideline to look for principles that will hold true in all situations.

ABSOLUTIST ETHICS

Kant

Categorical Imperative: Universal principles that hold true in every similar situation; a media professional may base his or her personal code on categorical imperatives, such as journalists' belief in freedom of the press.

Rawls

Veil of Ignorance: Everyone must be treated equally without regard to social or economic class; the media professional's loyalty and duty must be blind to all social distinctions.

SITUATION ETHICS

Aristotle

The Golden Mean: A midpoint between two extremes; for media practitioners, moderation should be the guiding principle as they weigh their professional needs against those of society.

Machiavelli

Enlighened Self-Interest: Success is an end unto itself; therefore, the end justifies the means; media professionals are justified in pursuing their goal without consideration of the consequences for others.

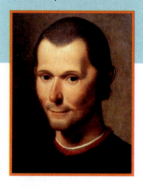

Mill

Utilitarian Principle: Behavior that generates the greatest good for the greatest number of people; the media professional must choose a course of action that places the importance of society over the well-being of the individual.

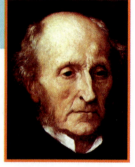

FIGURE 15.2 Ethical Philosophies Philosophers have dealt with the nature of ethics since ancient times.

Rawls's Veil of Ignorance

veil of ignorance
John Rawls's term associated with the idea that ethical behavior is possible only if everyone is treated equally.

Modern American philosopher John Rawls (1921–2002) built on Kant's ideas when he proposed the concept of a **veil of ignorance.** According to this perspective, ethical behavior is possible only if everyone is treated equally, without regard for social stature or economic class. For followers of Rawls, media justice must be blind. Practitioners must treat the poor as they do the rich, and the famous as the everyday person on the street. To be truly ethical, media practitioners must therefore wear a veil of ignorance that prevents them from recognizing these social distinctions. This philosophical perspective pertains to everything from the way journalists treat their sources to the way that movie producers depict minorities, religious people, or business executives.

Many media practitioners believe that absolutist ethics such as those proposed by Kant and Rawls are inadequate for handling the complexities of today's world. These practitioners subscribe to the second basic orientation, known as situation ethics.

Situation Ethics

The modern school of **situation ethics** was founded in the 1960s by Joseph Fletcher, an Episcopal priest who later renounced his faith and became an atheist. To those who subscribe to this school of thought, the most important aspect of ethical behavior is an appreciation that the moral quality of an action varies from one situation to another.[21] In this view, ethical choices can be made rationally, without a rigid adherence to a predetermined set of rules. Because this makes all actions relatively good or bad, situation ethics is sometimes referred to as **relativistic ethics.** Followers of situation ethics tend not to speak in terms of ethical and unethical media behavior. For them this black-and-white perspective is an oversimplification. They prefer to think in terms of degrees of ethicality. Thus they will speak of "more ethical" and "less ethical" choices.

One reporter spoke of the situation ethics of a teen suicide he covered. A boy had shot himself with a rifle, and the grieving family asked that the story be withheld from the newspaper. The reporter insisted on publishing the story, explaining that teen suicides were important news. Rather than sticking to a set rule about publication, however, the reporter did agree to let the mother read the story beforehand and, at her request, removed certain details, such as the fact that the boy had shot himself in the head. Later, the reporter felt that the mother's input improved the story.[22]

The philosophers most often cited in discussions on situational ethics include Aristotle, John Stuart Mill, and Niccolò Machiavelli.

Aristotle and the Golden Mean

Aristotle, a Greek philosopher who lived in the fourth century BC, proposed that ethical behavior was based on a **golden mean,** a midpoint between extremes. Aristotle's views were influenced both by his studies with Plato, the founder of the Greek Academy, and later by his work as a tutor for Alexander the Great. Under Plato, Aristotle developed a special interest in zoology and botany as well as philosophy. He noted that moderation was the key to health in living things. Too much or too little food can kill an animal, and too much or too little water can kill most plants. Ethical behavior, like health, could also be achieved by seeking a midpoint between excess and defect. As a tutor to Alexander the Great, Aristotle composed a treatise on ethics for the 13-year-old prince. The simplicity and clarity of the idea of the golden mean might be attributed to the way Aristotle had to approach this topic for young Alexander.

The golden mean has become a guiding principle of situational media ethics as practitioners navigate a daily path between their professional needs and those of society. Aristotle's idea, in practice, requires the media practitioner to first identify the extremes. In the reporting of a story for a television newsmagazine, for example, one extreme might be producing a facts-only, dull-as-dishwater story that will make people switch channels, while the other extreme is producing a story that is highly entertaining but bothers little with the facts. A midpoint between those extremes must then be found, resulting in a story that is both reasonably accurate and reasonably interesting.

situation ethics
Principle that ethical choices can be made according to the situation, without a rigid adherence to set rules.

relativistic ethics
Another name for situation ethics.

golden mean
Aristotle's term for describing ethical behavior as a midpoint between extremes.

Mill's Utilitarian Principle

John Stuart Mill, an influential English philosopher of the 1800s, was an economist as well as a philosopher, and many of his ideas deal with nation building. Ethical behavior, according to Mill, is that which is useful in generating the greatest good for the greatest number of people. Mill called his guideline the "greatest happiness principle," but because it appeared in his book *Utilitarianism* (1863), it is known today as the **utilitarian principle.**[23] For a utilitarian, the golden mean and universal rules apply only if those principles result in the greatest good for the most people. This can make for some hard choices. One reporter told the story of a small-town girl who had failed out of college and become a prostitute in a distant city. When the girl was murdered plying her trade, he had to publish the story, in spite of the grief and embarrassment it would cause the girl's family. The reporter reasoned that this girl's life and death would serve as an important warning for other young women in her community. That importance outweighed the suffering the story would bring to the girl's family.

Machiavellian Ethics

Another philosopher, Niccolò Machiavelli (1469–1527) of Florence, Italy, had a different idea about ethics. **Machiavellian ethics** are encapsulated in the expression "the end justifies the means": If your cause is ethical, such as the survival of the state, then the means you use to accomplish that end, including war, repression, and disinformation, are ethical also.[24] For Machiavelli, personal success was a noble end in itself. This led to the idea of **enlightened self-interest,** the idea that if you do what is right for yourself, it will probably also be right for the rest of the world in the long run. When today's investigative reporters go after a story at all cost, without consideration of the consequences to others, they are often accused of Machiavellian ethics, which is considered adhering to the least ethical of the various situation orientations.

> **utilitarian principle**
> John Stuart Mill's idea that actions are ethical only if they result in the greatest good for the most people.

> **Machiavellian ethics**
> The idea that the end justifies the means.

> **enlightened self-interest**
> Theory that holds that doing what is right for yourself will probably be right for others.

What are the basic philosophical ideas that underlie ethical decisions?

SELF QUIZ

CONSIDER THIS

Think about an ethical decision that you had to make. Which ethical principle or principles discussed here would have been most useful in that case?

CONFLICTING LOYALTIES

The basic philosophical perspectives are a good starting point for understanding media ethics, but they are complicated by the idea of conflicting loyalties and duties. Many theorists have pointed out the wide range of conflicting loyalties that influence the ethical decisions of media practitioners.[25] These practitioners may choose to be loyal to their own conscience, to their organization or firm, to their profession or art, or to society in general.

Duty to Personal Conscience

Many media practitioners develop a personal code of ethics over the years, one based on their individual beliefs. Daniel Schorr, a well-known television reporter, has said that personal integrity was always a key element in what he reported and how he reported it. Schorr even admits that he once withheld a major story from his organization because that story probably would have prevented thousands of Jews from slipping secretly out of the Soviet Union at a time when they were being persecuted there.[26]

Critics today often decry a lack of conscience on the part of media practitioners. Replacing it, they say, is a type of careerism in which professional success is the ultimate good, even if that success is attained by ignoring eth-

CYNTHIA TUCKER
ATLANTA CONSTITUTION

Cynthia Tucker is the Editorial Page Editor of the *Atlanta Constitution*. On the *Media World* DVD that accompanies this book she discusses the ethical standards of today's news profession (track 12).

ical considerations. Those who exploit sex, violence, and stereotypes in news and entertainment are often held up today as being deficient in conscience.

Duty to One's Organization or Firm

Most media practitioners feel a loyalty to the company or organization that signs their paychecks. To many, this feeling goes beyond a simple fear of losing their jobs to embrace a sense of fair play and a feeling of identity with the greater organization of which they are a part. Many journalists, for example, internalize the company policy of their firms. The Gannett Company publishes ethical guidelines for all 100 of its daily newspapers, and most employees accept these guidelines as things they believe in. Gannett's guidelines state that newspapers (1) should seek and report the truth, (2) serve the public interest, (3) exercise fair play, (4) maintain independence, and (5) act with integrity. These five general guidelines are accompanied by specifics that forbid such tactics as lying to get a story, misstating identity or intent, fabricating facts, plagiarizing others' work, altering photographs so as to mislead (see the Close-Up on Media Ethics box), and slanting the news.

Duty to One's Profession or Art

In today's world of corporate ownership, the loyalty that media practitioners feel to their companies might conflict with what they see as their duties to their profession. Most journalists see journalism as a noble undertaking, just as most filmmakers and musicians see themselves as artists. To them, their loyalty to their larger profession might be more important than even personal conscience. Thus, a reporter might publish a story that hurts a personal friend or a novelist might publish a book that embarrasses a family member if either writer feels it advances his or her profession or art in a broader sense.

CONSIDER THIS

Which of the loyalties discussed here is most important in your own ethical decision making? Why?

Duty to Society

Most media practitioners feel that they have a responsibility to society at large. This feeling recognizes the immense power of media within society today. It is the reason that the Communications Act of 1934 stipulated that broadcasters should operate in "the public interest, convenience, and necessity." In fact, an influential inquiry into media power in 1947, the Hutchins Commission, proposed that social responsibility was an essential element of free speech. That proposal has become one of the basic principles of media ethics today.

Some media outlets work with their communities to determine what their social responsibility is. For example, television stations in Portland, Oregon; Tampa, Florida; and Boston already have agreements with their local police departments setting rules for coverage of what they call "barricaded assailant situations." These agreements set distances for how close news helicopters can get to the scene and ban the live broadcast of special weapons and tactics (SWAT) teams in action. They also encourage the use of **pool cameras,** in which several TV news organizations share one camera crew. This avoids the chaotic congestion of a **media circus,** in which every imaginable outlet brings its own video crew. In exchange, the police agree to allow pool cameras better access and locations than they allow individual news crews' cameras.

SELF QUIZ How do conflicting loyalties affect media ethics?

pool cameras
One camera crew shared by several TV news organizations.

media circus
Chaos that results when crowds of journalists descend on the scene of a news event.

The Ethics of Photo Alteration

Ken Light, who teaches photojournalism and ethics at the University of California at Berkeley, was going through some of his old files one day and found a photo that he had taken of John Kerry more than 30 years before. Considering Kerry's run for president, Light thought the picture might be of general interest, so he sent it to Corbis, the online agency for stock photos. Within a week, the photo was circulating on the Internet, but it now looked dramatically different. Instead of just the young John Kerry, the photo included Jane Fonda, the actress/activist known as "Hanoi Jane" by the conservatives who hated her for her public stance against the war in Vietnam. The picture was circulated to identify Kerry with Fonda in the minds of voters. It appeared in several publications before it was exposed as a fake. Light was horrified by what had become of his original photo. "What if that photo had floated around two days before the general election and there wasn't time to say it's not true?" he said.[1]

The manipulation of photos for political purposes is hardly new. The Soviets and the Chinese were famous for removing the images of political figures who were out of favor—or had been executed—from photos of their groups of leaders. But it took a considerable amount of skill to pull it off in those predigital days, and often the result actually looked fake. With today's software packages such as Photoshop, which often come free with computers, scanners, printers and digital cameras, seamless manipulation of images is fast and easy. The Internet then allows the altered images to be transmitted worldwide in seconds.

Owen Franken, the photographer who took the original photograph of Fonda in 1972 that was blended with Light's photo of Kerry, was equally offended and was quick to point out how serious this ethical breach was. "The damage is not going to be undone later," he said, "by saying it was a doctored picture."[2]

[1] Quoted in Katie Hafner, "The Camera Never Lies, but the Software Can," *New York Times* online, March 11, 2004.
[2] Quoted in Hafner, "The Camera Never Lies."

Political enemies of John Kerry combined his photo with that of Jane Fonda.

TRUTH TELLING AND ITS COMPLICATIONS

Because of conflicting loyalties, different views toward absolute and situation ethics, and varying philosophical backgrounds, every ethical guideline has its complications. Take truth telling, for example. Every media code requires it, and on its face it seems like a worthwhile guideline. Even this

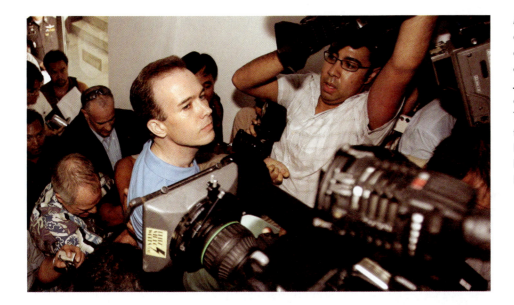

Media circuses occur when dozens of news organizations each bring their own video crews to a news event. Here John Mark Karr is confronted by camera crews as he leaves Thailand. Karr falsely confessed to the murder of six-year-old beauty queen JonBenet Ramsey but was eventually released after his return to the United States.

basic principle, though, is complicated by a difficult and complex philosophical question: What is truth?

In Entertainment

This quandary often arises in the entertainment media. Moviemakers, for example, will often try to tell an artistic rather than a historical truth. The movie *The Deer Hunter* (1978) contains a number of scenes in which Vietnamese people gather and place wagers on contests of Russian roulette. Nothing even remotely like this ever happened in Vietnam, but the scenes serve as a powerful metaphor for the arbitrary and sometimes commercial nature of war. In this movie, that metaphor serves as an artistic truth.

In Advertising

Advertisers also face continual criticism for playing fast and loose with the truth. Just like filmmakers, however, they often explain that they are trying to depict a different type of truth, one that shows the satisfaction the product will bring to the consumer rather than a literal depiction of the product's characteristics. Years ago, a floor wax company was fined by the Federal Trade Commission for using a sheet of glass over a floor in a TV commercial and claiming it was a waxed floor. The agency that made the ad insisted that it needed to make the floor look good under television photography. The set was designed to show the potential customer how she would feel with a terrifically shined floor.

In the News Media

The question of truth becomes paramount in the news media. Journalists are expected to present an objective form of truth. However, news gatherers do not have the means to discover truth that scientists, academics, or legal officials do. Scientists publish their findings in journals that are read by other experts, who then respond with their own data until the truth of the matter is determined. The same is true for academics looking for such things as historical truths. The process can take years, and no journalist has that kind of time. Legal officials such as judges and prosecutors have the power to subpoena sworn testimony and evidence to determine truth, but journalists have no such power. Generally, journalists have to rely on their sources, many of

Journalists are expected to present an objective form of truth. But journalists have to rely on their sources, many of whom have an agenda of their own.

whom have an agenda of their own. A journalist is expected to try as best as possible to uncover such agendas, but deadlines and limited finances are powerful restrictions.

The question of truth is also the basis of criticisms against staging the news. Journalists are expected to report on news, not set it up or make it happen. In Salt Lake City, a TV reporter was accused of staging news when he asked a group of high school students to come to the school parking lot and chew tobacco for the camera.[27] Even though he was asking them to do something that they did every day by themselves, he was also formally charged with contributing to the delinquency of a minor. An NBC reporter in Chicago was soundly criticized for talking a police officer into demonstrating how a criminal could get roughed up while being arrested and showing that demonstration on the evening news as an example of police brutality. The reporter insisted that he had evidence of real brutality and was just trying to illustrate it. Critics insisted it was an unethical inaccuracy.[28]

The Food Lion supermarket chain sued ABC News because of an undercover report about spoiled food.

A practice whereby reporters pretend to be what they are not (as the 19th-century reporter Nellie Bly sometimes did—see Chapter 4) is considered a legitimate part of investigative journalism by some and an ethical fault by others. In any event, it can be tempting, because it usually makes it easier for journalists to find the information they are looking for. But in 1997, a jury in North Carolina levied $5.5 million in punitive damages against ABC regarding a 1992 *Primetime Live* broadcast that accused the Food Lion supermarket chain of selling spoiled food. Food Lion did not challenge the truth of the accusation, only ABC's deceptive tactics in investigating the story: Undercover reporters infiltrated a Food Lion store by using faked résumés to gain employment and, once inside, used hidden cameras to catch Food Lion's unhealthful food-handling practices on film. Jury members later said that, with 70 current and former employees willing to speak out against

Why is truth telling complicated?

the store in recorded interviews, the subterfuge wasn't necessary. Eventually the award was reduced to $2 in token damages on appeal, but the jury's finding is still considered an important statement about the ethics of deceptive news gathering.[29]

Controversies *in Media Ethics*

Many ethical considerations within media have the potential to be controversial because there is often a conflict between ethics in theory and what media practitioners face in the real world. Media professionals often have to grapple with the difference between what philosophers say is right and what their jobs require. This section will look at three common controversial topics in the area of media ethics: stereotyping, conflicts of interest, and accountability.

STEREOTYPING

Stereotyping (which we touched on in Chapters 6 and 9, on movies and television) is the practice of representing a member of a group by using oversimplified characteristics. According to critics, stereotypes on television, in the movies, and so on show that the media are prejudiced and that they encourage prejudice in others (see Close-Up on Controversy). Puerto Rican community leaders were furious over a 1998 episode of the TV sitcom *Seinfeld* involving a series of mishaps at a Puerto Rican Day parade, ending with a car being thrown down a set of stairs. In the episode, the character Kramer remarks, "It's like this every day in Puerto Rico." Puerto Ricans said the remark was a slur. Jerry Seinfeld and the writers of the show apologized, saying they meant no offense.[30]

Similarly, Catholics were angered by an episode of the Fox network's *Ally McBeal* that included jokes about nuns having sex. One Catholic activist said, "Don't tie [such titillating nonsense] to a world religion, and certainly leave Catholics out of it, 'cause we're really sick and tired of it."[31] Fox also apologized, saying the network meant no offense and that the show was an equal-opportunity offender that made fun of all types of people, not just Catholics.

Many network executives grumble about "political correctness" in situations like these. They compare the pressure groups demanding changes today to the blacklisting groups of the 1950s. Giving in to the pressure groups of the McCarthy era, they note, was one of the least ethical actions that media had ever undertaken.

stereotyping
Representing a member of a group by using oversimplified characteristics.

CONSIDER THIS
Has the stereotyping of women in the media become less offensive in recent years? Support your point of view with examples.

CONFLICTS OF INTEREST

A **conflict of interest** occurs when some outside activity of a media professional—be it a business, social, or personal activity—influences the reality that is presented to the public. Critics objected, for example, when Larry King, in his *USA Today* column, called the 1997 Broadway play *Jekyll & Hyde* the best musical he had ever seen. The critics didn't mind his plugging the show, but he failed to mention that his nephew was the producer.[32] Worries about conflict of interest led the American Medical Association (AMA) to limit advertising by doctors promoting their practices. The AMA believes that such advertising makes the doctor a salesperson anxious to persuade rather than a neutral party eager to inform.[33]

Monetary conflicts of interest are often the most controversial. Junkets and freebies, for example, put a reporter's objectivity in question. Another blatant conflict of interest involves broadcast analysts who buy a stock, talk about it on the air as a good investment, and then sell it as soon as the price goes up. Critics claim that this practice has become so common that it is known on Wall Street as "pump and dump." Because of that, networks such as CNBC have developed rules requiring commentators to disclose their trading in any stock they discuss. For many critics, this is not enough, because the commentators' statements that they own the stock are just seen by audience members as one more reason to buy it.

Paying news sources to speak to reporters, the essential element of **checkbook journalism,** is viewed by many as unethical because it creates a conflict of interest. The credibility of the news is always suspect when the source has a financial interest in its publication. The potential for sleaze associated with checkbook journalism became evident in a 1997 case in which

conflict of interest
Clash that occurs when an outside activity influences what a media professional does.

checkbook journalism
Paying news sources for their stories.

The Guerrilla Girls' Guide to Female Stereotypes

The Guerrilla Girls are a group of anonymous women who appear in public wearing gorilla masks. They visit schools all over the country in jungle drag "to provoke their legions of fans to fight discrimination wherever it lurks."

The Guerrilla Girls say the goal of their book is to lessen the power of female stereotypes over women's lives.

The Guerrilla Girls believe that whatever life a woman leads, from biker chick to society girl, there's a stereotype she'll have to live up, or down, to. Their goal is to lessen the power of female stereotypes over women's lives. They believe that the media have mind-boggling power when it comes to generating new stereotypes and keeping alive the old standards. They want media practitioners and audiences to be aware of the ethical implications of that power.

Here are some sample stereotypes from the Guerrilla Girls' guide:

• Girl Next Door: She is the familiar, the unexotic, the undifferent, a mirror of conventional family values. She's almost always white. The Girl Next Door is pure, loyal, and would never think to question authority.

• Sitcom Mom: She's patient, always upbeat, and completely understanding. Her kids respect her. She never raises her voice. She exists only to pack a nutritious lunch and maybe crack a few jokes.

• Bimbo/Dumb Blonde: A beautiful, curvaceous blonde with tight clothes, high heels, and a not-so-high IQ. She is easily dominated and usually humiliated.

• Gold Digger: A woman whose ambition is to find a rich husband. In movies, the Gold Digger became a sexy, young, blonde showgirl on the make for a rich, usually older, man.

• Jewish American Princess/JAP: Her parents have treated her like royalty since the day she was born, and she expects you to do the same. Alternate versions include the BAP (Black American Princess), CAP (Chinese American Princess), and IAP (Italian American Princess).

• Lolita: A seductive adolescent girl, ready to have unlimited sex with older men. From Vladimir Nabokov's novel of the same name, about a college professor obsessed with a 12-year-old girl.

• Aunt Jemima: To white Americans she's a kindly, jovial black woman who wants nothing but to serve and dote on them. To African Americans, she's an uneducated, servile black woman who doesn't realize slavery is over. She's an offensive racial stereotype fabricated by white businessmen to sell their product.

• Femme Fatale/Vamp: An evil, conniving woman hell-bent on seducing men and leading them to ruin and damnation. Men find her irresistible and are reduced to helpless prey in her cunning clutches. If there were really as many of these evil women out there as the media suggest, it's a wonder there are any guys left standing.

• Diva/Prima Donna: A female singer who's larger than life and demands special treatment. She has extraordinary talent, legions of fans, and sycophant staffers who cater to her every need—the more ridiculous the better.

• Feminazi: A strident, controlling bitch who—Oh, horrible crime!—insists on equal rights for women. The term was coined by radio talk-show host Rush Limbaugh to describe women who support abortion rights. It was taken up by ultra-right-wing conservatives everywhere to refer to feminists in general. The Guerrilla Girls are still waiting for the day when everyone will think of the Feminist as a positive stereotype.

Source: The Guerrilla Girls, *Bitches, Bimbos and Ball Breakers: The Guerrilla Girls' Illustrated Guide to Female Stereotypes* (New York: Penguin, 2003).

the tabloid *Globe* paid former flight attendant Suzen Johnson for a story about her romance with Frank Gifford, the husband of TV's morning talk-show host Kathie Lee Gifford. When Johnson approached the *Globe,* the editors were interested in the basic idea of her story, but they did not like that the "romance" was just a flirtation. They then paid Johnson to fly to New York City and seduce Gifford in a hotel room set up with a hidden camera. The *Globe*'s reporting on this "news event" was picked up by many mainstream news organizations—sometimes as a story about the unsavory techniques of the tabloid press.

For many critics, corporate corruption of the news is a type of conflict of interest. Some protest, for example, when *Time* magazine reports on AOL, its corporate owner, or when ABC, which is owned by Disney, reports as news a gala celebration for a movie made by Disney.[34] Many critics howled when ABC also killed a *20/20* feature that focused on security lapses in the hiring of sex offenders at theme parks, including Walt Disney World. ABC officials responded that their decision not to run the story had nothing to do with ABC's Disney affiliation.

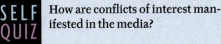

SELF QUIZ — How are conflicts of interest manifested in the media?

ANONYMITY AND WHO DESERVES IT

Chapter 14 discussed shield laws, which are designed to protect the confidentiality and anonymity of sources. But an ethical question lies at the base of this legal issue: When should anonymity be used? It's fairly clear that anonymity is justified when a whistle-blower brings in a story about government or corporate corruption, and the story is well documented and the whistle-blower would face dire consequences if his or her name were revealed. Watergate and other great journalistic stories of their day would never have come to light without anonymous sources. But other times, sources merely have a personal or professional grudge against a former boss, and they want anonymity so they can cause trouble without having to back up their claims. Because of this, the use of anonymous sources is always controversial. The *New York Times* revised its rules about confidential sources in 2006 and now stresses three principles. First, granting a source anonymity should be the "exception" rather than "routine." Second, before a confidential source makes it into the paper, at least one editor has to know the source's name. And third, readers are to be told why the *Times* believes a source is entitled to anonymity. When anonymous sources are used there now, wording such as this is used: "three Democratic aides, speaking on condition of anonymity to avoid reprisals from their bosses" or "two Pentagon officials who have worked on the project and were granted anonymity so they would describe the changes before an official announcement expected later this week."[35]

ACCOUNTABILITY

Who controls media practitioners, and who has the power to punish them for ethical lapses? In other words, to whom are they accountable? No answer to this question about **accountability**—the obligation to take responsibility, or account for, the consequences of one's actions—satisfies all parties involved. Most practitioners would say they are accountable to their own conscience, but that hardly satisfies most social critics. Practitioners are also directly accountable to corporate owners, editors, internal censors, news councils, competitors, and citizens' groups.

Most media practitioners are directly accountable to their employers and supervisors, and some are fired for ethical breaches. But critics feel that

accountability
The obligation to take responsibility, or account for, the consequences of one's actions. In media ethics, accountability involves the questions of who controls media practitioners and who has the power to punish them for ethical lapses.

corporate owners have their own ethical problems, most of which are caused by a single-minded devotion to making a profit. Owners of news organizations, however, point out that accountability to them works because integrity pays off. As one expert has pointed out: "In the end, what journalism companies are selling is their authority as a public asset. And that depends, especially with an ever more skeptical public, on proving you're in it for more than a buck."[36] In the same way, producers of entertainment media insist that the public will keep them honest because they will eventually stop supporting those who engage in unethical practices.

Media practitioners maintain that supervisors in all media companies monitor the ethical standards of those who work under them. In the words of one former editor: "Reporters are supposed to be aggressive and push hard for their stories. It is up to the editors to be the gatekeepers, and to see that what gets in the paper is right."[37] Critics respond that, looking over the ethical scandals of media history, it is obvious that many of them happened because of lax supervision. Janet Cooke's "Jimmy's World," the Pulitzer Prize–winning story of the nonexistent eight-year-old heroin addict, is an example; after the scandal broke, Cooke's editors said they would supervise reporters more diligently in the future. In the same way, after the Jayson Blair scandal broke at the *New York Times* in 2003, two top editors were forced to resign.

"In the end, what journalism companies are selling is their authority as a public asset. And that depends, especially with an ever more skeptical public, on proving you're in it for more than a buck."

standards and practices departments
Departments at television networks that oversee the ethics of their programming.

In the 1960s and 1970s, the television networks maintained large and powerful **standards and practices departments** to oversee the ethics of their programming. Creative personnel complained about the standards and practices "censors," saying that the "network suits" were in charge of deciding what was acceptable in terms of costumes, stories, and especially language. As networks became smaller and leaner in the 1980s and 1990s, most of those departments were cut down in size, and the result was an increase in the use of dialogue, plots, and visuals that had previously been unacceptable. It was not uncommon to hear street language and see partial nudity on late-night programs such as Howard Stern's TV program and even prime-time programs such as *NYPD Blue*. By 2007, however, because of heavy FCC fines and pressure from sponsors, networks and stations were controlling programming more carefully.

ombudsperson
Staff member whose job it is to oversee media employees' ethical behavior.

Some newspapers appoint a staff member known as an **ombudsperson** to oversee other employees' ethical behavior. The ombudsperson usually writes a regular column, which includes answers to reader complaints. He or she also investigates alleged ethical breaches and works with the paper's management to try to resolve them. The *Louisville Courier-Journal and Times* is credited with appointing the first U.S. newspaper ombudsperson in 1967. Some papers appoint a temporary ombudsperson if a particular ethical problem has arisen. They might assign a second reporter or outside expert to check the facts on a story, and publish a follow-up article if inaccuracy or unfairness is found. The *New York Times* hired a regular ombudsperson in 2003, following the Jayson Blair scandal.

Many critics have insisted that **news councils** should be established to ensure press accountability. News councils are independent agencies whose mission is to objectively monitor media performance. When they determine that an ethical breach has been committed, they issue reports and rely on the media to publicize them. News councils are fairly common in Europe. The British Press Council, for example, has been in operation since 1963. In the United States, a National News Council, supported by several foundations, was established in 1973 but had folded by 1984 because of lack of media support. News councils have never caught on nationally in the United States because the mainstream press generally refuses to support them. Media organizations decline to fund them, to cooperate with their investigations, or to give them the publicity they need to disseminate their findings. These organizations do not like the idea of an independent watchdog group that might grow in power to the point that it would interfere with First Amendment rights. Many of those in control of today's mainstream media remember the blacklisters of the 1950s, who also considered themselves independent watchdog groups. In spite of the resistance to the National News Council, however, there are several local news councils that have operated successfully for many years. The best known are the Minnesota News Council and the Washington News Council, which serves the state of Washington.

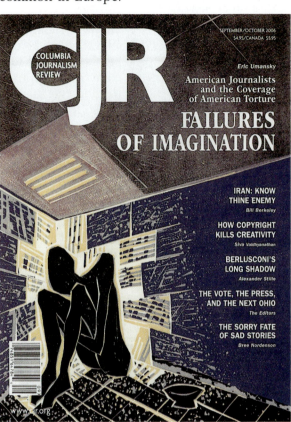

Media practitioners are also accountable to their profession. A few professional organizations, such as the Public Relations Society of America, have the power to revoke membership for ethical breaches. The majority of professional accountability, however, comes in the form of criticism in professional journals such as the *Columbia Journalism Review* and the *American Journalism Review*. To a certain extent, media producers are also accountable to critics who publish and broadcast in a variety of other media outlets. These critics write books and articles that explain ethical breaches that others might not have noticed.

The majority of professional accountability comes in the form of criticism in professional journals such as the *Columbia Journalism Review*.

Other criticism comes from competitors. When the former airline attendant was paid by the *Globe* to entrap Frank Gifford in a compromising position, mainstream media roundly condemned the practice. Even other members of the tabloid press were put off. The editor of the *National Enquirer* sniffed: "We've chased down the cheating spouse, we've tried to get the telling pictures, we've reported the news. But we've never created the lover. What's next? Is someone going to buy a case of vodka and deliver it to a celebrity who is a recovering alcoholic and then report to readers that the star went on a binge?"[38]

Media people are also accountable to **citizens' groups,** associations made up of members of the public to exert influence, sometimes by organizing boycotts of media outlets or their advertisers. Other times these groups rely on the power of negative publicity, including occasional full-page newspaper ads explaining why they are against a certain program or company. Coming together into groups gives individuals considerable power.

Nosotros, a group of Hispanic Americans, was able to have the "Frito Bandito," a cartoon character based on a stereotyped image of a Mexican bandit, banned from television commercials. A group of older people calling themselves the Gray Panthers successfully protested the depiction of the elderly on television, and gays have influenced how they are depicted through the Human Rights Campaign Fund and the Gay and Lesbian Alliance Against Defamation. Citizens' groups have even successfully challenged broadcast station licenses when they were up for renewal and used public relations tactics to lobby Congress.[39] Action for Smoking and Health, for example, led the drive against cigarette advertising on television, and Action for Children's Television was instrumental in convincing Congress of the need to require more educational programming. Again, many media practitioners refer to citizens' groups as "pressure groups," remembering that the blacklisters were also public-minded citizens who joined forces to exert pressure on the media.

SELF QUIZ

What is accountability, and how does it work in the media?

Summing Up

Ethics is the study of guidelines that help people determine right from wrong. Guidelines about media ethics derive from a variety of sources. One source is the field, where media practitioners work under deadlines, budgets, and the customs of their crafts.

The history of media is replete with scandals, controversies, and various interpretations of the concept of ethics. During the penny press and the yellow journalism eras, tactics that seemed unethical and purely commercial to some were defended as socially important by others. The electronic era ushered in new ethical concerns about the increased power of these new media. Today, the digital era and the capabilities of presenting unlimited information have created even more ethical concerns.

The second source of ethical guidelines is the realm of the philosopher, the thinker who has time to deliberate and make careful distinctions about ethical orientations, philosophies, and conflicting loyalties. At the most basic level, there are two primary ethical orientations: the absolutist orientation (which holds that there is either a right or a wrong response for every ethical decision) and the situation ethics orientation (which holds that ethical choices can be made without a rigid adherence to a predetermined value system).

The ideas of several philosophers form the backbone of discussions about contemporary media ethics. Under the realm of absolutist ethics, we have Immanuel Kant, who gave us the idea of the categorical imperative, which today advises media practitioners to look for principles that will hold true in all situations. Modern American philosopher John Rawls's veil of ignorance advances the absolutist idea that ethical behavior is possible only if everyone is treated equally, without regard for social stature or economic class.

Within the area of situational ethics we have the ideas of Aristotle, John Stuart Mill, and Niccolò Machiavelli. Aristotle's concept of the golden mean calls for finding a midpoint between extremes. Mill's utilitarian principle calls for actions that result in the greatest good for the most people. Machiavelli's idea that the end justifies the means is today interpreted by some to mean that if a cause is ethical, then the means used to accomplish that end will also be ethical. However, Machiavellian principles have been the rationalization for actions that many consider unethical.

These basic philosophical perspectives are complicated by the idea of conflicting loyalties, which include loyalties to personal conscience, to one's employers, to one's profession or art, and to society in general. Even an idea as basic as truth telling is complicated by philosophical questions about the nature of truth.

The third source of ethical guidelines is the controversies that erupt around them. There are a number of areas in which the tensions between critics and media professionals seem to be continual. One is the stereotyping of women and minorities. Conflicts of interest occur when a media professional's outside activities influence the reality that is presented to the public. Anonymity of sources becomes controversial when sources are not deserving of that anonymity. The question of accountability asks who controls media practitioners and who has the power to punish them for ethical lapses.

absolutist ethics *511*

accountability *521*

blacklisting *504*

categorical
  imperative *511*

checkbook
  journalism *519*

citizens' groups *523*

conflict of interest *519*

enlightened
  self-interest *514*

ethical codes *503*

ethics *498*

golden mean *513*

hoaxes *500*

Machiavellian ethics *514*

media circus *515*

objectivity *500*

ombudsperson *522*

pool cameras *515*

prescriptive codes *511*

proscriptive codes *511*

relativistic ethics *513*

situation ethics *513*

standards and practices
  departments *522*

stereotyping *519*

two-source rule *511*

utilitarian principle *514*

veil of ignorance *512*

Key Terms

These terms are defined and indexed in the Glossary of key terms at the back of the book.

HISTORY

Web Excursion

1. Media history includes many interesting scandals, and similar ones reappear from time to time. Search the Web for terms associated with the type of ethical lapses covered in the history portion of this chapter—terms such as "hoaxes," "conflict of interest," "sensationalism," and "blacklisting." Find the most current example of one of them, and compare it with its historical precedents.

INDUSTRY

Web Excursion

2. How do your own ethical standards compare with those of other people? Search the Web for ethical standards polls, or go directly to www.pbs.org/mediamatters* and move to the "Tough Calls" Ethical News Judgment Poll. See if your ethical standards are the same as those who have taken this online poll. The public, for example, prefers to have a reporter behave ethically even if it means missing a story about an illegal business practice. Write a brief reaction to the survey.

CONTROVERSIES

Web Excursion

3. How much does political point of view affect one's perceptions of ethical problems? Search the Web for liberal and conservative viewpoints about bias. You might want to go directly to AIM at www.aim.org* and FAIR at www.fair.org.* Find similar complaints from two different viewpoints and compare them.

Electronic Excursions

4. View track 18, *Pentagon Planning to Plant Misinformation in Foreign News Sources* (from NBC News Archive). This NBC news clip looks at the effects of the government planting false news stories abroad. Is it ever justifiable to fabricate news stories? Even in the case of national security? As a journalist, how would you handle suspect news leaks?

ONLINE LEARNING CENTER WWW.MHHE.COM/RODMAN2

You may access these and additional Web excursions at the Online Learning Center for the book (www.mhhe.com/rodman2). Visit the student portion of this Web site to also access the *Interactive Timeline of Mass Media Milestones,* chapter highlights, self quizzes, and recommended readings, movies, and documentaries for this chapter.

*Some Web site addresses may change. When they do, please search for the Web site by name or topic on your favorite search engine.

Chapter 1: Introduction

1 Andrea Thomas, a senior at Miami University, quoted in Stefanie Olsen, "The 'Millennials' Usher in a New Era," *CNET News*, online, November 18, 2005.

2 Meg Kissing, "The Millennials," *Milwaukee Journal Sentinel* online, June 5, 2005.

3 Neil Howe and William Strauss, *Millennials Rising: The Next Great Generation* (New York: Vintage, 2000). See also www.millennialsrising.com.

4 Seymour Papert of MIT's Media Lab, cited in Olsen, "The 'Millennials' Usher in a New Era."

5 Reports from the Centers for Disease Control and Prevention, cited in Kissing, "The Millennials."

6 For example, Claude Shannon, a mathematician, is credited with first providing the stimulus to social scientists to formulate their thinking about communication in model form. See Denis McQuail and Sven Windahl, *Communication Models for the Study of Mass Communication*, 2nd ed. (New York: Longman, 1993), pp. 6–7.

7 For more on this and other models of communication, see Ronald Adler and George Rodman, *Understanding Human Communication*, 9th ed. (New York: Oxford University Press, 2006), Chapter 1.

8 The term was coined in Herbert Schiller, *Mass Communication and the American Empire* (New York: Kelley, 1969).

9 The Pew Research Center for People and the Press Global Attitudes Survey, released in December 2002, cited in Michael E. Ross, "Anti-Americanism versus Hollywood," msnbc.com, March 12, 2003.

10 Paul Dergarabedian, president of Exhibitor Relations Co., a company that monitors film industry trends, quoted in Ross, "Anti-Americanism versus Hollywood."

11 Margaret DeFleur and Melvyn DeFleur, *Learning to Hate America* (Spokane, WA: Marquette Books, 2003).

12 "Antitrust Trial Set in Clear Channel Case," Associated Press online, April 8, 2004.

13 See the Freedom House Survey of Press Freedom, "Freedom of the Press 2006," at www.freedomhouse.org/research/pressurvey.htm.

14 Alexander Hamilton, "The Right to Criticize Public Men," in Calder M. Pickett, ed., *Voices of the Past: Key Documents in the History of American Journalism* (Columbus, OH: Grid, 1977), p. 71.

15 See for example, "Study Faults Media Coverage of WMD," *Editor & Publisher* online, March 9, 2004.

16 Greg Mitchell, "Where Was the Press When the First Iraq Prison Allegations Arose?" *Editor & Publisher*, May 13, 2004.

Chapter 2: Media Impact

1 Senator Joseph I. Lieberman, Democrat of Connecticut, quoted in John Leland, "Bigger, Bolder, Faster, Weirder," *New York Times* online, October 27, 2002.

2 "Video Game Blamed for Murder," *ABC News* online, September 6, 2003.

3 Raoul V. Mowatt, "New 'Grand Theft Auto': Looking for Trouble," *Chicago Tribune*, October 29, 2002.

4 John Roach, "Video Gamers Boost Visual Skills, Study Finds," *National Geographic News* online, May 28, 2003.

5 James Paul Gee, an education professor and author of *What Video Games Have to Teach Us about Learning and Literacy*, quoted in Mark Clayton, "Off to College to Major In ... Video Games?" *Christian Science Monitor* online, August 29, 2003.

6 Victoria Taplin of Chevy Chase, Maryland, quoted in Katie Hafner, "On Video Games, the Jury Is Out and Confused," *New York Times* online, June 5, 2003.

7 See, for example, Harold D. Lasswell, *Propaganda Technique in the World War* (New York: Peter Smith, 1927).

8 See, for example, Shearon Lowery and Melvin DeFleur, *Milestones in Mass Communication Research: Media Effects*, 3rd ed. (Boston: Allyn & Bacon, 1995).

9 Shearon Lowery and Melvin L. DeFleur, *Milestones in Mass Communication Research: Media Effects* (New York: Longman, 1983), p. 38.

10 Ibid., p. 40.

11 The team was headed by Hadley Cantril, head of the Office of Radio Research at Princeton, and funded by the Rockefeller Foundation.

12 The book in which this study was reported is Paul F. Lazarsfeld, Bernard Berelson, and Hazel Gaudet, *The People's Choice: How the Voter Makes Up His Mind in a Presidential Election* (New York: Columbia University Press, 1948).

13 Ibid., p. 151.

14 The results of these experiments were brought together in Carl I. Hovland, Arthur A. Lumsdaine, and Fred D. Sheffield, *Experiments on Mass Communication* (Princeton, NJ: Princeton University Press, 1949).

15 The findings of this study were published in Wilbur Schramm, Jack Lyle, and Edwin Parker, *Television in the Lives of Our Children* (Palo Alto, CA: Stanford University Press, 1961).

16 Ibid., p. 30.

17 Ibid., p. 13.

18 See, for example, W. Terrence Gordon, *Marshall McLuhan: Escape into Understanding* (New York: Basic Books, 1997).

19 Stanley J. Baran and Dennis K. Davis, *Mass Communication Theory: Foundations, Ferment and Future* (Belmont, CA: Wadsworth, 1995), p. 326.

20 See, for example, Paul Levinson, *Digital McLuhan: A Guide to the Information Millennium* (New York: Routledge, 1999).

21 Lowery and DeFleur, *Milestones*, p. 298.

22 Robert K. Baker and Sandra J. Ball, eds., *Violence and the Media* (Washington, DC: U.S. Government Printing Office, 1969).

23 L. Rowell Huesmann of the University of Michigan at Ann Arbor, quoted in Lawrie Mifflin, "Many Researchers Say Link Is Already Clear on Media and Youth Violence," *New York Times* online, May 9, 1999.

24 Joseph Turow, *Breaking Up America: Advertisers and the New Media World* (Chicago: University of Chicago Press, 1997).

25 See, for example, Sam Roberts, "Alone in the Wasteland," *New York Times*, December 24, 1995, Sec. 4, p. 3.

26 Joshua Meyrowitz, *No Sense of Place: The Impact of Electronic Media on Social Behavior* (New York: Oxford University Press, 1985).

27 See, for example, Edward Rothstein, "How Childhood Has Changed! (Adults, Too)," *New York Times,* February 14, 1998, p. B7.

28 See, for example, Maureen Dowd, "Leave It to Hollywood," *New York Times,* August 16, 1997, p. 21.

29 The name *bullet theory,* also referred to as *hypodermic needle theory,* was not used by the early researchers who performed these studies, but by later theorists. See Melvin L. DeFleur and Sandra Ball-Rokeach, *Theories of Mass Communication,* 5th ed. (New York: Longman, 1989), pp. 145–66.

30 See, for example, Peter M. Sandman, David M. Rubin, and David B. Sachsman, *Media: An Introductory Analysis of American Mass Communications,* 3rd ed. (Englewood Cliffs, NJ: Prentice Hall, 1982), pp. 4–5.

31 Werner J. Severin and James W. Tankard, Jr., *Communication Theories: Origins, Methods, and Uses in the Mass Media,* 4th ed. (New York: Longman, 1997), p. 322.

32 These and other social learning experiments are reported in Bandura's seminal book, *Social Learning Theory* (Englewood Cliffs, NJ: Prentice Hall, 1977).

33 See, for example, Jennifer Herrett-Skjellum and Mike Allen, "Television Programming and Sex Stereotyping: A Meta-Analysis," *Communication Yearbook* 19 (1996), pp. 157–85. This meta-analysis (the analysis of previously published findings) indicates (1) that television content contains numerous sexual stereotypes, and (2) exposure to televised material increases the acceptance of sexual stereotypes.

34 A recent study in the area of aggressive stimulation/catalytic theory is Kirstie M. Farrar, Marina Kremar, and Kristine L. Nowak, "Contextual Features of Violent Video Games, Mental Models, and Aggression," *Journal of Communication* 56, no. 2 (2006), pp. 387–405.

35 DeFleur and Ball-Rokeach, *Theories of Mass Communication,* pp. 172–86.

36 Diffusion of innovations theory is attributed primarily to Everett Rogers, *Diffusion of Innovations,* 3rd ed. (New York: Free Press, 1983).

37 See, for example, Leo Jeffres, and David Atkin, "Predicting Use of Technologies for Communication and Consumer Needs," *Journal of Broadcasting and Electronic Media* 40, no. 3 (Summer 1996), pp. 318–30. See also Tyrone L. Adams, "Follow the Yellow Brick Road: Using Diffusion of Innovations Theory to Enrich Virtual Organizations in Cyberspace," *Southern Communication Journal* 62, no. 2 (Winter 1997), pp. 133–48.

38 George Gerbner, L. Gross, M. Morgan, and N. Signorielli, "Living with Television: The Cultivation Perspective," in J. Bryant and D. Zillmann, eds., *Media Effects: Advances in Theory and Research* (Hillsdale, NJ: Erlbaum, 1994), pp. 17–41. See also Severin and Tankard, *Communication Theories,* pp. 299–303.

39 Dmitri Williams, "Virtual Cultivation: Online Worlds, Offline Perceptions," *Journal of Communication* 56, no. 1 (March 2006), p. 69. This study supports the idea that video games have the same effects as TV viewing in terms of perceptions of offline danger.

40 Donald Shaw and Maxwell McCombs, *The Emergence of American Political Issues: The Agenda-Setting Function of the Press* (St. Paul, MN: West, 1977), p. 7.

41 The way these theories converge can be seen in studies such as Hans-Bernd Brosius and Gabriel Weimann, "Who Sets the Agenda? Agenda-Setting as a Two-Step Flow," *Communication Research* 23, no. 5 (October 1996), pp. 561–80.

42 See, for example, James W. Dearing and Everett M. Rogers, *Agenda-Setting* (Thousand Oaks, CA: Sage, 1996), especially Chapter 5.

43 Baran and Davis, *Mass Communication Theory,* provides a concise, readable overview of uses and gratifications theory. See Chapter 10, "Using Media: Theories of the Active Audience," pp. 210–75.

44 Caren Deming and Mercilee Jenkins, "Bar Talk: Gender Discourse in *Cheers,*" in Leah R. Vande Berg and Lawrence A. Wenner, eds., *Television Criticism: Approaches and Applications* (New York: Longman, 1991), pp. 47–57. A similar type of study can be found in Jocelyn Steinke, "Connecting Theory and Practice: Using Women Scientist Role Models in Television Programming," *Journal of Broadcasting and Electronic Media* 42, no. 1 (Winter 1998), pp. 142–51.

45 See, for example, Justine Cassell and Henry Jenkins, eds., *From Barbie to Mortal Kombat: Gender and Computer Games* (Boston: MIT Press, 1999).

46 Simon Jones and Thomas Shumacher, "Muzak: On Functional Music and Power," *Critical Studies in Mass Communication* 9 (June 1992), pp. 156–69.

47 Some researchers call this a mass society point of view. See, for example, Baran and Davis, *Mass Communication Theory,* pp. 43–44.

48 Lowery and DeFleur, *Milestones,* p. 321.

49 See, for example, David Gauntlett, "Ten Things Wrong with the 'Effects Model'" in Roger Dickinson, Ramaswean Harindranath, and Olga Lineè, eds., *Approaches to Audiences: A Reader* (London: Arnold, 1998). Available online at www.leeds.ac.uk/ics/arts-dg2.htm.

50 Lowery and DeFleur, *Milestones,* p. 339.

51 Harold Schechter, "A Movie Made Me Do It," *New York Times,* December 3, 1995, Sec. 4, p. 15.

52 *People* online, August 5, 1998.

53 According to experts from the FBI's behavioral science unit; see Schechter, "A Movie Made Me Do It."

54 Quoted in Richard Corliss, "Bang, You're Dead: Revenge Fantasies Are Proliferating in Movies and on TV. But Should They Be Blamed for Littleton?" *Time* online, May 3, 1999.

Chapter 3: Books

1 Leigh Teabing, in Dan Brown, *The Da Vinci Code* (New York: Doubleday, 2003), p. 248.

2 Jeannie Kever, "Cracking the Da Vinci Code: Author Dan Brown Courted Controversy, Then Capitalized on It," *Houston Chronicle* online, April 16, 2005.

3 Paul Gessell, "Canadian Readers Believe Da Vinci Code," *Ottawa Citizen* online, June 24, 2005. The study was conducted by a professional research firm for the National Geographic Channel.

4 Carl E. Olson and Sandra Miesel, "A Da Vinci De-Coder," *The Catholic Answer,* May/June 2004. Available online at http://carl-olson.com/articles/tca_tdvc_apr04.html.

5 Charles A. Madison, *Book Publishing in America* (New York: McGraw-Hill, 1966), p. 3.

6 Cover line from Jack Woodford's *Three Gorgeous Hussies,* a paperback published by Avon, in Kenneth C. Davis, *Two-Bit Culture: The Paperbacking of America* (Boston: Houghton Mifflin, 1984), p. 223.

7 See, for example, Geoffrey O'Brien, *Hardboiled America: Lurid Paperbacks and the Masters of Noir,* expanded edition (New York: Da Capo Press, 1997).

8 Davis, *Two-Bit Culture,* p. 363.

9 Daniel Johnson, "Springtime for Bertelsmann," *The New Yorker,* April 27, 1998, p. 104.

10 Murdoch earlier canceled the BBC news channel on his satellite service in China because the Chinese government objected to the BBC's reports.

11 "A High-Tech Rescue for Out-of-Print Books," *New York Times,* June 4, 1998, p. G3.

12 See, for example, Thomas L. Friedman, "In Pakistan, It's Jihad 101," *New York Times,* November 13, 2001, p. A17.

13 Frank Rich, "Star of the Month Club," *New York Times,* March 23, 1997, Sec. 4, p. 15.

14 From the back cover of Tony Kornheiser, *Bald as I Wanna Be* (New York: Villard, 1997).

15 Victor Navasky, "Buying Books: Theory vs. Practice," *New York Times,* June 20, 1996, p. A21. Navasky is the publisher of *The Nation.* In this piece, he sings the praises of the superstore.

16 See Doreen Carvajal, "Falling Sales Hit Publishers for 2nd Year," *New York Times,* July 7, 1997; Porter Bibb, "In Publishing, Bigger Is Better," *New York Times,* March 31, 1998.

17 Mary B. W. Tabor, "In Bookstore Chains, Display Space Is for Sale," *New York Times,* January 15, 1996, p. A1.

18 Doreen Carvajal, "You Can't Read Books Fast Enough," *New York Times,* August 24, 1997.

19 In fact, some literary historians now claim that Joyce developed his complex prose style as a deliberate strategy to confuse potential censors. See, for example, Paul Vanderham, *James Joyce and Censorship: The Trials of Ulysses* (New York: NYU Press, 1998).

20 Fox claimed that it had trademarked that phrase. See "Windfall Publicity for Al Franken's Book," editorial, *New York Times* online, August 13, 2003.

21 Irving Kristol, "Pornography, Obscenity, and the Case for Censorship," in George Rodman, ed., *Mass Media Issues,* 4th ed. (Dubuque, IA: Kendall/Hunt, 1993), p. 443.

22 Kristol, "Pornography, Obscenity," p. 448.

23 Dinitia Smith and Motoko Rich, "A Second Ripple in Plagiarism Scandal," *New York Times* online, May 2, 2006.

24 Quoted in Edward Wyatt, "Author Is Kicked Out of Oprah Winfrey's Book Club," *New York Times* online, January 27, 2006.

25 Ibid.

Chapter 4: Newspapers

1 David Carr, "In Print, Staring Down a Daily Worry," *New York Times* online, May 22, 2006.

2 Michael Kinsley, "The Future of Newspapers," *Slate* online, January 7, 2006.

3 Katharine Q. Seelye, "At Newspapers, Some Clipping," *New York Times* online, October 10, 2005.

4 Ridder is quoted in Seelye, "At Newspapers, Some Clipping."

5 Katharine Q. Seelye, "*Washington Post* Has an Exit Jam after Buyouts," *New York Times* online, June 5, 2006.

6 "Something to Discover: The American Newspaper at a Crossroads," editorial, *Columbia Journalism Review* online, November/December 2005.

7 Kinsley, "The Future of Newspapers."

8 Pew Internet and American Life Project, January 2004.

9 Some historians say that *Publick Occurrences* wasn't the first real newspaper because it lasted only one issue, and continuous publication is, by definition, part of being a newspaper. See, for example, Michael Emery and Edwin Emery, *The Press in America,* 6th ed. (Englewood Cliffs: Prentice Hall, 1988), p. 23. Most authorities, however, give Harris the benefit of the doubt, since he at least *intended* his paper to continue publishing.

10 Some historians reserve the term *partisan press* to identify only the postrevolution press, during the turbulent years when the Constitution was written, up to the Alien and Sedition Acts, which expired under Jefferson.

11 Frank Luther Mott, *American Journalism,* 3rd ed. (New York: Macmillan, 1962), p. 529. Hearst is said to have denied sending such a telegram.

12 John Tebbel, *The Compact History of the American Newspaper* (New York: Hawthorne Books, 1969), p. 204.

13 Along with encouraging investigative journalism, Pulitzer also contributed to the improvement of news reporting by endowing the School of Journalism at Columbia University and the Pulitzer Prizes that bear his name.

14 Walter Goodman, "Adventures of Nellie Bly, Investigative Reporter," *New York Times,* April 28, 1997, p. C14. This is a review of the PBS documentary "The American Experience: Around the World in 72 Days," broadcast April 28, 1997.

15 Jerry M. Rosenberg, *Inside The Wall Street Journal: The Power and the History of Dow Jones & Company and America's Most Influential Newspaper* (New York: Macmillan, 1982).

16 For the complete wording, see "Canons of Journalism," in Calder M. Pickett, *Voices of the Past: Key Documents in the History of American Journalism* (Columbus, OH: Grid, 1977), pp. 261–63.

17 Goldman Sachs data, cited in Seelye, "At Newspapers, Some Clipping." Gannett and E. W. Scripps were the most profitable, with profit margins of 30 percent each, and Dow Jones was the least, at 9 percent.

18 Seelye, "At Newspapers, Some Clipping"

19 The *Wall Street Journal* and the *New York Times* also send their national editions by satellite to local printing plants for local distribution. The *Christian Science Monitor* is still printed at its home plant and distributed mostly by mail.

20 The Unification Church also owns the *Washington Times* newspaper and *Insight* and *The World & I* magazines, as well as many other media ventures in other countries. Among its nonmedia holdings is the University of Bridgeport in Connecticut. The Rev. Sun Myung Moon is a political conservative.

21 Thomas C. Leonard, *News for All: America's Coming-of-Age with the Press* (New York: Oxford University Press, 1995). Cited in Michael Janeway, "Read All About It," *New York Times Book Review,* November 12, 1995, p. 58.

22 "Newspapers Skipping a Generation," Research Brief, Center for Media Research online newsletter, February 13, 2003.

23 After years of expressing concern about newspaper monopolies, the U.S. Congress passed the Newspaper Preservation Act in 1970. This law allowed local papers to set up joint operating agreements, business arrangements in which two competing papers could share printing facilities and business staffs without violating federal antitrust laws. The idea was to encourage competing papers to stay alive by allowing them to enjoy some of the same economies of scale that a single chain owner would have. Joint operating agreements now exist in a handful of cities, usually with two papers that are owned by different chains. For example, Detroit's two dailies, the *Detroit News* (owned by MediaNews Group) and the *Detroit Free Press* (owned by Gannett) operate under a joint operating agreement.

24 See, for example, "Newsroom Diversity," *Jet,* April 19, 1999, p. 38. Both ASNE and associations such as Journalists of Color, Inc., associate newsroom diversity with accuracy.

25 Mark Fitzgerald, "Diversity Analysis Says Only 13% of Daily Newsrooms Reflect Populations of Their Communities," *Editor & Publisher,* May 13, 2004.

26 Mark Fitzgerald, "Minority Journalist Representation Nudges Up Slightly," *Editor & Publisher,* April 20, 2004.

27 "Women Still Underrepresented in Newsroom," *Editor & Publisher,* April 27, 2004.

Chapter 5: Magazines

1   Quoted in Jason Cohen, "Christy Haubegger: A Fresh Face in Niche Publishing," *Texas Monthly,* September, 1997, p. 125.

2   Quoted in Cohen, "Christy Haubegger."

3   Quoted in Jeff Garigliano, "The Essence of a Good Launch Strategy," *Folio: The Magazine for Magazine Management,* October 1, 1996, p. 29.

4   Quoted in Christy Haubegger, "The Legacy of Generation Ñ," *Newsweek,* July 12, 1999, p. 61.

5   Quoted in Lorraina Calvacca, "Christy Haubegger," *Folio: the Magazine for Magazine Management,* April 15, 1999, p. 54.

6   Quoted in Cohen, "Christy Haubegger."

7   Ibid.

8   Theodore Peterson, *Magazines in the Twentieth Century* (Urbana: University of Illinois Press, 1964), p. 13.

9   The life history of *Life* shows how reluctant the industry is to let go of a solid brand name. *Life* was a weekly until 1972 and came back as a monthly from 1978 until 2000, with occasional special issues after that. In 2003, Time Inc. reintroduced *Life* as a weekly newspaper supplement. See www.life.com.

10 Charles P. Daly, Patrick Henry, and Ellen Ryder, *The Magazine Publishing Industry* (Boston: Allyn & Bacon, 1997), pp. 11, 22. This is a carefully considered estimate by these authors.

11 This definition is established by *Folio,* the trade magazine for the magazine industry.

12 *Bacon's Magazine Directory* (Chicago: Bacon's Information Inc., 2004). Some of Bacon's classifications have been collapsed for this summary.

13 See, for example, Elliott Anderson and Mary Kinzie, eds., *The Little Magazine in America: A Modern Documentary History* (Pushcart Press, 1978).

14 From the first anniversary issue of *Playboy,* cited in Theodore Peterson, *Magazines in the Twentieth Century* (Urbana: University of Illinois Press, 1964), p. 316.

15 Adapted from Susan L. Taylor, "Ethnic Magazines Reflect Pride and Purpose," in Magazine Publishers of America, "Magazines: The Medium of the Moment," special advertising insert in the *New York Times,* October 8, 1998, p. 16.

16 Professor Samir Husni of the University of Mississippi, quoted in Christina Hoag, "Thalía Launches a Magazine," *Miami Herald,* April 12, 2004.

17 The list appeared in *Blender*'s May 2004 issue. Each of the songs had to be a hit to make the list. The bottom 10 were: 1. "We Built This City," Starship, 1985; 2. "Achy Breaky Heart," Billy Ray Cyrus, 1992; 3. "Everybody Have Fun Tonight," Wang Chung, 1986; 4. "Rollin'," Limp Bizkit, 2000; 5. "Ice Ice Baby," Vanilla Ice, 1990; 6. "The Heart of Rock & Roll," Huey Lewis & The News, 1984; 7. "Don't Worry, Be Happy," Bobby McFerrin, 1988; 8. "Party All the Time," Eddie Murphy, 1985; 9. "American Life," Madonna, 2003; 10. "Ebony and Ivory," Paul McCartney and Stevie Wonder, 1982.

18 Publicist Paul Wilmot, quoted in Robin Pogrebin, "Magazines Work to Make Headlines with Their Headlines," *New York Times,* July 6, 1998, p. D1.

19 Lorne Manly, "A Lad Mag and a Brand in Las Vegas," *New York Times* online, June 5, 2006.

20 Magazine Publishers of America, "Magazines: There's No Stopping Them," special advertising insert in the *New York Times,* October 8, 1998.

21 Ibid.

22 Kathy Peiss, *Hope in a Jar: The Making of America's Beauty Culture* (Minneapolis: Metropolitan Books, 1998).

23 Anorexia nervosa is an image disease in which the victim, usually a girl or young woman, sees herself as overweight when she isn't; it can lead the sufferer to starve herself to death.

24 Katherine Gilday, producer and director, *The Famine Within,* PBS documentary, 1990.

25 See, for example, Maureen Dowd, "Beach Blanket Lingo," *New York Times* online, June 27, 1999.

26 "Chrysler Relaxing Policy on Magazines," *New York Times,* October 17, 1997, p. D8.

Chapter 6: Movies

1   Edward Jay Epstein, "Downloading for Dollars: The Future of Hollywood Has Arrived," *Slate* online, November 28, 2005.

2   Patrick Goldstein, "In a Losing Race with the Zeitgeist," *Los Angeles Times* online, November 22, 2005.

3   Goldstein, "In a Losing Race." See also Sharon Waxman, "Study Finds Young Men Attending Fewer Films," *New York Times* online, October 8, 2005.

4   Anonymous executive quoted in Edward Jay Epstein, "The Popcorn Palace Economy," *Slate* online, January 2, 2006.

5   Production executive quoted by Goldstein, "In a Losing Race."

6   The term *peep show* used in this early context should not be confused with its modern meaning of a cheap, sexually explicit film.

7   We say Edison accomplished this, although, like many of the inventions Edison developed, the real work was done by scientists working under him—in this case William Dickson, who actually invented the first motion picture camera. Edison was a great inventor in his own right, but he was also an excellent manager of others (such as Dickson), and an astute businessman who bought other inventors' patents (such as Thomas Armat's intermittent movement and loop-forming devices) and improved on them.

8   Chaplin, Pickford, and Fairbanks later revolted against the star system by forming their own independent studio, United Artists.

9   The popularity of drive-ins peaked in 1958, when there were 4,000 of them. There are around 400 of them left today.

10 A 1970s version of Smell-o-Vision required a scratch-and-sniff card. 3-D would occasionally make a comeback in individual films, such as *Spy Kids 3-D* (2003).

11 Eric A. Taub, "Among Film's Ghosts, Its Future," *New York Times* online, June 19, 2003.

12 Statistics on worldwide movie production can be found at the Motion Picture Association of America's Web site, (www.mpaa.org).

13 The figure is from the Motion Picture Association of America's Web site, www.mpaa.org, accessed August 2006.

14 The eight-hour Russian epic *War and Peace* was produced in 1967 for $100 million, which would be equivalent to almost $500 million today.

15 Frank Rose, "Big Stars! Huge Explosions! 3% Margins!" *Fortune,* October 26, 1998, p. 52.

16 In one of the more arcane distinctions within the industry, the term *independent film* is used for movies produced with no connection to a studio, while *independent production* is reserved for films made by a studio subsidiary. See Ira Konigsberg, *The Complete Film Dictionary* (New York: Meridian, 1987).

17 Janet Maslin, quoted in Jaime Wolf, "The Blockbuster Script Factory," *New York Times Magazine,* August 23, 1998, p. 35.

18 Ricardo Montalban, interviewed on *Late Night with David Letterman,* January 23, 1998.

19 Peter Pasell, "Hollywood Bets Its All on Openings," *New York Times,* December 23, 1997, p. E1.

20 After the first two weeks, a blockbuster's split will slip to 70–30 for the second two weeks, and then to 50–50 for the third.

21 Bernard Weinraub, "Hollywood Feels Chill of Chinese Warning to Disney," *New York Times,* December 9, 1996, p. C11.

22 David Leonhardt, "What Netflix Could Teach Hollywood," *New York Times* online, June 7, 2006.

23 Robert G. Friedman, quoted in Bernard Weinraub, "Media," *New York Times,* August 12, 1996, p. D7.

24 See, for example, Nat Ives, "Agency to Study Marketing of Films," *New York Times* Online, January 14, 2003.

25 Sony's deception was discovered in 2001. It turned out that the made-up quotes appeared in ads for movies that had already been critically applauded, but the real pull quotes were not satisfactory to the studio.

26 Stuart Elliot, "A New Take on Product Placement," *New York Times* online, April 17, 2001.

27 Epstein, "The Popcorn Palace Economy."

28 Ibid.

29 From "Box-Office Greats" list at www.filmsite.org.

30 Edward Jay Epstein, "Multiplexities," *New Yorker,* July 13, 1998, p. 36.

31 Carol Kaesuk Yoon, "Scientists Find Lemmings Die as Dinners, Not Suicides," *New York Times* online, October 31, 2003.

32 Alan F. Kiepper, "What Does Hollywood Say Now?" *New York Times,* December 12, 1995, p. A27.

33 Molly Haskell, *From Reverence to Rape: The Treatment of Women in the Movies* (New York: Oxford University Press, 1974).

34 Marilyn Friedman, quoted in "Rhett and Scarlett: Rough Sex or Rape? Feminists Give a Damn," *New York Times,* February 19, 1995, Week in Review section. An entire book has been written about the significance of this one scene: Helen Taylor, *Scarlett's Women: Gone With the Wind and Its Female Fans* (New Brunswick, NJ: Rutgers University Press, 1989).

35 Susan Faludi, "The Fatal Detractions by Hollywood," *Philadelphia Inquirer,* November 12, 1991, p. 1E.

36 Michelle Goldberg, "Where Are the Female Directors?" Salon.com, August 22, 2002.

37 Tony Hillerman, quoted in John Clark, "Movies: No Reservations," *Los Angeles Times,* Calendar section, June 28, 1998, p. 8.

38 Sherman Alexie, "I Hated Tonto," *Los Angeles Times,* Calendar section, June 28, 1998, p. 9.

39 "Judge Overturns Ban on Film," *New York Times,* September 11, 1988, p. 34.

40 Richard Land, interview for *60 Minutes* on CBS, September 15, 1998.

Chapter 7: Recordings and the Music Industry

1 For example, the great epic poems of Homer, *The Iliad* and *The Odyssey,* were originally sung.

2 John Kruesi built the tinfoil cylinder phonograph for Edison from Edison's sketches.

3 Interesting media connection: The poem "Mary Had a Little Lamb" was written by Sara Josepha Hale, the magazine editor discussed in Chapter 5.

4 Jukeboxes are exempt from the performance rights groups' blanket fees. The industry has fought this exemption for years.

5 In Don McLean's 1971 song, "American Pie."

6 Christopher John Farley, "Hip-Hop Nation," *Time,* February 8, 1999, p. 56.

7 James H. Burnett III, "Music's Influence Moves from Street Corner to Boardroom," *Milwaukee Journal Sentinel* online, November 21, 2003.

8 Neil Strauss, "Rap Rules among the Grammy Award Nominations," *New York Times,* December 5, 2003, p. E3.

9 In deference to vinyl loyalists, we should point out that many purists prefer vinyl to CDs and are quite passionate about it.

10 Jefferson Graham, "RIAA Chief Says Illegal Song-Sharing 'Contained,'" *USA Today* online, June 13, 2006.

11 CEO Mitch Bainwol, quoted in Graham, "RIAA Chief."

12 Jefferson Graham, "RIAA Chief Says . . ."

13 Sony and Bertelsmann merged in 2004 to form Sony BMG, but in 2006 European regulators announced their intentions to reexamine the merger.

14 See, for example, Celia Colista and Glenn Leshner, "Traveling Music: Following the Path of Music through the Global Market," *Critical Studies in Mass Communication* 15, no. 2 (June 1998), p. 181.

15 This executive was quoted on condition of anonymity in Neil Strauss, "Restless Music Fans Hungry for the New," *New York Times,* January 28, 1998, p. C7.

16 Neil Strauss, "In Gangsta Rap, a Reality as Bad as the Fantasy," *New York Times,* March 3, 1998, p. E8.

17 Mark Crispin Miller, "Who Controls the Music?" *The Nation,* August 25/September 1, 1997, p. 11.

18 Courtney Love, "Courtney Love Does the Math," Salon.com, June 14, 2000.

19 Neil Strauss, "Are Pop Charts Manipulated?" *New York Times,* January 26, 1996, p. C15.

20 Cited in Neil Strauss, "Media," *New York Times,* February 17, 1997, p. 49.

21 Neil Strauss, "Restless Music Fans Hungry for the News," *New York Times,* January 28, 1998, p. C7.

22 See, for example, Peter Mock, "Why One-Hit Wonders Top the Pop Charts," *New York Times,* letter to the editor, February 2, 1998, p. A22.

23 Strauss, "Restless Music Fans," p. C1.

24 Gerald Marzorati, "How the Album Got Played Out," *New York Times Magazine,* February 22, 1998, p. 38.

25 Senator Joseph Lieberman (D., Conn.) quoted in James Kuhnhenn, "Clash Over Pop Music Renewed at a Hearing on Violent Lyrics," *Philadelphia Inquirer,* November 7, 1997, p. A10.

26 See, for example, Mary Billard, "Heavy Metal Goes on Trial," in George Rodman, ed., *Mass Media Issues,* 4th ed. (Dubuque, IA: Kendall/Hunt, 1993), p. 221. See also, in the same source, "Ozzy: Read My Lyrics," p. 232.

27 Roger Cohen, "Two 'Perfect Little Girls' Stun France in Suicide," *New York Times,* May 30, 1997, p. A4.

28 Neil Strauss, "R-Rated Rock Concerts? Marilyn Manson and Mom?" *New York Times,* December 1, 1997, p. E1.

29 "A Campaign against 'Degrading' Rock Lyrics," *New York Times,* May 31, 1996, p. C12.

30 Neil Strauss, "Wal-Mart's CD Standards Are Changing Pop Music," *New York Times,* November 12, 1996, p. A1.

31 Ibid.

Chapter 8: Radio

1 National Association of Broadcasters Website, www.nab.org, accessed August, 2006.

2 One such scientist was James Clerk Maxwell, a Scot who published a paper in 1873 that proposed the possibility of sending an electromagnetic signal through space.

3 There is a considerable amount of skepticism about this claim today. See, for example, Tom Lewis, *Empire of the Air: The Men Who Made Radio* (New York: Harper, 1991), pp. 105–7.

4 This claim has also been disputed. See "In Search of the Sarnoff 'Radio Music Box' Memo, *Journal of Broadcasting & Electronic Media* 37 (1993), pp. 325–35.

5 Trivia question: James Cox was soon forgotten, but what is his family known for today? Answer: Cox Communications, a media firm with major investments in broadcasting and cable television.

6 Other examples of meaningful call letters include WLS (World's Largest Store) and WGN (World's Greatest Network), both in Chicago.

7 Lydia Polgreen, "The Death of 'Local Radio,'" *Washington Monthly,* April 1999, p. 9.

8 David Colker, "Nobody Does Web Radio Better than BBC," *Los Angeles Times* online, July 10, 2005.

9 Richard Jones, quoted in Matthew Weiner, "Radio Retunes to the Future," *Telegraph* online, www.telegraph.co.uk, January 20, 2005.

10 "Media: Radio," *BusinessWeek* online, February 15, 1999.

11 Gerald Marzorati, "How the Album Got Played Out," *New York Times Magazine,* February 22, 1998, p. 38.

12 Jon Pareles, "Fracturing the Formula: A Hope for the Offbeat on Small FM," *New York Times* online, February 9, 1999.

13 Ibid.

14 Dan Rutherford, music promoter, cited in Ricardo Baca, "Free Range Radio: College Playlists Roam Outside the Corporate Fence," *Denver Post* online, July 27, 2003.

15 Stefan Lovgren, "The Resurgence of Hate Radio: Rwanda," *U.S. News & World Report,* May 18, 1998, p. 44.

16 Betsy Pisik, "Hateful Words a War Crime," *Washington Times* online, December 3, 2003.

17 "Commerce Department Report Shows Minority Ownership of Radio and Television Stations Remains Low," *Jet,* July 22, 1996, p. 36.

18 Charles Duhigg, "FCC Launches Payola Probes of 4 Radio Giants," *Los Angeles Times* online, April 20, 2006.

19 Quoted in Brian Ross, Richard Esposito, and Vic Walter, "100's of Radio Stations in Payola Probe," ABC News online, February 9, 2006.

20 Quoted in Chris Graham, "The Return of Payola," *Augusta Free Press* online, May 17, 2006.

Chapter 9: Television

1 According to Nielsen Media Research www.nielsenmedia .com, accessed August, 2006, the average American home watched more television during the 2004–2005 TV season than during any previous season. September to September, the average household in the United Stateds tuned into television 8 hours and 11 minutes per day. This is 2.7 percent higher than the previous season, 12.5 percent higher than 10 years earlier, and the highest levels ever reported since television viewing was first measured by Nielsen Media Research in the 1950s. In that same time frame, the average person watched television 4 hours and 32 minutes each day, the highest level in 15 years.

2 "Traditionally, women in TV households have spent the most time viewing television, averaging almost 5 hours a day. Men are next, hovering around the 4-hour mark. Teens and children have been viewing at about the same levels, just above the 3-hour mark." Quote from the Television Advertising Bureau's Web site www.tvb.org, accessed January 11, 2004. There are, however, very few "average" people. People of different ages, sexes, and other demographic characteristics tend to watch different amounts of television.

3 The kinescope was a specially designed film camera that ran at 30 frames a second, the same speed as a television image. A regular film camera runs at 24 frames a second; if it records from a television screen, it will produce an image with a line constantly cycling from top to bottom of the frame.

4 Marcus D. Pohlmann, *Black Politics in Conservative America,* 2nd ed. (New York: Longman, 1999), p. 247.

5 "Family Values on Fox," editorial, *New York Times* online, January 22, 2006.

6 Bill Carter, "Media," *New York Times,* March 31, 1997, p. D7.

7 Paramount Television Group, owned by Viacom, was joined by BHC Communications, a subsidiary of Chris-Craft Industries.

8 Joel Brinkley, "Building Your Next TV: Two Industries Fight for a $150 Billion Prize," *New York Times,* March 28, 1997, p. D1.

9 According to Nielsen Media Research, www.nielsenmedia .com, accessed August 2006, the average American household received 96.4 channels in 2005 but watched only 15.4 of them. Nielsen observes that "given an unlimited number of media options, the average person will still opt to use a relatively small number."

10 Technically, TBS gave up its legal right to the "superstation" designation in 1999 as part of the must-carry Supreme Court decisions (collectively known as Turner I and Turner II). While WTBS still calls itself the superstation, it does not satisfy the FCC requirements to be a superstation for carriage purposes. WGN now finds itself in the same situation.

11 Teresa Méndez, "Access for the Masses," *Christian Science Monitor* online, September 26, 2005.

12 Anthony Riddle, executive director of the Alliance for Community Media in Washington, DC, quoted in Méndez, "Access for the Masses."

13 Ralph Engelman, the chairman of the Journalism Department at Long Island University's Brooklyn campus, quoted in Felicia R. Lee, "Proposed Legislation May Affect Future of Public-Access Television," *New York Times* online, November 8, 2005.

14 As the older networks have found it increasingly difficult to achieve the high levels of profit they have become accustomed to, they have toyed with the idea of ending compensation to stations. New networks, such as Fox, The WB, and UPN, however, created competition that would have made it easy for a station to drop any network that refused to pay its affiliates to run its programming, so the traditional arrangement persists.

15 The FCC voted in June 2003 to increase the limit to 45 percent, but Congress and the courts intervened, blocking the FCC from putting the plan into effect.

16 Nielsen "flags" stations that hold contests for viewers during ratings periods so that readers of the report will know that results might have been affected by the contests.

17 Bill Carter, "A New Report Becomes a Weapon in Debate on Censoring TV Violence," *New York Times,* February 7, 1996,

p. C11. The following definition of violence was used: "Any overt depiction of the use of physical force or the credible threat of such force intended to physically harm an animate being or group of beings."

18   This trend is analyzed in Lawrie Mifflin, "Study Says Networks Have Cut Violence," *New York Times,* October 16, 1996, p. C11.

19   A line attributed to Alfred Hitchcock.

20   Jennifer Herrett-Skjellum and Mike Allen, "Television Programming and Sex Stereotyping: A Meta-Analysis," *Communication Yearbook* 19 (1996), pp. 157–85. This is a meta-analysis because it examines previously published findings.

21   Lawrie Mifflin, "U.S. Mandates Educational TV for Children," *New York Times,* August 9, 1996, p. A16.

22   Daniel Goleman, "How Viewers Grow Addicted to Television," *New York Times,* October 16, 1990, p. C1.

23   See, for example, Robert Kubey and Mihaly Csikszentmihalyi, *Television and the Quality of Life* (Mahwah, NJ: Erlbaum, 1990).

Chapter 10: The Internet

1   Danah Boyd, quoted in an interview with Sarah Wright, "Discussion: MySpace and Deleting Online Predators Act," MIT News Office, www.danah.org/papers/MySpaceDOPA .html. May 24, 2006.

2   Boyd, quoted in Wright, "Discussion: MySpace."

3   Henry Jenkins, quoted in Wright, "Discussion: MySpace."

4   Stefanie Olsen, "The 'Millennials' Usher in a New Era," CNET News online, November 18, 2005.

5   There were, of course, many advances in between the abacus and electronics that we don't have the space to cover here, including Pascal's mechanical calculator (1642), Jacquard's loom with punch cards (1801), and Babbage's "difference engine" (1822). See, for example, the Computer Society's History of Computing at www.computer.org.

6   The founding of ARPA in 1958 was a reaction to the launching of the first satellite, *Sputnik,* by the Soviet Union. The Eisenhower administration was worried that the United States was falling behind its great cold-war enemy in terms of scientific advancement.

7   CompuServe was founded in 1969 as a computer time-sharing company.

8   Steve Wozniak was the other founder of Apple Computer.

9   Tim Berners-Lee, on *Adam Smith's Money World,* PBS television program broadcast February 12, 1996. He did, however, win the first-ever Millennium Technology Prize, worth 1 million euros (US$1.2 million) from the Finnish Technology Award Foundation in April 2004. This award is considered the "Finnish Nobel Prize."

10   Elisabeth Rosenthal, "China Issues Rules to Limit E-Mail and Web Content," *New York Times* online, January 27, 2000.

11   Bob Tedeschi, "As Online Ads Grow, Eyeballs Are Valuable Again on the Web," *New York Times* online, June 26, 2006.

12   Other domain signifiers include .mil, for the U.S. military, and .int, for international institutions, such as the UN or NATO. New domain names such as .firm, .arts, and .web have been proposed. Anyone can register a .com, .net, or .org domain. The .net and .org domains might therefore imply that a site is part of a network or an organization when it is not. The domains .edu, .mil, and .gov are restricted to the groups they refer to.

13   The other protocols that define access to Internet resources include file transfer protocol (FTP, a program that lists files and allows the user to transfer them between systems); Telnet (which allows the user to connect with a remote host and appear as a terminal for that system); Gopher (an early type of search engine, requiring specialized commands); and Usenet (the protocol used for newsgroups and bulletin boards).

14   A Java program is known as an applet; JavaScript enables Java to work with HTML. Both are famous for making browsers crash.

15   Andrew Pollack, "What's in a Cyber Name? $7.5 Million for the Right Address," *New York Times* online, December 1, 1999.

16   "Eflowers Domain Name Sold," Associated Press story on www.infobeat.com, February 15, 1999.

17   The term *cyberspace* was originated by science fiction writer William Gibson in his 1984 novel, *Neuromancer.* Today, the prefix *cyber-* has become a central metaphor for anything occurring on the Internet, where young rebels are now called cyberpunks and intimacy of the online sort is called cybersex. The term *cyber* had appeared earlier, in the 1940s, in the work of Norbert Wiener when he created cybernetics, the science of automated systems. From the Greek *kybernan,* "to steer."

18   Jeri Clausing, "Cybersquatting Measure Attached to Satellite-TV Bill," *New York Times* online, November 11, 1999.

19   Flaming was analyzed by communication researchers in L. Martin, T. O'Shea, P. Fung, and R. Spears, "'Flaming' in Computer-Mediated Communication: Observations, Explanations, Implications," in M. Lea, ed., *Contexts of Computer-Mediated Communication* (New York: Harvester Wheatsheaf, 1992), pp. 89–112.

20   Technically, to be a true acronym, the resulting word should be pronounceable, such as NASA (an acronym for the National Aeronautics and Space Administration) or radar (an acronym for radio detecting and ranging). Otherwise, it would be an initialism.

21   Dave Barry, *Dave Barry in Cyberspace* (New York: Crown, 1996), p. 48.

22   The social significance of newsgroups is examined in S. Rafaeli, and R. J. LaRose, "Electronic Bulletin Boards and 'Public Goods' Explanations of Collaborative Mass Media," *Communication Research* 20 (1993), pp. 277–97.

23   See, for example, Nicola Doring, "Personal Home Pages on the Web: A Review of Research," *Journal of Computer-Mediated Communication,* Summer 2002, available online at www .ascusc.org/jcmc/vol7/issue3/ doering.html#Theories.

24   These figures come from Perseus Development Corporation, a company that designs software for online surveys, as cited in Emily Nussbaum, "My So-Called Blog," *New York Times Magazine,* January 11, 2004, p. 32.

25   Doring, "Personal Home Pages."

26   Smart mobs are also known as flash mobs. See, for example, Dean E. Murphy, "San Francisco Journal: Last Car. Geek Party. Spread the Word," *New York Times* online, January 29, 2004.

27   Steve Kelley, "Life Without Banners?" *Netguide,* April 1997, p. 39.

28   Earlier forms of distance learning included correspondence courses, which were conducted by mail.

29   Elaine K. Bailey and Morton Cotlar, "Teaching Via the Internet," *Communication Education* 43, no. 2 (April 1994), pp. 151–58.

30   Linus Torvalds, the creator of the Linux operating system, cited in David Diamond, "The Sharer," *New York Times* online, September 28, 2003.

31 "Minnesota Teenager Arrested in Internet Attack," Associated Press online, August 29, 2003.

32 The word *spam* began as the trademarked name of the popular mystery meat, which eventually became the focus of a skit by the British comedy team Monty Python. In the skit, a restaurant serves all its food with lots of Spam, and the waitress repeats the word several times in describing how much Spam is in the items. When she does this, a group of Vikings in the corner sing, "Spam, Spam, lovely Spam! Wonderful Spam!" over and over. So the term, when it was first used to describe unsolicited e-mail in 1978, suggested something that keeps repeating and repeating to great annoyance. From "Origin of the Word 'Spam' to Mean Net Abuse" on Brad Templeton's blog at www.templetons.com/brad/spamterm.html.

33 Controlling the Assault of Non-Solicited Pornography and Marketing Act of 2003 (CAN-SPAM Act). See summary of 108th Congress at www.spamlaws.com/federal/summ108.html.

34 Jeri Clausing, "Report Rings Alarm Bells about Privacy on the Internet," *New York Times* online, February 7, 2000.

35 "Target Practice," Snopes Urban Legends, www.snopes.com/politics/military/target.asp, accessed August 2006.

Chapter 11: Electronic News

1 Gerard Baker, "What Katie Did Next: Why Do They Care So Much?" *Times* (UK) online, April 10, 2006.

2 "Katie Couric's Years of Liberal Tilt," Media Research Web site, www.mediaresearch.org/projects/couric/welcome.asp, updated April 2006.

3 "With *Today* Host's Record of Silence on Conservative Falsehoods, Couric Chided Dean for *Accurate* Statement," Media Matters for America Web site, available at http://mediamatters.org/items/200601260003, posted January 26, 2006.

4 Kara Gavin, "U-M Study: Katie Couric's Colonoscopy Caused Cross-Country Climb in Colon Cancer Checks," University of Michigan Health Systems press release, www.med.umich.edu/opm/newspage/2003/couric.htm, July 14, 2003.

5 Joe Gandelman, "The Significance of Katie Couric's Move to CBS News," blog article, www.themoderatevoice.com/posts/1144303629.shtml, April 6, 2006.

6 Robert L. Hilliard and Michael C. Keith, *The Broadcast Century: A Biography of American Broadcasting,* 2nd ed. (Boston: Focal Press, 1997), p. 107.

7 Historian Daniel Boorstin originated this term in his book *The Image: A Guide to Pseudo Events in America* (New York: Harper & Row, 1964).

8 Erik Barnouw, *Tube of Plenty: The Evolution of American Television* (New York: Oxford University Press, 1975), p. 179.

9 The memoirs of Dwight D. Eisenhower, as cited in Barnouw, *Tube of Plenty,* p. 226.

10 NBC continued to cover the hearings, but many of their affiliates refused to pick them up.

11 Barnouw, *Tube of Plenty,* p. 387.

12 Videotext was a two-way interactive service that was used over cable systems. A similar type of service, teletext, was a one-way technology that operated over broadcast television.

13 A maxim usually attributed to John B. Bogart (1848–1921), city editor of the *New York Sun.*

14 Connie Chung, quoted in Dana Kennedy, "Women on the Verge," *Entertainment Weekly,* June 16, 1995, p. 16.

15 Jill Abramson, "When Will We Stop Saying 'First Woman to _____'?" *New York Times* online, April 9, 2006.

16 Bob Papper, a professor of telecommunications at Ball State college in Muncie, IN, directed the study that shows that women now make up more than 57 percent of local news anchors. The study was conducted for the Radio-Television News Directors Association (RTNDA). "Women Outnumber Men as News Anchors," Studio Briefing, online, January 18, 2006.

17 Howard Rosenberg, "In TV News, Taking Credit Is Called Business as Usual," *Los Angeles Times* online, June 2, 2003.

18 Surveys are conducted by such groups as the Radio and Television News Directors Association, at www.RTNDA.org.

19 Radio and Television News Directors Foundation Study, conducted in 2000 and reported at www.rtndf.org.

20 Steve Carney, "22% of Americans Get News from Talk Jocks," *Los Angeles Times* online, January 10, 2003.

21 Caryn James, "A Public Flooded with Images from Friend and Foe Alike," *New York Times* online, October 10, 2001.

22 Gallup News Service, "Poll Analyses: Public Remains Skeptical of News Media," www.gallup.com/poll/releases/pr030530.asp, May 30, 2003.

23 AIM Web site, www.aim.org, accessed January 14, 2000.

24 From Jim Rutenberg and Bill Carter, "Network Coverage a Target of Fire from Conservatives," *New York Times* online, November 7, 2001.

25 Bill Carter and Alessandra Stanley, "Networks Ask if 'Message' by bin Laden Is Really News," *New York Times* online, October 10, 2001.

26 Jeff Cohen, "The Centrist Bias of the U.S. Media," in George Rodman, ed., *Mass Media Issues,* 4th ed. (Dubuque, IA: Kendall/Hunt, 1993), p. 411.

27 Michael Josephson, president of the Josephson Institute of Ethics, quoted in Robert K. Elder, "Seeking Neutrality in the Media's War of Words," *Chicago Tribune* online, February 19, 2003.

28 Peter Dobrin, "Media's War Music Carries a Message," *Philadelphia Inquirer* online, March 30, 2003.

29 Peter Fish, quoted in Dobrin, "Media's War Music."

30 F. Marshall Maher, "When Journalists Attack: The *Boston Herald*'s Loose Cannon," *Extra!,* May/June 2003.

31 Av Westin, *Newswatch: How TV Decides the News* (New York: Simon & Schuster), 1982, flyleaf.

32 Quoted in Lori Robertson, "Poll Crazy," *American Journalism Review* online, January/February 2003.

33 David Warga, executive producer for the Naked News Network, quoted in "Toronto Station to Air 'Naked News,'" AP Entertainment Wire, February 14, 2003.

Chapter 12: Public Relations

1 John M. Broder, "Immigration, from a Simmer to a Scream," *New York Times* online, May 21, 2006.

2 "Hazy Days of Immigration," editorial, *New York Times* online, July 20, 2006.

3 Dan Pfeiffer, a spokesman for Senator Evan Bayh, Democrat of Indiana, quoted in Carl Hulse, "A Build-a-Protest Approach to Immigration," *New York Times* online, May 31, 2006.

4 The Sophists of the fifth century BC were later characterized by Plato as superficial manipulators of rhetoric.

5 Allan Nevins, quoted by Scott M. Cutlip, Allen H. Center, and Glen M. Broom, *Effective Public Relations,* 6th ed. (Englewood Cliffs, NJ: Prentice Hall, 1985), p. 25.

6 Andrew Jackson was known as "Old Hickory" because his soldiers thought of him as being as "tough as a hickory tree," particularly when it came to their welfare.

7   Dennis L. Wilcox, Phillip H. Ault and Warren K. Agee, *Public Relations,* 5th ed. (New York: Longman, 1998), p. 33.

8   Stuart Ewen, *PR! A Social History of Spin* (New York: Basic Books, 1996), p. 77.

9   One of the earliest publicity coups of the motion picture industry was the created image of Mary Pickford as "America's Sweetheart." Far from being the innocent little girl that audiences saw, she was an extremely talented actress and businesswoman, and cofounder of United Artists. Publicity agents, capitalizing on her international fame, later changed her nickname to "The World's Sweetheart."

10 Roger Babson, cited in Ewen, *PR!,* p. 131.

11 Deborah Stead, "Wagging the Dog: The Early Years," *New York Times,* September 6, 1998, Sec. 3, p. 10.

12 Other organizations at the forefront of the movement included the National Urban League, the Southern Christian Leadership Conference (Martin Luther King's organization), and the Student Nonviolent Coordinating Committee.

13 "A World without Gatekeepers," PR Central's Web site, www.prcentral.com, accessed April 21, 1999.

14 Wilcox et al., *Public Relations,* p. 48.

15 Quoted in Ewen, *PR!,* p. 11.

16 Ken Ringle, "ASCAP Changes Its Tune on Charging Girl Scouts," *Fresno Bee,* August 28, 1996, p. E3.

17 Steve Hartman, quoted in Trudy Lieberman, "Answer the &$%#* Question! Ever Wonder Why They Won't? They've Been Media-Trained. And the Public Is the Loser," *Columbia Journalism Review* online, January/February 2004.

18 Greg Critser of *Salon* magazine, quoted in Frank Rich, "Electric Kool-Aid Viagra," *New York Times,* August 12, 1998, p. A19.

19 On July 13, 2006, Joseph Wilson and his wife, Valerie Plame, filed a civil suit against Vice President Dick Cheney, his former chief of staff I. Lewis "Scooter" Libby, top presidential advisor Karl Rove, and other unnamed senior White House officials for their role in the public disclosure of Plame's classified CIA employment.

20 Howard Kurtz, *Spin Cycle: Inside the Clinton Propaganda Machine* (New York: Free Press, 1998), p. 92.

21 David Pogue, "Neuter Your Bunny Day," Pogue's Posts blog, NYTimes.com, June 14, 2006.

22 Jack Krumholtz, quoted in Mark Hosenball, "The Big Spin Game," *Newsweek,* January 19, 1998, p. 52.

23 Quoted in Hosenball, "The Big Spin Game."

24 Richard J. Mahoney, "On TV, a Backdrop Is Worth a Thousand Words," *New York Times,* August 30, 1998, Sec. 3, p. 12.

25 Diane Farsetta and Daniel Price, "Fake TV News: Widespread and Undisclosed," Center for Media and Democracy online, www.prwatch.org/fakenews/execsummary, posted April 6, 2006.

26 One of the most famous press kits was the "launch kit" for the Cartoon Network. It went out in two parts—first, a small box that contained a miniature crowbar painted black with the network logo on it in red. About a week later, a small wooden crate with the word *ACME* stenciled on the side showed up. This contained all the publicity photos, VNRs, fact sheets, and other materials normally associated with a launch kit. The strategy, while cute, backfired. Very few cable outlets were willing to open the crate, preferring to save it for posterity. The network had to repackage their launch kit into traditional packaging and resend it.

27 Wilcox et al., *Public Relations,* pp. 480–81.

28 See, for example, Edwin McDowell, "Marketers Line Up to Link Their Names to Events," *New York Times* online, July 16, 1999.

29 Allen Adamson, managing director of Landor Associates, the brand and corporate identity agency that is part of the Young & Rubicam Brands division of the WPP Group, quoted in Julie Bosman, "First Stadiums, Now Teams Take a Corporate Identity," *New York Times* online, March 22, 2006.

30 See, for example, J. David Pincus, Tony Rimmer, Robert E. Rayfield, and Fritz Cropp, "Newspaper Editors' Perceptions of Public Relations: How Business, News and Sports Editors Differ," *Journal of Public Relations Research* 5 (1993), pp. 27–45; see also Julie K. Henderson, "Negative Connotations in the Use of the Term 'Public Relations' in the Print Media," *Public Relations Review* 24 (Spring 1998), pp. 45–54.

31 Ewen, *PR!,* p. 83.

32 Wilcox et al., *Public Relations,* p. 40.

33 Eric Dexenhall, "Runaway Spin Cycle Washes Dirty Laundry," *Insight on News,* September 21, 1998, p. 28.

34 Robert L. Dilenschneider, "Spin: Can It Save You or Sink You?" *Vital Speeches of the Day,* December 1, 1999, p. 123.

35 David Beers and Catherine Capellaro, "Greenwash!" *Mother Jones,* March/April 1991, p. 38.

36 Michael Massing, "Wine's Unfortunate New Labels," *New York Times* online, February 9, 1999.

37 Trudy Lieberman, "Freebies for Newsfolk in the World of High Tech," *Columbia Journalism Review,* January/February 1998, pp. 62–65.

38 *TV Guide* study cited in Wilcox, et al., *Public Relations,* p. 62.

39 Stephen Engleberg, "A New Breed of Hired Hands Cultivates Grass-roots Anger," *New York Times,* May 17, 1993, p. A1.

40 Lou Harry, "Ya Gotta Have Hype!" *Philadelphia,* April 1991, p. 93.

Chapter 13: Advertising

1   Alex Bogusky, a partner in the ad firm Crispin Porter & Bogusky, quoted in Rob Walker, "Consumed: Poultry-Geist," *New York Times Magazine* online, May 23, 2004.

2   Yankelovich Partners studies, cited in Walker, "Consumed."

3   Larry Copeland, "Cities Consider Ads on Police Cars," *USA Today* online, October 30, 2002.

4   Today, that argument might be difficult to recognize because the brand-name, heavily advertised household products such as soap and packaged food are more expensive in the stores. If Ford and Carnegie were still around today, they might explain that the apparent lower cost of generic goods is true only because the advertised products have already created the demand—the mass market—for the goods, and the generic brands are hopping on for a free ride.

5   Many advertising professionals define *puffery* as exaggeration in a humorous context that is not meant to be taken seriously. See, for example, Laurence Urdang, ed., *Dictionary of Advertising Terms* (Chicago: Tatham-Laird & Kudner, 1977).

6   See, for example, Charles Goodrum and Helen Dalrymple, *Advertising in America: The First 200 Years* (New York: Abrams, 1990), p. 22.

7   Hoover is quoted in Robert L. Hilliard and Michael C. Keith, *The Broadcast Century: A Biography of American Broadcasting,* 2nd ed. (Boston: Focal Press, 1997), p. 42.

8   Ibid., p. 31.

9   Bob Garfield, "Class Consciousness Hurts Denny's Ads," *Advertising Age,* June 2, 1997, p. 49.

10 See, for example, Joseph Turow, *Breaking Up America: Advertisers and the New Media World* (Chicago: University of Chicago Press, 1997).

11 Peter Mayle, *Up the Agency: The Funny Business of Advertising* (New York: St. Martin's, 1990), p. 12.

12 This is from Michiko Kakutani, "Bananas for Rent," *New York Times Magazine,* November 9, 1997, p. 32.

13 Doreen Carvajal, "Diversity Pays Off in a Babel of Yellow Pages," *New York Times,* December 3, 1995, p. 1.

14 Guerrilla advertising, part of the larger concept of guerrilla marketing, can be part of a traditional campaign and is not confined to counteradvertising or parody.

15 See "FTC Files Suit against Exxon Over Ads," *New York Times,* September 18, 1996, p. D7.

16 Tom Kuntz, "Postage To-Do: The Flim-Flams Brought to You by the Mailman," *New York Times,* October 27, 1996.

17 Dave Barry, "Ask Mr. Language Person," *Miami Herald,* December 1, 1985. About the expression "part of this complete breakfast," Barry asks, "Don't they really mean 'adjacent to this complete breakfast,' or 'on the same table as this complete breakfast'? And couldn't they make essentially the same claim if, instead of Froot Loops, they put a can of shaving cream there, or a dead bat?"

18 "Consumer Group to Sue Cereal Maker," CorpWatch Web site, www.corpwatch.org/article.php?id=13128, June 18, 2006.

19 The study, conducted by Dartmouth Medical School, was cited with understandable concern in *New York Teacher,* January 19, 1998, p. 6.

20 "Hooking Teen-Age Smokers," editorial, *New York Times,* October 24, 1995, p. A26.

21 Gail Schiller, "In Risky Move, Newscasts Adopt Product Placements," Reuters online, March 15, 2006.

22 Gary Ruskin, executive director of Commercial Alert, quoted in Stuart Elliott, "On ABC, Sears Pays to Be Star of New Series," *New York Times* online, December 3, 2003.

23 For advocacy organizations, a brief disclosure at the end of a television program is not enough. Commercial Alert, for example, demands "concurrent, conspicuous and clear" disclosures, such as acknowledgments of sponsorship superimposed on screen, in a rolling scroll, as the placements occur.

24 "Miami Mayor Warns Paper to Be 'Nicer' or Lose Ads," *New York Times,* January 8, 1998, p. A16.

25 See, for example, Joe Tye, "Buying Silence: Self-Censorship of Smoking and Health in National Newsweeklies," in George Rodman, ed., *Mass Media Issues,* 4th ed. (Dubuque, IA: Kendall/Hunt, 1993), p. 304.

Chapter 14: Media Law

1   Greg Toppo, "Some U.S. Students Say Press Freedoms Go Too Far," *USA Today,* January 31, 2005.

2   Dennis Ryerson, editor of *The Indianapolis Star,* quoted in Warren Watson, "Leaving the First Amendment Behind," *Media Daily News* online, March 23, 2005.

3   Bill Maher, "Kids Say the Darndest, Most Stalinist Things," *Los Angeles Times* online, February 18, 2005.

4   John Milton, *Areopagitica,* quoted in George Rodman, *Mass Media Issues,* 4th ed. (Dubuque, IA: Kendall/Hunt, 1993), p. 33.

5   Benjamin Franklin, "An Apology for Printers," in Rodman, *Mass Media Issues,* p. 34.

6   What became the First Amendment was actually third in the list of amendments offered to the states for ratification. The first dealt with methods of assigning congressional seats to the individual states and was never ratified. The second, which barred congressional pay raises from taking effect during an intervening session of Congress, failed to gain a sufficient number of states required to ratify until 1992, when it became the Twenty-Seventh Amendment to the Constitution. Originally, the House passed 17 amendments, but the Senate combined several, and eliminated others. A Conference Committee eventually came out with the list of 12 amendments, of which our present First Amendment was listed third.

7   Samuel D. Warren and Louis D. Brandeis, "The Right to Privacy," *Harvard Law Review* 4, no. 5 (1890), p. 193. Legal scholars believe this is the most influential law review article ever written.

8   Max Frankel, "When Is Private Pain a Public Good?" *New York Times Magazine,* July 5, 1998, p. 12.

9   Charles A. Beard and Mary R. Beard, *The Rise of American Civilization* (New York: Macmillan, 1927), pp. 640, 641.

10 Oliver Wendell Holmes, "Clear and Present Danger," in Rodman, *Mass Media Issues,* p. 42.

11 Kent R. Middleton, Bill F. Chamberlin, and Matthew D. Bunker, *The Law of Public Communication,* 4th ed. (New York: Longman, 1997), p. 39. Six months after the original decision, the Supreme Court added "imminence" to the test. Justices Holmes and Brandeis modified their original standard to include the necessity that only immediate danger—or imminency—could serve as a condition to suppression of speech, in *Abrams v. United States,* 1919.

12 Libel laws in the United States and Britain are very different. In the United States, the person bringing the case has to prove not only that what was reported was false, but also that the publisher was at fault. In Britain, the burden falls the other way. The published statements are presumed to be false, and to win the defendant has to prove that what was said was true.

13 "Censored: Jordan," *The Economist,* September 12, 1998, p. 53.

14 "First Computer Wiretap Locates Hacker," *New York Times,* March 31, 1996, p. 20.

15 The hacker's name was Kevin Poulsen. See "Odds-on Favorite: Dark Dante Hacked His Way into Porsches and Prison," *Twenty-four Hours in Cyberspace* CD-ROM.

16 Some legal experts also include executive action, such as presidential decrees or gubernatorial orders, and equity law, which allows courts to make decisions that are fair and just, as additional types of law. See Middleton et al., *The Law of Public Communication,* p. 5.

17 *Miami Herald v. Tornillo,* 1974.

18 *Sony v. Universal Studios,* 1984.

19 The state of New York, where privacy actions are based on statutes, seems to be the major exception to this trend. See, for example, Donald M. Gillmor, Jerome A. Barron, Todd F. Simon, and Herbert A. Terry, *Fundamentals of Mass Communication Law* (St. Paul, MN: West, 1996), p. 84.

20 A fourth type of privacy action, called false light, is really a type of libel case. Discussing it here would muddy the waters; those who wish to pursue the matter can read Thomas L. Tedford, *Freedom of Speech in the United States* (State College, PA: Strata, 1997), pp. 106–7.

21 *Barber v. Time, Inc.,* 1942; cited in Middleton et al., *The Law of Public Communication,* p. 164.

22 Hoffman sued *Los Angeles* magazine over a computer-generated photograph in its March 1997 fashion feature that showed him wearing a butter-colored silk dress designed by Richard Tyler and Ralph Lauren, with the price listed. A federal judge awarded him $1.5 million in a nonjury trial.

23 Quoted in Dennis Hensley, "Alyssa's Witchy New World," *Cosmopolitan,* December 1998, p. 195.

24 "Photographers Convicted in Schwarzenegger Case," *New York Times,* February 24, 1998, p. A14.

25 Many states have nuances to their libel laws. For example, some states say that the truth must be communicated for "good motives" and justifiable ends. See Tedford, *Freedom of Speech,* p. 83.

26 Asked whether Mr. Farrakhan was involved in the slaying, Shabazz had replied, "Of course. Yes. Nobody kept it a secret. It was a badge of honor." See "Appeals Court Rejects Farrakhan Libel Suit," *New York Times,* December 18, 1997, p. B20. Farrakhan lost the case because the court found that he had failed to prove actual malice.

27 At first, the court applied the rule to officials like Sullivan; later the category was extended to other public people generally.

28 Benjamin Weiser, "Judge Rejects Libel Suit Over *Donnie Brasco* Film," *New York Times,* January 16, 1998, p. B8.

29 Don R. Pember, *Mass Media Law,* rev. ed. (New York: McGraw-Hill, 1998), p. 119.

30 These statistics are gathered by the Libel Defense Resource Center and are reported in Pember, *Mass Media Law,* p. 119.

31 Ibid., p. 120.

32 McDonald's sued David Morris and Helen Steel, two members of London Greenpeace (not affiliated with the international environmental group), over a leaflet they handed out in front of one of the chain's London restaurants. The six-page fact sheet was titled "What's Wrong With McDonald's—Everything They Don't Want You to Know." The pamphlet accused McDonald's of, among other things, promoting unhealthy food, exploiting workers and animals, and destroying the environment. See John Vidal, *McLibel: Burger Culture on Trial* (New York: New Press, 1997).

33 The 1976 act afforded a special protection of 75 years to works created prior to 1978, but which were not yet in the public domain. This was extended 20 years by the Sonny Bono Copyright Extension Act of 1998. The 1976 act also created special categories of copyright for works "created for hire"—in other words, by employees of movie studios for example—but those copyrights belong to the employer, not the originator. See Don R. Pember and Clay Calvert, *Mass Media Law 2005/2006* (New York: McGraw-Hill, 2005), p. 512.

34 Send to Register of Copyrights, Library of Congress, Washington, DC 20559.

35 The international treaty on copyright protection is known as the Berne Convention (for Berne, Switzerland, where it was first adopted in 1886 and amended during several sessions of the world intellectual property community since).

36 *Sony v. Universal Studios,* 1983.

37 Middleton et al., *The Law of Public Communication,* p. 245.

38 *Basic Books, Inc. v. Kinko's Graphics Corp.,* 1991.

39 Doris E. Long, professor of intellectual property at the John Marshall Law School in Chicago, quoted in Jill Braverman, *Chicago Tribune* online, Tech Section, November 20, 1998, accessed May 9, 1999.

40 As of this writing, the trademark office is still considering this request. See Roger Vincent, "Trump Seeks Trademark to Put 'You're Fired' to Work for Him," *Los Angeles Times* online, March 19, 2004.

41 The company was Symantec. "Cyberstrike," www .newmedianews.com. posted February 21, 1997.

42 Deborah Shapley, "Corporate Web Police Hunt Down E-Pirates," *New York Times,* May 19, 1997, p. D5.

43 See, for example, Charles Layton, "The Information Squeeze," in Joan Gorham, ed., *Annual Editions: Mass Media 04/05* (New York: McGraw-Hill, 2004), pp. 142–50.

44 "Rules of the Road on Pornography," editorial, *New York Times,* October 1, 1995, p. 12.

45 Walter Goodman, "Court TV: Case of the Curious Witness," *New York Times,* July 21, 1997, p. C15.

46 Quoted in Max Frankel, "Out of Focus," *New York Times Magazine,* November 5, 1995, p. 26.

47 Ibid., p. 26.

48 In Pennsylvania, for example, there is an ongoing (since 1979) "experimental rule," which allows cameras to be used in trial courts, with only nonjury trials allowed to be recorded. In the first appellate level, Superior Court, only Civil Division cases can be recorded. Presently, some states permit cameras and other recording devices in lower courts or appellate courts only. Some allow them at both levels, and some even restrict their use to certain judicial districts (Idaho). See www.ncsconline.org/WC/Publications/ KIS_CameraPub.pdf.

Chapter 15: Media Ethics

1 Reza Aslan, "Why I'm Offended by the Danish Cartoons of the Prophet," *Slate* online, February 8, 2006.

2 Flemming Rose, "Why I Published Those Cartoons," *Washington Post,* February 19, 2006, p. B1.

3 Rose, "Why I Published Those Cartoons."

4 Horace Greeley, "On Satanic Newspapers," in George Rodman, ed., *Mass Media Issues,* 4th ed. (Dubuque, IA: Kendall/Hunt, 1993), p. 39.

5 "Yellow Journalism and Anarchy," in Calder M. Pickett, *Voices of the Past: Key Documents in the History of American Journalism* (Columbus, OH: Grid, 1977), p. 191.

6 Joseph Pulitzer, "The Platform of the Post-Dispatch," in Rodman, *Mass Media Issues,* p. 40.

7 Theodore Roosevelt, "A President Denounces Some Reformers," in Pickett, *Voices of the Past,* p. 214.

8 David A. Weiss, "Media War in Mexico," letter to the editor, *New York Times Book Review,* August 31, 1997, p. 2.

9 The most famous list was published in *Red Channels: The Report of Communist Infiltration in Radio and Television* (New York: Counterattack: 1950).

10 Spiro Agnew, "Speeches on the Media," in Tom Goldstein, *One Hundred Years of Media Criticism* (New York: Columbia University Press, 1989), p. 69.

11 Ibid., p. 72.

12 Ibid., p. 66.

13 John Leo, "Bloopers of the Century," *Columbia Journalism Review* online, January/February 1999.

14 "Editor's Note," *New York Times,* online, May 11, 2003.

15 See "Secrets of the Cult," *Newsweek,* April 14, 1997, p. 29.

16 Pamela Mendels, "University Set Back in Fight against Term Paper Sites," *New York Times* online, December 16, 1998.

17 Sheryl Gay Stolber, "In Internet Drug Deals, a Regulation Dilemma," *New York Times* online, June 27, 1999.

18 "Online Bookseller Offers Refunds for Recommended Books," *CNN Interactive* online, February 10, 1999.

19 S. S. McClure, "About Three Articles in One Issue of *McClure's,*" in Pickett, *Voices of the Past,* p. 208.

20 Alex Kuczynski, "Reporter Fired for Lies about Her Illness," *New York Times* online, May 12, 1999.

21 See, for example, Joseph Fletcher, *Situation Ethics: The New Morality* (Louisville, KY: Westminster John Knox Press, 1966).

22 Mike Pride, "Out Here," *Brill's Content* online, November 1998.

23 Utilitarianism is the broader but related idea that acts are right or wrong depending on their consequences.

24 Niccolò Machiavelli, *The Prince,* translated by Daniel Donno (New York: Bantam, 1984).

25 See, for example, Clifford G. Christians, Kim B. Rotzoll, and Mark Fackler, *Media Ethics: Cases and Moral Reasoning,* 4th ed. (New York: Longman, 1995), p. 17.

26 Daniel Schorr, *Forgive Us Our Press Passes* (San Francisco: University of California, 1998).

27 "Chewing Out the TV News," *Newsweek,* January 19, 1998, p. 6.

28 Paul Starobin, "Why Those Hidden Cameras Hurt Journalism," *New York Times,* January 28, 1997, p. A21.

29 See, for example, Starobin, "Hidden Cameras . . ." Starobin is a contributing editor of the *Columbia Journalism Review.* He thinks ABC got what it deserved.

30 "NBC Apologizes for 'Seinfeld' Episode on the Puerto Rican Day Parade," *New York Times,* May 9, 1998, p. B3.

31 The Catholic League's William Donahue, quoted in an Info-beat news item, December 15, 1998.

32 As reported May 2, 1997, on *CBS Morning News.*

33 Randy Cohen, "Madison Avenue Medicine," *New York Times Magazine* online, June 27, 1999.

34 Mark Landler, "Your Media Ball, My Field," *New York Times,* August 11, 1996, Sec. 4, p. 5.

35 Byron Calame, "The Public Editor—Anonymity: Who Deserves It?" *New York Times* online, November 20, 2005.

36 Tom Rosenstiel, "Investing in Integrity Pays," *New York Times,* October 20, 1997, p. A19.

37 Bill Kovach, former newspaper editor and curator of the Nieman Foundation for Journalism at Harvard, quoted in Iver Peterson, "Repercussions from Flawed News Articles," *New York Times,* June 3, 1997, p. A12.

38 Steve Coz, editor and senior vice president of *The National Enquirer,* in "When Tabloids Cross the Line," op-ed piece, *New York Times,* May 29, 1997.

39 In 1964, for example, a citizens' group successfully challenged the license renewal of a TV station in Jackson, Mississippi, because of racial discrimination.

Glossary

A

absolutist ethics: Position from which there is a clear-cut right or wrong response for every ethical decision.

academic journals: Periodicals that publish research in a variety of scholarly fields; also called scholarly journals.

account executive: Employee who coordinates the agency's services for the client.

accountability: The obligation to take responsibility, or account for, the consequences of one's actions. In media ethics, accountability involves the questions of who controls media practitioners and who has the power to punish them for ethical lapses.

accreditation: Certification by an industry association.

acquisition editor: An editor who obtains books to be published.

actual malice: Reckless disregard for the truth of published, defamatory information.

ad broker: A liaison between advertisers and newspapers.

adjacency: The opportunity for an advertiser to place an ad near a particular article, at an extra cost.

administrative law: The rules and regulations of governmental agencies.

admonition: A judge's warning to jurors to consider only evidence presented in the courtroom.

adversarial relationship: A relationship in which two parties contend with or oppose each other. In the United States, the media are expected to have an adversarial relationship with the government so that they can serve a watchdog role.

advertising: According to the American Marketing Association: "any paid form of nonpersonal presentation and promotion of ideas, goods, or services by an identified sponsor."

advocacy ads: Ads designed to affect public opinion or government policy.

affiliates: Local stations that have a contractual relationship with the network but are not owned by the network.

agenda-setting theory: Theory that predicts that the amount of attention given to an issue in the media affects the level of importance assigned to it by the public.

a la carte pricing: Charging customers only for those cable channels they choose to receive.

aliterates: Those who are able to read but do not.

alternative press: Publications that provide a different viewpoint on the news, usually one that is politcally radical or otherwise out of the mainstream.

amplitude modulation (AM): Radio transmissions created by changing (modulating) the power (amplitude) of the carrier wave.

analog radio: Radio transmissions in which an electronic waveform represents the sound on a carrier wave.

analog recording: A recording technique in which representation of the sound wave is stored directly onto the recording medium.

anchor: The primary newsreader, who appears in the broadcast news studio.

antitrust laws: Laws that prohibit monopolistic practices in restraint of trade.

applied research: Media investigations devoted to practical, commercial purposes.

arrangers: Those who adapt a song for specific singers and other musical elements.

art director: The person who designs the physical look of a film.

artist and repertoire (A&R) executives: Specialists in the music industry who discover and develop the groups and performers.

artistic speech: Creative work, such as painting, dance, and literature.

attribution: The act of providing the source for information that appears in news reports.

audience research: The gathering of data about consumers targeted in an advertising campaign.

audio news release: Recorded material ready for insertion into radio broadcasts.

audiobooks: Books recorded on tape or some other medium.

Audion: A tube invented by Lee De Forest that was designed to pick up and amplify radio signals; also known as a vacuum tube.

Audit Bureau of Circulations: An association that verifies newspaper and magazine distribution.

auteur: A movie director with a distinctive style.

B

backgrounders: In-depth articles contained in press kits.

bait-and-switch advertising: Technique in which a seller provides bait in the form of an advertised bargain and a switch when the customer is talked into a more expensive product.

basic cable: Those channels that are supplied with the least expensive program package the cable provider offers.

beat reporters: Journalists who find and write stories in a specialized area.

best boy: The gaffer's (lighting director's) assistant.

bibliophiles: Book lovers; heavy readers.

billings: The gross dollar amount that an advertising agency's client spends.

blacklisting: The practice of keeping a particular type of person from working in media and other industries.

blind booking: Forcing theater owners to reserve movies without previewing them.

block booking: Forcing theater owners to show movies with unknown stars in order to get movies with established stars.

blockbuster: All types of huge events, especially in terms of media products.

blogs: See *weblogs*.

blow-in cards: Postcard-sized business reply cards, usually containing subscription solicitations, that are inserted into magazines during the production process.

blurb: Brief laudatory comments that can be placed on the cover of a book.

bots: Short for *robots*, which are software programs capable of carrying out automated searches over the Web; certain kinds of bots are called spiders or crawlers.

boutique agencies: Ad agencies that specialize in creative services.

broadcasting: Using wireless technology to instantaneously reach a wide audience.

browser: A software program that enables a user to move around the Internet.

bullet theory: Theory that implies that media effects flow directly from the media to an individual.

bulletin board services (BBSs): Early online news services.

byline: A line at the beginning of a news story giving the author's name.

C

call letters: Broadcast station identifications assigned by the FCC.

canned news: Press releases designed to be inserted into newspaper feature or editorial sections with no change.

casual readers: Those who enjoy reading but find the time to read only a few books a year.

categorical imperative: The ethical guideline to look for principles that will hold true in all situations.

catharsis theory: The idea that viewing violence actually reduces violent behavior.

censorship: Any action that prohibits an act of expression from being made public.

centrist bias: Failure of the news media to report on radical points of view.

chain: One company that owns the same type of company in more than one market area.

change of venue: The moving of a trial to a different location.

channel: A spot on the electromagnetic spectrum that the FCC licenses to a specific station.

channel allocation: The placement of assigned spots on the electromagnetic spectrum to individual broadcast stations.

chapbook: Inexpensive early form of paperback containing mostly stories to be read for pleasure.

chat: An application that allows Internet users to be part of live, real-time text conversations.

checkbook journalism: Paying news sources for their stories.

Chicano press: Part of Hispanic American newspaper industry that targets Mexican Americans.

cinematographer: The director of photography.

circulation department: (1) The division of a magazine company charged with finding and keeping subscribers, managing the subscriber list, and promoting single-copy sales. (2) The division of a print media company that manages distribution and sales.

circulation waste: That part of advertising received by people whom the advertiser has no interest in reaching.

citizens' groups: Associations made up of members of the public to exert influence, such as on the media.

civil law: Law that considers disputes between private parties.

clippings services: Businesses that collect newspaper articles of interest to a client.

clutter: The glut of ads that compete for the public's attention.

codex: A book written on parchment pages that were cut and bound on one side. Developed by the Romans in the first century AD, the codex was the first book to resemble today's familiar form.

colorizing: Adding color to black-and-white films.

commentaries: On-air discussions about the news.

commercial speech: Advertising.

common law: Precedents based on judges' rulings.

communication The process of human beings sharing messages.

community antenna television (CATV): The first cable television systems, designed to give viewers in hard-to-reach areas satisfactory reception from their nearest broadcast television stations.

community relations: Public relations activities designed to aid and to maintain a beneficial image with groups on the local, national, or global level.

compact discs (CDs): Plastic discs with digitally encoded music read by lasers.

complementary copy: Editorial material designed to be paired with nearby advertising.

conflict of interest: Clash that occurs when an outside activity influences what a media professional does.

conglomerates: Large companies that own many different types of businesses.

conservative bias: A point of view that is generally purported to be pro-big business, anti-big government, profamily, proreligion, and pro-Republican.

constitutional law: Basic laws of a country or state.

consumer advertising: Ads directed to the retail customer.

consumer magazine: Any magazine that advertises and reports on consumer products and the consumer lifestyle.

contempt: Willful disobedience of the rules of a court or legislative body.

content analysis: A research method in which observers systematically analyze media subject matter.

continuance: Postponement of a trial.

continuity supervisor: Film crew member in charge of making sure shots match up; sometimes called the script supervisor.

contributing editor: Title given to a magazine's highest-paid freelance writers, who sometimes polish others' work.

controlled circulation: A system of distribution in which magazines are sent free to desired readers.

convergence: The merging of technologies, industries, and content, especially within the realms of computer, telephone, and mass media.

copy editor: An editor who polishes a manuscript line by line and prepares it for typesetting.

copy research: Studies that test the effectiveness of ad content, or copy.

copyright: A legal right that grants to the owner of a work protection against unauthorized copying.

copyright law: Law that entitles the owner of a work to make and distribute reproductions of it.

corporate aid: Community relations activity in which a company helps society on a large scale.

Corporation for Public Broadcasting (CPB): The government entity whose main responsibility is to act as a buffer between the government and PBS so that there could be no political interference in programming decisions.

corrective ads: Ads designed to rectify an inaccurate impression.

correlation: A situation in which two things occur at the same time, or in close succession, more often than chance would lead you to expect.

counteradvertising: Ads designed to fight an image that is not in the public interest.

CPM: Cost per thousand; guideline for the price of each exposure of a customer to an ad.

credibility gap: The difference between what a government says and what the public believes to be true.

creeping bias: A subtle form of slanting that manifests itself in understated ways.

criminal law: Public law that deals with crimes and their prosecution.

crisis management: Public relations activity used to repair a client's public image following an emergency.

cross-merchandizing: Promoting a product in one form to sell it in some other form.

cultivation theory: Theory that the media shape how people view the world.

cultural imperialism: The displacement of a nation's customs with those of another country.

cultural studies: Research based on careful observation and thought rather than on controlled experiments or statistics.

cumulative effects theory: Theory that media have profound effects over time through redundancy.

cyber-: As a prefix, a metaphor for anything pertaining to the Internet.

cybersquatting: The practice of registering trademarked domain names with hopes of reselling them to those who own the trademarks.

D

dayparts: Time divisions that radio stations make in the day in order to schedule appropriate programming.

defamation: Communication that is false and injures a reputation.

demographic editions: Slightly different versions of the same magazine that go out to subscribers with different characteristics.

demographics: Measurements of audience characteristics that are easily observed and labeled, such as age, gender, income, occupation, and ethnicity.

demos: Demonstration recordings sent in to record companies by artists' agents, managers, or by the artists themselves.

deregulation: The repeal of government rules and regulations.

desensitization: A process by which viewers of media violence develop callousness or emotional neutrality in the face of a real-life act of violence.

desktop publishing: Using a personal computer to act as editor, publisher, and writer.

developmental editor: An editor who works directly with the author during the writing of a book, going over each chapter and suggesting major revisions.

diffusion of innovations theory: Theory that different types of people will adopt new ideas at different times.

digital radio: Signal transmissions by assigned numbers rather than analog waves.

digital recording: A recording technique in which sound is broken down electronically into a numerical code.

digital video recorders (DVRs): Specialized computers with oversized hard disks on which video signals are saved.

dime novels: Inexpensive fiction, popular in the 1860s, that sold for 10 cents; also called pulp novels.

direct broadcast satellite (DBS): Systems that deliver television programming to individual homes via satellite.

direct mail advertising: Advertising sent by mail.

director's cut: Version of film the director delivers to the studio.

directory: A type of search engine in which sites are arranged into categories by human editors.

display ads: Print ads that include artwork and fancy typefaces to capture the reader's attention.

distance learning: Taking classes away from a school facility, especially online.

docudramas: Fictional movies that dramatize real-life events.

documentary: A long-form filmed examination of a social problem or historical subject.

domain: The portion of an Internet address that identifies the network that handles the account.

E

e-books: Books that exist as digital files.

economies of scale: Savings that accrue with mass production.

editorial page: Section of newspaper reserved for opinion pieces.

electromagnetic spectrum: The range of frequencies that can be used for transmitting radio waves with electricity.

electronic news gathering (ENG): Reporting that uses portable field equipment.

elite stage (of media development): Phase of media evolution in which only the richest and best-educated members of the population make use of a particular medium.

embedded journalists: Nonmilitary reporters attached to a military unit.

enlightened self-interest: Theory that holds that doing what is right for yourself will probably be right for others.

entrepreneur: An individual who invests the time and money to start a new business.

ethical codes: Lists of guidelines issued by professional associations.

ethics: The study of guidelines that help people determine right from wrong in their voluntary conduct.

ethnic press: That part of the newspaper industry aimed at particular cultural groups.

exclusive: A story granted to just one news outlet.

executive producer: The person who finds the financing for a film and puts the package together.

external publics: Public relations term for groups outside the client organization.

F

fair comment: Defense against a charge of libel based on opinion or criticism.

fair use: Doctrine that allows the copying of a work for a noncommercial use.

feature news: Stories directed toward human interest and curiosity; also known as soft news.

feature syndicates: Brokers for newspaper entertainment and specialty items.

Federal Communications Commission (FCC): Government agency in charge of regulating all means of interstate telephone and radio communication.

Federalist Papers: Essays that explained the new federal government to early Americans; published in 1788 as *The Federalist*.

feedback: Messages that return from the receiver of a message to the source of that message.

firewall: A program that prevents unauthorized access to a computer or network.

First Amendment: The part of the U.S. Constitution's Bill of Rights that guarantees freedom of speech.

first-sale doctrine: The doctrine that allows purchasers of a copyrighted work to resell it or rent it out.

flacks: Derogatory term for public relations professionals.

flaming: Sending vicious personal attacks over the Internet.

flow theories: Explanations of the way effects travel from the mass media to their audiences.

focus groups: Small groups of potential consumers observed by a researcher.

format: Consistent programming formula with a recognizable sound and personality.

format clock: Graphic used by radio programmers showing each feature of the programming hour.

format wars: Rivalries in which companies selling specific types of recording and playback devices try to put competing companies with competing formats out of business.

fourth estate: The press as an unofficial fourth branch of government.

freebies: Anything given away by public relations practitioners to promote a favorable relationship with media gatekeepers.

frequency modulation (FM): Radio transmissions created by changing (modulating) the speed (frequency) at which sound waves are generated.

full-service agencies: Ad agencies that supply all advertising and marketing services.

G

gaffer: Lighting director.

gag order: Judicial command not to speak about trial proceedings.

gatekeepers: Those who determine which messages will be delivered to media consumers.

gender studies: Research that looks at how the media deal with male and female roles.

general assignment reporters: Journalists who can find and write stories in any area.

genre: Type of writing, such as romance or mystery.

geostationary: A term describing the placement of satellites so that they orbit the earth at the same speed that the earth rotates, effectively parking the satellites in one spot.

global village: Marshall McLuhan's idea that modern communications technologies will bring together people of different cultures.

golden mean: Aristotle's term for describing ethical behavior as a midpoint between extremes.

gramophone: Early playback device using a flat disc with lateral grooves cut on one side.

graphical user interface (GUI): A set of browser features such as icons and hot spots that allow users to navigate Web sites easily.

greenwashing: The public relations practice of covering up environmental problems by associating a client with beneficial environmental actions.

group ownership: The acquisition of the same type of business in more than one market area by one company.

guerrilla advertising: Advertising that uses unorthodox tactics.

H

hacker: One who uses programming skills to gain illegal access to computer networks or files.

handbills: Announcements on single sheets of paper.

hard news: Stories about current events that have impact on people's lives.

high-definition television (HDTV): Digital technology for transmitting television programs using more than double the standard number of scanning lines, creating a clearer, larger picture.

high-fidelity (hi-fi) sound: Recorded sound true to the original.

hip-hop: The backing music for rap; also refers to the culture of rap.

hoaxes: Purposeful deceptions of the public.

horizontal integration: Corporate growth through the acquisition of different types of businesses.

hosts: Internet computers that contain actual Web sites.

hybrid search engines: Search engines that use both robots and human editors.

hype: Dramatic publicity techniques.

hypertext fiction: Interactive stories that allow the reader to change the plot as the narrative is read.

hypertext links (hyperlinks): Highlighted words and images within a Web page that allow the user to move to another site by pointing and clicking a mouse button.

hypertext markup language (HTML): The basic computer language used to write hypertext transfer protocol (http).

hypertext transfer protocol (http): The protocol that enables computers to recognize links on the World Wide Web.

I

illiterates: Those who can't read because they never learned how.

image advertising: The promotion of an idea that becomes associated with a product.

importation: In cable television, the bringing in of additional signals from distant stations.

indecency: Offensive content with possible social value.

independent bookstores: Booksellers not owned by a chain and not part of a larger company.

independent films: Movies that are not made by one of the major studios.

independent label: Any recording industry company not owned by one of the major labels.

individual differences theory: Theory that predicts that people with different characteristics will be affected in different ways by the mass media.

infomercials: Program-length television commercials.

in-house agencies: Organizations built into a corporate structure.

institutional ads: Trade group image promotions for entire industries.

integrated marketing: Public relations and advertising working together.

internal publics: Public relations term for groups inside the client organization.

inverted pyramid: News style that packs the most important information into the first paragraph.

investigative journalism: Reporting that uncovers information that sources have tried to conceal.

J

Java: An advanced programming language used for animated images and advanced sound applications.

jazz journalism: Style of news presentation of the 1920s that paralleled the music of the era.

joint operating agreements: Business arrangements that allow two competing newspapers to share facilities.

jukebox: A coin-operated phonograph.

K

key grip: Member of film crew who sets up and moves cameras.

kinescopes: Poor-quality films taken directly from television monitors in the network studios; they were forerunners of videotapes.

kinetograph: Early motion picture camera invented by Thomas Edison.

kinetoscope: Early motion picture projector invented by Thomas Edison.

knowledge workers: Employees such as journalists, library professionals, and business analysts who use the Internet for research as part of their jobs.

L

laboratory experiment: Scientific method of isolating and observing variables in a controlled environment.

leaks: Unauthorized disclosures to the press.

libel: Published or broadcast defamation.

liberal bias: Point of view that is generally purported to be anti–big business, pro–big government, antifamily, antireligion, and anti-Republican.

line producers: People who lead the actual day-to-day work of making a film.

lines of resolution: Rows of lighted dots, or pixels, that make up a television picture image.

linking services: Online sites that connect the user to news sites.

list servers: Online discussion groups in which all messages are sent out to each member's e-mail address; also known as mailing lists, Listservs, or e-groups.

little magazines: Industry term for literary magazines with small circulations.

lobbying: Any attempt to influence the voting of legislators.

lurking: Reading newsgroup messages without responding.

lyricist: A professional who specializes in writing the words of a song.

M

Machiavellian ethics: The idea that the end justifies the means.

magazine: A collection of reading matter, issued regularly.

market: All the surrounding areas from which business tends to flow to a central point, usually a major city.

mass communication: Mediated messages transmitted to large, widespread audiences.

massively multiplayer online role-playing games (MMORPGs): Games such as EverQuest that allow many players to join in over the Internet.

media: Plural of *medium*.

media buyers: Advertising agency personnel who purchase ad time and space.

media circus: Chaos that results when crowds of journalists descend on the scene of a news event.

media criticism: The analysis used to assess the effects of media on individuals, on societies, and on cultures.

media ecology: School of cultural study that suggests that media make up an ecological system for humans.

media literacy: The ability to understand and make productive use of the media.

media relations: The practice of developing and maintaining contact with media gatekeepers; also called press relations.

mediated communication: Messages conveyed through an interposed device rather than face-to-face.

mediated interpersonal communication: The sharing of personal messages through an interposed device.

medium: An interposed device used to transmit messages.

megastores: Large bookstores that feature around 100,000 book titles and offer various amenities such as coffee bars and live readings.

mercantile press: Newspapers that provided news of business and shipping.

metacrawler: A type of search engine that combines results from a number of other search engines.

midlist authors: Authors who don't make it to the best-seller lists but still have respectable sales.

minimal-effects model: Model that predicts that media will have little influence on behavior.

mission statement: A brief explanation of how the magazine will be unique and what will make it successful.

mixed-effects model: Model that predicts that media can have a combination of influences.

moblogging: Posting photos from a cell phone directly onto the Web.

modeling: The imitation of behavior from media.

monopoly: An economic situation in which one company dominates an entire industry.

Morse code: Telegraph code of dots and dashes invented by Samuel Morse.

Motion Picture Patents Company: Company founded by Thomas Edison to control the movie equipment business; known as the Trust.

Moviola: Simple editing machine made up of two reels on which film is spooled over a small light.

MP3: The name for compressed digital audio files that enable music to be downloaded from the Internet.

muckraking: Investigative journalism conducted with the goal of bringing about social reform.

multiple system operators (MSOs): Companies that own several local cable service providers, usually in different areas of the country.

multistep flow: A complex interaction of media effects.

must-carry rules: FCC regulations that require cable systems to carry all local television stations within the system's area of coverage.

N

netiquette: A form of etiquette, or rules of acceptable behavior, for the Internet.

network: (1) A group of interconnected broadcast stations that share programming. (2) The parent company that supplies that programming. (3) Interconnected computers. (4) To make industry contacts for possible employment.

network affiliate: A local station that has a contractual relationship to show a network's programming.

network engineers: The people who design and build the systems that make up the Internet.

network managers: Those who provide the day-to-day maintenance of local systems and intranets.

news: The presentation of information that is timely, important, and interesting to its audience.

news councils: Independent agencies whose mission is to objectively monitor media performance.

news hole: Total amount of space in a newspaper that can be devoted to editorial content versus advertising.

news hook: The angle or approach that makes information newsworthy.

news on demand: Current information that users can access whenever they want it.

news ticker: Scrolling headlines on a screen.

news values: Characteristics that define news, including timeliness, importance, and interest.

newsgroups: Online bulletin boards, organized according to topic.

newsprint: Inexpensive paper used for newspapers.

newsreels: Short films covering current events that were shown in theaters before the advent of television.

nickelodeons: (1) Small early movie theaters. (2) Early jukeboxes set up in amusement arcades.

noise: Anything that interferes with the communication process.

O

objectivity: Writing style that separates fact from opinion; description according to the characteristics of the thing being described rather than the feelings of the one describing it.

off-network programs: Syndicated programs that were shown earlier on one of the television networks and are now begin licensed on a station-by-station basis.

oligopoly: An economic situation in which a small number of companies dominate an industry.

ombudsperson: Staff member whose job it is to oversee media employees' ethical behavior.

on spec: On speculation; in the publishing industry, finishing a work without a contract guaranteeing that it will be bought.

op-ed page: The section of the newspaper "opposite the editorial page" reserved for signed columns, opinion pieces, and guest editorials.

opinion leaders: Well-informed people who help others interpret media messages.

oral culture: A culture in which information is transmitted more by speech than writing.

organizational papers: Newspapers published as part of an organization's communication with members.

original syndication: The station-by-station licensing of new television programs that were not earlier shown on a network.

owned and operated stations (O&Os): Broadcast stations possessed by and run by the network; they usually carry everything the network provides.

P

paid circulation magazines: Magazines for which readers actually pay subscription fees and newsstand charges.

papyrus: A type of reed used to make an early form of paper.

parchment: An early form of paper made from animal skins.

parity statement: An assertion of equality that sounds like an assertion of superiority.

partisan press: Newspapers owned or supported by political parties.

pass-along circulation: Readership beyond the original purchaser of a publication.

patent: An exclusive right granted an inventor to manufacture, use, or sell an invention.

payola: A practice in which record companies paid radio station personnel to play certain records.

pay-per-view channels: Systems that allow cable TV subscribers to order recent feature films, sporting events, concerts, and other special events when scheduled.

peep shows: Amusement parlor boxes containing moving rolls of still pictures.

peg: An angle, or perspective, that makes information interesting to the audience.

penny press: Inexpensive, advertiser-supported newspapers that appeared in the 1830s.

periodical: Term for magazines based on the idea of their regular interval of publication.

persistence of vision: An aspect of human vision in which the brain retains images for a fraction of a second after they leave the field of sight; this allows for the illusion of movement from a series of still pictures.

personalized news services: News services that collect only information identified as being of interest to a client.

phonograph: Thomas Edison's name for his first recording device. Originally a trademark, the name eventually became generic for all home record players.

photo-offset printing: Technique in which a photo negative transfers ink onto paper.

pirate radio stations: Low-power, unlicensed, illegal stations.

pirating: The illegal copying and selling of movies.

pitching accounts: Presenting new ideas for ad campaigns to a prospective client.

pixels: Lighted dots that create a television picture image.

political speech: Messages about the meaning and correct course of government.

political/economic analysis: Theory that predicts that a culture's exchange system will influence its values.

pool cameras: One camera crew shared by several TV news organizations.

popular stage (of media development): Phase of media evolution in which a truly mass audience takes advantage of a particular medium.

portals: Sites from which people begin their Web surfing; they act as gateways to the rest of the Internet.

positioning: The process of finding specific customer types and creating advertising appeals for them.

postproduction: The final phase of moviemaking, which includes editing and other technical improvements to the film.

powerful-effects model: Model that predicts that media will have swift and potent influence.

premium cable channels: Cable channels that provide programming to subscribers for an additional fee, over and above their basic cable subscription fee; sometimes called pay cable.

preproduction: The planning phase of moviemaking.

prescriptive codes: Guidelines that stipulate specific behaviors to be followed.

press agents: People who work to generate publicity for a client.

press kit: A collection of publicity items given out to media gatekeepers.

press release: Brief document containing the information needed to write a news story; also called a news release.

prior restraint: Prevention of publication by the government.

privilege: Exemption given public officials to speak without fear of being sued for libel.

producer: In the music industry, the person who oversees the making of a master recording.

product placement: The inclusion of a product in a movie as a form of paid advertising.

production: The actual shooting phase of moviemaking.

professional journals: Periodicals that doctors, lawyers, engineers, and other occupational groups rely on for information in their fields.

program syndication: The sale of programs directly to stations or cable channels.

propaganda: Information that is spread for the purpose of promoting a doctrine or cause.

proscriptive codes: Guidelines that stress the things that should not be done.

protocols: Software codes that enable one computer to communicate with another.

pseudo events: Happenings that would not have occurred if media were not there to record them.

psychographics: Measurements of audience characteristics that are difficult to observe and label, such as the psychological (and sometimes hidden) dimensions of attitudes, beliefs, values, interests, and motivations.

Public Broadcasting Service (PBS): Government-sponsored association of public television stations designed to facilitate the sharing of programs.

public domain: The category of creative works on which the copyright has expired.

"public interest, convenience, and necessity": A phrase from the Radio Act of 1927 requiring that broadcasting be good for the community.

public journalism: Reporting that becomes involved in, rather than just covers, community issues.

public radio: Broadcast outlets that derive their income from sources other than the sale of advertising time; also known as noncommercial.

public relations: All the activities that maintain a beneficial relationship between an organization and its various publics.

public relations magazines: Magazines produced with the objective of making their parent organizations look good.

public service announcements (PSAs): Ads on public interest issues presented as a service to the community.

publicity stunt: Any action designed to create a human interest story; many are outlandish or outrageous.

publisher: In print industries, the person who runs an individual company and acts as its chief representative.

puffery: Exaggeration in advertising claims.

pulp novels: Paperback books printed on cheap paper made from wood pulp; another name for dime novels.

pulps: Magazines produced on cheap paper with a low cultural reach, such as *True Romance* and *True Confessions*.

R

rag content: Proportion of cotton or linen fiber in high-quality paper.

ragtime: Instrumental music with a steady, syncopated beat.

random sampling: Method that ensures that every member of the population being studied has an equal chance of being chosen.

rap: Music composed of rhymed speech over drumbeats.

rating: The percentage of all homes equipped with radios or televisions that are tuned to a particular station at a particular time.

regional editions: Slightly different versions of the same magazine produced for different geographic areas.

relativistic ethics: Another name for situation ethics.

reporting stations: The radio stations whose playlists are tracked weekly to determine airplay popularity for individual songs.

required readers: Those who read only what they have to for their job or studies.

residual news: Stories about events that are recurrent or long-lasting.

royalties: The author's share of the net amount of a work's revenues.

S

sampling: Measurements taken from a small percentage of the audience, chosen to represent the behavior of the rest of the audience; broadcast ratings are a form of sampling.

satellite news gathering (SNG): Reporting the news with equipment that enables transmission via satellite.

second unit directors: Movie directors in charge of shooting the scenes that do not require the stars.

seditious libel laws: Laws established in colonial America that made it illegal to criticize government or its representatives.

selective exposure: Process by which people seek out messages that are consistent with their attitudes.

selective perception: Process by which people with different attitudes interpret the same messages differently.

selective retention: Process by which people with different views remember the same event differently.

sensationalism: Use of exaggeration and lurid elements to produce a startling effect.

sequestering: Isolating members of a jury.

share: The percentage of homes in which the radio or television is in use and tuned to a particular station.

shield laws: Laws designed to ensure confidentiality of news sources.

shock jocks: Radio personalities who derive humor and ratings from lewd and tasteless comments, using tactics such as vulgarity, racism, sexism, and cynicism.

shoppers: Free-distribution newspapers consisting mostly of ads.

short wave: Long-distance radio broadcast band.

situation ethics: Principle that ethical choices can be made according to the situation, without a rigid adherence to set rules.

slander: Defamation that occurs in a transitory form, such as speech.

small press: A publisher with few employees and minimal facilities. Many small presses try to publish serious books, especially poetry and avant-garde fiction.

smart mobs: Crowds formed in response to cell phone postings.

social learning theory: Theory that people learn by observing others.

socialization: Process by which children learn the expectations, norms, and values of society.

sound bites: Short, carefully crafted statements designed to be picked up in news reports.

Soundscan: A point-of-sale computer system that determines sales for best-selling records lists.

spam: Unsolicited e-mail messages.

special interest magazines: Magazines aimed at specific readers with specific concerns and tastes.

specialized stage (of media development): Phase of media evolution in which a particular medium tends to break up into segments for audience members with diverse and specialized interests.

spectrum scarcity: Limited nature of broadcast frequencies.

split-run editions: Slightly different versions of the same magazine, as in demographic and regional editions.

sponsored magazines: Magazines published by associations, such as *National Geographic*.

spyware: Programs that track Internet users' activities and report them back to advertisers.

standards and practices departments: Departments at television networks that oversee the ethics of their programming.

statutory law: Collection of laws, or statues, written by legislative bodies, such as the U.S. Congress.

stereophonic sound: Recording technique in which tracks are placed individually in the right or left speaker.

stereotyping: Representing a member of a group by using oversimplified characteristics.

stringers: Independent journalists who are paid only for material used.

strip programming: A system of showing a program in the same time period five times a week.

stunt journalism: Reporting that includes a spectacular exploit to gain publicity for the story.

subliminal advertising: Promotional messages that the consumer is not consciously aware of.

subscription fulfillment companies: Businesses that specialize in soliciting magazine subscriptions.

sunshine laws: Laws that ensure that public meetings are conducted in the open.

superstation: A local station whose signal is delivered to cable systems via satellite.

survey methods: Research methods that rely on questionnaires to collect research data.

sustaining programming: Regular unsponsored broadcast shows designed to maintain audience contact until advertising can be sold for that time.

sweeps months: Those months in which local stations use the ratings to set their basic advertising rates for the next three-month period—currently, November, February, May, and July.

syndication: The process of selling media content to individual outlets.

synergy: A combination in which the whole is more than the sum of its parts.

T

tabloids: Newspapers characterized by a smaller size than a standard newspaper, a single fold, and abundant photographs.

target marketing: The process of breaking up the advertising audience into diverse segments to reach those individuals most likely to purchase a particular product.

technological determinism: Theory that states that the introduction of new technology changes society, sometimes in unexpected ways.

teleconference: A news conference in which newsmakers and reporters in various locations are joined by a satellite or an Internet hookup; also called a videoconference or a satellite media tour (SMT).

theory: A set of related statements that seek to explain and predict behavior.

thread: A connected series of messages in newsgroup or online discussion group postings.

tie-ins: Consumer products built around movie characters.

time shifting: Recording of a television program for playback at some later time.

Tin Pan Alley: District in New York City where songs were written "on order" for Broadway shows.

toll broadcasting: Early plan for radio revenue in which access to radio time would be by fee.

Top 40: Radio format in which the current 40 best-selling songs are played in rotation.

track: A single recorded sound source, used in multitrack recording.

trade advertising: Business-to-business promotions.

trade books: Fiction and nonfiction books sold to the general public.

trade cards: Illustrated cards with a business message on one side and artwork on the other.

trade magazines: Magazines that focus on a particular business and are usually essential reading for people in that business.

trade paperback: A quality paperback book with a larger trim size than the standard mass-market paperback.

trademark: A word, symbol, or device that identifies a seller's goods.

trailers: Brief previews of coming movies shown in theaters.

transistor: A durable, solid-state, miniature version of the large and fragile vacuum tubes used in early radios.

trial balloons: Leaks in which the source reveals that some action is being considered, in order to test public feeling about the action before going ahead with it.

turnkey networks: Companies that provide fully automated around-the-clock programming for radio stations.

tweeters: Small speakers that reproduce high sounds.

two-source rule: Common newspaper rule stating that nothing should be published as fact unless at least two sources confirm it.

two-step flow: Communication process in which media effects travel through opinion leaders.

U

ultra high frequency (UHF): Term used to describe stations transmitting on channels 14 and up.

underground press: Alternative newspapers of the 1960s and 1970s that passionately criticized cultural and political norms.

uniform resource locator (URL): An Internet address that connects the user to a Web site on a particular computer.

university press: A publisher that is affiliated with an institution of higher education and that publishes mostly academic books, especially original research by college professors.

Usenet: An application used to support newsgroups on the Internet.

user ID: The first part of an e-mail address.

uses and gratifications theory: Theory that looks at the ways media consumers choose media to meet their needs.

utilitarian principle: John Stuart Mill's idea that actions are ethical only if they result in the greatest good for the most people.

V

vanity press: A publisher that requires its authors to pay the full cost of producing their own books.

V-chip: An electronic device that can be set to recognize and block programs with a particular rating.

veil of ignorance: John Rawls's term associated with the idea that ethical behavior is possible only if everyone is treated equally.

vertical integration: A business model in which a company owns different parts of the same industry.

very high frequency (VHF): Term used to describe television stations that operate on channels 2 through 13.

Victrola: Early hand-cranked record player introduced by the Victor Company.

video news release (VNR): A ready-to-broadcast videotape designed for use in television news.

video on demand (VOD): Services that allow subscribers to order recent feature films, sporting events, concerts, news items, and special events at any time; television clips that users can access whenever they want to.

videocassette recorder (VCR): An improvement on the videotape recorder (VTR) that uses cassette tapes instead of reels.

videotape recorder (VTR): A device for recording sounds and images on reels of magnetic tape.

videotext: An experimental system for delivering electronic newspapers to homes via television sets.

virus: A program designed specifically to damage other software, and to propagate itself to other computers.

W

weblogs: Online journals or diaries; called blogs for short.

webmasters: Those who maintain either content or systems for large Web sites.

webzines: Magazines that appear only on the Internet, such as *Slate* and *Salon;* also called e-zines.

whitewashing: The practice of using public relations messages to cover up problems without correcting them.

wireless telegraphy: Name for early radio transmissions, before human voices could be carried on the airwaves.

woofers: Large speakers that reproduce low sounds.

World Wide Web: A simplified means of navigating the Internet based on hypertext links and graphical user interfaces.

Y

yellow journalism: A style of reporting characterized by unprecedented sensationalism; it reached its peak in the Hearst–Pulitzer circulation wars of the 1890s.

Z

zapping: Avoiding commercials by using the Pause button while videotaping or by fast-forwarding through them during playback.

zines: Low-cost self-published magazines put out by fans on a variety of topics; also called fanzines.

Complete Timeline of Mass Media Milestones

Chapter references 1 2 3 4 5 6 7 8 9 10 11 12 13 14 15

1400s

1456 In Germany, Johannes Gutenberg's printing press sets in motion a revolution in the way people communicate. Gutenberg's version of the Bible becomes the first book printed with movable metal type. 1 3

1500s

1530s The first press in the Americas is set up in Mexico City. 3

1600s

1638 The first press in the English colonies is set up at Harvard College. 3

1642 Massachusetts becomes the first colony to pass a law requiring that every child be taught to read. 3

1644 *Areopagitica*, written by John Milton, advances a religious argument for freedom of speech. 14

1663 *Edifying Monthly Discussions*, the first magazine, is published in Germany. 5

1690 Benjamin Harris's unlicensed *Publick Occurrences*, the first newspaper in America, angers the royal government and is shut down by the government after one issue. 1 4 14

1700s

1735 The trial and exoneration of John Peter Zenger establishes that colonists believe that newspapers should be allowed to print the truth about government. 4 14

1741 The first two American magazines are published: Andrew Bradford's *American Magazine* and Benjamin Franklin's *General Magazine*. 1 5

1773 The Boston Tea Party proves that American patriots know the value

of a well-staged public relations event. 12

1791 The First Amendment is ratified. More than any other event, this symbolized the U.S. government's commitment to free speech and created controversies about media freedom that continue to this day. 1 4 14

1800s

1827 The first black newspaper, *Freedom's Journal*, is published. 4

1828 Andrew Jackson becomes the first U.S. president elected with the help of a sophisticated public relations campaign. 12

1830s The Industrial Revolution begins in the United States, bringing with it urbanization and modernization, both of which created the need for new and different media. 1

1833 The penny press era begins with the establishment of Benjamin Day's *New York Sun*, establishing advertising as the primary support for newspapers. 4 13

1830s The penny newspapers' quest for large audiences leads to excesses such as hoaxes. 15

1841 Palmer Volney sets up shop as the first ad broker, relieving newspapers of some of the burden of finding and servicing advertising accounts. 13

1848 The Associated Press of New York becomes the first wire service. Wire services encourage the standard of objectivity because stories have to be written for all types of newspapers in a variety of locations. 1 4

1851 Harriet Beecher Stowe's *Uncle Tom's Cabin* becomes America's first national best seller and brings the realities of slavery to the attention of the American people. 3

1869 The first modern ad agency, N. W. Ayer & Son, is founded, dedicated to serving the client rather than the newspaper or magazine. 13

1872 Eadweard Muybridge's first successful photography of motion suggests the potential of motion pictures. 6

1873 The Comstock Law is passed, making a wide variety of immoral communication illegal. 🄔

1877 Thomas Edison first records the human voice. His phonograph sets in motion an industry that will revolutionize home entertainment. ❶ ❼

1878 E. W. Scripps begins the first modern newspaper chain, proving the economic benefits of the concentration of media ownership. ❹

1879 The Postal Act lowers postage for magazines, making it possible to distribute them through the mail. ❺

1880s The Linotype machine allows type to be set automatically. ❸

1883 *The Ladies' Home Journal* is founded. It will revolutionize the field of women's magazines. ❺

1889 Edison patents the first practical motion picture projector, leading to the huge international success of the silent film industry. ❶

1889 Discs and cylinders for recordings both become best sellers, setting off the first format war. ❼

1894 Edison's kinetoscope parlor opens for business in New York City, proving the popular appeal of the technology of motion pictures. ❻

1895 Newspaper circulation wars lead to sensational tactics of the yellow press. 🄕

1896 Guglielmo Marconi patents radio technology, moving electronics from "wired" to "wireless." ❶ ❽

1898 The Hearst–Pulitzer circulation war and yellow journalism reach their peaks during the Spanish–American War. ❹

1900s

1900 The first publicity agency, the Boston Publicity Bureau, is formed, establishing press agentry as a separate business enterprise. 🄒

1902 Ida Tarbell's series on Standard Oil in *McClure's Magazine* comes to symbolize the era of muckraking. ❺

The Ladies' Home Journal

1903 Edwin Porter directs *The Great Train Robbery,* the first movie to use editing techniques to tell a story. ❻

1906 Reginald Fessenden makes the first wireless voice transmission, which frees radio from the Morse code limitations of the telegraph. ❽

1906 The Victor Talking Machine Company sells the first Victrola, a popular record player designed as living room furniture. ❼

1906 The Pure Food and Drug Act is passed, largely as a reaction to false patent medicine claims. Such advertising would now be government regulated. 🄓

1906 The public relations profession is born when Ivy Ledbetter Lee is hired by the coal industry during a strike. 🄒

1906 Theodore Roosevelt denounces muckrakers who "fix their eyes only on that which is vile and debasing." 🄕

1907 Lee De Forest invents the Audion, the vacuum tube that picks up and amplifies radio signals. ❽

1909 Charles Pathé presents the first newsreels in Paris. ⑪

1910s

1912 The first Radio Act, which requires the licensing of radio operators, establishes the government's role in regulating broadcast communications. ❽

1914 The Federal Trade Commission (FTC) is established as a national watchdog of business, increasing the government regulation of advertising. 🄓

1915 *The Birth of a Nation,* the first modern feature film, is released to a huge popular success in spite of its overt racism. ❻

1916 Lee De Forest, in experiments testing his Audion tube, "broadcasts" the results of the 1916 presidential election. ❽ ⑪

1917 The Committee on Public Information (CPI) promotes U.S. involvement in World War I, making public relations an official part of government. ⑫

1918 The "clear and present danger" test of free speech is enunciated by Supreme Court justice Oliver Wendell Holmes. ⑭

1919 Jazz journalism begins with the *New York Daily News,* the first tabloid. ④

1920s

1920 What is probably the first commercial radio station, KDKA, goes on the air in Pittsburgh. ⑧

1920 First commercial radio news report. ⑪

1922 *Reader's Digest* is founded. It becomes one of the few mass circulation, general interest magazines to survive to this day. ⑤

1922 The first radio ad establishes advertising as the source of funding for broadcast media. ⑬

1923 *Time,* the first newsmagazine, is founded. It becomes the cornerstone of Henry Luce's Time–Life empire. ⑤

1923 Edward Bernays coins the term *public relations counsel,* establishing the public relations professional as part of corporate management decision making. ⑫

1923 The Canons of Journalism, the first of the print media codes, calls for fair and accurate reporting. ⑮

1924 The American Association of Advertising Agencies publishes its code of ethics, establishing industry standards of acceptable practices. ⑬

1926 The first book club, the Book-of-the-Month Club, is started. It ushers in a new way of marketing books and affecting literary tastes. ③

1927 *The Jazz Singer* becomes the first talkie. ⑥

1927 The Radio Act decrees that broadcasters must operate in the "public interest, convenience, and necessity." ⑧

1927 The jukebox is introduced by the Automatic Music Instrument Co. (AMI). ⑦

1927 Television is invented. ⑨

1929 The Payne Fund Studies look at the effects of movies on youngsters, especially in terms of modeling behavior. ②

1929 The National Association of Broadcasters (NAB) Ethics Code, the first of the electronic media codes, is established. ⑮

1930s

1930 The Motion Picture Production Code is adopted, limiting the sex and violence that can be portrayed in movies. ⑮

1934 The Federal Communications Commission (FCC) is established in the Communications Act, which still governs electronic communication today. ⑧

1935 The Biltmore Agreement ends the press–radio war. ⑪

1936 Edwin Armstrong invents FM, improving radio sound quality considerably. ⑧

1937 The *Hindenburg* explosion coverage shocks and amazes radio audience. ⑪

1938 The *War of the Worlds* broadcast creates a panic and demonstrates the power of radio. ⑧

1938 The Invasion from Mars study finds that many audience members panicked during the *War of the Worlds* broadcast because of individual differences. ②

1939 Television of broadcast quality is demonstrated for the first time at the New York World's Fair by RCA. ① ⑨

1939 Mass-market paperbacks are introduced to the United States by Pocket Books of New York City. ③

1954 *Seduction of the Innocent*, an unscientific but influential study of the dangers of comic books, damages that industry. **2**

1957 Obscenity is defined according to contemporary community standards by the U.S. Supreme Court. **14**

1958 The first stereo LPs are sold. Their greater capacity and superior sound make them an essential part of the stereo and high-fidelity movement. **7**

1958 The television quiz show scandals shock America, leading to network control of ethical choices in programming. **15**

1960s

1961 Activist movements adopt public relations strategies, proving that those tactics can be effective in promoting social change. **12**

1961 Wilbur Schramm and his Stanford University colleagues publish *Television in the Lives of Our Children*, concluding that for some children, under some conditions, some television is harmful. **2**

1940s

1940 First network TV newscasts. **11**

1940 The People's Choice study establishes the importance of the two-step flow in which people are influenced by other people as well as the media. **2**

1940 The Smith Act is passed, making it illegal to advocate the violent overthrow of the U.S. government. **14**

1941–1945 Radio news coverage of WWII. **11**

1941 The first television ad, for Bulova watches, costs $9 to air but demonstrates the visual effectiveness of television ads. **13**

1941 Technical standards for television broadcasting are established by the U.S. government. Other countries will establish standards as well. **9**

1942 The Office of War Information (OWI) supports U.S. involvement in World War II, further establishing the government–public relations link. **12**

1944 The American Soldier studies refute the direct, powerful model of media effects. **2**

1947 The Public Relations Society of America (PRSA) is founded to encourage professional conduct in the industry. **12**

1948 The golden age of television begins. **9**

1948 The U.S. government forces studios to sell their theaters in a move against vertical integration. **1 6**

1949 Hollywood begins to produce programming for television. **6**

1950s

1953 The Public Relations Society of America adopts a code of standards that seeks to improve the industry's ethics. **14**

1953 The first national rock-and-roll hit, Bill Haley's "Crazy Man Crazy," is released, establishing the economic and cultural potential of this new musical genre. **7**

1954 The first transistor portable radios are introduced. **8**

1963 The Beatles reach stardom and influence the style of popular music, clothing, and even the acceptable length of male hair all over the world. ⑦

1963 Coverage of the Kennedy and Oswald assassinations show the power and the danger of our new obsession with live TV news coverage. ⑪

1964 Marshall McLuhan publishes *Understanding Media,* an influential work that states that when it comes to media effects, "the medium is the message." ②

1966 All the U.S. television networks begin broadcasting all prime-time programs in color. ⑨

1967 Public Television is established as an alternative to commercial programming. ⑨

1968 The Motion Picture Association of America Ratings System goes into effect. ⑥

1969 The first large-scale government study into the effects of television is conducted by the National Commission on the Causes and Prevention of Violence. ②

1969 The U.S. Department of Defense sets up a computer network, called the Advanced Research Project Agency Network (ARPANET), connecting university, military, and defense contractor computers. ⑩

1970s

1971 The Pentagon Papers case brings about the first instance of prior restraint of a major U.S. newspaper. ⑭

1972 *Life* magazine ceases publication as a weekly; the move is seen as the end of the era of mass circulation general interest magazines. ⑤

1972 The surgeon general's report on the effects of television violence is issued. The report will be updated in 1982 and 1996, confirming that under some circumstances, violent TV encourages violence in society. ②

1974 Reporting on the Watergate scandal by the *New York Times* and the *Washington Post* leads to the resignation of President Richard Nixon. ④

1975 Sony introduces the Betamax home videocassette recorder (VCR) over the objections of the movie industry, which fears that it will lose revenues because of home recording. ⑦

1976 Time, Inc., launches Home Box Office (HBO), the first premium cable service. ⑨

1976 George Gerbner and his colleagues publish "The Scary World of TV's Heavy Viewer" in *Psychology Today,* establishing that unrealistic TV violence makes heavy viewers see the world as more dangerous than it actually is. ②

1979 Civilian researchers who had been excluded from ARPANET invent Usenet, which features discussion groups. ⑩

1979 CompuServe, the first successful general interest online service, begins service. ⑩

1980s

1980 CNN is founded. ⑪

1980 Janet Cooke, a reporter for the *Washington Post,* is forced to return a Pulitzer Prize when it is discovered that she made up facts and characters. ⑮

1982 *USA Today,* established by the Gannett Corporation and distributed by satellite to local printing plants, becomes the first national newspaper. Several innovations, such as brief stories and colorful charts, influence other newspapers. ④

1982 Compact discs (CDs) are introduced to the market and soon become the prominent home music format. ⑦

1982 Public relations professionals prove that they can bring a company back from the brink of disaster when they restore public confidence in Tylenol following a sabotage poisoning crisis. ⑫

1983 The National Association of Broadcasters (NAB) Code for

television programming is dropped after the U.S. government declares it an antitrust violation. **15**

1984 The *New England Journal of Medicine* becomes the first periodical on the Internet. **5**

1989 The Fox Network, the first competition to ABC, CBS, and NBC since the beginning of the American television industry, is established. **9**

1989 America Online begins operation, with simple point-and-click software that quickly makes it the most popular online service. **10**

1990s

1990s Home users begin communicating via the Internet, a new medium that brings interpersonal messages together with mass communication as never before. **1**

1992 Studios begin to use digital editing and special effects. **6**

1993 The World Wide Web, invented by Tim Berners-Lee, becomes public, allowing users to access Web pages easily. **10**

1993 Marc Andreessen, a student at the University of Illinois at Urbana-Champaign, creates Mosaic, the first Web browser, which makes it easier for nontechnical people to navigate on the Internet. **10**

1994 The first Internet ads appear, allowing unprecedented targeting of diverse audiences. **13**

1994 Amazon.com goes online and becomes one of the most successful Internet businesses practically overnight. **3**

1995 Newspapers establish their presence on the World Wide Web. **4** **11**

1995 Dozens of magazines establish a presence on the World Wide Web. **5**

1995 *Toy Story* becomes the first feature film produced entirely on a computer. **6**

1995 Warner Bros.' WB Network and Viacom's UPN start up, mostly to ensure these corporations that their production studios will have network customers in the future. **9**

1995 The Internet is turned over to the public sector, partly because there are so many civilians on it that it can no longer be used for national security purposes. **10**

1996 The first major convergence of the television and Internet industries is launched. **9**

1996 The Telecommunications Act of 1996 removes many of the restrictions on a wide range of communications industries, allowing cable television, long-distance telephone carriers, local telephone companies, information services, and Internet service providers to merge at will. It also removes most of the restrictions in radio and television station ownership, encouraging consolidation in the industry. **8** **14**

1997 MP3 files become available for downloading music from the Internet. This is seen as both a major threat and a potential benefit for the industry, depending on whether or not record companies will be paid for the music that is distributed this way. **7**

1998 A jury in North Carolina levies $5.5 million in punitive damages against ABC for deceptive tactics in investigating the Food Lion supermarket chain. **15**

1998 HDTV broadcasting officially begins, although few viewers have sets capable of receiving the new digital signals. **9**

1998 West Coast rapper/producer Dr. Dre discovers Marshall Mathers III, also known as Eminem. **7**

1998 The first Harry Potter book, *Harry Potter and the Sorcerer's Stone*, goes on sale in the United States and becomes a huge hit with young readers. **3**

1998 The Drudge Report breaks the Clinton–Lewinsky scandal online. **11**

1998 Kenneth Starr's Office of the Special Prosecutor releases its report on the Clinton–Lewinsky affair over the Internet. Within 48 hours, 25 million people access it, establishing the Internet as a true mass medium. **10**

1998 *Will and Grace*, a sitcom about a gay man and a straight woman who are roommates, premieres on NBC. Its popularity leads the way for a crop of new shows with gay lead characters. **9**

1998 Congress passes the Digital Millennium Copyright Act, making it a crime to break through any technology intended to secure digital copies of software, literary works, videos, and music.⑭

1999 *The Blair Witch Project,* which cost $30,000 to make, earns $140 million at the box office, largely because of Web-based promotion.⑥

1999 *Star Wars: The Phantom Menace* becomes the first Hollywood movie to be digitally distributed to theaters.⑥

1999 A school shooting in Littleton, Colorado, leaves 15 people dead. Extensive media coverage includes speculation that the murderers were influenced by video games and other violent media.②

1999 A settlement between tobacco companies and state attorneys general bans most forms of youth-oriented advertising of tobacco products throughout United States.⑬

1999 College student Shawn Fanning develops Napster, the first successful, free file-sharing program for exchanging music on the Internet. It is later closed down as illegal.⑦

1999 TiVo and Replay TV, the first two digital video recorders, are introduced.⑦

2000s

2000s The success of the Internet creates problems with the "ethics of unlimited information."⑮

2000 Several of the best-protected and most popular commercial sites are attacked and shut down for several hours by hackers, perhaps as a protest against the commercialization of the Internet.⑩

2000 George W. Bush and Albert Gore are both declared winners of the presidential election by network television, only to have the election results placed in a limbo that lasts more than a month.①

2001 America Online (AOL) purchases Time Warner, combining AOL's online services with Time

Warner's entertainment businesses. Within two years the new company will lose half its shareholder value.①

2001 Terrorists plan the September 11 attacks on the World Trade Center and the Pentagon for maximum media coverage.① ⑪

2002 The news media provide context for the U.S. invasion of Afghanistan.①

2002 Fox News overtakes CNN as the most-watched all-news television network.⑪

2002 Two companies, XM and Sirius, begin distributing digital radio services by satellite.⑧

2002 The U.S. government uses public relations tactics to change America's image in Arab and Islamic countries.⑫

2003 Having your own Weblog, or blog, becomes hip.⑩

2003 *Harry Potter and the Order of the Phoenix* sells 5 million copies in its first 24 hours, an all-time record for a book. Its one-day gross of $100 million exceeds that of *The Hulk,* the blockbuster action film that opened the same weekend.③

2003 Fox News sues Al Franken for using the phrase "fair and balanced" in the title of his book *Lies and the Lying Liars Who Tell Them: A Fair and Balanced Look at the Right.* The publicity increases sales of the book.③

2003 The music industry sues individuals for sharing music on the Internet.⑦

2003 Executives of a Rwanda radio station are convicted of genocide by an international tribunal and sentenced to life in prison for their role in the ethnic massacres of 1994.⑧

2003 The *New York Times* announces that a young reporter, Jayson Blair, has been guilty of plagiarism, factual errors, and fabrications.④

2003 Journalists are embedded with troops in the war in Iraq. News organizations are faulted for failing to cover the buildup to the war critically.⑪

2003 Hollywood declares war on file sharers of copyrighted films.⑥

2003 *The Matrix: Revolutions* has the first global movie opening as it is shown simultaneously on more than 18,000 screens in 96 countries.⑥

2003 Online worm attacks result in $82 billion worth of damage. Some computer experts call it "The Year of the Worm."⑩

2004 Janet Jackson and Justin Timberlake have a "wardrobe malfunction" during the Super Bowl that leads the Federal Communications Commission (FCC) to crack down on broadcast indecency.⑭

2004 The first federal law to address the spam problem becomes active, but is not effective.⑩

2004 Napster returns as a legal subscription service.⑦

2004 Howard Stern's show is removed from six radio stations owned by Clear Channel Communications.①

2004 Abuse of Iraqi prisoners by Americans becomes a scandal when photos of the abuse are published. ❶

2004 The U.S. government initiates an antitrust lawsuit against Clear Channel Communications, accusing the company of keeping artists that signed with other concert promoters off its radio playlists. ❶

2004 The United States builds Alhurra, an Arab-language news and entertainment cable television network that is beamed by satellite from the United States to the Middle East. ⑫

2004 NBC merges with Universal Entertainment, giving it both the Universal production facilities and the NBC television network and cable channels to distribute the programming that Universal produces. ❶

2004 Electronic game sales, at $17 billion a year, equal movie ticket receipts and surpass music industry revenues. ⑩

2004 Walt Disney Company refuses to distribute Michael Moore's controversial film *Fahrenheit 9/11,*

which is critical of the Bush administration, during an election year. ⑥

2004 Internet ads earn over $5 billion, asserting the power of the Internet as a potent source of advertising revenue for the foreseeable future. ⑬

2004 The video game becomes the new medium to be investigated for its harmful effects on children. ❷

2005 *The DaVinci Code* becomes one of the most widely read best sellers of all time, but is criticized as blasphemy by some Catholics. ❸

2005 Podcasting takes off. ❼

2005 Google Earth, a global mapping program using satellite imaging and aerial photography, is released. ⑩

2005 *Dateline NBC* presents the first of its specials trapping online predators. ⑩

2005 Cartoons depicting the prophet Muhammad are published in a Danish newspaper. Months later, 139 die in protest riots. ⑮

2006 Shareholder pressure forces the sale of Knight Ridder, one of the largest newspaper chains. ❹

2006 *Teen People* and *Elle Girl* convert to Web-only versions. ❺

2006 Howard Stern moves to Sirius Satellite Radio. ❽

2006 Fox Network syndicates a prime-time program, *Arrested Development,* to MSN, a Web site. ❾

2006 The social networking site MySpace becomes one of the top five Internet destinations. ⑩

2006 Katie Couric becomes the first female solo anchor of a broadcast television network newscast. ⑪

2006 Local Los Angeles DJs coordinate immigration reform protest marches that draw 500,000 marchers. ⑫

2006 *American Idol* logs more than 3,000 product placements in one three-month period. ⑬

2006 A chain takes control of a student newspaper for the first time when Gannett purchases the *FS View & Florida Flambeau* of Florida State University. ❹

Credits

Photo Credits

p. 436, © Bill Aron/PhotoEdit; p. 437, © Serge Attal/Getty Images; p. 442, Courtesy Advertising Archives; p. 444, © Liu Jin/Getty Images; p. 445, © Joel Gordon; p. 448, Courtesy American Legend; p. 450, Shards O' Glass courtesy The American Legacy Foundation, Arnold Worldwide, & Crispin Porter and Bogusky; p. 452, McGraw-Hill Companies/Christopher Kerrigan, Photographer; p. 454, © Joel W. Rogers/Corbis; p. 455, © AP/Wide World Photos; p. 456, © NBC/Courtesy Everett Collection **PO5** Chris Thomaidis/Getty Images; **Chapter 14** p. 463, © AP/Wide World Photos; p. 465, © The Granger Collection, New York; p. 466, Library of Congress (608421); p. 471, © Bettmann/Corbis; p. 472, Nick Koudis/Getty Images; p. 476, Steve Cole/Getty Images; p. 479, © Columbia Pictures/Courtesy Everett Collection; p. 481, © AP/Wide World Photos; p. 482, © David McNew/Getty Images; p. 485, © Pace Gregory/Corbis Sygma; p. 486, © XEROX CORPORATION. All rights reserved. Used with the express permission of Xerox Corporation.; p. 491, © AP/Wide World Photos; p. 492, Art Spiegelman/The New Yorker. © 1999 Condé Nast Publications, Inc. Reprinted by permission. All Rights Reserved.; **Chapter 15** p. 497, © Fayyaz Ahmed/epa/Corbis; p. 501, © Bettmann/Corbis; pp. 502, 503L© The Granger Collection, New York; p. 503R, © North Wind Picture Archives; pp. 504, 505, 506, © Bettmann/Corbis; p. 507L, Used by permission of The Washington Post; pp. 507R, 509, © AP/Wide World Photos; p. 512TL, © Bettmann/Corbis; p. 512TR, © Jane Reed/Harvard University News Office; pp. 512BL, 512BM, © Scala/Art Resource, NY; p. 512BR, © The Granger Collection, New York; p. 516L, © Ken Light/Corbis; p. 516M, © Owen Franken/Corbis; p. 516R, © The New York Times; p. 517, © Saeed Khan/AFP/Getty Images; p. 518, © AP/Wide World Photos; p. 520, From *Bitches, Bimbos and Ballbreakers* by The Guerilla Girls,

© 2003 by The Guerilla Girls, Inc. Used by permission of Viking Penguin, a division of Penguin Group (USA) Inc.; p. 523, Art © Raymond Verdaguer. Courtesy Columbia Journalism Review

Text and line art credits

Chapter 3 p. 79, cover from Alan Brinkley, *The Unfinished Nation,* 4th Edition. Copyright © 2004 The McGraw-Hill Companies. Reprinted with permission from The McGraw-Hill Companies; p. 79, cover from G. Dennis Rains, *Principles of Human Neuropsychology.* Copyright © 2002 The McGraw-Hill Companies **Chapter 6** p. 178, Quotation from Patrick Goldstein, "In a Losing Race with the Zeitgeist," *Los Angeles Times* online, November 22, 2005. Copyright 2005 *Los Angeles Times.* Reprinted by permission **Chapter 8** p. 246, The XM name and logo are registered trademarks of XM Satellite Radio Inc. Used with permission; p. 246, Logo courtesy SIRIUS Satellite Radio; p. 265, Real Rock 99.3 logo courtesy of KCGQ FM Real Rock 99.3, Cape Girardeau, MO **Chapter 9** p. 300, Fig. 9.2 Copyright © 2003 Nielsen Media Research. All rights reserved. Reprinted with permission **Chapter 10** p. 346, BBBOnLine Privacy Seal. Reprinted with permission of the Council of Better Business Bureaus, Inc.; p. 346, TRUSTe Privacy Seal. TRUSTe and the Privacy Seal are registered trademarks of TRUSTe, Inc. **Chapter 14** p. 484, Sony Electronics Inc. Used with permission; © Eveready Battery Company, Inc. 2006 Reprinted with permission; Logo used with permission from the McDonald's Corporation; Xerox Corporation. Used by permission; Jell-O is a trademark of Kraft Foods, reproduced with permission.

Index